ēm des tiefstandes ist kein unbo... ...ön
tille z' steh~/wie sumpfwass°/da... ...ang
edeckt v~ so gross ist/dass das feste land nur wie ein
mēre-als ein tropf~ des mēres nimst du theil an strö
~ sinkst langsam wied° zurück in unendlich lan
weite streck~ v~ bespülst fremde küst~ v~ weisst nicht
ies hebst du di~ empor v~ rauschest wiederum in die
ptest du/dass deine beweg° aus dir kome v~ dass es
u di~ bewegest v~ von d° stelle komest. abe mit alle
gegend~ gekom~/z' den~ das mēr v~ d° grosse win
st du in schwärzliche tief~/leuchtende fische zieh~ an di
pf~ dur~ spalt~ v~ dur~ schlingende schwankende
erum empor in hellgrüne wass° auf weissandig° kü
ed° zurück v~ eine geglättete breite woge hebt di~
~ v~ schlingend~ pflanz~ v~ langschwänzig~ fisch~ v
wass° v~ weiss~ sande v~ brechend° brandungswoge
über's mēr/wie d° mond/d° d° fluth entsteigt/v~ du
ässt di~ v~ d° wille z' eigen° beweg°. du willst hin
as das athm~ des mēres ist v~ sein ström~/das di
eine woge/die di~ an fremde küst~ wirft v~ di~ wi
st/dass es das leb~ des ganz~ war v~ d° tod jedes ei
m tode am tiefst~ orte d° erde/vom tode in deine° eigen
di~ hinaus/verzweifelst v~ todesangst fass~ di~ in all
imt. alle diese hell~ v~ dunkeln/warm~ lau~ v~ kalt
anzenthiere v~ thierpflanz~/alle diese nächtig~
ne/na~ hell° trocken° luft/na~ fest~ stein/na~ be-

THE RED BOOK

LIBER NOVUS

A Reader's Edition

THE RED BOOK

LIBER NOVUS

A Reader's Edition

C·G· JUNG

Edited and with an Introduction by
SONU SHAMDASANI

PREFACE BY ULRICH HOERNI

TRANSLATED BY MARK KYBURZ,
JOHN PECK, AND SONU SHAMDASANI

PHILEMON SERIES
A publication in arrangement with
the Foundation of the Works of C. G. Jung, Zürich

W. W. Norton & Company
New York · London

THE RED BOOK: A READER'S EDITION

PRINTED IN CHINA
FIRST EDITION

MANUFACTURING THROUGH ASIA-PACIFIC OFFSET, CHINA
ART DIRECTION BY LARRY VIGON
BOOK ADAPTATION AND COMPOSITION BY LAURA LINDGREN
FROM THE FACSIMILE EDITION DESIGNED BY ERIC BAKER ASSOCIATES

The Red Book: A Reader's Edition is a publication of the heirs of C. G. Jung and is one of the volumes of the Philemon Series, sponsored by the Philemon Foundation.

The Library of Congress has cataloged another edition as follows:
Jung, C. G. (Carl Gustav), 1875–1961.
The Red Book = Liber novus / C. G. Jung ; edited by Sonu Shamdasani ; translated by Mark Kyburz, John Peck, and Sonu Shamdasani.—1st ed.
p. cm.—(Philemon series)
ISBN 978-0-393-06567-1 (Hardcover)
1. Jung, C. G. (Carl Gustav), 1875–1961. 2. Psychoanalysts—Switzerland—Biography. 3. Jungian psychology. I. Shamdasani, Sonu, 1962– II. Title. III. Title: Liber novus.
BF109.J8A3 2009
150.19'54—dc22 2009018465

ISBN 978-0-393-08908-0

W. W. NORTON & COMPANY, 500 FIFTH AVENUE, NEW YORK, NY 10110
WWW.WWNORTON.COM

W. W. NORTON & COMPANY LTD., CASTLE HOUSE, 75/76 WELLS STREET, LONDON, W1T 3QT

1 2 3 4 5 6 7 8 9 0

Contents

Note: Black numbers refer to the translation. Red numbers refer to the plates in the facsimile edition.

THE YEARS, OF WHICH I HAVE SPOKEN TO YOU, when I pursued the inner images, were the most important time of my life. Everything else is to be derived from this. It began at that time, and the later details hardly matter anymore. My entire life consisted in elaborating what had burst forth from the unconscious and flooded me like an enigmatic stream and threatened to break me. That was the stuff and material for more than only one life. Everything later was merely the outer classification, the scientific elaboration, and the integration into life. But the numinous beginning, which contained everything, was then.

C. G. JUNG, 1957

Preface to the Reader's Edition

More than a decade has passed since the memorable decision of the former society of heirs of C. G. Jung to release *The Red Book* for publication. Much consideration was given to what kind of audience this multilayered work should be directed: Professional readers of works on the history of psychology? The general reader? Visually receptive people, orientated toward images? Lovers of calligraphy? Collectors of beautiful books? Which aspects should the format and design of the publication foreground? These questions weren't easy to answer, since even the physical appearance of the precious original seemed to contain a message. Many proposals were discussed and discarded. It was W. W. Norton that finally found the appropriate solution: a complete facsimile edition, which was presented in its original format in 2009. Overwhelming success proved that the publisher was right. The work rapidly spread worldwide and is already available in nine languages. Evidently, it was possible to design an edition that did justice not only to the many facets of the work but also to the different types of audience. The list of people to whom the credit for this success is due is now of considerable length. However, two names especially deserve to be mentioned, Jim Mairs (W. W. Norton) and Sonu Shamdasani (Philemon Foundation).

The present Reader's Edition contains the complete text of the original. It is specifically aimed toward those who would like to engage deeply with the literary documentation of Jung's inner development. It would undoubtedly accord with Jung's intention if this edition helps readers to make their reading more fruitful for their own development.

Ulrich Hoerni
Foundation of the Works of C. G. Jung
July 2012

Preface

Since 1962, the existence of C. G. Jung's *Red Book* has been widely known. Yet only with the present publication is it finally accessible to a broad public. Its genesis is described in Jung's *Memories, Dreams, Reflections*, and has been the subject of numerous discussions in the secondary literature. Hence I will only briefly outline it here.

The year 1913 was pivotal in Jung's life. He began a self-experiment that became known as his "confrontation with the unconscious" and lasted until 1930. During this experiment, he developed a technique to "get to the bottom of [his] inner processes," "to translate the emotions into images," and "to grasp the fantasies which were stirring . . . 'underground.' " He later called this method "active imagination." He first recorded these fantasies in his *Black Books*. He then revised these texts, added reflections on them, and copied them in a calligraphic script into a book entitled *Liber Novus* bound in red leather, accompanied by his own paintings. It has always been known as the *Red Book*.

Jung shared his inner experiences with his wife and close associates. In 1925 he gave a report of his professional and personal development in a series of seminars at the Psychological Club in Zürich in which he also mentioned his method of active imagination. Beyond this, Jung was guarded. His children, for example, were not informed about his self-experiment and they did not notice anything unusual. Clearly, it would have been difficult for him to explain what was taking place. It was already a mark of favor if he allowed one of his children to watch him write or paint. Thus for Jung's descendants, the *Red Book* had always been surrounded by an aura of mystery. In 1930 Jung ended his experiment and put the *Red Book* aside—unfinished. Although it had its honored place in his study, he let it rest for decades. Meanwhile the insights he had gained through it directly informed his subsequent writings. In 1959, with the help of the old draft, he tried to complete the transcription of the text into the *Red Book* and to finish an incomplete painting. He also started on an epilogue, but for unknown reasons both the calligraphic text and epilogue break off in midsentence.

Although Jung actively considered publishing the *Red Book*, he never took the necessary steps. In 1916 he privately published the *Septem Sermones ad Mortuos* (Seven Sermons to the Dead), a short work that arose out of his confrontation with the unconscious. Even his 1916 essay, "The Transcendent Function," in which he described the technique of active imagination, was not published until 1958. There are a number of reasons why he did not publish the *Red Book*. As he himself stated, it was unfinished. His growing interest in alchemy as a research topic distracted him. In hindsight, he described the detailed working out of his fantasies in the *Red Book* as a necessary but annoying "aestheticizing elaboration." As late as 1957 he declared that the *Black Books* and the *Red Book* were autobiographical records that he did not want published in his *Collected Works* because they were not of a scholarly character. As a concession, he allowed Aniela Jaffé to quote excerpts from the *Red Book* and the *Black Books* in *Memories, Dreams, Reflections*—a possibility which she made little use of.

In 1961, Jung died. His literary estate became the property of his descendants, who formed the Society of Heirs of C. G. Jung. The inheritance of Jung's literary rights brought an obligation and challenge to his heirs: to see through the publication of the German edition of his *Collected Works*. In his will, Jung had expressed the wish that the *Red Book* and the *Black Books* should remain with his family, without, however, giving more detailed instructions. Since the *Red Book* was not meant to be published in the *Collected Works*, the Society of Heirs concluded that this was Jung's final wish concerning the work, and that it was an entirely private matter. The Society of Heirs guarded Jung's unpublished writings like a treasure; no further publications were considered. The *Red Book* remained in Jung's study for more than twenty years, entrusted to the care of Franz Jung, who had taken over his father's house.

In 1983 the Society of Heirs placed the *Red Book* in a safe-deposit box, knowing that it was an irreplaceable document. In 1984 the newly appointed executive committee had five photographic duplicates made for family use. For the first time, Jung's descendants now had the opportunity to take a close look at it. This careful handling had its benefits. The *Red Book*'s well-preserved state is due, among other things, to the fact that it has only rarely been opened in decades.

When, after 1990, the editing of the German *Collected Works*—a *selection* of works—was drawing to a conclusion, the executive committee decided to start looking through all the accessible unpublished material with an eye to further publications. I took up this task, because in 1994, the Society of Heirs had placed the responsibility for archival and editorial questions on me. It turned out that there was an entire corpus of drafts and variants pertaining to the *Red Book*. From this it emerged that the missing part of the calligraphic text existed as a draft and that there was a manuscript entitled "Scrutinies," which continued where the draft ended, containing the *Seven Sermons*. Yet whether and how this substantial material could be published remained an open question. At first glance, the style and content appeared to have little in common with Jung's other works. Much was unclear and by the mid-1990s there was no one left who could have provided firsthand information on these points.

However, since Jung's time, the history of psychology had been gaining in importance and could now offer a new approach. While working on other projects I had come in contact with Sonu Shamdasani. In extensive talks we discussed the possibility of further Jung publications, both in general terms as well as with regard to the *Red Book*. The book had emerged within a specific context with which a reader at the turn of the twenty-first century is no longer familiar. But a historian of psychology would be able to present it to the modern reader as a historical document. With the help of primary sources he could embed it in the cultural context of its genesis, situate it within the history of science, and relate it to Jung's life and works. In 1999 Sonu Shamdasani developed a publication proposal following these guiding principles. On the basis of this proposal the Society of Heirs decided in spring 2000—not without discussion—

to release the *Red Book* for publication and to hand over the task of editing it to Sonu Shamdasani.

I have been asked repeatedly why, after so many years, the *Red Book* is now being published. Some new understandings on our part played a major role: Jung himself did not—as it had seemed—consider the *Red Book* a secret. On several occasions the text contains the address "dear friends"; it is, in other words, directed at an audience. Indeed, Jung let close friends have copies of transcriptions and discussed these with them. He did not categorically rule out publication; he simply left the issue unresolved. Moreover, Jung himself stated that he had gained the material for all his later works from his confrontation with the unconscious. As a record of this confrontation the *Red Book* is thus, beyond the private sphere, central to Jung's works. This understanding allowed the generation of Jung's grandchildren to look at the situation in a new light. The decision-making process took time. Exemplary excerpts, concepts, and information helped them to deal more rationally with an emotionally charged matter. Finally, the Society of Heirs decided democratically that the *Red Book* could be published. It was a long journey from that decision to the present publication. The result is impressive. This edition would not have been possible without the cooperation of many people who devoted their skill and energy to a common goal.

On behalf of the descendants of C. G. Jung, I would like to express my sincere thanks to all the contributors.

April 2009
Ulrich Hoerni
Foundation of the Works of C. G. Jung

Acknowledgments

Given the unpublished copies in circulation, the *Red Book* would in all likelihood have eventually entered the public domain at some stage, in some form. In what follows, I would like to thank those who have enabled the present historical edition to come about. A number of people collaborated and they have each in their own way contributed to its realization.

The former Society of Heirs of C. G. Jung (dissolved in 2008) decided in spring 2000 after intensive discussion to release the work for publication. On the behalf of the Society of Heirs, Ulrich Hoerni, formerly its manager and president and presently the vice president of its successor, the Foundation of the Works of C. G. Jung, planned the project with the support of the executive committee. Wolfgang Baumann, president from 2000 to 2004, signed the agreement in autumn 2000 that made possible the commencement of the work and committed the Society of Heirs to underwrite a major part of the costs. The Foundation of the Works of C. G. Jung would like to thank: Heinrich Zweifel, publisher, Zürich, for advice in the planning phase on technical issues; The Donald Cooper Fund of the Swiss Federal Institute for Technology for a significant donation; Rolf Auf der Maur for legal advice and contractual assistance; Leo La Rosa and Peter Fritz for contractual negotiations.

At a critical moment in 2003, the editorial work was supported by the Bogette Foundation and an anonymous donor. From 2004, the editorial work was supported by the Philemon Foundation, an organization established with the sole purpose of raising funds to enable Jung's unpublished works to see the light of day. In this regard, I am indebted to Stephen Martin. Whatever the shortcomings of this edition, the editorial apparatus and the translation could not have attained anything like the current level without the support of the Board of the Philemon Foundation: Tom Charlesworth, Gilda Frantz, Nancy Furlotti, Judith Harris, James Hollis, Stephen Martin, and Eugene Taylor. The Philemon Foundation would like to acknowledge the support of its donors, in particular, the MSST Foundation, Carolyn Grant Fay, Judith Harris and Tony Woolfson, and significant gifts toward the English translation from Nancy Furlotti and Laurence de Rosen.

My work on this project would not have been possible without the support of Maggie Baron and Ximena Roelli de Angulo through numerous tribulations. It commenced and was made possible by research on the intellectual history of Jung's work sponsored by the Wellcome Trust between 1993 and 1998, by the Institut für Grenzgebiete der Psychologie in 1999, and the Solon Foundation between 1998 and 2001. Throughout the project, the Wellcome Trust Centre for the History of Medicine at University College London (formerly the Wellcome Institute for the History of Medicine) has been an ideal environment for my research. Confidentiality agreements precluded discussing my work on this project with my friends and colleagues: I thank them for their forbearance over the last thirteen years.

Between late 2000 and early 2003 the Society of Heirs of C. G. Jung supported the editorial work, which initiated the project. Ulrich Hoerni collaborted with aspects of the research and made a corrected transcription of the calligraphic volume. Susanne Hoerni transcribed Jung's *Black Books*. Presentations were made to members of the Jung family in 1999, 2001, and 2003, which were hosted by Helene Hoerni Jung (1999, 2001) and Andreas and Vreni Jung (2003). Peter Jung provided counsel through the publication deliberations and early stages of the editorial work. Andreas and Vreni Jung assisted during countless visits to consult books and manuscripts in Jung's library, and Andreas Jung provided invaluable information from the Jung family archives.

This edition came about through Nancy Furlotti, and Larry and Sandra Vigon, who led me to Jim Mairs at Norton, who had been responsible for the facsimile edition of Larry Vigon's modern-day *Liber Novus, Dream*. In Jim Mairs, the work could not have found a better editor. The design and layout of the work provided numerous challenges, elegantly resolved by Eric Baker, Larry Vigon, and

Amy Wu. Carol Rose was tireless and ever-vigilant in copyediting the text. Austin O'Driscoll was of continuous assistance. For the Reader's Edition Laura Lindgren has designed an elegantly fitting layout and made a number of corrections. The calligraphic volume was scanned by Hugh Milstein and John Supra of Digital Fusion. The care and the precision of their work (focusing via sonar) met with and matched the care and precision of Jung's calligraphy in a remarkable fusion of the ancient and the modern. Dennis Savini made his photographic studio available for the scanning. At Mondadori Printing Nancy Freeman, Sergio Brunelli, and their colleagues took great care to ensure that the work was printed to the highest standards technically possible.

From 2006, I was joined by Mark Kyburz and John Peck on the translation—a collaboration that was a privileged instruction in the art of translation. Our regular conference calls provided the welcome opportunity to discuss the text at a microscopic level, and the humor brought much-needed levity to the constant immersion in the spirit of the depths. Their contributions to the later stages of the editorial work have been invaluable. John Peck picked up several significant allusions that were beyond my ken.

Ximena Roelli de Angulo, Helene Hoerni Jung, Pierre Keller, and the late Leonhard Schlegel provided crucial recollections of the atmosphere in Jung's circle in the twenties, and figures involved in it. Leonhard Schlegel provided critical insights into the Dada movement and the collisions between art and psychology in this period.

Erik Hornung provided consultation concerning Egyptological references. Felix Walder assisted with a digital close-up of image 155, Ulrich Hoerni deciphered its small inscriptions, and Guy Attewell recognized the Arabic inscription. Ulrich Hoerni provided references to the Mithraic Liturgy (note 1, p. 578). David Oswald pointed to the *Mutus Liber* as Jung's possible referent in note 314 (p. 429). Thomas Feitknecht drew my attention to and assisted with the J. B. Lang papers. Stephen Martin recovered Jung's letters to J. B. Lang. Paul Bishop, Wendy Doniger and Rachel McDermott responded to queries.

I would like to thank Ernst Falzeder for the reference in note 145 on p. 46, for transcribing Stockmayer's letters to Jung, and for extensively correcting the translation of the introduction and notes in the German edition.

I would like to thank the Foundation of the Works of C. G. Jung and the Paul and Peter Fritz Literary Agency for permission to cite from Jung's unpublished manuscripts and correspondences, and Ximena Roelli de Angulo for permission to cite from Cary Baynes's correspondence and diaries.

Responsibility for the establishment of the text, the introduction, and the apparatus remains my own. Like the donkey on page 126 (note 29), I am glad finally to be able to lay down this load.

Sonu Shamdasani

Liber Novus
The "Red Book" of C. G. Jung[1]

SONU SHAMDASANI

C. G. Jung is widely recognized as a major figure in modern Western thought, and his work continues to spark controversies. He played critical roles in the formation of modern psychology, psychotherapy, and psychiatry, and a large international profession of analytical psychologists work under his name. His work has had its widest impact, however, outside professional circles: Jung and Freud are the names that most people first think of in connection with psychology, and their ideas have been widely disseminated in the arts, the humanities, films, and popular culture. Jung is also widely regarded as one of the instigators of the New Age movement. However, it is startling to realize that the book that stands at the center of his oeuvre, on which he worked for over sixteen years, is only now being published.

There can be few *unpublished* works that have already exerted such far-reaching effects upon twentieth-century social and intellectual

1. The following draws, at times directly, on my reconstruction of the formation of Jung's psychology in *Jung and the Making of Modern Psychology: The Dream of a Science* (Cambridge: Cambridge University Press, 2003). Jung referred to the work both as *Liber Novus* and as *The Red Book*, as it has become generally known. Because there are indications that the former is its actual title, I have referred to it as such throughout for consistency. A number of these themes are elaborated more fully in my *C. G. Jung: A Biography in Books* (New York: W. W. Norton, 2012).

history as Jung's *Red Book*, or *Liber Novus* (New Book). Nominated by Jung to contain the nucleus of his later works, it has long been recognized as the key to comprehending their genesis. Yet aside from a few tantalizing glimpses, it has remained unavailable for study.

The Cultural Moment

The first few decades of the twentieth century saw a great deal of experimentation in literature, psychology, and the visual arts. Writers tried to throw off the limitations of representational conventions to explore and depict the full range of inner experience—dreams, visions, and fantasies. They experimented with new forms and utilized old forms in novel ways. From the automatic writing of the surrealists to the gothic fantasies of Gustav Meyrink, writers came into close proximity and collision with the researches of psychologists, who were engaged in similar explorations. Artists and writers collaborated to try out new forms of illustration and typography, new configurations of text and image. Psychologists sought to overcome the limitations of philosophical psychology, and they began to explore the same terrain as artists and writers. Clear demarcations among literature, art, and psychology had not yet been set; writers and artists borrowed from psychologists, and vice versa. A number of major psychologists, such as Alfred Binet and Charles Richet, wrote dramatic and fictional works, often under assumed names, whose themes mirrored those of their "scientific" works.[2] Gustav Fechner, one of the founders of psychophysics and experimental psychology, wrote on the soul life of plants and of the earth as a blue angel.[3] Meanwhile writers such as André Breton and Philippe Soupault assiduously read and utilized the works of psychical researchers and abnormal psychologists, such as Frederick Myers, Théodore Flournoy, and Pierre Janet. W. B. Yeats utilized spiritualistic auto-

2. See Jacqueline Carroy, *Les personnalités multiples et doubles: entre science et fiction* (Paris: PUF, 1993).
3. See Gustav Theodor Fechner, *The Religion of a Scientist*, ed. and tr. Walter Lowrie (New York: Pantheon, 1946).

matic writing to compose a poetic psychocosmology in *A Vision*.[4] On all sides, individuals were searching for new forms with which to depict the actualities of inner experience, in a quest for spiritual and cultural renewal. In Berlin, Hugo Ball noted:

> The world and society in 1913 looked like this: life is completely confined and shackled. A kind of economic fatalism prevails; each individual, whether he resists it or not, is assigned a specific role and with it his interests and his character. The church is regarded as a "redemption factory" of little importance, literature as a safety valve . . . The most burning question day and night is: is there anywhere a force that is strong enough to put an end to this state of affairs? And if not, how can one escape it?[5]

Within this cultural crisis Jung conceived of undertaking an extended process of self-experimentation, which resulted in *Liber Novus*, a work of psychology in a literary form.

We stand today on the other side of a divide between psychology and literature. To consider *Liber Novus* today is to take up a work that could have emerged only before these separations had been firmly established. Its study helps us understand how the divide occurred. But first, we may ask,

Who was C. G. Jung?

Jung was born in Kesswil, on Lake Constance, in 1875. His family moved to Laufen by the Rhine Falls when he was six months old. He was the oldest child and had one sister. His father was a pastor in the Swiss Reformed Church. Toward the end of his life, Jung wrote a memoir entitled "From the Earliest Experiences of

---

4. See Jean Starobinski, "Freud, Breton, Myers," in *L'oeuil vivante II: La relation critique* (Paris: Gallimard, 1970), and W. B. Yeats, *A Vision* (London: Werner Laurie, 1925). Jung possessed a copy of the latter.
5. Hugo Ball, *Flight Out of Time: A Dada Diary*, ed. John Elderfield, tr. A. Raimes (Berkeley: University of California Press, 1996), p. 1.

My Life," which was subsequently included in *Memories, Dreams, Reflections* in a heavily edited form.[6] Jung narrated the significant events that led to his psychological vocation. The memoir, with its focus on significant childhood dreams, visions, and fantasies, can be viewed as an introduction to *Liber Novus.*

In the first dream, he found himself in a meadow with a stone-lined hole in the ground. Finding some stairs, he descended into it, and found himself in a chamber. Here there was a golden throne with what appeared to be a tree trunk of skin and flesh, with an eye on the top. He then heard his mother's voice exclaim that this was the "man-eater." He was unsure whether she meant that this figure actually devoured children or was identical with Christ. This profoundly affected his image of Christ. Years later, he realized that this figure was a penis and, later still, that it was in fact a ritual phallus, and that the setting was an underground temple. He came to see this dream as an initiation "in the secrets of the earth."[7]

In his childhood, Jung experienced a number of visual hallucinations. He also appears to have had the capacity to evoke images voluntarily. In a seminar in 1935, he recalled a portrait of his maternal grandmother which he would look at as a boy until he "saw" his grandfather descending the stairs.[8]

One sunny day, when Jung was twelve, he was traversing the Münsterplatz in Basel, admiring the sun shining on the newly restored glazed roof tiles of the cathedral. He then felt the approach of a terrible, sinful thought, which he pushed away. He was in a state of anguish for several days. Finally, after convincing himself that it was God who wanted him to think this thought, just as it had been God who had wanted Adam and Eve to sin, he let himself contemplate it, and saw God on his throne unleashing an almighty turd on

---

6. On how this mistakenly came to be seen as Jung's autobiography, see my *Jung Stripped Bare by His Biographers, Even* (London, Karnac, 2004), ch. 1, "'How to catch the bird': Jung and his first biographers." See also Alan Elms, "The auntification of Jung," in *Uncovering Lives: The Uneasy Alliance of Biography and Psychology* (New York: Oxford University Press, 1994).
7. *Memories*, p. 30.
8. "Fundamental psychological conceptions," CW 18, §397.

the cathedral, shattering its new roof and smashing the cathedral. With this, Jung felt a sense of bliss and relief such as he had never experienced before. He felt that it was an experience of the "direct living God, who stands omnipotent and free above the Bible and Church."[9] He felt alone before God, and that his real responsibility commenced then. He realized that it was precisely such a direct, immediate experience of the living God, who stands outside Church and Bible, that his father lacked.

This sense of election led to a final disillusionment with the Church on the occasion of his First Communion. He had been led to believe that this would be a great experience. Instead, nothing. He concluded: "For me, it was an absence of God and no religion. Church was a place to which I no longer could go. There was no life there, but death."[10]

Jung's voracious reading started at this time, and he was particularly struck by Goethe's *Faust*. He was struck by the fact that in Mephistopheles, Goethe took the figure of the devil seriously. In philosophy, he was impressed by Schopenhauer, who acknowledged the existence of evil and gave voice to the sufferings and miseries of the world.

Jung also had a sense of living in two centuries, and felt a strong nostalgia for the eighteenth century. His sense of duality took the form of two alternating personalities, which he dubbed NO. 1 and 2. NO. 1 was the Basel schoolboy, who read novels, and NO. 2 pursued religious reflections in solitude, in a state of communion with nature and the cosmos. He inhabited "God's world." This personality felt most real. Personality NO. 1 wanted to be free of the melancholy and isolation of personality NO. 2. When personality NO. 2 entered, it felt as if a long dead yet perpetually present spirit had entered the room. NO. 2 had no definable character. He was connected to history, particularly with the Middle Ages. For NO. 2, NO. 1, with his failings and ineptitudes, was someone to be put up with.

9. *Memories*, p. 57.
10. Ibid., p. 73.

This interplay ran throughout Jung's life. As he saw it, we are all like this—part of us lives in the present and the other part is connected to the centuries.

As the time drew near for him to choose a career, the conflict between the two personalities intensified. NO. 1 wanted to pursue science, NO. 2, the humanities. Jung then had two critical dreams. In the first, he was walking in a dark wood along the Rhine. He came upon a burial mound and began to dig, until he discovered the remains of prehistoric animals. This dream awakened his desire to learn more about nature. In the second dream, he was in a wood and there were watercourses. He found a circular pool surrounded by dense undergrowth. In the pool, he saw a beautiful creature, a large radiolarian. After these dreams, he settled for science. To solve the question of how to earn a living, he decided to study medicine. He then had another dream. He was in an unknown place, surrounded by fog, making slow headway against the wind. He was protecting a small light from going out. He saw a large black figure threateningly close. He awoke, and realized that the figure was the shadow cast from the light. He thought that in the dream, NO. 1 was himself bearing the light, and NO. 2 followed like a shadow. He took this as a sign that he should go forward with NO. 1, and not look back to the world of NO. 2.

In his university days, the interplay between these personalities continued. In addition to his medical studies, Jung pursued an intensive program of extracurricular reading, in particular the works of Nietzsche, Schopenhauer, Swedenborg,[11] and writers on

11. Emmanuel Swedenborg (1688–1772) was a Swedish scientist and Christian mystic. In 1743, he underwent a religious crisis, which is depicted in his *Journal of Dreams*. In 1745, he had a vision of Christ. He then devoted his life to relating what he had heard and seen in Heaven and Hell and learned from the angels, and in interpreting the internal and symbolic meaning of the Bible. Swedenborg argued that the Bible had two levels of meaning: a physical, literal level, and an inner, spiritual level. These were linked by correspondences. He proclaimed the advent of a "new church" that represented a new spiritual era. According to Swedenborg, from birth one acquired evils from one's parents which are lodged in the natural man, who is diametrically opposed to the spiritual man. Man is destined for Heaven, and he cannot reach there without spiritual regeneration and a new birth. The means to this lay in charity and faith. See Eugene Taylor, "Jung on Swedenborg, redivivus," *Jung History*, 2, 2 (2007), pp. 27–31.

spiritualism. Nietzsche's *Thus Spoke Zarathustra* made a great impression on him. He felt that his own personality NO. 2 corresponded to Zarathustra, and he feared that his personality NO. 2 was similarly morbid.[12] He participated in a student debating society, the Zofingia society, and presented lectures on these subjects. Spiritualism particularly interested him, as the spiritualists appeared to be attempting to use scientific means to explore the supernatural, and prove the immortality of the soul.

The latter half of the nineteenth century witnessed the emergence of modern spiritualism, which spread across Europe and America. Through spiritualism, the cultivation of trances—with the attendant phenomena of trance speech, glossolalia, automatic writing, and crystal vision—became widespread. The phenomena of spiritualism attracted the interest of leading scientists such as Crookes, Zollner, and Wallace. It also attracted the interest of psychologists, including Freud, Ferenczi, Bleuler, James, Myers, Janet, Bergson, Stanley Hall, Schrenck-Notzing, Moll, Dessoir, Richet, and Flournoy.

During his university days in Basel, Jung and his fellow students took part in séances. In 1896, they engaged in a long series of sittings with his cousin Helene Preiswerk, who appeared to have mediumistic abilities. Jung found that during the trances, she would become different personalities, and that he could call up these personalities by suggestion. Dead relatives appeared, and she became completely transformed into these figures. She unfolded stories of her previous incarnations and articulated a mystical cosmology, represented in a mandala.[13] Her spiritualistic revelations carried on until she was caught attempting to fake physical apparitions, and the séances were discontinued.

On reading Richard von Krafft-Ebing's *Text-Book of Psychiatry* in 1899, Jung realized that his vocation lay in psychiatry, which represented a fusion of the interests of his two personalities. He under-

12. *Memories*, p. 120.
13. See CW 1, §66, fig. 2.

went something like a conversion to a natural scientific framework. After his medical studies, he took up a post as an assistant physician at Burghölzli hospital at the end of 1900. The Burghölzli was a progressive university clinic, under the directorship of Eugen Bleuler. At the end of the nineteenth century, numerous figures attempted to found a new scientific psychology. It was held that by turning psychology into a science through introducing scientific methods, all prior forms of human understanding would be revolutionized. The new psychology was heralded as promising nothing less than the completion of the scientific revolution. Thanks to Bleuler, and his predecessor Auguste Forel, psychological research and hypnosis played prominent roles at the Burghölzli.

Jung's medical dissertation focused on the psychogenesis of spiritualistic phenomena, in the form of an analysis of his séances with Helene Preiswerk.[14] While his initial interest in her case appeared to be in the possible veracity of her spiritualistic manifestations, in the interim, he had studied the works of Frederic Myers, William James, and, in particular, Théodore Flournoy. At the end of 1899, Flournoy had published a study of a medium, whom he called Hélène Smith, which became a best seller.[15] What was novel about Flournoy's study was that it approached her case purely from the psychological angle, as a means of illuminating the study of subliminal consciousness. A critical shift had taken place through the work of Flournoy, Frederick Myers, and William James.They argued that regardless of whether the alleged spiritualistic experiences were valid, such experiences enabled far-reaching insight into the constitution of the subliminal, and hence into human psychology as a whole. Through them, mediums became important subjects of the new psychology. With this shift, the methods used by the mediums—such as automatic writing, trance speech, and crystal vision—were appropriated by the psychologists, and became prominent

14. *On the Psychology and Pathology of So-called Occult Phenomena: A Psychiatric Study*, 1902, CW 1.
15. Théodore Flournoy, *From India to the Planet Mars: A Case of Multiple Personality with Imaginary Languages*, ed. Sonu Shamdasani, tr. D. Vermilye (Princeton: Princeton University Press, 1900/1994).

experimental research tools. In psychotherapy, Pierre Janet and Morton Prince used automatic writing and crystal gazing as methods for revealing hidden memories and subconscious fixed ideas. Automatic writing brought to light subpersonalities, and enabled dialogues with them to be held.[16] For Janet and Prince, the goal of holding such practices was to reintegrate the personality.

Jung was so taken by Flournoy's book that he offered to translate it into German, but Flournoy already had a translator. The impact of these studies is clear in Jung's dissertation, where he approaches the case purely from a psychological angle. Jung's work was closely modeled on Flournoy's *From India to the Planet Mars*, both in terms of subject matter and in its interpretation of the psychogenesis of Helene's spiritualistic romances. Jung's dissertation also indicates the manner in which he was utilizing automatic writing as a method of psychological investigation.

In 1902, he became engaged to Emma Rauschenbach, whom he married and with whom he had five children. Up till this point, Jung had kept a diary. In one of the last entries, dated May 1902, he wrote: "I am no longer alone with myself, and I can only artificially recall the scary and beautiful feeling of solitude. This is the shadow side of the fortune of love."[17] For Jung, his marriage marked a move away from the solitude to which he had been accustomed.

In his youth, Jung had often visited Basel's art museum and was particularly drawn to the works of Holbein and Böcklin, as well as to those of the Dutch painters.[18] Toward the end of his studies, he was much occupied with painting for about a year. His paintings from this period were landscapes in a representational style, and show highly developed technical skills and fine technical proficiency.[19] In

16. Pierre Janet, *Névroses et idées fixes* (Paris: Alcan, 1898); Morton Prince, *Clinical and Experimental Studies in Personality* (Cambridge, MA: Sci-Art, 1929). See my "Automatic writing and the discovery of the unconscious," *Spring: A Journal of Archetype and Culture* 54 (1993), pp. 100–131.

17. *Black Book 2*, p. 1 (*JFA*; all the *Black Books* are in the *JFA*).

18. *MP*, p. 164.

19. See Gerhard Wehr, *An Illustrated Biography of Jung*, tr. M. Kohn (Boston: Shambala, 1989), p. 47; Aniela Jaffé, ed., C. G. *Jung: Word and Image* (Princeton: Princeton University Press/Bollingen Series, 1979), pp. 42–43.

1902/3, Jung left his post at the Burghölzli and went to Paris to study with the leading French psychologist Pierre Janet, who was lecturing at the Collège de France. During his stay, he devoted much time to painting and visiting museums, going frequently to the Louvre. He paid particular attention to ancient art, Egyptian antiquities, the works of the Renaissance, Fra Angelico, Leonardo da Vinci, Rubens, and Frans Hals. He bought paintings and engravings and had paintings copied for the furnishing of his new home. He painted in both oil and watercolor. In January 1903, he went to London and visited its museums, paying particular attention to the Egyptian, Aztec, and Inca collections at the British Museum.[20]

After his return, he took up a post that had become vacant at the Burghölzli and devoted his research to the analysis of linguistic associations, in collaboration with Franz Riklin. With co-workers, they conducted an extensive series of experiments, which they subjected to statistical analyses. The conceptual basis of Jung's early work lay in the work of Flournoy and Janet, which he attempted to fuse with the research methodology of Wilhelm Wundt and Emil Kraepelin. Jung and Riklin utilized the associations experiment, devised by Francis Galton and developed in psychology and psychiatry by Wundt, Kraepelin, and Gustav Aschaffenburg. The aim of the research project, instigated by Bleuler, was to provide a quick and reliable means for differential diagnosis. The Burghölzli team failed to come up with this, but they were struck by the significance of disturbances of reaction and prolonged response times. Jung and Riklin argued that these disturbed reactions were due to the presence of emotionally stressed complexes, and used their experiments to develop a general psychology of complexes.[21]

This work established Jung's reputation as one of the rising stars of psychiatry. In 1906, he applied his new theory of complexes to study the psychogenesis of dementia praecox (later called schizophrenia) and to demonstrate the intelligibility of delusional for-

---

20. *MP*, p. 164, and unpublished letters, JFA.

21. "Experimental researches on the associations of the healthy," 1904, *CW* 2.

mations.[22] For Jung, along with a number of other psychiatrists and psychologists at this time, such as Janet and Adolf Meyer, insanity was not regarded as something completely set apart from sanity, but rather as lying on the extreme end of a spectrum. Two years later, he argued that "If we feel our way into the human secrets of the sick person, the madness also reveals its system, and we recognize in the mental illness merely an exceptional reaction to emotional problems which are not strange to us."[23]

Jung became increasingly disenchanted by the limitations of experimental and statistical methods in psychiatry and psychology. In the outpatient clinic at the Burghölzli, he presented hypnotic demonstrations. This led to his interest in therapeutics, and to the use of the clinical encounter as a method of research. Around 1904, Bleuler introduced psychoanalysis into the Burghölzli, and entered into a correspondence with Freud, asking Freud for assistance in his analysis of his own dreams.[24] In 1906, Jung entered into communication with Freud. This relationship has been much mythologized. A Freudocentric legend arose, which viewed Freud and psychoanalysis as the principal source for Jung's work. This has led to the complete mislocation of his work in the intellectual history of the twentieth century. On numerous occasions, Jung protested. For instance, in an unpublished article written in the 1930s, "The schism in the Freudian school," he wrote: "I in no way exclusively stem from Freud. I had my scientific attitude and the theory of complexes before I met Freud. The teachers that influenced me above all are Bleuler, Pierre Janet, and Théodore Flournoy."[25] Freud and Jung clearly came from quite different intellectual traditions, and were drawn together by shared interests in the psychogenesis of mental disorders and psychotherapy. Their intention was to form a scientific psychotherapy based on the new psychology and, in turn,

22. *On the Psychology of Dementia Praecox: An Attempt*, CW 3.
23. "The content of the psychoses," CW 3, §339.
24. Freud archives, Library of Congress. See Ernst Falzeder, "The story of an ambivalent relationship: Sigmund Freud and Eugen Bleuler," *Journal of Analytical Psychology* 52 (2007), pp. 343–68.
25. *JA*.

to ground psychology in the in-depth clinical investigation of individual lives.

With the lead of Bleuler and Jung, the Burghölzli became the center of the psychoanalytic movement. In 1908, the *Jahrbuch für psychoanalytische und psychopathologische Forschungen* (Yearbook for Psychoanalytic and Psychopathological Researches) was established, with Bleuler and Freud editors in chief and Jung as managing editor. Due to their advocacy, psychoanalysis gained a hearing in the German psychiatric world. In 1909, Jung received an honorary degree from Clark University for his association researches. The following year, an international psychoanalytic association was formed with Jung as the president. During the period of his collaboration with Freud, he was a principal architect of the psychoanalytic movement. For Jung, this was a period of intense institutional and political activity. The movement was riven by dissent and acrimonious disagreements.

The Intoxication of Mythology

In 1908, Jung bought some land by the shore of Lake Zürich in Küsnacht and had a house built, where he was to live for the rest of his life. In 1909, he resigned from the Burghölzli, to devote himself to his growing practice and his research interests. His retirement from the Burghölzli coincided with a shift in his research interests to the study of mythology, folklore, and religion, and he assembled a vast private library of scholarly works. These researches culminated in *Transformations and Symbols of the Libido*, published in two installments in 1911 and 1912. This work can be seen to mark a return to Jung's intellectual roots and to his cultural and religious preoccupations. He found the mythological work exciting and intoxicating. In 1925 he recalled, "it seemed to me I was living in an insane asylum of my own making. I went about with all these fantastic figures: centaurs, nymphs, satyrs, gods and goddesses, as though they were patients and I was analyzing them. I read a Greek or a Negro myth as if a lunatic were telling me his anamnesis."[26] The end of the nineteenth century had seen an explosion of scholarship in the newly founded disciplines of comparative religion and ethnopsychology. Primary texts were collected and translated for the first time and subjected to historical scholarship in collections such as Max Müller's *Sacred Books of the East.*[27] For many, these works represented an important relativization of the Christian worldview.

In *Transformations and Symbols of the Libido,* Jung differentiated two kinds of thinking. Taking his cue from William James, among others, Jung contrasted directed thinking and fantasy thinking. The former was verbal and logical, while the latter was passive, associative, and imagistic. The former was exemplified by science and the latter by mythology. Jung claimed that the ancients lacked a capacity for directed thinking, which was a modern acquisition. Fantasy thinking took place when directed thinking ceased. *Transformations and Symbols of the Libido* was an extended study of fantasy thinking, and of the continued presence of mythological themes in the dreams and fantasies of contemporary individuals. Jung reiterated the anthropological equation of the prehistoric, the primitive, and the child. He held that the elucidation of current-day fantasy thinking in adults would concurrently shed light on the thought of children, savages, and prehistoric peoples.[28] In this work, Jung synthesized nineteenth-century theories of memory, heredity, and the unconscious and posited a phylogenetic layer to the unconscious that was still present in everyone, consisting of mythological images. For Jung, myths were symbols of the libido and they depicted its typical movements. He used the comparative method of anthropology to draw together a vast panoply of myths, and then subjected them to analytic interpretation. He later termed his use of the comparative method "amplification." He claimed that there had to be typical myths, which corresponded to the ethnopsychological development

26. *Introduction to Jungian Psychology,* p. 24.
27. Jung possessed a complete set of this.
28. Jung, *The Psychology of the Unconscious,* CW B, §36. In his 1952 revision of this text, Jung qualified this (*Symbols of Transformation,* CW 5, §29).

of complexes. Following Jacob Burckhardt, Jung termed such typical myths "primordial images" (*Urbilder*). One particular myth was given a central role: that of the hero. For Jung, this represented the life of the individual, attempting to become independent and to free himself from the mother. He interpreted the incest motif as an attempt to return to the mother to be reborn. He was later to herald this work as marking the discovery of the collective unconscious, though the term itself came at a later date.[29]

In a series of articles from 1912, Jung's friend and colleague Alphonse Maeder argued that dreams had a function other than that of wish fulfillment, which was a balancing or compensatory function. Dreams were attempts to solve the individual's moral conflicts. As such, they did not merely point to the past, but also prepared the way for the future. Maeder was developing Flournoy's views of the subconscious creative imagination. Jung was working along similar lines, and adopted Maeder's positions. For Jung and Maeder, this alteration of the conception of the dream brought with it an alteration of all other phenomena associated with the unconscious.

In his preface to the 1952 revision of *Transformations and Symbols of the Libido*, Jung wrote that the work was written in 1911, when he was thirty-six: "The time is a critical one, for it marks the beginning of the second half of life, when a metanoia, a mental transformation, not infrequently occurs."[30] He added that he was conscious of the loss of his collaboration with Freud, and was indebted to the support of his wife. After completing the work, he realized the significance of what it meant to live without a myth. One without a myth "is like one uprooted, having no true link either with the past, or with the ancestral life which continues within him, or yet with contemporary human society."[31] As he further describes it:

29. "Address on the founding of the C. G. Jung Institute, Zürich, 24 April, 1948," CW *18*, §1131.
30. CW 5, p. xxvi.
31. Ibid., p. xxix.

> I was driven to ask myself in all seriousness: "what is the myth you are living?" I found no answer to this question, and had to admit that I was not living with a myth, or even in a myth, but rather in an uncertain cloud of theoretical possibilities which I was beginning to regard with increasing distrust . . . So in the most natural way, I took it upon myself to get to know "my" myth, and I regarded this as the task of tasks—for—so I told myself—how could I, when treating my patients, make due allowance for the personal factor, for my personal equation, which is yet so necessary for a knowledge of the other person, if I was unconscious of it?[32]

The study of myth had revealed to Jung his mythlessness. He then undertook to get to know his myth, his "personal equation."[33] Thus we see that the self-experimentation which Jung undertook was in part a direct response to theoretical questions raised by his research, which had culminated in *Transformations and Symbols of the Libido*.

"My Most Difficult Experiment"

In 1912, Jung had some significant dreams that he did not understand. He gave particular importance to two of these, which he felt showed the limitations of Freud's conceptions of dreams. The first follows:

> I was in a southern town, on a rising street with narrow half landings. It was twelve o'clock midday—bright sunshine. An old Austrian customs guard or someone similar passes by me, lost in thought. Someone says, "that is one who cannot die. He died already 30–40 years ago, but has not yet managed to decompose." I was very surprised. Here a striking figure came, a knight of powerful build, clad in yellowish armor. He looks solid and

32. Ibid.
33. Cf. *Introduction to Jungian Psychology*, p. 25.

> inscrutable and nothing impresses him. On his back he carries a red Maltese cross. He has continued to exist from the 12th century and daily between 12 and 1 o'clock midday he takes the same route. No one marvels at these two apparitions, but I was extremely surprised.
>
> I hold back my interpretive skills. As regards the old Austrian, Freud occurred to me; as regards the knight, I myself.
>
> Inside, a voice calls, "It is all empty and disgusting." I must bear it.[34]

Jung found this dream oppressive and bewildering, and Freud was unable to interpret it.[35] Around half a year later Jung had another dream:

> I dreamt at that time (it was shortly after Christmas 1912), that I was sitting with my children in a marvelous and richly furnished castle apartment—an open columned hall—we were sitting at a round table, whose top was a marvelous dark green stone. Suddenly a gull or a dove flew in and sprang lightly onto the table. I admonished the children to be quiet, so that they would not scare away the beautiful white bird. Suddenly this bird turned into a child of eight years, a small blond girl, and ran around playing with my children in the marvelous columned colonnades. Then the child suddenly turned into the gull or dove. She said the following to me: "*Only in the first hour of the night can I become human, while the male dove is busy with the twelve dead.*" With these words the bird flew away and I awoke.[36]

34. *Black Book 2*, pp. 25–26.
35. In 1925, he gave the following interpretation to this dream: "The meaning of the dream lies in the principle of the ancestral figure: not the Austrian officer—obviously he stood for the Freudian theory—but the other, the Crusader, is an archetypal figure, a Christian symbol living from the twelfth century, a symbol that does not really live today, but on the other hand is not wholly dead either. It comes out of the times of Meister Eckhart, the time of the culture of the Knights, when many ideas blossomed, only to be killed again, but they are coming again to life now. However, when I had this dream, I did not know this interpretation" (*Introduction to Jungian Psychology*, p. 42).
36. *Black Book 2*, pp. 17–18.

In *Black Book* 2, Jung noted that it was this dream that made him decide to embark on a relationship with a woman he had met three years earlier (Toni Wolff).[37] In 1925, he remarked that this dream "was the beginning of a conviction that the unconscious did not consist of inert material only, but that there was something living down there."[38] He added that he thought of the story of the *Tabula smaragdina* (emerald tablet), the twelve apostles, the signs of the Zodiac, and so on, but that he "could make nothing out of the dream except that there was a tremendous animation of the unconscious. I knew no technique of getting at the bottom of this activity; all I could do was just wait, keep on living, and watch the fantasies."[39]These dreams led him to analyze his childhood memories, but this did not resolve anything. He realized that he needed to recover the emotional tone of childhood. He recalled that as a child, he used to like to build houses and other structures, and he took this up again.

While he was engaged in this self-analytic activity, he continued to develop his theoretical work. At the Munich Psycho-Analytical Congress in September 1913, he spoke on psychological types. He argued that there were two basic movements of the libido: extraversion, in which the subject's interest was oriented toward the outer world, and introversion, in which the subject's interest was directed inward. Following from this, he posited two types of people, characterized by a predominance of one of these tendencies. The psychol-

37. Ibid., p. 17.
38. *Introduction to Jungian Psychology*, p. 42.
39. Ibid., pp. 40–41. E. A. Bennet noted Jung's comments on this dream: "At first he thought the 'twelve dead men' referred to the twelve days before Christmas for that is the dark time of the year, when traditionally witches are about. To say 'before Christmas' is to say 'before the sun lives again,' for Christmas day is at the turning point of the year when the sun's birth was celebrated in the Mithraic religion . . . Only much later did he relate the dream to Hermes and the twelve doves" (*Meetings with Jung: Conversations recorded by E. A. Bennet during the Years 1946–1961* [London: Anchor Press, 1982; Zürich, Daimon Verlag, 1985], p. 93). In 1951 in "The psychological aspects of the Kore," Jung presented some material from *Liber Novus* (describing them all as part of a dream series) in an anonymous form ("case Z."), tracing the transformations of the anima. He noted that this dream "shows the anima as elflike, i.e., only partially human. She can just as well be a bird, which means that she may belong wholly to nature and can vanish (i.e., become unconscious) from the human sphere (i.e., consciousness)" (CW 9, 1, §371). See also *Memories*, pp. 195–96.

ogies of Freud and Adler were examples of the fact that psychologies often took what was true of their type as generally valid. Hence what was required was a psychology that did justice to both of these types.[40]

The following month, on a train journey to Schaffhausen, Jung experienced a waking vision of Europe being devastated by a catastrophic flood, which was repeated two weeks later, on the same journey.[41] Commenting on this experience in 1925, he remarked: "I could be taken as Switzerland fenced in by mountains and the submergence of the world could be the debris of my former relationships." This led him to the following diagnosis of his condition: "I thought to myself, 'If this means anything, it means that I am hopelessly off.' "[42] After this experience, Jung feared that he would go mad.[43] He recalled that he first thought that the images of the vision indicated a revolution, but as he could not imagine this, he concluded that he was "menaced with a psychosis."[44] After this, he had a similar vision:

> In the following winter I was standing at the window one night and looked North. I saw a blood-red glow, like the flicker of the sea seen from afar, stretched from East to West across the northern horizon. And at that time someone asked me what I thought about world events in the near future. I said that I had no thoughts, but saw blood, rivers of blood.[45]

In the years directly preceding the outbreak of war, apocalyptic imagery was widespread in European arts and literature. For example, in 1912, Wassily Kandinsky wrote of a coming univer-

---

40. "On the question of psychological types," CW 6.
41. See below, p. 123.
42. *Introduction to Jungian Psychology*, pp. 47–48.
43. Barbara Hannah recalls that "Jung used to say in later years that his tormenting doubts as to his own sanity should have been allayed by the amount of success he was having at the same time in the outer world, especially in America" (C. G. *Jung: His Life and Work. A Biographical Memoir* [New York: Perigree, 1976], p. 109).
44. *Memories*, p. 200.
45. *Draft*, p. 8.

sal catastrophe. From 1912 to 1914, Ludwig Meidner painted a series of works known as the apocalyptic landscapes, with scenes of destroyed cities, corpses, and turmoil.[46] Prophecy was in the air. In 1899, the famous American medium Leonora Piper predicted that in the coming century there would be a terrible war in different parts of the world that would cleanse the world and reveal the truths of spiritualism. In 1918, Arthur Conan Doyle, the spiritualist and author of the Sherlock Holmes stories, viewed this as having been prophetic.[47]

In Jung's account of the fantasy on the train in *Liber Novus*, the inner voice said that what the fantasy depicted would become completely real. Initially, he interpreted this subjectively and prospectively, that is, as depicting the imminent destruction of his world. His reaction to this experience was to undertake a psychological investigation of himself. In this epoch, self-experimentation was used in medicine and psychology. Introspection had been one of the main tools of psychological research.

Jung came to realize that *Transformations and Symbols of the Libido* "could be taken as myself and that an analysis of it leads inevitably into an analysis of my own unconscious processes."[48] He had projected his material onto that of Miss Frank Miller, whom he had never met. Up to this point, Jung had been an active thinker and had been averse to fantasy: "as a form of thinking I held it to be altogether impure, a sort of incestuous intercourse, thoroughly immoral from an intellectual viewpoint."[49] He now turned to analyze his fantasies, carefully noting everything, and had to overcome considerable resistance in doing this: "Permitting fantasy in myself had the same effect as would be produced on a man if he came into

46. Gerda Breuer and Ines *Wagemann, Ludwig Meidner: Zeichner, Maler, Literat 1884–1966* (Stuttgart: Verlag Gerd Hatje, 1991), vol. 2, pp. 124–49. See Jay Winter, *Sites of Memory, Sites of Mourning: The Great War in European Cultural History* (Cambridge: Cambridge University Press, 1995), pp. 145–77.
47. Arthur Conan Doyle, *The New Revelation and the Vital Message* (London: Psychic Press, 1918), p. 9.
48. *Introduction to Jungian Psychology*, p. 28.
49. Ibid.

his workshop and found all the tools flying about doing things independently of his will."[50] In studying his fantasies, Jung realized that he was studying the myth-creating function of the mind.[51]

Jung picked up the brown notebook, which he had set aside in 1902, and began writing in it.[52] He noted his inner states in metaphors, such as being in a desert with an unbearably hot sun (that is, consciousness). In the 1925 seminar, he recalled that it occurred to him that he could write down his reflections in a sequence. He was "writing autobiographical material, but not as an autobiography."[53] From the time of the Platonic dialogues onward, the dialogical form has been a prominent genre in Western philosophy. In 387 CE, St. Augustine wrote his *Soliloquies,* which presented an extended dialogue between himself and "Reason," who instructs him. They commenced with the following lines:

> When I had been pondering many different things to myself for a long time, and had for many days been seeking my own self and what my own good was, and what evil was to be avoided, there suddenly spoke to me—what was it? I myself or someone else, inside or outside me? (this is the very thing I would love to know but don't).[54]

While Jung was writing in *Black Book 2*,

> I said to myself, "What is this I am doing, it certainly is not science, what is it?" Then a voice said to me, "That is art." This made the strangest sort of impression upon me, because it was not in any sense my impression that what I was writing was art.

50. Ibid.
51. *MP*, p. 23.
52. The subsequent notebooks are black, hence Jung referred to them as the *Black Books*.
53. *Introduction to Jungian Psychology*, p. 48.
54. St. Augustine, *Soliloquies and Immortality of the Soul*, ed. and tr. Gerard Watson (Warminster: Aris & Phillips, 1990), p. 23. Watson notes that Augustine "had been through a period of intense strain, close to a nervous breakdown, and the Soliloquies are a form of therapy, an effort to cure himself by talking, or rather, writing" (p. v).

> Then I came to this, "Perhaps my unconscious is forming a personality that is not I, but which is insisting on coming through to expression." I don't know why exactly, but I knew to a certainty that the voice that had said my writing was art had come from a woman . . . Well I said very emphatically to this voice that what I was doing was not art, and I felt a great resistance grow up within me. No voice came through, however, and I kept on writing. This time I caught her and said, "No it is not," and I felt as though an argument would ensue.[55]

He thought that this voice was "the soul in the primitive sense," which he called the anima (the Latin word for soul).[56] He stated that "In putting down all this material for analysis, I was in effect writing letters to my anima, that is part of myself with a different viewpoint from my own. I got remarks of a new character—I was in analysis with a ghost and a woman."[57] In retrospect, he recalled that this was the voice of a Dutch patient whom he knew from 1912 to 1918, who had persuaded a psychiatrist colleague that he was a misunderstood artist. The woman had thought that the unconscious was art, but Jung had maintained that it was nature.[58] I have previously argued that the woman in question—the only Dutch woman in Jung's circle at this time—was Maria Moltzer, and that the psychiatrist in question was Jung's friend and colleague Franz Riklin, who increasingly forsook analysis for painting. In 1913, he became a student of Augusto Giacometti's, the uncle of Alberto Giacometti, and an important early abstract painter in his own right.[59]

55. Ibid., p. 42. In Jung's account here, it seems that this dialogue took place in the autumn of 1913, though this is not certain, because the dialogue itself does not occur in the *Black Books*, and no other manuscript has yet come to light. If this dating is followed, and in the absence of other material, it would appear that the material the voice is referring to is the November entries in *Black Book 2*, and not the subsequent text of *Liber Novus* or the paintings.
56. Ibid., p. 44.
57. Ibid., p. 46.
58. *MP*, p. 171.
59. Riklin's painting generally followed the style of Augusto Giacometti: semi-figurative and fully abstract works, with soft floating colors. Private possession, Peter Riklin. There is one painting of Riklin's from 1915/6, *Verkündigung*, in the Kunsthaus in

The November entries in *Black Book 2* depict Jung's sense of his return to his soul. He recounted the dreams that led him to opt for his scientific career, and the recent dreams that had brought him back to his soul. As he recalled in 1925, this first period of writing came to an end in November: "Not knowing what would come next, I thought perhaps more introspection was needed . . . I devised such a boring method by fantasizing that I was digging a hole, and by accepting this fantasy as perfectly real."[60] The first such experiment took place on December 12, 1913.[61]

As indicated, Jung had had extensive experience studying mediums in trance states, during which they were encouraged to produce waking fantasies and visual hallucinations, and had conducted experiments with automatic writing. Practices of visualization had also been used in various religious traditions. For example, in the fifth of the spiritual exercises of St. Ignatius of Loyola, individuals are instructed on how to "see with the eyes of the imagination the length, breadth and depth of hell," and to experience this with full sensory immediacy.[62] Swedenborg also engaged in "spirit writing." In his spiritual diary, one entry reads:

> 26 JAN. 1748.—Spirits, if permitted, could possess those who speak with them so utterly, that they would be as though they were entirely in the world; and indeed, in a manner so manifest, that they could communicate their thoughts through their medium, and even by letters; for they have sometimes, and indeed often, directed my hand when writing, as though it were

---

Zürich, which was donated by Maria Moltzer in 1945. Giacometti recalled: "Riklin's psychological knowledge was extraordinarily interesting and new to me. He was a modern magician. I had the feeling that he could do magic" (*Von Stampa bis Florenz: Blätter der Erinnerung* [Zürich: Rascher, 1943], pp. 86–87).

60. *Introduction to Jungian Psychology*, p. 51.

61. The vision that ensued is found below in *Liber Primus*, chapter 5, "Descent into Hell in the Future," p. 147.

62. St. Ignatius of Loyola, "The spiritual exercises," in *Personal Writings*, tr. J. Munitiz and P. Endean (London: Penguin, 1996), p. 298. In 1939/40, Jung presented a psychological commentary on the spiritual exercises of St. Ignatius of Loyola at the ETH (*Philemon Series*, forthcoming).

quite their own; so that they thought it was not I, but themselves writing.[63]

From 1909 onward in Vienna, the psychoanalyst Herbert Silberer conducted experiments on himself in hypnagogic states. Silberer attempted to allow images to appear. These images, he maintained, presented symbolic depictions of his previous train of thought. Silberer corresponded with Jung and sent him offprints of his articles.[64]

In 1912, Ludwig Staudenmaier (1865–1933), a professor of experimental chemistry, published a work entitled *Magic as an Experimental Science*. Staudenmaier had embarked on self-experimentations in 1901, commencing with automatic writing. A series of characters appeared, and he found that he no longer needed to write to conduct dialogues with them.[65] He also induced acoustic and visual hallucinations. The aim of his enterprise was to use his self-experimentation to provide a scientific explanation of magic. He argued that the key to understanding magic lay in the concepts of hallucinations and the "under consciousness" (*Unterbewußtsein*), and gave particular importance to the role of personifications.[66] Thus we see that Jung's procedure closely resembled a number of historical and contemporary practices with which he was familiar.

From December 1913 onward, he carried on in the same procedure: deliberately evoking a fantasy in a waking state, and then entering into it as into a drama. These fantasies may be understood as a type of dramatized thinking in pictorial form. In reading his fantasies, the impact of Jung's mythological studies is clear. Some of the figures and conceptions derive directly from his readings, and the form and style bear witness to his fascination with the world

63. This passage was reproduced by William White in his *Swedenborg: His Life and Writings*, vol. 1 (London: Bath, 1867), pp. 293–94. In Jung's copy of this work, he marked the second half of this passage with a line in the margin.

64. See Silberer, "Bericht über eine Methode, gewisse symbolische Halluzinations-Erscheinungen hervorzurufen und zu beobachten," *Jahrbuch für psychoanalytische und psychopathologische Forschungen* 2 (1909), pp. 513–25.

65. Staudenmaier, *Die Magie als experimentelle Naturwissenschaft* (Leipzig: Akademische Verlagsgesellschaft, 1912), p. 19.

66. Jung had a copy of Staudenmaier's book, and marked some passages in it.

of myth and epic. In the *Black Books*, Jung wrote down his fantasies in dated entries, together with reflections on his state of mind and his difficulties in comprehending the fantasies. The *Black Books* are not diaries of events, and very few dreams are noted in them. Rather, they are the records of an experiment. In December 1913, he referred to the first of the black books as the "book of my most difficult experiment."[67]

In retrospect, he recalled that his scientific question was to see what took place when he switched off consciousness. The example of dreams indicated the existence of background activity, and he wanted to give this a possibility of emerging, just as one does when taking mescalin.[68]

In an entry in his dream book on April 17, 1917, Jung noted: "since then, frequent exercises in the emptying of consciousness."[69] His procedure was clearly intentional—while its aim was to allow psychic contents to appear spontaneously. He recalled that beneath the threshold of consciousness, everything was animated. At times, it was as if he heard something. At other times, he realized that he was whispering to himself.[70]

From November 1913 to the following July, he remained uncertain of the meaning and significance of his undertaking, and concerning the meaning of his fantasies, which continued to develop. During this time, Philemon, who would prove to be an important figure in subsequent fantasies, appeared in a dream. Jung recounted:

67. *Black Book* 2, p. 58.
68. *MP*, p. 381.
69. "Dreams," *JFA*, p. 9.
70. *MP*, p. 145. To Margaret Ostrowski-Sachs, Jung said "The technique of active imagination can prove very important in difficult situations—where there is a visitation, say. It only makes sense when one has the feeling of being up against a blank wall. I experienced this when I separated from Freud. I did not know what I thought. I only felt, 'It is not so.' Then I conceived of 'symbolic thinking' and after two years of active imagination so many ideas rushed in on me that I could hardly defend myself. The same thoughts recurred. I appealed to my hands and began to carve wood—and then my way became clear" (From *Conversations with C. G. Jung* [Zürich: Juris Druck Verlag, 1971], p. 18).

> There was a blue sky, like the sea, covered not by clouds but by flat brown clods of earth. It looked as if the clods were breaking apart and the blue water of the sea were becoming visible between them. But the water was the blue sky. Suddenly there appeared from the right a winged being sailing across the sky. I saw that it was an old man with the horns of a bull. He held a bunch of four keys, one of which he clutched as if he were about to open a lock. He had the wings of the kingfisher with its characteristic colors. Since I did not understand this dream image, I painted it in order to impress it upon my memory.[71]

While he was painting this image, he found a dead kingfisher (which is very rarely found in the vicinity of Zürich) in his garden by the lake shore.[72]

The date of this dream is not clear. The figure of Philemon first appears in the *Black Books* on January 27, 1914, but without kingfisher wings. To Jung, Philemon represented superior insight, and was like a guru to him. He would converse with him in the garden. He recalled that Philemon evolved out of the figure of Elijah, who had previously appeared in his fantasies:

> Philemon was a pagan and brought with him an Egypto-Hellenic atmosphere with a Gnostic coloration . . . It was he who taught me psychic objectivity, the reality of the psyche. Through the conversations with Philemon, the distinction was clarified between myself and the object of my thought . . . Psychologically, Philemon represented superior insight.[73]

On April 20, Jung resigned as president of the International Psychoanalytical Association. On April 30, he resigned as a lecturer in the medical faculty of the University of Zürich. He recalled that he felt that he was in an exposed position at the university and

71. *Memories*, p. 207.
72. Ibid.
73. Ibid., pp. 207–8.

felt that he had to find a new orientation, as it would otherwise be unfair to teach students.[74] In June and July, he had a thrice-repeated dream of being in a foreign land and having to return home quickly by ship, followed by the descent of an icy cold.[75]

On July 10, the Zürich Psychoanalytical Society voted by 15 to 1 to leave the International Psychoanalytic Association. In the minutes, the reason given for the secession was that Freud had established an orthodoxy that impeded free and independent research.[76] The group was renamed the Association for Analytical Psychology. Jung was actively involved in this association, which met fortnightly. He also maintained a busy therapeutic practice. Between 1913 and 1914, he had between one and nine consultations per day, five days a week, with an average of between five and seven.[77]

The minutes of the Association for Analytical Psychology offer no indications of the process that Jung was going through. He does not refer to his fantasies, and continues to discuss theoretical issues in psychology. The same holds true in his surviving correspondences during this period.[78] Each year, he continued his military service duties.[79] Thus he maintained his professional activities and familial responsibilities during the day, and dedicated his evenings to his self-explorations.[80] Indications are that this partitioning of activities continued during the next few years. Jung recalled that during this period his family and profession "always remained a joyful reality and a guarantee that I was normal and really existed."[81]

The question of the different ways of interpreting such fantasies was the subject of a talk that he presented on July 24 before the Psycho-Medical Society in London, "On psychological understand-

74. Ibid., p. 219.
75. See below, p. 124.
76. *MZS*.
77. Jung's appointment books, *JFA*.
78. This is based on a comprehensive study of Jung's correspondences in the ETH up to 1930 and in other archives and collections.
79. These were: 1913, 16 days; 1914, 14 days; 1915, 67 days; 1916, 34 days; 1917, 117 days (Jung's military service books, *JFA*).
80. See below, p. 151.
81. *Memories*, p. 214.

ing." Here, he contrasted Freud's analytic-reductive method, based on causality, with the constructive method of the Zürich school. The shortcoming of the former was that through tracing things back to antecedent elements, it dealt with only half of the picture, and failed to grasp the living meaning of phenomena. Someone who attempted to understand Goethe's *Faust* in such a manner would be like someone who tried to understand a Gothic cathedral under its mineralogical aspect.[82] The living meaning "only lives when we experience it in and through ourselves."[83] Inasmuch as life was essentially new, it could not be understood merely retrospectively. Hence the constructive standpoint asked, "how, out of this present psyche, a bridge can be built into its own future."[84] This paper implicitly presents Jung's rationale for not embarking on a causal and retrospective analysis of his fantasies, and serves as a caution to others who may be tempted to do so. Presented as a critique and reformulation of psychoanalysis, Jung's new mode of interpretation links back to the symbolic method of Swedenborg's spiritual hermeneutics.

On July 28, Jung gave a talk on "The importance of the unconscious in psychopathology" at a meeting of the British Medical Association in Aberdeen.[85] He argued that in cases of neurosis and psychosis, the unconscious attempted to compensate the one-sided conscious attitude. The unbalanced individual defends himself against this, and the opposites become more polarized. The corrective impulses that present themselves in the language of the unconscious should be the beginning of a healing process, but the form in which they break through makes them unacceptable to consciousness.

A month earlier, on June 28, Archduke Franz Ferdinand, the heir to the Austro-Hungarian empire, was assassinated by Gavrilo Princip, a nineteen-year-old Serb student. On August 1, war broke out. In 1925 Jung recalled, "I had the feeling that I was an over-

82. Jung, "On psychological understanding," *CW* 3, §396.
83. Ibid., §398.
84. Ibid., §399.
85. *CW* 3.

compensated psychosis, and from this feeling I was not released till August 1st 1914."[86] Years later, he said to Mircea Eliade:

> As a psychiatrist I became worried, wondering if I was not on the way to "doing a schizophrenia," as we said in the language of those days . . . I was just preparing a lecture on schizophrenia to be delivered at a congress in Aberdeen, and I kept saying to myself: "I'll be speaking of myself! Very likely I'll go mad after reading out this paper." The congress was to take place in July 1914—exactly the same period when I saw myself in my three dreams voyaging on the Southern seas. On July 31st, immediately after my lecture, I learned from the newspapers that war had broken out. Finally I understood. And when I disembarked in Holland on the next day, nobody was happier than I. Now I was sure that no schizophrenia was threatening me. I understood that my dreams and my visions came to me from the subsoil of the collective unconscious. What remained for me to do now was to deepen and validate this discovery. And this is what I have been trying to do for forty years.[87]

At this moment, Jung considered that his fantasy had depicted not what would happen to *him*, but to Europe. In other words, that it was a precognition of a collective event, what he would later call a "big" dream.[88] After this realization, he attempted to see whether and to what extent this was true of the other fantasies that he experienced, and to understand the meaning of this correspondence between private fantasies and public events. This effort makes up much of the subject matter of *Liber Novus*. In *Scrutinies*, he wrote that the outbreak of the war had enabled him to understand much of what he had previously experienced, and had given him the courage

86. *Introduction to Jungian Psychology*, p. 48.
87. *Combat* interview (1952), C. G. *Jung Speaking: Interviews and Encounters*, eds. William McGuire and R.F.C. Hull (Bollingen Series, Princeton: Princeton University Press, 1977), pp. 233–34. See below, p. 125.
88. See below, p. 125.

to write the earlier part of *Liber Novus*.[89] Thus he took the outbreak of the war as showing him that his *fear* of going mad was misplaced. It is no exaggeration to say that had war not been declared, *Liber Novus* would in all likelihood not have been compiled. In 1955/56, while discussing active imagination, Jung commented that "the reason why the involvement looks very much like a psychosis is that the patient is integrating the same fantasy-material to which the insane person falls victim because he cannot integrate it but is swallowed up by it."[90]

It is important to note that there are around twelve separate fantasies that Jung may have regarded as precognitive:

1–2. OCTOBER, 1913
Repeated vision of flood and death of thousands, and the voice that said that this will become real.
3. AUTUMN 1913
Vision of the sea of blood covering the northern lands.
4–5. DECEMBER 12, 15, 1913
Image of a dead hero and the slaying of Siegfried in a dream.
6. DECEMBER 25, 1913
Image of the foot of a giant stepping on a city, and images of murder and bloody cruelty.
7. JANUARY 2, 1914
Image of a sea of blood and a procession of dead multitudes.
8. JANUARY 22, 1914
His soul comes up from the depths and asks him if he will accept war and destruction. She shows him images of destruction, military weapons, human remains, sunken ships, destroyed states, etc.
9. MAY 21, 1914
A voice says that the sacrificed fall left and right.

---

89. See below, p. 474.
90. *Mysterium Coniunctionis*, CW 14, §756. On the myth of Jung's madness, first promoted by Freudians as a means of invalidating his work, see my *Jung Stripped Bare by His Biographers, Even*.

10–12. JUNE–JULY 1914
Thrice-repeated dream of being in a foreign land and having to return quickly by ship, and the descent of the icy cold.[91]

Liber Novus

Jung now commenced writing the draft of *Liber Novus.* He faithfully transcribed most of the fantasies from the *Black Books,* and to each of these added a section explaining the significance of each episode, combined with a lyrical elaboration. Word-by-word comparison indicates that the fantasies were faithfully reproduced, with only minor editing and division into chapters. Thus the sequence of the fantasies in *Liber Novus* nearly always exactly corresponds to the *Black Books.* When it is indicated that a particular fantasy happened "on the next night," etc., this is always accurate, and not a stylistic device. The language and content of the material were not altered. Jung maintained a "fidelity to the event," and what he was writing was not to be mistaken for a fiction. The draft begins with the address to "My friends," and this phrase occurs frequently. The main difference between the *Black Books* and *Liber Novus* is that the former were written for Jung's personal use, and can be considered the records of an experiment, while the latter is addressed to a public and presented in a form to be read by others.

In November 1914, Jung closely studied Nietzsche's *Thus Spoke Zarathustra,* which he had first read in his youth. He later recalled, "then suddenly the spirit seized me and carried me to a desert country in which I read Zarathustra."[92] It strongly shaped the structure

91. See below, pp. 123–24, 147, 161, 196, 264, 375, 468.
92. James Jarrett, ed., *Nietzsche's Zarathustra: Notes of the Seminar Given in 1934–9* (Bollingen Series, Princeton: Princeton University Press, 1988), p. 381. On Jung's reading of Nietzsche, see Paul Bishop, *The Dionysian Self:* C. G. *Jung's Reception of Nietzsche* (Berlin: Walter de Gruyter); Martin Liebscher, "Die 'unheimliche Ähnlichkeit.' Nietzsches Hermeneutik der Macht und analytische Interpretation bei Carl Gustav Jung," in *Ecce Opus. Nietzsche-Revisionen im 20. Jahrhundert,* eds. Rüdiger Görner and Duncan Large (London/Göttingen: Vandenhoeck & Ruprecht, 2003), pp. 37–50; "Jungs Abkehr von Freud im Lichte seiner Nietzsche-Rezeption," in *Zeitenwende-Wertewende,* ed. Renate Reschke (Berlin 2001), pp. 255–60; and Graham Parkes, "Nietzsche and Jung:

and style of *Liber Novus*. Like Nietzsche in *Zarathustra*, Jung divided the material into a series of books comprised of short chapters. But whereas Zarathustra proclaimed the death of God, *Liber Novus* depicts the rebirth of God in the soul. There are also indications that he read Dante's *Commedia* at this time, which also informs the structure of the work.[93] *Liber Novus* depicts Jung's descent into Hell. But whereas Dante could utilize an established cosmology, *Liber Novus* is an attempt to shape an individual cosmology. The role of Philemon in Jung's work has analogies to that of Zarathustra in Nietzsche's work and Virgil in Dante's.

In the *Draft*, about 50 percent of the material is drawn directly from the *Black Books*. There are about thirty-five new sections of commentary. In these sections, he attempted to derive general psychological principles from the fantasies, and to understand to what extent the events portrayed in the fantasies presented, in a symbolic form, developments that were to occur in the world. In 1913, Jung had introduced a distinction between interpretation on the objective level in which dream objects were treated as representations of real objects, and interpretation on the subjective level in which every element concerns the dreamers themselves.[94] As well as interpreting his fantasies on the subjective level, one could characterize his procedure here as an attempt to interpret his fantasies on the "collective" level. He does not try to interpret his fantasies reductively, but sees them as depicting the functioning of general psychological principles in him (such as the relation of introversion to extraversion, thinking and pleasure, etc.), and as depicting literal or symbolic events that are going to happen. Thus the second layer of the *Draft* represents the first major and extended attempt to

Ambivalent Appreciations," in *Nietzsche and Depth Psychology*, ed. Jacob Golomb, Weaver Santaniello, and Ronald Lehrer (Albany: SUNY Press, 1999), pp. 69, 213.

93. In *Black Book 2*, Jung cited certain cantos from "Purgatorio" on December 26, 1913 (p. 104). See below, note 213, p. 198.

94. In 1913 Maeder had referred to Jung's "excellent expression" of the "objective level" and the "subjective level." ("Über das Traumproblem," *Jahrbuch für psychoanalytische und psychopathologische Forschungen* 5, 1913, pp. 657–58). Jung discussed this in the Zürich Psychoanalytical Society on 30 January 1914, MZS.

develop and apply his new constructive method. The second layer is itself a hermeneutic experiment. In a critical sense, *Liber Novus* does not require supplemental interpretation, for it contains its own interpretation.

In writing the *Draft*, Jung did not add scholarly references, though unreferenced citations and allusions to works of philosophy, religion, and literature abound. He had self-consciously chosen to leave scholarship to one side. Yet the fantasies and the reflections on them in *Liber Novus* are those of a scholar and, indeed, much of the self-experimentation and the composition of *Liber Novus* took place in his library. It is quite possible that he might have added references if he had decided to publish the work.

After completing the handwritten *Draft*, Jung had it typed, and edited it. On one manuscript, he made alterations by hand (I refer to this manuscript as the *Corrected Draft*). Judging from the annotations, it appears that he gave it to someone (the handwriting is not that of Emma Jung, Toni Wolff, or Maria Moltzer) to read, who then commented on Jung's editing, indicating that some sections which he had intended to cut should be retained.[95] The first section of the work—untitled, but effectively *Liber Primus*—was composed on parchment. Jung then commissioned a large folio volume of over 600 pages, bound in red leather, from the bookbinders, Emil Stierli. The spine bears the title, *Liber Novus.* He then inserted the parchment pages into the folio volume, which continues with *Liber Secundus.* The work is organized like a medieval illuminated manuscript, with calligraphic writing, headed by a table of abbreviations. Jung titled the first book "The Way of What Is to Come," and placed beneath this some citations from the book of Isaiah and from the gospel according to John. Thus it was presented as a prophetic work.

In the *Draft*, Jung had divided the material into chapters. In the course of the transcription into the red leather folio, he altered some of the titles to the chapters, added others, and edited the material

95. For example, by page 39 of the *Corrected Draft*, "Awesome! Why cut?" is written in the margin. Jung evidently took this advice, and retained the original passages. See below, p. 151, second paragraph.

once again. The cuts and alterations were predominantly to the second layer of interpretation and elaboration, and not to the fantasy material itself, and mainly consisted in shortening the text. It is this second layer that Jung continually reworked. In the transcription of the text in this edition, this second layer has been indicated, so that the chronology and composition are visible. As Jung's comments in the second layer sometimes implicitly refer forward to fantasies that are found later in the text, it is also helpful to read the fantasies straight through in chronological sequence, followed by a continuous reading of the second layer.

Jung then illustrated the text with some paintings, historiated initials, ornamental borders, and margins. Initially, the paintings refer directly to the text. At a later point, the paintings become more symbolic. They are active imaginations in their own right. The combination of text and image recalls the illuminated works of William Blake, whose work Jung had some familiarity with.[96]

A preparatory draft of one of the images in *Liber Novus* has survived, which indicates that they were carefully composed, starting from pencil sketches that were then elaborated.[97] The composition of the other images likely followed a similar procedure. From the paintings of Jung's which have survived, it is striking that they make an abrupt leap from the representational landscapes of 1902/3 to the abstract and semifigurative from 1915 onward.

Art and the Zürich School

Jung's library today contains few books on modern art, though some books were probably dispersed over the years. He possessed a catalogue of the graphic works of Odilon Redon, as well as a study

96. In 1921, he cited from Blake's *The Marriage of Heaven and Hell* (CW 6, §422n, §460); in *Psychology and Alchemy*, he refers to two of Blake's paintings (CW 12, figs. 14 and 19). On November 11, 1948, he wrote to Piloo Nanavutty, "I find Blake a tantalizing study, since he has compiled a lot of half- or undigested knowledge in his fantasies. According to my idea, they are an artistic production rather than an authentic representation of unconscious processes" (*Letters* 2, pp. 513–14).

97. See below, Appendix A.

of him.[98] He likely encountered Redon's work when he was in Paris. Strong echoes of the symbolist movement appear in the paintings in *Liber Novus*.

In October of 1910, Jung went on a bicycle tour of northern Italy, together with his colleague Wolfgang Stockmayer.[99] In April 1914, he visited Ravenna, and the frescos and mosaics there made a deep impression on him. These works seemed to have had an impact on his paintings: the use of strong colors, mosaic-like forms, and two-dimensional figures without the use of perspective.

In 1913 when he was in New York, he likely attended the Armory Show, which was the first major international exhibition of modern art in America (the show ran to March 15, and Jung left for New York on March 4). He referred to Marcel Duchamp's painting *Nude Descending a Staircase* in his 1925 seminar, which had caused a furor there.[100] Here, he also referred to having studied the course of Picasso's paintings. Given the lack of evidence of extended study, Jung's knowledge of modern art probably derived more immediately from direct acquaintance.

During the First World War, there were contacts between the members of the Zürich school and artists. Both were part of avant-garde movements and intersecting social circles.[101] In 1913, Erika Schlegel came to Jung for analysis. She and her husband, Eugen Schlegel, had been friendly with Toni Wolff. Erika Schlegel was Sophie Taeuber's sister, and became the librarian of the Psychological Club. Members of the Psychological Club were invited to some of the Dada events. At the celebration of the opening of the Gallery Dada on March 29, 1917, Hugo Ball notes members of the Club in

98. Redon, *Oeuvre graphique complet* (Paris: Secrétariat, 1913); André Mellerio, *Odilon Redon: Peintre, Dessinateur et Graveur* (Paris: Henri Floury, 1923). There is also one book on modern art, which was harshly critical of it: Max Raphael, *Von Monet zu Picasso: Grundzüge einer Ästhetik und Entwicklung der Modernen Malerei* (Munich: Delphin Verlag, 1913).
99. See Jung to Freud, October 20, 1910, *The Freud/Jung Letters*, ed. William McGuire, tr. R. Mannheim and R. F. C. Hull (Princeton: Bollingen Series, Princeton University Press, 1974), p. 359.
100. *Introduction to Jungian Psychology*, p. 59.
101. See Rainer Zuch, *Die Surrealisten und C. G. Jung: Studien zur Rezeption der analytischen Psychologie im Surrealismus am Beispeil von Max Ernst, Victor Brauner und Hans Arp* (Weimar: VDG, 2004).

the audience.[102] The program that evening included abstract dances by Sophie Taeuber and poems by Hugo Ball, Hans Arp, and Tristan Tzara. Sophie Taeuber, who had studied with Laban, arranged a dance class for members of the Club together with Arp. A masked ball was also held and she designed the costumes.[103] In 1918, she presented a marionette play, *King Deer,* in Zürich. It was set in the woods by the Burghölzli. Freud Analytikus, opposed by Dr. Oedipus Complex, is transformed into a parrot by the Ur-Libido, parodically taking up themes from Jung's *Transformations and Symbols of the Libido* and his conflict with Freud.[104] However, relations between Jung's circle and some of the Dadaists became more strained. In May 1917, Emmy Hennings wrote to Hugo Ball that the "psycho-Club" had now gone away.[105] In 1918, Jung criticized the Dada movement in a Swiss review, which did not escape the attention of the Dadaists.[106] The critical element that separated Jung's pictorial work from that of the Dadaists was his overriding emphasis on meaning and signification.

Jung's self-explorations and creative experiments did not occur in a vacuum. During this period, there was great interest in art and painting within his circle. Alphonse Maeder wrote a monograph on Ferdinand Hodler[107] and had a friendly correspondence with him.[108] Around 1916, Maeder had a series of visions or waking fantasies, which he published pseudonymously. When he told Jung of these events, Jung replied, "What, you too?"[109] Hans Schmid also wrote and painted his fantasies in something akin to *Liber Novus.* Moltzer

102. *Flight Out of Time,* p. 102.

103. Greta Stroeh, "Biographie," in *Sophie Taeuber: 15 Décembre 1989–Mars 1990, Musée d'art moderne de la ville de Paris* (Paris: Paris-musées, 1989), p. 124; Aline Valangin interview, Jung biographical archive, Countway Library of Medicine, p. 29.

104. The puppets are in the Bellerive museum, Zürich. See Bruno Mikol, "Sur le théatre de marionnettes de Sophie Taeuber-Arp," in *Sophie Taeuber: 15 Décembre 1989–Mars 1990, Musée d'art moderne de la ville de Paris,* pp. 59–68.

105. Hugo Ball and Emmy Hennings, *Damals in Zürich: Briefe aus den Jahren 1915–1917* (Zürich: Die Arche, 1978), p. 132.

106. Jung, "On the unconscious," CW 10, §44; Pharmouse, *Dada Review* 391 (1919); Tristan Tzara, *Dada,* nos. 4–5 (1919).

107. *Ferdinand Holder: Eine Skizze seiner seelischen Entwicklung und Bedeutung für die schweizerisch-nationale Kultur* (Zürich: Rascher, 1916).

108. Maeder papers.

109. Maeder interview, Jung biographical archive, Countway Library of Medicine, p. 9.

was keen to increase the artistic activities of the Zürich school. She felt that more artists were needed in their circle and considered Riklin as a model.[110] J. B. Lang, who was analyzed by Riklin, began to paint symbolic paintings. Moltzer had a book that she called her Bible, in which she put pictures with writings. She recommended that her patient Fanny Bowditch Katz do the same thing.[111]

In 1919, Riklin exhibited some of his paintings as part of the "New Life" at the Kunsthaus in Zürich, described as a group of Swiss Expressionists, alongside Hans Arp, Sophie Taeuber, Francis Picabia, and Augusto Giacometti.[112] With his personal connections, Jung could easily have exhibited some of his works in such a setting, had he so liked. Thus his refusal to consider his works as art occurs in a context where there were quite real possibilities for him to have taken this route.

On some occasions, Jung discussed art with Erika Schlegel. She noted the following conversation:

> I wore my pearl medallion (the pearl embroidery that Sophie had made for me) at Jung's yesterday. He liked it very much, and it prompted him to talk animatedly about art—for almost an hour. He discussed Riklin, one of Augusto Giacometti's students, and observed that while his smaller works had a certain aesthetic value, his larger ones simply dissolved. Indeed, he vanished wholly in his art, rendering him utterly intangible.

110. Franz Riklin to Sophie Riklin, May 20, 1915, Riklin papers.

111. On August 17, 1916, Fanny Bowditch Katz, who was in analysis with her at this time, noted in her diary: "Of her [i.e., Moltzer] book—her Bible—pictures and each with writing—which I must also do." According to Katz, Moltzer regarded her paintings as "purely subjective, not works of art" (July 31, Countway Library of Medicine). On another occasion, Katz notes in her diary that Moltzer "spoke of Art, real art, being the expression of religion" (August 24, 1916). In 1916, Moltzer presented psychological interpretations of some of Riklin's paintings in a talk at the Psychological Club (in my *Cult Fictions: Jung and the Founding of Analytical Psychology* [London: Routledge, 1998], p. 102). On Lang, see Thomas Feitknecht, ed., *"Die dunkle und wilde Seite der Seele". Hermann Hesse. Briefwechsel mit seinem Psychoanalytiker Josef Lang, 1916–1944* (Frankfurt: Suhrkampf, 2006).

112. *"Das Neue Leben," Erst Ausstellung*, Kunsthaus Zürich. J. B. Lang noted an occasion at Riklin's house at which Jung and Augusto Giacometti were also present (Diary, December 3, 1916, p. 9, Lang papers, Swiss Literary Archives, Berne).

> His work was like a wall over which water rippled. He could therefore not analyze, as this required one to be pointed and sharp-edged, like a knife. He had fallen into art in a manner of speaking. But art and science were no more than the servants of the creative spirit, which is what must be served.
>
> As regards my own work, it was also a matter of making out whether it was really art. Fairy tales and pictures had a religious meaning at bottom. I, too, know that somehow and sometime it must reach people.[113]

For Jung, Franz Riklin appears to have been something like a doppelganger, whose fate he was keen to avoid. This statement also indicates Jung's relativization of the status of art and science to which he had come through his self-experimentation.

Thus, the making of *Liber Novus* was by no means a peculiar and idiosyncratic activity, nor the product of a psychosis. Rather, it indicates the close intersections between psychological and artistic experimentation with which many individuals were engaged at this time.

The Collective Experiment

In 1915, Jung held a lengthy correspondence with his colleague Hans Schmid on the question of the understanding of psychological types. This correspondence gives no direct signs of Jung's self-experimentation, and indicates that theories he developed during this period did not stem solely from his active imaginations, but also in part consisted of conventional psychological theorizing.[114] On March 5, 1915, Jung wrote to Smith Ely Jeliffe:

> I am still with the army in a little town where I have plenty of practical work and horseback riding . . . Until I had to join the

113. March 11, 1921, Notebooks, Schlegel papers.
114. *The Question of Psychological Types: The Correspondence of* C. G. *Jung and Hans Schmid-Guisan 1915–1916*, ed. John Beebe and Ernst Falzeder, tr. Ernst Falzeder with Tony Woolfson, Philemon Series, Princeton University Press, forthcoming.

> army I lived quietly and devoted my time to my patients and to my work. I was especially working about the two types of psychology and about the synthesis of unconscious tendencies.[115]

During his self-explorations, he experienced states of turmoil. He recalled that he experienced great fear, and sometimes had to hold the table to keep himself together,[116] and "I was frequently so wrought up that I had to eliminate the emotions through yoga practices. But since it was my purpose to learn what was going on within myself, I would do them only until I had calmed myself and could take up again the work with the unconscious."[117]

He recalled that Toni Wolff had become drawn into the process in which he was involved, and was experiencing a similar stream of images. Jung found that he could discuss his experiences with her, but she was disorientated and in the same mess.[118] Likewise, his wife was unable to help him in this regard. Consequently, he noted, "that I was able to endure at all was a case of brute force."[119]

The Psychological Club had been founded at the beginning of 1916, through a gift of 360,000 Swiss francs from Edith Rockefeller McCormick, who had come to Zürich to be analyzed by Jung in 1913. At its inception, it had approximately sixty members. For Jung, the aim of the Club was to study the relation of individuals to the group, and to provide a naturalistic setting for psychological observation to overcome the limitations of one-to-one analysis, as well as to provide a venue where patients could learn to adapt to social situations. At the same time, a professional body of analysts continued to meet together as the Association for Analytical Psychology.[120] Jung participated fully in both of these organizations.

---

115. John Burnham, *Jeliffe: American Psychoanalyst and Physician & His Correspondence with Sigmund Freud and* C. G. *Jung*, ed. William McGuire (Chicago: University of Chicago Press, 1983), pp. 196–97.
116. *MP*, p. 174.
117. *Memories*, p. 201.
118. *MP*, p. 174.
119. *Memories*, p. 201.
120. On the formation of the Club, see my *Cult Fictions: C. G. Jung and the Founding of Analytical Psychology*.

Jung's self-experimentation also heralded a change in his analytic work. He encouraged his patients to embark upon similar processes of self-experimentation. Patients were instructed on how to conduct active imagination, to hold inner dialogues, and to paint their fantasies. He took his own experiences as paradigmatic. In the 1925 seminar, he noted: "I drew all my empirical material from my patients, but the solution of the problem I drew from the inside, from my observations of the unconscious processes."[121]

Tina Keller, who was in analysis with Jung from 1912, recalls that Jung "often spoke of himself and his own experiences":

> In those early days, when one arrived for the analytic hour, the so-called "red book" often stood open on an easel. In it Dr. Jung had been painting or had just finished a picture. Sometimes he would show me what he had done and comment upon it. The careful and precise work he put into these pictures and into the illuminated text that accompanied them were a testimony to the importance of this undertaking. The master thus demonstrated to the student that psychic development is worth time and effort.[122]

In her analyses with Jung and Toni Wolff, Keller conducted active imaginations and also painted. Far from being a solitary endeavor, Jung's confrontation with the unconscious was a collective one, in which he took his patients along with him. Those around Jung formed an avant-garde group engaged in a social experiment that they hoped would transform their lives and the lives of those around them.

121. *Introduction to Jungian Psychology*, p. 35.

122. "C. G. Jung: Some memories and reflections," *Inward Light* 35 (1972), p. 11. On Tina Keller, see Wendy Swan, C. G. *Jung and Active Imagination* (Saarbrücken: VDM, 2007).

The Return of the Dead

Amid the unprecedented carnage of the war, the theme of the return of the dead was widespread, such as in Abel Gance's film *J'accuse*.[123] The death toll also led to a revival of interest in spiritualism. After nearly a year, Jung began to write again in the *Black Books* in 1915, with a further series of fantasies. He had already completed the handwritten draft of *Liber Primus* and *Liber Secundus*.[124] At the beginning of 1916, Jung experienced a striking series of parapsychological events in his house. In 1923, he narrated this event to Cary de Angulo (later Baynes). She recorded it as follows:

> One night your boy began to rave in his sleep and throw himself about saying he couldn't wake up. Finally your wife had to call you to get him quiet & this you could only do by cold cloths on him—finally he settled down and went on sleeping. Next morning he woke up remembering nothing, but seemed utterly exhausted, so you told him not to go to school, he didn't ask why but seemed to take it for granted. But quite unexpectedly he asked for paper and colored pencils and set to work to make the following picture—a man was angling for fishes with hook and line in the middle of the picture. On the left was the Devil saying something to the man, and your son wrote down what he said. It was that he had come for the fisherman because he was catching his fishes, but on the right was an angel who said, "No you can't take this man, he is taking only bad fishes and none of the good ones." Then after your son had made that picture he was quite content. The same night, two of your daughters thought that they had seen spooks in their rooms. The next day you wrote out the "Sermons to the Dead," and you knew after that nothing more would disturb your family, and nothing did.

123. See Winter, *Sites of Memory, Sites of Mourning*, pp. 18, 69, and 133–44.
124. There is a note added in *Black Book 5* at this point: "In this time the I and II parts [of the *Red Book*] were written. Directly after the beginning of the war" (p. 86). The main script is in Jung's hand, and 'of the Red Book' was added by someone else.

> Of course I knew you were the fisherman in your son's picture, and you told me so, but the boy didn't know it.[125]

In *Memories*, Jung recounted what followed:

> Around five o'clock in the afternoon on Sunday the front doorbell began ringing frantically . . . Everyone immediately looked to see who was there, but there was no one in sight. I was sitting near the doorbell, and not heard it but saw it moving. We all simply stared at one another. The atmosphere was thick, believe me! Then I knew something had to happen. The whole house was as if there was a crowd present, crammed full of spirits. They were packed deep right up to the door and the air was so thick it was scarcely possible to breathe. As for myself, I was all aquiver with the question: "For God's sake, what in the world is this?" Then they cried out in chorus, "We have come back from Jerusalem where we found not what we sought." That is the beginning of the *Septem Sermones.*
>
> Then it began to flow out of me, and in the course of three evenings the thing was written. As soon as I took up the pen, the whole ghastly assemblage evaporated. The room quieted and the atmosphere cleared. The haunting was over.[126]

The dead had appeared in a fantasy on January 17, 1914, and had said that they were about to go to Jerusalem to pray at the holiest graves.[127] Their trip had evidently not been successful. The *Septem Sermones ad Mortuos* is a culmination of the fantasies of this period. It is a psychological cosmology cast in the form of a gnostic creation myth. In Jung's fantasies, a new God had been born in his soul, the God who is the son of the frogs, Abraxas. Jung understood this symbolically. He saw this figure as representing the uniting of the Christian God with Satan, and hence as depicting a transformation

125. *CFB.*
126. *Memories*, pp. 215–16.
127. See below, p. 334.

of the Western God-image. Not until 1952 in *Answer to Job* did Jung elaborate on this theme in public.

Jung had studied the literature on Gnosticism in the course of his preparatory reading for *Transformations and Symbols of the Libido*. In January and October 1915, while on military service, he studied the works of the Gnostics. After writing the *Septem Sermones* in the *Black Books*, Jung recopied it in a calligraphic script into a separate book, slightly rearranging the sequence. He added the following inscription under the title: "The seven instructions of the dead. Written by Basilides in Alexandria, the city where the East touches the West."[128] He then had this privately printed, adding to the inscription: "Translated from the Greek original into German." This legend indicates the stylistic effects on Jung of late-nineteenth-century classical scholarship. He recalled that he wrote it on the occasion of the founding of the Psychological Club, and regarded it as a gift to Edith Rockefeller McCormick for founding the Club.[129] He gave copies to friends and confidants. Presenting a copy to Alphonse Maeder, he wrote:

> I could not presume to put my name to it, but chose instead the name of one of those great minds of the early Christian era which Christianity obliterated. It fell quite unexpectedly into my lap like a ripe fruit at a time of great stress and has kindled a light of hope and comfort for me in my bad hours.[130]

On January 16, 1916, Jung drew a mandala in the *Black Books* (see Appendix A). This was the first sketch of the "Systema Munditotius." He then proceeded to paint this. On the back of it, he wrote in English: "This is the first mandala I constructed in the year 1916, wholly unconscious of what it meant." The fantasies in the *Black*

128. The historical Basilides was a Gnostic who taught in Alexandria in the second century. See note 81, pp. 508–9.
129. *MP*, p. 26.
130. January 19, 1917, *Letters* 1, pp. 33–34. Sending a copy of the *Sermones* to Jolande Jacobi, Jung described them as "a curiosity from the workshop of the unconscious" (October 7, 1928, JA).

Books continued. The Systema Munditotius is a pictorial cosmology of the *Sermones*.

Between June 11 and October 2, 1917, Jung was on military service in Chateau d'Oex, as commander of the English prisoners of war. Around August, he wrote to Smith Ely Jeliffe that his military service had taken him completely away from his work and that, on his return, he hoped to finish a long paper about the types. He concluded the letter by writing: "With us everything is unchanged and quiet. Everything else is swallowed by the war. The psychosis is still increasing, going on and on."[131]

At this time, he felt that he was still in a state of chaos and that it only began to clear toward the end of the war.[132] From the beginning of August to the end of September, he drew a series of twenty-seven mandalas in pencil in his army notebook, which he preserved.[133] At first, he did not understand these mandalas, but felt that they were very significant. From August 20, he drew a mandala on most days. This gave him the feeling that he had taken a photograph of each day and he observed how these mandalas changed. He recalled that he received a letter from "this Dutch woman that got on my nerves terribly."[134] In this letter, this woman, that is, Moltzer, argued that "the fantasies stemming from the unconscious possessed artistic worth and should be considered as art."[135] Jung found this troubling because it was not stupid, and, moreover, modern painters were attempting to make art out of the unconscious. This awoke a doubt in him whether his fantasies were really spontaneous and natural. On the next day, he drew a mandala, and a piece of it was broken off, leaving the symmetry:

> Only now did I gradually come to what the mandala really is: "Formation, transformation, the eternal mind's eternal rec-

131. John C. Burnham, *Jeliffe: American Psychoanalyst and Physician*, p. 199.
132. *MP*, p.172.
133. See Appendix A.
134. *Memories*, p. 220.
135. Ibid.

> reation." And that is the self, the wholeness of the personality, which, when everything is well, is harmonious, but which can bear no self deception. My mandala images were cryptograms on the state of my self, which were delivered to me each day.[136]

The mandala in question appears to be the mandala of August 6, 1917.[137] The second line is from Goethe's *Faust*. Mephistopheles is addressing Faust, giving him directions to the realm of the Mothers:

> MEPHISTOPHELES
> A glowing tripod will finally show you
> that you are in the deepest, most deepest ground.
> By its light you will see the Mothers:
> the one sits, others stand and walk,
> as it may chance. Formation, transformation
> the eternal mind's eternal recreation.
> Covered in images of all creatures,
> they do not see you, since they only see shades.
> Then hold your heart, since the danger is great,
> and go straight to that tripod,
> touch it with the key![138]

The letter in question has not come to light. However, in a subsequent unpublished letter from November 21, 1918, while at Chateau d'Oex, Jung wrote that "M. Moltzer has again disturbed me with letters."[139] He reproduced the mandalas in *Liber Novus*. He noted that it was during this period that a living idea of the self first came to him: "The self, I thought, was like the monad which I am, and which is my world. The mandala represents this monad, and

136. Ibid., p. 221.
137. See Appendix A.
138. *Faust*, 2, act 1. 6287f.
139. Unpublished letter, *JFA*. There also exists an undated painting by Moltzer that appears to be a quadrated mandala, which she described in brief accompanying notes as "A pictorial presentation of Individuation or of the Individuation process" (Library, Psychological Club, Zürich).

corresponds to the microcosmic nature of the soul."[140] At this point, he did not know where this process was leading, but he began to grasp that the mandala represented the goal of the process: "Only when I began to paint the mandalas did I see that all the paths I took, all the steps I made, all led back to the one point, that is, to the center. The mandala became the expression of all paths."[141] In the 1920s, Jung's understanding of the significance of the mandala deepened.

The *Draft* had contained fantasies from October 1913 to February 1914. In the winter of 1917, Jung wrote a fresh manuscript called *Scrutinies*, which began where he had left off. In this, he transcribed fantasies from April 1913 until June 1916. As in the first two books of *Liber Novus*, Jung interspersed the fantasies with interpretive commentaries.[142] He included the *Sermones* in this material, and now added Philemon's commentaries on each sermon. In these, Philemon stressed the compensatory nature of his teaching: he deliberately stressed precisely those conceptions that the dead lacked. *Scrutinies* effectively forms *Liber Tertius* of *Liber Novus*. The complete sequence of the text would thus be:

Liber Primus: The Way of What Is to Come
Liber Secundus: The Images of the Erring
Liber Tertius: Scrutinies

During this period, Jung continued transcribing the *Draft* into the calligraphic volume and adding paintings. The fantasies in the *Black Books* became more intermittent. He portrayed his realization of the significance of the self, which took place in the autumn of

140. *Memories*, p. 221. The immediate sources that Jung drew on for his concept of the self appear to be the Atman/Brahman conception in Hinduism, which he discussed in 1921 *Psychological Types*, and certain passages in Nietzsche's *Zarathustra*. (See note 29, p. 477).
141. Ibid.
142. On page 23 of the manuscript of *Scrutinies*, a date is indicated: "27/11/17," which suggests that they were written in the latter half of 1917, and thus after the mandala experiences at Chateau d'Oex.

1917, in *Scrutinies*.[143] This contains Jung's vision of the reborn God, culminating in the portrayal of Abraxas. He realized that much of what was given to him in the earlier part of the book (that is, *Liber Primus* and *Liber Secundus*) was actually given to him by Philemon.[144] He realized that there was a prophetic wise old man in him, to whom he was not identical. This represented a critical disidentification. On January 17, 1918, Jung wrote to J. B. Lang:

> The work on the unconscious has to happen first and foremost for us ourselves. Our patients profit from it indirectly. The danger consists in the prophet's delusion which often is the result of dealing with the unconscious. It is the devil who says: Disdain all reason and science, mankind's highest powers. That is never appropriate even though we are forced to acknowledge [the existence of] the irrational.[145]

Jung's critical task in "working over" his fantasies was to differentiate the voices and characters. For example, in the *Black Books*, it is Jung's "I" who speaks the *Sermones* to the dead. In *Scrutinies*, it is not Jung's "I" but Philemon who speaks them. In the *Black Books*, the main figure with whom Jung has dialogues is his soul. In some sections of *Liber Novus*, this is changed to the serpent and the bird. In one conversation in January 1916, his soul explained to him that when the Above and Below are not united, she falls into three parts—a serpent, the human soul, and the bird or heavenly soul, which visits the Gods. Thus Jung's revision here can be seen to reflect his understanding of the tripartite nature of his soul.[146]

During this period, Jung continued to work over his material, and there is some indication that he discussed it with his colleagues.

---

143. See below, p. 461f.
144. See below, p. 474.
145. Private possession, Stephen Martin. The reference is to Mephistopheles' statement in *Faust*, (1.1851f.)
146. See below, p. 577.

In March 1918 he wrote to J. B. Lang, who had sent him some of his own fantasies:

> I would not want to say anything more than telling you to continue with this approach because, as you have observed correctly yourself, it is very important that we experience the contents of the unconscious before we form any opinions about it. I very much agree with you that we have to grapple with the knowledge content of gnosis and neo-Platonism, since these are the systems that contain the materials which are suited to form the basis of a theory of the unconscious spirit. I have already been working on this myself for a long time, and also have had ample opportunity to compare my experiences at least partially with those of others. That's why I was very pleased to hear pretty much the same views from you. I am glad that you have discovered all on your own this area of work which is ready to be tackled. Up to now, I lacked workers. I am happy that you want to join forces with me. I consider it very important that you extricate your own material uninfluenced from the unconscious, as carefully as possible. My material is very voluminous, very complicated, and in part very graphic, up to almost completely worked through clarifications. But what I completely lack is comparative modern material. Zarathustra is too strongly consciously formed. Meyrink retouches aesthetically; furthermore, I feel he is lacking in religious sincerity.[147]

The Content

Liber Novus thus presents a series of active imaginations together with Jung's attempt to understand their significance. This work of understanding encompasses a number of interlinked threads: an attempt to understand himself and to integrate and develop the various components of his personality; an attempt to understand the

147. Private possession, Stephen Martin.

structure of the human personality in general; an attempt to understand the relation of the individual to present-day society and to the community of the dead; an attempt to understand the psychological and historical effects of Christianity; and an attempt to grasp the future religious development of the West. Jung discusses many other themes in the work, including the nature of self-knowledge; the nature of the soul; the relations of thinking and feeling and the psychological types; the relation of inner and outer masculinity and femininity; the uniting of opposites; solitude; the value of scholarship and learning; the status of science; the significance of symbols and how they are to be understood; the meaning of the war; madness, divine madness, and psychiatry; how the Imitation of Christ is to be understood today; the death of God; the historical significance of Nietzsche; and the relation of magic and reason.

The overall theme of the book is how Jung regains his soul and overcomes the contemporary malaise of spiritual alienation. This is ultimately achieved through enabling the rebirth of a new image of God in his soul and developing a new worldview in the form of a psychological and theological cosmology. *Liber Novus* presents the prototype of Jung's conception of the individuation process, which he held to be the universal form of individual psychological development. *Liber Novus* itself can be understood on one hand as depicting Jung's individuation process, and on the other hand as his elaboration of this concept as a general psychological schema. At the beginning of the book, Jung refinds his soul and then embarks on a sequence of fantasy adventures, which form a consecutive narrative. He realized that until then, he had served the spirit of the time, characterized by use and value. In addition to this, there existed a spirit of the depths, which led to the things of the soul. In terms of Jung's later biographical memoir, the spirit of the times corresponds to personality NO. 1, and the spirit of the depths corresponds to personality NO. 2. Thus this period could be seen as a return to the values of personality NO. 2. The chapters follow a particular format: they begin with the exposition of dramatic visual fantasies. In them Jung encounters a series of figures in various settings and enters into conversation with them. He is confronted with unexpected happenings and shocking statements. He then attempts to understand what had transpired, and to formulate the significance of these events and statements into general psychological conceptions and maxims. Jung held that the significance of these fantasies was due to the fact that they stemmed from the mythopoeic imagination which was missing in the present rational age. The task of individuation lay in establishing a dialogue with the fantasy figures—or contents of the collective unconscious—and integrating them into consciousness, hence recovering the value of the mythopoeic imagination which had been lost to the modern age, and thereby reconciling the spirit of the time with the spirit of the depth. This task was to form a leitmotif of his subsequent scholarly work.

"A New Spring of Life"

In 1916, Jung wrote several essays and a short book in which he began to attempt to translate some of themes of *Liber Novus* into contemporary psychological language, and to reflect on the significance and the generality of his activity. Significantly, in these works he presented the first outlines of the main components of his mature psychology. A full account of these papers is beyond the scope of this introduction. The following overview highlights elements that link most directly with *Liber Novus*.

In his works between 1911 and 1914, he had principally been concerned with establishing a structural account of general human functioning and of psychopathology. In addition to his earlier theory of complexes, we see that he had already formulated conceptions of a phylogenetically acquired unconscious peopled by mythic images, of a nonsexual psychic energy, of the general types of introversion and extraversion, of the compensatory and prospective function of dreams, and of the synthetic and constructive approach to fantasies. While he continued to expand and develop these conceptions in detail, a new project emerges here: the attempt to provide a temporal account of higher development, which he termed the individuation process. This was a pivotal theoretical result of his self-experimentation. The full elaboration of the individuation process, and its historical and cross-cultural comparison, would come to occupy him for the rest of his life.

In 1916, he presented a lecture to the association for analytical psychology entitled "The structure of the unconscious," which was first published in a French translation in Flournoy's *Archives de Psychologie*.[148] Here, he differentiated two layers of the unconscious. The first, the personal unconscious, consisted in elements acquired during one's lifetime, together with elements that could equally well be conscious.[149] The second was the impersonal unconscious or collective psyche.[150] While consciousness and the personal unconscious were developed and acquired in the course of one's lifetime, the collective psyche was inherited.[151] In this essay, Jung discussed the curious phenomena that resulted from assimilating the unconscious. He noted that when individuals annexed the contents of the collective psyche and regarded them as personal attributes, they experienced extreme states of superiority and inferiority. He borrowed the term "godlikeness" from Goethe and Alfred Adler to characterize this state, which arose from fusing the personal and collective psyche, and was one of the dangers of analysis.

Jung wrote that it was a difficult task to differentiate the personal and collective psyche. One of the factors one came up against was the persona—one's "mask" or "role." This represented the segment of the collective psyche that one mistakenly regarded as individual. When one analyzed this, the personality dissolved into the collective psyche, which resulted in the release of a stream of fantasies: "All the treasures of mythological thinking and feeling are unlocked."[152] The difference between this state and insanity lay in the fact that it was intentional.

---

148. After his separation with Freud, Jung found that Flournoy was of continued support to him. See Jung in Flournoy, *From India to the Planet Mars*, p. ix.
149. CW 7, §§444–46.
150. Ibid., §449.
151. Ibid., §459.
152. Ibid., §468.

Two possibilities arose: one could attempt to regressively restore persona and return to the prior state, but it was impossible to get rid of the unconscious. Alternatively, one could accept the condition of godlikeness. However, there was a third way: the hermeneutic treatment of creative fantasies. This resulted in a synthesis of the individual with the collective psyche, which revealed the individual lifeline. This was the process of individuation. In a subsequent undated revision of this paper, Jung introduced the notion of the anima, as a counterpart to that of the persona. He regarded both of these as "subject-imagoes." Here, he defined the anima as "how the subject is seen by the collective unconscious."[153]

The vivid description of the vicissitudes of the state of godlikeness mirror some of Jung's affective states during his confrontation with the unconscious. The notion of the differentiation of the persona and its analysis corresponds to the opening section of *Liber Novus,* where Jung sets himself apart from his role and achievements and attempts to reconnect with his soul. The release of mythological fantasies is precisely what ensued in his case, and the hermeneutic treatment of creative fantasies was what he presented in layer two of *Liber Novus*. The differentiation of the personal and impersonal unconscious provided a theoretical understanding of Jung's mythological fantasies: it suggests that he did not view them as stemming from his personal unconscious but from the inherited collective psyche. If so, his fantasies stemmed from a layer of the psyche that was a collective human inheritance, and were not simply idiosyncratic or arbitrary.

In October of the same year, Jung presented two talks to the Psychological Club. The first was titled "Adaptation." This took two forms: adaptation to outer and inner conditions. The "inner" was understood to designate the unconscious. Adaptation to the "inner" led to the demand for individuation, which was contrary to adaptation to others. Answering this demand and the corresponding break with conformity led to a tragic guilt that required

153. Ibid., §521.

expiation and called for a new "collective function," because the individual had to produce values that could serve as a substitute for his absence from society. These new values enabled one to make reparation to the collective. Individuation was for the few. Those who were insufficiently creative should rather reestablish collective conformity with a society. The individual had not only to create new values, but also socially recognizable ones, as society had a "*right to expect realizable values.*"[154]

Read in terms of Jung's situation, this suggests that his break with social conformity to pursue his "individuation" had led him to the view that he had to produce socially realizable values as an expiation. This led to a dilemma: would the form in which Jung embodied these new values in *Liber Novus* be socially acceptable and recognizable? This commitment to the demands of society separated Jung from the anarchism of the Dadaists.

The second talk was on "Individuation and collectivity." He argued that individuation and collectivity were a pair of opposites related by guilt. Society demanded imitation. Through the process of imitation, one could gain access to values that were one's own. In analysis, "Through imitation the patient learns individuation, because it reactivates his own values."[155] It is possible to read this as a comment on the role of imitation in the analytic treatments of those of his patients whom Jung had now encouraged to embark on similar processes of development. The claim that this process evoked the patient's preexisting values was a counter to the charge of suggestion.

In November, while on military service at Herisau, Jung wrote a paper on "The transcendent function," which was published only in 1957. There, he depicted the method of eliciting and developing fantasies that he later termed active imagination, and explained its therapeutic rationale. This paper can be viewed as an interim prog-

154. CW 18, §1098.
155. CW 18, §1100.

ress report on Jung's self-experimentation, and may profitably be considered as a preface to *Liber Novus*.

Jung noted that the new attitude gained from analysis became obsolete. Unconscious materials were needed to supplement the conscious attitude, and to correct its one-sidedness. But because energy tension was low in sleep, dreams were inferior expressions of unconscious contents. Thus other sources had to be turned to, namely, spontaneous fantasies. A recently recovered dream book contains a series of dreams from 1917 to 1925.[156] A close comparison of this book with the *Black Books* indicates that his active imaginations did not derive directly from his dreams, and that these two streams were generally independent.

Jung described his technique for inducing such spontaneous fantasies: "The training consists first of all in systematic exercises for eliminating critical attention, thus producing a vacuum in consciousness."[157] One commenced by concentrating on a particular mood, and attempting to become as conscious as possible of all fantasies and associations that came up in connection with it. The aim was to allow fantasy free play, without departing from the initial affect in a free associative process. This led to a concrete or symbolic expression of the mood, which had the result of bringing the affect nearer to consciousness, hence making it more understandable. Doing this could have a vitalizing effect. Individuals could draw, paint, or sculpt, depending on their propensities:

> Visual types should concentrate on the expectation that an inner image will be produced. As a rule such a fantasy-image will actually appear—perhaps hypnagogically—and should be carefully noted down in writing. Audio-verbal types usually hear inner words, perhaps mere fragments or apparently meaningless sentences to begin with . . . Others at such times simply hear

156. *JFA*.
157. CW 8, §155.

> their "other" voice . . . Still rarer, but equally valuable, is automatic writing, direct or with the planchette.[158]

Once these fantasies had been produced and embodied, two approaches were possible: creative formulation and understanding. Each needed the other, and both were necessary to produce the transcendent function, which arose out of the union of conscious and unconscious contents.

For some people, Jung noted, it was simple to note the "other" voice in writing and to answer it from the standpoint of the I: "It is exactly as if a dialogue were taking place between two human beings . . . "[159] This dialogue led to the creation of the transcendent function, which resulted in a widening of consciousness. This depiction of inner dialogues and the means of evoking fantasies in a waking state represents Jung's own undertaking in the *Black Books*. The interplay of creative formulation and understanding corresponds to Jung's work in *Liber Novus*. Jung did not publish this paper. He later remarked that he never finished his work on the transcendent function because he did it only halfheartedly.[160]

In 1917, Jung published a short book with a long title: *The Psychology of the Unconscious Processes: An Overview of the Modern Theory and Method of Analytical Psychology*. In his preface, dated December 1916, he proclaimed the psychological processes that accompanied the war had brought the problem of the chaotic unconscious to the forefront of attention. However, the psychology of the individual corresponded to the psychology of the nation, and only the transformation of the attitude of the individual could bring about cultural renewal.[161] This articulated the intimate interconnection between individual and collective events that was at the center of *Liber Novus*. For Jung, the conjunction between his precognitive visions and the

158. Ibid., §§170–71. A planchette is a small wooden board on coasters used to facilitate automatic writing.
159. Ibid., §186.
160. *MP*, p. 380.
161. CW 7, pp. 3–4.

outbreak of war had made apparent the deep subliminal connections between individual fantasies and world events—and hence between the psychology of the individual and that of the nation. What was now required was to work out this connection in more detail.

Jung noted that after one had analyzed and integrated the contents of the personal unconscious, one came up against mythological fantasies that stemmed from the phylogenetic layer of the unconscious.[162] *The Psychology of the Unconscious Processes* provided an exposition of the collective, suprapersonal, absolute unconscious—these terms being used interchangeably. Jung argued that one needed to separate oneself from the unconscious by presenting it visibly as something separate from one. It was vital to differentiate the I from the non-I, namely, the collective psyche or absolute unconscious. To do this, "*man must necessarily stand upon firm feet* in his I-function; *that is, he must fulfil his duty toward life completely, so that he may in every respect be a vitally living member of society.*"[163] Jung had been endeavoring to accomplish these tasks during this period.

The contents of this unconscious were what Jung in *Transformations and Symbols of the Libido* had called typical myths or primordial images. He described these "dominants" as "the ruling powers, the Gods, that is, images of dominating laws and principles, average regularities in the sequence of images, that the brain has received from the sequence of secular processes."[164] One needed to pay particular attention to these dominants. Particularly important was the "*detachment of the mythological or collective psychological contents from the objects of consciousness, and their consolidation as psychological realities outside the*

162. In his 1943 revision of this work, Jung added that the personal unconscious "corresponds to the figure of the *shadow* so frequently met with in dreams" (CW 7, §103). He added the following definition of this figure: "By *shadow* I understand the 'negative' side of the personality, the sum of all those hidden unpleasant qualities, the insufficiently developed functions and the contents of the personal unconscious" (Ibid., §103n). Jung described this phase of the individuation process as the encounter with the shadow (see CW 9, pt. 2, §§13–19).

163. "The psychology of the unconscious processes," in Jung, *Collected Papers on Analytical Psychology*, ed. Constance Long (London: Baillière, Tindall & Cox, 1917, 2nd ed.), pp. 416–47.

164. Ibid., p. 432.

individual psyche."[165] This enabled one to come to terms with activated residues of our ancestral history. The differentiation of the personal from the nonpersonal resulted in a release of energy.

These comments also mirror his activity: his attempt to differentiate the various characters which appeared, and to "consolidate them as psychological realities." The notion that these figures had a psychological reality in their own right, and were not merely subjective figments, was the main lesson that he attributed to the fantasy figure of Elijah: psychic objectivity.[166]

Jung argued that the era of reason and skepticism inaugurated by the French Revolution had repressed religion and irrationalism. This in turn had serious consequences, leading to the outbreak of irrationalism represented by the world war. It was thus a historical necessity to acknowledge the irrational as a psychological factor. The acceptance of the irrational forms one of the central themes of *Liber Novus*.

In *The Psychology of the Unconscious Processes*, Jung developed his conception of the psychological types. He noted that it was a common development that the psychological characteristics of the types were pushed to extremes. By what he termed the law of enantiodromia, or the reversal into the opposite, the other function entered in, namely, feeling for the introvert, and thinking for the extravert. These secondary functions were found in the unconscious. The development of the contrary function led to individuation. As the contrary function was not acceptable to consciousness, a special technique was required to come to terms with it, namely the production of the transcendent function. The unconscious was a danger when one was not at one with it. But with the establishment of the transcendent function, the disharmony ceased. This rebalancing gave access to the productive and beneficent aspects of the unconscious. The unconscious contained the wisdom and experience of untold ages, and thus formed an unparalleled guide. The

165. Ibid., p. 435.
166. *Introduction to Jungian Psychology*, p. 103.

development of the contrary function appears in the "Mysterium" section of *Liber Novus*.[167] The attempt to gain the wisdom stored in the unconscious is portrayed throughout the book, in which Jung asks his soul to tell him what she sees and the meaning of his fantasies. The unconscious is here viewed as a source of higher wisdom. He concluded the essay by indicating the personal and experiential nature of his new conceptions: "Our age is seeking a new spring of life. I found one and drank of it and the water tasted good."[168]

The Way to the Self

In 1918, Jung wrote a paper entitled "On the unconscious," where he noted that all of us stood between two worlds: the world of external perception and the world of perception of the unconscious. This distinction depicts his experience at this time. He wrote that Friedrich Schiller had claimed that the approximation of these two worlds was through art. By contrast, Jung argued, "I am of the opinion that the union of rational and irrational truth is to be found not so much in art as in the symbol *per se*; for it is the essence of the symbol to contain both the rational and irrational."[169] Symbols, he maintained, stemmed from the unconscious, and the creation of symbols was the most important function of the unconscious. While the compensatory function of the unconscious was always present, the symbol-creating function was present only when we were willing to recognize it. Here, we see him continuing to eschew viewing his productions as art. It was not art but symbols which were of paramount importance here. The recognition and recuperation of this symbol-creating power is portrayed in *Liber Novus*. It depicts Jung's attempt to understand the psychological nature of symbolism and to view his fantasies symbolically. He concluded that what was unconscious at any given epoch was only relative, and

167. See below, pp. 174–207.
168. *Collected Papers on Analytical Psychology*, p. 444. This sentence appeared only in the first edition of Jung's book.
169. CW 10, §24.

changing. What was required now was the "remolding of our views in accordance with the active forces of the unconscious."[170] Thus the task confronting him was one of translating the conceptions gained through his confrontation with the unconscious, and expressed in a literary and symbolic manner in *Liber Novus*, into a language that was compatible with the contemporary outlook.

The following year, he presented a paper in England before the Society of Psychical Research, of which he was an honorary member, on "The psychological foundations of the belief in spirits."[171] He differentiated between two situations in which the collective unconscious became active. In the first, it became activated through a crisis in an individual's life and the collapse of hopes and expectations. In the second, it became activated at times of great social, political, and religious upheaval. At such moments, the factors suppressed by the prevailing attitudes accumulate in the collective unconscious. Strongly intuitive individuals become aware of these and try to translate them into communicable ideas. If they succeeded in translating the unconscious into a communicable language, this had a redeeming effect. The contents of the unconscious had a disturbing effect. In the first situation, the collective unconscious might replace reality, which is pathological. In the second situation, the individual may feel disorientated, but the state is not pathological. This differentiation suggests that Jung viewed his own experience as falling under the second heading—namely, the activation of the collective unconscious due to the general cultural upheaval. Thus his initial fear of impending insanity in 1913 lay in his failure to realize this distinction.

In 1918, he presented a series of seminars to the Psychological Club on his work on typology, and was engaged in extensive scholarly research on this subject at this time. He developed and expanded the themes articulated in these papers in 1921 in *Psychological Types*. As regards the working over of themes of *Liber Novus*,

---

170. CW 10, §48.
171. CW 8.

the most important section was chapter 5, "The type problem in poetry." The basic issue discussed here was how the problem of opposites could be resolved through the production of the uniting or reconciling symbol. This forms one of the central themes of *Liber Novus*. Jung presented detailed analysis of the issue of the resolution of the problem of opposites in Hinduism, Taoism, Meister Eckhart, and, in present times, in the work of Carl Spitteler. This chapter can also be read in terms of a meditation on some of the historical sources that directly informed his conceptions in *Liber Novus*. It also heralded the introduction of an important method. Rather than directly discussing the issue of the reconciliation of opposites in *Liber Novus*, he sought out historical analogies and commented upon them.

In 1921, the "self" emerged as a psychological concept. Jung defined it as follows:

> Inasmuch as the I is only the center of my field of consciousness, it is not identical with the totality of my psyche, being merely a complex among other complexes. Hence I discriminate between the *I* and the *self*, since the I is only the subject of my consciousness, while the self is the subject of my totality: hence it also includes the unconscious psyche. In this sense the self would be an (ideal) greatness which embraces and includes the I. In unconscious fantasy the self often appears as the superordinated or ideal personality, as Faust is in relation to Goethe and Zarathustra to Nietzsche.[172]

He equated the Hindu notion of Brahman/Atman with the self. At the same time, Jung provided a definition of the soul. He argued that the soul possessed qualities that were complementary to the persona, containing those qualities that the conscious attitude lacked. This complementary character of the soul also affected its sexual character, so that a man had a feminine soul, or anima, and a

172. *Psychological Types*, CW 6, §706.

woman had a masculine soul, or animus.[173] This corresponded to the fact that men and women had both masculine and feminine traits. He also noted that the soul gave rise to images that were assumed to be worthless from the rational perspective. There were four ways of using them:

> The first possibility of making use of them is *artistic*, if one is in any way gifted in that direction; a second is *philosophical speculation*; a third is *quasi-religious*, leading to heresy and the founding of sects; and a fourth way of employing the *dynamis* of these images is to squander it in every form of licentiousness.[174]

From this perspective, the psychological utilization of these images would represent a "fifth way." For it to succeed, psychology had to distinguish itself clearly from art, philosophy, and religion. This necessity accounts for Jung's rejection of the alternatives.

In the subsequent *Black Books*, he continued to elaborate his "mythology." The figures developed and transformed into one another. The differentiation of the figures was accompanied by their coalescence, as he came to regard them as aspects of underlying components of the personality. On January 5, 1922, he had a conversation with his soul concerning both his vocation and *Liber Novus*:

> [I:] I feel that I must speak to you. Why do you not let me sleep, as I am tired? I feel that the disturbance comes from you. What induces you to keep me awake?
> [Soul:] Now is no time to sleep, but you should be awake and prepare important matters in nocturnal work.The great work begins.
> [I:] What great work?
> [Soul:] The work that should now be undertaken. It is a great

173. Ibid., §§804–5.
174. CW 6, §426.

and difficult work. There is no time to sleep, if you find no time during the day to remain in the work.

[I:] But I had no idea that something of this kind was taking place.

[Soul:] But you could have told by the fact that I have been disturbing your sleep for a long time. You have been too unconscious for a long time. Now you must go to a higher level of consciousness.

[I:] I am ready. What is it? Speak!

[Soul:] You should listen: to no longer be a Christian is easy. But what next? For more is yet to come. Everything is waiting for you. And you? You remain silent and have nothing to say. But you should speak. Why have you received the revelation? You should not hide it. You concern yourself with the form? Is the form important, when it is a matter of revelation?

[I:] But you are not thinking that I should publish what I have written? That would be a misfortune. And who would understand it?

[Soul:] No, listen! You should not break up a marriage, namely the marriage with me, no person should supplant me . . . I want to rule alone.

[I:] So you want to rule? From whence do you take the right for such a presumption?

[Soul:] This right comes to me because I serve you and your calling. I could just as well say, you came first, but above all your calling comes first.

[I:] But what is my calling?

[Soul:] The new religion and its proclamation.

[I:] Oh God, how should I do this?

[Soul:] Do not be of such little faith. No one knows it as you do. There is no one who could say it as well as you could.

[I:] But who knows, if you are not lying?

[Soul:] Ask yourself if I am lying. I speak the truth.[175]

175. *Black Book 7*, p. 92c.

His soul here pointedly urged him to publish his material, at which he balked. Three days later, his soul informed him that the new religion "expresses itself only in the transformation of human relations. Relations do not let themselves be replaced by the deepest knowledge. Moreover a religion does not consist only in knowledge, but at its visible level in a new ordering of human affairs. Therefore expect no further knowledge from me. You know everything that is to be known about the manifested revelation, but you do not yet live everything that is to be lived at this time." Jung's "I" replied, "I can fully understand and accept this. However, it is dark to me, how the knowledge could be transformed into life. You must teach me this." His soul said, "There is not much to say about this. It is not as rational as you are inclined to think. The way is symbolic."[176]

Thus the task confronting Jung was how to realize and embody what he had learned through his self-investigation into life. During this period the themes of the psychology of religion and the relation of religion to psychology became increasingly prominent in his work, starting from his seminar in Polzeath in Cornwall in 1923. He attempted to develop a psychology of the religious-making process. Rather than proclaiming a new prophetic revelation, his interest lay in the psychology of religious experiences. The task was to depict the translation and transposition of the numinous experience of individuals into symbols, and eventually into the dogmas and creeds of organized religions, and, finally, to study the psychological function of such symbols. For such a psychology of the religion-making process to succeed, it was essential that analytical psychology, while providing an affirmation of the religious attitude, did not succumb to becoming a creed.[177]

---

176. Ibid., p. 95. In a seminar the following year, Jung took up the theme of the relation of individual relations to religion: "No individual can exist without individual relationships, and that is how the foundation of your Church is laid. Individual relations lay the form of the invisible Church" (*Notes on the Seminar in Analytical Psychology conducted by Dr. C. G. Jung*, Polzeath, England, July 14–July 27, 1923, arranged by members of the class, p. 82).

177. On Jung's psychology of religion, see James Heisig, *Imago Dei: A Study of Jung's Psychology of Religion* (Lewisburg: Bucknell University Press, 1979), and Ann Lammers, *In God's Shadow: The Collaboration between Victor White and C. G. Jung* (New York: Paulist Press,

In 1922, Jung wrote a paper on "The relation of analytical psychology to poetic art works." He differentiated two types of work: the first, which sprang entirely from the author's intention, and the second, which seized the author. Examples of such symbolic works were the second part of Goethe's *Faust* and Nietzsche's *Zarathustra*. He held that these works stemmed from the collective unconscious. In such instances, the creative process consisted in the unconscious activation of an archetypal image. The archetypes released in us a voice that was stronger than our own:

> Whoever speaks in primordial images speaks with a thousand voices; he enthrals and overpowers . . . he transmutes our personal destiny into the destiny of mankind, and evokes in us all those beneficent forces that ever and anon have enabled humanity to find a refuge from every peril and to outlive the longest night.[178]

The artist who produced such works educated the spirit of the age, and compensated the one-sidedness of the present. In describing the genesis of such symbolic works, Jung seemingly had his own activities in mind. Thus while Jung refused to regard *Liber Novus* as "art," his reflections on its composition were nevertheless a critical source of his subsequent conceptions and theories of art. The implicit question that this paper raised was whether psychology could now serve this function of educating the spirit of the age and compensating the one-sidedness of the present. From this period onward, he came to conceive of the task of his psychology in precisely such a manner.[179]

1994). See also my "'In Statu Nascendi,'" *Journal of Analytical Psychology* 44 (1999), pp. 539–45.

178. CW 15, §130.

179. In 1930, Jung expanded upon this theme, and described the first type of work as "psychological," and the latter as "visionary." "Psychology and poetry," CW 15.

Publication Deliberations

From 1922 onward, in addition to discussions with Emma Jung and Toni Wolff, Jung had extensive discussions with Cary Baynes and Wolfgang Stockmayer concerning what to do with *Liber Novus*, and around its potential publication. Because these discussions took place when he was still working on it, they are critically important. Cary Fink was born in 1883. She studied at Vassar College, where she was taught by Kristine Mann, who became one of Jung's earliest followers in the United States. In 1910, she married Jaime de Angulo, and completed her medical training at Johns Hopkins in 1911. In 1921, she left him, and went to Zürich with Kristine Mann. She entered analysis with Jung. She never practiced analysis, and Jung highly respected her critical intelligence. In 1927, she married Peter Baynes. They were subsequently divorced in 1931. Jung asked her to make a fresh transcription of *Liber Novus*, because he had added a lot of material since the previous transcription. She undertook this in 1924 and 1925, when Jung was in Africa. Her typewriter was heavy, so she first copied it by hand and then typed it out.

These notes recount her discussions with Jung and are written in the form of letters to him, but were not sent.

> OCTOBER 2, 1922
>
> In another book of Meyrink's the "White Dominican," you said he made use of exactly the same symbolism that had come to you in the first vision that revealed to your unconscious. Furthermore you said, he had spoken of a "Red Book" which contained certain mysteries and the book that you are writing about the unconscious, you have called the "Red Book".[180] Then you said

180. See Meyrink, *The White Dominican*, tr. M. Mitchell (1921/1994), ch. 7. The "founding father" informs the hero of the novel, Christopher, that "whoever possesses the Cinnabar-red Book, the plant of immortality, the awakening of the spiritual breath, and the secret of bringing the right hand to life, will dissolve with the corpse . . . It is called the Cinnabar book because, according to ancient belief in China, that red is the colour of the garments of those who have reached the highest stage of perfection and stayed behind on earth for the salvation of mankind" (p. 91). Jung was particularly interested

you were in doubt as to what to do about that book. Meyrink you said could throw his into novel form and it was all right, but you could only command the scientific and philosophical method and that stuff you couldn't cast into that mold. I said you could use the Zarathustra form and you said that was true, but you were sick of that. I am too. Then you said you had thought of making an autobiography out of it. That would seem to me by far the best, because then you would tend to write as you spoke which was in a very colorful way. But apart from any difficulty with the form, you said you dreaded making it public because it was like selling your house. But I jumped upon you with both feet there and said it wasn't a bit like that because you and the book stood for a constellation of the Universe, and that to take the book as being purely personal was to identify yourself with it which was something you would not think of permitting to your patients . . .Then we laughed over my having caught you red-handed as it were. Goethe had been caught in the same difficulty in the 2nd part of Faust in which he had gotten into the unconscious and found it so difficult to get the right form that he had finally died leaving the Mss. as such in his drawer. So much of what you had experienced you said, would be counted as sheer lunacy that if it were published you would lose out altogether not only as a scientist, but as a human being, but not I said if you went at it from the Dichtung und Wahrheit [Poetry and Truth] angle, then people could make their own selection as to which was which.[181] You objected to presenting any of it as Dichtung when it was *all* Wahrheit, but it does not seem to me falseness to make use of that much of a mask in order to

in Meyrink's novels. In 1921, when referring to the transcendent function and unconscious fantasies, he noted that examples where such material had been subjected to aesthetic elaboration could be found in literature, and that "I would single out two works of Meyrink for special attention: *The Golem and The Green Face*," *Psychological Types*, CW 6, §205. He regarded Meyrink as a "visionary" artist ("Psychology und poetry" [1930], CW 15, §142) and was also interested in Meyrink's alchemical experiments (*Psychology and Alchemy* [1944], CW 12, §341n).

181. The reference is to Goethe's autobiography, *From My Life: Poetry and Truth*, tr. R. Heitner (Princeton: Princeton University Press, 1994).

protect yourself from Philistia—and after all, as I said Philistia has its rights, confronted with the choice of you as a lunatic, and themselves as inexperienced fools they *have* to choose the former alternative, but if they can place you as a poet, their faces are saved. Much of your material you said has come to you as runes & the explanation of those runes sounds like the veriest nonsense, but that does not matter if the end product is sense. In your case I said, apparently you have become conscious of more of the steps of creation than ever anyone before. In most cases the mind evidently drops out of the irrelevant stuff automatically and delivers the end product, whereas you bring along the whole business, matrix process and product. Naturally it is frightfully more difficult to handle. Then my hour was up.

JANUARY 1923

What you told me some time ago set me thinking, and suddenly the other day while I was reading the "Vorspiel auf dem Theater" [prelude in the theater],[182] it came to me that you too ought to make use of that principle which Goethe has handled so beautifully all through Faust, namely, the placing in opposition of the creative and eternal with the negative and transient. You may not see right away what this has to do with the Red Book, but I will explain. As I understand it in this book you are going to challenge men to a new way of looking at their souls, at any rate there is going to be in it a good deal that will be out of the grasp of the ordinary man, just as at one period of your own life you would scarcely have understood it. In a way it is a "jewel" you are giving to the world is it not? My idea is that it needs a sort of protection in order not to be thrown into the gutter and finally made away with by a strangely clad Jew.

The best protection you could devise, it seems to me, would be to put in incorporate the book itself an exposition of the

182. The reference is to the beginning of *Faust*: a dialogue among the director, poet, and a merry person.

forces that will attempt to destroy it. It is one of your great gifts ~~strength~~ of seeing the black as well as the white of every given situation, so you will know better than most of the people who attack the book, what it is that they want to destroy. Could you not take the wind out of their sails by writing their criticism for them? Perhaps that is the very thing you have done in the introduction. Perhaps you would rather assume towards the public the attitude of "Take or leave it, and be blessed or be damned whichever you prefer." That would be all right, whatever there is of truth in it is going to survive in any case. But I would like to see you do the other thing if it did not call for too much effort.

JANUARY 26, 1924

You had the night before had a dream in which I appeared in a disguise and was to do work on the Red Book and you had been thinking about it all that day and during Dr. Wharton's hour preceding mine especially (pleasant for her I must say) . . . As you had said you had made up your mind to turn over to me all of your unconscious material represented by the Red Book etc. to see what I as a stranger and impartial observer would say about it. You thought I had a good critique and an impartial one. Toni you said was deeply interwoven with it and besides did not take any interest in the thing in itself, nor in getting it into usable form. She is lost in "bird fluttering" you said. For yourself, you said you had always known what to do with your ideas, but here you were baffled. When you approached them you became enmeshed as it were and could no longer be sure of anything. You were certain some of them had great importance, but you could not find the appropriate form—as they were now you said they might come out of a madhouse. So then you said I was to copy down the contents of the Red Book—once before you had had it copied, but you had since then added a great deal of material, so you wanted it done again and you would explain things to me as I went along, for you understood nearly everything in it you said. In this way we could come to discuss many things which never came up in

> my analysis and I could understand your ideas from the foundation. You told me then something more of your own attitude toward the "Red Book." You said some of it hurt your sense of the fitness of things terribly, and that you had shrunk from putting it down as it came to you, but that you had started on the principle of "voluntariness" that is of making no corrections and so you had stuck to that. Some of the pictures were absolutely infantile, but were intended so to be. There were various figures speaking, Elias, Father Philemon, etc. but all appeared to be phases of what you thought ought to be called "the master." You were sure that this latter was the same who inspired Buddha, Mani, Christ, Mahomet—all those who may be said to have communed with God.[183] But the others had identified with him. You absolutely refused to. It could not be for you, you said, you had to remain the psychologist—the person who understood the process. I said then that the thing to be done was to enable the world to understand the process also without their getting the notion that they had the Master caged as it were at their beck & call. They had to think of him as a pillar of fire perpetually moving on and forever out of human grasp. Yes, you said it was something like that. Perhaps it cannot yet be done. As you talked I grew more and more aware of the immeasurability of the ideas which are filling you. You said they had the shadow of eternity upon them and I could feel the truth of it.[184]

On January 30, she noted that Jung said of a dream which she had told him:

> That it was a preparation for the Red Book, because the Red Book told of the battle between the world of reality and the world of the spirit. You said in that battle you had been very nearly torn asunder but that you had managed to keep your feet

183. In reference to this, see the inscription to Image 154 below, note 282, p. 412.
184. *CFB*.

> on the earth & make an effect on reality. That you said for you was the test of any idea, and that you had no respect for any ideas however winged that had to exist off in space and were unable to make an impression on reality.[185]

There is an undated fragment of a letter draft to an unidentified person in which Cary Baynes expresses her view of the significance of *Liber Novus*, and the necessity of its publication:

> I am absolutely thunderstruck, for example, as I read the Red Book, and see all that is told there for the *Right Way* for us of today, to find how Toni has kept it out of her system. She wouldn't have an unconscious spot in her psyche had she digested even as much of the Red Book as I have read & that I should think was not a third or a fourth. And another difficult thing to understand is why she has no interest in seeing him publish it. There are people in my country who would read it from cover to cover without stopping to breathe scarcely, so does it re-envisage and clarify the things that are today, staggering everyone who is trying to find the clue to life . . . he has put into it all the vigor and color of his speech, all the directness and simplicity that come when as at Cornwall the fire burns in him.[186]
>
> Of course it may be that as he says, if he published it as it is, he would forever be hors du combat in the world of rational science, but then there must be some way around that, some way of protecting himself against stupidity, in order that the people who would want the book need not go without for the time it will take the majority to get ready for it. I always knew he must be able to write the fire that he can speak—and here it is. His published books are doctored up for the world at large, or rather they are written out of his head & this out of his heart.[187]

185. Ibid.
186. The reference is to the Polzeath seminar.
187. I suspect that this may have been written to her ex-husband, Jaime de Angulo. On July 10, 1924, he wrote to her: "I daresay you have been as busy as I have, with that material

These discussions vividly portray the depth of Jung's deliberations concerning the publication of *Liber Novus*, his sense of its centrality in comprehending the genesis of his work, and his fear that the work would be misunderstood. The impression that the style of the work would make on an unsuspecting public strongly concerned Jung. He later recalled to Aniela Jaffé that the work still needed a suitable form in which it could be brought into the world because it sounded like prophecy, which was not to his taste.[188]

There appears to have been some discussion concerning these issues in Jung's circle. On May 29, 1924, Cary Baynes noted a discussion with Peter Baynes in which he argued that *Liber Novus* could be understood only by someone who had known Jung. By contrast, she thought that the book

> was the record of the passage of the universe through the soul of a man, and just as a person stands by the sea and listens to that very strange and awful music and cannot explain why his heart aches, or why a cry of exaltation wants to leap from his throat, so I thought it would be with the *Red Book*, and that a man would be perforce lifted out of himself by the majesty of it, and swung to heights he had never been before.[189]

There are further signs that Jung circulated copies of *Liber Novus* to confidantes, and that the material was discussed together with the possibilities of its publication. One such colleague was Wolfgang Stockmayer. Jung met Stockmayer in 1907. In his unpublished obituary, Jung nominated him as the first German to be interested in his work. He recalled that Stockmayer was a true friend. They traveled together in Italy and Switzerland, and there was seldom a year in which they did not meet. Jung commented:

---

of Jung's . . . I read your letter, the one in which you announced it, and you warned me not to tell anyone, and you added that you ought not to tell me, but you knew I would feel so proud of you" (*CFB*).

188. *MP*, p. 169.

189. *CFB*.

> He distinguished himself through his great interest and equally great understanding for pathological psychic processes. I also found with him a sympathetic reception for my broader viewpoint, which became of importance for my later comparative psychological works.[190]

Stockmayer accompanied Jung in "the valuable penetration of our psychology" into classical Chinese philosophy, the mystical speculations of India and Tantric yoga.[191]

On December 22, 1924, Stockmayer wrote to Jung:

> I often long for the *Red Book*, and I would like to have a transcript of what is available; I failed to do so when I had it, as things go. I recently fantasized about a kind of journal of "Documents" in a loose form for materials from the "forge of the unconscious," with words and colors.[192]

It appears that Jung sent some material to him. On April 30, 1925, Stockmayer wrote to Jung:

> In the meantime we have gone through "Scrutinies," and it is the same impression as with the great wandering.[193] A selected collective milieu for such from the Red Book is certainly worth trying out, although your commentary would be quite desired. Since a certain adjacent center of yours lies here, ample access to sources is of great significance, consciously and unconsciously. And I obviously fantasize about "facsimiles," which you will understand: you need not fear extraversion magic from me. Painting also has great appeal.[194]

190. "Stockmayer obituary," JA.
191. Ibid.
192. *JA*. Jung's letters to Stockmayer have not come to light.
193. The reference is to *Liber Secundus* of *Liber Novus*; see note 4, p. 212 below.
194. *JA*.

Jung's manuscript "Commentaries" (see Appendix B) was possibly connected with these discussions.

Thus figures in Jung's circle held differing views concerning the significance of *Liber Novus* and whether it should be published, which may have had bearings on Jung's eventual decisions. Cary Baynes did not complete the transcription, getting as far as the first twenty-seven pages of *Scrutinies*. For the next few years, her time was taken up with the translation of Jung's essays into English, followed by the translation of the *I Ching*.

At some stage, which I estimate to be in the mid-twenties, Jung went back to the *Draft* and edited it again, deleting and adding material on approximately 250 pages. His revisions served to modernize the language and terminology.[195] He also revised some of the material that he had already transcribed into the calligraphic volume of *Liber Novus*, as well as some material that was left out. It is hard to see why he undertook this unless he was seriously considering publishing it.

In 1925, Jung presented his seminars on analytical psychology to the Psychological Club. Here, he discussed some of the important fantasies in *Liber Novus*. He described how they unfolded and indicated how they formed the basis of the ideas in *Psychological Types* and the key to understanding its genesis. The seminar was transcribed and edited by Cary Baynes. That same year, Peter Baynes prepared an English translation of the *Septem Sermones ad Mortuos*, which was privately published.[196] Jung gave copies to some of his English-speaking students. In a letter that is presumably a reply to one from Henry Murray thanking him for a copy, Jung wrote:

> I am deeply convinced, that those ideas that came to me, are really quite wonderful things. I can easily say that (without blushing), because I know, how resistant and how foolishly obstinate I was, when they first visited me and what a trouble it

195. E.g., substituting "Zeitgeist" for "Geist der Zeit" (spirit of the times), "Idee" (Idea) for "Vordenken" (Forethinking).
196. London: Stuart and Watkins, 1925.

> was, until I could read this symbolic language, so much superior to my dull conscious mind.[197]

It is possible that Jung may have considered the publication of the *Sermones* as a trial for the publication of *Liber Novus*. Barbara Hannah claims that he regretted publishing it and that "he felt strongly that it should only have been written in the *Red Book*."[198]

At some point, Jung wrote a manuscript entitled "Commentaries," which provided a commentary on chapters 9, 10, and 11 of *Liber Primus* (see Appendix B). He had discussed some of these fantasies in his 1925 seminar, and he goes into more detail here. From the style and conceptions, I would estimate that this text was written in the mid-twenties. He may have written—or intended to write—further "commentaries" for other chapters, but these have not come to light. This manuscript indicates the amount of work he put into understanding each and every detail of his fantasies.

Jung gave a number of people copies of *Liber Novus*: Cary Baynes, Peter Baynes, Aniela Jaffé, Wolfgang Stockmayer, and Toni Wolff. Copies may also have been given to others. In 1937, a fire destroyed Peter Baynes's house, and damaged his copy of *Liber Novus*. A few years later, he wrote to Jung asking if by chance he had another copy, and offered to translate it.[199] Jung replied: "I will try whether I can procure another copy of the Red Book. Please don't worry about translations. I am sure there are 2 or 3 translations already. But I don't know of what and by whom."[200] This supposition was presumably based on the number of copies of the work in circulation.

Jung let the following individuals read and/or look at *Liber Novus*: Richard Hull, Tina Keller, James Kirsch, Ximena Roelli de Angulo (as a child), and Kurt Wolff. Aniela Jaffé read the *Black Books*, and

197. May 2, 1925, Murray papers, Houghton Library, Harvard University, original in English. Michael Fordham recalled being given a copy by Peter Baynes when he had reached a suitably "advanced" stage in his analysis, and being sworn to secrecy about it (personal communication, 1991).

198. C. G. *Jung: His Life and Work. A Biographical Memoir*, p. 121.

199. November 23, 1941, *JA*.

200. January 22, 1942, C. G. *Jung Letters 1*, p. 312.

Tina Keller was also allowed to read sections of the *Black Books*. Jung most likely showed the book to other close associates, such as Emil Medtner, Franz Riklin Sr., Erika Schlegel, Hans Trüb, and Marie-Louise von Franz. It appears that he allowed those people to read *Liber Novus* whom he fully trusted and whom he felt had a full grasp of his ideas. Quite a number of his students did not fit into this category.

The Transformation of Psychotherapy

Liber Novus is of critical significance for grasping the emergence of Jung's new model of psychotherapy. In 1912, in *Transformation and Symbols of the Libido*, he considered the presence of mythological fantasies—such as are present in *Liber Novus*—to be the signs of a loosening of the phylogenetic layers of the unconscious, and indicative of schizophrenia. Through his self-experimentation, he radically revised this position: what he now considered critical was not the presence of any particular content, but the attitude of the individual toward it and, in particular, whether an individual could accommodate such material in their worldview. This explains why he commented in his afterword to *Liber Novus* that to the superficial observer, the work would seem like madness, and could have become so, if he had failed to contain and comprehend the experiences.[201] In *Liber Secundus*, chapter 15, he presents a critique of contemporary psychiatry, highlighting its incapacity to differentiate religious experience or divine madness from psychopathology. If the content of visions or fantasies had no diagnostic value, he held that it was nevertheless critical to view them carefully.[202]

Out of his experiences, he developed new conceptions of the aims and methods of psychotherapy. Since its inception at the end of the nineteenth century, modern psychotherapy had been primarily concerned with the treatment of functional nervous disorders,

201. See below, p. 554.
202. Cf. Jung's comments after a talk on Swedenborg at the Psychological Club, Jaffé papers, ETH.

or neuroses, as they came to be known. From the time of the First World War onward, Jung reformulated the practice of psychotherapy. No longer solely preoccupied with the treatment of psychopathology, it became a practice to enable the higher development of the individual through fostering the individuation process. This was to have far-reaching consequences not only for the development of analytical psychology but also for psychotherapy as a whole.

To demonstrate the validity of the conceptions that he derived in *Liber Novus*, Jung attempted to show that the processes depicted within it were not unique and that the conceptions which he developed in it were applicable to others. To study the productions of his patients, he built up an extensive collection of their paintings. So that his patients were not separated from their images, he would generally ask them to make copies for him.[203]

During this period, he continued to instruct his patients as to how to induce visions in a waking state. In 1926, Christiana Morgan came to Jung for analysis. She had been drawn to his ideas on reading *Psychological Types*, and turned to him for assistance with her problems with relationships and her depressions. In a session in 1926, Morgan noted Jung's advice to her on how to produce visions:

> Well, you see these are too vague for me to be able to say much about them. They are only the beginning. You only use the retina of the eye at first in order to objectify. Then instead of keeping on trying to force the image out you just want to look in. Now when you see these images you want to hold them and see where they take you—how they change. And you want to try to get into the picture yourself—to become one of the actors. When I first began to do this I saw landscapes. Then I learned how to put myself into the landscape, and the figures would talk to me and I would answer them . . . People said he has an artistic temperament. But it was only that my unconscious was sway-

203. These paintings are available for study at the picture archive at the C. G. Jung Institute, Küsnacht.

> ing me. Now I learn to act its drama as well as the drama of the outer life & so nothing can hurt me now. I have written 1000 pages of material from the unconscious (Told the vision of a giant who turned into an egg).[204]

He described his own experiments in detail to his patients, and instructed them to follow suit. His role was one of supervising them in experimenting with their own stream of images. Morgan noted Jung saying:

> Now I feel as though I ought to say something to you about these phantasies . . . The phantasies now seem to be rather thin and full of repetitions of the same motives. There isn't enough fire and heat in them. They ought to be more burning . . . You must be in them more, that is you must be your own conscious critical self in them—imposing your own judgments and criticisms . . . I can explain what I mean by telling you of my own experience. I was writing in my book and suddenly saw a man standing watch over my shoulder. One of the gold dots from my book flew up and hit him in the eye. He asked me if I would take it out. I said no—not unless he told me who he was. He said he wouldn't. You see I knew that. If I had done what he asked then he would have sunk into the unconscious and I would have missed the point of it ie.: why he had appeared from the unconscious at all. finally he told me that he would tell me the meaning of certain hieroglyphs which I had had a few days previous. This he did and I took the thing out of his eye and he vanished.[205]

Jung went so far as to suggest that his patients prepare their own *Red Books*. Morgan recalled him saying:

---

204. July 8, 1926, analysis notebooks, Countway Library of Medicine. The vision referred to at the end is found in *Liber Secundus*, ch. 11, p. 295 below.

205. Ibid., October 12, 1926. The episode referred to here is the appearance of magician "Ha." See below, p. 325, note 155.

> I should advise you to put it all down as beautifully as you can—in some beautifully bound book. It will seem as if you were making the visions banal—but then you need to do that—then you are freed from the power of them. If you do that with these eyes for instance they will cease to draw you. You should never try to make the visions come again. Think of it in your imagination and try to paint it. Then when these things are in some precious book you can go to the book & turn over the pages & for you it will be your church—your cathedral—the silent places of your spirit where you will find renewal. If anyone tells you that it is morbid or neurotic and you listen to them—then you will lose your soul—for in that book is your soul.[206]

In a letter to J. A. Gilbert in 1929, he commented on his procedure:

> I found sometimes, that it is of great help in handling such a case, to encourage them, to express their peculiar contents either in the form of writing or of drawing and painting. There are so many incomprehensible intuitions in such cases, phantasy fragments that rise from the unconscious, for which there is almost no suitable language. I let my patients find their own symbolic expressions, their "mythology."[207]

Philemon's Sanctuary

In the 1920s, Jung's interest increasingly shifted from the transcription of *Liber Novus* and the elaboration of his mythology in the *Black Books* to working on his tower in Bollingen. In 1920, he purchased some land on the upper shores of Lake Zürich in Bollingen. Prior to this, he and his family sometimes spent holidays camping around Lake Zürich. He felt the need to represent his innermost thoughts in stone and to build a completely primitive dwelling: "Words and

206. Ibid., July 12, 1926.
207. December 20, 1929, *JA* (original in English).

paper, however, did not seem real enough to me; something more was needed."[208] He had to make a confession in stone. The tower was a "representation of individuation." Over the years, he painted murals and made carvings on the walls. The tower may be regarded as a three-dimensional continuation of *Liber Novus*: its "*Liber Quartus*." At the end of *Liber Secundus*, Jung wrote: "I must catch up with a piece of the Middle Ages—within myself. We have only finished the Middle Ages of—others. I must begin early, in that period when the hermits died out."[209] Significantly, the tower was deliberately built as a structure from the Middle Ages, with no modern amenities. The tower was an ongoing, evolving work. He carved this inscription on its wall: "Philemonis sacrum—Fausti poenitentia" (Philemon's Shrine—Faust's Repentance). (One of the murals in the tower is a portrait of Philemon.) On April 6, 1929, Jung wrote to Richard Wilhelm: "Why are there no worldly cloisters for men, who should live outside the times!"[210]

On January 9, 1923, Jung's mother died. On December 23/24, December, 1923, he had the following dream:

> I am on military service. Marching with a battalion. In a wood by Ossingen I come across excavations at a crossroads: 1 meter high stone figure of a frog or a toad with a head. Behind this sits a boy with a toad's head. Then the bust of a man with an anchor hammered into the region of his heart, Roman. A second bust from around 1640, the same motif. Then mummified corpses. finally there comes a barouche in the style of the seventeenth century. In it sits someone who is dead, but still alive. She turns her head, when I address her as "Miss"; I am aware that "Miss" is a title of nobility.[211]

208. *Memories*, p. 250.
209. See below, p. 457.
210. *JP*.
211. *Black Book 7*, p. 120.

A few years later, he grasped the significance of this dream. He noted on December 4, 1926:

> Only now do I see for that the dream of 23/24 December 1923 means the death of the anima ("She does not know that she is dead"). This coincides with the death of my mother . . . Since the death of my mother, the A. [Anima] has fallen silent. Meaningful![212]

A few years later, he had a few further dialogues with his soul, but his confrontation with the anima had effectively reached a closure at this point. On January 2, 1927, he had a dream set in Liverpool:

> Several young Swiss and I are down by the docks in Liverpool. It is a dark rainy night, with smoke and clouds. We walk up to the upper part of town, which lies on a plateau. We come to a small circular lake in a centrally located garden. In the middle of this there is an island. The men speak of a Swiss who lives here in such a sooty, dark dirty city. But I see that on the island stands a magnolia tree covered with red flowers illuminated by an eternal sun, and think, "Now I know, why this Swiss fellow lives here. He apparently also knows why." I see a city map: [Plate].[213]

Jung then painted a mandala based upon this map.[214] He attached great significance to this dream, commenting later:

> This dream represented my situation at the time. I can still see the grayish-yellowish raincoats, glistening with the wetness of the rain. Everything was extremely unpleasant, black and opaque, just as I felt then. But I had had a vision of unearthly beauty, and that was why I was able to live at all . . . I saw that

212. Ibid., p. 121.
213. Ibid., p. 124. For the illustration, see Appendix A, p. 560.
214. See image 159, the facsimile edition of this work, .

> here the goal had been reached. One could not go beyond the center. The center is the goal, and everything is directed toward that center. Through this dream I understood that the self is the principle and archetype of orientation and meaning.[215]

Jung added that he himself was the one Swiss. The "I" was not the self, but from there one could see the divine miracle. The small light resembled the great light. Henceforth, he stopped painting mandalas. The dream had expressed the unconscious developmental process, which was not linear, and he found it completely satisfying. He felt utterly alone at that time, preoccupied with something great that others didn't understand. In the dream, only he saw the tree. While they stood in the darkness, the tree appeared radiantly. Had he not had such a vision, his life would have lost meaning.[216]

The realization was that the self is the goal of individuation and that the process of individuation was not linear, but consisted in a circumambulation of the self. This realization gave him strength, for otherwise the experience would have driven him or those around him crazy.[217] He felt that the mandala drawings showed him the self "in its saving function" and that this was his salvation. The task now was one of consolidating these insights into his life and science.

In his 1926 revision of *The Psychology of the Unconscious Processes*, he highlighted the significance of the midlife transition. He argued that the first half of life could be characterized as the natural phase, in which the prime aim was establishing oneself in the world, gaining an income, and raising a family. The second half of life could be characterized as the cultural phase, which involved a revaluation of earlier values. The goal in this period was one of conserving previous values together with the recognition of their opposites. This meant that individuals had to develop the undeveloped and neglected aspects of their personality.[218] The individuation process was now

---

215. *Memories*, p. 224.
216. *MP*, pp. 159–60.
217. Ibid., p. 173.
218. CW 7, §§114–17.

conceived as the general pattern of human development. He argued that there was a lack of guidance for this transition in contemporary society, and he saw his psychology as filling this lacuna. Outside of analytical psychology, Jung's formulations have had an impact on the field of adult developmental psychology. Clearly, his crisis experience formed the template for this conception of the requirements of the two halves of life. *Liber Novus* depicts Jung's reappraisal of his previous values, and his attempt to develop the neglected aspects of his personality. Thus it formed the basis of his understanding of how the midlife transition could be successfully navigated.

In 1928 he published a small book, *The Relations between the I and the Unconscious*, which was an expansion of his 1916 paper "The structure of the unconscious." Here, he expanded upon the "interior drama" of the transformation process, adding a section dealing in detail with the process of individuation. He noted that after one had dealt with the fantasies from the personal sphere, one met with fantasies from the impersonal sphere. These were not simply arbitrary, but converged upon a goal. Hence these later fantasies could be described as processes of initiation, which provided their nearest analogy. For this process to take place, active participation was required: "When the conscious mind participates actively and experiences each stage of the process . . . then the next image always starts off on the higher level that has been won, and purposiveness develops."[219]

After the assimilation of the personal unconscious, the differentiation of the persona, and the overcoming of the state of godlikeness, the next stage that followed was the integration of the anima for men and of the animus for women. Jung argued that just as it was essential for a man to distinguish between what he was and how he appeared to others, it was equally essential to become conscious of "his invisible relations to the unconscious" and hence to differentiate himself from the anima. He noted that when the anima was unconscious, it was projected. For a child, the first bearer of the

219. Ibid., §386.

soul-image was the mother, and thereafter, the women who aroused a man's feelings. One needed to objectify the anima and to pose questions to her, by the method of inner dialogue or active imagination. Everyone, he claimed, had this ability to hold dialogues with him- or herself. Active imagination would thus be one form of inner dialogue, a type of dramatized thinking. It was critical to disidentify from the thoughts that arose, and to overcome the assumption that one had produced them oneself.[220] What was most essential was not interpreting or understanding the fantasies, but experiencing them. This represented a shift from his emphasis on creative formulation and understanding in his paper on the transcendent function. He argued that one should treat the fantasies completely literally while one was engaged in them, but symbolically when one interpreted them.[221] This was a direct description of Jung's procedure in the *Black Books*. The task of such discussions was to objectify the effects of the anima and to become conscious of the contents that underlay these, thereby integrating these into consciousness. When one had become familiar with the unconscious processes reflected in the anima, the anima then became a function of the relationship between consciousness and the unconscious, as opposed to an autonomous complex. Again, this process of the integration of the anima was the subject of *Liber Novus* and the *Black Books*. (It also highlights the fact that the fantasies in *Liber Novus* should be read symbolically and not literally. To take statements from them out of context and to cite them literally would represent a serious misunderstanding.) Jung noted that this process had three effects:

> The first effect is that the range of consciousness is increased by the inclusion of a great number and variety of unconscious contents. The second is a gradual diminution of the dominating influence of the unconscious. The third is an *alteration in the personality*.[222]

220. Ibid., §323.
221. Ibid., §353.
222. Ibid., §358.

After one had achieved the integration of the anima, one was confronted with another figure, namely the "mana personality." Jung argued that when the anima lost her "mana" or power, the man who assimilated it must have acquired this, and so became a "mana personality," a being of superior will and wisdom. However, this figure was "a *dominant* of the collective unconscious, the recognized archetype of the powerful man in the form of hero, chief, magician, medicine man, and saint, the lord of men and spirits, the friend of Gods."[223] Thus in integrating the anima, and attaining her power, one inevitably identified with the figure of the magician, and one faced the task of differentiating oneself from this. He added that for women, the corresponding figure was that of the Great Mother. If one gave up the claim to victory over the anima, possession by the figure of the magician ceased, and one realized that the mana truly belonged to the "mid-point of the personality," namely, the self. The assimilation of the contents of the mana personality led to the self. Jung's description of the encounter with the mana personality, both the identification and subsequent disidentification with it, corresponds to his encounter with Philemon in *Liber Novus.* Of the self, Jung wrote: "It might as well be called 'God in us.' The beginnings of our whole psychic life seem to be inextricably rooted to this point, and all our highest and deepest purposes seem to be striving toward it."[224] Jung's description of the self conveys the significance of his realization following his Liverpool dream:

> The *self* could be characterized as a kind of compensation for the conflict between inner and outer . . . the self is also the goal of life, because it is the most complete expression of that fateful combination we call individuality . . . With the experiencing of the self as something irrational, as an indefinable being to which the I is neither opposed nor subjected, but in a relation of dependence, and around which it revolves, very much as the

223. Ibid., §377.
224. Ibid., §399.

earth revolves about the sun—then the goal of individuation has been reached.[225]

The Confrontation with the World

Why did Jung stop working on *Liber Novus*? In his afterword, written in 1959, he wrote:

> My acquaintance with alchemy in 1930 took me away from it. The beginning of the end came in 1928, when [Richard] Wilhelm sent me the text of the "Golden flower," an alchemical treatise. There the contents of this book found their way into actuality and I could no longer continue working on it.[226]

There is one more completed painting in *Liber Novus*. In 1928, Jung painted a mandala of a golden castle (Page 163, facsimile edition). After painting it, it struck him that the mandala had something Chinese about it. Shortly afterward, Richard Wilhelm sent him the text of *The Secret of the Golden Flower*, asking him to write a commentary on it. Jung was struck by it and the timing:

> The text gave me an undreamed-of confirmation of my ideas about the mandala and the circumambulation of the center. This was the first event which broke through my isolation. I became aware of an affinity; I could establish ties with someone and something.[227]

The significance of this confirmation is indicated in the lines that he wrote beneath the painting of the Yellow Castle.[228] Jung was struck by the correspondences between the imagery and conceptions of this text and his own paintings and fantasies. On May

225. Ibid., §405.
226. See below, p. 555.
227. *Memories*, pp. 222–23.
228. See below, p. 422, note 307.

25, 1929, he wrote to Wilhelm: "Fate appears to have given us the role of two bridge pillars which carry the bridge between East and West."[229] Only later did he realize that the alchemical nature of the text was important.[230] He worked on his commentary during 1929. On September 10, 1929, he wrote to Wilhelm: "I am thrilled by this text, which stands so close to our unconscious."[231]

Jung's commentary on *The Secret of the Golden Flower* was a turning point. It was his first public discussion of the significance of the mandala. For the first time, Jung anonymously presented three of his own paintings from *Liber Novus* as examples of European mandalas, and commented on them.[232] To Wilhelm, he wrote on October 28, 1929, concerning the mandalas in the volume: "the images amplify one another precisely through their diversity. They give an excellent image of the effort of the unconscious European spirit to grasp Eastern eschatology."[233] This connection between the "European unconscious spirit" and Eastern eschatology became one of the major themes in Jung's work in the 1930s, which he explored through further collaborations with the Indologists Wilhelm Hauer and Heinrich Zimmer.[234] At the same time, the form of the work was crucial: rather than revealing the full details of his own experiment, or those of his patients, Jung used the parallels with the Chinese text as an indirect way of speaking about it, much as he had begun to do in chapter 5 of *Psychological Types*. This allegorical method now became his preferred form. Rather than write directly

229. *JA*.
230. Foreword to the second German edition, "Commentary to 'The Secret of the Golden Flower,'" *CW* 13, p. 4.
231. Wilhelm appreciated Jung's commentary. On October 24, 1929, he wrote to him: "I am again struck most deeply by your comments" (*JA*).
232. See images 105, 159, and 163 in the facsimile edition. These pictures, together with two more, were again anonymously reproduced in 1950 in Jung, ed., *Gestaltungen des Unbewussten: Psychologischen Abhandlungen*, vol. 7 [Forms of the Unconscious: Psychological Treatises] (Zürich: Rascher, 1950).
233. *JA*.
234. On this issue, see *The Psychology of Kundalini Yoga: Notes of the Seminar Given in 1932 by* C. G. *Jung*, ed. Sonu Shamdasani (Bollingen Series, Princeton: Princeton University Press, 1996).

of his experiences, he commented on analogous developments in esoteric practices, and most of all in medieval alchemy.

Shortly afterward, Jung abruptly left off working on *Liber Novus*. The last full-page image was left unfinished, and he stopped transcribing the text. He later recalled that when he reached this central point, or Tao, his confrontation with the world commenced, and he began to give many lectures.[235] Thus the "confrontation with the unconscious" drew to a close, and the "confrontation with the world" began. Jung added that he saw these activities as a form of compensation for the years of inner preoccupation.[236]

The Comparative Study of the Individuation Process

Jung had been familiar with alchemical texts from around 1910. In 1912, Théodore Flournoy had presented a psychological interpretation of alchemy in his lectures at the University of Geneva and, in 1914, Herbert Silberer published an extensive work on the subject.[237] Jung's approach to alchemy followed the work of Flournoy and Silberer, in regarding alchemy from a psychological perspective. His understanding of it was based on two main theses: first, that in meditating on the texts and materials in their laboratories, the alchemists were actually practicing a form of active imagination. Second, that the symbolism in the alchemical texts corresponded to that of the individuation process with which Jung and his patients had been engaged.

---

235. *MP*, p. 15.
236. On February 8, 1923, Cary Baynes noted a discussion with Jung in the previous spring which has bearings on this: "You [Jung] said that no matter how marked off from the crowd an individual might be with special gifts, he yet had not fulfilled all his duties, psychologically speaking, unless he could function successfully in collectivity. By functioning in collectivity we both meant what is commonly called 'mixing' with people in a social way, not professional or business relationships. Your point was that if an individual kept away from these collective relationships, he lost something he could not afford to lose" (*CFB*).
237. *Problems of Mysticism and Its Symbolism*, tr. S. E. Jeliffe (New York: Moffat Yard, 1917).

In the 1930s, Jung's activity shifted from working on his fantasies in the *Black Books* to his alchemy copy books. In these, he presented an encyclopedic collection of excerpts from alchemical literature and related works, which he indexed according to key words and subjects. These copy books formed the basis of his writings on the psychology of alchemy.

After 1930, Jung put *Liber Novus* to one side. While he had stopped working directly on it, it still remained at the center of his activity. In his therapeutic work, he continued to attempt to foster similar developments in his patients, and to establish which aspects of his own experience were singular, and which had some generality and applicability to others. In his symbolic researches, Jung was interested in parallels to the imagery and conceptions of *Liber Novus*. The question that he pursued was the following: was something akin to the individuation process to be found in all cultures? If so, what were the common and differential elements? In this perspective, Jung's work after 1930 could be considered as an extended amplification of the contents of *Liber Novus*, and an attempt to translate its contents into a form acceptable to the contemporary outlook. Some of the statements made in *Liber Novus* closely correspond to positions that Jung would later articulate in his published works, and represent their first formulations.[238] On the other hand, much did not directly find its way into the *Collected Works*, or was presented in a schematic form, or through allegory and indirect allusion. Thus *Liber Novus* enables a hitherto unsuspected clarification of the most difficult aspects of Jung's *Collected Works*. One is simply not in a position to comprehend the genesis of Jung's late work, nor to fully understand what he was attempting to achieve, without studying *Liber Novus*. At the same time, the *Collected Works* can in part be considered an indirect commentary on *Liber Novus*. Each mutually explicates the other.

Jung saw his "confrontation with the unconscious" as the source of his later work. He recalled that all his work and every-

238. These are indicated in the footnotes to the text.

thing that he subsequently achieved came from these imaginings. He had expressed things as well as he was able, in clumsy, handicapped language. He often felt as if "gigantic blocks of stone were tumbling down upon [him]. One thunderstorm followed another." He was amazed it hadn't broken him as it had done others, such as Schreber.[239]

When asked by Kurt Wolff in 1957 on the relation between his scholarly works and his biographical notes of dreams and fantasies, Jung replied:

> That was the primal stuff that compelled me to work on it, and my work is a more or less successful attempt to incorporate this incandescent matter into the worldview of my time. The first imaginings and dreams were like fiery, molten basalt, from which the stone crystallized, upon which I could work.[240]

He added that "it has cost me 45 years so to speak, to bring the things that I once experienced and wrote down into the vessel of my scientific work."[241]

In Jung's own terms, *Liber Novus* could be considered to contain, among other things, an account of stages of his process of individuation. In subsequent works, he tried to point out the general schematic common elements to which he could find parallels in his patients and in comparative research. The later works thus present a skeletal outline, a basic sketch, but left out the main body of detail. In retrospect, he described the *Red Book* as an attempt to formulate things in terms of revelation. He had hope that this would free him, but found that it didn't. He then realized that he had to return to the human side and to science. He had to draw conclusions from the insights. The elaboration of the material in the *Red Book* was vital,

239. *Memories*, p. 201, *MP*, p. 144.
240. *Erinnerungen, Träume, Gedanken von* C. G. *Jung*, ed. Aniela Jaffé (Olten: Walter Verlag, 1988), p. 201.
241. Ibid.

but he also had to understand the ethical obligations. In doing so, he had paid with his life and his science.[242]

In 1930, he commenced a series of seminars on the fantasy visions of Christiana Morgan at the Psychological Club in Zürich, which can in part be regarded as an indirect commentary on *Liber Novus*. To demonstrate the empirical validity of the conceptions that he derived in the latter, he had to show that processes depicted within it were not unique.

With his seminars on Kundalini Yoga in 1932, Jung commenced a comparative study of esoteric practices, focusing on the spiritual exercises of Ignatius of Loyola, Patanjali's Yoga sutras, Buddhist meditational practices, and medieval alchemy, which he presented in an extensive series of lectures at the Swiss Federal Institute of Technology (ETH).[243] The critical insight that enabled these linkages and comparisons was Jung's realization that these practices were all based on different forms of active imagination—and that they all had as their goal the transformation of the personality—which Jung understood as the process of individuation. Thus Jung's ETH lectures provide a comparative history of active imagination, the practice that formed the basis of *Liber Novus*.

In 1934, he published his first extended case description of the individuation process, which was that of Kristine Mann, who had painted an extensive series of mandalas. He referred to his own undertaking:

> I have naturally used this method on myself too and can affirm that one can paint very complicated pictures without having the least idea of their real meaning. While painting them, the picture seems to develop out of itself and often in opposition to one's conscious intentions.[244]

242. *MP*, p. 148.
243. These lectures are currently being prepared for publication. For further details, see www.philemonfoundation.org.
244. "A study in the process of individuation," *CW* 9, 1, §622.

He noted that the present work filled a gap in his description of his therapeutic methods, as he had written little about active imagination. He had used this method since 1916, but only sketched it in *The Relations of the I to the Unconscious* in 1928, and first mentioned the mandala in 1929, in his commentary on *The Secret of the Golden Flower*:

> For at least thirteen years I kept quiet about the results of these methods in order to avoid any suggestion. I wanted to assure myself that these things—mandalas especially—really are produced spontaneously and were not suggested to the patient by my own fantasy.[245]

Through his historical studies, he convinced himself that mandalas had been produced in all times and places. He also noted that they were produced by patients of psychotherapists who were not his students. This also indicates one consideration that may have led him not to publish *Liber Novus*: to convince himself, and his critics, that the developments of his patients and especially their mandala images were not simply due to suggestion. He held that the mandala represented one of the best examples of the universality of an archetype. In 1936, he also noted that he himself had used the method of active imagination over a long period of time, and observed many symbols that he had been able to verify only years later in texts that had been unknown to him.[246] However, from an evidential standpoint, given the breadth of his learning, Jung's own material would not have been a particularly convincing example of his thesis that images from the collective unconscious spontaneously emerged without prior acquaintance.

In *Liber Novus,* Jung articulated his understanding of the historical transformations of Christianity, and the historicity of symbolic formations. He took up this theme in his writings on the psychology of alchemy and on the psychology of Christian dogmas, and most of

245. Ibid., §623.
246. "On the psychological aspects of the Kore figure," CW 9, 1, §334.

all in *Answer to Job*. As we have seen, it was Jung's view that his prewar visions were prophetic that led to the composition of *Liber Novus*. In 1952, through his collaboration with the Nobel Prize–winning physicist Wolfgang Pauli, Jung argued that there existed a principle of acausal orderedness that underlay such "meaningful coincidences," which he called synchronicity.[247] He claimed that under certain circumstances, the constellation of an archetype led to a relativization of time and space, which explained how such events could happen. This was an attempt to expand scientific understanding to accommodate events such as his visions of 1913 and 1914.

It is important to note that the relation of *Liber Novus* to Jung's scholarly writings did not follow a straight point-by-point translation and elaboration. As early as 1916, Jung sought to convey some of the results of his experiments in a scholarly language, while continuing with the elaboration of his fantasies. One would do best to regard *Liber Novus* and the *Black Books* as representing a private opus that ran parallel to and alongside his public scholarly opus; whilst the latter was nourished by and drew from the former, they remained distinct. After ceasing to work on *Liber Novus*, he continued to elaborate his private opus—his own mythology—in his work on the tower, and in his stone carvings and paintings. Here, *Liber Novus* functioned as a generating center, and a number of his paintings and carvings relate to it. In psychotherapy, Jung sought to enable his patients to recover a sense of meaning in life through facilitating and supervising their own self-experimentation and symbol creation. At the same time, he attempted to elaborate a general scientific psychology.

The Publication of *Liber Novus*

While Jung had stopped working directly on *Liber Novus*, the question of what to do with it remained, and the issue of its eventual

247. See C. A. Meier, ed., *Atom and Archetype: The Pauli/Jung Letters*, with a preface by Beverley Zabriskie, tr. D. Roscoe (Princeton: Princeton University Press, 2001).

publication remained open. On April 10, 1942, Jung replied to Mary Mellon concerning a printing of the *Sermones*: "Concerning the printing of the 'Seven Sermones' I should wish you to wait for a while. I had in mind to add certain material, but I have hesitated for years to do it. But at such an occasion one might risk it."[248] In 1944, he had a major heart attack and did not see this plan through.

In 1952, Lucy Heyer put forward a project for a biography of Jung. At Olga Froebe's suggestion and on Jung's insistence, Cary Baynes began collaborating with Lucy Heyer on this project. Cary Baynes considered writing a biography of Jung based on *Liber Novus*.[249] To Jung's disappointment, she withdrew from the project. After several years of interviews with Lucy Heyer, Jung terminated her biographical project in 1955, because he was dissatisfied with her progress. In 1956, Kurt Wolff proposed another biographical project, which became *Memories, Dreams, Reflections*. At some stage, Jung gave Aniela Jaffé a copy of the draft of *Liber Novus*, which had been made by Toni Wolff. Jung authorized Jaffé to cite from *Liber Novus* and the *Black Books* in *Memories, Dreams, Reflections*.[250] In his interviews with Aniela Jaffé, Jung discussed *Liber Novus* and his self-experimentation. Unfortunately, she did not reproduce all his comments.

On October 31, 1957, she wrote to Jack Barrett of the Bollingen Foundation concerning *Liber Novus*, and informed him that Jung had suggested that it and the *Black Books* be given to the library of the University of Basel with a restriction of 50 years, 80 years, or longer, as "he hates the idea that anybody should read this material without knowing the relations to his life, etc." She added that she had decided not to use much of this material in *Memories*.[251] In one early

248. *JP*. It is likely that Jung had Philemon's commentaries in mind—see below, pp. 514–36.
249. Olga Froebe-Kapteyn to Jack Barrett, January 6, 1953, Bollingen archives, Library of Congress.
250. Jung to Jaffé, October 27, 1957, Bollingen archives, Library of Congress.
251. Bollingen archives, Library of Congress. Jaffé gave a similar account to Kurt Wolff, mentioning 30, 50, or 80 years as the possible restriction (undated; received October 30, 1957), Kurt Wolff papers, Beinecke Library, Yale University. On reading the first sections of the protocols of Aniela Jaffé's interviews with Jung, Cary Baynes wrote to Jung on January 8, 1958, that "it is the right introduction to the Red Book, and so I can die in peace on that score!" (*CFB*)

manuscript of *Memories*, Jaffé had included a transcription of the draft typescript of most of *Liber Primus*.[252] But it was omitted from the final manuscript, and she did not cite from *Liber Novus* or the *Black Books*. In the German edition of *Memories*, Jaffé included Jung's epilogue to *Liber Novus* as an appendix. Jung's flexible date stipulations concerning access to *Liber Novus* were similar to that which he gave around the same time concerning the publication of his correspondence with Freud.[253]

On October 12, 1957, Jung told Jaffé that he had never finished the *Red Book*.[254] According to Jaffé, in the spring of the year 1959 Jung, after a time of lengthy ill-health, took up *Liber Novus* again, to complete the last remaining unfinished image. Once again, he took up the transcription of the manuscript into the calligraphic volume. Jaffé notes, "However, he still could not or would not complete it. He told me that it had to do with death."[255] The calligraphic transcription breaks off midsentence, and Jung added an afterword, which also broke off midsentence. The postscript and Jung's discussions of its donation to an archive suggest that Jung was aware that the work would eventually be studied at some stage. After Jung's death, *Liber Novus* remained with his family, in accordance with his will.

In her 1971 Eranos lecture, "The creative phases in Jung's life," Jaffé cited two passages from the draft of *Liber Novus*, noting that "Jung placed a copy of the manuscript at my disposal with permission to quote from it as occasion arose."[256] This was the only time

252. Kurt Wolff papers, Beinecke Library, Yale University. The prologue was omitted, and it was given the title of the first chapter, "Der Wiederfindung der Seele" (the recovery of the soul). Another copy of this section was heavily edited by an unidentified hand, which may have been part of preparing this for publication at this time (*JFA*).

253. One may note that the publication of the *Freud/Jung Letters*, crucial as this was in its own right, while *Liber Novus* and the bulk of Jung's other correspondences remained unpublished, regrettably heightened the mistaken Freudocentric view of Jung: as we see, in *Liber Novus*, Jung is moving in a universe that is as far away from psychoanalysis as could be imagined.

254. *MP*, p. 169.

255. Jung/Jaffé, *Erinnerungen, Träume, Gedanken von* C. G. *Jung* (Olten: Walter Verlag, 1988), p. 387. Jaffé's other comments here are inaccurate.

256. Jaffé, "The creative phases in Jung's life," *Spring: An Annual of Archetypal Psychology and Jungian Thought*, 1972, p. 174.

she did so. Pictures from *Liber Novus* were also shown in a BBC documentary on Jung narrated by Laurens van der Post in 1972. These created widespread interest in it. In 1975, after the much acclaimed publication of *The Freud/Jung Letters*, William McGuire, representing Princeton University Press, wrote to the lawyer of the Jung estate, Hans Karrer, with a publication proposal for *Liber Novus* and a collection of photographs of Jung's stone carvings, paintings, and the tower. He proposed a facsimile edition, possibly without the text. He wrote that "we are uninformed of the number of its pages, the relative amount of text and pictures, and the content and interest of the text."[257] No one in the press had actually seen or read the work or knew much about it. This request was denied.

In 1975, some reproductions from the calligraphic volume of *Liber Novus* were displayed at an exhibition commemorating Jung's centenary in Zürich. In 1977, nine paintings from *Liber Novus* were published by Jaffé in *C. G. Jung: Word and Image* and in 1989 a few other

257. McGuire papers, Library of Congress. In 1961, Aniela Jaffé had shown *Liber Novus* to Richard Hull, Jung's translator, and he had written his impressions to McGuire: "She [AJ] showed us the famous Red Book, full of real mad drawings with commentaries in monkish script; I'm not surprised Jung keeps it under lock and key! When he came in and saw it lying—fortunately closed—on the table, he snapped at her: 'Das soll nicht hier sein. Nehmen Sie's weg!' (That should not be here. Take it away!), although she had written me earlier that he had given permission for me to see it. I recognized several of the mandalas that are included in *On Mandala Symbolism*. It would make a marvellous facsimile edition, but I didn't feel it wise to raise the subject, or to suggest the inclusion of drawings in the autobiography (which Mrs. Jaffé urged me to do). It really should form part, sometime, of his opus: just as the autobiography is an essential supplement to his other writings, so is the Red Book to the autobiography. The Red Book made a profound impression on me; there can be no doubt that Jung has gone through everything that an insane person goes through, and more. Talk of Freud's self-analysis: Jung is a walking asylum in himself! The only difference between him and a regular inmate is his astounding capacity to stand off from the terrifying reality of his visions, to observe and understand what was happening, and to hammer out of his experience a system of therapy that works. But for this unique achievement he'd be as mad as a hatter. The raw material of his experience is Schreber's world over again; only by his powers of observation and detachment, and his drive to understand, can it be said of him what Coleridge said in his Notebooks of a great metaphysician (and what a motto it would make for the autobiography!): He looked at his own Soul with Telescope / What seemed all irregular, he saw & shewed to be beautiful Constellations & he added to the Consciousness hidden worlds within worlds / "(March 17, 1961, Bollingen archives, Library of Congress). The citation from Coleridge was indeed used as a motto for *Memories, Dreams, Reflections*.

related paintings were published by Gerhard Wehr in his illustrated biography of Jung.[258]

In 1984, *Liber Novus* was professionally photographed, and five facsimile editions were prepared. These were given to the five families directly descendent from Jung. In 1992, Jung's family, who had supported the publication of Jung's *Collected Works* in German (completed in 1995), commenced an examination of Jung's unpublished materials. As a result of my researches, I found one transcription and a partial transcription of *Liber Novus* and presented them to the Jung heirs in 1997. Around the same time, another transcription was presented to the heirs by Marie-Louise von Franz. I was invited to present reports on the subject and its suitability for publication, and made a presentation on the subject. On the basis of these reports and discussions, the heirs decided in May 2000 to release the work for publication.

The work on *Liber Novus* was at the center of Jung's self-experimentation. It is nothing less than the central book in his oeuvre. With its publication, one is now in a position to study what took place there on the basis of primary documentation as opposed to the fantasy, gossip, and speculation that makes up too much of what is written on Jung, and to grasp the genesis and constitution of Jung's later work. For nearly a century, such a reading has simply not been possible, and the vast literature on Jung's life and work that has arisen has lacked access to the single most important documentary source. This publication marks a caesura, and opens the possibility of a new era in the understanding of Jung's work. It provides a unique window into how he recovered his soul and, in so doing, constituted a psychology. Thus this introduction does not end with a conclusion, but with the promise of a new beginning.

258. Aniela Jaffé, ed., C. G. *Jung: Word and Image*, figures 52–57, 77–79, together with a related image, fig. 59; Gerhard Wehr, *An Illustrated Biography of Jung*, pp. 40, 140–41.

Translators' Note

MARK KYBURZ, JOHN PECK, AND SONU SHAMDASANI

At the outset of *Liber Novus,* Jung experiences a crisis of language. The spirit of the depths, who immediately challenges Jung's use of language along with the spirit of the time, informs Jung that on the terrain of his soul his achieved language will no longer serve. His own powers of knowing and speaking can no longer account for why he utters what he says or under what compulsion he speaks. All such attempts become arbitrary in the depth realm, even murderous. He is made to understand that what he might say on these occasions is both "madness" and, instructively, what is.[1] Indeed, in a broader perspective, the language that he will find for his inner experience would compose a vast Commedia: "Do you believe, man of this time, that laughter is lower than worship? Where is your measure, false measurer? The sum of life decides in laughter and in worship, not your judgment."[2]

In translating this accumulated record of Jung's imaginal encounters with his inner figures, from a sixteen-year period beginning just before the First World War, we have let Jung remain a man who was pulled loose from his moorings but also caught up in the maelstrom that has gone by the name of literary modernism. We have tried neither to further modernize nor to render more archaic the language and forms in which he couched his personal record.

The language in *Liber Novus* pursues three main stylistic registers, and each poses distinct difficulties for a translator. One of them faithfully reports the fantasies and inner dialogues of Jung's imaginal encounters, while a second remains firmly and discerningly conceptual. Still a third writes in a mantic and prophetic, or Romantic and dithyrambic, mode. The relation between these reportorial, reflective, and Romantic aspects of Jung's language remains comedic in a manner that Dante or Goethe would have recognized.

1. See below, p. 122.
2. See below, p. 122.

That is, within each chapter the descriptive, conceptual, and mantic registers consistently rub against each other, while at the same time no single register is affected by its partners. All three stylistic registers serve psychic promptings, and each chapter shares a polyphonic mode with the others. In the *Scrutinies* section from 1917 this polyphony matures, its voices commingling in various ratios.

A reader will quickly infer that this design was not premeditated, but rather grew from the experiment to which Jung arduously submitted. The "Editorial Note" diagrams the textual evolution of this composition. Here we need only observe that Jung each time sets down an initial protocol layer of narrative encounter, usually with dialogue, and then, in the "second layer," a lyrical elaboration of and commentary on that encounter. The first layer avoids an elevated tone, whereas the second welcomes elevation and modulates into sermonic, mantic-prophetic reflections on the episode's meaning, which in turn unpack events discursively. This mode of composition—which is unique in Jung's works—was no temperamental arrangement. Instead, as the episodes accumulated and their stakes mounted, it grew into an experiment that was as much literary as it was psychological and spiritual. In Jung's extensive published and unpublished corpus, there is no other text that was subjected to such careful and continual linguistic revision as *Liber Novus*.

These three linguistic registers already present themselves as virtual models for a possible translation. Our practice has been to let them cohabit within the exploratory frameworks alive in Jung's own day. The task before him was to find a language rather than use one ready at hand. The mantic and conceptual registers can themselves be considered as translations of the descriptive register. That is, these registers move from a literal level to symbolic ones that amplify it, in a modern analogue to Dante's "modi diversi" in his letter to Can Grande della Scala.[3] In a very real sense, *Liber Novus* was composed through intertextual translation. The book's rhetoric, its manner

3. See the translation and discussion of this letter in Lucia Boldrini, *Joyce, Dante, and the Poetics of Literary Relations* (New York: Cambridge University Press, 2001), pp. 30–35.

of address, emerges from this interanimating structure of internal translation or transvaluation. A critical task for any translation of the work, therefore, is conveying this compositional texture intact.

The fact that painted images of an accomplished and hybrid kind illuminate the medieval format of a folio in scribal hand compounds any reflections on the linguistic task. The novel language required a renewed ancient script. A polyphonic style couches itself multimedia fashion within a symbolic throwback-yet-forward movement, medieval and anticipatory, into retrievals of psychic reality. Verbal and visual images press in on Jung from the root past and present while aiming toward the beyond: a layered medium emerges, whose polyphonic style mirrors within its language that same composite layering.

Faced with the task of translating a text composed nearly a hundred years ago, translators usually have the benefit of prior models to consult, as well as decades of scholarly commentary and criticism. Without such exemplars at hand, we were left to imagine how the work might have been translated in previous decades. Consequently, our translation sidesteps several unpublished or hypothetical models for rendering *Liber Novus* into English. There is Peter Baynes's strikingly archaizing *Septem Sermones* of 1925, which draws largely upon a Victorian idiom. Or the conceptually rationalizing version that R.F.C. Hull might have attempted had he been allowed to translate it alongside his other volumes in the Bollingen Series of Jung's *Collected Works*;[4] or the elegant literary rendering from the hand of someone like R. J. Hollingdale. Our version therefore occupies an actual position in a largely virtual sequence. Consideration of these virtual models highlighted questions of how to pitch the language within historical shifts in English prose, how to convey the myriad convergences and divergences between the language of *Liber Novus* and Jung's *Collected Works*, and how to render in English a work simultaneously echoing Luther's German and Nietzsche's

4. On the issue of Hull's translations of Jung, see Shamdasani, *Jung Stripped Bare by His Biographers, Even*, pp. 47–51.

parody of the same in *Thus Spoke Zarathustra*. Because our version takes this position, accordingly when we have cited Jung's *Collected Works* we have freshly rendered or discreetly modified the published translations.

Liber Novus was coeval with the literary ferment that Mikhail Bakhtin called the dialogical prose imagination.[5] The Anglo-Welsh writer and artist David Jones, author of *In Parenthesis* and *The Anathemata*, referred to the rupture of the First World War, and its effects on the historical sense of writers, artists, and thinkers, simply as "The Break."[6] In concert with other experimental writing from these decades, *Liber Novus* excavates archaeological layers of literary adventure, with hard-won consciousness as both shovel and precious shard. While Jung actively considered publishing *Liber Novus* for many years, he chose not to make a name for himself in this literary manner—as much for style as for content—by releasing it. By 1921 with *Psychological Types* he already found that his sanctum could furnish him his main themes, through translation into a scholarly idiom.

Jung enunciates the tension among his three stylistic registers, already addressing a future readership—which shifts from an inner circle of friends to a wider public between different layers of the text. This is graphically apparent in the frequent pronomial shifts between the versions, which show the manner in which he was constantly reimagining the potential readers of the text. Jung coherently adopted this dialogical stance—polyphonic in Bakhtin's later terms—once again mindful of a hypothetical future audience yet also aloof from the question of audience altogether, not from pride but simply in view of the aims to be served. Paintings and fantasies from this private treasury entered anonymously as crypted intertexts into Jung's later work, nestling as hermetic clues to the undisclosed whole of his effort.

5. See *The Dialogic Imagination: Four Essays,* ed. Michael Holquist, tr. Caryl Emerson and Michael Holquist (Austin: University of Texas Press, 1981).
6. David Jones, *Dai Greatcoat: A Self-Portrait of David Jones in his Letters,* ed. Rene Hague (London: Faber & Faber, 1980, pp.41ff.).

Indeed, we can imagine Jung laughing when he wrote of "3. Case Z" in the last section of his essay on "The Psychological Aspects of the Kore" (1941).[7] There he summarizes as anonymous twelve episodes from encounters with his own soul in *Liber Novus*, calling them "a dream-series." The comments he appends to these propel the adventurer he had been, and the subject he became in that adventure, into the discourse of a would-be science. The comedy is both spacious and exquisite: this respectful host to the anima also wields the diagnostic pointer in all seriousness. His language flexibly straddled both contexts, but also kept certain veils in place while doing so. This linguistic strategy mirrored Jung's larger aims in remaining fruitfully dual and contextual. Declaring his mysteries to be particular, not to be aped in any way, he nonetheless also offered them as a template of formative spiritual process, and, in so doing, attempted to develop an idiom that could be taken up by others to articulate their experiences.

This is one way of paraphrasing the considerable anomaly of the language that Jung had to find through sleepless nights from 1913 onward. That language shifted its shape, altered its scale, and weighed both megrims and tons. Therefore it comes as no surprise that in his more elevated passages Jung relied on the resonance of the Luther Bible, itself a translation that had achieved rocklike stability within German culture. *Ein feste Burg*, "a mighty fortress:" thus our own reliance here on the King James Version of the Bible (KJV) for comparable tonalities in English. Yet a paradox rises immediately: what Jung counted on in that resonance had transplanted an alien spirit into the Germanic *Heimat* or home, as one may likewise say of the KJV's deep embedding of the same implant in Anglo-Saxon culture. Franz Rosenzweig, translating parts of the Old Testament with Martin Buber in the mid-1920s, identified Luther's Bible as the great space-maker within Germanic spirit, precisely through Luther's close-in moves toward his source: "For the comfort of our souls, we must retain such words, must put up with them, and so give the Hebrew some room where it does better than Ger-

7. CW 9, 1.

man can."[8] Thus our own practice of not smoothing out Jung's several modes, or making them run more fluently than need be, or even regularizing his punctuation. Think of Dante's "shaggy" diction, or of still another maxim from Luther in Rosenzweig's notes: "The mud will cling to the wheel."[9]

Yet even these profound allowances for archaic and original speech across abysses of meaning fail to approximate the destabilizing experience, in and through language, to which Jung testifies. His later comments in the published memoir, on his reservations about high-flown style,[10] in effect cover his tracks in *Liber Novus*. The original experience sent speech into a spin that animates the book's initiatic dimension. Language too undergoes a descent into hell and the realm of the dead, which divests one of speech even as it renews the capacity for utterance.

The following instances give some idea of this factor's range, mapping the stresses in any sincere ventriloquism such as Jung risked by undertaking a controlled séance with himself and his ground, with pen in hand. Hölderlin's hair-breadth space warps and Isaiah's tongue-borne burning coal both move in this league, along with Plato on "right frenzy" or divine madness: (1)"My soul spoke to me in a whisper, urgently and alarmingly: 'Words, words, do not make too many words. Be silent and listen: have you recognized your madness, and do you admit it? Have you noticed that all your foundations are all completely mired in madness?' "[11] (2) Jung's soul: "There are hellish webs of words, only words . . . Be tentative with words, value them . . . for you are the first who gets snared in them. For words have meanings. With words you pull up the underworld. Word, the paltriest and the mightiest. In words the emptiness and the fullness flow together. Hence the word is an image of

8. Martin Buber and Franz Rosenzweig, *Scripture and Translation*, tr. Lawrence Rosenwald with Everett Fox (Bloomington and Indianapolis: Indiana University Press, 1994), p. 49, citing Luther's Preface to his *German Psalter*.
9. Ibid., p. 69.
10. See above, p. 74.
11. See below, p. 347.

the God."[12] (3) "But if the word is a symbol, it means everything. When the way enters death and we are surrounded by rot and horror, the way rises in the darkness and leaves the mouth as the saving symbol, the word."[13] (4) The dead woman: "Let me have the word—oh, that you cannot hear! How difficult—give me the word!"[14] It then materializes in Jung's hand as HAP, the phallus. (5) Jung's soul: "You possess the word that should not be allowed to remain concealed."[15] (6) Jung: "What is my word? It is the stammering of a minor . . ." Soul: "They do not see the fire, they do not believe your words, but they see your mark and unknowingly suspect you to be the messenger of the burning agony . . .You stutter, you stammer."[16] In the protocols for his memoir, Jung recalls bringing to the original experiences in *Liber Novus* only a "highly clumsy speech."[17] Yet one instance (7) strongly belies that later emphasis: "I knew that Philemon had intoxicated me and given me a language that was foreign to me and of a different sensitivity. All of this faded when the God arose and only Philemon kept that language."[18]

This last instance indicates that Jung later attributed the mantic, dithyrambic speech of layer two in everything before the *Scrutinies* section to Philemon. The literal intoxication described here is linguistic, a dramatized, ventriloquial version of Platonic divine madness. It therefore underscores our attempt to faithfully render the stylistic registers of *Liber Novus* so as to present a vital aspect of Jung's literary experiment, as he grapples with attempting to find the most fitting idiom in which to cast the transformations of inner experience. Jung's search for the soul, then, stands at one with the search for appropriately dialogical and differentiated language.

These instances in all their oscillations affect a reading of Jung's *Collected Works*, and counsel caution with applying its conceptual

12. See below, p. 351.
13. See below, p. 392.
14. See below, p. 484.
15. See below, p. 506.
16. See below, p. 506.
17. *MP*, p. 148.
18. See below, p. 112.

tools to the task of reading and understanding *Liber Novus*. To take but one example, one begins to see that it is too neat to equate the opposed yet related depths of Logos and Eros with the conceptual and lyrical-mantic registers found in *Liber Novus*. Jung's "Commentary" on the Elijah-Salome relationship included here shows that relationship to be developmental, a mystery play of "the formative process" that kindles love for the lowest in us.[19] The modal span for language in *Liber Novus* thus animates that mystery play but does not correspond directly to opposed psychological functions.

This complex respect for language instructs translators of *Liber Novus* in navigating the underworld/redemptive tensions spanned by its rhetoric. The great force behind the mantic tension in that rhetoric occupied Jung in the brief Epilogue he inscribed in the calligraphic volume in 1959, two years before his death. Once again plying the seas of those illuminated pages, he seems to have found any further summing-up to be unnecessary. Breaking off in midsentence, he left the book to stand on its own, as one strand of discourse within his whole effort. That counterpoint required no comment, any more than did the three registers of language within the book itself. Ordeal was Commedia after all, calling for no retrospective theoretical justification. *Liber Novus* would survive the gropings and peltings of reception. Jung had remarked in 1957 to Aniela Jaffé that so much rubbish had been said about him that any more rubbish didn't disturb him.[20] That lifted pen therefore confidently consigned the book to its depth trajectory, steeply expanding into the quarry it had become, with both his *Collected Works* and the lakeside tower at Bollingen as its final extractions.

In this note we have attempted to convey only the general principles that have guided this translation. A full discussion of the choices that confronted us and a justification of the decisions taken would fill a volume as ample as this one.

---

19. See Appendix B.
20. *MP*, p. 183.

Editorial Note

SONU SHAMDASANI

Liber Novus is an unfinished manuscript corpus, and it is not completely clear how Jung intended to complete it, or how he would have published it, had he decided to do so. We have a series of manuscripts, of which no single version can be taken as final. Consequently, the text could be presented in a variety of ways. This note indicates the editorial rationale behind the present edition.

The following is the sequence of extant manuscripts for *Liber Primus* and *Liber Secundus*:

Black Books 2–5 (November 1913–April 1914)
Handwritten Draft (Summer 1914–1915)
Typed Draft (circa 1915)
Corrected Draft (with one layer of changes circa 1915; one layer of changes circa mid-1920s)
Calligraphic Volume (1915–1930, resumed in 1959, left incomplete)
Cary Baynes's transcription (1924–1925)
Yale Manuscript. Liber Primus, minus the prologue (identical with *Typed Draft*)
Copy-Edited Draft of Liber Primus minus the prologue, with corrections in unknown hands (circa late 1950s; edited version of the *Typed Draft*)

For *Scrutinies*, we have:

Black Books 5–6 (April 1914–June 1916)
Calligraphic Septem Sermones (1916)
Printed Septem Sermones (1916)
Handwritten Draft (circa 1917)
Typed Draft (circa 1918)
Cary Baynes's transcription (1925) (27 pages, incomplete)

The arrangement presented here starts with a revision of Cary Baynes's transcription and a fresh transcription of the remaining material in the calligraphic volume together with the *Typed Draft* of *Scrutinies*, with line-by-line comparisons with all extant versions. The last thirty pages are completed from the *Draft*. The main variations between the different manuscripts concern the "second layer" of the text. These changes represent Jung's continued work of comprehending the psychological significance of the fantasies. As Jung considered *Liber Novus* to be an "attempt at an elaboration in terms of the revelation," the changes between the different versions present this "attempt at an elaboration," and therefore are an important part of the work itself. Thus the notes indicate significant changes between the different versions, and they present material that clarifies the meaning or context of a particular section. Each manuscript layer is important and interesting, and a publication of all of them—which would run to several thousand pages—would be a task for the future.[1]

The criterion for including passages from the earlier manuscripts has been simply the question: does this inclusion help the reader comprehend what is taking place? Aside from the intrinsic importance of these changes, noting them in the footnotes serves a second purpose—it shows how carefully Jung worked at continually revising the text.

The *Corrected Draft* has two layers of corrections by Jung. The first set of corrections appears to have been done after the *Draft* was typed and before the transcription into the calligraphic volume, as it appears that it was this manuscript that Jung transcribed.[2] A further set of corrections on approximately 200 pages of the typescript appears to have been made *after* the calligraphic volume, and I would estimate that these were done sometime in the mid-1920s. These

1. Interested readers may compare this edition with the sections from the *Draft* in the Kurt Wolff papers at Yale University and with Cary Baynes's transcription at the Contemporary Medical Archives at the Wellcome Collection, London. It is quite possible that other manuscripts may yet come to light.
2. There are also some paint marks on this manuscript.

corrections modernize the language, and bring the terminology into relation with Jung's terminology from the period of *Psychological Types*. Additional clarifications are also added. Jung even corrected material in the *Draft* that was deleted in the calligraphic volume. I have presented some of the significant changes in the footnotes. From them, it is possible for a reader to see how Jung would have revised the whole text, had he completed this layer of corrections.

Subdivisions have been added in *Liber Secundus*, chapter 21, "The Magician," and in *Scrutinies* for ease of reference. These are indicated by numbers in scrolled brackets: { }. Where possible, the date of each fantasy has been given from the *Black Books*. The second layer added in the draft is indicated by [2], and the manuscript reverts to the sequence of the fantasies in the *Black Books* at the beginning of the following chapter. In the passages where subdivisions have been added, the reversion to the sequence of the *Black Books* is indicated by [1].

The various manuscripts have different systems of paragraphing. In the *Draft*, paragraphs often consist of one or two sentences, and the text is presented like a prose poem. At the other extreme, in the calligraphic volume, there are lengthy passages of text with no paragraph breaks. The most logical paragraphing appears in Cary Baynes's transcription. She frequently took her cue for paragraph breaks from the presence of colored initials. Because it is unlikely that she would have reparagraphed the text without Jung's approval, her layout has formed the point of departure for this edition. In some instances, the paragraphing has been brought closer into line with the *Draft* and the calligraphic volume. In the second half of her transcription, Cary Baynes transcribed the *Draft*, because the calligraphic volume had not been completed. Here, I have paragraphed the text in the same manner as established before. I believe that this presents the text in the clearest and easiest-to-follow form.

In the calligraphic volume, Jung illustrated certain initials and wrote some in red and blue, and sometimes increased the size of the text. The layout here attempts to follow these conventions. Because the initials in question aren't always the same in English and German, the choice of which initial to set in red in the English has been governed by its corresponding location in the text. The bolding and increase of font size has been rendered by italics. The remainder of the text beyond that which Jung transcribed in the calligraphic volume has been set following the same conventions, to maintain consistency. In the case of the *Septem Sermones*, the font coloring has followed Jung's printed version of 1916.

The decision to include *Scrutinies* in sequence with and as part of *Liber Novus* is based on the following editorial rationale: The material in the *Black Books* commences in November 1913. *Liber Secundus* closes with material from April 19, 1914, and *Scrutinies* commences with material from the same day. The *Black Books* run consecutively until July 21, 1914, and recommence on June 3, 1915. In the hiatus, Jung wrote the *Handwritten Draft*. When Cary Baynes transcribed *Liber Novus* between 1924 and 1925, the first half of her transcription followed *Liber Novus* itself to the point reached by Jung in his own transcription into the calligraphic volume. It continues by following the draft, and then proceeds 27 pages into *Scrutinies*, ending midsentence.

At the end of *Liber Secundus*, Jung's soul has ascended to Heaven following the reborn God. Jung now thinks that Philemon is a charlatan, and comes to his "I," whom he must live with and educate. *Scrutinies* continues directly from this point with a confrontation with his "I." The ascent of the reborn God is referred to, and his soul returns and explains why she had disappeared. Philemon reappears, and instructs Jung on how to establish the right relation to his soul, the dead, the Gods, and the daimons. In *Scrutinies* Philemon fully emerges and takes on the significance that Jung attached to him both in the 1925 seminar and in *Memories*. Only in *Scrutinies* do certain episodes in *Liber Primus* and *Liber Secundus* become clear. By the same token, the narrative in *Scrutinies* makes no sense if one has not read *Liber Primus* and *Liber Secundus*.

At two places in *Scrutinies*, *Liber Primus* and *Liber Secundus* are mentioned in a way that strongly suggests that they are all part of the same work:

And then the War broke out. This opened my eyes about what I had experienced before and it also gave me the courage to say all that I have written in the earlier part of this book.[3]

Since the God has ascended to the upper realms, ΦΙΛΗΜΩΝ has also become different. He first appeared to me as a magician who lived in a distant land, but then I felt his nearness and, since the God has ascended, I knew that ΦΙΛΗΜΩΝ had intoxicated me and given me a language that was foreign to me and of a different sensitivity. All of this faded when the God arose and only ΦΙΛΗΜΩΝ kept that language. But I felt that he went on other ways than I did. Probably the greater part of what I have written in the earlier part of this book was given to me by ΦΙΛΗΜΩΝ.[4]

These references to the "earlier part of this book" suggest that all of this indeed constitutes one book, and that *Scrutinies* was considered by Jung to be part of *Liber Novus.*

This view is supported by the number of internal connections between the texts. One example is the fact that the mandalas in *Liber Novus* are closely connected to the experience of the self and the realization of its centrality depicted only in *Scrutinies.* Another example occurs in *Liber Secundus,* chapter 15; when Ezechiel and his fellow Anabaptists arrive, they tell Jung that they are going to Jerusalem's holy places because they are not at peace, not having fully finished with life. In *Scrutinies,* the dead reappear, telling Jung that they have been to Jerusalem, but did not find what they sought there. At that point, Philemon appears and the *Septem Sermones* begin. Perhaps Jung intended to transcribe *Scrutinies* into the calligraphic volume and illustrate it; there are ample blank pages.

On January 8, 1958, Cary Baynes asked Jung: "Do you remember that you had me copy quite a bit of the Red Book itself while you were in Africa? I got as far as the beginning of the *Prüfungen* [*Scruti-*

3. See below, p. 474.
4. See below, p. 483.

nies]. This goes beyond what Frau Jaffé put at K. W.'s [Kurt Wolff] disposal and he would like to read it. Is that OK?"[5] Jung replied on January 24, "I have no objections against your lending your notes of the 'Red Book' to Mr. Wolff."[6] Here Cary Baynes, too, seems to have regarded *Scrutinies* as part of *Liber Novus*.

In citations in the notes, ellipses have been indicated by three periods. No emphases have been added.

5. *JA*.
6. *JA*.

Note to the Reader's Edition

Since the publication of the original edition of this work, which included a facsimile reproduction of the calligraphic pages on a one to one scale, there has been a clamor for a more portable reader's edition as a complement to facilitate close study of the work. Judging by Jung's privately printed edition of the *Septem Sermones ad Mortuous*, a text-only edition would likely have been one of the forms of publication that he contemplated at some stage. This edition reproduces the complete translation, introduction, and notes of the original edition of the work, now laid out in one column, similar to the format of Jung's handwritten manuscript and typescript. Cross-references in the text to the facsimile plates have been retained, to enable readers to quickly find the corresponding location and images, when read alongside the original edition. Aside from a few corrections, the text is unchanged. References to Jung's 1925 seminar have been updated to the revised edition of 2012.

Abbreviations and a Note on Pagination

[HI]: Historiated initial: an initial filled with a miniature representation of a single figure or complete scene.

IMAGE 000: Indicates the page number on which the image appears in the facsimile edition.

Where passages in the notes are cited from the *Corrected Draft*, words deleted are given in strikeout, and words added are given in square brackets.

[2]: "Layer two" added in the *Draft*.

{00}: Subdivisions added in long sections for ease of reference

OB: Ornamental border.

BP: Bas de page.

Introduction to Jungian Psychology: C. G. Jung, *Introduction to Jungian Psychology: Notes of the Seminar Given By Jung on Analytical Psychology in 1925*, original edition edited by William McGuire, revised edition edited by Sonu Shamdasani (Princeton: Bollingen/Philemon Series, Princeton University Press) 2012.

CFB: Cary Baynes Papers, Contemporary Medical Archives, Wellcome Library, London.

CW: *The Collected Works of C. G. Jung*, ed. Sir Herbert Read, Michael Fordham, Gerhard Adler, tr. R.F.C. Hull (Princeton: Bollingen Series, Princeton University Press, 1953–1983), 21 vols.

JA: Jung collection, History of Science Collections, Swiss Federal Institute of Technology Archive, Zürich.

JFA: Jung family archives.

Letters: C. G. *Jung Letters*, sel. and ed. by Gerhard Adler in collaboration with Aniela Jaffé, tr. R. F. C. Hull (Princeton: Bollingen Series, Princeton University Press, 1973, 1975), 2 vols.

Memories: *Memories, Dreams, Reflections*, C. G. Jung/Aniela Jaffé, tr. Richard and Clara Winston (London: Flamingo, 1962/1983).

MP: Protocols of Aniela Jaffé's interviews with Jung for *Memories, Dreams, Reflections*, Library of Congress, Washington, D.C. (original in German).

MAP: Minutes of the Association for Analytical Psychology, Psychological Club, Zürich (original in German).

MZS: Minutes of the Zürich Psychoanalytical Society, Psychological Club, Zürich (original in German).

To facilitate moving between the plates in the facsimile edition and the translation here, the following devices are used:

In the *Liber Primus* translation, the numbers at the end of the left-hand running head refer to the folios of the facsimile. For instance, fol. ii(v)/fol. iii(r) indicates the material in the translation is from folio ii, verso, and folio iii, recto, of the facsimile. The break from one page to the next in the facsimile is indicated by a red slash / in the text of the translation and the folio numbers divided by a slash / in the margins of the page.

In *Liber Secundus*, page numbers are used: 3/5 in the running head refers to pages 3 through 5 of the facsimile. A red slash in the text and 3/4 in the margin indicate the break between pages 3 and 4 of the facsimile.

Liber Primus

[fol. i(r)][1]

The Way of What Is to Come

Isaias dixit: quis credidit auditui nostro et brachium Domini cui revelatum est? et ascendet sicut virgultum coram eo et sicut radix de terra sitienti non est species ei neque decor et vidimus eum et non erat aspectus et desideravimus eum: despectum et novissimum virorum virum dolorum et scientem infirmitatem et quasi absconditus vultus eius et despectus unde nec reputavimus eum. vere languores nostros ipse tulit et dolores nostros ipse portavit et nos putavimus eum quasi leprosum et percussum a Deo et humiliatum. Cap. liii/i-iv.

parvulus enim natus est nobis filius datus est nobis et factus est principatus super umerum eius et vocabitur nomen eius Admirabilis consiliarius Deus fortis Pater futuri saeculi princeps pacis. caput ix/vi.

[Isaiah said: Who hath believed our report? and to whom is the arm of the Lord revealed? For he shall grow up before him as a tender plant, and as a root out of a dry ground: he hath no form nor comeliness; and when we shall see him, there is no beauty that we should desire him. He is despised and rejected of men; a man of sorrows, and acquainted with grief: and we hid as it were our faces from him; he was despised, and we esteemed him not. Surely he hath borne our griefs, and carried our sorrows: yet we did esteem him stricken, smitten of God, and afflicted. (Isaiah 53: 1–4)][2]

[For unto us a child is born, unto us a son is given: and the government shall be upon his shoulder: and his name shall be called

1. Medieval manuscripts were numbered by folios instead of pages. The front side of the folio is the recto (the right-hand page of an open book), and the back is the verso (the left-hand of an open book). In *Liber Primus*, Jung followed this practice. He reverted to contemporary pagination in *Liber Secundus*.
2. In 1921, Jung cited the first three verses of this passage (from Luther's Bible), noting: "The birth of the Savior, the development of the redeeming symbol, takes place where one does not expect it, and from precisely where a solution is most improbable" (*Psychological Types*, CW 6, §439).

Wonderful, Counsellor, The mighty God, The everlasting Father, The Prince of Peace. (Isaiah 9:6)][3]

Ioannes dixit: et Verbum caro factum est et habitavit in nobis et vidimus gloriam eius gloriam quasi unigeniti a Patre plenum gratiae et veritatis. Ioann. Cap. i/xiiii.

[John said: And the Word was made flesh, and dwelt among us (and we beheld his glory, the glory as of the only begotten of the Father), full of grace and truth. (John 1:14)]

Isaias dixit: laetabitur deserta et invia et exultabit solitudo et florebit quasi lilium. germinans germinabit et exultabit laetabunda et laudans. tunc aperientur oculi caecorum et aures sordorum patebunt. tunc saliet sicut cervus claudus aperta erit lingua mutorum: quia scissae sunt in deserto aquae et torrentes in solitudine et quae erat arida in stagnum et sitiens in fontes aquarum. in cubilibus in quibus prius dracones habitabant orietur viror calami et iunci. et erit ibi semita et via sancta vocabitur. non transibit per eam pollutus et haec erit vobis directa via ita ut stulti non errent per eam. Cap. xxxv.

[Isaiah said: The wilderness and the solitary place shall be glad for them; and the desert shall rejoice, and blossom as the rose. It shall blossom abundantly, and rejoice even with joy and singing . . . Then the eyes of the blind shall be opened, and the ears of the deaf shall be unstopped. Then shall the lame man leap as a hart, and the tongue of the dumb sing: for in the wilderness shall waters break out, and streams in the desert. And the parched ground shall become a pool, and the thirsty land springs of water: in the habitation of dragons, where each lay, shall be grass with reeds and rushes. And an highway

3. In 1921, Jung cited this passage, noting: "The nature of the redeeming symbol is that of a child, that is the childlikeness or presuppositionlessness of the attitude belongs to the symbol and its function. This 'childlike' attitude necessarily brings with it another guiding principle in place of self-will and rational intentions, whose 'godlikeness' is synonymous with 'superiority.' Since it is of an irrational nature, the guiding principle appears in a miraculous form. Isaiah expresses his connection very well (9:5) . . .These honorific titles reproduce the essential qualities of the redeeming symbol. The criterion of 'godlike' effect is the irresistible power of the unconscious impulses" (*Psychological Types*, CW 6, §442–43).

shall be there, and a way, and it shall be called The way of holiness; the unclean shall not pass over it; but it shall be for those: the wayfaring men, though fools, shall not err therein. (Isaiah 35:1–8)][4]

manu propria scriptum a C. G. *Jung anno Domini mcmxv in domu sua Kusnach Turicense*

[Written by C. G. Jung with his own hand in his house in Küsnacht/Zürich in the year 1915.]

/ [HI i(v)] [2] If I speak in the spirit of this time,[5] I must say: no one and nothing can justify what I must proclaim to you. Justification is superfluous to me, since I have no choice, but I must. I have learned that in addition to the spirit of this time there is still another spirit at work, namely that which rules the depths of everything contemporary.[6] The spirit of this time would like to hear of use and value. I also thought this way, and my humanity still thinks this way. But that other spirit forces me nevertheless to speak, beyond justification, use, and meaning. Filled with human pride and blinded by the presumptuous spirit of the times, I long sought to hold that other spirit away from me. But I did not consider that the spirit of the depths from time immemorial and for all the future possesses a greater power than the spirit of this time, who changes with the generations. The spirit of the depths has subjugated all pride and arrogance to the power of judgment. He took away my belief in science, he robbed me of the joy of explaining and ordering fol. i(r) /i(v)

4. In 1955/56, Jung noted that the union of the opposites of the destructive and constructive powers of the unconscious paralleled the Messianic state of fulfillment depicted in this passage (*Mysterium Coniunctionis*, CW 14, §258).
5. In Goethe's *Faust*, Faust says to Wagner: "What you call the spirit of the times / is fundamentally the gentleman's own mind, / in which the times are reflected" (*Faust* 1, lines 577–79).
6. The *Draft* continues: "And then one whom I did not know, but who evidently had such knowledge, said to me: 'What a strange task you have! You must disclose your innermost and lowermost.' / This I resisted since I hated nothing more than that which seemed to me unchaste and insolent" (p. 1).

things, and he let devotion to the ideals of this time die out in me. He forced me down to the last and simplest things.

The spirit of the depths took my understanding and all my knowledge and placed them at the service of the inexplicable and the paradoxical. He robbed me of speech and writing for everything that was not in his service, namely the melting together of sense and nonsense, which produces the supreme meaning.

But the supreme meaning is the path, the way and the bridge to what is to come. That is the God yet to come. It is not the coming God himself, but his image which appears in the supreme meaning.[7] *God is an image, and those who worship him must worship him in the image of the supreme meaning.*

The supreme meaning is not a meaning and not an absurdity, it is image and force in one, magnificence and force together.

The supreme meaning is the beginning and the end. It is the bridge of going across and fulfillment.[8]

The other Gods died of their temporality, yet the supreme meaning never dies, it turns into meaning and then into absurdity, and out of the fire and blood of their collision the supreme meaning rises up rejuvenated anew.

The image of God has a shadow. The supreme meaning is real and casts a shadow. For what can be actual and corporeal and have no shadow?

The shadow is nonsense. It lacks force and has no continued existence through itself. But nonsense is the inseparable and undying brother of the supreme meaning.

Like plants, so men also grow, some in the light, others in the shadows. There are many who need the shadows and not the light.

The image of God throws a shadow that is just as great as itself.

The supreme meaning is great and small, it is as wide as the space of the starry Heaven and as narrow as the cell of the living body.

---

7. In *Transformations and Symbols of the Libido* (1912), Jung interpreted God as a symbol of the libido (CW B, §111). In his subsequent work, Jung laid great emphasis on the distinction between the God image and the metaphysical existence of God (cf. passages added to the revised retitled 1952 edition, *Symbols of Transformation*, CW 5, §95).

8. The terms *hinübergehen* (going across), *Übergang* (going-across), *Untergang* (down-going), and *Brücke* (bridge) feature in Nietzsche's *Zarathustra* in relation to the passage from man to the *Übermensch* (superman). For example, "What is great in man is that he is a bridge and not a goal: what can be loved in man is that he is a going-across and a down-going. / I love those who do not know how to live except their lives be a down-going, for they are those who are going over" (tr. R. Hollingdale [Harmondsworth: Penguin, 1984], p. 44, tr. mod; words are as underlined in Jung's copy).

The spirit of this time in me wanted to recognize the greatness and extent of the supreme meaning, but not its littleness. The spirit of the depths, however, conquered this arrogance, and I had to swallow the small as a means of healing the immortal in me. It completely burnt up my innards since it was inglorious and unheroic. It was even ridiculous and revolting. But the pliers of the spirit of the depths held me, and I had to drink the bitterest of all draughts.[9]

The spirit of this time tempted me with the thought that all this belongs to the shadowiness of the God-image. This would be pernicious deception, since the shadow is nonsense. But the small, narrow, and banal is not nonsense, but one of both of the essences of the Godhead.

I resisted recognizing that the everyday belongs to the image of the Godhead. I fled this thought, I hid myself behind the highest and coldest stars.

But the spirit of the depths caught up with me, and forced the bitter drink between my lips.[10]

The spirit of this time whispered to me: "This supreme meaning, this image of God, this melting together of the hot and the cold, that is you and only you." But the spirit of the depths spoke to me: "[11] You are an image of the unending world, all the last mysteries of becoming and passing away live in you. If you did not possess all this, how could you know?"

For the sake of my human weakness, the spirit of the depths gave me this word. Yet this word is also superfluous, since I do not speak it freely, but because I must. I speak because the spirit robs me of joy and life if I do not speak.[12] I am the serf who brings it and does not

9. Jung seems to be referring to episodes that occur later in the text: the healing of Izdubar (*Liber Secundus*, ch. 9), and the drinking of the bitter drink prepared by the solitary (*Liber Secundus*, ch. 20).
10. The *Draft* continues: "Who drinks this drink will never again thirst for this world nor for the afterlife since he drank crossing and completion. He drank the hot melting river of life which congeals to hard ore in his soul and awaits new melting and mixture" (p. 4).
11. The calligraphic volume has: "~~this supreme meaning~~."
12. The *Draft* continues: "He who knows understands me and sees that I am not lying. May each one inquire of his own depth whether he needs what I say" (p. 4).

know what he carries in his hand. It would burn his hands if he did not place it where his master orders him to lay it.

The spirit of our time spoke to me and said: "What dire urgency could be forcing you to speak all this?" This was an awful temptation. I wanted to ponder what inner or outer bind could force me into this, and because I found nothing that I could grasp, I was near to making one up. But with this the spirit of our time had almost brought it about that instead of speaking, I was thinking again about reasons and explanations. But the spirit of the depths spoke to me and said: "To understand a thing is a bridge and possibility of returning to the path. But to explain a matter is arbitrary and sometimes even murder. Have you counted the murderers among the scholars?"

But the spirit of this time stepped up to me and laid before me huge volumes which contained all my knowledge. Their pages were made of ore, and a steel stylus had engraved inexorable words in them, and he pointed to these inexorable words and spoke to me, and said: "What you speak, that is madness."

It is true, it is true, what I speak is the greatness and intoxication and ugliness of madness.

But the spirit of the depths stepped up to me and said: "What you speak is. The greatness is, the intoxication is, the undignified, sick, paltry dailiness is. It runs in all the streets, lives in all the houses, and rules the day of all humanity. Even the eternal stars are commonplace. It is the great mistress and the one essence of God. One laughs about it, and laughter, too, is. Do you believe, man of this time, that laughter is lower than worship? Where is your measure, false measurer?[13] The sum of life decides in laughter and in worship, not your judgment."

I must also speak the ridiculous. You coming men! You will recognize the supreme meaning by the fact that he is laughter and worship, a bloody laughter and a bloody worship. A sacrificial blood binds the poles. Those who know this laugh and worship in the same breath.

13. Lit. *Vermessener.* This also carries the connotation of the adjective *vermessen*, that is, a lack or loss of measure, and thus implies overconfidence, presumptuousness.

After this, however, my humanity approached me and said: "What solitude, what coldness of desolation you lay upon me when you speak such! Reflect on the destruction of being and the streams of blood from the terrible sacrifice that the depths demand."[14]

But the spirit of the depths said: "No one can or should halt sacrifice. Sacrifice is not destruction, sacrifice is the foundation stone of what is to come. Have you not had monasteries? Have not countless thousands gone into the desert? You should carry the monastery in yourself. The desert is within you. The desert calls you and draws you back, and if you were fettered to the world of this time with iron, the call of the desert would break all chains. Truly, I prepare you for solitude."

After this, my humanity remained silent. Something happened to my spirit, however, which I must call mercy.

My speech is imperfect. Not because I want to shine with words, but out of the impossibility of finding those words, I speak in images. With nothing else can I express the words from the depths.

The mercy which happened to me gave me belief, hope, and sufficient daring, not to resist further the spirit of the depths, but to utter his word. But before I could pull myself together to really do it, I needed a visible sign that would show me that the spirit of the depths in me was at the same time the ruler of the depths of world affairs.

[15]It happened in October of the year 1913 as I was leaving alone for a journey, that during the day I was suddenly overcome in broad daylight by a vision: I saw a terrible flood that covered all the northern and low-lying lands between the North Sea and the Alps. It reached from England up to Russia, and from the coast of the North Sea right up to the Alps. I saw yellow waves, swimming rubble, and the death of countless thousands.

This vision lasted for two hours, it confused me and made me ill. I was not able to interpret it. Two weeks passed then the vision returned, still more violent than before, and an inner voice spoke:

14. A reference to the vision that follows.
15. The *Corrected Draft* has: "I Beginning" (p. 7).

"Look at it, it is completely real, and it will come to pass. You cannot doubt this." I wrestled again for two hours with this vision, but it held me fast. It left me exhausted and confused. And I thought my mind had gone crazy.[16]

From then on the anxiety toward the terrible event that stood directly before us kept coming back. Once I also saw a sea of blood over the northern lands.

In the year 1914 in the month of June, at the beginning and end of the month, and at the beginning of July, I had the same dream three times: I was in a foreign land, and suddenly, overnight and right in the middle of summer, a terrible cold descended from space. All seas and rivers were locked in ice, every green living thing had frozen.

The second dream was thoroughly similar to this. But the third dream at the beginning of July went as follows:

I was in a remote English land.[17] It was necessary that I return to my homeland with a fast ship as speedily as possible.[18] I reached home quickly.[19] In my homeland I found that in the middle of summer a terrible cold had fallen from space, which had turned every living thing into ice. There stood a leaf-bearing but fruitless tree, whose leaves had turned into sweet grapes full of healing juice through the working of the frost.[20] I picked some grapes and gave them to a great waiting throng.[21]

16. Jung discussed this vision on several occasions, stressing different details: in his 1925 seminar *Introduction to Jungian Psychology* (p. 44f), to Mircea Eliade (see above, p. 28), and in *Memories* (pp. 199–200). Jung was on the way to Schaffhausen, where his mother-in-law lived; her fifty-seventh birthday was on October 17. The journey by train takes about one hour.

17. The *Draft* continues: "with a friend (whose lack of farsightedness and whose improvidence I had in reality often noted)" (p. 8).

18. The *Draft* continues: "my friend, however, wanted to return on a small and slower ship, which I considered stupid and imprudent" (p. 8).

19. The *Draft* continues: "and there I found, strangely enough, my friend, who had evidently taken the same faster ship without my noticing" (pp. 8–9).

20. Ice wine is made by leaving grapes on the vine until they are frozen by frost. They are then pressed, and the ice is removed, leading to a highly concentrated delectable sweet wine.

21. The *Draft* continues: "This was my dream. All my efforts to understand it were in vain. I labored for days. Its impression, however, was powerful" (p. 9). Jung also recounted this dream in *Memories* (p. 200).

In reality, now, it was so: At the time when the great war broke out between the peoples of Europe, I found myself in Scotland,[22] compelled by the war to choose the fastest ship and the shortest route home. I encountered the colossal cold that froze everything, I met up with the flood, the sea of blood, and found my barren tree whose leaves the frost had transformed into a remedy. And I plucked the ripe fruit and gave it to you and I do not know what I poured out for you, what bitter-sweet intoxicating drink, which left on your tongues an aftertaste of blood.

Believe me:[23] *It is no teaching and no instruction that I give you. On what basis should I presume to teach you? I give you news of the way of* this *man, but not of your own way. My path is not your path, therefore I / cannot teach you.*[24] *The* fol. i(v)
way is within us, but not in Gods, nor in teachings, nor in laws. Within us is the /ii(r)
way, the truth, and the life.

Woe betide those who live by way of examples! Life is not with them. If you live according to an example, you thus live the life of that example, but who should live your own life if not yourself? So live yourselves.[25]

The signposts have fallen, unblazed trails lie before us.[26] *Do not be greedy to gobble up the fruits of foreign fields. Do you not know that you yourselves are the fertile acre which bears everything that avails you?*

Yet who today knows this? Who knows the way to the eternally fruitful climes of the soul? You seek the way through mere appearances, you study books and give ear to all kinds of opinion. What good is all that?

There is only one way and that is your way.[27]

You seek the path? I warn you away from my own. It can also be the wrong way for you.

May each go his own way.

---

22. See introduction, p. 28.
23. In the *Draft*, this is addressed to "my friends" (p. 9).
24. Cf. the contrast to John 14:6: "Jesus said unto him, I am the way, the truth and the life: no man cometh unto the Father, but by me."
25. The *Draft* continues: "This is not a law, but notice of the fact that the time of example and law, and of the straight line drawn in advance has become overripe" (p. 10).
26. The *Draft* continues: "My tongue shall wither if I serve up laws, if I prattle to you about teachings. Those who seek such will leave my table hungry" (p. 10).
27. The *Draft* continues: "only one law exists, and that is your law. Only one truth exists, and that is your truth" (p. 10).

I will be no savior, no lawgiver, no master teacher unto you. You are no longer little children.[28]

Giving laws, bettering, making things easier, has all become wrong and evil. May each one seek out his own way. The way leads to mutual love in community. Men will come to see and feel the similarity and commonality of their ways.

Laws and teachings held in common compel people to solitude, so that they may escape the pressure of undesirable contact, but solitude makes people hostile and venomous.

Therefore give people dignity and let each of them stand apart, so that each may find his own fellowship and love it.

Power stands against power, contempt against contempt, love against love. Give humanity dignity, and trust that life will find the better way.

The *one eye of the Godhead is blind, the one ear of the Godhead is deaf, the order of its being is crossed by chaos. So be patient with the crippledness of the world and do not overvalue its consummate beauty.*[29]

28. The *Draft* continues: "One should not turn people into sheep, but sheep into people. The spirit of the depth demands this, who is beyond present and past. Speak and write for those who want to listen and read. But do not run after men, so that you do not soil the dignity of humanity—it is a rare good. A sad demise in dignity is better than an undignified healing. Whoever wants to be a doctor of the soul sees people as being sick. He offends human dignity. It is presumptuous to say that man is sick. Whoever wants to be the soul's shepherd treats people like sheep. He violates human dignity. It is insolent to say that people are like sheep. Who gives you the right to say that man is sick and a sheep? Give him human dignity so he may find his ascendancy or downfall, his way" (p. 11).
29. The *Draft* continues: "This is all, my dear friends, that I can tell you about the grounds and aims of my message, which I am burdened with like the patient donkey with a heavy load. He is glad to put it down" (p. 12).

Refinding the Soul

[HI ii(r)][30]

Cap i.[31]

[2] When I had the vision of the flood in October of the year 1913, it happened at a time that was significant for me as a man. At that time, in the fortieth year of my life, I had achieved everything that I had wished for myself. I had achieved honor, power, wealth, knowledge, and every human happiness. Then my desire for the increase of these trappings ceased, the desire ebbed from me and horror came over me.[32] The vision of the flood seized me and I felt the spirit of the depths, but I did not understand him.[33] Yet he drove me on with unbearable inner longing and I said:

[1][34] "My soul, where are you? Do you hear me? I speak, I call you—are you there? I have returned, I am here again. I have shaken the dust of all the lands from my feet, and I have come to you, I am with you. After long years of long wandering, I have come to you again. Should I tell you everything I have seen, experienced, and drunk in? Or do you not want to hear about all the noise of life and the world?

30. In the text, Jung identifies the white bird as his soul. For Jung's discussion of the dove in alchemy, see *Mysterium Coniunctionis* (1955/56) (CW 14, §81).
31. The *Corrected Draft* has: "*First Nights*" (p. 13).
32. The *Handwritten Draft* has: "Dear Friends!" (p. 1). The *Draft* has "Dear Friends!" (p. 1). In his lecture at the *ETH* on June 14, 1935, Jung noted: "A point exists at about the thirty-fifth year when things begin to change, it is the first moment of the shadow side of life, of the going down to death. It is clear that Dante found this point and those who have read *Zarathustra* will know that Nietzsche also discovered it. When this turning point comes people meet it in several ways: some turn away from it; others plunge into it; and something important happens to yet others from the outside. If we do not see a thing Fate does it to us" (Barbara Hannah, ed., *Modern Psychology Vol. 1 and 2: Notes on Lectures given at the Eidgenössiche Technische Hochschule, Zürich, by Prof. Dr. C. G. Jung, October 1933–July 1935, 2nd ed.* [Zürich: privately printed, 1959], p. 223).
33. On October 27, 1913, Jung wrote to Freud breaking off relations with him and resigning as editor of the *Jahrbuch für Psychoanalytische und Psychopathologische Forschungen* (William McGuire, ed., *The Freud/Jung Letters*, tr. R. Mannheim and R.F.C. Hull [Princeton: Princeton University Press/Bollingen Series, 1974], p. 550).
34. November 12, 1913. After "longing," the *Draft* has "at the beginning of the following month, I seized my pen and began writing this" (p. 13).

But one thing you must know: the one thing I have learned is that one must live this life.

This life is the way, the long sought-after way to the unfathomable, which we call divine.[35] There is no other way, all other ways are false paths. I found the right way, it led me to you, to my soul. I return, tempered and purified. Do you still know me? How long the separation lasted! Everything has become so different. And how did I find you? How strange my journey was! What words should I use to tell you on what twisted paths a good star has guided me to you? Give me your hand, my almost forgotten soul. How warm the joy at seeing you again, you long disavowed soul. Life has led me back to you. Let us thank the life I have lived for all the happy and all the sad hours, for every joy, for every sadness. My soul, my journey should continue with you. I will wander with you and ascend to my solitude."[36]

[2] The spirit of the depths forced me to say this and at the same time to undergo it against myself, since I had not expected it then. I still labored misguidedly under the spirit of this time, and thought differently about the human soul. I thought and spoke much of the soul. I knew many learnèd words for her, I had judged her and turned her into a scientific object.[37] I did not consider that my soul cannot be the object of my judgment and knowledge; much more are my judgment and knowledge the objects of my soul.[38] Therefore the spirit of the depths forced me to speak to my soul, to call upon

35. This affirmation occurs a number of times in Jung's later writings—see for example, Jane Pratt, "Notes on a talk given by C. G. Jung: 'Is analytical psychology a religion?'" *Spring Journal of Archetypal Psychology and Jungian Thought* (1972), p. 148.

36. Jung later described his personal transformation at this time as an example of the beginning of the second half of life, which frequently marked a return to the soul, after the goals and ambitions of the first half of life had been achieved (*Symbols of Transformation* [1952], CW 5, p. xxvi); see also "The turning point of life" (1930, CW 8).

37. Jung is referring here to his earlier work. For example, he had written in 1905, "Through the associations experiment we are at least given the means to pave the way for the experimental research of the mysteries of the sick soul" ("The psychopathological meaning of the associations experiment," CW 2, §897).

38. In *Psychological Types* (1921) Jung noted that in psychology, conceptions are "a product of the subjective psychological constellation of the researcher" (CW 6, §9). This reflexivity formed an important theme in his later work (see my *Jung and the Making of Modern Psychology: The Dream of a Science*, §1).

her as a living and self-existing being. I had to become aware that I had lost my soul.

From this we learn how the spirit of the depths considers the soul: he sees her as a living and self-existing being, and with this he contradicts the spirit of this time for whom the soul is a thing dependent on man, which lets herself be judged and arranged, and whose circumference we can grasp. I had to accept that what I had previously called my soul was not at all my soul, but a dead system.[39] Hence I had to speak to my soul as to something far off and unknown, which did not exist through me, but through whom I existed.

He whose desire turns away from outer things, reaches the place of the soul.[40] If he does not find the soul, the horror of emptiness will overcome him, and fear will drive him with a whip lashing time and again in a desperate endeavor and a blind desire for the hollow things of the world. He becomes a fool through his endless desire, and forgets the way of his soul, never to find her again. He will run after all things, and will seize hold of them, but he will not find his soul, since he would find her only in himself. Truly his soul lies in things and men, but the blind one seizes things and men, yet not his soul in things and men. He has no knowledge of his soul. How could he tell her apart from things and men? He could find his soul in desire itself, but not in the objects of desire. If he possessed his desire, and his desire did not possess him, he would lay a hand on his soul, since his desire is the image and expression of his soul.[41]

If we possess the image of a thing, we possess half the thing.

The image of the world is half the world. He who possesses the world but not its image possesses only half the world, since his soul

39. The *Draft* continues: "a dead system that I had contrived, assembled from so-called experiences and judgments" (p. 16).

40. In 1913, Jung called this process the introversion of the libido ("On the question of psychological types," CW 6).

41. In 1912, Jung had written, "It is a common error *to judge longing in terms of the quality of the object* . . . Nature is only beautiful on account of the longing and love accorded to it by man. The aesthetic attributes emanating therefrom apply first and foremost to the libido, which alone accounts for the beauty of nature" (*Transformations and Symbols of the Libido*, CW B, §147).

is poor and has nothing. The wealth of the soul exists in images.[42] He who possesses the image of the world, possesses half the world, even if his humanity is poor and owns nothing.[43] But hunger makes the soul into a beast that devours the unbearable and is poisoned by it. My friends, it is wise to nourish the soul, otherwise you will breed dragons and devils in your heart.[44]

Soul and God

[HI ii(r)2][45]

Cap. ii.

On the second night I called out to my soul:[46]

"I am weary, my soul, my wandering has lasted too long, my search for myself outside of myself. Now I have gone through events and find you behind all of them. For I made discoveries on my err-

42. In *Psychological Types*, Jung articulated this primacy of the image through his notion of *esse in anima* (CW 6, §66ff, §711ff). In her diary notes, Cary Baynes commented on this passage: "What struck me especially was what you said about the "Bild" [image] being half the world. That is the thing that makes humanity so dull. They have missed understanding that thing. The world, that is the thing that holds them rapt. 'Das Bild', they have never seriously considered unless they have been poets" (February 8, 1924, *CFB*).
43. The *Draft* continues: "He who strives only for things will sink into poverty as outer wealth increases, and his soul will be afflicted by protracted illness" (p. 17).
44. The *Draft* continues: "This parable about refinding the soul, my friends, is meant to show you that you have only seen me as half a man, since my soul had lost me. I am certain that you did not notice this; because how many are with their souls today? Yet without the soul, there is no path that leads beyond these times" (p. 17). In her diary notes Cary Baynes commented on this passage: "February 8th [1924]. I came to your conversation with your soul. All that you say is said in the right way and is sincere. It is no cry of the young man awakening into life but that of the mature man who has lived fully and richly in ways of the world and yet knows almost abruptly one night, say, that he has missed the essence. The vision came at the height of your power, when you could have gone on just as you were with perfect worldly success. I do not know how you were strong enough to give it heed. I am really for everything you say and understand it. Everyone who has lost the connection with his soul or has known how to give it life ought to have a chance to see this book. Every word so far lives for me and strengthens me just where I feel weak, but as you say the world is very far away from it in mood today. That does not matter too much, a book can swing even a whole world if it is written in fire and blood" (*CFB*).
45. In 1945, Jung commented on the symbolism of the bird and serpent in connection with the tree, "The philosophical tree" (ch. 12, CW 13).
46. November 14, 1913.

ing through events, humanity, and the world. I found men. And you, my soul, I found again, first in images within men and then you yourself. I found you where I least expected you. You climbed out of a dark shaft. You announced yourself to me in advance in dreams.[47] They burned in my heart and drove me to all the boldest acts of daring, and forced me to rise above myself. You let me see truths of which I had no previous inkling. You let me undertake journeys, whose endless length would have scared me, if the knowledge of them had not been secure in you.

I wandered for many years, so long that I forgot that I possessed a soul.[48] Where were you all this time? Which Beyond sheltered you and gave you sanctuary? Oh, that you must speak through me, that my speech and I are your symbol and expression! How should I decipher you?

Who are you, child? My dreams have represented you as a child and as a maiden.[49] I am ignorant of your mystery.[50] Forgive me if I speak as in a dream, like a drunkard—are you God? Is God a child, a maiden?[51] Forgive me if I babble. No one else hears me. I speak to you quietly, and you know that I am neither a drunkard nor someone deranged, and that my heart twists in pain from the wound, whose darkness delivers speeches full of mockery: "You are lying to yourself! You spoke so as to deceive others and make them believe in you. You want to be a prophet and chase after your ambition." The wound still bleeds, and I am far from being able to pretend that I do not hear the mockery.

47. The *Draft* continues: "which were dark to me, and which I sought to grasp in my own inadequate way" (p. 18).

48. The *Draft* continues: "I belonged to men and things. I did not belong to myself." In *Black Book 2*, Jung states that he wandered for eleven years (p. 19). He had stopped writing in this book in 1902, taking it up again in the autumn of 1913.

49. *Black Book 2* continues: "And I found you again only through the soul of the woman" (p. 8).

50. *Black Book 2* continues: "Look, I bear a wound that is as yet not healed: my ambition to make an impression" (p. 8).

51. *Black Book 2* continues: "I must tell myself most clearly: does *He* use the image of a child that lives in every man's soul? Were Horus, Tages, and Christ not children? Dionysus and Heracles were also divine children. Did Christ, the God of man, not call himself the *son* of man? What was his innermost thought in doing so? Should the *daughter of man* be God's name?" (p. 9).

How strange it sounds to me to call you a child, you who still hold the all-without-end in your hand.[52] I went on the way of the day, and you went invisibly with me, putting the pieces together meaningfully, and letting me see the whole in each part.

You took away where I thought to take hold, and you gave me where I did not expect anything and time and again you brought about fate from new and unexpected quarters. Where I sowed, you robbed me of the harvest, and where I did not sow, you give me fruit a hundredfold. And time and again I lost the path and found it again where I would never have foreseen it. You upheld my belief, when I was alone and near despair. At every decisive moment you let me believe in myself."

[2] Like a tired wanderer who had sought nothing in the world apart from her, shall I come closer to my soul. I shall learn that my soul finally lies behind everything, and if I cross the world, I am ultimately doing this to find my soul. Even the dearest are themselves not the goal and end of the love that goes on seeking, they are symbols of their own souls.

My friends, do you guess to what solitude we ascend?

I must learn that the dregs of my thought, my dreams, are the speech of my soul. I must carry them in my heart, and go back and forth over them in my mind, like the words of the person dearest to me. Dreams are the guiding words of the soul. Why should I henceforth not love my dreams and not make their riddling images into objects of my daily consideration? You think that the dream is foolish and ungainly. What is beautiful? What is ungainly? What is clever? What is foolish? The spirit of this time is your measure, but

52. The *Draft* continues: "How thick the earlier darkness was! How impetuous and how egotistic my passion was, subjugated by all the daimons of ambition, the desire for glory, greed, uncharitableness, and zeal! How ignorant I was at the time! Life tore me away, and I deliberately moved away from you and I have done so for all these years. I recognize how good all of this was. But I thought that you were lost, even though I sometimes thought that I was lost. But you were not lost. I went on the way of the day. You went invisibly with me and guided me step by step, putting the pieces together meaningfully" (pp. 20–21).

the spirit of the depths surpasses it at both ends. Only the spirit of this time knows the difference between large and small. But this difference is invalid, like the spirit which recognizes it. / fol. ii(r) /ii(v)

The spirit of the depths even taught me to consider my action and my decision as dependent on dreams. Dreams pave the way for life, and they determine you without you understanding their language.[53] One would like to learn this language, but who can teach and learn it? Scholarliness alone is not enough; there is a knowledge of the heart that gives deeper insight.[54] The knowledge of the heart is in no book and is not to be found in the mouth of any teacher, but grows out of you like the green seed from the dark earth. Scholarliness belongs to the spirit of this time, but this spirit in no way grasps the dream, since the soul is everywhere that scholarly knowledge is not.

But how can I attain the knowledge of the heart? You can attain this knowledge only by living your life to the full. You live your life fully if you also live what you have never yet lived, but have left for others to live or to think.[55] You will say: "But I cannot live or think everything that others live or think." But you should say: "The life that I could still live, I should live, and the thoughts that I could still think, I should think." It appears as though you want to flee

53. In 1912, Jung endorsed Maeder's notion of the prospective function of the dream ("An attempt at an account of psychoanalytic theory," CW 4, §452). In a discussion in the Zürich Psychoanalytical Society on January 31, 1913, Jung said: "The dream is not only the fulfillment of infantile desires, but also symbolizes the future . . . The dream provides the answer through the symbol, which one must understand" (*MZS*, p. 5). On the development of Jung's dream theory, see my *Jung and the Making of Modern Psychology: The Dream of a Science*, §2.

54. This echoes Blaise Pascal's famous statement, "The heart has its reasons of which reason knows nothing" (*Pensées*, 423 [London: Penguin, 1660/1995], p. 127). Jung's copy of Pascal's work contains a number of marginal marks.

55. In 1912, Jung argued that scholarliness was insufficient if one wanted to become a "knower of the human soul." To do this, one had to "hang up exact science and put away the scholar's gown, to say farewell to his study and wander with human heart through the world, through the horror of prisons, mad houses and hospitals, through drab suburban pubs, in brothels and gambling dens, through the salons of elegant society, the stock exchanges, the socialist meetings, the churches, the revivals and ecstasies of the sects, to experience love, hate and passion in every form in one's body" ("New paths of psychology," CW 7, §409).

from yourself so as not to have to live what remains unlived until now.[56] But you cannot flee from yourself. It is with you all the time and demands fulfillment. If you pretend to be blind and dumb to this demand, you feign being blind and deaf to yourself. This way you will never reach the knowledge of the heart.

The knowledge of your heart is how your heart is.

From a cunning heart you will know cunning.

From a good heart you will know goodness.

So that your understanding becomes perfect, consider that your heart is both good and evil. You ask, "What? Should I also live evil?"

The spirit of the depths demands: "The life that you could still live, you should live. Well-being decides, not your well-being, not the well-being of the others, but only well-being."

Well-being is between me and others, in society. I, too, lived—which I had not done before, and which I could still do. I lived into the depths, and the depths began to speak. The depths taught me the other truth. It thus united sense and nonsense in me.

I had to recognize that I am only the expression and symbol of the soul. In the sense of the spirit of the depths, I am as I am in this visible world a symbol of my soul, and I am thoroughly a serf, completely subjugated, utterly obedient. The spirit of the depths taught me to say: "I am the servant of a child." Through this dictum I learn above all the most extreme humility, as what I most need.

The spirit of this time of course allowed me to believe in my reason. He let me see myself in the image of a leader with ripe thoughts. But the spirit of the depths teaches me that I am a servant, in fact the servant of a child. This dictum was repugnant to me and I hated

56. In 1931, Jung commented on the pathogenic consequences of the unlived life of parents upon their children: "What usually has the strongest psychic effect on the child is the life which the parents . . . have not lived. This statement would be rather too perfunctory and superficial if we did not add by way of qualification: that part of their lives which might have been lived had not certain somewhat threadbare excuses prevented the parents from doing so" ("Introduction to Frances Wickes, 'Analyse der Kinderseele,'" CW 17, §87).

it. But I had to recognize and accept that my soul is a child and that my God in my soul is a child.[57]

If you are boys, your God is a woman.
If you are women, your God is a boy.
If you are men, your God is a maiden.
The God is where you are not.
So: *it is wise that one has a God; this serves for your perfection.*
A maiden is the pregnant future.
A boy is the engendering future.
A woman is: having given birth.
A man is: having engendered.

So: *if you are childlike beings now, your God will descend from the height of ripeness to age and death.*

But if you are developed beings, having engendered or given birth, in body or in soul, so your God rises from the radiant cradle, to the incalculable height of the future, to the maturity and fullness of the coming time.

He *who still has his life before him is a child.*
He who lives life in the present is developed.
If you thus live all that you can live, you are developed.
He who is a child in this time, his God dies.
He who is developed in this time, his God continues to live.
The spirit of the depths teaches this mystery.
Prosperous and woeful are those whose God is developed!
Prosperous and woeful are those whose God is a child!
What is better, that man has life ahead of him, or that God does?

57. In the 1925 seminar, Jung explained his thoughts at this time: "These ideas about the anima and animus led me ever further afield into metaphysical problems, and more things crept up for reexamination. At that time I was on the Kantian basis that there were things that could never be solved and that therefore should not be speculated about, but it seemed to me that if I could find such definite ideas about the anima, it was quite worthwhile to try to formulate a conception of God. But I could arrive at nothing satisfactory and thought for a time that perhaps the anima figure was the deity. I said to myself that perhaps men had had a female God originally, but growing tired of being governed by women, they had then overthrown this God. I practically threw the whole metaphysical problem into the anima and conceived of it as the dominating spirit of psyche. In this way I got into a psychological argument with myself about the problem of God" (*Introduction to Jungian Psychology*, p. 50).

I know no answer. Live; the unavoidable decides.

The spirit of the depths taught me that my life is encompassed by the divine child.[58] *From his hand everything unexpected came to me, everything living.*

This child is what I feel as an eternally springing youth in me.[59]

In childish men you feel the hopeless transience. All that you saw passing is yet to come for him. His future is full of transience.

But the transience of the things coming toward you has never yet experienced a human meaning.

Your continuing to live is a living onward. You engender and give birth to what is to come, you are fecund, you live onward.

The childish is unfruitful, what is to come to him is what already has been engendered and already withered. It does not live onward.[60]

My God is a child, so wonder not that the spirit of this time in me is incensed to mockery and scorn. There will be no one who will laugh at me as I laughed at myself.

Your God should not be a man of mockery, rather you yourself will be the man of mockery. You should mock yourself and rise above this. If you have still not learned this from the old holy books, then go there, drink the blood and eat the flesh of him who was

58. In 1940, Jung presented a study of the motif of the divine child, in a collaborative volume with the Hungarian classicist Karl Kérenyi (see "On the psychology of the child archetype," CW 9, 1). Jung wrote that the child motif occurs frequently in the individuation process. It does not represent one's literal childhood, as is emphasized by its mythological nature. It compensates the onesidedness of consciousness and paves the way for the future development of the personality. In certain conditions of conflict, the unconscious psyche produces a symbol that unites the opposites. The child is such a symbol. It anticipates the self, which is produced through the synthesis of the conscious and unconscious elements of the personality. The typical fates that befall the child indicate the kind of psychic events accompanying the genesis of the self. The wonderful birth of the child indicates that this happens psychically as opposed to physically.

59. In 1940, Jung wrote: "an essential aspect of the child motif is its futural character. The child is potential future" ("On the psychology of the child archetype," CW 9, 1, §278).

60. The *Draft* continues: "My friends, as you can see, mercy is granted to the developed, not the childish. I thank my God for this message. Do not let the teachings of Christianity deceive you! Its teachings are good for the most mature minds of bygone time. Today, it serves immature minds. Christianity no longer promises us grace, and yet we still need mercy. That which I tell you is the way of what is to come, my way to mercy" (p. 27).

mocked[61] and tormented for the sake of our sins, so that you totally become his nature, deny his being-apart-from-you; you should be he himself, not Christians but Christ, otherwise you will be of no use to the coming God.

Is there any one among you who believes he can be spared the way? Can he swindle his way past the pain of Christ? I say: "Such a one deceives himself to his own detriment. He beds down on thorns and fire. No one can be spared the way of Christ, since this way leads to what is to come. You should all become Christs.[62]

You do not overcome the old teaching through doing less, but through doing more. Every step closer to my soul excites the scornful laughter of my devils, those cowardly ear-whisperers and poison-mixers. It was easy for them to laugh, since I had to do strange things.

On the Service of the Soul
[HI ii(v)]
Cap. iii.

[63]On the following night I had to write down all the dreams that I could recollect, true to their wording.[64] The meaning of this act was dark to me. Why all this? Forgive the fuss that rises in me. Yet you want me to do this. What strange things are happening to me? I know too much not to see on what swaying bridges I go. Where are you leading me? Forgive my excessive apprehension, brimful of knowledge. My foot hesitates to follow you. Into what mist and darkness does your path lead? Must I also learn to do without meaning? If this is what you demand, then so be it. This hour belongs to

61. I.e., Christ. Cf. Jung, "Transformation symbolism in the mass" (1942, CW 11).
62. In *Answer to Job* Jung noted: "Through the indwelling of the third divine person in man, namely the Holy Ghost, a christification of the many arises" (1952, CW 11, §758).
63. November 15, 1913.
64. In *Black Book 2*, Jung wrote down here the two pivotal dreams he had when he was nineteen years old which led him to turn to natural science (p. 13f); they are described in *Memories*, p. 105f.

you. What is there, where there is no meaning? Only nonsense, or madness, it seems to me. Is there also a supreme meaning? Is that your meaning, my soul? I limp after you on crutches of understanding. I am a man and you stride like a God. What torture! I must return to myself, to my smallest things. I saw the things of my soul as small, pitiably small. You force me to see them as large, to make them large. Is that your aim? I follow, but it terrifies me. Hear my doubts, otherwise I cannot follow, since your meaning is a supreme meaning, and your steps are the steps of a God.

I understand, I must not think either; should thought, too, no longer be? I should give myself completely into your hands—but who are you? I do not trust you. Not once to trust, is that my love for you, my joy in you? Do I not trust every valiant man, and not you, my soul? Your hand lies heavy on me, but I will, I will. Have I not sought to love men and trust them, and should I not do this with you? Forget my doubts, I know it is ignoble to doubt you. You know how difficult it is for me to set aside the beggar's pride I take in my own thought. I forgot that you are also one of my friends, and have the first right to my trust. Should what I give them not belong to you? I recognize my injustice. It seems to me that I despised you. My joy at finding you again was not genuine. I also recognize that the scornful laughter in me was right.

I must learn to love you.[65] Should I also set aside self-judgment? I am afraid. Then the soul spoke to me and said: "This fear testifies against me!" It is true, it testifies against you. It kills the holy trust between you and me.

---

65. In *Black Book 2,* Jung noted here: "Here, someone stands beside me and whispers terrible things into my ear: 'You write to be printed and circulated among people. You want to cause a stir through the unusual. Nietzsche did this better than you. You are imitating Saint Augustine'" (p. 20). The reference is to Augustine's *Confessions* (400 CE), a devotional work written when he was forty-five years old, in which he narrates his conversion to Christianity in an autobiographical form (*Confessions*, tr. H. Chadwick [Oxford: Oxford University Press, 1991]). The *Confessions* are addressed to God, and recount the years of his wandering from God and the manner of his return. Echoing this in the opening sections of *Liber Novus,* Jung addresses his soul and recounts the years of his wandering away from her, and the manner of his return. In his published works, Jung frequently cited Augustine, and referred to his *Confessions* several times in *Transformations and Symbols of the Libido.*

[2] *How hard is fate! If you take a step toward your soul, you will at first miss the meaning. You will believe that you have sunk into meaninglessness, into eternal disorder. You will be right! Nothing will deliver you from disorder and meaninglessness, since this is the other half of the world.*

Your God is a child, so long as you are not childlike. Is the child order, meaning? Or disorder, caprice? Disorder and meaninglessness are the mother of order and meaning. Order and meaning are things that have become and are no longer becoming.

You open the gates of the soul to let the dark flood of chaos flow into your order and meaning. If you marry the ordered to the chaos you produce the divine child, the supreme meaning beyond meaning and meaninglessness.

You are afraid to open the door? I too was afraid, since we had forgotten that God is terrible. Christ taught: God is love.[66] *But you should know that love is also terrible.*

I spoke to a loving soul and as I drew nearer to her, I was overcome by horror, and I heaped up a wall of doubt, and did not anticipate that I thus wanted to protect myself from my fearful soul.

You dread the depths; it should horrify you, since the way of what is to come leads through it. You must endure the temptation of fear and doubt, and at the same time acknowledge to the bone that your fear is justified and your doubt is reasonable. How otherwise / could it be a true temptation and a true overcoming? fol. ii(v) /iii(r)

Christ totally overcomes the temptation of the devil, but not the temptation of God to good and reason.[67] *Christ thus succumbs to cursing.*[68]

You still have to learn this, to succumb to no temptation, but to do everything of your own will; then you will be free and beyond Christianity.

I have had to recognize that I must submit to what I fear; yes, even more, that I must even love what horrifies me. We must learn such from that saint who was dis-

66. The first letter of John: "God is love. Whoever lives in love lives in God, and God in him" (1 John 4:16).
67. Christ was tempted by the devil for forty days in the desert (Luke 4:1–13).
68. Matthew 21:18-20 : "Now in the morning as he returned into the city, he hungered. And when he saw a fig tree in the way, he came to it, and found nothing thereon, but leaves only, and said unto it, Let no fruit grow on thee henceforward for ever. And presently the fig tree withered away. And when the disciples saw it, they marveled, saying, How soon is the fig tree withered away!" In 1944 Jung wrote: "The Christian—my Christian—knows no curse formulas; indeed he does not even sanction the cursing of the innocent fig-tree by the rabbi Jesus" ("Why I have not adopted the 'Catholic truth'?" CW 18, §1468).

gusted by the plague infections; she drank the pus of plague boils and became aware that it smelled like roses. The acts of the saint were not in vain.[69]

In everything regarding your salvation and the attainment of mercy, you are dependent on your soul. Thus no sacrifice can be too great for you. If your virtues hinder you from salvation, discard them, since they have become evil to you. The slave to virtue finds the way as little as the slave to vices.[70]

If you believe that you are the master of your soul, then become her servant. If you were her servant, make yourself her master, since she needs to be ruled. These should be your first steps.

During six further nights, the spirit of the depths was silent in me, since I swayed between fear, defiance, and nausea, and was wholly the prey of my passion. I could not and did not want to listen to the depths. But on the seventh night, the spirit of the depths spoke to me: "Look into your depths, pray to your depths, waken the dead."[71]

But I stood helpless and did not know what I could do. I looked into myself, and the only thing I found within was the memory of earlier dreams, all of which I wrote down without knowing what good this would do. I wanted to throw everything away and return to the light of day. But the spirit stopped me and forced me back into myself.

---

69. The *Draft* continues: "They may serve for your redemption" (p. 34).
70. In *Thus Spoke Zarathustra*, Nietzsche wrote: "And even when one has all the virtues, there is still one thing to remember: to send even these virtues to sleep at the proper time" ("Of the chairs of virtue," p. 56). In 1939 Jung commented on the Eastern notion of liberation from virtues and vices ("Commentary to the 'Tibetan Book of Great Liberation,'" CW 11, §826).
71. November 22, 1913. In *Black Book 2*, this sentence reads "says a voice" (p. 22). On November 21 Jung had given a presentation to the Zürich Psychoanalytical Society on "Formulations on the psychology of the unconscious."

The Desert
[HI iii(r)]
Cap. iv.

[72]Sixth night. My soul leads me into the desert, into the desert of my own self. I did not think that my soul is a desert, a barren, hot desert, dusty and without drink. The journey leads through hot sand, slowly wading without a visible goal to hope for? How eerie is this wasteland. It seems to me that the way leads so far away from mankind. I take my way step by step, and do not know how long my journey will last.

Why is my self a desert? Have I lived too much outside of myself in men and events? Why did I avoid my self? Was I not dear to myself? But I have avoided the place of my soul. I was my thoughts, after I was no longer events and other men. But I was not my self, confronted with my thoughts. I should also rise up above my thoughts to my own self. My journey goes there, and that is why it leads away from men and events into solitude. Is it solitude, to be with oneself? Solitude is true only when the self is a desert.[73] Should I also make a garden out of the desert? Should I people a desolate land? Should I open the airy magic garden of the wilderness? What leads me into the desert, and what am I to do there? Is it a deception that I can no longer trust my thoughts? Only life is true, and only life leads me into the desert, truly not my thinking, that would like to return to thoughts, to men and events, since it feels uncanny in the desert. My soul, what am I to do here? But my soul spoke to me and said, "Wait." I heard the cruel word. Torment belongs to the desert.[74]

---

72. November 28, 1913.
73. *Black Book 2* continues: "I hear the words: 'An anchorite in his own desert.' The monks in the Syrian desert occur to me" (p. 33).
74. *Black Book 2* continues: "I think of Christianity in the desert. Physically, those ancients went into the desert. Did they also enter into the desert of their own self? Or was their self not as barren and desolate as mine? There they wrestled with the devil. I wrestle with waiting. It seems to me not less since it is truly a hot hell" (p. 35).

Through giving my soul all I could give, I came to the place of the soul and found that this place was a hot desert, desolate and unfruitful. No culture of the mind is enough to make a garden out of your soul. I had cultivated my spirit, the spirit of this time in me, but not that spirit of the depths that turns to the things of the soul, the world of the soul. The soul has its own peculiar world. Only the self enters in there, or the man who has completely become his self, he who is neither in events, nor in men, nor in his thoughts. Through the turning of my desire from things and men, I turned my self away from things and men, but that is precisely how I became the secure prey of my thoughts, yes, I wholly became my thoughts.

[2] I also had to detach myself from my thoughts through turning my desire away from them. And at once, I noticed that my self became a desert, where only the sun of unquiet desire burned. I was overwhelmed by the endless infertility of this desert. Even if something could have thrived there, the creative power of desire was still absent. Wherever the creative power of desire is, there springs the soil's own seed. But do not forget to wait. Did you not see that when your creative force turned to the world, how the dead things moved under it and through it, how they grew and prospered, and how your thoughts flowed in rich rivers? If your creative force now turns to the place of the soul, you will see how your soul becomes green and how its field bears wonderful fruit.

Nobody can spare themselves the waiting and most will be unable to bear this torment, but will throw themselves with greed back at men, things, and thoughts, whose slaves they will become from then on. Since then it will have been clearly proved that this man is incapable of enduring beyond things, men, and thoughts, and they will hence become his master and he will become their fool, since he cannot be without them, not until even his soul has become a fruitful field. Also he whose soul is a garden, needs things, men, and thoughts, but he is their friend and not their slave and fool.

Everything to come was already in images: to find their soul, the ancients went into the desert.[75] This is an image. The ancients lived their symbols, since the world had not yet become real for them. Thus they went into the solitude of the desert to teach us that the place of the soul is a lonely desert. There they found the abundance of visions, the fruits of the desert, the wondrous flowers of the soul. Think diligently about the images that the ancients have left behind. They show the way of what is to come. Look back at the collapse of empires, of growth and death, of the desert and monasteries, they are the images of what is to come. Everything has been foretold. But who knows how to interpret it?

When you say that the place of the soul is not, then it is not. But if you say that it is, then it is. Notice what the ancients said in images: the word is a creative act. The ancients said: in the beginning was the Word.[76] Consider this and think upon it.

The words that oscillate between nonsense and supreme meaning are the oldest and truest.

Experiences in the Desert
[HI iii(r) 2]

[77]After a hard struggle I have come a piece of the way nearer to you. How hard this struggle was! I had fallen into an undergrowth of doubt, confusion, and scorn. I recognize that I must be alone with my soul. I come with empty hands to you, my soul. What do you want to hear? But my soul spoke to me and said, "If you come to a friend, do you come to take?" I knew that this should not be so, but it seems to me that I am poor and empty. I would like to sit down

75. Around 285, St. Anthony went to live as a hermit in the Egyptian desert, and other hermits followed, whom he and Pachomius organized into a community. This formed the basis of Christian monasticism, which spread to the Palestinian and Syrian deserts. In the fourth century, there were thousands of monks in the Egyptian desert.

76. John 1:1: "In the beginning was the Word, and the Word was with God, and the Word was God."

77. December 11, 1913.

near you and at least feel the breath of your animating presence. My way is hot sand. All day long, sandy, dusty paths. My patience is sometimes weak, and once I despaired of myself, as you know.

My soul answered and said, "You speak to me as if you were a child complaining to its mother. I am not your mother." I do not want to complain, but let me say to you that mine is a long and dusty road. You are to me like a shady tree in the wilderness. I would like to enjoy your shade. But my soul answered, "You are pleasure-seeking. Where is your patience? Your time has not yet run its course. Have you forgotten why you went into the desert?"

My faith is weak, my face is blind from all that shimmering blaze of the desert sun. The heat lies on me like lead. Thirst torments me, I dare not think how unendingly long my way is, and above all, I see nothing in front of me. But the soul answered, "You speak as if you have still learned nothing. Can you not wait? Should everything fall into your lap ripe and finished? You are full, yes, you teem with intentions and desirousness!—Do you still not know that the way to truth stands open only to those without intentions?"

I know that everything you say, Oh my soul, is also my thought. But I hardly live according to it. The soul said, "How, tell me, do you then believe that your thoughts should help you?" I would always like to refer to the fact that I am a human being, just a human being who is weak and sometimes does not do his best. But the soul said, "Is this what you think it means to be human?" You are hard, my soul, but you are right. How little we still commit ourselves to living. We should grow like a tree that likewise does not know its law. We tie ourselves up with intentions, not mindful of the fact that intention is the limitation, yes, the exclusion of life. We believe that we can illuminate the darkness with an intention, and in that way aim past the light.[78] How can we presume to want to know in advance, from where the light will come to us?

78. In "Commentary on 'The Secret of the Golden Flower'" (1929), Jung criticized the Western tendency to turn everything into methods and intentions. The cardinal lesson, as presented by the Chinese texts and by Meister Eckhart, was that of allowing psychic events to happen of their own accord: "Letting things happen, the action

Let me bring only one complaint before you: I suffer from scorn, my own scorn. But my soul said to me, "Do you think little of yourself?" I do not believe so. My soul answered, "Then listen, do you think little of me? Do you still not know that you are not writing a book to feed your vanity, but that you are speaking with me? How can you suffer from scorn if you address me with those words that I give you? Do you know, then, who I am? Have you grasped me, defined me, and made me into a dead formula? Have you measured the depths of my chasms, and explored all the ways down which I am yet going to lead you? Scorn cannot challenge you if you are not vain to the marrow of your bones." Your truth is hard. I want to lay down my vanity before you, since it blinds me. See, that is why I also believed my hands were empty when I came to you today. I did not consider that it is you who fills empty hands if only they want to stretch out, yet they do not want to. I did not know that I am your vessel, empty without you but brimming over with you.

[2] This was my twenty-fifth night in the desert. This is how long it took my soul to awaken from a shadowy being to her own life, until she could approach me as a free-standing being separate from me. And I received hard but salutary words from her. I needed that taking in hand, since I could not overcome the scorn within me.

The spirit of this time considers itself extremely clever, like every such spirit of the time. But wisdom is simpleminded, not just simple. Because of this, the clever person mocks wisdom, since mockery is his weapon. He uses the pointed, poisonous weapon, because he is struck by naive wisdom. If he were not struck, he would not need the weapon. Only in the desert do we become aware of our terrible simplemindedness, but we are afraid of admitting it. "That is why we are scornful. But mockery / does not attain simplemindedness. The mockery falls on the mocker, and fol. iii(r)/iii(v)
in the desert where no one hears and answers, he suffocates from his own scorn.

The cleverer you are, the more foolish your simplemindedness. The totally clever are total fools in their simplemindedness. We cannot save ourselves from the

through non-action, the 'letting go of oneself' of Meister Eckhart, became the key for me that succeeded in opening the door to the way: One must be able to psychically let things happen" (CW 13, §20).

cleverness of the spirit of this time through increasing our cleverness, but through accepting what our cleverness hates most, namely simplemindedness. Yet we also do not want to be artificial fools because we have fallen into simplemindedness, rather we will be clever fools. That leads to the supreme meaning. Cleverness couples itself with intention. Simplemindedness knows no intention. Cleverness conquers the world, but simplemindedness, the soul. So take on the vow of poverty of spirit in order to partake of the soul.[79]

Against this the scorn of my cleverness rose up.[80] *Many will laugh at my foolishness. But no one will laugh more than I laughed at myself.*

So I overcame scorn. But when I had overcome it, I was near to my soul, and she could speak to me, and I was soon to see the desert becoming green.

Descent into Hell in the Future
[HI iii(v)]
Cap. v.

[81]In the following night, the air was filled with many voices. A loud voice called, "I am falling." Others cried out confused and

79. Christ preached: "Blessed are the poor in spirit, for theirs is the kingdom of heaven" (Matthew 5:3). In a number of Christian communities, members take a vow of poverty. In 1934, Jung wrote: "Just as in Christianity the vow of worldly poverty turned the mind away from the riches of this earth, so spiritual poverty seeks to renounce the false riches of the spirit in order to withdraw not only from the sorry remnants—which today call themselves the protestant 'churches'—of a great past, but also from all the allurements of exotic aromas; in order, finally, to turn back to itself, where, in the cold light of consciousness, the blank barrenness of the world reaches to the very stars" ("On the archetypes of the collective unconscious," CW 9, 1, §29).
80. The *Draft* continues: "This, too, is an image of the ancients, that they lived in things symbolically: they renounced wealth in order to have a share of the voluntary poverty of their souls. Therefore I had to grant my soul my most extreme poverty and need. And the scorn of my cleverness rose up against this" (p. 47).
81. December 12 1913. The *Corrected Draft* has: ~~"IV The Mystery Play. First Night."~~ (p. 34). *Black Book 2* continues: "The battle of late was the battle with scorn. A vision that caused me three sleepless nights and three days of torment has likened me to G. Keller's druggist of Chamounix (from start to finish). I know and acknowledge this style. I have learned that one must give one's heart to men, but one's intellect to the spirit of humanity, God. Then His work can be beyond vanity, since there is no more hypocritical whore than the intellect when it replaces the heart" (p. 41). Gottfried Keller (1819–1890) was a Swiss writer. See "Der Apotheker von Chamounix: Ein Buch Romanzen," in Gottfried Keller, *Gesammelte Gedichte: Erzählungen aus dem Nachlass* (Zürich: Artemis Verlag, 1984), pp. 351–417.

excited during this: "Where to? What do you want?" Should I entrust myself to this confusion? I shuddered. It is a dreadful deep. Do you want me to leave myself to chance, to the madness of my own darkness? Whither? Whither? You fall, and I want to fall with you, whoever you are.

The spirit of the depths opened my eyes and I caught a glimpse of the inner things, the world of my soul, the many-formed and changing. [Image iii(v) 1]

I see a gray rock face along which I sink into great depths.[82] I stand in black dirt up to my ankles in a dark cave. Shadows sweep over me. I am seized by fear, but I know I must go in. I crawl through a narrow crack in the rock and reach an inner cave whose bottom is covered with black water. But beyond this I catch a glimpse of a luminous red stone which I must reach. I wade through the muddy water. The cave is full of the frightful noise of shrieking voices.[83] I take the stone, it covers a dark opening in the rock. I hold the stone in my hand, peering around inquiringly. I do not want to listen to the voices, they keep me away.[84] But I want to know. Here something wants to be uttered. I place my ear to the opening. I hear the flow of underground waters. I see the bloody head of a man on the dark stream. Someone wounded, someone slain floats there. I take in this image for a long time, shuddering. I see a large black scarab floating past on the dark stream.

---

82. The *Draft* continues: "A dwarf clad entirely in leather stood before it, minding the entrance" (p. 48).

83. The *Corrected Draft* continues: "The stone must be conquered, it is the stone ~~of the torment~~, of the red light" (p. 35). The *Corrected Draft* has: "It is a six-sided crystal that gives off a cold, reddish light" (p. 35). Albrecht Dieterich refers to the representation of the underworld in Aristophanes' *The Frogs* (which he understood to be of Orphic origin) as having a large lake and a place with serpents (*Nekyia: Beiträge zur Erklärung der neuentdeckten Petrusapokalypse* [Leipzig: Teubner, 1893], p. 71). Jung underlined these motifs in his copy. Dieterich referred to his description again on page 83, which Jung marked by the margin, and underlined "Darkness and Mud." Dieterich also referred to an Orphic representation of a stream of mud in the underworld (p. 81). In his list of references in the back of his copy, Jung noted, "81 Mud."

84. *Black Book 2* continues: "This dark hole—I want to know where it leads and what it says? An oracle? Is it the place of Pythia?" (p. 43).

In the deepest reach of the stream shines a red sun, radiating through the dark water. There I see—and a terror seizes me—small serpents on the dark rock walls, striving toward the depths, where the sun shines. A thousand serpents crowd around, veiling the sun. Deep night falls. A red stream of blood, thick red blood springs up, surging for a long time, then ebbing. I am seized by fear. What did I see?[85] [Image iii(v) 2]

Heal the wounds that doubt inflicts on me, my soul. That too is to be overcome, so that I can recognize your supreme meaning. How far away everything is, and how I have turned back! My spirit is a spirit of torment, it tears asunder my contemplation, it would dismantle everything and rip it apart. I am still a victim of my thinking. When can I order my thinking to be quiet, so that my thoughts, those unruly hounds, will crawl to my feet? How can I ever hope to hear your voice louder, to see your face clearer, when all my thoughts howl?

I am stunned, but I want to be stunned, since I have sworn to you, my soul, to trust you even if you lead me through madness. How shall I ever walk under your sun if I do not drink the bitter draught of slumber to the lees? Help me so that I do not choke on my own knowledge. The fullness of my knowledge threatens to fall in on me. My knowledge has a thousand voices, an army roaring like lions; the air trembles when they speak, and I am their defenseless

85. Jung narrated this episode in his 1925 seminar, stressing different details. He commented: "When I came out of the fantasy, I realized that my mechanism had worked wonderfully well, but I was in great confusion as to the meaning of all those things I had seen. The light in the cave from the crystal was, I thought, like the stone of wisdom. The secret murder of the hero I could not understand at all. The beetle of course I knew to be an ancient sun symbol, and the setting sun, the luminous red disk, was archetypal. The serpents I thought might have been connected with Egyptian material. I could not then realize that it was all so archetypal, I need not seek connections. I was able to link the picture up with the sea of blood I had previously fantasized about. / Though I could not then grasp the significance of the hero killed, soon after I had a dream in which Siegfried was killed by myself. It was a case of destroying the hero ideal of my efficiency. This has to be sacrificed in order that a new adaptation can be made; in short, it is connected with the sacrifice of the superior function in order to get at the libido necessary to activate the inferior functions" (*Introduction to Jungian Psychology*, p. 52f). (The killing of Siegfried occurs below in ch. 7.) Jung also anonymously cited and discussed this fantasy in his *ETH* lecture on June 14, 1935 (*Modern Psychology, vols. 1. and 2*, p. 223).

sacrifice. Keep it far from me, science that clever knower,[86] that bad prison master who binds the soul and imprisons it in a lightless cell. But above all protect me from the serpent of judgment, which only appears to be a healing serpent, yet in your depths is infernal poison and agonizing death. I want to go down cleansed into your depths with white garments and not rush in like some thief, seizing whatever I can and fleeing breathlessly. Let me persist in divine[87] astonishment, so that I am ready to behold your wonders. Let me lay my head on a stone before your door, so that I am prepared to receive your light.

[2] When the desert begins to bloom, it brings forth strange plants. You will consider yourself mad, and in a certain sense you will in fact be mad.[88] To the extent that the Christianity of this time lacks madness, it lacks divine life. Take note of what the ancients taught us in images: madness is divine.[89] But because the ancients

86. In the *Corrected Draft*, "science" is deleted (p. 37).
87. In the *Corrected Draft*, "more blessed" is substituted (p. 38).
88. In the *Corrected Draft*, this sentence is substituted by: "Madness grows" (p. 38).
89. The theme of divine madness has a long history. Its locus classicus was Socrates's discussion of it in the *Phaedrus*: madness, "provided it comes as a gift of heaven, is the channel by which we receive the greatest blessings" (Plato, *Phaedrus and Letters VII and VIII*, tr. W. Hamilton [London: Penguin, 1986], p. 46, line 244). Socrates distinguished four types of divine madness: (1) inspired divination, such as by the prophetess at Delphi; (2) instances in which individuals, when ancient sins have given rise to troubles, have prophesied and incited to prayer and worship; (3) possession by the Muses, since the technically skilled untouched by the madness of the Muses will never be a good poet; and (4) the lover. In the Renaissance, the theme of divine madness was taken up by the Neoplatonists such as Ficino and by humanists such as Erasmus. Erasmus's discussion is particularly important, as it fuses the classical Platonic conception with Christianity. For Erasmus, Christianity was the highest type of inspired madness. Like Plato, Erasmus differentiated between two types of madness: "Thus as long as the soul uses its bodily organs aright, a man is called sane; but truly, when it bursts its chains and tries to be free, practising running away from its prison, then one calls it insanity. If this happens through disease or a defect of the organs, then by common consent it is, plainly, insanity. And yet men of this kind, too, we find foretelling things to come, knowing tongues and writings which they had never studied beforehand—altogether showing forth something divine" (*In Praise of Folly*, tr. M. A. Screech [London: Penguin, 1988], pp. 128–29). He adds that if insanity "happens through divine fervor, it may not be the same kind of insanity, but it is so like it that most people make no distinction." For lay people, the two forms of insanity appeared the same. The happiness that Christians sought was "nothing other than a certain kind of madness." Those who experience this "experience something which is very like madness. They speak incoherently and unnaturally, utter sound without sense, and their

lived this image concretely in events, it became a deception for us, since we became masters of the reality of the world. It is unquestionable: if you enter into the world of the soul, you are like a madman, and a doctor would consider you to be sick. What I say here can be seen as sickness, but no one can see it as sickness more than I do.

This is how I overcame madness. If you do not know what divine madness is, suspend judgment and wait for the fruits.[90] But know that there is a divine madness which is nothing other than the overpowering of the spirit of this time through the spirit of the depths. Speak then of sick delusion when the spirit of the depths can no longer stay down and forces a man to speak in tongues instead of in human speech, and makes him believe that he himself is the spirit of the depths. But also speak of sick delusion when the spirit of this time does not leave a man and forces him to see only the surface, to deny the spirit of the depths and to take himself for the spirit of the times. The spirit of this time is ungodly, the spirit of the depths is ungodly, balance is godly.

Because I was caught up in the spirit of this time, precisely what happened to me on this night had to happen to me, namely that the spirit of the depths erupted with force, and swept away the spirit of this time with a powerful wave. But the spirit of the depths had gained this power, because I had spoken to my soul during 25 nights in the desert and I had given her all my love and submission. But

faces suddenly change expression . . . in fact they are truly beside themselves" (ibid., pp. 129–33). In 1815, the philosopher F.W.J. Schelling discussed divine madness in a manner that has a certain proximity to Jung's discussion, noting that "The ancients did not speak in vain of a divine and holy madness." Schelling related this to the "inner self-laceration of nature." He held that "nothing great can be accomplished without a constant solicitation of madness, which should always be overcome, but should never be entirely lacking." On the one hand, there were sober spirits in whom there was no trace of madness, together with men of understanding who produced cold intellectual works. On the other, "there is one kind of person that governs madness and precisely in this overwhelming shows the highest force of the intellect. The other kind of person is governed by madness and is someone who is really mad" (*The Ages of the World*, tr. J. Wirth [Albany: SUNY Press, 2000], pp. 102–4).

90. An application of William James's notion of the pragmatic rule. Jung read James's *Pragmatism* in 1912, and it had a strong impact on his thinking. In his foreword to his Fordham University lectures, Jung stated that he had taken James's pragmatic rule as his guiding principle (CW 4, p. 86). See my *Jung and the Making of Modern Psychology: The Dream of a Science*, pp. 57–61.

during the 25 days, I gave all my love and submission to things, to men, and to the thoughts of this time. I went into the desert only at night.

Thus can you differentiate sick and divine delusion. Whoever does the one and does without the other you may call sick since he is out of balance.

But who can withstand fear when the divine intoxication and madness comes to him? Love, soul, and God are beautiful and terrible. The ancients brought over some of the beauty of God into this world, and this world became so beautiful that it appeared to the spirit of the time to be fulfillment, and better than the bosom of the Godhead. The frightfulness and cruelty of the world lay under wraps and in the depths of our hearts. If the spirit of the depths seizes you, you will feel the cruelty and cry out in torment. The spirit of the depths is pregnant with iron, fire, and death. You are right to fear the spirit of the depths, as he is full of horror.

You see in these days what the spirit of the depths bore. You did not believe it, but you would have known it if you had taken counsel with your fear.[91]

Blood shone at me from the red light of the crystal, and when I picked it up to discover its mystery, there lay the horror uncovered before me: in the depths of what is to come lay murder. The blond hero lay slain. The black beetle is the death that is necessary for renewal; and so thereafter, a new sun glowed, the sun of the depths,

91. The *Draft* continues: "The spirit of the depths was so alien to me that it took me twenty-five nights to comprehend him. And even then he was still so alien that I could neither see nor ask. He had to come to me as a stranger from far away and from an unheard-of side. He had to call me. I could not address him, knowing him and his nature. He announced himself with a loud voice, as in a warlike turmoil with the manifold clamoring of the voices of this time. The spirit of this time arose in me against this stranger, and uttered a battle cry together with his many serfs. I heard the noise of this battle in the air. Then the spirit of the depths burst forth and led me to the site of the innermost. But he had reduced the spirit of this time to a dwarf who was clever and bustling, yet was a dwarf. And the vision showed me the spirit of this time as made of leather, that is, pressed together, sere and lifeless. He could not prevent me from entering the dark underworld of the spirit of the depths. To my astonishment I realized that my feet sank into the black muddy water of the river of death. [The *Corrected Draft* adds: "for that is where death is," p. 41] The mystery of the shining red crystal was my next destination" (pp. 54–55).

full of riddles, a sun of the night. And as the rising sun of spring quickens the dead earth, so the sun of the depths quickened the dead, and thus began the terrible struggle between light and darkness. Out of that burst the powerful and ever unvanquished source of blood. This was what was to come, which you now experience in your life, and it is even more than that. (I had this vision on the night of 12 December 1913.)

Depths and surface should mix so that new life can develop. Yet the new life does not develop outside of us, but within us. What happens outside us in these days is the image that the peoples live in events, to bequeath this image immemorially to far-off times so that they might learn from it for their own way, just as we learned from the images that the ancients had lived before us in events.

Life does not come from events, but from us. Everything that happens outside has already been.

Therefore whoever considers the event from outside always sees only that it already was, and that it is always the same. But whoever looks from inside, knows that everything is new. The events that happen are always the same. But the creative depths of man are not always the same. Events signify nothing, they signify only in us. We create the meaning of events. The meaning is and always was artificial. We make it.

Because of this we seek in ourselves the meaning of events, so that the way
fol. iii(v) /iv(r) *of / what is to come becomes apparent and our life can flow again.*

That which you need comes from yourself, namely the meaning of the event. The meaning of events is not their particular meaning. This meaning exists in learnèd books. Events have no meaning.

The meaning of events is the way of salvation that you create. The meaning of events comes from the possibility of life in this world that you create. It is the mastery of this world and the assertion of your soul in this world.

This meaning of events is the supreme meaning, that is not in events, and not in the soul, but is the God standing between events and the soul, the mediator of life, the way, the bridge and the going across.[92]

92. *The Draft* continues: "My soul is my supreme meaning, my image of God, neither God himself nor the supreme meaning. God becomes apparent in the supreme meaning of the human community" (p. 58).

I would not have been able to see what was to come if I could not have seen it in myself.

Therefore I take part in that murder; the sun of the depths also shines in me after the murder has been accomplished; the thousand serpents that want to devour the sun are also in me. I myself am a murderer and murdered, sacrificer and sacrificed.[93] The upwelling blood streams out of me.

You all have a share in the murder.[94] In you the reborn one will come to be, and the sun of the depths will rise, and a thousand serpents will develop from your dead matter and fall on the sun to choke it. Your blood will stream forth. The peoples demonstrate this at the present time in unforgettable acts, that will be written with blood in unforgettable books for eternal memory.[95]

But I ask you, when do men fall on their brothers with mighty weapons and bloody acts? They do such if they do not know that their brother is themselves. They themselves are sacrificers, but they mutually do the service of sacrifice. They must all sacrifice each other, since the time has not yet come when man puts the bloody knife into himself, in order to sacrifice the one he kills in his brother. But whom do people kill? They kill the noble, the brave, the heroes. They take aim at these and do not know that with these they mean themselves. They should sacrifice the hero in themselves, and because they do not know this, they kill their courageous brother.

The time is still not ripe. But through this blood sacrifice, it should ripen. So long as it is possible to murder the brother instead

93. In "Transformation symbolism in the mass," (1942), Jung commented on the motif of the identity of the sacrificer and the sacrificed, with particular reference to the visions of Zosimos of Panapolis, a natural philosopher and alchemist of the third century. Jung noted: "What I sacrifice is my egotistical claim, and by doing this I give up myself. Every sacrifice is therefore, to a greater or lesser degree, a self-sacrifice" (CW 11, §397). Cf. also the Katha Upanishad, ch. 2, verse 19. Jung cited the next two verses of the Katha Upanishad on the nature of the self in 1921 (CW 6, §329). There is a line in the margin of Jung's copy by these verses in the *Sacred Books of the East*, vol. XV, pt. 2, p. 11. In "Dreams," Jung noted in connection with a dream "My intensive unconscious relation to India in the Red Book" (p. 9).

94. Jung elaborated the theme of collective guilt in "After the catastrophe" (1945, CW 10).

95. The reference is to the events of World War I. The autumn of 1914 (when Jung wrote this section of "layer two") saw the battle of the Marne and the first battle of Ypres.

of oneself, the time is not ripe. Frightful things must happen until men grow ripe. But anything else will not ripen humanity. Hence all this that takes place in these days must also be, so that the renewal can come. Since the source of blood that follows the shrouding of the sun is also the source of the new life.[96]

As the fate of the peoples is represented to you in events, so will it happen in your heart. If the hero in you is slain, then the sun of the depths rises in you, glowing from afar, and from a dreadful place. But all the same, everything that up till now seemed to be dead in you will come to life, and will change into poisonous serpents that will cover the sun, and you will fall into night and confusion. Your blood also will stream from many wounds in this frightful struggle. Your shock and doubt will be great, but from such torment the new life will be born. Birth is blood and torment. Your darkness, which you did not suspect since it was dead, will come to life and you will feel the crush of total evil and the conflicts of life that still now lie buried in the matter of your body. But the serpents are dreadful evil thoughts and feelings.

You thought you knew that abyss? Oh you clever people! It is another thing to experience it. Everything will happen to you. Think of all the frightful and devilish things that men have inflicted on their brothers. That should happen to you in your heart. Suffer it yourself through your own hand, and know that it is your own heinous and devilish hand that inflicts the suffering on you, but not your brother, who wrestles with his own devils.[97]

---

96. In his lecture at the *ETH* on June 14, 1935, Jung commented (partially in reference to this fantasy, which he referred to anonymously): "The sun motif appears in many places and times and the meaning is always the same—that a new consciousness has been born. It is the light of illumination which is projected into space. This is a psychological event; the medical term 'hallucination' makes no sense in psychology. / The Katabasis plays a very important role in the Middle Ages and the old masters conceived of the rising sun in this Katabasis as of a new light, the lux moderna, the jewel, the lapis" (*Modern Psychology*, p. 231).

97. *The Draft* continues: "My friends, I know that I speak in riddles. But the spirit of the depths has granted me a view of many things in order to help my weak comprehension. I want to tell you more about my visions so that you better understand which things the spirit of the depths would like you to see. May those be well who can see these things! Those who cannot must live them as blind fate, in images" (p. 61).

I would like you to see what the murdered hero means. Those nameless men who in our day have murdered a prince are blind prophets who demonstrate in events what then is valid only for the soul.[98] Through the murder of princes we will learn that the prince in us, the hero, is threatened.[99] Whether this should be seen as a good or a bad sign need not concern us. What is awful today is good in a hundred years, and in two hundred years is bad again. But we must recognize what is happening: there are nameless ones in you who threaten your prince, the hereditary ruler.

But our ruler is the spirit of this time, which rules and leads in us all. It is the general spirit in which we think and act today. He is of frightful power, since he has brought immeasurable good to this world and fascinated men with unbelievable pleasure. He is bejewelled with the most beautiful heroic virtue, and wants to drive men up to the brightest solar heights, in everlasting ascent.[100]

The hero wants to open up everything he can. But the nameless spirit of the depths evokes everything that man cannot. Incapacity prevents further ascent. Greater height requires greater virtue. We do not possess it. We must first create it by learning to live with our incapacity. We must give it life. For how else shall it develop into ability?

We cannot slay our incapacity and rise above it. But that is precisely what we wanted. Incapacity will overcome us and demand its share of life. Our ability will desert us, and we will believe, in the sense of the spirit of this time, that it is a loss. Yet it is no loss but a gain, not for outer trappings, however, but for inner capability.

---

98. In *The Relations between the I and the Unconscious* (1927), Jung refers to the destructive and anarchic aspects that are constellated in societies being enacted by prophetically inclined individuals though spectacular crimes such as regicide (CW 7, §240).

99. Political assassinations were frequent at the beginning of the twentieth century. The particular event referred to here is the assassination of Archduke Franz Ferdinand. Martin Gilbert describes this event, which played a critical role in the events that led to the outbreak of the First World War, as "a turning point in the history of the twentieth century" (*A History of the Twentieth Century: Volume One: 1900–1933* [London: William Morrow, 1977], p. 308).

100. The *Draft* continues: "When I was aspiring to my highest worldly power, the spirit of the depths sent me nameless thoughts and visions, that wiped out the heroic aspiration in me as our time understands it" (p. 62).

The one who learns to live with his incapacity has learned a great deal. This will lead us to the valuation of the smallest things, and to wise limitation, which the greater height demands. If all heroism is erased, we fall back into the misery of humanity and into even worse. Our foundations will be caught up in excitement since our highest tension, which concerns what lies outside us, will stir them up. We will fall into the cesspool of our underworld, among the rubble of all the centuries in us.[101]

The heroic in you is the fact that you are ruled by the thought that this or that is good, that this or that performance is indispensable, this or that cause is objectionable, this or that goal must be attained in headlong striving work, this or that pleasure should be ruthlessly repressed at all costs. Consequently you sin against incapacity. But incapacity exists. No one should deny it, find fault with it, or shout it down.[102]

Splitting of the Spirit

[HI iv(r)]

Cap. vi.

But on the fourth night I cried, "To journey to Hell means to become Hell oneself.[103] It is all frightfully muddled and interwoven.

---

101. The *Draft* continues: "Everything that we have forgotten will be revived, each human and divine passion, the black serpents and the reddish sun of the depths" (p. 64).

102. On June 9, 1917, there was a discussion on the psychology of the world war in the Association for Analytical Psychology following a presentation by Jules Vodoz on the *Song of Roland*. Jung argued that "Hypothetically, the World War can be raised to the subjective level. In detail, the authoritarian principle (taking action on the basis of principles) clashes with the emotional principle. The collective unconscious enters into allegiance with the emotional." Concerning the hero, he said: "The hero—the beloved figure of the people, should fall. All heroes bring themselves down by carrying the heroic attitude beyond a certain limit, and hence lose their footing" (*MAP*, vol. 2, p. 10). The psychological interpretation of the First World War on the subjective level describes what is developed in this chapter. The connection between individual and collective psychology which he articulates here forms one of the leitmotifs of his later work (cf. *Present and Future* [1957], CW 10).

103. December 16, 1913. In *Beyond Good and Evil,* Nietzsche wrote: "Anyone who fights with monsters should take care that he does not in the process become a monster. And if you

On this desert path there is not just glowing sand, but also horrible tangled invisible beings who live in the desert. I didn't know this. The way is only apparently clear, the desert is only apparently empty. It seems inhabited by magical beings who murderously attach themselves to me and daimonically change my form. I have evidently taken on a completely monstrous form in which I can no longer recognize myself. It seems to me that I have become a monstrous animal form for which I have exchanged my humanity. This way is surrounded by hellish magic, invisible nooses have been thrown over me and ensnare me."

But the spirit of the depths approached me and said, "Climb down into your depths, sink!"

But I was indignant at him and said, "How can I sink? I am unable to do this myself."

Then the spirit spoke words to me that appeared ridiculous, and he said, "Sit yourself down, be calm."

But I cried out indignantly: "How frightful, it sounds like nonsense, do you also demand this of me? You overthrew the mighty Gods who mean the most to us. My soul, where are you? Have I entrusted myself to a stupid animal, do I stagger like a drunkard to the grave, do I stammer stupidities like a lunatic? Is this your way, my soul? The blood boils in me and I would strangle you if I could seize you. You weave the thickest darknesses and I am like a madman caught in your net. But I yearn, teach me."

But my soul spoke to me saying, "My path is light."

Yet I indignantly answered, "Do you call light what we men call the worst darkness? Do you call day night?"

To this my soul spoke a word that roused my anger: "My light is not of this world."

I cried, "I know of no other world."

The soul answered, "Should it not exist because you know nothing of it?" I: "But our knowledge? Does our knowledge also not hold

---

gaze for long into an abyss, the abyss gazes back into you" (tr. Marion Faber [Oxford: Oxford University Press], 1998, §146, p. 68).

good for you? What is it going to be, if not knowledge? Where is security? Where is solid ground? Where is light? Your darkness is not only darker than night, but bottomless as well. If it's not going to be knowledge, then perhaps it will do without speech and words too?"

My soul: "No words."

I: "Forgive me, perhaps I'm hard of hearing, perhaps I misinterpret you, perhaps I ensnare myself in self-deceit and monkey business, and I am a rascal grinning at myself in a mirror, a fool in my own madhouse. Perhaps you stumble over my folly?"

My soul: "You delude yourself, you do not deceive me. Your words are lies to you, not me."

I: "But could I wallow in raging nonsense, and hatch absurdity and perverse monotony?"

My soul: "Who gives you thoughts and words? Do you make them? Are you not my serf, a recipient who lies at my door and picks up my alms? And you dare think that what you devise and speak could be nonsense? Don't you know yet that it comes from me and belongs to me?"

So I cried full of anger, "But then my indignation must also come from you, and in me you are indignant against yourself." My soul then spoke the ambiguous words: "That is civil war."[104]

I was afflicted with pain and rage, and I answered back, "How painful, my soul, to hear you use hollow words; I feel sick. Comedy and drivel—but I yearn. I can also crawl through mud and the most despised banality. I can also eat dust; that is part of Hell. I do not yield, I am defiant. You can go on devising torments, spider-legged monsters, ridiculous, hideous, frightful theatrical spectacles. Come close, I am ready. Ready, my soul, you who are a devil, to wrestle with you too. You donned the mask of a God, and I worshiped you. Now you wear the mask of a devil, a frightful one, the mask of the banal, of eternal mediocrity! Only one favor! Give me a moment to step back and consider! Is the struggle with this mask worthwhile?

104. *Black Book 2* continues: "Are you neurotic? Are we neurotic?" (p. 53).

Was the mask of God worth worshiping? I cannot do it, the lust for battle burns in my limbs. No, I cannot leave the battlefield defeated. I want to seize you, crush you, monkey, buffoon. Woe if the struggle is unequal, my hands grab at air. But your blows are also air, and I perceive trickery."

I find myself again on the desert path. It was a desert vision, a vision of the solitary who has wandered down long roads. There lurk invisible robbers and assassins and shooters of poison darts. Suppose the murderous arrow is sticking in my heart?

[2] As the first vision had predicted to me, the assassin appeared from the depths, and came to me just as in the fate of the peoples of this time a nameless one appeared and leveled the murder weapon at the prince.[105]

I felt myself transformed into a rapacious beast. My heart glowered in rage against the high and beloved, against my prince and hero, just as the nameless one of the people, driven by greed for murder, lunged at his dear prince. Because I carried the murder in me, I foresaw it.[106]

Because I carried the war in me, I foresaw it. I felt betrayed and lied to by my king. Why did I feel this way? He was not as I had wished him to be. He was other than I expected. He should be the king in my sense, not in his sense. He should be what I called ideal. My soul appeared to me hollow, tasteless and meaningless. But in reality what I thought of her was valid for my ideal.

It was a / vision of the desert, I struggled with mirror images fol. iv(r)/iv(v)
of myself. It was civil war in me. I myself was the murderer and the murdered. The deadly arrow was stuck in my heart, and I did not know what it meant. My thoughts were murder and the fear of death, which spread like poison everywhere in my body.

105. See note 99, p. 155.

106. The *Draft* continues: "My friends, if you knew what depths of the future you carry inside you! Those who look into their own depths, look at what is to come" (p. 70).

And thus was the fate of the people: The murder of one was the poisonous arrow that flew into the hearts of men, and kindled the fiercest war. This murder is the indignation of incapacity against will, a Judas betrayal that one would like someone else to have committed.[107] We are still seeking the goat that should bear our sin.[108]

Everything that becomes too old becomes evil, the same is true of your highest. Learn from the suffering of the crucified God that one can also betray and crucify a God, namely the God of the old year. If a God ceases being the way of life, he must fall secretly.[109]

The God becomes sick if he oversteps the height of the zenith. That is why the spirit of the depths took me when the spirit of this time had led me to the summit.[110]

Murder of the Hero

[HI iv(v)][111]

Cap. vii.

On the following night, however, I had a vision:[112] I was with a youth in high mountains. It was before daybreak, the Eastern sky was already light. Then Siegfried's horn resounded over the moun-

107. The *Draft* continues: "But just as Judas is a necessary link in the chain of the work of redemption, so is our Judas betrayal of the hero also a necessary passageway to redemption" (p. 71). In *Transformations and Symbols of the Libido* (1912), Jung discussed the view of the Abbé Oegger, in Anatole France's story *Le jardin d'Épicure*, who maintained that God had chosen Judas as an instrument to complete Christ's work of redemption (CW B, §52).
108. Cf. Leviticus 16:7–10: "And he shall take the two goats, and present them before the Lord at the door of the tabernacle of the congregation. And Aaron shall cast lots upon the two goats; one lot for the Lord, and the other lot for the scapegoat. And Aaron shall bring the goat upon which the Lord's lot fell, and offer him for a sin offering. But the goat, on which the lot fell to be the scapegoat, shall be presented alive before the Lord, to make an atonement with him, and to let him go for a scapegoat into the wilderness."
109. The *Draft* continues: "this is what the ancients taught us" (p. 72).
110. The *Draft* continues: "Those who wander in the desert experience everything that belongs to the desert. The ancients have described this to us. From them we can learn. Open the ancient books and learn what will come to you in solitude. Everything will be given to you and you will be spared nothing, the mercy and the torment" (p. 72).
111. This refers to the mourning for the death of the hero.
112. December 18, 1913. *Black Book 2* has: "The following night was terrible. I soon awoke from a frightful dream" (p. 56). The *Draft* has: "a mighty dream vision rose from the depths" (p. 73).

tains with a jubilant sound.[113] We knew that our mortal enemy was coming. We were armed and lurked beside a narrow rocky path to murder him. Then we saw him coming high across the mountains on a chariot made of the bones of the dead. He drove boldly and magnificently over the steep rocks and arrived at the narrow path where we waited in hiding. As he came around the turn ahead of us, we fired at the same time and he fell slain. Thereupon I turned to flee, and a terrible rain swept down. But after this[114] I went through a torment unto death and I felt certain that I must kill myself, if I could not solve the riddle of the murder of the hero.[115]

Then the spirit of the depths came to me and spoke these words:

"The highest truth is one and the same with the absurd." This statement saved me, and like rain after a long hot spell, it swept away everything in me which was too highly tensed.

---

113. Siegfried was a heroic prince who appears in old German and Norse epics. In the twelfth-century *Niebelunglied*, he is described as follows: "And in what magnificent style Siegfried rode! He bore a great spear, stout of shaft and broad of head; his handsome sword reached down to his spurs; and the fine horn which this lord carried was of the reddest gold" (tr. A. Hatto [London: Penguin, 2004], p. 129). His wife, Brunhild, is tricked into revealing the only place where he could be wounded and killed. Wagner reworked these epics in *The Ring of the Niebelung*. In 1912, in *Transformations and Symbols of the Libido*, Jung presented a psychological interpretation of Siegfried as a symbol of the libido, principally citing Wagner's libretto of *Siegfried* (CW B, §568f).

114. The *Draft* continues: "After this dream vision" (p. 73).

115. In *Black Book 2*, Jung noted: "I strode light-footedly up an incredibly steep path and later helped my wife, who followed me at a slower pace, to ascend. Some people mocked us, but I didn't mind, since this showed that they didn't know that I had murdered the hero" (p. 57). Jung recounted this dream in the 1925 seminar, stressing different details. He preceded it with the following remarks: "Siegfried was not an especially sympathetic figure to me, and I don't know why my unconscious got engrossed in him. Wagner's Siegfried, especially, is exaggeratedly extraverted and at times actually ridiculous. I never liked him. Nevertheless the dream showed him to be my hero. I could not understand the strong emotion I had with the dream." After narrating the dream, Jung concluded: "I felt an enormous pity for him [Siegfried], as though I myself had been shot. I must then have had a hero I did not appreciate, and it was my ideal of force and efficiency I had killed. I had killed my intellect, helped on to the deed by a personification of the collective unconscious, the little brown man with me. In other words, I deposed my superior function . . . The rain that fell is a symbol of the release of tension; that is, the forces of the unconscious are loosed. When this happens, the feeling of relief is engendered. The crime is expiated because, as soon as the main function is deposed, there is a chance for other sides of the personality to be born into life" (*Introduction to Jungian Psychology*, pp. 61–62). In *Black Book 2*, and in his later remarks about this dream in *Memories* (p. 204), Jung said that he felt that he would have to kill himself if he could not solve this riddle.

Then I had a second vision:[116] I saw a merry garden, in which forms walked clad in white silk, all covered in colored light, some reddish, the others blueish and greenish.[117] [Image iv(v)]

I know, I have stridden across the depths. Through guilt I have become a newborn.[118]

[2] We also live in our dreams, we do not live only by day. Sometimes we accomplish our greatest deeds in dreams.[119]

In that night my life was threatened since I had to kill my lord and God, not in single combat, since who among mortals could kill a God in a duel? You can reach your God only as an assassin,[120] if you want to overcome him.

But this is the bitterest for mortal men: our Gods want to be overcome, since they require renewal. If men kill their princes, they do so because they cannot kill their Gods, and because they do not know that they should kill their Gods in themselves.

If the God grows old, he becomes shadow, nonsense, and he goes down. The greatest truth becomes the greatest lie, the brightest day becomes darkest night.

As day requires night and night requires day, so meaning requires absurdity and absurdity requires meaning.

---

116. The *Draft* continues: "and I fell asleep again. A second dream vision rose in me" (pp. 73–74).

117. The *Draft* continues: "These lights pervaded my mind and senses. And once again I fell asleep like a convalescent" (p. 74). Jung recounted this dream to Aniela Jaffé, and commented that after he had been confronted with the shadow, as in the Siegfried dream, this dream expressed the idea that he was one thing and something else at the same time. The unconscious reached beyond one, like a saint's halo. The shadow was like the light-colored sphere that surrounded the people. He thought this was a vision of the beyond, where men are complete. (*MP*, p. 170).

118. The *Draft* continues: "The world in-between is a world of the simplest things. It is not a world of intention and imperatives, but a perchance-world with indefinite possibilities. Here the next ways are all small, no broad, straight highroads, no Heaven above them, no Hell beneath" (p. 74). In October of 1916, Jung gave some talks to the Psychological Club, "Adaptation, individuation, and collectivity," in which he commented on the importance of guilt: "the first step in individuation is tragic guilt. The accumulation of guilt demands expiation" (CW 18, §1094).

119. The *Draft* has here, in addition: "Are you smiling? The spirit of this time would want to make you believe that the depths are no world and no reality" (p. 74).

120. The *Draft* continues: "a Judas" (p. 75).

Day does not exist through itself, night does not exist through itself.

The reality that exists through itself is day and night.

So the reality is meaning and absurdity.

Noon is a moment, midnight is a moment, morning comes from night, evening turns into night, but evening comes from the day and morning turns into day.

So meaning is a moment and a transition from absurdity to absurdity, and absurdity only a moment and a transition from meaning to meaning.[121]

Oh that Siegfried, blond and blue-eyed, the German hero, had to fall by my hand, the most loyal and courageous! He had everything in himself that I treasured as the greater and more beautiful; he was my power, my boldness, my pride. I would have gone under in the same battle, and so only assassination was left to me. If I wanted to go on living, it could only be through trickery and cunning.

Judge not! Think of the blond savage of the German forests, who had to betray the hammer-brandishing thunder to the pale Near-Eastern God who was nailed to the wood like a chicken marten. The courageous were overcome by a certain contempt for themselves. But their life force bade them to go on living, and they betrayed their beautiful wild Gods, their holy trees and their awe of the German forests.[122]

What does Siegfried mean for the Germans! What does it tell us that the Germans suffer Siegfried's death! That is why I almost preferred to kill myself in order to spare him. But I wanted to go on living with a new God.[123]

---

121. The *Draft* continues: "My dream vision showed me that I was not alone when I committed the deed. I was helped by a youth, that is, one who was younger than me; a rejuvenated version of myself" (p. 76).

122. The *Draft* continues: "Siegfried had to die, just like Wotan" (p. 76). In 1918, Jung wrote of the effects of the introduction of Christianity into Germany: "Christianity split the Germanic barbarian into his upper and lower halves and enabled him, by repressing the dark side, to domesticate the brighter half and fit it for culture. But the lower, darker half still awaits redemption and a second domestication. Until then, it will remain associated with vestiges of prehistory, with the collective unconscious, which must indicate a peculiar and increasing activation of the collective unconscious" ("On the unconscious," CW 10, §17). He expanded on this situation in "Wotan" (1936, CW 10).

123. In the *Draft*, this sentence reads: "We want to continue living with a new God, a hero beyond Christ" (p. 76). To Aniela Jaffé, he recounted that he had thought of himself

After death on the cross Christ went into the underworld and became Hell. So he took on the form of the Antichrist, the dragon. The image of the Antichrist, which has come down to us from the ancients, announces the new God, whose coming the ancients had foreseen.

Gods are unavoidable. The more you flee from the God, the more surely you fall into his hand.

The rain is the great stream of tears that will come over the peoples, the tearful flood of released tension after the constriction of death had encumbered the peoples with horrific force. It is the mourning of the dead in me, which precedes burial and rebirth. The rain is the fructifying of the earth, it begets the new wheat, the young, germinating God.[124]

The Conception of the God

[HI iv(v) 2]

Cap. viii.

On the second night thereafter, I spoke to my soul and said, "This new world appears weak and artificial to me. Artificial is a bad word, but the mustard seed that grew into a tree, the word that was conceived in the womb of a virgin, became a God to whom the earth was subject."[125]

---

as an overcoming hero, but the dream indicated that the hero had to be killed. This exaggeration of the will was represented by the Germans at that time, such as by the Siegfried line. A voice within him said, "If you do not understand the dream, you must shoot yourself!" (*MP*, p. 98, *Memories*, p. 204) The original Siegfried line was a defensive line established by the Germans in northern France in 1917 (this was actually a subsection of the Hindenburg Line).

124. The theme of the dying and resurrecting God features prominently in James Frazer's *The Golden Bough: A Study in Magic and Religion* (London: Macmillan, 1911–15), which Jung drew upon in *Transformations and Symbols of the Libido* (1912).

125. December 20, 1913. A reference to Christ's parable of the mustard seed. Matthew 13:31-32: "The kingdom of heaven is like to a grain of mustard seed, which a man took, and sowed in his field: Which indeed is the least of all seeds: but when it is grown, it is the greatest among herbs, and becometh a tree" (Cf. Luke 13:18–20, Mark 4:30–32).

As I spoke thus, the spirit of the depths suddenly erupted. He filled me with intoxication and mist and spoke these words with a powerful voice: [OB iv (v)] *"I have received your sprout, you who are to come!*

I have received it in deepest need and lowliness.

I covered it in shabby patchwork and bedded down on poor words.

And mockery worshiped it, your child, your wondrous child, the child of one who is to come, who should announce the father, a fruit that is older than the tree on which it grew.

In pain will you conceive and joyful is your birth.

Fear is your herald, doubt stands to your right, disappointment to your left.

We passed by in our ridiculousness and senselessness when we caught sight of you.

Our eyes were blinded and our knowledge fell silent when we received your radiance.

You new spark of an eternal fire, into which night were you born?

You will wring truthful prayers from your believers, and they must speak of your glory in tongues that are atrocious to them.

You will come over them in the hour of their disgrace, and will become known to them in what they hate, fear, and abhor.[126]

Your voice, the rarest pleasing sound, will be heard amid the stammerings of wretches, rejects, and those condemned as worthless.

Your realm will be touched by the hands of those who also worshiped before the most profound lowliness, and whose longing drove them through the mud tide of evil.

You will give your gifts to those who pray to you in terror and doubt, and your light will shine upon those whose knees must bend before you unwillingly and who are filled with resentment.

Your life is with he who has overcome himself / [OB v(r)] *and who has disowned his self-overcoming.*[127] fol. iv(v) /v(r)

126. In Mark 16:17, Christ stated that those who believe shall speak with new tongues. The issue of speaking in tongues is discussed in 1 Corinthians 14, and is central in the Pentecostal movement.

127. The theme of self-overcoming is an important one in the work of Nietzsche. In *Thus Spoke Zarathustra*, Nietzsche writes: "I teach you the Superman. Man is something that should be overcome. What have you done to overcome him? All creatures hitherto have created something beyond themselves: *and do you want to be the ebb of this great tide, and return*

I also know that the salvation of mercy is given only to those who believe in the highest and faithlessly betray themselves for thirty pieces of silver.[128]

Those who will dirty their pure hands and cheat on their best knowledge against error and take their virtues from a murderer's grave are invited to your great banquet.

The constellation of your birth is an ill and changing star.

These, Oh child of what is to come, are the wonders that will bear testimony that you are a veritable God."

[2] When my prince had fallen, the spirit of the depths opened my vision and let me become aware of the birth of the new God.

The divine child approached me out of the terrible ambiguity, the hateful-beautiful, the evil-good, the laughable-serious, the sick-healthy, the inhuman-human and the ungodly-godly.[129]

I understood that the God[130] whom we seek in the absolute was not to be found in absolute beauty, goodness, seriousness, elevation, humanity or even in godliness. Once the God was there.

I understood that the new God would be in the relative. If the God is absolute beauty and goodness, how should he encompass the fullness of life, which is beautiful and hateful, good and evil, laughable and serious, human and inhuman? How can man live in the womb of the God if the Godhead himself attends only to one-half of him?[131]

If we have risen near the heights of good and evil, then our badness and hatefulness lie in the most extreme torment. Man's torment is so great and the air of the heights so weak that he can hardly live anymore. The good and the beautiful freeze to the ice of the absolute idea,[132] and the bad and hateful become mud puddles full of crazy life.

---

to the animals rather than overcome man? ("Zarathustra's prologue 3," p. 41; underlined as in Jung's copy). For Jung's discussion of this theme in Nietzsche, see Nietzsche's *Zarathustra: Notes of the Seminar Given in 1934–9*, vol. 2, ed. James Jarrett (Princeton: Princeton University Press, 1988, pp. 1502–8).

128. Judas betrayed Christ for thirty pieces of silver (Matthew 26:14–16).

129. See note 58, p. 136.

130. This conception of the encompassing nature of the new God is fully developed further ahead in *Scrutinies* (Sermon 2, p. 516f).

131. The theme of the integration of evil into the Godhead played an important role in Jung's works; see *Aion* (1951, CW 9, 2, ch. 5), and *Answer to Job* (1952, CW 11).

132. The conception of the absolute idea was developed by Hegel. He understood it as the culmination and the self-differentiating unity of the dialectical sequence that gives

Therefore after his death Christ had to journey to Hell, otherwise the ascent to Heaven would have become impossible for him. Christ first had to become his Antichrist, his underworldly brother.

No one knows what happened during the three days Christ was in Hell. I have experienced it.[133] The men of yore said that he had preached there to the deceased.[134] What they say is true, but do you know how this happened?

It was folly and monkey business, an atrocious Hell's masquerade of the holiest mysteries. How else could Christ have saved his Antichrist? Read the unknown books of the ancients, and you will learn much from them. Notice that Christ did not remain in Hell, but rose to the heights in the beyond.[135]

Our conviction of the value of the good and beautiful has become strong and unshakable, that is why life can extend beyond this and still fulfil everything that lay bound and yearning. But the bound

---

rise to the cosmos. Cf. *Hegel's Logic* (tr. W. Wallace [London: Thames and Hudson, 1975]). Jung refers to this in 1921 in *Psychological Types* (CW 6, §735).

133. This sentence is cut in the *Corrected Draft* and replaced with "but this can be guessed:" (p. 68).

134. 1 Peter 4:6 states: "For this reason the gospel was preached also to those who are dead, that they might be judged according to men in the flesh, but live according to God in the spirit."

135. The theme of Christ's descent into Hell features in several apocryphal gospels. In the "Apostles Creed," it is stated that "He descended into Hell. The third day He arose again from the dead." Jung commented on the appearance of this motif in medieval alchemy (*Psychology and Alchemy*, 1944, CW 12, §61n, 440, 451; *Mysterium Coniunctionis*, 1955/56, CW 14, 475). One of the sources which Jung referred to (CW 12, §61n) was Albrecht Dieterich's *Nekyía: Beiträge zur Erklärung der neuentdeckten Petrusapokalypse*, which commented on an apocalyptic fragment from the Gospel of St. Peter, in which Christ gives a detailed description of Hell. Jung's copy of this work has numerous markings in the margins, and in the rear are two additional pieces of paper with a list of page references and remarks. In 1951 he gave the following psychological interpretation of the motif of Christ's descent into Hell: "The scope of the integration is suggested by the 'descensus ad infernos,' the descent of Christ's soul to Hell, whose work of redemption also encompasses the dead. The psychological equivalent of this forms the integration of the collective unconscious which represents an essential part of the individuation process" (*Aion*, CW 9, 2, §72). In 1938 he noted: "The three days descent into Hell during death describes the sinking of the vanished value into the unconscious, where, by conquering the power of darkness, it establishes a new order, and then rises up to heaven again, that is, attains supreme clarity of consciousness" ("Psychology and religion," CW 11, §149). The "unknown books of the ancients" refer to the apocryphal gospels.

and yearning is also the hateful and bad. Are you again indignant about the hateful and the bad?

Through this you can recognize how great are their force and value for life. Do you think that it is dead in you? But this dead can also change into serpents.[136] These serpents will extinguish the prince of your days.

Do you see what beauty and joy came over men when the depths unleashed this greatest war? And yet it was a frightful beginning.[137]

If we do not have the depths, how do we have the heights? Yet you fear the depths, and do not want to confess that you are afraid of them. It is good, though, that you fear yourselves; say it out loud that you are afraid of yourselves. It is wisdom to fear oneself. Only the heroes say that they are fearless. But you know what happens to the hero.

With fear and trembling, looking around yourselves with mistrust, go thus into the depths, but do not do this alone; two or more is greater security since the depths are full of murder. Also secure yourselves the way of retreat. Go cautiously as if you were cowards,

---

136. The *Draft* continues: "But the serpent is also life. In the image furnished by the ancients, the serpent put an end to the childlike magnificence of paradise; they even said that Christ himself had been a serpent" (p. 83). Jung commented on this motif in 1950 in *Aion*, CW 9, 2, §291.

137. The *Corrected Draft* has: "a beginning of Hell" (p. 70). In 1933 Jung recalled: "At the outbreak of war I was in Inverness, and I returned through Holland and Germany. I came right through the armies going west, and I had the feeling that it was what one would call in German a *Hochzeitsstimmung*, a feast of love all over the country. Everything was decorated with flowers, it was an outburst of love, they all loved each other and everything was beautiful. Yes, the war was important, a big affair, but the main thing was the brotherly love all over the country, everybody was everybody else's brother, one could have everything anyone possessed, it did not matter. The peasants threw open their cellars and handed out what they had. That happened even in the restaurant and buffet at the railroad station. I was very hungry, I had had nothing to eat for about twenty-four hours, and they had some sandwiches left, and when I asked what they cost, they said, 'Oh nothing, just take them!' And when I first crossed the border into Germany, we were led into an enormous tent full of beer and sausages and bread and cheese, and we paid nothing, it was one great feast of love. I was absolutely bewildered" (*Visions Seminars* 2, ed. Claire Douglas [Princeton: Princeton University Press, 1997], pp. 974–75).

so that you pre-empt the soul murderers.[138] The depths would like to devour you whole and choke you in mud.

He who journeys to Hell also becomes Hell; therefore do not forget from whence you come. The depths are stronger than us; so do not be heroes, be clever and drop the heroics, since nothing is more dangerous than to play the hero. The depths want to keep you; they have not returned very many up to now, and therefore men fled from the depths and attacked them.

What if the depths, due to the assault, now change themselves into death? But the depths indeed have changed themselves into death; therefore when they awoke they inflicted a thousandfold death.[139] We cannot slay death, as we have already taken all life from it. If we still want to overcome death, then we must enliven it.

Therefore on your journey be sure to take golden cups full of the sweet drink of life, red wine, and give it to dead matter, so that it can win life back. The dead matter will change into black serpents. Do not be frightened, the serpents will immediately put out the sun of your days, and a night with wonderful will-o'-the-wisps will come over you.[140]

Take pains to waken the dead. Dig deep mines and throw in sacrificial gifts, so that they reach the dead. Reflect in good heart upon evil, this is the way to the ascent. But before the ascent, everything is night and Hell.

What do you think of the essence of Hell? Hell is when the depths come to you with all that you no longer are or are not yet capable of. Hell is when you can no longer attain what you could

138. The phrase "Soul murderer" had been used by Luther and Zwingli, and more recently by Daniel Paul Schreber in his 1903 *Memoirs of my Nervous Illness*, eds. and tr. Ida Macalpine and Richard Hunter (Folkestone: William Dawson, 1955). Jung discussed this work in 1907 in "On the psychology of dementia praecox" (*CW* 3), and drew Freud's attention to it. In discussions concerning Schreber in the Association for Analytical Psychology on July 9 and 16 of 1915 following presentations by Schneiter, Jung drew attention to Gnostic parallels to Schreber's imagery (*MAP*, vol. 1., p. 88f).

139. The reference is to the carnage of World War I.

140. This refers back to the vision in chapter 5, "Descent into Hell in the Future." In 1940 Jung wrote: "the threat to one's inmost self from dragons and serpents points to the danger of the newly acquired consciousness being swallowed up again by the instinctive soul, the unconscious" ("On the psychology of the child archetype," *CW* 9,1, §282).

attain. Hell is when you must think and feel and do everything that you know you do not want. Hell is when you know that your having to is also a wanting to, and that you yourself are responsible for it. Hell is when you know that everything serious that you have planned with yourself is also laughable, that everything fine is also brutal, that everything good is also bad, that everything high is also low, and that everything pleasant is also shameful.

But the deepest Hell is when you realize that Hell is also no Hell, but a cheerful Heaven, not a Heaven in itself, but in this respect a Heaven, and in that respect a Hell.

That is the ambiguity of the God: he is born from a dark ambiguity and rises to a bright ambiguity. Unequivocalness is simplicity and leads to death.[141] But ambiguity is the way of life.[142] If the left foot does not move, then the right one does, and you move. The God wills this.[143]

You say: the Christian God is unequivocal, he is love.[144] But what is more ambiguous than love? Love is the way of life, but your love is only on the way of life if you have a left and a right.

Nothing is easier than to play at ambiguity and nothing is more difficult than living ambiguity. He who plays is a child; his God is old and dies. He who lives is awakened; his God is young and goes on. He who plays hides from the inner death. He who lives feels the going onward and immortality. So leave the play to the players. Let fall what wants to fall; if you stop it, it will sweep you away. There is a true love that does not concern itself with neighbors.[145]

---

141. The *Corrected Draft* has instead "to an end" (p. 73).
142. In 1952, Jung wrote to Zwi Werblowsky concerning the intentional ambiguity of his writings: "The language I speak must be equivocal, that is, *ambiguous*, to do justice to psychic nature with its double aspect. I strive consciously and deliberately for ambiguous expressions, because it is superior to unequivocalness and corresponds to the nature of being" (*Letters* 2, pp. 70–71).
143. The *Draft* continues: "Look at the images of the Gods that the ancients and the men of old left behind: their nature is ambiguous and equivocal" (p. 87).
144. I John 4:16: "God is love; and he that dwelleth in love dwelleth in God, and God in him."
145. The *Draft* continues: "Whoever reverses this word and others that I speak, is a player, since he doesn't respect the spoken word. Know that you attain yourself from what you read in a book. You read as much into a book as out of it" (p. 88).

When the hero was slain and the meaning recognized in the absurdity, when all tension came rushing down from gravid clouds, when everything had become cowardly and looked to its own rescue, I became aware of the birth of the God.[146] Opposing me, the God sank into my heart when I was confused by mockery and worship, by grief and laughter, by yes and no.

The one arose from the melting together of the two. He was born as a child from my own human soul, which had conceived him with resistance like a virgin. Thus it corresponds to the image that the ancients have given to us.[147] But when the mother, my soul, was pregnant with the God, I did not know it. It even seemed to me as if my soul herself was the God, although he lived only in her body.[148]

And thus the image of the ancients is fulfilled: I pursued my soul to kill the child in it. For I am also the worst enemy of my God.[149] But I also recognized that my enmity is decided upon in the God. He is mockery and hate and anger, since this is also a way of life.

I must say that the God could not come into being before the hero had been slain. The hero as we understand him has become an enemy of the God, since the hero is perfection. The Gods envy the perfection of man, because perfection has no need of the Gods. But since no one is perfect, we need the Gods. The Gods love perfection because it is the total way of life. But the Gods are not with him who wishes to be perfect, because he is an imitation of perfection.[150]

Imitation was a way of life when men still needed the heroic prototype.[151] The monkey's manner is a way of life for monkeys, and

146. The *Corrected Draft* has "~~birth of the new~~ [conception of a] God" (p. 74).

147. The reference is to the Virgin Mary.

148. See note 57, p. 135.

149. This seems to refer to the wounding of Izdubar in *Liber Secundus*, ch. 8, "First Day." See below, p. 277f.

150. The importance of wholeness above perfection is an important theme in Jung's later work. Cf. *Aion*, 1951, CW 9, 2, §123; *Mysterium Coniunctionis*, 1955/56, CW 14, §616.

151. In 1916, Jung wrote: "Man has one ability which, though it is of the greatest utility for collective purposes, is the most pernicious for individuation, and that is *imitation*. *Collective psychology can hardly dispense with imitation*" ("The structure of the unconscious," CW 7, §463). In "On the psychology of the child archetype" (1940) Jung wrote about the danger of identifying with the hero: "This identity is often very extremely stubborn and dangerous for the equilibrium of the soul. If the identity can be dissolved, the

for man as long as he is like a monkey. Human apishness has lasted a terribly long time, but the time will come when a piece of that apishness will fall away from men.

That will be a time of salvation and the dove, and the eternal fire, and redemption will descend.

Then there will no longer be a hero, and no one who can imitate him. Because from that time henceforth all imitation is cursed. The new God laughs at imitation and discipleship. He needs no imitators and no pupils. He forces men through himself. The God is his own follower in man. He imitates himself.

We think that there is singleness within us, and communality outside us. Outside of us is the communal in relation to the external, while singleness refers to us. We are single if we are in ourselves, but communal in relation to what is outside us. But if we are outside of ourselves, then we are single and selfish in the communal. Our self suffers privation if we are outside ourselves, and thus it satisfies its needs with communality. Consequently, communality is distorted into singleness. If we are in ourselves, we fulfil the need of the self, we prosper, and through this we become aware of the needs of the communal and can fulfil them.[152]

If we set a God outside of ourselves, he tears us loose from the self, since the God is more powerful than we are. Our self falls into privation. But if the God moves into the self, he snatches us from what is outside us.[153] We arrive at singleness in ourselves. So the God becomes communal in reference to what is outside us, but single in relation to us. No one has my God, but my God has everyone, including myself. The Gods of all individual men always have all other men, including myself. So it is always only the one God despite

figure of the hero, through the reduction of consciousness to a human level, can gradually be differentiated into a symbol of the self" (CW 9, 1, §303).

152. Jung dealt with the issue of the conflict between individuation and collectivity in 1916 in "Individuation and collectivity" (CW 18).

153. Cf. Jung's comments in "Individuation and collectivity" that "The individual must now consolidate himself by cutting himself off from God and becoming wholly himself. Thereby and at the same time he also separates himself from society. Outwardly he plunges into solitude, but inwardly into Hell, distance from God" (CW 18, §1103).

his multiplicity. You arrive at him in yourself and only through your self seizing you. It seizes you in the advancement of your life.

The hero must fall for the sake of our redemption, since he is the model and demands imitation. But the measure of imitation is fulfilled.[154] We should become reconciled to solitude in ourselves and to the God outside of us. If we enter into this solitude then the life of the God begins. If we are in ourselves, then the space around us is free, but filled by the God.

Our relations to men go through this empty space and also through the God. But earlier it went through selfishness since we were outside ourselves. Therefore the spirit foretold to me that the cold of outer space will spread across the earth.[155] With this he showed me in an image that the God will step between men and drive every individual with the whip of icy cold to the warmth of his own monastic hearth. Because people were beside themselves, going into raptures like madmen.

Selfish desire ultimately desires itself. You find yourself in your desire, so do not say that desire is vain. If you desire yourself, you produce the divine son in your embrace with yourself. Your desire is the father of the God, your self is the mother of the God, but the son is the new God, your master.

If you embrace your self, then it will appear to you as if the world has become cold and empty. The coming God moves into this emptiness.

If you are in your solitude, and all the space around you has become cold and unending, then you have moved far from men, and at the same time you have come near to them as never before. Selfish desire only apparently led you to men, but in reality it led you away from them and in the end to yourself, which to you and to others was the most remote. But now, if you are in solitude, your God leads you to the God of others, and through that to the true neighbor, to the neighbor of the self in others.

---

154. This is an interpretation of the murder of Siegfried in *Liber Primus*, ch. 7, "Murder of the Hero."

155. This refers to the dream mentioned in the prologue, p. 124.

If you are in yourself, you become aware of your incapacity. You will see how little capable you are of imitating the heroes and of being a hero yourself. So you will also no longer force others to become heroes. Like you, they suffer from incapacity. Incapacity, fol. v(r) /v(v) too, wants to live, but it will overthrow your Gods. [BP v (r)]/

Mysterium. Encounter

[HI v(v)]

Cap. ix.

On the night when I considered the essence of the God, I became aware of an image: I lay in a dark depth. An old man stood before me. He looked like one of the old prophets.[156] A black serpent lay at his feet. Some distance away I saw a house with columns. A beautiful maiden steps out of the door. She walks uncertainly and I see that she is blind. The old man waves to me and I follow him to the house at the foot of the sheer wall of rock. The serpent creeps behind us. Darkness reigns inside the house. We are in a high hall with glittering walls. A bright stone the color of water lies in the background. As I look into its reflection, the images of Eve, the tree, and the serpent appear to me. After this I catch sight of Odysseus and his journey on the high seas. Suddenly a door opens on the right, onto a garden full of bright sunshine. We step outside and the old man says to me, "Do you know where you are?"

I: "I am a stranger here and everything seems strange to me, anxious as in a dream. Who are you?"

156. December 21, 1913. In *Black Book* 2 Jung noted: "with a gray beard and wearing an Oriental robe" (p. 231).

E: "I am Elijah[157] and this is my daughter Salome."[158]

I: "The daughter of Herod, the bloodthirsty woman?"

E: "Why do you judge so? You see that she is blind. She is my daughter, the daughter of the prophet."

I: "What miracle has united you?"

E: "It is no miracle, it was so from the beginning. My wisdom and my daughter are one."

I am shocked, I am incapable of grasping it.

E: "Consider this: her blindness and my sight have made us companions through eternity."

I: "Forgive my astonishment, am I truly in the underworld?"

S: "Do you love me?"

I: "How can I love you? How do you come to this question? I see only one thing, you are Salome, a tiger, your hands are stained with the blood of the holy one. How should I love you?"

S: "You will love me."

I: "I? Love you? Who gives you the right to such thoughts?"

S: "I love you."

I: "Leave me be, I dread you, you beast."

S: "You do me wrong. Elijah is my father, and he knows the deepest mysteries. The walls of his house are made of precious stones. His

157. Elijah was one of the prophets of the Old Testament. He first appears in 1 Kings 17, bearing a message from God to Ahab, the king of Israel. In 1953, the Carmelite Père Bruno wrote to Jung asking how one established the existence of an archetype. Jung replied by taking Elijah as an example, describing him as a highly mythical personage, which did not prevent him from probably being a historical figure. Drawing together descriptions of him throughout history, Jung described him as a "living archetype" who represented the collective unconscious and the self. He noted that such a constellated archetype gave rise to new forms of assimilation, and represented a compensation on the part of the unconscious (CW 18, §§1518–31).

158. Salome was the daughter of Herodias and the stepdaughter of King Herod. In Matthew 14 and Mark 6, John the Baptist had told King Herod that it was unlawful for him to be married to his brother's wife, and Herod put him in prison. Salome (who is not named, but simply called the daughter of Herodias) danced before Herod on his birthday, and he promised to give her anything she wished for. She requested the head of John the Baptist, who was then beheaded. In the late nineteenth and early twentieth centuries, the figure of Salome fascinated painters and writers, including Guillaume Apollinaire, Gustave Flaubert, Stéphane Mallarmé, Gustave Moreau, Oscar Wilde, and Franz von Stuck, featuring in many works. See Bram Dijkstra, *Idols of Perversity: Fantasies of Feminine Evil in Fin-de-Siècle Culture* (New York: Oxford University Press, 1986), pp. 379–98.

wells hold healing water and his eyes see the things of the future. And what wouldn't you give for a single look into the infinite unfolding of what is to come? Are these not worth a sin for you?"

I: "Your temptation is devilish. I long to be back in the upper world. It is dreadful here. How oppressive and heavy is the air!"

E: "What do you want? The choice is yours."

I: "But I do not belong to the dead. I live in the light of day. Why should I torment myself here with Salome? Do I not have enough of my own life to deal with?"

E: "You heard what Salome said."

I: "I cannot believe that you, the prophet, can recognize her as a daughter and a companion. Is she not engendered from heinous seed? Was she not vain greed and criminal lust?"

E: "But she loved a holy man."

I: "And shamefully shed his precious blood."

E: "She loved the prophet who announced the new God to the world. She loved him, do you understand that? For she is my daughter."

I: "Do you think that because she is your daughter, she loved the prophet in John, the father?"

E: "By her love shall you know her."

I: "But how did she love him? Do you call that love?"

E: "What else was it?"

I: "I am horrified. Who wouldn't be horrified if Salome loved him?"

E: "Are you cowardly? Consider this, I and my daughter have been one since eternity."

I: "You pose dreadful riddles. How could it be that this unholy woman and you, the prophet of your God, could be one?"

E: "Why are you amazed? But you see it, we are together."

I: "What my eyes see is exactly what I cannot grasp. You, Elijah, who are a prophet, the mouth of God, and she, a bloodthirsty horror. You are the symbol of the most extreme contradiction."

E: "We are real and not symbols."

I see how the black serpent writhes up the tree, and hides in the branches. Everything becomes gloomy and doubtful. Elijah rises, I follow and we go silently back through the hall.[159] Doubt tears me apart. It is all so unreal and yet a part of my longing remains behind. Will I come again? Salome loves me, do I love her? I hear wild music, a tambourine, a sultry moonlit night, the bloody-staring head of the holy one[160]—fear seizes me. I rush out. I am surrounded by the dark night. It is pitch black all around me. Who murdered the hero? Is this why Salome loves me? Do I love her, and did I therefore murder the hero? She is one with the prophet, one with John, but also one with me? Woe, was she the hand of the God? I do not love her, I fear her. Then the spirit of the depths spoke to me and said: "Therein you acknowledge her divine power." Must I love Salome?[161]

---

159. *Black Book* 2 continues: "The crystal shines dimly. I think again of the image of Odysseus, how he passed the rocky island of the Sirens on his lengthy odyssey. Should I, should I not?" (p. 74).

160. I.e., the head of John the Baptist.

161. In the 1925 Seminar, Jung recounted: "I used the same technique of the descent, but this time I went much deeper. The first time I should say I reached a depth of about one thousand feet, but this time it was a cosmic depth. It was like going to the moon, or like the feeling of a descent into empty space. First the picture was of a crater, or a ring-chain of mountains, and my feeling association was that of one dead, as if oneself were a victim. It was the mood of the land of the hereafter. I could see two people, an old man with a white beard and a young girl who was very beautiful. I assumed them to be real and listened to what they were saying. The old man said he was Elijah and I was quite shocked, but she was even more upsetting because she was Salome. I said to myself that there was a queer mixture: Salome and Elijah, but Elijah assured me that he and Salome had been together since eternity. This also upset me. With them was a black serpent who had an affinity for me. I stuck to Elijah as being the most reasonable of the lot, for he seemed to have a mind. I was exceedingly doubtful about Salome. We had a long conversation but I did not understand it. Of course I thought of the fact of my father being a clergyman as being the explanation of my having figures like this. How about this old man then? Salome was not to be touched upon. It was only much later that I found her association with Elijah quite natural. Whenever you take journeys like this you find a young girl with an old man" (*Introduction to Jungian Psychology*, pp. 68–69). Jung then refers to examples of this pattern in the work of Melville, Meyrink, Rider Haggard, and the Gnostic legend of Simon Magus (see note 154, p. 552), Kundry and Klingsor from Wagner's *Parsifal* (see below, p. 363f), and Francesco Colonna's *Hypnerotomachia*. In *Memories*, he noted: "In myths the snake is a frequent counterpart of the hero. There are numerous accounts of their affinity . . . Therefore the presence of the snake was an indication of a hero-myth" (p. 206). Of Salome, he said: "Salome is an anima figure, blind because, though connecting the conscious and the unconscious, she does not see the operation of the unconscious. Elijah is the personification of the cognitional element, Salome of the erotic. Elijah is the figure of the old prophet filled with wisdom. One could speak of these two figures as personifications of Logos and Eros very specifically shaped. This is practical for intellectual play, but as Logos and Eros are purely speculative terms, not scientific in any sense, but irrational, it is very much better to leave the figures as they are, namely as events, experiences" (*Introduc-*

[2] [162]*This play that I witnessed is my play, not your play. It is my secret, not yours. You cannot imitate me. My secret remains virginal and my mysteries are inviolable, they belong to me and cannot belong to you. You have your own.*[163]

He who enters into his own must grope through what lies at hand, he must sense his way from stone to stone. He must embrace the worthless and the worthy with the same love. A mountain is nothing, and a grain of sand holds kingdoms, or also nothing. Judgment must fall from you, even taste, but above all pride, even when it is based on merit. Utterly poor, miserable, humiliated, ignorant, go on through the gate. Turn your anger against yourself, since only you stop yourself from looking and from living. The mystery play is soft like air and thin smoke, and you are raw matter that is disturbingly heavy. But let your hope, which is your highest good and highest ability, lead the way and serve you as a guide in the world of darkness, since it is of like substance with the forms of that world.[164] [Image v (v)][165]

The scene of the mystery play is a deep place like the crater of a volcano. My deep interior is a volcano, that pushes out the fiery-molten mass of the unformed and the undifferentiated. Thus my

tion to Jungian Psychology, pp. 96–97). In 1955/56, Jung wrote: "For purely psychological reasons I have elsewhere attempted to equate the masculine consciousness with the concept of *Logos* and the feminine with that of *Eros*. By Logos I meant discrimination, judgment, insight, and by Eros I meant the placing into relation" (*Mysterium Coniunctionis*, CW 14, §224). On Jung's reading of Elijah and Salome in terms of Logos and Eros respectively, see Appendix B, "Commentaries."

162. *The Corrected Draft* has: "*Guiding Reflection*" (p. 86). The *Draft* and *Corrected Draft* have "This, my friend, is a mystery play in which the spirit of the depths cast me. I had recognized ~~the birth of the new God~~ [the conception], and therefore the spirit of the depths allowed me to participate in the underworld ceremonies, which were supposed to instruct me about the God's intentions and works. Through these rituals I was supposed to be initiated into the mysteries of redemption" (*Corrected Draft*, p. 86).

163. The *Draft* continues: "In the renewed world you can have no outer possessions, unless you create them out of yourselves. You can enter only into your own mysteries. The spirit of the depths has other things to teach you than me. I only have to bring you tidings of the new God and of the ceremonies and mysteries of his service. But this is the way. It is the gate to darkness" (p. 100).

164. The *Draft* continues: "The mystery play took place at the deepest bottom of my interior, which is that other world. You have to bear this in mind, it is also a world and its reality is large and frightening. You cry and laugh and tremble and sometimes you break out in a cold sweat for fear of death. The mystery play represents my self and through me the world to which I belong is represented. Thus, my friends, you learn much about the world, and through it about yourself, by what I say to you here. But you have not learned anything about your mysteries in this way; indeed, your way is darker than before, since my example will stand obstructively in your path. You may follow me, not on my way, but on yours" (p. 102).

165. This depicts the scene in the fantasy.

interior gives birth to the children of chaos, of the primordial mother. He who enters the crater also becomes chaotic matter, he melts. The formed in him dissolves and binds itself anew with the children of chaos, the powers of darkness, the ruling and the seducing, the compelling and the alluring, the divine and the devilish. These powers stretch beyond my certainties and limits on all sides, and connect me with all forms and with all distant beings and things, through which inner tidings of their being and their character develop in me.

Because I have fallen into the source of chaos, into the primordial beginning, I myself become smelted anew in the connection with the primordial beginning, which at the same time is what has been and what is becoming. At first I come to the primordial beginning in myself. But because I am a part of the matter and formation of the world, I also come into the primordial beginning of the world in the first place. I have certainly participated in life as someone formed and determined, but only through my formed and determined consciousness and through this in a formed and determined piece of the whole world, but not in the unformed and undetermined aspects of the world that likewise are given to me. Yet it is given only to my depths, not to my surface, which is a formed and determined consciousness.

The powers of my depths are predetermination and pleasure.[166] Predetermination or forethinking[167] is Prometheus,[168] who, without determined thoughts, brings the chaotic to form[169] and definition, who digs the channels and holds the object before pleasure. Forethinking also comes before thought. But pleasure is the force that desires and destroys forms without form and definition. It loves the form in itself that it takes hold of, and destroys the forms that it does not take. The forethinker is a seer, but pleasure is blind. It does

166. This is a subjective interpretation of the figures of Elijah and Salome.
167. In the *Corrected Draft*, "Predetermination or forethought" is replaced by "The Idea." This substitution occurs throughout the rest of this section (p. 89).
168. In Greek mythology, Prometheus created mankind out of clay. He could foretell the future, and his name signifies "forethought." In 1921, Jung wrote an extended analysis of Carl Spitteler's epic poem *Prometheus und Epimetheus* (1881) together with Goethe's *Prometheus Fragment* (1773); see *Psychological Types*, CW 6, ch. 5.
169. The *Corrected Draft* has: "Boundary" (p. 89).

not foresee, but desires what it touches. Forethinking is not powerful in itself and therefore does not move. But pleasure is power, and therefore it moves. Forethinking needs pleasure to be able to come to form. Pleasure needs forethinking to come to form, which it requires.[170] If pleasure lacked forming, pleasure would dissolve in manifoldness and become splintered and powerless through unending division, lost to the unending. If a form does not contain and compress pleasure within itself, it cannot reach the higher, since it always flows like water from above to below. All pleasure, when left alone, flows into the deep sea and ends in the deathly stillness of dispersal into unending space. Pleasure is not older than forethinking, and forethinking is not older than pleasure. Both are equally old and in nature intimately one. Only in man does the separate existence of both principles become apparent.

Apart from Elijah and Salome I found the serpent as a third principle.[171] It is a stranger to both principles although it is associated with both. The serpent taught me the unconditional difference in essence between the two principles in me. If I look across from forethinking to pleasure, I first see the deterrent poisonous serpent. If I feel from pleasure across to forethinking, likewise I feel first the cold cruel serpent.[172] The serpent is the earthly essence of man of which he is not conscious. Its character changes according to peoples and lands, since it is the mystery that flows to him from the nourishing earth-mother.[173]

170. The *Draft* continues: "Therefore the forethinker approached me as Elijah, the prophet, and pleasure as Salome" (p. 103).

171. The *Draft* continues: "The animal of deadly horror, which lay between Adam and Eve" (p. 105).

172. The *Corrected Draft* continues: "The serpent is not only a separating but also a unifying principle" (p. 91).

173. When commenting on this in the 1925 seminar, Jung noted that there were many accounts in mythology of the relation between a hero and a serpent, so the presence of the serpent indicated that "it will again be a hero myth" (p. 94). He showed a diagram of a cross with Rational/Thinking (Elijah) at the top, Feeling (Salome) at the bottom, Irrational / Intuition (Superior) at the left, and Sensation / Inferior (Serpent) at the right (p. 95). He interpreted the black serpent as the introverting libido: "The serpent leads the psychological movement apparently astray into the kingdom of shadows, dead and wrong images, but also into earth, into concretization . . . Inasmuch as the serpent leads into the shadows, it has the function of the anima; it leads you into the depths, it

The earthly (numen loci) separates forethinking and pleasure in man, but not in itself. The serpent has the weight of the earth in itself, but also its changeability and germination from which everything that becomes emerges. It is always the serpent that causes man to become enslaved now to one, now to the other principle, so that it becomes error. One cannot live with forethinking alone, or with pleasure alone. You need both. But you cannot be in forethinking and in pleasure at the same time, you must take turns being in forethinking and pleasure, obeying the prevailing law, unfaithful to the other so to speak. But men prefer one or the other. Some love thinking and establish the art of life on it. They practice their thinking and their circumspection, so they lose their pleasure. Therefore they are old and have a sharp face. The others love pleasure, they practice their feeling and living. Thus they forget thinking. Therefore they are young and blind. Those who think base the world on thought, those who feel, on feeling. You find truth and error in both.

The way of life writhes like the serpent from right to left and from left to right, from thinking to pleasure and from pleasure to thinking. Thus the serpent is an adversary and a symbol of enmity, but also a wise bridge that connects right and left through longing, much needed by our life.[174]

The place where Elijah and Salome live together is a dark space and a bright one. The dark space is the space of forethinking. It is dark, so he who lives there requires vision.[175] This space is limited, so forethinking does not lead into the extended distance, but into the depth of the past and the future. The crystal is the formed thought that reflects what is to come in what has gone before.

Eve / and the serpent show me that my next step leads to pleasure and from there again on lengthy wanderings like Odysseus. He fol. v(v) /vi(r)

connects the Above and Below . . . the serpent is also the symbol of wisdom" (*Introduction to Jungian Psychology*, pp. 102–3).

174. The *Draft* continues: "By following Elijah and Salome, I follow the two principles inside me and through me in the world, of which I am part" (p. 106).

175. The *Corrected Draft* continues: "that is, of thinking. And without thinking one cannot grasp an idea" (p. 92).

went astray when he played his trick at Troy.[176] The bright garden is the space of pleasure. He who lives there needs no vision;[177] he feels the unending.[178] A thinker who descends into his forethinking finds his next step leading into the garden of Salome. Therefore the thinker fears his forethought, although he lives on the foundation of forethinking. The visible surface is safer than the underground. Thinking protects against the way of error, and therefore it leads to petrification.

A thinker should fear Salome, since she wants his head, especially if he is a holy man. A thinker cannot be a holy person, otherwise he loses his head. It does not help to hide oneself in thought. There the solidification overtakes you. You must turn back to motherly forethought to obtain renewal. But forethought leads to Salome.

[179]Because I was a thinker and caught sight of the hostile principle of pleasure from forethinking, it appeared to me as Salome. If I had been one who felt, and had groped my way toward forethinking, then it would have appeared to me as a serpent-encoiled daimon, if I had actually seen it. But I would have been blind. Therefore I would have felt only slippery, dead, dangerous, allegedly overcome, insipid, and mawkish things, and I would have pulled back with the same shudder I felt in turning from Salome.

The thinker's passions are bad, therefore he has no pleasure. The thoughts of one who feels[180] are bad, therefore he has no thoughts. He who prefers to think than to feel,[181] leaves his feeling[182] to rot in darkness. It does not grow ripe, but in moldiness produces sick tendrils that do not reach the light. He who prefers to feel than

176. The *Draft* continues: "What would Odysseus have been without his wandering?" (p. 107). The *Corrected Draft* adds: "There would have been no odyssey" (p. 92).

177. The *Corrected Draft* continues: "Than much rather the pleasure to enjoy the garden" (p. 92).

178. The *Corrected Draft* continues: "It is strange that Salome's garden lies so close to the dignified and mysterious hall of ideas. Does a thinker therefore experience awe or perhaps even fear of the idea, because of its proximity to paradise?" (p. 92).

179. The *Draft* continues: "I was a forethinker. What could astonish me more than the intimate community of forethinking and pleasure, these inimical principles?" (p. 108).

180. The *Corrected Draft* has instead: "One who has pleasure" (p. 94).

181. The *Corrected Draft* has instead: "Pleasure" (p. 94).

182. The *Corrected Draft* has instead: "Pleasure" (p. 94).

to think leaves his thinking in darkness, where it spins its nets in gloomy places, desolate webs in which mosquitos and gnats become enmeshed. The thinker feels the disgust of feeling, since the feeling in him is mainly disgusting. The one who feels thinks the disgust of thinking, since the thinking in him is mainly disgusting. So the serpent lies between the thinker and the one who feels. They are each other's poison and healing.

In the garden it had to become apparent to me that I loved Salome. This recognition struck me, since I had not thought it. What a thinker does not think he believes does not exist, and what one who feels does not feel he believes does not exist. You begin to have a presentiment of the whole when you embrace your opposite principle, since the whole belongs to both principles, which grow from one root.[183]

Elijah said: "You should recognize her through her love!" Not only do you venerate the object, but the object also sanctifies you. Salome loved the prophet, and this sanctified her. The prophet loved God, and this sanctified him. But Salome did not love God, and this profaned her. But the prophet did not love Salome, and this profaned him. And thus they were each other's poison and death. May the thinking person accept his pleasure, and the feeling person accept his own thought. Such leads one along the way.[184]

---

183. The *Draft* continues: "as one of your poets has said: 'the shaft bears two irons'" (p. 110).

184. In 1913, Jung presented his paper "On the question of psychological types," in which he noted that the libido or psychic energy in an individual was characteristically directed toward the object (extraversion) or toward the subject (introversion); CW 6. Commencing in the summer of 1915 he had extensive correspondence with Hans Schmid on this question, in which he now characterized the introverts as being dominated by the function of thinking, and the extraverts as being dominated by the function of feeling. He also characterized the extraverts as being dominated by the pleasure-pain mechanism, seeking out the love of the object, and unconsciously seeking tyrannical power. Introverts unconsciously sought inferior pleasure, and had to see that the object was also a symbol of their pleasure. On August 7, 1915, he wrote to Schmid: "*The opposites should be evened out in the individual himself*" (*The Question of Psychological Types*, forthcoming). This linkage between thinking and introversion and feeling and extraversion was maintained in his discussion of this subject in 1917 in *The Psychology of the Unconscious Processes*. In *Psychological Types* (1921), this model had expanded to encompass two main attitude types of introverts and extraverts further subdivided by the predominance of one of the four psychological functions of thinking, feeling, sensation, and intuition.

Instruction

[HI vi(r)]

Cap. x.

On the following night,[185] I was led to a second image: I am standing in the rocky depth that seems to me like a crater. Before me I see the house with columns. I see Salome walking along the length of the wall toward the left, touching the wall like a blind person. The serpent follows her. The old man stands at the door and waves to me. Hesitantly I draw closer. He calls Salome back. She is like someone suffering. I cannot detect any sacrilege in her nature. Her hands are white and her face has a gentle expression. The serpent lies before them. I stand before them clumsily like a stupid boy, overwhelmed by uncertainty and ambiguity. The old man eyes me searchingly and says: "What do you want here?"

I: "Forgive me, it is not obtrusiveness or arrogance that leads me here. I am here perchance, not knowing what I want. A longing that stayed behind in your house yesterday has brought me here. You see, prophet, I am tired, my head is as heavy as lead. I am lost in my ignorance. I have toyed with myself enough. I played hypocritical games with myself and they all would have disgusted me, were it not clever to perform what others expect from us in the world of men. It seems to me as if I were more real here. And yet I do not like being here."

Wordlessly Elijah and Salome step inside the house. I follow them reluctantly. A feeling of guilt torments me. Is it bad conscience? I would like to turn back, but I cannot. I stand before the play of fire in the shining crystal. I see in splendor the mother of God with the child. Peter stands in front of her in admiration—then Peter alone with the key—the Pope with a triple crown—a Buddha sitting rigidly in a circle of fire—a many-armed bloody Goddess[186]—it is Salome

185. December 22, 1913. On December 19, 1913, Jung gave a talk "On the psychology of the unconscious" to the Zürich Psychoanalytical Society.

186. The *Draft* continues: "Kali" (p. 113).

desperately wringing her hands[187]—it takes hold of me, she is my own soul, and now I see Elijah in the image of the stone.

Elijah and Salome stand smiling before me.

I: "These visions are full of torment, and the meaning of these images is dark to me, Elijah; please shed some light."

Elijah turns away silently, and leads the way toward the left. Salome enters a colonnade to the right. Elijah leads me into an even darker room. A burning red lamp hangs from the ceiling. I sit down exhausted. Elijah stands before me leaning on a marble lion in the middle of the room.

E: "Are you anxious? Your ignorance is to blame for your bad conscience. Not-knowing is guilt, but you believe that it is the urge toward forbidden knowledge that causes your feeling of guilt. Why do you think you are here?"

I: "I don't know. I sank into this place when unknowingly I tried resisting the not-known. So here I am, astonished and confused, an ignorant fool. I experience strange things in your house, things that frighten me and whose meaning is dark to me."

E: "If it were not your law to be here, how would you be here?"

I: "I'm afflicted by fatal weakness, my father."

E: "You are evasive. You cannot extricate yourself from your law."

I: "How can I extricate myself from what is unknown to me, which I cannot reach with either feeling or presentiment?"

E: "You are lying. Do you not know that you yourself recognized what it means if Salome loves you?"

I: "You are right. A doubtful and uncertain thought arose in me. But I have forgotten it again."

---

187. *Black Book* 2 continues: "now that white shape of a girl with black hair—my own soul—and now that white shape of a man, which also appeared to me at the time—it resembles Michelangelo's sitting Moses—it is Elijah" (p. 84). Michelangelo's Moses is in the Church of San Pietro in Vincoli in Rome. It was the subject of a study by Freud that was published in 1914 (*The Standard Edition of the Complete Psychological Works of Sigmund Freud*, ed. James Strachey in collaboration with Anna Freud assisted by Alix Strachey and Alan Tyson, tr. J. Strachey, 24 vols. [London: The Hogarth Press and the Institute of Psycho-analysis, 1953–1974], vol. 13). The third-person pronoun "it" identifies Salome with Kali, whose many hands wring each other; cf. note 196, p. 190.

E: "You have not forgotten it. It burned deep inside you. Are you cowardly? Or can you not differentiate this thought from your own self, enough so that you wished to claim it for yourself?"

I: "The thought went too far for me, and I shun far-fetched ideas. They are dangerous, since I am a man, and you know how much men are accustomed to seeing thoughts as their very own, so that they eventually confuse them with themselves."

E: "Will you therefore confuse yourself with a tree or animal, because you look at them and because you exist with them in one and the same world? Must you be your thoughts, because you are in the world of your thoughts? But your thoughts are just as much outside your self as trees and animals are outside your body."[188]

I: "I understand. My thought world was for me more word than world. I thought of my thought world: it is I."

E: "Do you say to your human world and every being outside of you: you are I?"

I: "I stepped into your house, my father, with the fear of a schoolboy. But you taught me salutary wisdom[189]: I can also consider my thoughts as being outside my self. That helps me to return to that terrible conclusion that my tongue is reluctant to express. I thought that Salome loves me because I resemble John or you. This thought seemed unbelievable to me. That's why I rejected it and thought that she loves me because I am really quite opposite to you, that she loves her badness in my badness. This thought was devastating."

Elijah is silent. Heaviness lies on me. Then Salome steps in, comes over to me and lays her arm around my shoulder. She takes me for her father in whose chair I sat. I dare neither move nor speak.

S: "I know that you are not my father. You are his son, and I am your sister."

---

188. Jung mentioned this conversation in the 1925 seminar and commented: "Only then I learned psychological objectivity. Only then could I say to a patient, 'Be quiet, something is happening.' There *are* such things as mice in a house. You cannot say you are wrong when you have a thought. For the understanding of the unconscious we must see our thoughts as events, as phenomena" (*Introduction to Jungian Psychology*, p. 103).

189. The *Corrected Draft* has instead: "Truth" (p. 100).

I: "You, Salome, my sister? Was this the terrible attraction that emanated from you, that unnamable horror of you, of your touch? Who was our mother?"

S: "Mary."

I: "Is it a hellish dream? Mary, our mother? What madness lurks in your words? The mother of our Savior, our mother? When I crossed your threshold today, I foresaw calamity. Alas! It has come. Are you out of your senses, Salome? Elijah, protector of the divine law, speak: is this a devilish spell cast by the rejected? How can she say such a thing? Or are both of you out of your senses? You are symbols and Mary is a symbol. I am simply too confused to see through you now."

E: "You may call us symbols for the same reason that you can also call your fellow men symbols, if you wish to. But we are just as real as your fellow men. You invalidate nothing and solve nothing by calling us symbols."

I: "You plunge me into a terrible confusion. Do you wish to be real?"

E: "We are certainly what you call real. Here we are, and you have to accept us. The choice is yours."

I am silent. Salome has removed herself. Uncertainly I look around. Behind me a high golden red flame burns on a round altar. The serpent has encircled the flame. Its eyes glitter with golden reflections. Swaying I turn to the exit. As I step out into the hall, I see a powerful lion going before me. Outside, it is a wide cold starry night.

[2] [190]It is no small matter to acknowledge one's yearning. For this many need to make a particular effort at honesty. All too many

190. The *Corrected Draft* has: "Guiding Reflection" (p. 103). In the *Draft* and *Corrected Draft*, a lengthy passage occurs. What follows here is a paraphrase: I wonder whether this is real, an underworld, or the other reality, and whether it was the other reality that had forced me here. I see here that Salome, my pleasure, moves to the left, the side of the impure and bad. This movement follows the serpent, which represents the resistance and the enmity against this movement. Pleasure goes away from the door. Forethinking [*Corrected Draft*: "the Idea," throughout this passage] stands at the door, knowing the entrance to the mysteries. Therefore desire melts into the many, if forethinking does not direct it and force it toward its goal. If one meets a man who only desires, then

do not want to know where their yearning is, because it would seem to them impossible or too distressing. And yet yearning is the way of life. If you do not acknowledge your yearning, then you do not follow yourself, but go on foreign ways that others have indicated to you. So you do not live your life but an alien one. But who should live your life if you do not live it? It is not only stupid to exchange your own life for an alien one, but also a hypocritical game, because you can never really live the life of others, you can only pretend to do it, deceiving the other and yourself, since you can only live your own life.

If you give up your self, you live it in others; thereby you become selfish to others, and thus you deceive others. Everyone thus believes that such a life is possible. It is, however, only apish imitation. Through giving in to your apish appetite, you infect others, because the ape stimulates the apish. So you turn yourself and others into apes. Through reciprocal imitation you live according to the average expectation. The image of the hero was set up for all in every age through the appetite for imitation. Therefore the hero was murdered, since we have all been aping him. Do you know why you cannot abandon apishness? For fear of loneliness and defeat.

To live oneself means: to be one's own task. Never say that it is a pleasure to live oneself. It will be no joy but a long suffering, since you must become your own creator. If you want to create yourself, then

---

one will find resistance against his desire behind it. Desire without forethinking gains much but keeps nothing, therefore his desire is the source of constant disappointment. Thus Elijah calls Salome back. If pleasure is united with forethinking, the serpent lies before them. To succeed in something, you first need to deal with the resistance and difficulty, otherwise joy leaves behind pain and disappointment. Therefore I drew nearer. I had first to overcome the difficulty and the resistance to gain what I desired. When desire overcomes the difficulty, it becomes seeing and follows forethinking. Therefore I see that Salome's hands are pure, with no trace of crime. My desire is pure if I first overcome the difficulty and resistance. If I weigh up pleasure and forethinking, I am like a fool, blindly following his longing. If I follow my thinking, I forsake my pleasure. The ancients said in images that the fool finds the right way. Forethinking has the first word, therefore Elijah asked me what I wanted. You should always ask yourself what you desire, since all too many do not know what they want. I did not know what I wanted. You should confess your longing and what you long for to yourself. Thus you satisfy your pleasure and nourish your forethinking at the same time (*Corrected Draft*, pp. 103–4).

you do not begin with the best and the highest, but with the worst and the deepest. Therefore say that you are reluctant to live yourself. The flowing together of the stream of life is not joy but pain, since it is power against power, guilt, and shatters the sanctified.

The image of the mother of God with the child that I foresee, indicates to me the mystery of the transformation.[191] If forethinking and pleasure unite in me, a third arises from them, the divine son, who is the supreme meaning, the symbol, the passing over into a new creation. I do not myself become the supreme meaning[192] or the symbol, but the symbol becomes in me such that it has its substance, and I mine. Thus I stand like Peter in worship before the miracle of the transformation and the becoming real of the God in me.

Although I am not the son of the God myself, I represent him nevertheless as one who was a mother to the God, and one therefore to whom in the name of the God the freedom of the binding and loosing has been given. The binding and loosing take place in me.[193] But insofar as it takes place in me, and I am a part of the world, it also takes place through me in the world, and no one can hinder it. It doesn't take place according to the way of my will but in the way of unavoidable effect. I am not master over you, but the being of the God in me. I lock the past with one key, with the other I open the future. This takes place through my transformation. The miracle of transformation commands. I am its servant, just as the Pope is.

You see how incredible it was to believe such of oneself.[194] It applies not to me, but to the symbol. The symbol becomes my lord

191. The *Corrected Draft* has: "in his outer appearance, in the misery of earthly reality" (p. 107).

192. The *Corrected Draft* has instead: "the son of God" (p. 107).

193. Cf. Matthew 18:18. Christ: "Whatsoever ye shall bind on earth shall be bound in heaven: and whatsoever ye shall loose on earth shall be loosed in heaven."

194. The *Draft* and *Corrected Draft* continue: "The Pope in Rome has become an image ~~and symbol~~ for us of how God becomes human and how he [God] becomes the visible lord of men. Thus the coming God will become the lord of the world. This happens first [here] in me. The supreme meaning becomes my lord and infallible commander, though not only in me, but perhaps in many others whom I don't know" (*Corrected Draft*, pp. 108–9).

and unfailing commander. It will fortify its reign and change itself into a fixed and riddling image, whose meaning turns completely inward, and whose pleasure radiates outward like blazing fire,[195] a Buddha in the flames.[196] Because I sink into my symbol to such an extent, the symbol changes me from my one into my other, and that cruel Goddess of my interior, my womanly pleasure, my own other, the tormented tormentor, that which is to be tormented. I have interpreted these images, as best I can, with poor words.

[197]In the moment of your bewilderment, follow your forethinking and not your blind desire, since forethinking leads you to the difficulties that should always come first. They come nevertheless.

---

195. The *Corrected Draft* has: "thus I become, like the Buddha sitting in the flames" (p. 109).

196. The *Corrected Draft* continues: "Where the idea is, pleasure always is too. If the idea is inside, pleasure is outside. Therefore an air of evil pleasure envelops me. A lecherous and bloodthirsty Godhead gives me this false air. This happens because I must altogether suffer the becoming of the God and can therefore not separate it from myself at first. But as long as it is not separated from me, I am so seized by the idea that I am it, and therefore I am also the woman associated with the idea from the beginning. In that I receive the idea and represent it in the manner of Buddha, my pleasure is like the Indian Kali, since she is Buddha's other side. Kali, however, is Salome and Salome is my soul" (p. 109).

197. In the *Draft*, a lengthy passage occurs here, a paraphrase of which follows: The numbness is like a death. I needed total transformation. Through this my meaning, like that of the Buddha, went completely inside. Then the transformation happened. I then went over to pleasure, as I was a thinker. As a thinker, I rejected my feeling, but I had rejected part of life. Then my feeling became a poisonous plant, and when it awakened, it was sensuality instead of pleasure, the lowest and commonest form of pleasure. This is represented by Kali. Salome is the image of his pleasure, that suffers pain, since it was shut out for too long. It then became apparent that Salome, i.e., my pleasure, was my soul. When I recognized this, my thinking changed and ascended to the idea, and then the image of Elijah appeared. This prepared me for the mystery play, and showed me in advance the way of transformation that I had to undergo in the Mysterium. The flowing together of the forethinking with pleasure produces the God. I recognized that the God in me wanted to become a man, and I considered this and honored this, and I became the servant of the God, but for no one other than myself. [*Corrected Draft*: it would be madness and presumption to assume that I also did this for others, p. 110]. I sank into the contemplation of the wonder of transformation, and first turned into the lower level of my pleasure, and then through this I recognized my soul. The smiles of Elijah and Salome indicate that they were happy at my appearance, but I was in deep darkness. When the way is dark, so is the idea that gives light. When the idea in the moment of confusion allows the words and not the blind longing, then the words lead you to difficulty. Whereas it leads you to the right. That is why Elijah turns left, to the side of the unholy and evil, and Salome turns right to the side of the correct and good. She doesn't go to the garden, the place of pleasure, but remains in the house of the father (pp. 125–27).

If you look for a light, you fall first into an even deeper darkness. In this darkness you find a light with a weak reddish flame that gives only a low brightness, but it is enough for you to see your neighbor. It is exhausting to reach this goal that seems to be no goal. And so it is good: I am paralyzed and therefore ready to accept. My fore-thinking rests on the lion, my power.[198]

I held to the sanctified form, and didn't want to allow the chaos to break through its dams. I believed in the order of the world and hated everything disorganized and unformed. Therefore above all I had to realize that my own law had brought me to this place. As the God developed in me, I thought he was a part of my self. I thought that my "I" included him and therefore I took him for my thought. But I also considered that my thoughts were parts of my "I." Thus I entered into my thoughts, and into the thinking about the God, in that I took him / for a part of my self. fol. vi(r)/vi(v)

On account of my thoughts, I had left myself; therefore my self became hungry and made God into a selfish thought. If I leave myself, my hunger will drive me to find my self in my object, that is, in my thought. Therefore you love reasonable and orderly thoughts, since you could not endure it if your self was in disordered, that is, unsuitable thoughts. Through your selfish wish, you pushed out of your thoughts everything that you do not consider ordered, that is, unfitting. You create order according to what you know, you do not know the thoughts of chaos, and yet they exist. My thoughts are not my self, and my I does not embrace the thought. Your thought has this meaning and that, not just one, but many meanings. No one knows how many.

198. In the *Draft*, a passage occurs, a paraphrase of which follows: If I am strong, so also are my intentions and presuppositions. My own thought weakens and goes over into the idea. The idea becomes strong; it is supported by its own strength. I recognize this in the fact that Elijah is supported by the lions. The lion is of stone. My pleasure is dead and turned to stone, because I did not love Salome. This gave my thought the coldness of stone, and from this the idea took its solidity, which it needed to subjugate my thought. It needed to be subjugated as it strove against Salome, since she appeared bad to it (p. 128).

My thoughts are not my self, but exactly like the things of the world, alive and dead.[199] Just as I am not damaged through living in a partly chaotic world, so too I am not damaged if I live in my partly chaotic thought world. Thoughts are natural events that you do not possess, and whose meaning you only imperfectly recognize.[200] Thoughts grow in me like a forest, populated by many different animals. But man is domineering in his thinking, and therefore he kills the pleasure of the forest and that of the wild animals. Man is violent in his desire, and he himself becomes a forest and a forest animal. Just as I have freedom in the world, I also have freedom in my thoughts. Freedom is conditional.

To certain things of the world I must say: you should not be thus, but you should be different. Yet first I look carefully at their nature, otherwise I cannot change it. I proceed in the same way with certain thoughts. You change those things of the world that, not being useful in themselves, endanger your welfare. Proceed likewise with your thoughts. Nothing is complete, and much is in dispute. The way of life is transformation, not exclusion. Well-being is a better judge than the law.

But as I became aware of the freedom in my thought world, Salome embraced me and I thus became a prophet, since I had found pleasure in the primordial beginning, in the forest, and in the wild animals. It stands too close to reason for me to set myself on a par with my visions, and for me to take pleasure in seeing. I am in danger of believing that I myself am significant since I see the significant. This will always drive us crazy, and we transform the vision into foolishness and monkey business, since we cannot desist from imitation.[201]

---

199. In 1921 Jung wrote: "The peculiar reality of unconscious contents, therefore, gives us the same right to describe them as objects as outer things" (*Psychological Types*, CW 6, §280).

200. The *Draft* and *Corrected Draft* have: "~~I would have to consider myself mad,~~ [: It would be more than inconsistent,] if I thought that I had produced the thoughts of the Mysterium" (*Corrected Draft*, p. 115).

201. The *Draft* continues: "I recognized the father because I was a thinker, and thus I did not know the mother, but saw love in the guise of pleasure and called it pleasure, and therefore this was Salome to me. Now I learn that Mary is the mother, the innocent

Just as my thinking is the son of forethinking, so is my pleasure the daughter of love, of the innocent and conceiving mother of God. Aside from Christ Mary gave birth to Salome. Therefore Christ in the gospel of the Egyptians says to Salome: "Eat every herb, but do not eat the bitter." And when Salome wanted to know, Christ spoke to her: "If you crush the covering of shame, and when the two become one, and the male with the female, neither male nor female."[202]

Forethinking is the procreative, love is the receptive.[203] Both are beyond this world. Here are understanding and pleasure, we only suspect the other. It would be madness to claim that they are in this world. So much that is riddling and cunning coils around this light. I won the power back again from the depths, and it went before me like a lion.[204]

---

and love-receiving, and not pleasure, who bears the seed of evil in her heated and seductive nature. / If Salome, evil pleasure, is my sister, then I must be a thinking saint, and my intellect has met with a sad fate. I must sacrifice my intellect and confess to you that what I told you about pleasure, namely that it is the principle opposed to forethought, is incomplete and prejudiced. I observed as a thinker from the vantage point of my thinking, otherwise I could have recognized that Salome, as Elijah's daughter, is an offspring of thought and not the principle itself, which Mary, the innocent Virgin Mother, now appears as" (p. 133).

202. The gospel of the Egyptians is one of the apocryphal gospels that features a dialogue between Christ and Salome. Christ states that he has come to undo the work of the female, namely, lust, birth, and decay. To Salome's question of how long shall death prevail, Christ answered, as long as women bear children. Here, Jung is referring to the following passage: "she said, 'Then I have done well in not giving birth,' imagining that it is not permitted to bear children; the Lord answered, 'Eat of every herb, but the bitter one eat not.'" The dialogue continues: "When Salome asked when it shall be made known the Lord said, 'When you tread under foot the covering of shame and when out of two is made one, and the male with the female, neither male nor female'"(*The Apocryphal New Testament*, ed. J. K. Elliot [Oxford: Oxford University Press, 1999], p. 18). Jung cites this logion, available to him from Clement in the *Stromateis*, as an example of the union of opposites in *Visions* (1932, vol. 1., p. 524), and as an example of the coniunctio of male and female in "On the psychology of the child archetype" (1940, CW 9, 1, §295) and *Mysterium Coniunctionis* (1955–56, CW 14, §528).

203. The *Draft* and *Corrected Draft* have: "~~but~~ when the mystery play showed me this, I didn't understand, but I thought I had produced an incredible thought. ~~I am mad to believe this, And I believed it.~~ Therefore I was seized by fear, and I wanted to explain my arbitrary thoughts to Elijah and Salome, and thus invalidate them" (*Corrected Draft*, p. 118).

204. The *Draft* continues: "The image of the cool starry night and of the vast sky opens up my eye to the infinity of the inner world, which I as a desirous man feel is still too cold. I cannot pull the stars down to myself, but only watch them. Therefore my impetuous desire feels that that world is nightly and cold" (p. 135).

Resolution

[HI vi(v)][205]

Cap. xi.

[206]On the third night, deep longing to continue experiencing the mysteries seized me. The struggle between doubt and desire was great in me. But suddenly I saw that I stood before a steep ridge in a wasteland. It is a dazzling bright day. I catch sight of the prophet high above me. His hand makes an averting movement, and I abandon my decision to climb up. I wait below, gazing upward. I look: to the right it is dark night; to the left it is bright day. The rock separates day and night. On the dark side lies a big black serpent, on the bright side a white serpent. They thrust their heads toward each other, eager for battle. Elijah stands on the heights above them. The serpents pounce on one another and a terrible wrestling ensues. The black serpent seems to be stronger; the white serpent draws back. Great billows of dust rise from the place of struggle. But then I see: the black serpent pulls itself back again. The front part of its body has become white. Both serpents curl about themselves, one in light, the other in darkness.[207]

Elijah: "What did you see?"

I: "I saw the fight of two formidable serpents. It seemed to me as if the black would overcome the white serpent; but behold, the black one withdrew and its head and the top part of its body had turned white."

E: "Do you understand that?"

---

205. This depicts a scene in the fantasy that follows.

206. December 25, 1913.

207. In the 1925 seminar, Jung said: "A few evenings later, I felt that things should continue, so again I tried to follow the same procedure, but it would not descend. I remained on the surface. Then I realized that I had a conflict in myself about going down, but I could not make out what *it* was, I only felt that two dark principles were fighting each other, two serpents" (*Introduction to Jungian Psychology*, p. 104). He then recounted the fantasy that ensued.

I: "I have thought it over, but I cannot understand it. Should it mean that the power of the good light will become so great that even the darkness that resists it will be illumined by it?"

Elijah climbs before me into the heights, to a very high summit; I follow. On the peak we come to some masonry made of huge blocks. It is a round embankment on the summit.[208] Inside lies a large courtyard, and there is a mighty boulder in the middle, like an altar. The prophet stands on this stone and says: "This is the temple of the sun. This place is a vessel, that collects the light of the sun."

Elijah climbs down from the stone, his form becomes smaller in descending, and finally becomes dwarflike, unlike himself.

I ask: "Who are you?"

"I am Mime,[209] and I will show you the wellsprings. The collected light becomes water and flows in many springs from the summit into the valleys of the earth." He then dives down into a crevice. I follow him down into a dark cave. I hear the rippling of a spring. I hear the voice of the dwarf from below: "Here are my wells, whoever drinks from them becomes wise."

But I cannot reach down. I lose courage. I leave the cave and, doubting, pace back and forth in the square of the yard. Everything appears to me strange and incomprehensible. It is solitary and deathly silent here. The air is clear and cool as on the remotest heights, a wonderful flood of sunlight all around, the great wall surrounds me. A serpent crawls over the stone. It is the serpent of the prophet. How did it come out of the underworld into the world above? I follow it and see how it crawls into the wall. I feel weird all over: a little house stands there with a portico, minuscule, snuggling against the rock. The serpents become infinitely small. I feel as if I

208. In the 1925 seminar, Jung added: "I thought, 'Ha, this is a Druidic sacred place'" (Ibid.).

209. In Wagner's *Ring of the Nibelung*, the Nibelung dwarf Mime is the brother of Alberich and a master craftsman. Alberich stole the Rhinegold from the Rhinemaidens; through renouncing love, he was able to forge a ring out of it that conferred limitless power. In *Siegfried*, Mime, who lives in a cave, brings up Siegfried so that he will kill Fafner the giant, who has transformed into a dragon and now has the ring. Siegfried slays Fafner with the invincible sword that Mime has fashioned, and kills Mime, who had intended to kill him after he had recovered the ring.

too am shrinking. The walls enlarge into a huge mountain and I see that I am below on the foundation of the crater in the underworld, and I stand before the house of the prophet.[210] He steps out of the door of his house.

I: "I notice, Elijah, that you have shown me and let me experience all sorts of strange things and allowed me to come before you today. But I confess that it is all dark to me. Your world appears to me today in a new light. Just now it was as if I were separated by a starry distance from your place, which I still wanted to reach today. But behold: it seems to be one and the same place."

E: "You wanted to come here far too much. I did not deceive you, you deceived yourself. He sees badly who wants to see; you have overreached yourself."

I: "It is true, I eagerly longed to reach you, to hear more. Salome startled me and led me into bewilderment. I felt dizzy, because what she said seemed to me to be monstrous and like madness. Where is Salome?"

E: "How impetuous you are! What is up with you? Step over to the crystal and prepare yourself in its light."

A wreath of fire shines around the stone. I am seized with fear at what I see: The coarse peasant's boot? The foot of a giant that crushes an entire city? I see the cross, the removal of the cross, the mourning. How agonizing this sight is! No longer do I yearn—I see the divine

210. In the 1925 seminar, Jung interpreted this episode as follows: "the fight of the two snakes: the white means a movement into the day, the black into the kingdom of darkness, with moral aspects too. There was a real conflict in me, a resistance to going down. My stronger tendency was to go up. Because I had been so impressed the day before with the cruelty of the place I had seen, I really had a tendency to find a way to the conscious by going up, as I did on the mountain . . . Elijah said that it was just the same below or above. Compare Dante's *Inferno*. The Gnostics express this same idea in the symbol of the reversed cones. Thus the mountain and the crater are similar. There was nothing of conscious structure in these fantasies, they were just events that happened. So I assume that Dante got his ideas from the same archetypes" (*Introduction to Jungian Psychology*, pp. 104–5). McGuire suggests that Jung is referring to Dante's conception "of the conical form of the cavity of Hell, with its circles, mirroring in reverse the form of Heaven, with its spheres" (Ibid.). In *Aion*, Jung also noted that serpents were a typical pair of opposites, and that the conflict between serpents was a motif found in medieval alchemy (1951, CW 9, 2, §181).

child, with the white serpent in his right hand, and the black serpent in his left hand. I see the green mountain, the cross of Christ on it, and a stream of blood flowing from the summit of the mountain—I can look no longer, it is unbearable—I see the cross and Christ on it in his last hour and torment—at the foot of the cross the black serpent coils itself—it has wound itself around my feet—I am held fast and I spread my arms wide. Salome draws near. The serpent has wound itself around my whole body, and my countenance is that of a lion.

Salome says, "Mary was the mother of Christ, do you understand?"

I: "I see that a terrible and incomprehensible power forces me to imitate the Lord in his final torment. But how can I presume to call Mary my mother?"

S: "You are Christ."

I stand with outstretched arms like someone crucified, my body taut and horribly entwined by the serpent: "You, Salome, say that I am Christ?"[211]

---

211. In the 1925 seminar, Jung recounted that after Salome's declaration that he was Christ: "In spite of my objections she maintained this. I said, 'this is madness,' and became filled with skeptical resistance" (*Introduction to Jungian Psychology*, p. 104). He interpreted this event as follows: "Salome's approach and her worshiping of me is obviously that side of the inferior function which is surrounded by an aura of evil. One is assailed by the fear that perhaps this is madness. This is how madness begins, this is madness . . . You cannot get conscious of these unconscious facts without giving yourself to them. If you can overcome your fear of the unconscious and can let yourself go down, then these facts take on a life of their own. You can be gripped by these ideas so much that you really go mad, or nearly so. These images have so much reality that they recommend themselves, and such extraordinary meaning that one is caught. They form part of the ancient mysteries; in fact it is such fantasies that made the mysteries. Compare the mysteries of Isis as told in Apuleius, with the initiation and deification of the initiate . . . One gets a peculiar feeling from being put through such an initiation. The important part that led up to the deification was the snake's encoiling of me. Salome's performance was deification. The animal face which I felt mine transformed into was the famous [Deus] Leontocephalus of the Mithraic mysteries, the figure which is represented with a snake coiled around the man, the snake's head resting on the man's head, and the face of the man that of a lion . . . In this deification mystery you make yourself into the vessel, and are a vessel of creation in which the opposites reconcile." He added: "All this is Mithraic symbolism from beginning to end" (Ibid., pp. 105–8). In *The Golden Ass*, Lucian undergoes an initiation into the mysteries of Isis. The significance of this episode is that it is the only direct description of such an initiation that has survived. Of the event itself, Lucian states: *"I approached the very gates of death and set foot on Prosperine's threshold, yet was permitted to return, rapt through all the elements. At midnight I saw the sun shining as if it were noon; I entered the presence of the gods of the under-world and the gods of the upper-world, stood near and worshiped them."* After this, he was presented on a pulpit in the temple in front of a crowd. He wore garments which included designs of serpents

It is as if I stood alone on a high mountain with stiff outstretched arms. The serpent squeezes my body in its terrible coils and the blood streams from my body, spilling down the mountainside. Salome bends down to my feet and wraps her black hair round them. She lies thus for a long time. Then she cries, "I see light!" Truly, she sees, her eyes are open. The serpent falls from my body and lies languidly on the ground. I stride over it and kneel at the feet of the prophet, whose form shines like a flame.

E: "Your work is fulfilled here. Other things will come. Seek untiringly, and above all write exactly what you see."

Salome looks in rapture at the light that streams from the prophet. Elijah transforms into a huge flame of white light. The serpent wraps itself around her foot, as if paralyzed. Salome kneels before the light in wonderstruck devotion. Tears fall from my eyes, and I hurry out into the night, like one who has no part in the glory of the mystery. My feet do not touch the ground of this earth, and it is as if I were melting into air.[212]

[2] [213]My longing[214] led me up to the overbright day, whose light is the opposite to the dark space of forethinking.[215] The opposite

---

and winged lions, held a torch, and wore "a palm tree chaplet with its leaves sticking all out like rays of light" (*The Golden Ass*, tr. R. Graves [Harmondsworth: Penguin, 1984], p. 241). Jung's copy of a German translation of this work has a line in the margin by this passage.

212. In "On the psychology of the Kore figure" (1951), Jung described these episodes as follows: "In an underground house, actually in the underworld, there lives an old magician and prophet with his 'daughter.' She is, however, not really his daughter; she is a dancer, a very loose person, but is blind and seeks healing" (CW 9, 1, §360). This description of Elijah draws him together with the later description of Philemon. Jung noted that this "shows the unknown woman as a mythological figure in the beyond (that means in the unconscious). She is *soror* or *filia mystica* of a hierophant or 'philosopher,' evidently a parallel to those mystic syzigies which are to be met with in the figures of Simon Magus and Helen, Zosimus and Theosebia, Comarius and Cleopatra, etc. Our dream-figure fits in best with Helen" (Ibid., §372).

213. The *Corrected Draft* has: "Guiding Reflection" (p. 127). In *Black Book 2*, Jung copied the following citations from Dante's *Commedia* in German translation (p. 104): "And I to him: 'I am one who, when love / Breathes on me, notices, and in the manner / That he dictates within, I utter words'" (Purgatorio 24, 52–54); "And then, in the same manner as a flame / Which follows the fire whatever shape it takes, / The new form follows the spirit exactly" (Purgatorio 25, 97–99). Tr. C. H. Sisson (Manchester: Carcanet, 1980), pp. 259, 265.

214. The *Draft* has: "the news of the desire revived by the mother" (p. 143).

215. The *Corrected Draft* has: "of the primordial image" (p. 127).

principle is, as I think I understand it, heavenly love, the mother. The darkness that surrounds forethinking[216] appears to be due to the fact that it is invisible in the interior and takes place in the depths.[217] But the brightness of love seems to come from the fact that love is visible life and action. My pleasure was with forethinking and had its merry garden there, surrounded by darkness and night. I climbed down to my pleasure, but ascended to my love. I see Elijah high above me: this indicates that forethinking stands nearer to love than I, a man, do. Before I ascend to love, a condition must be fulfilled, which represents itself as the fight between two serpents. Left is day, right is night. The realm of love is light, the realm of forethinking is dark. Both principles have separated themselves strictly, and are even hostile to one another and have taken on the form of serpents. This form indicates the daimonic nature of both principles. I recognize in this struggle a repetition of that vision where I saw the struggle between the sun and the black serpent.[218]

At that time, the loving light was annihilated, and blood began to pour out. This was the great war. But the spirit of the depths[219] wants this struggle to be understood as a conflict in every man's own nature.[220] Since after the death of the hero our urge to live could no longer imitate anything, it therefore went into the depths of every man and excited the terrible conflict between the powers of the depths.[221] Forethinking is singleness, love is togetherness. Both

---

216. The *Corrected Draft* has: "The idea or the primordial image" (p. 127).
217. The *Corrected Draft* has: "lives" (p. 127).
218. I.e., in ch. 5, "Descent into Hell in the Future."
219. The *Corrected Draft* has: "the spirit" (p. 127).
220. The *Draft* continues: "Therefore they all say that they are fighting for the good and for peace, but one cannot fight one another over the good. But since men don't know that the conflict lies within themselves, the Germans thus believe that the English and the Russians are wrong; but the English and the Russians say that the Germans are wrong. But no one can judge history in terms of right and wrong. Because one-half of mankind is wrong, every man is half wrong. Therefore a conflict resides in his own soul. But man is blind and always knows only his half. The German has in him the English and the Russian whom he fights outside of himself. Likewise, the English and the Russian has in him the German whom he fights. But man appears to see the outer quarrel, not the one within, which alone is the wellspring of the great war. But before man can ascend to light and love, the great battle is needed" (p. 145).
221. In December 1916, in his preface to *The Psychology of the Unconscious Processess,* Jung wrote: "The psychological processes, which accompany the present war, above all the

need one another, and yet they kill one another. Since men do not
fol. vi(v) /vii(r) know that the conflict occurs inside themselves, they go mad, / and one lays the blame on the other. If one-half of mankind is at fault, then every man is half at fault. But he does not see the conflict in his own soul, which is however the source of the outer disaster. If you are aggravated against your brother, think that you are aggravated against the brother in you, that is, against what in you is similar to your brother.

As a man you are part of mankind, and therefore you have a share in the whole of mankind, as if you were the whole of mankind. If you overpower and kill your fellow man who is contrary to you, then you also kill that person in yourself and have murdered a part of your life. The spirit of this dead man follows you and does not let your life become joyful. You need your wholeness to live onward.

If I myself endorse the pure principle, I step to one side and become onesided. Therefore my forethinking in the principle[222] of the heavenly mother becomes an ugly dwarf who lives in a dark cave like an unborn in the womb. You do not follow him, even if he says to you that you could drink wisdom from his source. But forethinking[223] appears to you there as dwarfish cleverness, false and of the night, just as the heavenly mother appears to me down there as Salome. That which is lacking in the pure principle appears as the serpent. The hero strives after the utmost in the pure principle, and therefore he finally falls for the serpent. If you go to thinking,[224] take your heart with you. If you go to love, take your head with you. Love is empty without thinking, thinking hollow without love. The

---

incredible brutalization of public opinion, the mutual slanderings, the unprecedented fury of destruction, the monstrous flood of lies, and man's incapacity to call a halt to the bloody demon—are suited like nothing else to powerfully push in front of the eyes of thinking men the problem of the restlessly slumbering chaotic unconscious under the ordered world of consciousness. This war has pitilessly revealed to civilized man that he is still a barbarian . . . *But the psychology of the individual corresponds to the psychology of the nation. What the nation does is done also by each individual, and so long as the individual does it, the nation also does it.* Only the change in the attitude of the individual is the beginning of the change in the psychology of the nation" (CW 7, p. 4).

222. The *Corrected Draft* has: "the prophet, the personification of the idea" (p. 131).
223. The *Corrected Draft* has: "Idea" (p. 131).
224. The *Corrected Draft* has "Idea" substituted throughout this paragraph (p. 131).

serpent lurks behind the pure principle. Therefore I lost courage, until I found the serpent that at once led me across to the other principle. In climbing down I become smaller.

Great is he who is in love, since love is the present act of the great creator, the present moment of the becoming and lapsing of the world. Mighty is he who loves. But whoever distances himself from love, feels himself powerful.

In your forethinking you recognize the nullity of your current being as a smallest point between the infinity of what has passed and of what is to come. The thinker is small, he feels great if he distances himself from thinking. But if we speak about appearances, it is the other way around. To whoever is in love, form is a trifling. But his field of vision ends with the form given to him. To whoever is in thinking, form is unsurpassable and the height of Heaven. But at night he sees the diversity of the innumerable worlds and their never-ending cycles. Whoever is in love is a full and overflowing vessel, and awaits the giving. Whoever is in forethinking is deep and hollow and awaits fulfillment.

Love and forethinking are in one and the same place. Love cannot be without forethinking, and forethinking cannot be without love. Man is always too much in one or the other. This comes with human nature. Animals and plants seem to have enough in every way, only man staggers between too much and too little. He wavers, he is uncertain how much he must give here and how much there. His knowledge and ability is insufficient, and yet he must still do it himself. Man doesn't only grow from within himself, for he is also creative[225] from within himself. The God becomes revealed in him.[226] Human nature is little skilled in divinity, and therefore man fluctuates between too much and too little.[227]

225. The *Corrected Draft* adds "conscious" and deletes "From within himself" (p. 133).

226. The *Draft* and *Corrected Draft* have instead: "The divine creative power becomes [in him] ~~a person~~ [a personal consciousness] from the [unconscious] collective" (pp. 133–34).

227. The *Draft* and *Corrected Draft* have: "But why, you ask, does ~~forethinking~~ [the idea] appear to you in the guise of a Jewish prophet and ~~your~~ [the] pleasure in the guise of the heathen Salome? My friend, do not forget, that I too am one who thinks and wants

The spirit of this time has condemned us to haste. You have no more futurity and no more past if you serve the spirit of this time. We need the life of eternity. We bear the future and the past in the depths. The future is old and the past is young. You serve the spirit of this time, and believe that you are able to escape the spirit of the depths. But the depths do not hesitate any longer and will force you into the mysteries of Christ.[228] It belongs to this mystery that man is not redeemed through the hero, but becomes a Christ himself. The antecedent example of the saints symbolically teaches us this.

Whoever wants to see will see badly. It was my will that deceived me. It was my will that provoked the huge uproar among the daimons. Should I therefore not want anything? I have, and I have fulfilled my will as well as I could, and thus I fed everything in me that strived. In the end I found that I wanted myself in everything, but without looking for myself. Therefore I no longer wanted to seek myself outside of myself, but within. Then I wanted to grasp myself, and then I wanted to go on again, without knowing what I wanted, and thus I fell into the mystery.

Should I therefore not want anything anymore? You wanted this war. That is good. If you had not, then the evil of this war would be small.[229] But with your wanting you make the evil great. If you do not succeed in producing the greatest evil out of this war, you will never learn the violent deed and learn to overcome fighting what lies

---

in the spirit of this time, and is completely under the spell of the serpent. I am just now through my initiation into the mysteries of the spirit ~~of the depths~~ about to not entirely discard all the ancientness lacked by those thinking in the spirit of this time, but to readopt it into my being human, to make my life whole. For I have become poor and far removed from God. I must take in the divine and the mundane, since the spirit of this time had nothing else to give me; on the contrary he took the little that I possessed of real life. But in particular he made me hasty and greedy, since he is merely the present and he forced me to hunt down everything present to fill the moment" (pp. 134–35).

228. The *Draft* and *Corrected Draft* have: "Just as the ~~old prophets~~ [ancients] stood before the Mysterium of Christ, I also stand as yet before ~~the~~ [this] Mysterium ~~of Christ~~, [insofar as I reassume the past] although I live two thousand years ~~after him~~ [later] and at one time believed I was a Christian. But I had never been a Christ" (p. 136).

229. In *Thus Spoke Zarathustra*, Nietzsche wrote: "To redeem the past and to transform every 'It was' into an 'I wanted it thus!'—that alone do I call redemption!" ("Of redemption," p. 161).

outside you.[230] Therefore it is good if you want this greatest evil with your whole heart.[231] You are Christians and run after heroes, and wait for redeemers who should take the agony on themselves for you, and totally spare you Golgotha. With that you[232] pile up a mountain of Calvary over all Europe. If you succeed in making a terrible evil out of this war and throw innumerable victims into this abyss, this is good, since it makes each of you ready to sacrifice himself. For as I, you draw close to the accomplishment of Christ's mystery.

You already feel the fist of the iron one on your back. This is the beginning of the way. If blood, fire, and the cry of distress fill this world, then you will recognize yourself in your acts: Drink your fill of the bloody atrocities of the war, feast upon the killing and destruction, then your eyes will open, you will see that you yourselves are the bearers of such fruit.[233] You are on the way if you will all this. Willing creates blindness, and blindness leads to the way. Should we will error? You should not, but you do will that error which you take for the best truth, as men have always done.

The symbol of the crystal signifies the unalterable law of events that comes of itself. In this seed you grasp what is to come. I saw something terrible and incomprehensible. (It was on the night of Christmas day of the year 1913.) I saw the peasant's boot, the sign of the horrors of the peasant war,[234] of murdering incendiaries and of bloody cruelty. I knew to interpret this sign for myself as nothing but the fact that something bloody and dreadful lay before us. I saw the foot of a giant that crushed a whole city. How could I interpret this sign otherwise? I saw that the way to self-sacrifice began here.

230. On February 11, 1916, Jung said in a discussion at the Association for Analytical Psychology: "We abuse the will, natural growth is subjugated to the will . . . War teaches us: The will is of no use—we will see where this leads. We are completely subject to the absolute power of the becoming" (*MAP*, vol. 1, p. 106).

231. The *Draft* and *Corrected Draft* have: "Since ~~you are~~ [we are] inwardly still ancient Jews and heathens with unholy Gods" (p. 137).

232. The *Corrected Draft* has: "we ourselves" (p. 138).

233. The *Corrected Draft* has: "and we called ourselves Christians, imitators of Christ. To be Christ onself is the true following of Christ" (p. 139).

234. This may refer to the German peasants' rebellion of 1525.

They will all become terribly enraptured by these tremendous experiences, and in their blindness will want to understand them as outer events. It is an inner happening; that is the way to the perfection of the mystery of Christ,[235] so that the peoples learn self-sacrifice.

May the frightfulness become so great that it can turn men's eyes inward, so that their will no longer seeks the self in others but in themselves.[236] I saw it, I know that this is the way. I saw the death of Christ and I saw his lament; I felt the agony of his dying, of the great dying. I saw a new God, a child, who subdued daimons in his hand.[237] The God holds the separate principles in his power, he unites them. The God develops through the union of the principles in me. He is their union.

If you will one of these principles, so you are in one, but far from your being other. If you will both principles, one and the other, then you excite the conflict between the principles, since you cannot want both at the same time. From this arises the need, the God appears in it, he takes your conflicting will in his hand, in the hand of a child whose will is simple and beyond conflict. You cannot learn this, it can only develop in you. You cannot will this, it takes the will from your hand and wills itself. Will yourself, that leads to the way.[238]

---

235. In 1918, in his preface to the second edition of *The Psychology of the Unconscious Processes*, Jung wrote: "The spectacle of this catastrophe threw man back on himself by making him feel his complete impotence; it turned him inward, and, with everything rocking, he seeks something that guarantees him a hold. Too many still seek outward . . . But still too few seek inward, to their own selves, and still fewer ask themselves whether the ends of human society might not best be served if each man tries to abolish the old order in himself, and to practice in his own person and in his own inward state those precepts, those victories which he preaches at every street-corner, instead of always expecting these things of his fellow men" (CW 7, p. 5).

236. The *Draft* has: "If this doesn't happen, Christ will not be overcome and the evil must become even greater. Therefore, my friend, I say this to you so that you can tell your friends, and that the word may spread among the people" (p. 157).

237. The *Draft* continues: "I saw that a new God had come to be out of Christ the Lord, a young Hercules" (p. 157).

238. A long passage occurs here in the *Draft* and *Corrected Draft*, a paraphrase of which follows: The God holds love in his right, forethinking ["the idea," substituted throughout] in his left. Love is on our favorable side, forethinking on the unfavorable. This should recommend love to you, insofar as you are a part of this world, and especially if you are a thinker. ~~The God possesses both.~~ Their unity is God. ~~The~~ God develops through the uniting of both principles in ~~you~~ [me]. You [I] do not become God through this, or become divine, but God becomes human. He becomes apparent in you

But fundamentally you are terrified of yourself, and therefore you prefer to run to all others rather than to yourself. I saw the mountain of the sacrifice, and the blood poured in streams from its sides. When I saw how pride and power satisfied men, how beauty beamed from the eyes of women when the great war broke out, I knew that mankind was on the way to self-sacrifice.

The spirit of the depths[239] has seized mankind and forces self-sacrifice upon it. Do not seek the guilt here or there. The spirit of the depths clutched the fate of man unto itself, as it clutched mine. He leads mankind through the river of blood to the mystery. In the

---

and through you, as a child. ~~The divine will come to you as childlike or childish, insofar as you are a developed man. The childish man has an old God, the old God who we know and whose death we have seen. If you are grown up, you can only become more childlike. You have youth before you and all the mysteries of what is to come. The childish has death before him since he must first become grown up. You will become grown up insofar as you overcome the God of the ancients and of your childhood.~~ You overcome him not through setting him aside, obeying the ~~spirit of the time~~ [: Zeitgeist]. The spirit of this time sways between yes and no like a drunkard ["since he is the uncertainty of the present general consciousness"]. ~~You~~ ["One," throughout] can only overcome the old God through becoming him yourself and experiencing his suffering and dying yourself. You overcome him and become yourself, as one who seeks himself and no longer imitates heroes. You free yourself, when you free yourself from the old God and his model. When you have become the model, then you no longer need his. ~~In that the God held love and forethinking in the form of the serpent in his hands, it was shown to me that he had seized the human will.~~ ["God unifies the opposition between love and the idea, and holds it in his hands."] Love and forethinking existed from eternity, but they were not willed. Everyone always wills the spirit of this time, which thinks and desires. He who wills the spirit of the depths, wills love and forethinking. If you will both, you become God. If you do this, the God is born and seizes possession of the will of men and holds his will in his child's hand. ~~The spirit of the depths appears in you as thoroughly childish. If you don't want the spirit of the depths, he is to you a torment. Willing leads to the way.~~ Love and forethinking are in the world of the beyond, so long as you do not will them and your willing ~~lies between them like the serpent~~ ["keeps them separate"]. If you will both, the struggle breaks out in you between willing love and willing ~~forethinking~~ ["recognition"]. You will see that you can't will both at the same time. In this need the God will be born, ~~as you have experienced in the Mysterium~~, and he will take the divided will in his hands, in the hands of a child, whose will is simple and beyond being split. What is this divine-childish willing? You can't learn it through description, it can only become in you. Nor can you will it. You cannot learn or empathize it from what I say. ~~It is unbelievable how men can falsify themselves and lie to themselves. Let this be a warning. What I say is my mystery and not yours, my way and not yours, since my self belongs to me and not to you. You should not learn my way but your own. My way leads to me and not to you~~ (pp. 142–45).

239. The *Corrected Draft* has "The great spirit" (p. 146).

mystery man himself becomes the two principles, the lion and the serpent.

Because I also want my being other, I must become a Christ. I am made into Christ, I must suffer it. Thus the redeeming blood flows. Through the self-sacrifice my pleasure is changed and goes above into its higher principle. Love is sighted, but pleasure is blind. Both principles are one in the symbol of the flame. The principles strip themselves of human form.[240]

240. A long passage appears here in the *Corrected Draft*, a paraphrase of which follows: As ~~you saw how~~ pride and power filled men and how beauty streamed out of the eyes of women when the war gripped the people, ~~you knew~~ that mankind was on the way. You knew that this war was not only adventure, criminal acts and killing, but the mystery of self-sacrifice. The ["great," changed throughout] spirit ~~of the depths~~ has seized humanity and forced him through the war to self-sacrifice. ~~Do not seek the guilt here or there.~~ ["Guilt doesn't lie outside"] ~~—It is the spirit of the depths who leads the people into the Mysterium, just as he led me.~~ He leads the people to the river of blood, just as he led me. I experienced in the Mysterium ~~what the people were forced to do in actuality~~ ["which happened outside on a large scale"]. ~~I did not know it, but the Mysterium taught me how my willing laid itself at the feet of the crucified God.~~ I ~~experienced~~ [wanted] Christ's self-sacrifice. The Mysterium of ~~Christ~~ completed itself in front of my eyes. ~~My forethinking~~ ["The idea standing above me"] forced me to this, but I resisted. ~~My highest desire, my lions, my hottest and strongest passion~~, I wanted to rise up against the mysterious will to self-sacrifice. So I was like a lion encircled by the serpent, ["an image of fate eternally renewing itself"]. Salome came to me from the right, the favorable side. ~~Pleasure awakened in me.~~ I experienced that my pleasure comes to me when I accomplish the self-sacrifice. I hear that Maria, ~~the symbol of love~~, is also ~~the~~ [my] mother ~~of Christ~~, since love has also borne Christ. Love brings the self-sacrificer and self-sacrifice. Love is also the mother of my self-sacrifice. In that I hear and accept this, I experience that I become Christ, since I recognize that love makes me into Christ. But I still doubt, since it is nearly impossible for the thinker to differentiate himself from his thought and accept that what happens in his thought is also something outside of himself. ~~It is outside him in the inner world. I become Christ in the Mysterium, rather I see, how I was made into Christ and yet am completely myself, so that I could still doubt when my pleasure told me that I was Christ.~~ [Salome,] My pleasure said to me, ["that I am Christ"] because love, which is higher than pleasure, which however is still in me hidden in pleasure, had led me to self-sacrifice and made me into Christ. Pleasure came near to me, encircled me in rings and forced me to experience the torment of Christ and to spill my blood for the world. My willing, which earlier served the ~~spirit of this time~~ ["Zeitgeist," substituted throughout] went under to the spirit of the depths, and just as it was previously determined by the spirit of the time, it is now determined by the spirit of the depths, by forethinking ["Idea," substituted throughout] and pleasure. It determined me through the willing of self-sacrifice, and to the spilling of blood, my life's essence. Mark that it is my bad pleasure which leads me to self-sacrifice. Its innermost is love, which will be freed from pleasure through sacrifice. Here the wonder happened that my previously blind pleasure became sighted. My pleasure was blind, and it was love. Since my strongest willing willed self-sacrifice, my pleasure changed, it went into a higher principle, which in God is one with forethinking. Love is sighted, but pleasure is blind. Pleasure always wants

The mystery showed me in images what I should afterward live. I did not possess any of those boons that the mystery showed me, for I still had to earn all of them.[241]

finis. part. prim. (End of part one)

what is closest, and feels through the multiplicity, going from one to another, without a goal, just seeking and never fulfilled. Love wants what is furthest, the best and the fulfilling. And I saw something further, namely that the forethinking in me had the form of an old prophet, which showed that it was pre-Christian, and transformed itself into a principle that no longer appeared in a human form, but in the absolute form of a pure white light. ~~So the human relative transformed itself into the divine absolute through the Mysterium of Christ.~~ Forethinking and pleasure united in me in a new form and the willing in me, which appeared foreign and dangerous, the willing of the spirit of the depths, ~~lay paralyzed at the feet~~ of the shining flame. I became one with my will. This happened in me, I just saw it in ~~the mystery play. Through this much was made known that I didn't previously know~~ ["like in a play"]. But I found everything doubtful. I felt as if he was melting in the air, since the land of ~~the Mysterium~~ [that spirit] was still foreign to me. ~~The Mysterium showed me the things which lay before me and had to be fulfilled. But I did not know how and when.~~ But that image of the sighted Salome, who knelt in rapture before the white flame, was a strong feeling that came to the side of my will and led me through everything that came after. What happened was my wandering with myself, through whose suffering I had to earn ~~what served for the completion of the Mysterium I had seen~~ ["I had first seen"] (pp. 146–50).

241. Gilles Quispel reports that Jung told the Dutch poet Roland Horst that he had written *Psychological Types* on the basis of thirty pages of *The Red Book* (cited in Stephan Hoeller, *The Gnostic Jung and the Seven Sermons to the Dead* [Wheaton, IL: Quest, 1985], p. 6). It is likely that he had in mind these preceding three chapters of the "Mysterium." What is presented here develops the notions of the conflict between opposing functions, the identification with the leading function, and the development of the reconciling symbol as a resolution of the conflict of opposites, which are the central issues in chapter 5 of *Psychological Types* (CW 6), the "Type Problem in Poetry." In his 1925 seminar, Jung said: "I found that the unconscious is working out enormous collective fantasies. Just as, before, I was passionately interested in working out myths, now I became just as much interested in the material of the unconscious. This is in fact the only way of getting at myth formation. And so the first chapter of the *Psychology of the Unconscious* became most correctly true. I watched the creation of myths going on, and got an insight into the structure of the unconscious, forming thus the concept that plays such a role in the *Types*. I drew all my empirical material from my patients, but the solution of the problem I drew from the inside, from my observations of the unconscious processes. I have tried to fuse these two currents of outer and inner experience in the book of the *Types*, and have termed the process of the fusion of the two currents the transcendent function" (*Introduction to Jungian Psychology*, p. 35).

Liber Secundus

The Images of the Erring[1]

[HI 1][2, 3] *nolite audire verba prophetarum, qui prophetant vobis et decipiunt vos: visionem cordis sui loquuntur, non de ore Domini. audivi quae dixerunt prophetae prophetantes in nomine meo mendacium, atque dicentes: somniavi, somniavi. usquequo istud est in corde prophetarum vaticinantium mendacium et prophetantium seductionem cordis sui? qui volunt facere ut obliviscatur populus meus nominis mei propter somnia eorum, quae narrat unusquisque ad proximum suum: sicut obliti sunt patres eorum nominis mei propter Baal. propheta, qui habet somnium, narret somnium et qui habet sermonem meum, loquatur sermonem meum vere: quid paleis ad triticum? dicit dominus.*

["Hearken not unto the words of the prophets that prophesy unto you: they make you vain: they speak a vision of their own heart, and not out of the mouth of the Lord." (Jeremiah 23: 16)]

["I have heard what the prophets said, that prophesy lies in my name, saying, I have dreamed, I have dreamed. How long shall this be in the heart of the prophets that prophesy lies? Yea, they are prophets of the deceit of their own heart; Which think to cause my people to forget my name by their dreams which they tell every man to his neighbour, as their fathers have forgotten my name for Baal. The prophet that hath a dream, let him tell a dream; and he that hath my word, let him speak my word faithfully. What is the chaff to the wheat? saith the Lord" (Jeremiah 23: 25–28)]. / 1/2

1. *The Handwritten Draft* has: "The Adventures of the Wandering" (p. 353).
2. In his essay on Picasso in 1932, Jung described the paintings of schizophrenics—meaning here only those in which a psychic disturbance would probably produce schizoid symptoms, rather than people who suffered from this condition—as follows: "From a purely formal point of view, the main characteristic is one of *fragmentation*, which expresses itself in the so-called lines of fracture, that is, a type of psychic fissure which runs right through the picture"(CW 15, §208).
3. These passages in Latin from the Bible were cited by Jung in *Psychological Types* (1921) (from Luther's *Bible*) and introduced with the following comments: "The form in which Christ presented the content of his unconscious to the world became accepted and was delared valid for all. Thereafter all individual fantasies became otiose and worthless, and were persecuted as heretical, as the fate of the Gnostic movement and of all later heresies testifies. The prophet Jeremiah is speaking just in this vein when he warns" (CW 6, §81).

The Red One[4]

Cap. i.

[HI 2][5] [2] The door of the Mysterium has closed behind me. I feel that my will is paralyzed and that the spirit of the depths possesses me. I know nothing about a way. I can therefore neither want this nor that, since nothing indicates to me whether I want this or that. I wait, without knowing what I'm waiting for. But already in the following night I felt that I had reached a solid point.[6]

[1] [7]I find that I am standing on the highest tower of a castle. The air tells me so: I am far back in time. My gaze wanders widely over solitary countryside, a combination of fields and forests. I am wearing a green garment. A horn hangs from my shoulder. I am the tower guard. I look out into the distance. I see a red point out there. It comes nearer on a winding road, disappearing for a while in forests and reappearing again: it is a horseman in a red coat, the red horseman. He is coming to my castle: he is already riding through the gate. I hear steps on the stairway, the steps creak, he knocks: a strange fear comes over me: there stands the Red One, his long shape wholly shrouded in red, even his hair is red. I think: in the end he will turn out to be the devil.

The Red One: "I greet you, man on the high tower. I saw you from afar, looking and waiting. Your waiting has called me."

I: "Who are you?"

T. R.: "Who am I? You think I am the devil. Do not pass judgment. Perhaps you can also talk to me without knowing who I am. What sort of a superstitious fellow are you, that immediately you think of the devil?"

---

4. The *Corrected Draft* has: "*V The Great Wandering I. The Red One*" (p. 157).
5. This depicts Jung's "I" in the opening scene of this fantasy.
6. The previous paragraph was added in the *Draft* (p. 167).
7. December 26, 1913.

I: "If you have no supernatural ability, how could you feel that I stood waiting on my tower, looking out for the unknown and the new? My life in the castle is poor, since I always sit here and no one climbs up to me."

T. R.: "So what are you waiting for?"

I: "I await all kinds of things, and especially I'm waiting for some of the world's wealth, which we don't see here, to come to me."

T. R.: "So, I have come to absolutely the right place. I have wandered a long time through the world, seeking those like you who sit upon a high tower on the lookout for things unseen."

I: "You make me curious. You seem to be a rare breed. Your appearance is not ordinary, and then too—forgive me—it seems to me that you bring with you a strange air, something worldly, something impudent, or exuberant, or—in fact—something pagan."

T. R.: "You don't offend me, on the contrary, you hit your nail on the head. But I'm no old pagan as you seem to think."

I: "I don't want to insist on that. You are also not pompous and Latin enough. You have nothing classical about you. You seem to be a son of our time, but as I must remark, a rather unusual one. You're no real pagan, but the kind of pagan who runs alongside our Christian religion."

T. R.: "You're truly a good diviner of riddles. You're doing better than many others who have totally mistaken me."

I: "You sound cool and sneering. Have you never broken your heart over the holiest mysteries of our Christian religion?"

T. R.: "You're an unbelievably ponderous and serious person. Are you always so urgent?"

I: "I would before God always like to be as serious and true to myself as I try to be. However, that certainly becomes difficult in your presence. You bring a certain gallows air with you, and you're bound to be from the black school of Salerno,[8] where pernicious arts are taught by pagans and the descendants of pagans."

8. Salerno is a town in southwest Italy, founded by the Romans. Jung may have been referring to the Academia Segreta, which was established in the 1540s and promoted alchemy.

T. R.: "You're superstitious and too German. You take literally what the scriptures say, otherwise you could not judge me so hard."

2/3 / I: "A hard judgment is the last thing I would want. But my nose does not play tricks on me. You're evasive, and don't want to reveal yourself. What are you hiding?"

(The Red One seems to get redder, his garments shine like glowing iron.)

T. R.: "I hide nothing from you, you true-hearted soul. I simply amuse myself with your weighty seriousness and your comic veracity. This is so rare in our time, especially in men who have understanding at their disposal."

I: "I believe you cannot fully understand me. You apparently compare me with those whom you know. But I must say to you for the sake of truth that I neither really belong to this time nor to this place. A spell has banished me to this place and time for years. I am really not what you see before you."

T. R.: "You say astounding things. Who are you then?"

I: "That is irrelevant. I stand before you as that which I presently am. Why am I here and like this, I do not know. But I do know that I must be here to justify myself according to my best knowledge. I know just as little who you are, as you know who I am."

T. R.: "That sounds very strange. Are you something of a saint? Hardly a philosopher, since you have no aptitude for scholarly language. But a saint? Surely that. Your solemnity smells of fanaticism. You have an ethical air and a simplicity that smacks of stale bread and water."

I: "I can say neither yes nor no: you speak as one trapped in the spirit of this time. It seems to me that you lack the terms of comparison."

T. R.: "Perhaps you attended the school of the pagans? You answer like a sophist.[9] How can you then measure me with the yardstick of the Christian religion, if you are no saint?"

I: "It seems to me, though, that one can apply this yardstick even if one is no saint. I believe I have learned that no one is allowed to avoid the mysteries of the Christian religion unpunished. I repeat: he whose heart has not been broken over the Lord Jesus Christ drags a pagan around in himself, who holds him back from the best."

T. R.: "Again this old tune? What for, if you are not a Christian saint? Are you not a damned sophist after all?"

I: "You are ensnared in your own world. But you certainly seem to think that one can assess the worth of Christianity correctly without being a downright saint."

T. R.: "Are you a doctor of theology, who examines Christianity from the outside and appreciates it historically, and therefore a sophist after all?"

I: "You're stubborn. What I mean is that it's hardly a coincidence that the whole world has become Christian. I also believe that it was the task of Western man to carry Christ in his heart and to grow with his suffering, death, and resurrection."

T. R.: "Well, there are also Jews who are good people and yet had no need for your solemn gospels."

I: "You are, it seems to me, no good reader of people: have you never noticed that the Jew himself lacks something—one in his head, another in his heart, and he himself feels that he lacks something?"

T. R.: "Indeed I'm no Jew, but I must come to the Jew's defense: you seem to be a Jew hater."

I: "Well, now you speak like all those Jews who accuse anyone of Jew hating who does not have a completely favorable judgment,

9. The Sophists were Greek philosophers in the fourth and fifth centuries BCE, centered in Athens, and included figures such as Protagoras, Gorgias, and Hippias. They gave lectures and took on students for fees, and paid particular attention to teaching rhetoric. Plato's attack in a number of dialogues gave rise to the modern negative connotation of the term as one who plays with words.

while they themselves make the bloodiest jokes about their own kind. Since the Jews only too clearly feel that particular lack and yet do not want to admit it, they are extremely sensitive to criticism. Do you believe that Christianity left no mark on the souls of men? And do you believe that one who has not experienced this most intimately can still partake of its fruit?"[10]

T. R.: "You argue your case well. But your solemnity?! You could make matters much easier for yourself. If you're no saint, I really don't see why you have to be so solemn. You wholly spoil the fun. What the devil is troubling you? Only Christianity with its mourn-
3/4 ful escape from the world can make people / so ponderous and sullen."

I: "I think there are still other things that bespeak seriousness."

T. R.: "Oh, I know, you mean life. I know this phrase. I too live and don't let my hair turn white over it. Life doesn't require any seriousness. On the contrary, it's better to dance through life."[11]

I: "I know how to dance. Yes, would we could do it by dancing! Dancing goes with the mating season. I know that there are those who are always in heat, and those who also want to dance for their Gods. Some are ridiculous and others enact Antiquity, instead of honestly admitting their utter incapacity for such expression."

T. R.: "Here, my dear fellow, I doff my mask. Now I grow somewhat more serious, since this concerns my own province. It's conceivable that there is some third thing for which dancing would be the symbol."

The red of the rider transforms itself into a tender reddish flesh color. And behold—Oh miracle—my green garments everywhere burst into leaf.

---

10. The *Draft* continues:"No one can flout the spiritual development of many centuries and reap what they have not sowed" (p. 172).

11. In Nietzsche's *Thus Spoke Zarathustra*, Zarathustra admonishes the overcoming of the spirit of gravity, and urges "You Higher Men, the worst thing about you is: none of you has learned to dance as a man ought to dance—to dance beyond yourselves!" ("Of the higher men," p. 306).

I: "Perhaps too there is a joy before God that one can call dancing. But I haven't yet found this joy. I look out for things that are yet to come. Things came, but joy was not among them."

T. R.: "Don't you recognize me, brother, I am joy!"

I: "Could you be joy? I see you as through a cloud. Your image fades. Let me take your hand, beloved, who are you, who are you?"

Joy? Was he joy?

[2] Surely this red one was the devil, but my devil. That is, he was my joy, the joy of the serious person, who keeps watch alone on the high tower—his red-colored, red-scented, warm bright red joy.[12] Not the secret joy in his thoughts and in his looking, but that strange joy of the world that comes unsuspected like a warm southerly wind with swelling fragrant blossoms and the ease of living. You know it from your poets, this seriousness, when they expectantly look toward what happens in the depths, sought out first of all by the devil because of their springlike joy.[13] It picks up men like a wave and drives them forth. Whoever tastes this joy forgets himself.[14] And there is nothing sweeter than forgetting oneself. And not a few have forgotten what they are. But even more have taken root so firmly that not even the rosy wave is able to uproot them. They are petrified and too heavy, while the others are too light.

I earnestly confronted my devil and behaved with him as with a real person. This I learned in the Mysterium: to take seriously every unknown wanderer who personally inhabits the inner world, since they are real because they are effectual.[15] It does not help that we say

12. In a seminar in 1939, Jung discussed the historical transformation of the figure of the devil. He noted that "When he appears red, he is of a fiery, that is, passionate nature, and causes wantonness, hate, or unruly love"; see *Children's Dreams: Notes from the Seminar Given in 1936–1940*, eds. Lorenz Jung and Maria Meyer-Grass, tr. Ernst Falzeder and Tony Woolfson (Princeton: Princeton University Press/Philemon Series, 2008), p.174.

13. The *Draft* continues: "You have heard from Faust about how commanding this kind of joy is" (p. 175). The reference is to Goethe's *Faust*.

14. The *Draft* has: "As you have known from Faust, there are many who forget who they were because they let themselves be swept away" (p. 175).

15. Jung elaborated this point in 1928 while presenting the method of active imagination: "As against this, the scientific credo of our time has developed a superstitious phobia

in the spirit of this time: there is no devil. There was one with me. This took place in me. I did with him what I could. I could speak with him. A religious conversation is inevitable with the devil, since he demands it, if one does not want to surrender to him unconditionally. Because religion is precisely what the devil and I cannot agree about. I must have it out with him, as I cannot expect that he as an independent personality would accept my standpoint without further ado.

I would be fleeing if I did not try to come to an understanding with him. If ever you have the rare opportunity to speak with the devil, then do not forget to confront him in all seriousness. He is your devil after all. The devil as the adversary is your own other standpoint; he tempts you and sets a stone in your path where you least want it.

Taking the devil seriously does not mean going over to his side, or else one becomes the devil. Rather it means coming to an understanding. Thereby you accept your other standpoint. With that the devil fundamentally loses ground, and so do you. And that may be well and good.

Although the devil very much abhors religion for its particular solemnity and candor, it has become apparent, however, that it is precisely through religion that the devil can be brought to an understanding. What I said about dancing struck him because I spoke about something that belonged in his own domain. He fails to take seriously only what concerns others because that is the peculiarity of all devils. In such a manner, I arrive at his seriousness, and with
4/5 this we reach common / ground where understanding is possible. The devil is convinced that dancing is neither lust nor madness, but an expression of joy, which is something proper to neither one nor the other. In this I agree with the devil. Therefore he humanizes himself before my eyes. But I turn green like a tree in spring.

---

about fantasy. *But the real is what works.* The fantasies of the unconscious work—there can be no doubt about that" (*The Relations between the I and the Unconscious,* CW 7, §353).

Yet that joy is the devil, or that the devil is joy, has got to worry you. I pondered this for over a week, and I fear that it has not been enough. You dispute the fact that your joy is your devil. But it seems as if there is always something devilish about joy. If your joy is no devil for you, then possibly it is for your neighbors, since joy is the most supreme flowering and greening of life. This knocks you down, and you must grope for a new path, since the light in that joyful fire has completely gone out for you. Or your joy tears your neighbor away and throws him off course, since life is like a great fire that torches everything in its vicinity. But fire is the element of the devil.

When I saw that the devil is joy, surely I would have wanted to make a pact with him. But you can make no pact with joy, because it immediately disappears. Therefore you cannot capture the devil either. Yes, it belongs to his essence that he cannot be captured. He is stupid if he lets himself be caught, and you gain nothing from having yet one more stupid devil. The devil always seeks to saw off the branch on which you sit. That is useful and protects you from falling asleep and from the vices that go along with it.

The devil is an evil element. But joy? If you run after it, you see that joy also has evil in it, since then you arrive at pleasure and from pleasure go straight to Hell, your own particular Hell, which turns out differently for everyone.[16]

Through my coming to terms with the devil, he accepted some of my seriousness, and I accepted some of his joy. This gave me courage. But if the devil has gotten more earnest, one must brace oneself.[17] It is always a risky thing to accept joy, but it leads us to life and its disappointment, from which the wholeness of our life becomes.[18]

---

16. The *Draft* continues: "Every attentive person knows their Hell, but not all know their devil. There are not only joyful devils, but also sad ones" (p. 178).
17. The *Draft* continues: "On a later adventure I discovered how seriousness suits the devil. While seriousness certainly makes him more dangerous for you, it doesn't agree with him, believe me" (pp. 178–79).
18. The *Draft* continues: "With this newly gained joy I took off on adventures without knowing where the way would lead. I could have known, however, that the devil always tempts us first through women. While I might have had clever thoughts as a thinker, it was not so in life. There I was even fatuous and prejudiced. And so quite ready to be caught in a fox trap" (p. 179).

The Castle in the Forest[19]

Cap. ii.

[HI 5] [20]In the second night thereafter, I am walking alone in a dark forest and I notice that I have lost my way.[21] I am on a dark cart track and stumble through the darkness. I finally come to quiet, dark swamp water, and a small old castle stands at its center. I think it would be good to ask here for the night's lodgings. I knock on the door, I wait a long time, it begins to rain. I have to knock again. Now I hear someone coming: the door opens. A man in an old fashioned garment, a servant, asks what I want. I ask about lodgings for the night, and he lets me enter a dark vestibule. Then he leads me up an old, worn-out stairway. At the top I come to a wider and higher hall-like space with white walls, lined with black chests and wardrobes.

I am led into a kind of reception room. It is a simple space with old upholstered furniture. The dim light of an antiquated lamp lights the room only very meagerly. The servant knocks on a side door and then quietly opens it. I scan it swiftly: it's a scholar's study, with bookshelves on all four walls and a large writing desk, at which an old man sits wearing a long black robe. He beckons me to draw closer. The air in the room is heavy and the old man seems careworn. He is not without dignity—he seems to be one of those who have as much dignity as one can be granted. He has that modest-fearful look of scholarly men who have long since been squashed to nothing by the abundance of knowledge. I think that he is a
5/6 real / scholar who has learned great modesty before the immensity of knowledge and has given himself tirelessly to the material of science and research, anxiously and equably appraising, as if he personally had to represent the working out of scientific truth.

19. The *Handwritten Draft* has: "*Second Adventure*" (p. 383).
20. December 28, 1913.
21. Dante's *Inferno* begins with the poet getting lost in a dark wood. There is a slip of paper in Jung's copy by this page.

He greets me embarrassed, as if absent and defensive. I do not wonder about this since I look like an ordinary person. Only with difficulty can he turn his gaze away from his work. I repeat my request for lodgings for the night. After a longer pause the old man remarks, "So, you want to sleep, then please yourself." I notice that he is absentminded, and therefore ask him to instruct the servant to show me a chamber. To this he says, "You are demanding, wait, I cannot just drop everything!" He sinks again into his book. I wait patiently. After a while he looks up astonished: "What do you want here? Oh—forgive me—I totally forgot that you are waiting here. I'll call the servant straightaway." The servant comes and leads me to a small chamber on the same floor with bare white walls and a large bed. He wishes me good night and withdraws.

As I am tired, I undress immediately and go to bed, after I have snuffed out the candle. The sheet is uncommonly rough and the pillow hard. My errant way has led me to a strange place: a small old castle whose scholarly owner is apparently spending the evening of his life alone with his books. No one else seems to be living in the house apart from the servant who lives over there in the tower. An ideal though solitary existence, I think, this life of the old man with his books. And here my thoughts linger for a long time, until I finally notice that another thought doesn't let go of me, namely that the old man has hidden his beautiful daughter here—a vulgar idea for a novel—an insipid, worn-out theme—but the romantic can be felt in every limb—a real novelistic idea—a castle in a forest—solitary night—an old man petrified in his books, protecting a costly treasure and enviously hiding it from all the world—what ridiculous thoughts come to me! Is it Hell or purgatory that I must also contrive such childish dreams on my wanderings? But I feel impotent to elevate my thoughts to something a bit stronger or more beautiful. I suppose I must allow these thoughts to come. What good would it do to push them away—they will come again—better to swallow this stale drink than keep it in the mouth. So what does this boring heroine look like? Surely blonde, pale—blue eyes—hoping longingly that every lost wanderer is her savior from the paternal prison—Oh,

I know this hackneyed nonsense—I'd rather sleep—why the devil must I plague myself with such empty fantasies?

Sleep does not come. I toss and turn—sleep still does not come—must I finally harbor this unsaved soul in myself? And is it this that will not let me sleep? Have I such a novelistic soul? That's all I needed—this would be agonizingly ridiculous. Does this bitterest of all drinks never end? It must already be midnight—and still sleep does not come. What in the wide world, then, won't let me sleep? Is it something to do with this chamber? Is the bed bewitched? It's terrible, what sleeplessness can drive a man to—even the most absurd and superstitious theories. It seems to be cool, I'm freezing—perhaps that's what keeps me from sleeping—it's really uncanny here—Heaven knows what goes on here—weren't those steps just now? No, that must have been outside—I roll over, firmly closing my eyes, I simply must sleep. Wasn't that the door just now? My God, someone is standing there! Am I seeing straight?—a slim girl, pale as death, standing at the door? For Heaven's sake, what is this? She's coming nearer!

"Have you come at last?" she asks quietly. Impossible—this is a cruel mistake—the novel wants to become real—does it want to grow into some silly ghost story? To what nonsense am I damned? Is it my soul that harbors such novelistic brilliance? Must this, too, happen to me? I am truly in Hell—the worst awakening after death, to be resurrected in a lending library! Have I held the men of my time and their taste in such contempt that I must live in Hell and write out the novels that I have already spat on long ago? Does the lower half of average human taste also claim holiness and invulner-
6/7 ability, so that we might not say any bad word / about it without having to atone for the sin in Hell?

She says, "Oh, so you too think me common? Do you too let yourself be deluded by the wretched delusion that I belong in a novel? You as well, whom I hoped had thrown off appearances and striven after the essence of things?"

I: "Forgive me, but are you real? It's the sorriest likeness to those foolishly threadbare scenes in novels for me to assume that you are not simply some unfortunate product of my sleepless brain. Is my doubt then truly confirmed by a situation that conforms so thoroughly with a sentimental romance?"

She: "You wretch, how can you doubt that I am real?"

She falls to her knees at the foot of my bed, sobbing and holding her face in her hands. My God, in the end is she really real, and do I do her an injustice? My pity awakens.

I: "But for Heaven's sake, tell me one thing: in all earnestness must I assume that you are real?"

She weeps and does not answer.

I: "Who are you, then?"

She: "I am the old man's daughter. He holds me here in unbearable captivity, not out of envy or hate, but out of love, since I am his only child and the image of my mother. who died young."

I scratch my head: is this not some hellish banality? Word for word, pulp fiction from the lending library! Oh you Gods, where have you led me? It's enough to make one laugh, it's enough to make one weep—to be a beautiful sufferer, a tragic shattered person is difficult, but to become an ape, you beautiful and great ones? To you the banal and eternally ridiculous, the unutterably hackneyed and emptied out, is never set like a gift of Heaven in uplifted praying hands.

But still she lies there, crying—yet what if she were real? Then she would be worth feeling sorry for, every man would have compassion for her. If she is a decent girl, what must it have cost her to enter into the room of a strange man! And to overcome her shame in this way?

I: "My dear child, I believe you, despite everything, that you are real. What can I do for you?"

She: "Finally, finally a word from a human mouth!"

She gets up, her face beaming. She is beautiful. A deep purity rests in her look. She has a beautiful and unworldly soul, one that wants to come into the life of reality, to all reality worthy of pity, to the bath of filth and the well of health. Oh this beauty of the soul! To see it climb down into the underworld of reality—what a spectacle!

She: "What can you do for me? You have already done much for me. You spoke the redeeming word when you no longer placed the banal between you and me. Know then: I was bewitched by the banal."

I: "Woe is me, you now become very fairy-tale-like."

She: "Be reasonable, dear friend, and do not stumble now over the fabulous, since the fairy tale is the great mother of the novel, and has even more universal validity than the most-avidly read novel of your time. And you know that what has been on everyone's lips for millennia, though repeated endlessly, still comes nearest the ultimate human truth. So do not let the fabulous come between us."[22]

I: "You are clever and do not seem to have inherited the wisdom of your father. But tell me, what do you think of the divinity, of the so-called ultimate truths? I found it very strange to seek them in banality. According to their nature, they must be quite uncommon. Think only of our great philosophers."

She: "The more uncommon these highest truths are, the more inhuman must they be and the less they speak to you as something valuable or meaningful concerning human essence and being. Only
7/8 what is human and what you call banal and hackneyed / contains
the wisdom that you seek. The fabulous does not speak against me but for me, and proves how universally human I am and how much I too not only need redemption but also deserve it. For I can live in the world of reality as well or better than many others of my sex."

I: "Strange maiden, you are bewildering—when I saw your father, I hoped he would invite me to a scholarly conversation. He did

22. In "Wish fulfillment and symbolism in fairy tales" (1908), Jung's colleague Franz Riklin argued that fairy tales were the spontaneous inventions of the primitive human soul and the general tendency to wish fulfillment (tr. W. A. White, *The Psychoanalytic Review* [1913], p. 95). In *Transformations and Symbols of the Libido,* Jung viewed fairy tales and myths alike as representing primordial images. In his later work, he viewed them as expressions of archetypes, as in "On the archetypes of the collective unconscious" (CW 9, 1, §6). Jung's pupil Marie-Louise von Franz developed the psychological interpretation of fairy tales in a series of works. See her *The Interpretation of Fairy Tales* (Boston: Shambala, 1996).

not, and I was aggrieved at him because of this, since his distracted slackness hurt my dignity. But with you I find it much better. You give me matters to ponder. You are uncommon."

She: "You are mistaken, I am very common."

I: "I can't believe that. How beautiful and worthy of adoration is the expression of your soul in your eyes. Happy and enviable is the man who will free you."

She: "Do you love me?"

I: "By God, I love you—but—unfortunately I am already married."

She: "So—you see: even banal reality is a redeemer. I thank you, dear friend, and I bring you greetings from Salome."

With these words her shape dissolves into darkness. Dim moonlight penetrates the room. Where she stood something shadowy lies—it is a profusion of red roses.[23]

[2][24] If no outer adventure happens to you, then no inner adventure happens to you either. The part that you take over from the devil—joy, that is—leads you into adventure. In this way you will find your lower as well as your upper limits. It is necessary for you to know your limits. If you do not know them, you run into the artificial barriers of your imagination and the expectations of your fellow men. But your life will not take kindly to being hemmed in by artificial barriers. Life wants to jump over such barriers and you will fall out with yourself. These barriers are not your real limits, but

23. In "On the psychological aspects of the Kore figure" (1951), Jung described this episode as follows: "A lonely house in a wood, where an old scholar is living. Suddenly his daughter appears, a kind of ghost, complaining that people always only consider her as a fantasy" (CW 9, I, §361). Jung commented (following his remarks concerning the Elijah and Salome episode above, note 212, p. 198) "Dream iii. presents the same theme, but on a more fairy tale-like plane. The anima is here characterized as a ghostly being" (Ibid., §373).

24. The *Draft* continues: "My friend, you learn nothing about my outer visible life. You only hear about my inner life, the counterpart of my outer life. If you therefore think that I have but my inner life and that is my only life, then you are mistaken. For you must know that your inner life does not become richer at the expense of your outer one, but poorer. If you do not live on the outside, you will not become richer within, but merely more burdened. This is not to your advantage and it is the beginning of evil. Likewise, your outer life will not become richer and more beautiful at the expense of your inner one, but only poorer and poorer. Balance finds the way" (p. 188).

arbitrary limitations that do unnecessary violence to you. Therefore try to find your real limits. One never knows them in advance, but one sees and understands them only when one reaches them. And this happens to you only if you have balance. Without balance you transgress your limits without noticing what has happened to you. You achieve balance, however, only if you nurture your opposite. But that is hateful to you in your innermost core, because it is not heroic.

My spirit reflected on everything rare and uncommon, it pried its way into unfound possibilities, toward paths that lead into the hidden, toward lights that shine in the night. And as my spirit did this, everything ordinary in me suffered harm without my noticing it, and it began to hanker after life, since I did not live it. Hence this adventure. I was smitten by the romantic. The romantic is a step backward. To reach the way, one must sometimes also take a few steps backward.[25]

In the adventure I experienced what I had witnessed in the Mysterium. What I saw there as Salome and Elijah became in life the old scholar and his pale, locked-up daughter. What I live is a distorted likeness of the Mysterium. Following the romantic way I reached the awkwardness and ordinariness of life, where I run out of thoughts and almost forget myself. What I formerly loved I must now experience as feeble and wasted, and what I formerly derided I had to envy as towering and helplessly crave. I accepted the absurdity of this adventure. No sooner had this happened than I also saw how the maiden transformed herself and signified an autonomous meaning. One inquires into the desire of the ridiculous, and that is enough for it to change.

What about masculinity? Do you know how much femininity man lacks for completeness? Do you know how much masculinity woman lacks for completeness? You seek the feminine in women and the masculine in men. And thus there are always only

25. The *Draft* continues: "I returned to my middle ages where I was still romantic, and there I experienced the adventure" (p. 190).

men and women. But where are people? You, man, should not seek the feminine in women, but seek and recognize it in yourself, as you / possess it from the beginning. It pleases you, however, to play 8/9
at manliness, because it travels on a well-worn track. You, woman, should not seek the masculine in men, but assume the masculine in yourself, since you possess it from the beginning. But it amuses you and is easy to play at femininity, consequently man despises you because he despises his femininity. But humankind is masculine and feminine, not just man or woman. You can hardly say of your soul what sex it is. But if you pay close attention, you will see that the most masculine man has a feminine soul, and the most feminine woman has a masculine soul. The more manly you are, the more remote from you is what woman really is, since the feminine in yourself is alien and contemptuous.[26]

If you take a piece of joy from the devil and set off on adventures with it, you accept your pleasure. But pleasure immediately attracts everything you desire, and then you must decide whether your pleasure spoils or enhances you. If you are of the devil, you will grope in blind desire after the manifold, and it will lead you astray. But if you remain with yourself, as a man who is himself and not of the devil, then you will remember your humanity. You will not behave toward women per se as a man, but as a human being, that is to say, as if you were of the same sex as her. You will recall your femininity. It may seem to you then as if you were unmanly, stupid, and feminine so to speak. But you must accept the ridiculous, otherwise you will suffer distress, and there will come a time, when you are least observant, when it will suddenly round on you and make you ridiculous. It is

26. In 1921 in *Psychological Types*, Jung wrote: "A very feminine woman has a masculine soul, and a very masculine man has a feminine soul. The contrast is due to the fact that for example a man is not in all things wholly masculine, but also normally has certain feminine traits. The more masculine his outer attitude is, the more his feminine traits are obliterated: instead, they appear in the unconscious" (CW 6, §804). He designated the man's feminine soul as the anima, and the woman's masculine soul as the animus, and described how individuals projected their soul images onto members of the opposite sex (§ 805).

bitter for the most masculine man to accept his femininity, since it appears ridiculous to him, powerless and tawdry.

Yes, it seems as if you have lost all virtue, as if you have fallen into debasement. It seems the same way to the woman who accepts her masculinity.[27] Yes, it seems to you like enslavement. You are a slave of what you need in your soul. The most masculine man needs women, and he is consequently their slave. Become a woman yourself,[28] and you will be saved from slavery to woman. You are abandoned without mercy to woman so long as you cannot fend off mockery with all your masculinity. It is good for you once to put on women's clothes: people will laugh at you, but through becoming a woman you attain freedom from women and their tyranny. The acceptance of femininity leads to completion. The same is valid for the woman who accepts her masculinity.

The feminine in men is bound up with evil. I find it on the way of desire. The masculine in the woman is bound up with evil. Therefore people hate to accept their own other. But if you accept it, that which is connected with the perfection of men comes to pass: namely, that when you become the one who is mocked, the white bird of the soul comes flying. It was far away, but your humiliation attracted it.[29] The mystery draws near to you, and things happen around you like miracles. A gold luster shines, since the sun has risen from its grave. As a man you have no soul, since it is in the woman; as a woman you have no soul, since it is in the man. But if you become a human being, then your soul comes to you.

If you remain within arbitrary and artificially created boundaries, you will walk as between two high walls: you do not see

27. For Jung, the integration of the anima for the man and of the animus for the woman was necessary for the development of the personality. In 1928, he described this process, which required withdrawing the projections from members of the opposite sex, differentiating from them, and becoming conscious of them in *The Relations between the I and the Unconscious*, part 2, ch. 2, CW 7, §296ff. See also *Aion* (1951), CW 9, 2, §20ff.

28. Instead of this phrase, the *Corrected Draft* has: "But if he accepts the feminine in himself, he frees himself from slavery to woman" (p. 178).

29. Albrecht Dieterich noted: "Often enough popular belief deems the soul a bird from the start" (*Abraxas. Studien zur Religionsgeschichte des spätern Altertums* [Leipzig, 1891], p. 184).

the immensity of the world. But if you break down the walls that confine your view, and if the immensity and its endless uncertainty inspire you with fear, then the ancient sleeper awakens in you, whose messenger is the white bird. Then you need the message of the old tamer of chaos. There in the whirl of chaos dwells eternal wonder. Your world begins to become wonderful. Man belongs not only to an ordered world, he also belongs in the wonder-world of his soul. Consequently you must make your ordered world horrible, so that you are put off by being too much outside yourself.

Your soul is in great need, because drought weighs on its world. If you look outside yourselves, you see the far-off forest and mountains, and above them your vision climbs to the realms of the stars. And if you look into yourselves, you will see on the other hand the nearby as far-off and infinite, since the world of the inner is as infinite as the world of the outer. Just as you become a part of the manifold essence of the world through your bodies, so you become a part of the manifold essence of the inner world through your soul. This inner world is truly infinite, in no way poorer than the outer one. Man lives in two worlds. A fool lives here or there, but never here and there.

[30]Perhaps you think that a man who consecrates his life to research leads a spiritual life and that his soul lives in / larger mea- 9/10
sure than anyone else's. But such a life is also external, just as external as the life of a man who lives for outer things. To be sure, such a scholar does not live for outer things but for outer thoughts—not for himself, but for his object. If you say of a man that he has totally lost himself to the outer and wasted his years in excess, you must also say the same of this old man. He has thrown himself away in all the books and thoughts of others. Consequently his soul is in great need, it must humiliate itself and run into every stranger's room to beg for the recognition that he fails to give her.

30. The *Draft* and *Corrected Draft* have: "Inasmuch I was this old man, buried in books ~~and barren science~~, just and appraising, wresting grains of sand from the infinite desert, my [self] ~~so-called soul, namely my inner self~~, suffered greatly" (p. 180).

Therefore you see those old scholars running after recognition in a ridiculous and undignified manner. They are offended if their name is not mentioned, cast down if another one says the same thing in a better way, irreconcilable if someone alters theirs views in the least. Go to the meetings of scholars and you will see them, these lamentable old men with their great merits and their starved souls famished for recognition and their thirst which can never be slaked. The soul demands your folly, not your wisdom.

Therefore, because I rise above gendered masculinity and yet do not exceed the human, the feminine that is contemptible to me transforms itself into a meaningful being. This is the most difficult thing—to be beyond the gendered and yet remain within the human. If you rise above the gendered with the help of a general rule, you become the same as that rule and overreach the human. Therefore you become dry, hard, and inhuman.

You may go past the gendered for human reasons, and never for the sake of a general rule that remains the same in the most diverse situations, and therefore never has a perfect validity for each single situation. If you act from your humanity, you act from that particular situation without general principle, with only what corresponds to the situation. Thus you do justice to the situation, perhaps at the expense of a general rule. That should not be too painful for you, because you are not the rule. There is something else that is human, something all too human, and whoever has ended up there will do well to remember the blessing of the general rule.[31] For the general rule also has meaning and has not been set up for fun. It comprises much venerable work of the human spirit. Such persons are not capable of a general principle above the gendered, but only their imagination is capable of what they have lost. They have become their own imagination and arbitrariness, to their own detriment.

31. *Human, All Too Human* was the title of a work of Nietzsche's, published in three installments from 1878. He described psychological observation as the reflection on the "human, all too human" (tr. R. J. Hollingdale [Cambridge: Cambridge University Press, 1996], p. 31).

They need to remember the gendered, so that they wake from their dreams to reality.

It is as agonizing as a sleepless night to fulfill the beyond from the here and now, namely the other and the opposing in myself. It sneaks up like a fever, like a poisonous fog. And when your senses are excited and stretched to the utmost, the daimonic comes as something so insipid and worn out, so mild and stale, that it makes you sick. Here you would gladly stop feeling across to your beyond. Startled and disgusted, you long for the return of the supernal beauties of your visible world. You spit out and curse everything that lies beyond your lovely world, since you know that it is the disgust, scum, refuse of the human animal who stuffs himself in dark places, creeps along sidewalks, sniffs out every blessèd angle, and from the cradle to the grave enjoys only what has already been on everyone's lips.

But here you may not stop—do not place your disgust between your here-and-now and your beyond. The way to your beyond leads through Hell and in fact through your own wholly particular Hell, whose bottom consists of knee-deep rubble, whose air is the spent breath of millions, whose fires are dwarflike passions, and whose devils are chimerical sign-boards.

Everything odious and disgusting is your own particular Hell. How can it be otherwise? Every other Hell was at least worth seeing or full of fun. But that is never Hell. Your Hell is made up of all the things that you always ejected from your sanctuary with a curse and a kick of the foot. When you step into your own Hell, never think that you come like one suffering in beauty, or as a proud pariah, but you come like a stupid and curious fool and gaze in wonder at the
scraps that have fallen from your table.[32] / 10/11

32. In October 1916, in his talk before the Psychological Club on "Individuation and Collectivity," Jung noted that through individuation, "the individual must now consolidate himself by cutting himself off from the divine and become wholly himself. Thereby and at the same time he also separates himself from society. Outwardly he plunges into solitude, but inwardly into hell, distance from God" (CW 18, §1103).

You really want to rage, but you see at the same time how well rage suits you. Your hellish absurdity stretches for miles. Good for you if you can swear! You will find that profanity is lifesaving. Thus if you go through Hell, you should not forget to give due attention to whatever crosses your path. Quietly look into everything that excites your contempt or rage; thereby you accomplish the miracle that I experienced with the pale maiden. You give soul to the soulless, and thereby it can come to something out of horrible nothingness. Thus you will redeem your other into life. Your values want to draw you away from what you presently are, to get you ahead of and beyond yourself. Your being, however, pulls you to the bottom like lead. You cannot at the same time live both, since both exclude each other. But on the way you can live both. Therefore the way redeems you. You cannot at the same time be on the mountain and in the valley, but your way leads you from mountain to valley and from valley to mountain. Much begins amusingly and leads into the dark. Hell has levels.[33]

One of the Lowly[34]

Cap. iii.

[HI 11] In the following night,[35] I found myself wandering once more, in a homely, snow-covered country. A gray evening sky covers the sun. The air is moist and frosty. Someone who does not look trustworthy has joined me. Most notably, he has only one eye and a few scars on his face. He is poor and dirtily clothed, a tramp. He has a black stubble beard that has not seen a razor for a long time. I have a good walking stick for any eventuality. "It's damned cold," he remarks after a while. I agree. After a longer pause he asks: "Where are you going?"

33. In Dante's *Commedia,* Hell has nine levels.
34. The *Handwritten Draft* has: "*Third Adventure*" (p. 440). The *Corrected Draft* has "The Rogue," which is then covered over with paper (p. 186).
35. December 29, 1913.

I: "I'm going to the next village, where I plan to stay overnight."

He: "I'd like to do that too, but will hardly manage to get a bed."

I: "Have you no money? Well, let us see. Are you out of work?"

He: "Yes, times are bad. Until a few days ago, I was working for a locksmith. But then he had no more work. Now I'm traveling and looking for work."

I: "Wouldn't you work for a farmer? There is always a shortage of farm labor."

He: "Working for a farmer doesn't suit me. That means getting up early in the morning—the work is hard and wages are low."

I: "But it's always much more beautiful in the country than in a town."

He: "It's boring in the country, one meets nobody."

I: "Well, but there are also villagers."

He: "But there is no mental stimulation, the farmers are clods."

I look at him astonished. What, he still wants mental stimulation? Better that he honestly earn his keep, and when he has done that he can think of stimulation. / 11/12

I: "But tell me, what kind of mental stimulation is there in the city?"

He: "You can go to the cinema in the evenings. That's great and it's cheap. You get to see everything that happens in the world."

I have to think of Hell, where there are also cinemas for those who despised this institution on earth and did not go there because everyone else found it to their taste.

I: "What interested you most about the cinema?"

He: "One sees all sorts of stunning feats. There was one man who ran up houses. Another carried his head under his arm. Another even stood in the middle of a fire and wasn't burnt. Yes, it's really remarkable, the things that people can do."

And that's what this fellow calls mental stimulation! But wait—that does seem remarkable: didn't the saints also carry their heads under their arms?[36] Didn't Saint Francis and Saint Ignatius levitate—and what about the three men in the fiery furnace?[37] Isn't it a blasphemous idea to consider the *Acta Sanctorum* as historical cinema?[38] Oh, today's miracles are simply somewhat less mythical than technical. I regard my companion with feeling—he lives the history of the world—and I?

I: "Certainly, it's very well done. Did you see anything else like this?"

He: "Yes, I saw how the King of Spain was murdered."

I: "But he wasn't murdered at all."

He: "Well, that doesn't matter; in that case it was one of those damned capitalist kings. At least they got one of them. If all of them were taken out, the people would be free."

Not a word more dare I say: *Wilhelm Tell*, a work by Friedrich Schiller—the man is standing right in the thick of it, in the stream of heroic story. One who announces the murder of the tyrant to a sleeping people.[39]

We have arrived at the inn, a country tavern—a reasonably clean parlor—a few men sit with beer in the corner. I am recognized as a "gentleman" and led into the better corner where a chequered cloth covers the end of a table. The other sits down at the far end of the table, and I decide to have him served a proper evening meal. He is already looking at me full of expectation and hunger—with his one eye.

---

36. The emblem of the city of Zürich bears this motif, showing the late-third-century martyrs Felix, Regula, and Exuperantius.
37. This appears to be a reference to Shadrach, Meshach, and Abednego in Daniel 3, whom Nebuchadnezzar ordered to be placed into a furnace for refusing to worship the golden idol that he had erected. They were unscathed by the fire, which led Nebuchadnezzar to decree that he would cut up anyone who henceforth spoke against their God.
38. The *Acta Sanctorum* is a collection of the lives and legends of the saints arranged according to their feast days. Published by Jesuits in Belgium known as the Bollandist Fathers, it began in 1643 and ran to sixty-three folio volumes.
39. In *Wilhelm Tell* (1805), Friedrich Schiller dramatized the revolt of the Swiss cantons against the rule of the Austrian Habsburg empire at the beginning of the fourteenth century, which led to the founding of the Swiss confederation. In act 4, scene 3, Wilhelm Tell kills Gessler, the imperial representative. Stüssi, the ranger, announces, "The tyrant of the land is dead. From now henceforth we suffer no oppression. We are free men" (tr. W. Mainland [Chicago: University of Chicago Press, 1973], p. 119).

I: "Where did you lose your eye?"

He: "In a brawl. But I also got my knife into the other fellow pretty nicely. After that he got three months. They gave me six. But it was beautiful in prison. At the time the building was completely new. I worked in the locksmith's. There wasn't much to do and yet there was enough to eat. Prison really isn't all that bad."

I look around to make sure that no one is listening to me talking with a former convict. But no one seems to have noticed. I seem to have ended up in well-to-do company. Are there also prisons in Hell for those who never saw the inside of one while they were alive? Incidentally—mustn't it be a peculiarly beautiful feeling to hit bottom in reality at least once, where there is no going down any further, but only upward beckons at best? Where for once one stands before the whole height of reality?

He: "So after that there I was, out on the street, since they banished me. Then I went to France. It was lovely there."

What demands beauty makes! Something can be learned from this man.

I: "Why did you have this brawl?"

He: "It was over a woman. She was carrying his bastard but I wanted to marry her. She was already due. After that she didn't want to anymore. I haven't heard from her."

I: "How old are you now?"

He: "I'll be thirty-five in spring. Once I find a proper job we can get married right off. I'll find myself one, I will. There's something wrong with my lungs, though. But that'll soon get better again."

/ He has a coughing fit. I think that the prospects are not good 12/13
and silently admire the poor devil's unswerving optimism.

After dinner I go to bed in a humble room. I hear how the other settles into his lodging for the night next door. He coughs several times. Then he falls still. Suddenly I awaken again at an uncanny moan and gurgle mixed with a half-stifled cough. I listen tensely—no doubt, it's him. It sounds like something dangerous. I jump up and throw something on. I open the door of his room. Moonlight floods it. The man lies still dressed on a sack of straw. A dark stream of blood is flowing from his mouth and forming a puddle on the floor. He moans half choking and coughs out blood. He wants to get up but sinks back again—I hurry to support him but I see that the hand of death lies on him. He is sullied with blood twice over. My hands are covered with it. A rattling sigh escapes from him. Then every stiffness loosens, a gentle shudder passes over his limbs. And then everything is deathly still.

Where am I? Are there also cases of death in Hell for those who have never thought about death? I look at my bloodstained hands—as if I were a murderer . . . Is it not the blood of my brother that sticks to my hands? The moon paints my shadow black on the white walls of the chamber. What am I doing here? Why this horrible drama? I look inquiringly at the moon as a witness. How does this concern the moon? Has it not already seen worse? Has it not shone a hundred thousand times into broken eyes? This is certainly of no avail to its eternal craters—one more or less. Death? Does it not uncover the terrible deceit of life? Therefore it is probably all the same to the moon, whether and how one passes away. Only we kick up a fuss about it—with what right?

What did this one do? He worked, lazed about, laughed, drank, ate, slept, gave his eye for the woman, and for her sake forfeited his good name; furthermore, he lived the human myth after a fashion, he admired the wonder-workers, praised the death of the tyrant, and vaguely dreamed of the freedom of the people. And then—then he miserably died—like everyone else. That is generally valid. I sat down on the floor. What shadows over the earth! All lights gutter out in final despondency and loneliness. Death has entered—and there is no one left to grieve. This is a final truth and no riddle. What delusion could make us believe in riddles?

[2] We stand on the spiky stones of misery and death.

A destitute joins me and wants admittance into my soul, and I am thus not destitute enough. Where was my destitution when I did not live it? I was a player at life, one who thought earnestly about life and lived it easily. The destitute was far away and forgotten. Life had become difficult and murkier. Winter kept on going, and the destitute stood in snow and froze. I join myself with him, since I need him. He makes living light and easy. He leads to the depths, to the ground where I can see the heights. Without the depths, I do not have the heights. I may be on the heights, but precisely because of that I do not become aware of the heights. I therefore need the bottommost for my renewal. If I am always on the heights, I wear them out and the best becomes atrocious to me.

But because I do not want to have it, my best becomes a horror to me. Because of that I myself become a horror, a horror to myself and to others, and a bad spirit of torment. Be respectful and know that your best has become a horror, with that you save yourself and others from useless torment. A man who can no longer climb down from his heights is sick, and he brings himself and others to torment. If you have reached your depths, then you see your height light up brightly over you, worthy of desire and far-off, as if unreachable, since secretly you would prefer not to reach it since it seems unattainable to you. For you also love to praise your heights when you are low and to tell yourself that you would have only left them with pain, and that you did not live so long as you missed them. It is a good thing that you have almost become the other nature that makes you speak this way. But at bottom you know that it is not quite true.

At your low point you are no longer distinct from your fellow beings. You are not ashamed and do not regret it, since insofar as you live the life of your fellow beings and descend to their lowliness / you also climb into the holy stream of common life, where 13/14
you are no longer an individual on a high mountain, but a fish among fish, a frog among frogs.

Your heights are your own mountain, which belongs to you and you alone. There you are individual and live your very own life. If you live your own life, you do not live the common life, which is always continuing and never-ending, the life of history and the inalienable and ever-present burdens and products of the human race. There you live the endlessness of being, but not the becoming.

Becoming belongs to the heights and is full of torment. How can you become if you never are? Therefore you need your bottommost, since there you are. But therefore you also need your heights, since there you become.

If you live the common life at your lowest reaches, then you become aware of your self. If you are on your heights, then you are your best, and you become aware only of your best, but not that which you are in the general life as a being. What one is as one who becomes, no one knows. But on the heights, imagination is at its strongest. For we imagine that we know what we are as developing beings, and even more so, the less we want to know what we are as beings. Because of that we do not love the condition of our being brought low, although or rather precisely because only there do we attain clear knowledge of ourselves.

Everything is riddlesome to one who is becoming, but not to one who is. He who suffers from riddles should take thought of his lowest condition; we solve those riddles from which we suffer, but not those which please us.

To be that which you are is the bath of rebirth. In the depths, being is not an unconditional persistence but an endlessly slow growth. You think you are standing still like swamp water, but slowly you flow into the sea that covers the earth's greatest deeps, and is so vast that firm land seems only an island imbedded in the womb of the immeasurable sea.

As a drop in the ocean you take part in the current, ebb and flow. You swell slowly on the land and slowly sink back again in interminably slow breaths. You wander vast distances in blurred currents and wash up on strange shores, not knowing how you got there. You mount the billows of huge storms and are swept back again into the depths. And you do not know how this happens to you. You had thought that your movement came from you and that it needed your decisions and efforts, so that you could get going and make progress. But with every conceivable effort you would never have achieved that movement and reached those areas to which the sea and the great wind of the world brought you.

From endless blue plains you sink into black depths; luminous fish draw you, marvelous branches twine around you from above. You slip through columns and twisting, wavering, dark-leaved plants, and the sea takes you up again in bright green water to white, sandy coasts, and a wave foams you ashore and swallows you back again, and a wide smooth swell lifts you softly and leads you again to new regions, to twisting plants, to slowly creeping slimy polyps, and to green water and white sand and breaking surf.

But from far off your heights shine to you above the sea in a golden light, like the moon emerging from the tide, and you become aware of yourself from afar. And longing seizes you and the will for your own movement. You want to cross over from being to becoming, since you have recognized the breath of the sea, and its flowing, that leads you here and there without your ever adhering; you have also recognized its surge that bears you to alien shores and carries you back, and gargles you up and down.

You saw that it was the life of the whole and the death of each individual. You felt yourself entwined in the collective death, from death to the earth's deepest place, from death in your own strangely breathing depths. Oh—you long to be beyond; despair and mortal fear seize you in this death that breathes slowly and streams back and forth eternally. All this light and dark, warm, tepid, and cold water, all these wavy, swaying, twisting plantlike animals and bestial plants, all these nightly wonders become a horror to you, and you long for the sun, for light dry air, for firm stones, for a fixed place and straight lines, for the motionless and firmly held, for rules and preconceived purpose, for singleness and your own intent.

The knowledge of death came to me that night, from the dying that engulfs the world. I saw how we live toward death, how the swaying golden wheat sinks together under the scythe of the reaper, / like 14/15
a smooth wave on the sea-beach. He who abides in common life becomes aware of death with fear. Thus the fear of death drives him toward singleness. He does not live there, but he becomes aware of life and is happy, since in singleness he is one who becomes, and has overcome death. He overcomes death through overcoming common

life. He does not live his individual being, since he is not what he is, but what he becomes.

One who becomes grows aware of life, whereas one who simply exists never will, since he is in the midst of life. He needs the heights and singleness to become aware of life. But in life he becomes aware of death. And it is good that you become aware of collective death, since then you know why your singleness and your heights are good. Your heights are like the moon that luminously wanders alone and through the night looks eternally clear. Sometimes it covers itself and then you are totally in the darkness of the earth, but time and again it fills itself out with light. The death of the earth is foreign to it. Motionless and clear, it sees the life of the earth from afar, without enveloping haze and streaming oceans. Its unchanging form has been solid from eternity. It is the solitary clear light of the night, the individual being, and the near fragment of eternity.

From there you look out, cold, motionless, and radiating. With otherworldly silvery light and green twilights, you pour out into the distant horror. You see it but your gaze is clear and cold. Your hands are red from living blood, but the moonlight of your gaze is motionless. It is the life blood of your brother, yes, it is your own blood, but your gaze remains luminous and embraces the entire horror and the earth's round. Your gaze rests on silvery seas, on snowy peaks, on blue valleys, and you do not hear the groaning and howling of the human animal.

The moon is dead. Your soul went to the moon, to the preserver of souls.[40] Thus the soul moved toward death.[41] I went into the inner death and saw that outer dying is better than inner death. And I decided to die outside and to live within. For that reason I turned away[42] and sought the place of the inner life.

---

40. In *Transformations and Symbols of the Libido* (1912), Jung cited beliefs in different cultures that the moon was the gathering place of departed souls (CW B, §496). In *Mysterium Coniunctionis* (1955/56), Jung commented on this motif in alchemy (CW 14, §155).
41. The *Draft* continues: "I accepted the rogue, and lived and died with him. Since I lived him, I became his murderer, since we kill what we live" (p. 217).
42. The *Corrected Draft* continues: "from death" (p. 200).

The Anchorite

Cap. iv. Dies I.[43]

[HI 15] On the following night,[44] I found myself on new paths; hot dry air flowed around me, and I saw the desert, yellow sand all around, heaped up in waves, a terrible irascible sun, a sky as blue as tarnished steel, the air shimmering above the earth, on my right side a deeply cut valley with a dry river bed, some languid grass and dusty brambles. In the sand I see the tracks of naked feet that lead up from the rocky valley to the plateau. I follow them along a high dune. Where it falls off, the tracks move off to the other side. They appear to be fresh, and old half-worn-away footprints run alongside. I pursue them attentively: again they follow the slope of the dune, now they flow into another set of footprints—but it is the same / set 15/16
that I have already followed, the one ascending from the valley.

Henceforth I follow the footprints downward in astonishment. I soon reach the hot red rocks corroded by the wind. On the stone the footprints are lost but I see where the rock falls off in layers and I climb down. The air glows and the rock burns my soles. Now I have reached the bottom; there are the tracks again. They lead along the winding of the valley, a short distance. Suddenly I stand before a small hut covered in reeds and made of mud bricks. A rickety

43. (First Day.) The *Handwritten Draft* has: "*Fourth Adventure: First Day*" (p. 476). The *Corrected Draft* has: "Dies I. Evening" (p. 201).

44. December 30, 1913. In *Black Book* 3, Jung noted: "All kinds of things lead me far away from my scientific endeavor, which I thought I had subscribed to firmly. I wanted to serve humanity through it, and now, my soul, you lead me to these new things. Yes, it is the in-between world, the pathless, the manifold-dazzling. I forgotthat I had reached a new world, which had been alien to me previously. I see neither way nor path. What I believed about the soul has to become true here, namely that she knows her own way better, and that no intention can prescribe her a better one. I feel that a large chunk of science has been broken off. I suppose it must be like this, for the sake of the soul and her life. I find the thought that this must occur only for me agonizing, and that perhaps no one will gain insight from my work. But my soul demands this achievement. I should be able to do this just for myself without hope—for the sake of God. This is truly a hard way. But what else did those anchorites of the first centuries of Christianity do? And were they the worst or least capable of those living at the end? Hardly, since they came to the most relentless conclusions with regard to the psychological necessity of their time. They left wife and child, wealth, glory and science—and turned toward the desert—for God's sake. So be it" (pp. 1–2).

wooden plank forms the door where a cross has been painted in red. I open it quietly. A haggard man covered in a white linen mantle is sitting on a mat with his back leaning against the wall. Across his knees lies a book in yellow parchment, with beautiful black handwriting—a Greek gospel, without doubt. I am with an anchorite of the Libyan desert.[45]

I: "Am I disturbing you, father?"

A: "You do not disturb me. But do not call me father. I am a man like you. What is your desire?"

I: "I come without desire, I have come to this place in the desert by chance, and found tracks in the sand up there that led me in a circle to you."

A: "You found the tracks of my daily walks at daybreak and sunset."

I: "Excuse me if I interrupt your devotion, it is a rare opportunity for me to be with you. I have never before seen an anchorite."

A: "There are several others whom you can see further down in this valley. Some have huts like me, others live in the graves that the ancients have hollowed out in these rocks. I live uppermost in the valley, because it is most solitary and quiet here, and because here I am closest to the peace of the desert."

I: "Have you already been here long?"

A: "I have lived here for perhaps ten years, but really, I can no longer remember exactly how long it is. It could also be a few more years. Time passes so quickly."

I: "Time passes quickly? How is that possible? Your life must be frightfully monotonous."

45. In the next chapter, the anchorite is identified as Ammonius. In a letter of December 31, 1913, Jung noted that the anchorite came from the third century (*JFA*). There are three historical figures named Ammonius in Alexandria from this period: Ammonius, a Christian philosopher in the third century, once thought to have been responsible for the medieval divisions of the gospels; Ammonius Cetus, who was born a Christian but turned to Greek philosophy and whose work presents a transition from Platonism to Neoplatonism; a Neoplatonic Ammonius in the fifth century, who tried to reconcile Aristotle and the Bible. At Alexandria, there was accommodation between Neoplatonism and Christianity, and some of the pupils of the latter Ammonius converted to Christianity.

A: "Time certainly passes quickly for me. Much too quickly even. It seems you are a pagan?"

I: "Me? No—not exactly. I was raised in the Christian faith."

A: "Well, then, how can you ask whether time drags on for me? You must know what preoccupies a man who is grieving. Only idlers grow bored."

I: "Again, forgive me, my curiosity is great, what then do you occupy yourself with?"

A: "Are you a child? To begin with you see that I am reading, and that I keep regular hours."

I: "But I can see nothing at all with which you could occupy yourself here. You must have read this book from cover to cover often enough. And if it is the gospels, as I suppose, then I am sure you already know them by heart."

A: "How childishly you speak! Surely you know that one can read a book many times—perhaps you almost know it by heart, and nevertheless it can be that, when you look again at the lines before you, certain things appear new or even new thoughts occur to you that you did not have before. Every word can work productively in your spirit. And finally if you have once left the book for a week and you take it up again after your spirit has experienced various different changes, then a number of things will dawn on you."

I: "I have difficulty grasping this. The book remains one and the same, certainly a wonderfully profound, yes, even divine matter, but surely not rich enough to fill countless years."

A: "You are astonishing. How, then, do you read this holy book? Do you really always see only one and the same meaning in it? Where do you come from? You are truly a pagan."

I: "I beg you, please don't hold it against me if I read like a pagan. Let me talk with you. I am here to learn from you. Consider me as an ignorant student, which I am in these matters."

A: "If I call you a pagan, don't take it as an insult. I used to be
a pagan, too, exactly like you as I / well remember. Therefore how 16/17
can I blame you for your ignorance?"

I: "Thank you for your patience. But it matters very much to me to know how you read and what you take from this book."

A: "Your question is not easy to answer. It's easier to explain colors to a blind person. You must know one thing above all: a succession of words does not have only one meaning. But men strive to assign only a single meaning to the sequence of words, in order to have an unambiguous language. This striving is worldly and constricted, and belongs to the deepest layers of the divine creative plan. On the higher levels of insight into divine thoughts, you recognize that the sequence of words has more than one valid meaning. Only to the all-knowing is it given to know all the meanings of the sequence of words. Increasingly we try to grasp a few more meanings."

I: "If I understand you correctly, you think that the holy writings of the New Testament also have a doubleness, an exoteric and an esoteric meaning, as a few Jewish scholars contend concerning their holy books."

A: "This bad superstition is far from me. I observe that you are wholly inexperienced in divine matters."

I: "I must confess my deep ignorance about these things. But I am eager to experience and understand what you think about the multifaceted meaning of the sequence of words."

A: "Unfortunately I am in no position to tell you everything I know about it. But at least I will try to make the elements clear to you. Because of your ignorance I will therefore begin elsewhere this time: What you need to know is that before I became acquainted with Christianity, I was a rhetorician and philosopher in the city of Alexandria. I had a great throng of students, including many Romans, a few barbarians, and also some Gauls and Britons. I taught them not only the history of Greek philosophy but also the new systems, among them the system of Philo, whom we call the Jew.[46] He was a clever head, but fantastically abstract, as the Jews are

46. Philo Judeaus, also called Philo of Alexandria (20 BCE–50 CE), was a Greek-speaking Jewish philosopher. His works presented a fusion of Greek philosophy and Judaism. For Philo, God, to whom he referred by the Platonic term "To On" (the One), was

wont to be when they devise systems; moreover he was a slave of his own words. I added my own, and wove an atrocious web of words in which I ensnared not only my listeners, but also myself. We rioted terribly among words and names, our own miserable creatures, and accorded divine potency to them. Yes, we even believed in their reality, and believed that we possessed the divine and had committed it to words."

I: "But Philo Judeaus, if this is who you mean, was a serious philosopher and a great thinker. Even John the Evangelist included some of Philo's thoughts in the gospel."

A: "You are right. It is to Philo's credit that he furnished language like so many other philosophers. He belongs to the language artists. But words should not become Gods."[47]

I: "I fail to understand you here. Does it not say in the gospel according to John: God was the Word. It appears to make quite explicit the point which you have just now rejected."

A: "Guard against being a slave to words. Here is the gospel: read from that passage where it says: In him was the life. What does John say there?"[48]

I: "'And life was the light of men and the light shines in the darkness and the darkness has not understood it. But it became a person

transcendent and unknowable. Certain powers reached down from God to the world. The facet of God knowable through reason is the divine Logos. There has been much debate on the precise relation between Philo's concept of the Logos and John's gospel. On June 23, 1954, Jung wrote to James Kirsch, "The gnosis from which John the Evangelist emanated, is definitely Jewish, but its essence is Hellenistic, in the style of Philo Judaeus, the founder of the teachings of the Logos" (*JA*).

47. In 1957, Jung wrote: "Until now it has not truly and fundamentally been noted that our time, despite the prevalence of irreligiosity, is so to speak congenitally charged with the attainment of the Christian epoch, namely with the *supremacy of the word*, that Logos which the central figure of Christian faith represents. The word has literally become our God and has remained so" (*Present and Future*, CW 10, §554).

48. John 1:1–10: "In the beginning was the Word, and the Word was with God, and the Word was God. The same was in the beginning with God. All things were made by him; and without him was not any thing made that was made. In him was life; and the life was the light of men. And the light shineth in darkness; and the darkness comprehended it not. There was a man sent from God, whose name was John. The same came for a witness, to bear witness of the Light, that all men through him might believe. He was not that Light, but was sent to bear witness of that Light. That was the true Light, which lighteth every man that cometh into the world. He was in the world, and the world was made by him, and the world knew him not."

sent from God, by the name of John, who came as a witness and to be a witness of the light. The genuine light, which illuminates each person, came into the world: He was in the world, and the world became through him, and the world did not recognize him.'—That is what I read here. But what do you make of this?"

A: "I ask you, was this ΛΟΓΟΣ [Logos] a concept, a word? It was a light, indeed a man, and lived among men. You see, Philo only lent John the word so that John would have at his disposal the word 'ΛΟΓΟΣ' alongside the word 'light' to describe the son of man. John gave to living men the meaning of the ΛΟΓΟΣ, but Philo gave ΛΟΓΟΣ as the dead concept that usurped life, even the divine life. Through this the dead does not gain life, and the living is killed. And this was also my atrocious error."

I: "I see what you mean. This thought is new to me and seems
17/18 worth consideration. Until now it always seemed to me / as if it were exactly that which was meaningful in John, namely that the son of man is the ΛΟΓΟΣ, in that he thus elevates the lower to the higher spirit, to the world of the ΛΟΓΟΣ. But you lead me to see the matter conversely, namely that John brings the meaning of the ΛΟΓΟΣ down to man."

A: "I learned to see that John has in fact even done the great service of having brought the meaning of the ΛΟΓΟΣ up to man."

I: "You have peculiar insights that stretch my curiosity to the utmost. How is that? Do you think that the human stands higher than the ΛΟΓΟΣ?"

A: "I want to answer this question within the scope of your understanding: if the human God had not become important above everything, he would not have appeared as the son in the flesh, but in the ΛΟΓΟΣ."[49]

I: "That makes sense to me, but I confess that this view is surprising to me. It is especially astonishing to me that you, a Christian

49. John 1:14: "And the Word was made flesh, and dwelt among us (and we beheld his glory, the glory as of the only begotten of the Father), full of grace and truth."

anchorite, have come to such views. I would not have expected this of you."

A: "As I have already noticed, you have a completely false idea of me and my essence. Let me give you a small example of my preoccupation. I've spent many years alone with the process of unlearning. Have you ever unlearned anything?—Well, then you should know how long it takes. And I was a successful teacher. As you know, for such people to unlearn is difficult or even impossible. But I see that the sun has gone down. Soon it will be completely dark. Night is the time of silence. I want to show you your place for the night. I need the morning for my work, but after midday you can come to me again if you like. Then we will continue our conversation."

He leads me out of the hut, the valley is covered in blue shadows. The first stars are already glittering in the sky. He leads me around the corner of a rock: we are standing at the entrance of a[50] grave cut into the stone. We step in. Not far from the entrance lies a heap of reeds covered with mats. Next to it there is a pitcher of water, and on a white cloth there are dried dates and black bread.

A: "Here is your place and your supper. Sleep well, and do not forget your morning prayer, when the sun rises."

[2] The solitary lives in endless desert full of awesome beauty. He looks at the whole and at inner meaning. He loathes manifold diversity if it is near him. He looks at it from afar in its totality. Consequently silvery splendor and joy and beauty cloak diversity for him. What is near him must be simple and innocent, since close at hand the manifold and complicated tear and break through the silvery splendor. No cloudiness of the sky, no haze or mist is allowed to be around him, otherwise he cannot look at the distant manifold in the whole. Consequently the solitary loves the desert above all, where everything nearby is simple and nothing turbid or blurred lies between him and the far-away.

50. The *Draft* has: "Egyptian" (p. 227). In an Egyptian context, the water, dates, and bread would be offerings to the dead.

The life of the solitary would be cold were it not for the immense sun, which makes the air and rocks glow. The sun and its eternal splendor replace for the solitary his own life warmth.

His heart longs for the sun.

He wanders to the lands of the sun.

He dreams of the flickering splendor of the sun, of the hot red stones spread out
18/19 *at midday, of the golden hot rays of dry sand.* /

The solitary seeks the sun and no one else is so ready to open his heart as he is. Therefore he loves the desert above all, since he loves its deep stillness.

He needs little food since the sun and its glow nourish him. Consequently the solitary loves the desert above all since it is a mother to him, giving him food and invigorating warmth at regular hours.

In the desert the solitary is relieved of care and therefore turns his whole life to the sprouting garden of his soul, which can flourish only under a hot sun. In his garden the delicious red fruit grows that bears swelling sweetness under a tight skin.

You think that the solitary is poor. You do not see that he strolls under laden fruit trees and that his hand touches grain a hundredfold. Under dark leaves the overfull reddish blossoms swell toward him from abundant buds, and the fruit almost bursts with thronging juices. Fragrant resins drip from his trees and under his feet thrusting seed breaks open.

If the sun sinks onto the plane of the sea like an exhausted bird, the solitary envelops himself and holds his breath. He does not move and is pure expectancy until the miracle of the renewal of light rises in the East.

Brimful delicious expectation is in the solitary.[51]

The horror of the desert and of withered evaporation surround him, and you do
19/20 *not understand how the solitary can live.* /

But his eye rests on the garden, and his ears listen to the source, and his hand touches velvet leaves and fruit, and his breath draws in sweet perfumes from blossom-rich trees.

51. The *Draft* continues: "Walking around in a circle I happen to return to myself and to him, the solitary one, who lives down in the depths hidden from the light, held securely by the warm bosom of the rock, above him the glowing desert and sharp resplendent skies" (p. 229).

He cannot tell you, since the splendor of his garden is so abundant. He stammers when he speaks of it, and he appears to you to be poor in spirit and in life. But his hand does not know where it should reach, in all this indescribable fullness.

He gives you a small insignificant fruit, which has just fallen at his feet. It appears worthless to you, but if you consider it, you will see that this fruit tastes like a sun which you could not have dreamt of. It gives off a perfume which confuses your senses and makes you dream of rose gardens and sweet wine and whispering palm trees. And you hold this one fruit in your hands dreaming, and you would like the tree in which it grows, the garden in which this tree stands, and the sun which brought forth this garden.

And you yourself want to be that solitary who strolls with the sun in his garden, his gaze resting on pendant flowers and his hand brushing a hundredfold of grain and his breath drinking the perfume from a thousand roses.

Dull from the sun and drunk from fermenting wines, you lie down in ancient graves, whose walls resound with many voices and many colors of a thousand solar years.

When you grow, then you see everything living again as it was. And / when 20/21
you sleep, you rest, like everything that was, and your dreams echo softly again from distant temple chants.

You sleep down through the thousand solar years, and you wake up through the thousand solar years, and your dreams full of ancient lore adorn the walls of your bedchamber.

You also see yourself in the totality.

You sit and lean against the wall, and look at the beautiful, riddlesome totality. The Summa[52] lies before you like a book, and an unspeakable greed seizes you to devour it. Consequently you lean back and stiffen and sit for a long time. You are completely incapable of grasping it. Here and there a light flickers, here and there a fruit falls from high trees which you can grasp, here and there your foot strikes gold. But what is it, if you compare it with the totality, which lies spread out tangibly close to you? You stretch out your hand, but it remains hanging in invisible webs. You want to see it

52. Latin for "whole."

exactly as it is but something cloudy and opaque pushes itself exactly in between. You would like to tear a piece out of it; it is smooth and impenetrable like polished steel. So you sink back against the wall, and when you have crawled through all the glowing hot crucibles of the Hell of doubt, you sit once more and lean back, and look at the wonder of the Summa that lies spread out before you. Here and there a light flickers, here and there a fruit falls. For you it is all too little. But you begin to be satisfied with yourself, and you pay no attention to the years passing away. What are years? What is hurrying time to him that sits under a tree? Your time passes like a breath of air and you wait for the next light, the next fruit.

The writing lies before you and always says the same, if you believe in words. But if you believe in things in whose places only words stand, you never come to the end. And yet you must go an endless road, since life flows not only down a finite path but also an infinite one. But the unbounded makes you[53] anxious since the unbounded is fearful and your humanity rebels against it. Consequently you seek limits and restraints so that you do not lose yourself, tumbling into infinity. Restraint becomes imperative for you. You cry out for the word which has one meaning and no other, so that you escape boundless ambiguity. The word becomes your God, since it protects you from the countless possibilities of interpretation. The word is protective magic against the daimons of the unending, which tear at your soul and want to scatter you to the winds. You are saved if you can say at last: that is that and only that. You speak the magic word, and the limitless is finally banished. Because of that men seek and make words.[54]

He who breaks the wall of words overthrows Gods and defiles temples. The solitary is a murderer. He murders the people, because he thus thinks and thereby breaks down ancient sacred walls. He

53. The *Draft* has "to you," and the *Corrected Draft* has "to me" (p. 232). Throughout this section, the *Corrected Draft* substitutes "to me" for "to you," and "I" for "you" (p. 214).
54. In 1940, Jung commented on protective word magic ("Transformation symbolism in the mass," CW 11, §442).

calls up the daimons of the boundless. And he sits, leans back, and does not hear the groans of mankind, whom the fearful fiery smoke has seized. And yet you cannot find the new words if you do not shatter the old words. But no one should shatter the old words, unless he finds the new word that is a firm rampart against the limitless and grasps more life in it than in the old word. A new word is a new God for old men. Man remains the same, even if you create a new model of God for him. He remains an imitator. What was word, shall become man. The word created the world and came before the world. It lit up like a light in the darkness, and the darkness did not comprehend it.[55] And thus the word should become what the darkness can comprehend, since what use is the light if the darkness does not comprehend it? But your darkness should grasp the light.

The God of words is cold and dead and shines from afar like the moon, mysteriously and inaccessibly. Let the word return to its / creator, to man, and thus the word will be heightened in man. 21/22
Man should be light, limits, measure. May he be your fruit, for which you longingly reach. The darkness does not comprehend the word, but rather man; indeed, it seizes him, since he himself is a piece of the darkness. Not from the word down to man, but from the word up to man: that is what the darkness comprehends. The darkness is your mother; she behooves reverence, since the mother is dangerous. She has power over you, since she gave birth to you. Honor the darkness as the light, and you will illumine your darkness.

If you comprehend the darkness, it seizes you. It comes over you like the night with black shadows and countless shimmering stars. Silence and peace come over you if you begin to comprehend the darkness. Only he who does not comprehend the darkness fears the night. Through comprehending the dark, the nocturnal, the abyssal in you, you become utterly simple. And you prepare to sleep through

55. See note 48, above, p. 245.

the millennia like everyone else, and you sleep down into the womb of the millennia, and your walls resound with ancient temple chants. Since the simple is what always was. Peace and blue night spread over you while you dream in the grave of the millennia.

Dies II.[56]

Cap. v.

[HI 22][57, 58] I awaken, the day reddens the East. A night, a wonderful night in the distant depths of time lies behind me. In what far-away space was I? What did I dream? Of a white horse? It seems to me as if I had seen this white horse on the Eastern sky over the rising sun. The horse spoke to me: What did it say? It said: "Hail him who is in darkness since the day is over him." There were four white horses, each with golden wings. They led the carriage of the sun, on which Helios stood with flaring mane.[59] I stood down in the gorge, astonished and frightened. A thousand black serpents crawled swiftly into their holes. Helios ascended, rolling upward toward the wide paths of the sky. I knelt down, raised my hands suppliantly, and called: "Give us your light, you are flame-curled, entwined, crucified and revived; give us your light, your light!" This cry woke me. Didn't Ammonius say yesterday evening: "Do not forget to say your morning prayer when the sun rises." I thought that perhaps he secretly
22/23 worships the sun. /

Outside a fresh morning wind rises. Yellow sand trickles in fine veins down the rocks. The redness expands across the sky and I see the first rays shoot up to the firmament. Solemn calm and solitude on all sides. A large lizard lies on a stone and awaits the sun. I stand as if spellbound and laboriously remember everything from yester-

56. The *Corrected Draft* has "(The Anchorite). Second Day. Morning" (p. 219).
57. In "The Philosophical Tree" (1945), Jung noted: "A man who is rooted below as well as above is sort of like an upright and inverted tree. The goal is not the heights but the center" (CW 13, §333). He also commented on "The inverted tree" (§410f).
58. January 1, 1914.
59. In Greek mythology, Helios was the sun God, and he drove a chariot led by four horses across the sky.

day, especially what Ammonius said. But what did he say? That the sequences of words have many meanings, and that John brought the ΛΟΓΟΣ to man. But that does not sound properly Christian. Is he perhaps a Gnostic?[60] No, that seems impossible to me, since they were really the worst of all the idolators of words, as he would probably put it.

The sun—what fills me with such inner exaltation? I should not forget my morning prayer—but where has my morning prayer gone? Dear sun, I have no prayer, since I do not know how one must address you. Have I already prayed to the sun? But Ammonius really meant that I should pray to God at the break of day. He probably does not know—we have no more prayers. How should he know about our nakedness and poverty? What has happened to our prayers? I miss them here. This must really be because of the desert. It seems as if there ought to be prayers here. Is this desert so very bad? I think it is no worse than our cities. But why then do we not pray there? I must look toward the sun, as if it had something to do with this. Alas—one can never escape the age-old dreams of mankind.

What shall I do this whole long morning? I do not understand how Ammonius could have endured this life for even a year. I go back and forth on the dried-up river bed and finally sit down on a boulder. Before me there are a few yellow grasses. Over there a small dark beetle is crawling along, pushing a ball in front of it—a scarab.[61] You dear little animal, are you still toiling away in order to live your beautiful myth? How seriously and undiscouraged it works! If only you had a notion that you are performing an old myth, you would

---

60. During this period, Jung was engaged with the study of Gnostic texts, in which he found historical parallels to his own experiences. See Alfred Ribi, *Die Suche nach den eigenen Wurzeln: Die Bedeutung von Gnosis, Hermetik und Alchemie für* C. G. *Jung und Marie-Louise von Franz und deren Einfluss auf das moderne Verständnis dieser Disziplin* (Bern: Peter Lang, 1999).

61. *In Synchronicity as a Principle of Acausal Connection* (1952), Jung wrote: "The scarab is a classical rebirth symbol. According to the description in the ancient Egyptian book *Am-Tuat*, the dead sun God transforms himself at the tenth station into Khepri, the scarab, and as such mounts the barge at the twelfth station, which raises the rejuvenated sun into the morning sky" (CW 8, §843).

probably renounce your fantasies as we men have also given up playing at mythology.

The unreality nauseates one. What I say sounds very odd in this place, and the good Ammonious would certainly not agree with it. What am I actually doing here? No, I don't want to condemn him in advance, since I still haven't really understood what he actually means. He has a right to be heard. By the way, I thought differently yesterday. I was even very thankful to him that he wanted to teach me. But I'm being critical once again, and superior, and may well learn nothing. His thoughts are not that bad at all; they are even good. I don't know why I always want to put the man down.

Dear beetle, where have you gone? I can no longer see you—Oh, you're already over there with your mythical ball. These little animals stick to things, quite unlike us—no doubt, no change of mind, no hesitation. Is this so because they live their myth?

Dear scarab, my father, I honor you, blessèd be your work—in eternity—Amen.

What nonsense am I talking? I'm worshiping an animal—that must be because of the desert. It seems absolutely to demand prayers.

How beautiful it is here! The reddish color of the stones is wonderful; they reflect the glow of a hundred thousand past suns—these small grains of sand have rolled in fabulous primordial oceans, over them swam primordial monsters with forms never beheld before. Where were you, man, in those days? On this warm sand lay your childish primordial animal ancestors, like children snuggling up to their mother.

O mother stone, I love you, I lie snuggled up against your warm body, your late
23/24 *child. Blessèd be you, ancient mother.*

/ Yours is my heart and all glory and power—Amen.

What am I saying? That was the desert. How everything appears so animated to me! This place is truly terrible. These stones—are they stones? They seem to have gathered here deliberately. They're lined up like a troop transport. They've arranged themselves by size, the large ones stand apart, the small ones close ranks and gather in groups that precede the large ones. Here the stones form states.

Am I dreaming or am I awake? It's hot—the sun already stands high—how the hours pass! Truly, the morning is nearly over—and how astonishing it has been! Is it the sun or is it these living stones, or is it the desert that makes my head buzz?

I go up the valley and before long I reach the hut of the anchorite. He is sitting on his mat lost in deep reflection.

I: "My father, I am here."

A: "How have you spent your morning?"

I: "I was surprised when you said yesterday that time passes quickly for you. I don't question you anymore and this will no longer surprise me. I've learned a lot. But only enough to make you an even greater riddle than you were before. Why, all the things that you must experience in the desert, you wonderful man! Even the stones are bound to speak to you."

A: "I'm happy that you have learned to understand something of the life of an anchorite. That will make our difficult task easier. I don't want to intrude on your mysteries, but I feel that you come from a strange world that has nothing to do with mine."

I: "You speak truthfully. I'm a stranger here, more foreign than any you've ever seen. Even a man from Britain's remotest coast is closer to you than I am. Therefore have patience, master—and let me drink from the source of your wisdom. Although the thirsty desert surrounds us, an invisible stream of living water flows here."

A: "Have you said your prayer?"

I: "Master, forgive me: I've tried, but I found no prayer. Yet I dreamed that I prayed to the rising sun."

A: "Don't worry yourself because of that. If you do find a word, your soul has nevertheless found inexpressible words to greet the break of day."

I: "But it was a heathen prayer to Helios."

A: "Let that suffice for you."

I: "But Oh master, I've prayed not only to the sun in a dream, but in my absentmindedness also to the scarab and the earth."

A: "Be astonished at nothing, and in no case condemn or regret it. Let us go to work. Do you want to ask something about the conversation we had yesterday?"

I: "I interrupted you yesterday when you spoke of Philo. You wanted to explain your notion of the various meanings of particular sequences of words."

A: "Well, I'll continue my account of how I was freed from the awful predicament of spinning words. A man my father had set free once came to me; this man, whom I'd been attached to since my childhood, spoke to me and said:

"Oh Ammonius, are you well?" "Certainly," I said, "as you can see, I am learnèd and have great success."

He: "I mean, are you happy and are you fully alive?"

I laughed: "As you can see, all is well."

The old man replied: "I saw how you lectured. You seemed to be anxious at the judgment of your listeners. You wove witty jokes into the lecture to please your listeners. You heaped up learnèd expressions to impress them. You were restless and hasty, as if still compelled to snatch up all knowledge. You are not in yourself."

Although these words at first seemed laughable to me, they
24/25 still made an impression on me, and reluctantly I had to / credit
the old man, since he was right.

Then he said: "Dear Ammonius, I have delightful tidings for you: God has become flesh in his son and has brought us all salvation." "What are you saying," I called, "you probably mean Osiris,[62] who shall appear in the mortal body?"

"No," he replied, "this man lived in Judea and was born from a virgin."

62. Osiris was the Egyptian God of life, death, and fertility. Seth was the God of the desert. Osiris was murdered and dismembered by his brother Seth. Osiris's body was recovered and put back together by his wife, Isis, and he was resurrected. Jung discussed Osiris and Seth in *Transformations and Symbols of the Libido* (1912) (CW B, §358f).

I laughed and answered: "I already know about this; a Jewish trader has brought tidings of our virgin queen to Judea, whose image appears on the walls of one of our temples, and reported it as a fairy tale."

"No," the old man insisted, "he was the Son of God."

"Then you mean Horus,[63] the son of Osiris, don't you?" I answered.

"No, he was not Horus, but a real man, and he was hung from a cross."

"Oh, but this must be Seth, surely, whose punishments our old ones have often described."

But the old man stood by his conviction and said: "He died and rose up on the third day."

"Well, then he must be Osiris," I replied impatiently.

"No," he cried, "he is called Jesus the anointed one."

"Ah, you really mean this Jewish God, whom the poor honor at the harbor, and whose unclean mysteries they celebrate in cellars."

"He was a man and yet the Son of God," said the old man staring at me intently.

"That's nonsense, dear old man," I said, and showed him to the door. But like an echo from distant rock faces the words returned to me: a man and yet the Son of God. It seemed significant to me, and this phrase was what brought me to Christianity.

I: "But don't you think that Christianity could ultimately be a transformation of your Egyptian teachings?"

A: "If you say that our old teachings were less adequate expressions of Christianity, then I'm more likely to agree with you."

I: "Yes, but do you then assume that the history of religions is aimed at a final goal?"

63. Horus, Osiris's son, was the Egyptian God of the sky. He fought against Seth.

A: "My father once bought a black slave at the market from the region of the source of the Nile. He came from a country that had heard of neither Osiris nor the other Gods; he told me many things in a more simple language that said the same as we believed about Osiris and the other Gods. I learned to understand that those uneducated Negroes unknowingly already possessed most of what the religions of the cultured peoples had developed into complete doctrines. Those able to read that language correctly could thus recognize in it not only the pagan doctrines but also the doctrine of Jesus. And it's with this that I now occupy myself. I read the gospels and seek their meaning which is yet to come. We know their meaning as it lies before us, but not their hidden meaning which points to the future. It's erroneous to believe that religions differ in their innermost essence. Strictly speaking, it's always one and the same religion. Every subsequent form of religion is the meaning of the antecedent."

I: "Have you found out the meaning which is yet to come?"

A: "No, not yet; it's very difficult, but I hope I'll succeed. Sometimes it seems to me that I need the stimulation of others, but I realize that those are temptations of Satan."

I: "Don't you believe that you'd succeed if you were nearer men?"

A: "Perhaps you're right."

He looks at me suddenly as if doubtful and suspicious. "But," he continues, "I love the desert, do you understand? This yellow, sunglowing desert. Here you can see the countenance of the sun every day, you are alone, you can see glorious Helios—no, that is pagan—what's wrong with me? I'm confused—you are Satan—I recognize you—give way, adversary!"

25/26 / He jumps up incensed and wants to lunge at me. But I am far away in the twentieth century.[64]

64. The *Corrected Draft* continues: "and I am unreal to myself as in a dream" (p. 228). Christian anchorites were perpetually on guard against the appearance of Satan. A famous example of temptations by the devil occurs in Athanasius's life of St. Anthony. In 1921 Jung noted that St. Anthony warned his monks "how cleverly the Devil disguised himself in order to bring holy men to their downfall. The Devil is naturally the voice of the anchorite's own unconscious, that rises up against the forcible sup-

[2][HI 26] *He who sleeps in the grave of the millennia dreams a wonderful dream. He dreams a primordially ancient dream. He dreams of the rising sun.*

If you sleep this sleep and dream this dream in this time of the world, you will know that the sun will also rise at this time. For the moment we are still in the dark, but the day is upon us.

He who comprehends the darkness in himself, to him the light is near. He who climbs down into his darkness reaches the staircase of the working light, fire-maned Helios.

His chariot ascends with four white horses, his back bears no cross, and his side no wound, but he is safe and his head blazes in the fire.

Nor is he a man of mockery, but of splendor and unquestionable force.

I do not know what I speak, I speak in a dream. Support me for I stagger, drunk with fire. I drank fire in this night, since I climbed down through the centuries and plunged into the sun far at the bottom. And I rose up drunk from the sun, with a burning countenance and my head is ablaze.

Give me your hand, a human hand, so that you / can hold me to the earth with 26/27
it, for whirling veins of fire swoop me up, and exultant longing tears me toward the zenith.

But day is about to break, actual day, the day of this world. And I remain concealed in the gorge of the earth, deep down and solitary, and in the darkening shadows of the valley. That is the shadow and heaviness of the earth.

How can I pray to the sun, that rises far in the East over the desert? Why should I pray to it? I drink the sun within me, so why should I pray to it? But the desert, the desert in me demands prayers, since the desert wants to satisfy itself with what is alive. I want to beg God for it, the sun, or one of the other immortals.

I beg because I am empty and am a beggar. In the day of this world, I forget that I drank the sun and am drunk from its active light and singeing power. But I stepped into the shadows of the earth, and saw that I am naked and have nothing to cover my pov-

pression of his nature" (*Psychological Types*, CW 6, §82). St. Anthony's experiences were elaborated by Flaubert in his *Temptation of Anthony*, a work with which Jung was familiar (*Psychology and Alchemy*, CW 12, §59).

erty. No sooner do you touch the earth than your inner life is over; it flees from you into things.

And a wondrous life arises in things. What you thought was dead and inanimate betrays a secret life and silent, inexorable intent. You have got caught up in a hustle and bustle where everything goes its own way with strange gestures, beside you, above you, beneath you, and through you; even the stones speak to you, and magical threads spin from you to things and from things to you. Far and near work within you and you work in a dark manner upon the near and the far. And you are always helpless and a prey.

But if you watch closely, you will see what you have never seen before, namely that things live your life, and that they live off you: the rivers bear your life to the valley, one stone falls upon another with your force, plants and animals also grow through you and they are the cause of your death. A leaf dancing in the wind dances with you; the irrational animal[65] guesses your thought and represents you. The whole earth sucks its life from you and everything reflects you again.

Nothing happens in which you are not entangled in a secret manner; for everything has ordered itself around you and plays your innermost. Nothing in you is hidden to things, no matter how remote, how precious, how secret it is. It inheres in things. Your dog robs you of your father, who passed away long ago, and looks at you as he did. The cow in the meadow has intuited your mother, and charms you with total calm and security. The stars whisper your deepest mysteries to you, and the soft valleys of the earth rescue you in a motherly womb.

Like a stray child you stand pitifully among the mighty, who hold the threads of your life. You cry for help and attach yourself to the first person that comes your way. Perhaps he can advise you, perhaps he knows the thought that you do not have, and which all things have sucked out of you.

---

65. An inversion of Aristotle's definition of man as the "rational animal."

I know that you would like to hear the tidings of he whom things have not lived, but who lived and fulfilled himself. For you are a son of the earth, sucked dry by the suckling earth, that can suck nothing out of itself, but suckles only from the sun. Therefore you would like to have tidings of the son of the sun, which shines and does not suckle.

/ You would like to hear of the son of God, who shone and gave, who begot, and 27/28
to whom life was born again, as the earth bears the sun green and colorful children.

You would like to hear of him, the radiating savior, who as a son of the sun cut through the webs of the earth, who sundered the magic threads and released those in bondage, who owned himself and was no one's servant, who sucked no one dry, and whose treasure no one exhausted.

You would like to hear of him who was not darkened by the shadow of earth, but illuminated it, who saw the thoughts of all, and whose thoughts no one guessed, who possessed in himself the meaning of all things, and whose meaning no thing could express.

The solitary fled the world; he closed his eyes, plugged his ears and buried himself in a cave within himself, but it was no use. The desert sucked him dry, the stones spoke his thoughts, the cave echoed his feelings, and so he himself became desert, stone, and cave. And it was all emptiness and desert, and helplessness and barrenness, since he did not shine and remained a son of the earth who sucked a book dry and was sucked empty by the desert. He was desire and not splendor, completely earth and not sun.

Consequently he was in the desert as a clever saint who very well knew that otherwise he was no different from the other sons of the earth. If he would have drunk of himself, he would have drunk fire.

The solitary went into the desert to find himself. But he did not want to find himself, but rather the manifold meaning of holy scripture. You can suck the immensity of the small and the great into yourself, and you will become emptier and emptier, since immense fullness and immense emptiness are one and the same.[66]

66. See Jung's description of the Pleroma, p. 509f, below.

He wanted to find what he needed in the outer. But you find manifold meaning only in yourself, not in things, since the manifoldness of meaning is not something that is given at the same time, but is a succession of meanings. The meanings that follow one another do not lie in things, but lie in you, who are subject to many changes, insofar as you take part in life. Things also change, but you do not notice this if you do not change. But if you change, the countenance of the world alters. The manifold sense of things is your manifold sense. It is useless to fathom it in things. And this probably explains why the solitary went into the desert, and fathomed the thing but not himself.

And therefore what happened to every desirous solitary also happened to him: the devil came to him with smooth tongue and clear reasoning and knew the right word at the right moment. He lured him to his desire. I had to appear to him as the devil, since I had accepted my darkness. I ate the earth and I drank the sun, and I
28/29 became a greening tree that stands alone and grows.[67] /

Death.[68]

Cap. vi.

[HI 29] On the following night,[69] I wandered to the northern land and found myself under a gray sky in misty-hazy cool-moist air. I strive to those lowlands where the weak currents, flashing in broad mirrors, stream toward the sea, where all haste of flowing becomes more and more dampened, and where all power and all striving unites with the immeasurable extent of the sea. The trees become

67. The *Draft* and *Corrected Draft* continue: "But I saw solitude and its beauty, and I seized the life of the inanimate and the meaning of the meaningless. I also understood this side of my manifoldness. And thus my tree grew in the solitude and quiet, eating the earth with roots reaching far down and drinking the sun with branches reaching high up. The solitary [alien] guest entered my soul. But my greening life flooded me. [Thus I wandered, following the nature of the water]. ~~The solitude grew and extended around me. I did not know how unlimited the solitude was, and I wandered and looked. I wanted to fathom the depths of solitude and I went so far until every last sound of life died~~" (p. 235).

68. The *Handwritten Draft* has: *"Fifth Adventure: Death"* (p. 557).

69. January 2, 1914.

sparse, wide swamp meadows accompany the still, murky water, the horizon is unending and lonely, draped by gray clouds. Slowly, with restrained breath, and with the great and anxious expectation of one gliding downward wildly on the foam and pouring himself into endlessness, I follow my brother, the sea. It flows softly and almost imperceptibly, and yet we continually approach the supreme embrace, entering the womb of the source, the boundless expansion and immeasurable depths. Lower yellow hills rise there. A broad dead lake widens at their feet. We wander along the hills quietly and they open up to a dusky, unspeakably remote horizon, where the sky and the sea are fused into infinity.

Someone is standing there, on the last dune. He is wearing a black wrinkled coat; he stands motionless and looks into the distance. I go up to him—he is gaunt and with a deeply serious look in his eyes. I say to him:

"Let me stand beside you for a while, dark one. I recognized you from afar. There is only one who stands this way, so solitary and at the last corner of the world."

He answered: "Stranger, you may well stand by me, if it is not too cold for you. As you can see, I am cold and my heart has never beaten."

"I know, you are ice and the end; you are the cold silence of the stones; and you are the highest snow on the mountains and the most extreme frost of outer space. I must feel this and that's why I stand near you."

"What leads you here to me, you living matter? The living are never guests here. Well, they all flow past here sadly in dense crowds, all those above in the land of the clear day who have taken their departure, / never to return again. But the living never come 29/30
here. What do you seek here?"

"My strange and unexpected path led me here as I happily followed the way of the living stream. And thus I found you. I gather this is your place, your rightful place?"

"Yes, here it leads into the undifferentiable, where none is equal or unequal, but all are one with one another. Do you see what approaches there?"

"I see something like a dark wall of clouds, swimming toward us on the tide."

"Look more closely, what do you recognize?"

"I see densely pressed multitudes of men, old men, women, and children. Between them I see horses, oxen and smaller animals, a cloud of insects swarms around the multitude, a forest swims near, innumerable faded flowers, an utterly dead summer. They are already near; how stiff and cool they all look, their feet do not move, no noise sounds from their closed ranks. They are clasping themselves rigidly with their hands and arms; they are gazing beyond and pay us no heed—they are all flowing past in an enormous stream. Dark one, this vision is awful."

"You wanted to stay by me, so get hold of yourself. Look!"

I see: "The first rows have reached the point where the surf and the stream flow together violently. And it looks as if a wave of air were confronting the stream of the dead together with the surging sea, whirling them up high, scattering them in black scraps, and dissolving them in murky clouds of mist. Wave after wave approaches, and ever new droves dissolve into black air. Dark one, tell me, is this the end?"

"Look!"

The dark sea breaks heavily—a reddish glow spreads out in it—it is like blood—a sea of blood foams at my feet—the depths of the sea glow—how strange I feel—am I suspended by my feet? Is it the sea or is it the sky? Blood and fire mix themselves together in a ball—red light erupts from its smoky shroud—a new sun escapes from the bloody sea, and rolls gleamingly toward the uttermost depths—it disappears under my feet.[70]

I look around me, I am all alone. Night has fallen. What did Ammonius say? Night is the time of silence.

---

70. Cf. the vision in *Liber Primus*, ch. 5, "Descent into Hell in the Future," p. 147.

[2] [HI 30] I looked around me and I saw that the solitude expanded into the immeasurable, and pierced me with horrible coldness. The sun still glowed in me, but I could feel myself stepping into the great shadow. I follow the stream that makes its way into the depths, slowly and unperturbed, into the depths of what is to come.

And thus I went out in that night (it was the second night of the year 1914), and anxious expectation filled me. I went out to embrace the future. The path was wide and what was to come was awful. It was the enormous dying, a sea of blood. From it the new sun arose, awful and a reversal of that which we call day. We have seized the darkness and its sun will shine above us, bloody and burning like a great downfall.

When I comprehended my darkness, a truly magnificent night came over me and my dream plunged me into the depths of the millennia, and from it my phoenix ascended.

But what happened to my day? Torches were kindled, bloody anger and disputes erupted. As darkness seized the world, the terrible war arose and the darkness destroyed the light of the world, since it was incomprehensible to the darkness and good for nothing anymore. And so we had to taste Hell.

I saw which vices the virtues of this time changed into, how your mildness became hard, your goodness became brutality, your love became hate, and your understanding became madness. Why did you want to comprehend the darkness! But you had to or else it would have seized you. Happy the man who anticipates this grasp.

Did you ever think of the evil in you? Oh, you spoke of it, you mentioned it, and you confessed it smilingly, as a generally human vice, or a recurring misunderstanding. But did you know / what 30/31
evil is, and that it stands precisely right behind your virtues, that it is also your virtues themselves, as their inevitable substance?[71] You

71. In 1940 Jung wrote: "Evil is relative, partly avoidable, partly fate; the same goes for virtue and one often does not know which is worst" ("Attempt at a psychological interpretation of the dogma of the trinity," CW 11, §291).

locked Satan in the abyss for a millennium, and when the millennium had passed, you laughed at him, since he had become a children's fairy tale.[72] But if the dreadful great one raises his head, the world winces. The most extreme coldness draws near.

With horror you see that you are defenseless, and that the army of your vices falls powerless to its knees. With the power of daimons, you seize the evil, and your virtues cross over to him. You are completely alone in this struggle, since your Gods have become deaf. You do not know which devils are greater, your vices, or your virtues. But of one thing you are certain, that virtues and vices are brothers.

[73]We need the coldness of death to see clearly. Life wants to live and to die, to begin and to end.[74] You are not forced to live eternally, but you can also die, since there is a will in you for both. Life and death must strike a balance in your existence.[75] Today's men need a large slice of death, since too much incorrectness lives in them, and too much correctness died in them. What stays in balance is correct, what disturbs balance is incorrect. But if balance has been attained, then that which preserves it is incorrect and that which disturbs it is correct. Balance is at once life and death. For the completion of life a balance with death is fitting. If I accept death, then my tree

---

72. In the *Corrected Draft*, this sentence is replaced with: "Evil is one-half of the world, one of the two pans of the scale" (p. 242).
73. The *Draft* continues: "In this bloody battle death steps up to you, just like today where mass killing and dying fill the world. The coldness of death penetrates you. When I froze to death in my solitude, I saw clearly and saw what was to come, as clearly as I could see the stars and the distant mountains on a frosty night" (p. 260).
74. *In Transformations and Symbols of the Libido* (1912), Jung had argued that the libido was not only a Schopenhauerian life urge, but contained the contrary striving toward death within itself (CW B, §696).
75. The *Draft* continues: "To live what is right and to let what is false die, that is the art of life" (p. 261). In 1934 Jung wrote: "Life is an energetic process like any other. But every energetic process is in principle irreversible and therefore unequivocally directed toward a goal, and the goal is the state of rest . . . From the middle of life, only he who is willing to die with life remains living. Since what takes place in the secret hour of life's midday is the reversal of the parabola, the *birth of death* . . . Not wanting to live is identical with not wanting to die. Becoming and passing away is the same curve" ("Soul and death," CW 8, §800). See my "'The boundless expanse': Jung's reflections on life and death," *Quadrant: Journal of the C. G. Jung Foundation for Analytical Psychology* 38 (2008), pp. 9–32.

greens, since dying increases life. If I plunge into the death encompassing the world, then my buds break open. How much our life needs death!

Joy at the smallest things comes to you only when you have accepted death. But if you look out greedily for all that you could still live, then nothing is great enough for your pleasure, and the smallest things that continue to surround you are no longer a joy. Therefore I behold death, since it teaches me how to live.

If you accept death, it is altogether like a frosty night and an anxious misgiving, but a frosty night in a vineyard full of sweet grapes.[76] You will soon take pleasure in your wealth. Death ripens. One needs death to be able to harvest the fruit. Without death, life would be meaningless, since the long-lasting rises again and denies its own meaning. To be, and to enjoy your being, you need death, and limitation enables you to fulfill your being.

[HI 31] When I see the lamentation and nonsense of the earth and consequently enter death with a covered head, then everything I see will indeed turn to ice. But in the shadow world the other rises, the red sun.[77] It rises secretly and unexpectedly, and my world revolves like a satanic apparition. I suspect blood and murder. Blood and murder alone are still exalted, and have their own peculiar beauty; one can assume the beauty of bloody acts of violence.

But it is the unacceptable, the awfully repulsive, that which I have forever rejected that rises in me. For if the wretchedness and poverty of this life ends, another life begins in what is opposed to me. This is opposed to such an extent that I cannot conceive it. For it is opposed not according to the laws of reason, but thoroughly and according to its own nature. Yes, it is not only opposed, but repulsive, invisibly and cruelly repulsive, something that takes my breath away, that drains the power from my muscles, that confuses my

76. See above, note 20, p. 124.
77. A reference to the vision above.

senses, stings me poisonously from behind in the heel, and always strikes just where I did not suspect I possessed a vulnerable spot.[78]

It does not confront me like a strong enemy, manly and dangerously, but I perish on a dung heap, while peaceful chickens cackle around me, amazedly and mindlessly laying their eggs. A dog passes, lifts his leg over me, then trots off calmly. I curse the hour of my birth seven times, and if I do not choose to kill myself on the spot, I prepare to experience the hour of my second birth. The ancients said: *Inter faeces et urinas nascimur.*[79] For three nights I was assaulted by the horrors of birth. On the third night, junglelike laughter pealed forth, for which nothing is too simple. Then life began to stir
31/32 again. /

The Remains of Earlier Temples[80]

Cap. vii.

[HI 32][81, 82]Yet another new adventure occurred: wide meadows spread out before me—a carpet of flowers—soft hills—a fresh green wood in the distance. I come across two strange journeymen—probably two completely accidental companions: an old monk and a tall gangly thin man with a childish gait and discolored red clothes. As they draw near, I recognize the tall one as the red rider. How he has changed! He has grown old, his red hair has become gray, his fiery red clothes are worn out, shabby, poor. And the other? He has

78. In *Transformations and Symbols of the Libido* (1912), Jung commented on the motif of the wounded heel (CW B, §461).
79. "We are born between faeces and urine," a saying widely attributed to St. Augustine, among others.
80. The *Handwritten Draft* has instead: "*Sixth Adventure*" (p. 586). The *Corrected Draft* has instead: "*6. Degenerate Ideals*" (p. 247).
81. The mosaic form resembles the mosaics at Ravenna, which Jung visited in 1913 and 1914, and which made a lasting impression on him.
82. January 5, 1914.

a paunch and appears not to have fallen on bad times. But his face seems familiar: by all the Gods, it's Ammonius!

What changes! And where are these utterly different people coming from? I approach them and bid them good day. Both look at me frightened and make the sign of the cross. Their horror prompts me to look down at myself. I am fully covered in green leaves, which spring from my body. I greet them a second time, laughing.

Ammonius exclaims horrified: "Apage, Satanas!"[83]

The Red One: "Damned pagan riffraff!"

I: "But my dear friends, what's wrong with you? I'm the Hyperborean stranger, who visited you, Oh Ammonius, in the desert.[84] And I'm the watchman whom you, Red One, once visited."

Ammonius: "I recognize you, you supreme devil. My downfall began with you."

The Red One looks at him reproachfully and gives him a poke in the ribs. The monk sheepishly stops. The Red One turns haughtily toward me.

R: "Already at that time I couldn't help thinking that you lacked a noble disposition, notwithstanding your hypocritical seriousness. Your damned Christian play-act—"

At this moment Ammonius pokes him in the ribs and the Red One falls into an embarrassed silence. And thus both stand before me, sheepish and ridiculous, and yet pitiable.

I: "Wherefrom, man of God? What outrageous fate has led you here, let alone in the company of the Red One?"

A: "I would prefer not to tell you. But it does not appear to be a
dispensation of God that one can escape. So know then that you, evil
spirit, have done me a terrible deed. You seduced me with / your 32/33
accursed curiosity, desirously stretching my hand after the divine

83. "Be gone, Satan"—a common expression in the Middle Ages.

84. The Hyperboreans were a race in Greek mythology who lived in a land of sunshine beyond the north wind, worshiping Apollo. Nietzsche referred on several occasions to the free spirits as Hyperboreans, *The Antichrist*, §1 (*Twilight of the Idols/The Antichrist*, tr. R. Hollingdale [London: Penguin, 1990], p. 127).

mysteries, since you made me conscious at that time that I really knew nothing about them. Your remark that I probably needed the closeness of men to arrive at the higher mysteries stunned me like infernal poison. Soon thereafter I called the brothers of the valley together and announced to them that a messenger of God had appeared to me—so terribly had you blinded me—and commanded me to form a monastery with the brothers.

"When Brother Philetus raised an objection, I refuted him with reference to the passage in the holy scriptures where it is said that it is not good for man to be alone.[85] So we founded the monastery, near the Nile, from where we could see the passing ships.

"We cultivated fat fields, and there was so much to do that the holy scriptures fell into oblivion. We became voluptuous, and one day I was filled with such terrible longing to see Alexandria again. I talked myself into believing that I wanted to visit the bishop there. But first I was intoxicated so much by life on the ship, and then by the milling crowds on the streets of Alexandria, that I became completely lost.

"As in a dream I climbed onto a large ship bound for Italy. I felt an insatiable greed to see the world. I drank wine and saw that women were beautiful. I wallowed in pleasure and wholly turned into an animal. When I climbed ashore in Naples, the Red One stood there, and I knew that I had fallen into the hands of evil."

R: "Be silent, old fool, if I had not been present, you would have become an outright pig. When you saw me, you finally pulled yourself together, cursed the drinking and the women, and returned to the monastery.

"Now hear my story, damned hobgoblin: I too fell into your snare, and your pagan arts also enticed me. After the conversation at that time, where you caught me in the fox trap with your remark

85. A reference to Genesis 2:18: "And the Lord God said, It is not good that the man should be alone; I will make him an help meet for him." There is one reference to a Philetus in the Bible, 2 Timothy 2:16–18: "But shun profane and vain babblings: for they will increase unto more ungodliness. And their word will eat as doth a canker: of whom is Hymenaeus and Philetus; Who concerning the truth have erred, saying that the resurrection is past already; and overthrow the faith of some."

about dancing, I became serious, so serious that I went into the monastery, prayed, fasted, and converted myself.

"In my blindness I wanted to reform the Church liturgy, and with the bishop's approval I introduced dancing.

"I became Abbot and, as such, alone had the sole right to dance before the altar, like David before the ark of the covenant.[86] But little by little, the brothers also began to dance; indeed, even the congregation of the faithful and finally the whole city danced.

"It was terrible. I fled into solitude and danced all day until I dropped, but in the morning the hellish dance began again.

"I sought to escape from myself, and strayed and wandered around at night. In the daytime I kept myself secluded, and danced alone in the forests and deserted mountains. And thus gradually I came to Italy. Down there in the south, I no longer felt as I had felt in the north; I could mingle with the crowds. Only in Naples did I somewhat find my way again, and there I also found this ragged man of God. His appearance gave me strength. Through him I could regain my health. You've heard how he took heart from me, too, and found his way again."

A: "I must confess I did not fare so badly with the Red One; he's a toned-down type of devil."

R: "I must add that the monk is hardly the fanatical type, although I've developed a deep aversion against the whole Christian religion since my experience in the monastery."

I: "Dear friends, it does my heart good to see you enjoying yourselves together."

Both: "We are not pleased, mocker and adversary, clear off, you robber, pagan!"

I: "But why are you traveling together, if you're not enjoying each other's company and friendship?"

A: "What can be done? Even the devil is necessary, since otherwise one has nothing that commands a sense of respect with people."

86. In Chronicles 1:15, David dances before the ark of the covenant.

R: "Well, I need to come to an arrangement with the clergy, or else I will lose my clientele."

I: "Therefore the necessities of life have brought you together! So let's make peace and be friends."

Both: "But we can never be friends."

I: "Oh, I see, the system is at fault. You probably want to die out first? Now let me pass, you old ghosts!"

[2] [HI 33] When I had seen death and all the terrible solemnity that is gathered around it, and had become ice and night myself,
an angry life and impulse rose up in me. My thirst for the rushing
water of the deepest knowledge[87] began to clink with wine glasses;
from afar I heard drunken laughter, laughing women and street
33/34 noise. Dance music, / stamping and cheering poured forth from
all over; and instead of the rose-scented south wind, the reek of the
human animal streamed over me. Luscious-lewd whores giggled and
rustled along the walls, wine fumes and kitchen steam and the foolish cackling of the human crowd drew near in a cloud. Hot sticky
tender hands reached out for me, and I was swaddled in the covers of a sickbed. I was born into life from below, and I grew up as
heroes do, in hours rather than years. And after I had grown up, I
found myself in the middle land, and saw that it was spring.

[HI 34] But I was no longer the man I had been, for a strange being grew through me. This was a laughing being of the forest, a leaf green daimon, a forest goblin and prankster, who lived alone in the forest and was itself a greening tree being, who loved nothing but greening and growing, who was neither disposed nor indisposed toward men, full of mood and chance, obeying an invisible law and greening and wilting with the trees, neither beautiful nor ugly, neither good nor bad, merely living, primordially old and yet completely young, naked and yet naturally clothed, not man but nature, frightened, laughable, powerful, childish, weak, deceiving

87. The *Corrected Draft* has "the wisdom" instead of "the deepest knowledge" (p. 251).

and deceived, utterly inconstant and superficial, and yet reaching deep down, down to the kernel of the world.

I had absorbed the life of both of my friends; a green tree grew from the ruins of the temple. They had not withstood life, but, seduced by life, had become their own monkey business. They had got caught in the muck, and so they called the living a devil and traitor. Because both of them believed in themselves and in their own goodness, each in his own way, they ultimately became mired in the natural and conclusive burial ground of all outlived ideals. The most beautiful and the best, like the ugliest and the worst, end up someday in the most laughable place in the world, surrounded by fancy dress and led by fools, and go horror-struck to the pit of filth.

After the cursing comes laughter, so that the soul is saved from the dead.

Ideals are, according to their essence, desired and pondered; they exist to this extent, but only to this extent. Yet their effective being cannot be denied. He who believes he is really living his ideals, or believes he can live them, suffers from delusions of grandeur and behaves like a lunatic in that he stages himself as an ideal; but the hero has fallen. Ideals are mortal, so one should prepare oneself for their end: at the same time it probably costs you your neck. For do you not see that it was you who gave meaning, value, and effective force to your ideal? If you have become a sacrifice to the ideal, then the ideal cracks open, plays carnival with you, and goes to Hell on Ash Wednesday. The ideal is also a tool that one can put aside anytime, a torch on dark paths. But whoever runs around with a torch by day is a fool. How much my ideals have come down, and how freshly my tree greens!

[88]When I turned green, they stood there, the sad remains of earlier temples and rose gardens, and I recognized with a shudder their inner affinity. It seemed to me that they had established an indecent

88. The *Draft* and *Corrected Draft* have: "I had become a victim of my sanctuaries and beauties, and so I died miserable and depressed [therefore death came to me]" (p. 254).

alliance. But I understood that this alliance had already existed for a long time. At a time when I still claimed that my sanctuaries were of crystal purity, and when I compared my friends to the perfume of the roses of Persia,[89] both of them formed an alliance of mutual silence. They seemed to scatter, but secretly they worked together. The solitary silence of the temple lured me far away from men to the supernatural mysteries in which I lost myself to the point of surfeit. And while I struggled with God, the devil prepared himself for my reception, and tore me just as far to his side. There, too, I found no boundaries other than surfeit and disgust. I did not live, but was driven; I was a slave to my ideals.[90]

And thus they stood there, the ruins, quarreling with one another and unable to reconcile themselves to their common misery. Within myself I had become one as a natural being, but I was a hobgoblin[91] who frightened the solitary wanderer, and who avoided the places of men. But I greened and bloomed from within myself. I had still not become a man again who carried within himself the conflict between a longing for the world and a longing for the spirit. I did not live either of these longings, but I lived myself, and was a merrily greening tree in a remote spring forest. And thus I learned to live without the world and spirit; and I was amazed how well I could live like this.

But what about men, what about mankind? There they stood,
the two deserted bridges that should lead across to mankind: one
leads from above to below, and men glide down on it, which pleases
34/35 them. / The other leads from below to above and mankind groans
upward on it. This causes them trouble. We drive our fellow men
to trouble and joy. If I myself do not live, but merely climb, it gives

89. In Persia, the crushed petals of rose were steam-distilled to make rose oil, from which perfumes were made.

90. In 1926, Jung wrote: "The transition from morning to afternoon is a *transvaluation of earlier values*. From this comes the necessity to appreciate the value of the opposite of our former ideals, to recognize the error in former truth and to feel how much antagonism and even hatred lay in what had formerly passed for love for us" (*The Unconscious in Normal and Sick Psychic Life*, CW 7, §115).

91. The *Corrected Draft* has: "green creature" (p. 255).

others undeserved pleasure. If I simply enjoy myself, it causes others undeserved trouble. If I merely live, I am far removed from men. They no longer see me, and when they see me, they are astonished and shocked. I myself, however, quite simply living, greening, blooming, fading, stand like a tree always in the same spot and let the suffering and the joy of men pass over me with equanimity. And yet I am a man who cannot excuse himself from the discord of the human heart.

But my ideals can also be my dogs, whose yapping and squabbling do not disturb me. But at least then I am a good and a bad dog to men. But I have not yet achieved what should be, namely that I live and yet am a man. It seems to be nearly impossible to live as a man. As long as you are not conscious of your self you can live; but if you become conscious of your self, you fall from one grave into another. All your[92] rebirths could ultimately make you[93] sick. The Buddha therefore finally gave up on rebirth, for he had had enough of crawling through all human and animal forms.[94] After all the rebirths you still remain the lion crawling on the earth, the ΧΑΜΑΙ ΛΕΩΝ [Chameleon], a caricature, one prone to changing colors, a crawling shimmering lizard, but precisely not a lion, whose nature is related to the sun, who draws his power from within himself, who does not crawl around in the protective colors of the environment, and who does not defend himself by going into hiding. I recognized the chameleon and no longer want to crawl on the earth and change colors and be reborn; instead I want to exist from my own force, like the sun which gives light and does not suck light. That belongs to

92. The *Corrected Draft* has: "my" (p. 257).

93. The *Corrected Draft* has: "me" (p. 257).

94. The *Corrected Draft* continues: "like a chameleon" (p. 258). A passage occurs here in the *Draft*, a paraphrase of which follows: It is our chameleon nature that forces us through these transformations. So long as we are chameleons, we need an annual journey in the bath of rebirth. Therefore I looked at the outdating of my ideals with horror, since I loved my natural greenness and mistrusted my chameleon skin, which changed colors according to the environment. The chameleon does this cleverly. One calls this change a progress through rebirth. So you experience 777 rebirths. The Buddha did not need quite so long to see that even rebirths are vain (pp. 275–76). There was a belief that the soul had to go through 777 reincarnations (Ernest Woods, *The New Theosophy* [Wheaton, IL: The Theosophical Press, 1929], p. 41).

the earth. I recall my solar nature and would like to rush to my rising. But ruins[95] stand in my way. They say: "With regard to men you should be this or that." My chameleonesque skin shudders. They obtrude upon me and want to color me. But that should no longer be. Neither good nor evil shall be my masters. I push them aside, the laughable survivors, and go on my way again, which leads me to the East. The quarreling powers that for so long stood between me and myself lie behind me.

Henceforth I am completely alone. I can no longer say to you: "Listen!" or "you should," or "you could," but now I talk only with myself. Now no one else can do anything more for me, nothing whatsoever. I no longer have a duty toward you, and you no longer have duties toward me, since I vanish and you vanish from me. I no longer hear requests and no longer make requests of you. I no longer fight and reconcile myself with you, but place silence between you and me.

Your call dies away in the distance, and you cannot find my footprints. Together with the west wind, which comes from the plains of the ocean, I journey across the green countryside, I roam through the forests, and bend the young grass. I talk with trees and the forest wildlife, and the stones show me the way. When I thirst and the source does not come to me, I go to the source. When I starve and the bread does not come to me, I seek my bread and take it where I find it. I provide no help and need no help. If at any time necessity confronts me, I do not look around to see whether there is a helper nearby, but I accept the necessity and bend and writhe and struggle. I laugh, I weep, I swear, but I do not look around me.

On this way, no one walks behind me, and I cross no one's path. I am alone, but I fill my solitariness with my life. I am man enough, I am noise, conversation, comfort, and help enough unto myself. And so I wander to the far East. Not that I know anything about what my distant goal might be. I see blue horizons before me: they

95. The *Draft* has instead: "the vestige of my ideal" (p. 277).

suffice as a goal. I hurry toward the East and my rising—I will my rising. / [Image 36][96] / 35/37

First Day

Cap. viii.[97]

[HI 37] But on the third night,[98] a desolate mountain range blocks my way, though a narrow valley gorge allows me to enter. The way leads inevitably between two high rock faces. My feet are bare and injure themselves on the jagged rocks. Here the path becomes slippery. One-half of the way is white, the other black. I step onto the black side and recoil horrified: it is hot iron. I step onto the white half: it is ice. But so it must be. I dart across and onward, and finally the valley widens into a mighty rocky basin. A narrow path winds up along vertical rocks to the mountain ridge at the top.

As I approach the top, a mighty booming resounds from the other side of the mountain like ore being pounded. The sound gradually swells, and echoes thunderously in the mountain. As I reach the pass, I see an enormous man approach from the other side.

Two bull horns rise from his great head, and a rattling suit of armor covers his chest. His black beard is ruffled and decked with exquisite stones. The giant is carrying a sparkling double axe in his hand, like those used to strike bulls. Before I can recover from my amazed fright, the giant is standing before me. I look at his face: it is

96. Image legend: "This image was printed on Christmas 1915." The depiction of Izdubar strongly resembles an illustration of him in Wilhelm Roscher's *Ausführliches Lexikon der Griechischen und Römischen Mythologie*, of which Jung possessed a copy ([Leipzig: Teubner, 1884–1937], vol. 2, p. 775). Izdubar was an early name given the figure now known as Gilgamesh. This was based on a mistranscription. In 1906 Peter Jensen noted: "It has now been established that Gilgamesch is the chief protagonist of the epic, and not Gistchubar or Izdubar as assumed previously" (*Das Gilgamesch-Epos in der Weltliteratur* [Strassburg: Karl Trübner, 1906], p. 2). Jung had discussed the Gilgamesh epic in 1912 in *Transformations and Symbols of the Libido*, using the corrected form, and cited Jensen's work several times.

97. The *Handwritten Draft* has instead: "*Seventh Adventure. First Day*" (p. 626). The *Corrected Draft* has instead: "7. The Great Encounter. First Day. The Hero from the East" (p. 262).

98. January 8, 1914.

faint and pale and deeply wrinkled. His almond-shaped eyes look at me astonished. Horror takes hold of me: this is Izdubar, the mighty, the bull-man. He stands and looks at me: his face speaks of consuming inner fear, and his hands and knees tremble. Izdubar, the powerful bull trembling? Is he frightened? I call out to him:

"Oh, Izdubar, most powerful, spare my life and forgive me for lying like a worm in your path."

Iz: "I do not want your life. Where do you come from?"

I: "I come from the West."

Iz: "You come from the West? Do you know of the Western lands? Is this the right way to the Western lands?"[99]

I: "I come from a Western land, whose coast washes against the great Western sea."

Iz: "Does the sun sink in that sea? Or does it touch the solid land in its decline?"

I: "The sun sinks far beyond the sea."

Iz: "Beyond the sea? What lies there?"

I: "There is nothing but empty space there. As you know, the earth is round and moreover it turns around the sun."

Iz: "Damned one, where do you get such knowledge? So there is no immortal land where the sun goes down to be reborn? Are you speaking the truth?"

His eyes flicker with fury and fear. He steps a thundering pace closer. I tremble.

I: "Oh, Izdubar, most powerful one, forgive my presumptuousness, but I'm really speaking the truth. I come from a land where this is proven science and where people live who travel round the world with their ships. Our scholars know through measurement how far the sun is from each point of the surface of the earth. It is a celestial body that lies unspeakably far out in unending space."

99. In Egyptian mythology, the Western lands (the Western bank of the Nile) were the land of the dead.

Iz: "Unending—did you say? Is the space of the world unending, and we can never reach the sun?"

I: "Most powerful one, insofar as you are mortal, you can never reach the sun."

I see him overcome with suffocating fear.

Iz: "I am mortal—and I shall never reach the sun, and never reach immortality?"

He smashes his axe with a powerful, clanging blow on the rock.

Iz: "Be gone, miserable weapon. You are not much use. How should you be of use against infinity, against the eternal void, / and 37/38
against the unreplenishible? There is no one left for you to conquer. Smash yourself, what's it worth!"

(In the West the sun sinks into the lap of glowing clouds in bright crimson.)

"So go away, sun, thrice-damned God, and wrap yourself in your immortality!"

(He snatches the smashed piece of his axe from the ground and hurls it toward the sun.)

"Here you have your sacrifice, your last sacrifice!"

He collapses and sobs like a child. I stand shaking and hardly dare stir.

Iz: "Miserable worm, where did you suckle on this poison?"

I: "Oh Izdubar, most powerful one, what you call poison is science. In our country we are nurtured on it from youth, and that may be one reason why we haven't properly flourished and remain so dwarfish. When I see you, however, it seems to me as if we are all somewhat poisoned."[100]

Iz: "No stronger being has ever cut me down, no monster has ever resisted my strength. But your poison, worm, which you have placed in my way has lamed me to the marrow. Your magical poi-

100. In *The Gay Science*, Nietzsche argued that thinking originated through the cultivation and uniting of several impulses which had the effect of poisons: the impulse to doubt, to negate, to wait, to collect, and to dissolve ("On the doctrine of poisons," tr. Walter Kaufmann [New York: Vintage, 1974] book 3, section 113).

son is stronger than the army of Tiamat."[101] (He lies as if paralyzed, stretched out on the ground.) "You Gods, help, here lies your son, cut down by the invisible serpent's bite in his heel. Oh, if only I had crushed you when I saw you, and never heard your words."

I: "Oh Izdubar, great and pitiable one, had I known that my knowledge could cut you down, I would have held my tongue. But I wanted to speak the truth."

Iz: "You call poison truth? Is poison truth? Or is truth poison? Do not our astrologers and priests also speak the truth? And yet theirs does not act like poison."

I: "Oh Izdubar, night is falling, and it will get cold up here. Shall I not fetch you help from men?"

Iz: "Let it be, and answer me instead."

I: "But we cannot philosophize here, of all places. Your wretched condition demands help."

Iz: "I say to you, let it be. If I should perish this night, so be it. Just give me an answer."

I: "I'm afraid, my words are weak, if they are to heal."

Iz: "They cannot bring about something more grave. The disaster has already happened. So tell me what you know. Perhaps you even have a magic word that counteracts the poison."

I: "My words, Oh most powerful one, are poor and have no magical power."

Iz: "No matter, speak!"

I: "I don't doubt that your priests speak the truth. It is certainly a truth, only it runs contrary to our truth."

Iz: "Are there then two sorts of truth?"

I: "It seems to me to be so. Our truth is that which comes to us from the knowledge of outer things. The truth of your priests is that which comes to you from inner things."

Iz (half sitting up): "That was a salutary word."

---

101. In Babylonian mythology, Tiamat, the mother of the Gods, waged war with an army of demons.

I: "I'm fortunate that my weak words have relieved you. Oh, if only I knew many more words that could help you. It has now grown cold and dark. I'll make a fire to warm us."

Iz: "Do that, as it might help." (I gathered wood and lit a big fire.) "The holy fire warms me. Now tell me, how did you make a fire so swiftly and mysteriously?"

I: "All I need are matches. Look, they are small pieces of wood with a special substance at the tip. Rubbing them against the box produces fire."

Iz: "That is astonishing, where did you learn this art?"

I: "Everyone has matches where I come from. But this is the least of it. We can also fly with the help of useful machines." / 38/39

Iz: "You can fly like birds? If your words did not contain such powerful magic, I would say to you, you were lying."

I: "I'm certainly not lying. Look, I also have a timepiece, for example, which shows the exact time of day."

Iz: "This is wonderful. It is clear that you come from a strange and marvelous land. You certainly come from the blessed Western lands. Are you immortal?"

I: "I—immortal? There is nothing more mortal than we are."

Iz: "What? You are not even immortal and yet you understand such arts?"

I: "Unfortunately our science has still not yet succeeded in finding a method against death."

Iz: "Who then taught you such arts?"

I: "In the course of the centuries men have made many discoveries, through precise observation and the science of outer things."

Iz: "But this science is the awful magic that has lamed me. How can it be that you are still alive even though you drink from this poison every day?"

I: "We've grown accustomed to this over time, because men get used to everything. But we're still somewhat lamed. On the other hand, this science also has great advantages, as you've seen. What we've lost in terms of force, we've rediscovered many times through mastering the force of nature."

Iz: "Isn't it pathetic to be so wounded? For my part, I draw my own force from the force of nature. I leave the secret force to the cowardly conjurers and womanly magicians. If I crush another's skull to pulp, that will stop his awful magic."

I: "But don't you realize how the touch of our magic has worked upon you? Terribly, I think."

Iz: "Unfortunately, you are right."

I: "Now you perhaps see that we had no choice. We had to swallow the poison of science. Otherwise we would have met the same fate as you have: we'd be completely lamed, if we encountered it unsuspecting and unprepared. This poison is so insurmountably strong that everyone, even the strongest, and even the eternal Gods, perish because of it. If our life is dear to us, we prefer to sacrifice a piece of our life force rather than abandon ourselves to certain death."

Iz: "I no longer think that you come from the blessed Western lands. Your country must be desolate, full of paralysis and renunciation. I yearn for the East, where the pure source of our life-giving wisdom flows."

We sit silently at the flickering fire. The night is cold. Izdubar groans and looks up at the starry sky above.

Iz: "Most terrible day of my life—unending—so long—so long—wretched magical art—our priests know nothing, or else they could have protected me from it—even the Gods die, he says. Have you no Gods anymore?"

I: "No, words are all we have."

Iz: "But are these words powerful?"

I: "So they claim, but one notices nothing of this."

Iz: "We do not see the Gods either and yet we believe that they exist. We recognize their workings in natural events."

I: "Science has taken from us the capacity of belief."[102]

Iz: "What, you have lost that, too? How then do you live?"

102. The issue of the relation of science to belief was critical in Jung's psychology of religion. See "Psychology and religion" (1938), CW 11.

I: "We live thus, with one foot in the cold and one foot in the hot, and for the rest, come what may!"

Iz: "You express yourself darkly."

I: "So it also is with us, it is dark."

Iz: "Can you bear it?"

I: "Not particularly well. I personally don't find myself at ease with it. For that reason, I've set out to the East, to the land of the rising sun, to seek the light that we lack. Where then does the sun rise?"

Iz: "The earth is, as you say, completely round. Thus the sun rises nowhere."

I: "I mean, do you have the light that we lack?"/ 39/40

Iz: "Look at me: I flourish in the light of the Eastern world. From this you can measure how fruitful this light is. But if you come from such a dark land, then beware of such an overpowering light. You could go blind just as we all are somewhat blind."

I: "If your light is as fantastic as you are, then I will be careful."

Iz: "You do well by this."

I: "I long for your truth."

Iz: "As I long for the Western lands. I warn you."

Silence descends. It is late at night. We fall asleep next to the fire.

[2] [HI 40] I wandered toward the South and found the unbearable heat of solitude with myself. I wandered toward the North and found the cold death from which all the world dies. I withdrew to my Western land, where the men are rich in knowing and doing, and I began to suffer from the sun's empty darkness. And I threw everything from me and wandered toward the East, where the light rises daily. I went to the East like a child. I did not ask, I simply waited.

Cheerful flowery meadows and lovely spring forests hemmed my path. But in the third night, the heaviness came. It stood before me like a range of cliffs full of sorrowful desolation, and everything tried to deter me from following my life's path. But I found the entrance and the narrow way. The torment was great, since it was not for nothing that I had pushed the two dissipated and dissolute ones away from me. I unsuspectingly absorb what I reject. What I accept enters that part of my soul which I do not know; I accept what I do to myself, but I reject what is done to me.

So the path of my life led me beyond the rejected opposites, united in smooth and—alas!—extremely painful sides of the way which lay before me. I stepped on them but they burned and froze my soles. And thus I reached the other side. But the poison of the serpent, whose head you crush, enters you through the wound in your heel; and thus the serpent becomes more dangerous than it was before. Since whatever I reject is nevertheless in my nature. I thought it was without, and so I believed that I could destroy it. But it resides in me and has only assumed a passing outer form and stepped toward me. I destroyed its form and believed that I was a conqueror. But I have not yet overcome myself.

The outer opposition is an image of my inner opposition. Once I realize this, I remain silent and think of the chasm of antagonism in my soul. Outer oppositions are easy to overcome. They indeed exist, but nevertheless you can be united with yourself. They will indeed burn and freeze your soles, but only your soles. It hurts, but you continue and look toward distant goals.

As I rose to the highest point and my hope wanted to look out toward the East, a miracle happened: as I moved toward the East, one from the East hurried toward me and strove toward the sinking light. I wanted light, he wanted night. I wanted to rise, he wanted to sink. I was dwarfish like a child, while he was enormous like an elementally powerful hero. Knowledge lamed me, while he was blinded by the fullness of the light. And so we hurried toward each other; he, from the light; I, from the darkness; he, strong; I, weak; he, God; I, serpent; he, ancient; I, utterly new; he, unknowing; I, knowing; he, fantastic; I, sober; he, brave, powerful; I, cowardly, cunning. But we were both astonished to see one another on the border between morning and evening.

I was a child and grew like a greening tree and let the wind and
distant cries and commotion of opposites / blow calmly through 40/41
my branches, I was a boy and mocked fallen heroes, I was a youth pushing aside their clutching grips left and right, and so I did not anticipate the Powerful, Blind, and Immortal One, who wandered longingly after the sinking sun, who wanted to cleave the ocean down to its bottom so he could descend into the source of life. That which hurries toward the rising is small, that which approaches the descent is great. Hence I was small, since I simply came from the depths of my descent. I had been where he yearned to be. He who descends is great, and it would be easy for him to smash me. A God who looks like the sun does not hunt worms. But the worm aims at the heel of the Powerful One and will prepare him for the descent that he needs. His power is great and blind. He is marvelous to look at and frightening. But the serpent finds its spot. A little poison and the great one falls. The words of the one who rises have no sound and taste bitter. It is not a sweet poison, but one that is fatal for all Gods.

Alas, he is my dearest, most beautiful friend, he who rushes across, pursuing the sun and wanting to marry himself with the immeasurable mother as the sun does. How closely akin, indeed how completely one are the serpent and the God! The word which was our deliverer has become a deadly weapon, a serpent that secretly stabs.

No longer do outer opposites stand in my way, but my own opposite comes toward me, and rises up hugely before me, and we block each other's way. The word of the serpent certainly defeats the danger, but my way remains barred, since I then had to fall from paralysis into blindness, just as the Powerful One fell into paralysis to escape his blindness. I cannot reach the blinding power of the sun, just as he, the Powerful One, cannot reach the ever-fruitful womb of darkness. I seem to be denied power, while he is denied rebirth, but I escape the blindness that comes with power and he escapes the nothingness that comes with death. My hope for the fullness of the light shatters, just as his longing for boundless conquered life shatters. I had felled the strongest, and the God climbs down to mortality.

[OB 41] *The Mighty One fell, he lies on the ground.*[103]

Power must subside for the sake of life.

The circumference of outer life should be made smaller.

Much more secrecy, solitary fires, fire, caverns, dark wide forests, sparsely peopled settlements, quietly flowing streams, silent winter and summer nights, small ships and carriages, and secure in dwellings the rare and precious.

From afar wanderers walk along solitary roads, looking here and there.

41/42 *Hurrying becomes impossible, patience grows.* /

[OB 42] *The noise of the days of the world falls silent, and the warming fire blazes inside.*

Sitting at the fire, the shades of those gone before wail softly and give news of the past.

Come to the solitary fire, you blind and lame ones and hear of both kinds of truth: the blind will be lamed and the lamed will be blinded, yet the shared fire warms both in the lengthening night.

An old secret fire burns between us, giving sparse light and ample warmth.

The primordial fire that conquers every necessity shall burn again, since the night of the world is wide and cold, and the need is great.

The well-protected fire brings together those from far away and those who are cold, those who do not see one another and cannot reach one another, and it conquers suffering and shatters need.

The words uttered at the fire are ambiguous and deep and show life the right way.

The blind shall be lamed, so that he will not run into the abyss, and the lamed shall be blind, so that he will not look at things beyond his reach with longing and contempt.

103. The *Draft* continues: "This is what I saw in the dream" (p. 295).

Both may be aware of their deep helplessness so that they will respect the holy fire again, as well as the shades sitting at the hearth, and the words that encircle the flames.

The ancients called the saving word the Logos, an expression of divine reason.[104] So much unreason / was in man that he needed reason to be saved. If one waits long enough, one sees how the Gods all change into serpents and underworld dragons in the end. This is also the fate of the Logos: in the end it poisons us all. In time, we were all poisoned, but unknowingly we kept the One, the Powerful One, the eternal wanderer in us away from the poison. We spread poison and paralysis around us in that we want to educate all the world around us into reason. 42/43

Some have their reason in thinking, others in feeling. Both are servants of Logos, and in secret become worshipers of the serpent.[105]

You can subjugate yourself, shackle yourself in irons, whip yourself bloody every day: you have crushed yourself, but not overcome yourself. Precisely through this you have helped the Powerful One, strengthened your paralysis, and promoted his blindness. He would like to see it in others, and inflict it on them, and would like to force the Logos on you and others, longingly and tyrannically with blind obstinacy and vacant stubborness. Give him a taste of Logos. He is afraid, and he already trembles from afar since he suspects that he has become outdated, and that a tiny droplet of the poison of Logos will paralyze him. But because he is your beautiful, much loved brother, you will act slavishly toward him and you would like to spare him as you have spared none of your fellow men. You spared no merry and no powerful means to strike your fellow men with the poisoned arrow. Paralyzed game is an unworthy prey. The powerful huntsman, who wrestles the bull to the ground and tears the

104. See *Liber Secundus*, ch. 4, p. 268f.
105. In *Psychological Types* (1921), Jung considered thinking and feeling to be the rational functions (CW 6, §731).

lion to pieces and strikes the army of Tiamat, is your bow's worthy target.[106]

If you live as he whom you are, He will come running against you impetuously, and you can hardly miss him. He will lay violent hands on you and force you into slavery if you do not remember your terrible weapon, which you have always used in his service against yourself. You will be cunning, terrible, and cold if you make the beautiful and much loved fall. But you should not kill him, even if he suffers and writhes in unbearable agony. Bind the holy Sebastian to a tree and slowly and rationally shoot arrow after arrow into his twitching flesh.[107] When you do so, remind yourself that each arrow that strikes him spares one of your dwarfish and lame brothers. So you may shoot many arrows. But there is a misunderstanding that occurs all too frequently and is almost ineradicable: Men always want to destroy the beautiful and much loved outside of themselves, but never within themselves.

He, the beautiful and most loved one, came to me from the East, from just that place which I was seeking to reach. Admiringly I saw his power and magnificence, and I recognized that he was striving for precisely what I had abandoned, namely my dark human milling crowd of abjection. I recognized the blindness and unknowingness of his striving which worked against my desire, and I opened his eyes and lamed his powerful limbs with a poisoned stab. And he lay crying like a child, as that which he was, a child, a primordial grown child that required human Logos. So he lay before me, helpless, my blind God, who had become half-seeing and paralyzed. And com-

106. The *Draft* continues: "As David, you may slay him, Goliath, with a cunning and impudent slingshot" (p. 299). In *Transformations and Symbols of the Libido* (CW B, §383f), Jung discussed the Babylonian creation myth in which Marduk, the God of spring, battles with Tiamat and her army. Marduk slayed Tiamat, and from this he created the world. Thus "the mighty huntsman" corresponds to Marduk.

107. St. Sebastian was a Christian martyr persecuted by the Romans who lived in the third century. He was often depicted tied to a tree and shot with arrows. The earliest such representation is in the Basilica Sant'Apollinaire Nuova in Ravenna.

passion seized me, since it was plain to me that I should not let him die, he who approached me from the rising, from that place where he could be well, but which I could never reach. He whom I sought I now possessed. The East could give me nothing other than him, the sick and fallen one.

You need to undertake only half of the way, he will undertake the other half. If you go beyond him, blindness will befall you. If he goes beyond you, paralysis will befall him. Therefore, and insofar as it is the manner of the Gods to go beyond mortals, they become paralyzed, and become as helpless as children. Divinity and humanity should remain preserved, if man should remain before the God, and the God remain before man. The high-blazing flame is the middle way, whose luminous course runs between the human and the divine.

The divine primordial power is blind, since its face has become human. The human is the face of the Godhead. If the God comes near you, then plead for your life to be spared, since the God is loving horror. The ancients said: it is terrible to fall into the hands of the living God.[108] They spoke thus because they knew, since they were still close to the ancient forest, and they turned green like the trees in a childlike manner and ascended far away toward the East. / 43/44

Consequently they fell into the hands of the living God. They learned to kneel and to lie with their faces down, to beg for pity, and they learned to live in servile fear and to be grateful. But he who saw him, the terrible beautiful one with his black velvet eyes and the long eyelashes, the eyes that do not see but merely gaze lovingly and fearfully, he has learned to cry out and whimper, so that he can at least reach the ear of the Godhead. Only your fearful cry can stop the God. And then you see that the God also trembles,

108. This refers to Hebrews 10:31: "It is a fearful thing to fall into the hands of the living God."

since he stands confronting his face, his observing gaze in you, and he feels unknown power. The God is afraid of man.

If my God is lamed, I must stand by him, since I cannot abandon the much-loved. I sense that he is my lot, my brother, who abided and grew in the light while I was in the darkness and fed myself with poison. It is good to know such things: if we are surrounded by night, our brother stands in the fullness of the light, doing his great deeds, tearing up the lion and killing the dragon. And he draws his bow against ever more distant goals, until he becomes aware of the sun wandering high up in the sky and wants to catch it. But when he has discovered his valuable prey, then your longing for the light also awakens. You discard the fetters and take yourself to the place of the rising light. And thus you rush toward each other. He believed he could simply capture the sun and encountered the worm of the shadows. You thought that in the East you could drink from the source of the light, and catch the horned giant, before whom you fall to your knees. His essence is blind excessive longing and tempestuous force. My essence is seeing limitation and the incapacity of cleverness. He possesses in abundance what I lack. Consequently I will also not let him go, the Bull God, who once wounded Jacob's hip and whom I have now lamed.[109] I want to make his force my own.

It is therefore prudent to keep alive the severely afflicted so that his force continues to support me. We miss nothing more than divine force. We say, "Yes, indeed, this is how it should or could be. This or that should be achieved." We speak thus and stand thus, and look about us embarrassed, to see whether somehow something

109. This refers to Jacob's wrestling with the angel in Genesis 32:24–29: "And Jacob was left alone; and there wrestled a man with him until the breaking of the day. And when he saw that he prevailed not against him, he touched the hollow of his thigh; and the hollow of Jacob's thigh was out of joint, as he wrestled with him. And he said, Let me go, for the day breaketh. And he said, I will not let thee go, except thou bless me. And he said unto him, What is thy name? And he said, Jacob. And he said, Thy name shall be called no more Jacob, but Israel: for as a prince hast thou power with God and with men, and hast prevailed. And Jacob asked him, and said, Tell me, I pray thee, thy name. And he said, Wherefore is it that thou dost ask after my name? And he blessed him there."

will occur. And should something happen, we look on and say: "Yes, indeed, we understand, it is this or that, or it is similar to this or that." And thus we speak and stand and look around to see whether somewhere something might happen. Something always happens, but we do not happen, since our God is sick. We have seen him dead with the venomous gaze of the Basilisk on his face, and we have understood that he is dead. We must think of his healing. And yet again I feel it quite clearly that my life would have broken in half had I failed to heal my God. Hence I abided with him in the long cold night. [Image 44] / [Image 45][110] / 44/46

Second Day

Cap. ix.

[HI 46] No dream gave me the saving word.[111] Izdubar lay silent and stiff all night, until daybreak.[112] I paced the mountain ridge, pondering, and looked back to my Western lands, where there is so much knowledge and so much possibility of help. I love Izdubar, and I do not want him to wither away miserably. But where should help come from? No one will travel the hot-cold path. And I? I am afraid

---

110. Image legend: "Arthava-veda 4,1,4." *Arthava-veda* 4,1,4 is a charm to promote virility: "Thee, the plant, which the Gandharva dug up for Varuna, when his virility had decayed, thee, that causest strength, we dig up. / Ushas (Aurora), Sûrya (the sun), and this charm of mine; the bull Pragâpati (the lord of creatures) shall with his lusty fire arouse him! / This herb shall make thee so very full of lusty strength, that thou shalt, when thou art excited, exhale heat as a thing on fire! / The fire of the plants, and the essence of the bulls shall arouse him! Do thou, O Indra, controller of bodies, place the lusty force of men into this person! / Thou (O herb) art the first-born sap of the waters and also of the plants. Moreover thou art the brother of Soma, and the lusty force of the antelope buck! / Now, O Agni, now, O Savitar, now, O goddess Sarasvatî, now, O Brahmanaspati, do thou stiffen the pasas as a bow! / I stiffen thy pasas as a bowstring upon the bow. Embrace thou (women) as the antelope buck the gazelle with ever unfailing (strength)! / The strength of the horse, the mule, the goat and the ram, moreover the strength of the bull bestow upon him, O controller of bodies (Indra)!" (*Sacred Books of the East* 42, pp. 31–32) The connection is to the healing of Izdubar, the wounded bull God.

111. The *Handwritten Draft* has instead: "I have slept little; unclear dreams upset me more than they have prompted the redeeming word" (p. 686).

112. January 9, 1914.

to return to that path. And in the East? Was there possibly help there? But what about the unknown dangers that loomed there? I do not want to go blind. What use would that be to Izdubar? I cannot carry this lamed one as a blind man either. Yes, if I were powerful like Izdubar. What use is science here?

Toward evening I went up to Izdubar and spoke to him: "Izdubar, my prince, listen! I will not let you decline. The second evening is falling. We have no food and we are bound to die if I cannot find help. We cannot expect any help from the West, but help is possible from the East. Did you meet anyone on your way whom we could call on for help?"

Iz: "Let it be, may death come when it will."

I: "My heart bleeds at the thought of leaving you here without having done the upmost to help you."

Iz: "What help is your magical power to you? If you were strong, as I am, you could carry me. But your poison can only destroy and not help."

I: "If we were in my land, swift wagons could bring us help."

Iz: "If we were in my land, your poisoned barb would not have reached me."

I: "Tell me, do you know of no help from the side of the East?"

Iz: "The way there is long and lonely, and when you reach the plains after crossing the mountains, you will meet the powerful sun which will blind you."

I: "But what if I wandered by night and if I sheltered from the sun during the day?"

Iz: "In the night all the serpents and dragons crawl out of their holes and you, unarmed, will inevitably fall victim to them. Let it be! How would this help? My legs have withered and are numb. I prefer not to bring home the booty of this journey."

I: "Should I not risk everything?"

Iz: "Useless! Nothing is gained if you die."

I: "Let me think it over a bit, perhaps a saving thought will yet come to me."

I withdraw and sit down on a rock high above on the ridge of the mountain. And this speech began in me: Great Izdubar, you are in a hopeless position—and I no less.[113] What can be done? It is not always necessary to act; sometimes thinking is better. I am basically convinced that Izdubar is hardly real in the ordinary sense, but is a fantasy. It would help if the situation were considered from another angle . . . considered . . . considered . . . it is remarkable that even here thoughts echo; one must be quite alone. But this will hardly last. He will of course not accept that he is a fantasy, but instead claim that he is completely real and that he can only be helped in a real way: nevertheless, it would be worth trying this means once. I will appeal to him:

I: "My prince, Powerful One, listen: a thought came to me that might save us. I think that you are not at all real, but only a fantasy."

Iz: "I am terrified by this thought. It is murderous. Do you even mean to declare me unreal / —now that you have lamed me so 46/47
pitifully?"

I: "Perhaps I have not made myself clear enough, and have spoken too much in the language of the Western lands. I do not mean to say that you are not real at all, of course, but only as real as a fantasy. If you could accept this, much would be gained."

Iz: "What would be gained by this? You are a tormenting devil."

I: "Pitiful one, I will not torment you. The hand of the doctor does not seek to torment even if it causes grief. Can you really not accept that you are a fantasy?"

Iz: "Woe betide me! In what magic do you want to entangle me? Should it help me if I take myself for a fantasy?"

I: "You know that the name one bears means a lot. You also know that one often gives the sick new names to heal them, for with the new name, they come by a new essence. Your name is your essence."

Iz: "You are right, our priests also say this."

113. The *Draft* continues: "thus spoke another voice in me, like an echo" (p. 309).

I: "So are you prepared to admit that you are a fantasy?"

Iz: "If it helps—yes."

The inner voice now spoke to me as follows: while admittedly he is a fantasy now, the situation remains extremely complex. A fantasy cannot be simply negated and treated with resignation either. It calls for action. Anyway, he is a fantasy—and thus considerably more volatile—I think I can see a way forward: I can take him on my back for now. I went to Izdubar and said to him:

"A way has been found. You have become light, lighter than a feather. Now I can carry you." I put my arms round him and lift him up from the ground; he is lighter than air, and I struggle to keep my feet on the ground since my load lifts me up into the air.

Iz: "That was a masterstroke. Where are you carrying me?"

I: "I am going to carry you down into the Western land. My comrades will happily accommodate such a large fantasy. Once we have crossed the mountains and have reached the houses of hospitable men, I can calmly go about finding a means to restore you completely again."

Carrying him on my back, I climb down the small rock path with great care, more in danger of being whirled aloft by the wind than of losing balance because of my load and plunging down the mountainside. I hang on to my all too lightweight load. finally we reach the bottom of the valley and the way of the hot and cold pain. But this time I am blown by a whistling East wind down through the narrow rocks and across the fields toward inhabited places, making no contact with the painful way. Spurred on, I hasten through beautiful lands. I see two people ahead of me: Ammonius and the Red One. When we are right behind them, they turn round and run off into the fields with horrified cries. I must have proved a strange sight indeed.

Iz: "Who are these misshapen ones? Are these your comrades?"

I: "These are not men, they are so-called relics of the past which one still often encounters in the Western lands. They used to be very important. They're now used mostly as shepherds."

Iz: "What a wondrous country! But look, isn't that a town? Don't you want to go there?"

I: "No, God forbid. I don't want a crowd to gather, since the enlightened live there. Can't you smell them? They're actually dangerous, since they cook the strongest poisons from which even I must protect myself. The people there are totally paralyzed, wrapped in a brown poisonous vapor and can only move with artificial means. / But 47/48
you need not worry. Night has almost fallen and no one will see us. Moreover, no one would admit to having seen me. I know an out of the way house here. I have close friends there who will take us in for the night."

Izdubar and I come to a quiet dark garden and a secluded house. I hide Izdubar under the drooping branches of a tree, go up to the door of the house, and knock. I ponder the door: it is much too small. I will never be able to get Izdubar through it. Yet—a fantasy takes up no space! Why did this excellent thought not occur to me earlier? I return to the garden and with no difficulty squeeze Izdubar into the size of an egg and put him in my pocket. Then I walk into the welcoming house where Izdubar should find healing.

[2][HI 48][114] Thus my God found salvation. He was saved precisely by what one would actually consider fatal, namely by declaring him a figment of the imagination. How often has it been assumed that the Gods have been brought to their end in this way.[115] This was obviously a serious mistake, since this was precisely what saved the God. He did not pass away, but became a living fantasy, whose workings I could feel on my own body: my inherent heaviness

114. This refers to a scene in the text describing how Jung reduced Izdubar to the size of an egg so he could secretly carry Izdubar into the house and enable his healing. Jung said to Aniela Jaffé concerning these sections that some of the fantasies were driven by fear, such as the chapter on the devil and the chapter on Gilgamesh-Izdubar. From one perspective it was stupid that he had to find a way to help the giant, but he felt that if he didn't do so, he would have failed. He paid for the ridiculous solution through realizing that he had captured a God. Many of these fantasies were a hellish combination of the sublime and the ridiculous (*MP*, p. 147–48).

115. In the *Draft*, this sentence reads: "Like many other Gods and on numerous previous occasions, the God was declared to be a fantasy, and it was thus assumed that he had been dealt with" (p. 314).

faded and the hot and cold way of pain no longer burned and froze my soles. The weight no longer kept me pressed to the ground, but instead the wind carried me lightly like a feather, while I carried the giant.[116]

One used to believe that one could murder a God. But the God was saved, he forged a new axe in the fire, and plunged again into the flood of light of the East to resume his ancient cycle.[117] But we clever men crept around lamed and poisoned, and did not even know that we lacked something. But I loved my God, and took him to the house of men, since I was convinced that he also really lived as a fantasy, and should therefore not be left behind, wounded and sick. And hence I experienced the miracle of my body losing its heaviness when I burdened myself with the God.

St. Christopher, the giant, bore his burden with difficulty, despite the fact that he bore only the Christ child.[118] But I was as small as a child and bore a giant, and yet my burden lifted me up. The Christ child became an easy burden for the giant Christopher, since Christ himself said, "My yoke is sweet, and my burden is light."[119] We should not bear Christ as he is unbearable, but we should be Christs, for then our yoke is sweet and our burden easy. This tangible and apparent world is one reality, but fantasy is the other reality. So long as we leave the God outside us apparent and tangible, he is unbearable and hopeless. But if we turn the God into fantasy, he is in us and is easy to bear. The God outside us increases the weight of everything heavy, while the God within us lightens

116. The *Draft* continues: "We men apparently believed that there is no such thing as a fantasy, and if we declared something to be fantastic, then it would be well and truly destroyed" (p. 314). In 1932, Jung commented on the contemporary disparagement of fantasy ("The development of the personality," CW 17, §302).

117. This seems to refer to the following chapter.

118. St. Christopher (Greek for "Christ bearer") was a martyr in the third century. According to legend, he had sought a hermit to inquire as to how he could serve Jesus. The hermit suggested he help carry people across a dangerous crossing in a river, which he did. On one occasion, a small child asked to be taken across. He found that the child was heavier than anyone else, and the child revealed himself to be Christ, bearing the sins of the world.

119. Matthew 11:30.

everything heavy. Hence all Christophers have stooped backs and short breath, since the world is heavy.

[HI 48/2] Many have wanted to get help for their sick God and were then devoured by the serpents and dragons lurking on the way to the land of the sun. They perished in the overbright day and have become dark men, since their eyes have been blinded. Now they go around like shadows and speak of the light but see little. But their God is in everything that they do not see: He is in the dark Western lands and he sharpens seeing eyes and he assists those cooking the poison and he guides serpents to the heels of the blind perpetrators. Therefore, if you are clever, take the God with you, then you know where he is. If you do not have him with you in the Western lands, he will come running to you at night with clanking armor and a crushing battle axe.[120] If you do not have him with you in the land of the dawn, then you will step unawares on the divine worm who awaits your unsuspecting heel. / 48/49

[HI 49] You gain everything from the God whom you bear, but not his weapon, since he crushed it. He who conquers needs weapons. But what else do you want to conquer? You cannot conquer more than the earth. And what is the earth? It is round all over and hangs like a drop in the cosmos. You will not reach the sun, and your power will not even extend to the barren moon; you will conquer neither the sea, nor the snow on the poles, nor the sands of the desert, but only a few spots on the green earth. You will not conquer anything for any length of time. Your power will turn into dust tomorrow, for above all—at the very least—you must conquer death. So do not be a fool, throw down your weapon. God himself smashed his weapon. Armor is enough to protect you from fools who still suffer from the need to conquer. God's armor will make you invulnerable and invisible to the worst fools.

120. I.e., as Izdubar came to Jung.

Take your God with you. Bear him down to your dark land where people live who rub their eyes each morning and yet always see only the same thing and never anything else. Bring your God down to the haze pregnant with poison, but not like those blinded ones who try to illuminate the darkness with lanterns which it does not comprehend. Instead, secretly carry your God to a hospitable roof. The huts of men are small and they cannot welcome the God despite their hospitality and willingness. Hence do not wait until rawly bungling hands of men hack your God to pieces, but embrace him again, lovingly, until he has taken on the form of his first beginning. Let no human eye see the much loved, terribly splendid one in the state of his illness and lack of power. Consider that your fellow men are animals without knowing it. So long as they go to pasture, or lie in the sun, or suckle their young, or mate with each other, they are beautiful and harmless creatures of dark Mother Earth. But if the God appears, they begin to rave, since the nearness of God makes people rave. They tremble with fear and fury and suddenly attack one another in fratricidal struggles, since one senses the approaching God in the other. So conceal the God that you have taken with you. Let them rave and maul each other. Your voice is too weak for those raging to be able to hear. Thus do not speak and do not show the God, but sit in a solitary place and sing incantations in the ancient manner:

Set the egg before you, the God in his beginning.
And behold it.
And incubate it with the magical warmth of your gaze.

49/50 HERE THE INCANTATIONS BEGIN. /

The Incantations[121]

Cap. x.

[Image 50][122]

Christmas has come. The God is in the egg.

I have prepared a rug for my God, an expensive red rug from the land of morning.

He shall be surrounded by the shimmer of magnificence of his Eastern land.

I am the mother, the simple maiden, who gave birth and did not know how.

I am the careful father, who protected the maiden.

I am the shepherd, who received the message as he guarded his herd at night on the dark fields.[123]

/ [Image 51] 50/51

I am the holy animal that stood astonished and cannot grasp the becoming of the God.

I am the wise man who came from the East, suspecting the miracle from afar.[124]

And I am the egg that surrounds and nurtures the seed of the God in me.

/ [Image 52] 51/52

The solemn hours lengthen.

And my humanity is wretched and suffers torment.

Since I am a giver of birth.

---

121. The chapter title is missing in the calligraphic volume, and is given here following the *Draft*.

122. Images 50–64 symbolically depict the regeneration of Izdubar.

123. Luke 2:8–11: "And there were in the same country shepherds abiding in the field, keeping watch over their flock by night. And, lo, the angel of the Lord came upon them, and the glory of the Lord shone round about them: and they were sore afraid. And the angel said unto them, Fear not: for, behold, I bring you good tidings of great joy, which shall be to all people. For unto you is born this day in the city of David a Savior, which is Christ the Lord."

124. Matthew 2:1–2: "Now when Jesus was born in Bethlehem of Judaea in the days of Herod the king, behold, there came wise men from the east to Jerusalem, Saying, Where is he that is born King of the Jews? For we have seen his star in the east, and are come to worship him."

Whence do you delight me, Oh God?
He is the eternal emptiness and the eternal fullness.[125]
Nothing resembles him and he resembles everything.
Eternal darkness and eternal brightness.
Eternal below and eternal above.
Double nature in one.
Simple in the manifold.
Meaning in absurdity.
Freedom in bondage.
Subjugated when victorious.
Old in youth.
Yes in no.

52/53 / [Image 53]

Oh
light of the middle way,
enclosed in the egg,
embryonic,
full of ardor, oppressed.
Fully expectant,
dreamlike, awaiting lost memories.
As heavy as stone, hardened.
Molten, transparent.
Streaming bright, coiled on itself.

53/54 / [Image 54][126, 127]

Amen, you are the lord of the beginning.

---

125. The attributes of the God in this section are elaborated as the attributes of Abraxas in the second and third sermons in *Scrutinies.* See below, p. 517f.

126. In "Dreams," Jung noted on January 3, 1917: "In Lib. nov. snake image III incent" [stimulus to snake image III in *Liber Novus*] (p. 1). This notation appears to refer to this image.

127. Image legend: "brahmaṇaspati." Julius Eggling notes that "Brihaspati or Brahmanaspati, the lord of prayer or worship, takes the place of Agni, as the representative of the priestly dignity . . . In Rig-Veda X, 68,9 . . . Brihaspati is said to have found (avindat) the dawn, the sky and the fire (agni), and to have chased away the darkness with his light (arka, sun), he seems rather to represent the element of light and fire generally" (*Sacred Books of the East* 12, p. xvi). See above note to image 45, note 110, p. 291.

Amen, you are the star of the East.
Amen, you are the flower that blooms over everything.

Amen, you are the deer that breaks out of the forest.
Amen, you are the song that sounds far over the water.
Amen, you are the beginning and the end.

/ [Image 55][128] 54/55

One word that was never spoken.
One light that was never lit up.
An unparalleled confusion.
And a road without end.

/ [Image 56] 55/56

I forgive myself these words, as you also forgive me for wanting your blazing light.

/ [Image 57] 56/57

Rise up, you gracious fire of old night.
I kiss the threshold of your beginning.
My hand prepares the rug and spreads abundant red flowers before you.
Rise up my friend, you who lay sick, break through the shell.
We have prepared a meal for you.
Gifts have been prepared for you.
Dancers await you.

---

128. The solar barge is a common motif in ancient Egypt. The barge was seen as the typical means of movement of the sun. In Egyptian mythology, the Sun God struggled against the monster Aphophis, who attempted to swallow the solar barge as it traveled across the heavens each day. In *Transformations and Symbols of the Libido* (1912) Jung discussed the Egyptian "living sun-disc" (CW B, §153) and the motif of the sea monster (§ 549f). In his 1952 revision of this text, he noted that the battle with the sea monster represented the attempt to free ego-consciousness from the grip of the unconscious (*Symbols of Transformation*, CW 5, §539). The solar barge resembles some of the illustrations in the *Egyptian Book of the Dead* (ed. E. A. Wallis Budge [London: Arkana, 1899 / 1985]), i.e., the vignettes on pp. 390, 400, and 404). The oarsman is usually a falcon-headed Horus. The night journey of the Sun God through the underworld is depicted in the *Amduat*, which has been seen as symbolic process of transformation. See Theodor Abt and Erik Hornung, *Knowledge for the Afterlife. The Egyptian Amduat—A Quest for Immortality* (Zürich: Living Human Heritage Publications, 2003).

We have built a house for you.
Your servants stand ready.
We drove herds together for you on green fields.
We filled your cup with red wine.
We set out fragrant fruit on golden dishes.
We knock at your prison and lay our ears against it.
The hours lengthen, tarry no longer.
We are wretched without you and our song is worn out.

57/58 / [Image 58][129]

We are miserable without you and wear out our songs.
We spoke all the words that our heart gave us.
What else do you want?
What else shall we fulfill for you?
We open every door for you.
We bend our knees where you want us to.
We go to all points of the compass according to your wish.
We carry up what is below, and we turn what is above into what is below, as you command.
We give and take according to your wish.
We wanted to turn right, but go left, obedient to your sign. We rise and we fall, we sway and we remain still, we see and we are blind, we hear and we are deaf, we say yes and no, always hearing your word.

129. In "Dreams," Jung wrote: "17 I 1917. Tonight: awful and formidable avalanches come crashing down the mountainside, like utterly nightmarish clouds; they will fill the valley on whose rim I am standing on the opposite side. I know that I must take flight up the mountain to avoid the dreadful catastrophe. This dream is explained in the Black Book in strange terms, in an entry bearing the same date. On 17 I 1917 I produced a drawing with red spots on page 58 of Lib. Nov. On 18 I 1917 I read about the current formation of huge sunspots" (p. 2). The following is a paraphrase of the entry in *Black Book* 6 for January 17, 1917: Jung asks what it is that fills him with fear and horror, what is falling down from the high mountain. His soul tells him to help the Gods and to sacrifice to them. She tells him that the worm crawls up to Heaven, it begins to cover the stars and with a tongue of fire he eats the dome of the seven blue heavens. She tells him that he will also be eaten, and that he should crawl into the stone and wait in the narrow casing until the torrent of fire is over. Snow falls from the mountains because the fiery breath falls down from above the clouds. The God is coming, Jung should get ready to receive him. Jung should hide himself in stone, as the God is a terrible fire. He should remain quiet and look within, so that the God does not consume him in flames (p. 152f).

We do not comprehend and we live the incomprehensible.
We do not love and we live the unloved.
And we evolve around ourselves again and comprehend
and live the understandable.
We love and live the loved, true to your law. / 58/59

Come to us, we who are willing from our own will.
Come to us, we who understand you from our own spirit.
Come to us, we who will warm you at our own fire.
Come to us, we who will heal you with our own art.
Come to us, we who will produce you out of our own body.
Come, child, to father and mother.

[Image 59][130] / 59/60
We asked earth.
We asked Heaven.
We asked the sea.
We asked the wind.
We asked the fire.
We looked for you with all the peoples.
We looked for you with all the kings.
We looked for you with all the wise.
We looked for you in our own heads and hearts.
And we found you in the egg. [Image 60]/ 60/61

I have slain a precious human sacrifice for you,
a youth and old man.
I have cut my skin with a knife.

130. Image legend: "hiraṇyagarbha." In the *Rig Veda*, hiraṇyagarbha was the primal seed from which Brahma was born. In Jung's copy of vol. 32 of the *Sacred Books of the East* (Vedic Hymns) the only section that is cut is the opening one, a hymn "To the Unknown God." This begins "In the beginning there arose the Golden Child (Hira*n*yagarbha); as soon as born, he alone was the lord of all that is. He established the earth and this heaven:—Who is the God to whom we shall offer sacrifice?" (p. 1). In Jung's copy of the Upanishads in the *Sacred Books of the East*, there is a piece of paper inserted near page 311 of the Maitrâyana-Brâhmana-Upanishad, a passage describing the Self, which begins, "And the same Self is also called . . . Hira*n*yagarbha" (vol. 15, pt. 2).

I have sprinkled your altar with my own blood.
I have banished my father and mother so that you can live with me.
I have turned my night into day and went about at midday
like a sleepwalker.
I have overthrown all the Gods, broken the laws, eaten the impure.
I have thrown down my sword and dressed in women's clothing.
I shattered my firm castle and played like a child in the sand.
I saw warriors form into line of battle and I destroyed my suit of armor
with a hammer.
I planted my field and let the fruit decay.
I made small everything that was great and made everything great
that was small.
I exchanged my furthest goal for the nearest, and so I am ready.

[Image 61][131]

61/62 / [HI 62] However, I am not ready, since I have still not accepted that which chokes my heart. That fearful thing is the enclosing of the God in the egg. I am happy that the great endeavor has been successful, but my fear made me forget the hazards involved. I love and admire the powerful. No one is greater than he with the bull's horns, and yet I lamed, carried, and made him smaller with ease. I almost slumped to the ground with fear when I saw him, and now I rescue him with a cupped hand. These are the powers that make you afraid and conquer you; these have been your Gods and your rulers since time immemorial: yet you can put them in your pocket. What is blasphemy compared to this? I would like to be able to blaspheme against the God: That way I would at least have a God whom I could insult, but it is not worth blaspheming against an egg that one carries in one's pocket. That is a God against whom one cannot even blaspheme.

I hated this pitifulness of the God. My own unworthiness is already enough. It cannot bear my encumbering it with the pitifulness of the God. Nothing stands firm: you touch yourself and you

131. The face of the monster is similar to HI 29.

turn to dust. You touch the God and he hides terrified in the egg. You force the gates of Hell: the sound of cackling masks and the music of fools approaches you. You storm Heaven: stage scenery totters and the prompter in the box falls into a swoon. You notice: you are not true, it is not true above, it is not true below, left and right are deceptions. Wherever you grasp is air, air, air.

But I have caught him, he who has been feared since time immemorial; I have made him small and my hand surrounds him. That is the demise of the Gods: man puts them in his pocket. That is the end of the story of the Gods. Nothing remains of the Gods other than an egg. And I possess this egg. Perhaps I can eradicate this last one and with this finally exterminate the race of Gods. Now that I know that the Gods have yielded to my power—what are the Gods to me now? Old and overripe, they have fallen and been buried in an egg.

But how did this happen? I felled the Great One, I mourned him, I did not want to leave him, since I loved him because no mortal being rivals him. Out of love I devised the trick that relieved him of heaviness and freed him from the confines of space. I took from him—out of love—form and corporeality. I enclosed him lovingly in the maternal egg. Should I slay him, the defenseless one whom I loved? Should I shatter the delicate shell of his grave, and expose him to the weightlessness and unboundedness of the winds of the world? But did I not sing the incantations for his incubation? Did I not do this out of love for him? Why do I love him? I do not want to tear the love for the Great One from my heart. I want to love my God, the defenseless and hopeless one. I want to care for him, like a child.

Are we not sons of the Gods? Why should Gods not be our children? If my father the God should die, a God child should arise from my maternal heart. Since I love the God and do not want to leave him. Only he who loves the God can make him fall, and the God submits to his vanquisher and nestles in his hand and dies in the heart of him who loves him and promises him birth.

My God, I love you as a mother loves the unborn whom she carries in her heart. Grow in the egg of the East, nourish yourself from my love, drink the juice of my life so that you will become a radiant God. We need your light, Oh child. Since we go in darkness, light up our paths. May your light shine before us, may your fire warm the coldness of our life. We do not need your power but life.

62/63 / What does power avail us? We do not want to rule. We want to live, we want light and warmth, and hence we need yours. Just as the greening earth and every living body needs the sun, so we as spirits need your light and your warmth. A sunless spirit becomes the para-
63/64 site of the body. But the God feeds the spirit. [Image 63] / [Image
64/65 64][132, 133] /

The Opening of the Egg.[134]

Cap. xi.

[HI 65] [135]*On the evening of the third day, I kneel down on the rug and carefully open the egg. Something resembling smoke rises up from it and suddenly Izdubar is*

132. In "Dreams," Jung noted on February 4, 1917: "Started work on the Opening of the Egg (Image)" (p. 5). This indicates that the image depicts the regeneration of Izdubar from the egg. Concerning the solar barge in this image, cf. image 55 in the facsimile edition and above, note 128, p. 301.
133. Image legend: "çatapatha-brâhmanam 2,2,4." Satapatha-brâhmana 2,2,4 (*Sacred Books of the East*, vol. 12) provides the cosmological justification behind the Agnihotra. It commences by describing how Prajapati, desiring to be reproduced, produced Agni from his mouth. Prajapati offered himself to Agni, and saved himself from Death as he was about to be devoured. The Agnihotra (lit. fire healing) is a Vedic ritual performed at sunrise and sunset. The performers purify themselves, light a sacred fire, and chant verses and a prayer to Agni.
134. The *Draft* has instead: "Third Day" (p. 329).
135. January 10, 1914. In *Black Book* 3, Jung wrote: "It appears as if something has been achieved through this memorable event. But it is incalculable where this will all lead. I hardly dare say that Izdubar's fate is grotesque and tragic, for that is what our most precious life is. Fr. Th. Vischer's (A[uch]. E[iner]) is the first attempt to elevate this truth to a system. He rightly deserves a place among the immortal. What lies in the middle is the truth. It has many faces; one is certainly comical, another sad, a third evil, a fourth tragic, a fifth funny, a sixth is a grimace, and so forth. Should one of these faces become particularly obtrusive, we thus recognize that we have deviated from certain truth and approach an extreme that constitutes a definite impasse should we decide to pursue this route. It is a murderous task to write the wisdom of real life, particularly if one has committed many years to serious scientific research. What proves to be most difficult is to grasp the playfulness of life (the childish, so to speak). All the manifold sides of life, the great, the beautiful, the serious, the black, the devilish, the good, the ridiculous, the grotesque are fields of application which each tend to wholly absorb the beholder or describer. / Our time requires something capable of regulating the mind. Just as the concrete world has expanded from the limitedness of

standing before me, enormous, transformed, and complete. His limbs are whole and I find no trace of damage on them. It's as if he had awoken from a deep sleep. He says:

"Where am I? How narrow it is here, how dark, how cool—am I
in the grave? Where was I? It seemed to me as if I had been outside in the uni-
verse—over and under me was an endlessly dark star-glittering sky—
and I was in a passion of unspeakable yearning.
Streams of fire broke from my radiating body—
I surged through blazing flames—
I swam in a sea that wrapped me in living fires—
Full of light, full of longing, full of eternity—
I was ancient and perpetually renewing myself—
Falling from the heights to the depths,
and whirled glowing from the depths to the heights—
hovering around myself amidst glowing clouds—
as raining embers beating down like the foam of the surf, engulfing
/ myself in stifling heat— 65/66
Embracing and rejecting myself in a boundless game—
Where was I? I was completely sun."[136]

I: "Oh Izdubar! Divine one! How wonderful! You are healed!"

---

the ancient outlook to the immeasurable diversity of our modern outlook, the world of intellectual possibilities has developed to unfathomable diversity. Infinitely long paths, paved with thousands of thick volumes, lead from one specialization to another. Soon no one will be able to walk down these paths anymore. And then only specialists will remain. More than ever we require the living truth of the life of the mind, of something capable of providing firm guidance" (pp. 74–77). Vischer's work was *Auch Einer: Eine Reisebekanntschaft* (Stuttgart, 1884). In 1921, Jung wrote: "Vischer's novel, *Auch Einer,* gives a deep insight into this side of the introverted state of the soul, and also into the underlying symbolism of the collective unconscious" (*Psychological Types,* CW 6, §627). In 1932 Jung commented on Vischer in *The Psychology of Kundalini Yoga,* p. 54. On *Auch Einer,* see Ruth Heller, "Auch Einer: the epitome of F. Th. Vischer's Philosophy of Life," *German Life and Letters* 8 (1954) pp. 9–18.

136. Roscher notes that "As a God, Izdubar is associated with the Sun-God" (*Ausführliches Lexikon der Griechischen und Römischen Mythologie,* vol. 2, p. 774). The incubation and rebirth of Izdubar follows the classic pattern of solar myths. In *Das Zeitalter des Sonnengottes,* Leo Frobenius pointed out the widespread motif of a woman becoming pregnant through a process of immaculate conception and giving birth to the Sun God, who develops in a remarkably short period of time. In some forms, he incubates in an egg. Frobenius related this to the setting and rising of the sun in the sea ([Berlin, G. Reimer, 1904], pp. 223–63). Jung cited this work on a number of occasions in *Transformations and Symbols of the Libido* (1912).

"Healed? Was I ever sick? Who speaks of sickness? I was sun, completely sun. I am the sun."

An inexpressible light breaks from his body, a light that my eyes cannot grasp. I must cover my face and cast my gaze to the ground.

I: "You are the sun, the eternal light—most powerful one, forgive me for carrying you."

Everything is quiet and dark. I look around me: the empty egg shell is lying on the rug. I feel myself, the floor, the walls: everything is as usual, utterly plain and utterly real. I would like to say that everything around me has turned to gold. But it is not true—everything is as it always has been. Here reigned eternal light, immeasurable and overpowering.[137]

[2] [HI 66] It happened that I opened the egg and that the God left the egg. He was healed and his figure shone transformed, and I knelt like a child and could not grasp the miracle. He who had been pressed into the core of the beginning rose up, and no trace of illness could be found on him. And when I thought that I had caught the mighty one and held him in my cupped hands, he was the sun itself.

I wandered toward the East where the sun rises. I probably wanted to rise, too, as if I were the sun. I wanted to embrace the sun and rise with it into daybreak. But it came toward me and stood in my way. It told me that I had no chance of reaching the beginning. But I lamed the one who wanted to rush down in order to set with the sun in the womb of the night; he was deprived of all hope of reaching the blessed Western lands.

But behold! I caught the sun without realizing it and carried it in my hand. He who wanted to go down with the sun found me

137. In *Psychological Types* (1921), Jung commented on the motif of the renewed God: "The renewed God signifies a renewed attitude, that is, a renewed possibility for intensive life, a recovery of life, because psychologically God always denotes the greatest value, thus the greatest sum of the libido, the greatest intensity of life, the optimum of psychological life's activity" (CW 6, §301).

through his downgoing. I became his nocturnal mother who incubated the egg of the beginning. And he rose up, renewed, reborn to greater splendor.

While he rises, however, I go down. When I conquered the God, his force streamed into me. But when the God rested in the egg and awaited his beginning, my force went into him. And when he rose up radiantly, I lay on my face. He took my life with him. All my force was now in him. My soul swam like a fish in his sea of fire. But I lay in the frightful cool of the shadows of the earth and sank down deeper and deeper to the lowest darkness. All light had left me. The God rose in the Eastern lands and I fell into the horror of the underworld. I lay there like a child-bearer cruelly mauled and bleeding her life into the child, uniting life and death in a dying glance, the day's mother, the night's prey. My God had torn me apart terribly, he had drunk the juice of my life, he had drunk my highest power into him and became marvelous and strong like the sun, an unblemished God who bore no stigma or flaw. He had taken my wings from me, he had robbed me of the swelling force of my muscles, and the power of my will disappeared with him. He left me powerless and groaning.

/ I did not know what was happening to me, since simply every- 66/67
thing powerful, beautiful, blissful, and superhuman had leaked from my maternal womb; none of the radiant gold remained. Cruelly and unthinkably the sunbird spread its wings and flew up into infinite space. I was left with the broken shells and the miserable casing of his beginning; the emptiness of the depths opened beneath me.

Woe betide the mother who gives birth to a God! If she gives birth to a wounded and pain-stricken God, a sword will pierce her soul. But if she gives birth to an unblemished God, then Hell will open to her, from which monstrous serpents will rise convulsively to suffocate the mother with miasma. Birth is difficult, but a thousand times more difficult is the hellish afterbirth.[138] All the drag-

138. In the next chapter, Jung finds himself in Hell.

ons and monstrous serpents of eternal emptiness follow behind the divine son.

What remains of human nature when the God has become mature and has seized all power? Everything incompetent, everything powerless, everything eternally vulgar, everything adverse and unfavorable, everything reluctant, diminishing, exterminating, everything absurd, everything that the unfathomable night of matter encloses in itself, that is the afterbirth of the God and his hellish and dreadfully deformed brother.

The God suffers when man does not accept his darkness. Consequently men must have a suffering God, so long as they suffer from evil. To suffer from evil means: you still love evil and yet love it no longer. You still hope to gain something, but you do not want to look closely for fear that you might discover that you still love evil. The God suffers because you continue to suffer from loving evil. You do not suffer from evil because you recognize it, but because it affords you secret pleasure, and because you believe it promises the pleasure of an unknown opportunity.

So long as your God suffers, you have sympathy with him and with yourself. You thus spare your Hell and prolong his suffering. If you want to make him well without engaging in secret sympathy with yourself, evil puts a spoke in your wheel—the evil whose form you generally recognize, but whose hellish strength in yourself you do not know. Your unknowing stems from the previous harmlessness of your life, from the peaceful passage of time, and from the absence of the God. But if the God draws near, your essence starts to seethe and the black mud of the depths whirls up.

Man stands between emptiness and fullness. If his strength combines with fullness, it becomes fully formative. There is always something good about such formation. If his strength combines with emptiness, it has a dissolving and destructive effect, since emptiness can never be formed, but only strives to satisfy itself at the cost of fullness. Combined thus human force turns emptiness into evil. If your force shapes fullness, it does so because of its association with fullness. But to ensure that your formation continues to exist, it must remain tied to your strength. Through constant shaping, you gradually lose your force, since ultimately all force is associated with the shapeliness that has been given form. Ultimately, where you mistakenly imagine that you are rich, you have actually become poor, and you stand amidst your forms like a beggar. That is when the blinded man is seized by an increasing desire to give shape to things, since he believes that manifold increased formation will satisfy his desire. Because he has spent his force, he becomes desirous; he begins to compel others into his service and takes their force to pursue his own designs.

In this moment, you need evil. When you notice that your strength is coming to an end and desire sets in, you must withdraw it from what has been formed into your emptiness; through this association with the emptiness you will succeed in dissolving the formation in you. You will thus regain your freedom, in that you have saved your strength from oppressive association with the object. So long as you persist with the standpoint of the good, you cannot dissolve your formation, precisely because it is what is good. You cannot dissolve good with good. You can dissolve good only with evil. For your good also leads ultimately to death through its progressive binding of your force by progressively binding your force. You are entirely unable to live without evil.

Your shaping first produces an image of your formation within
you. This image remains in you and / it is the first and unmedi- 67/68
ated expression of your shaping. It then produces precisely through this image an outer one, which can exist without you and outlive you. Your strength is not directly linked to your outer formation, but only through the image that remains in you. When you set about dissolving your formation with evil, you do not destroy the outer shape, or else you would be destroying your own work. But what you do destroy is the image that you have formed in yourself. For it is this image that clings to your force. You will need evil to dissolve your formation, and to free yourself from the power of what has been, to the same extent which this image fetters your strength.

Hence their formation causes many good persons to bleed to death, because they cannot attend to evil in the same measure. The better one is and the more attached one is to one's formation, the more one will lose one's force. But what happens when the good person has lost their force completely to their formation? Not only will they seek to force others into the service of their formation with unconscious cunning and power, but they will also become bad in their goodness without knowing it, since their longing for satisfaction and strengthening will make them more and more selfish. But because of this the good ones will ultimately destroy their own work, and all those whom they forced into the service of their own work will become their enemies, because they will have alienated them. But you will also secretly begin to hate whoever alienates you from yourself against your own wishes, even if this were in the best interest of things. Unfortunately, the good person who has bound his strength will all too easily find slaves for his service, since there are more than plenty who yearn for nothing more strongly than to be alienated from themselves under a good pretext.

You suffer from evil because you love it secretly and are unaware of your love. You wish to escape your predicament, and you begin to hate evil. And once more you are bound to evil through your hate, since whether you love or hate it, it makes no difference: you are bound to evil. Evil is to be accepted. What we want remains in our hands. What we do not want, and yet is stronger than us, sweeps us away and we cannot stop it without damaging ourselves, for our force remains in evil. Thus we probably have to accept our evil without love and hate, recognizing that it exists and must have its share in life. In doing so, we can deprive it of the power it has to overwhelm us.

When we have succeeded in making a God, and if through this creation our whole force has entered into this design, we are filled with an overwhelming desire to rise with the divine sun and to become a part of its magnificence. But we forget that we are then no more than hollow forms, since giving form to God has sapped us completely. We are not only poor but have become sluggish matter throughout, which would never be entitled to share in divinity.

Like a terrible suffering or an inescapable devilish persecution, the misery and neediness of our matter creeps up on us. The powerless matter begins to suckle and would like to swallow its shape back into itself again. But since we are always enamored of our own design, we believe that the God calls us to him, and we make desperate attempts to follow the God into the higher realm, or we turn preachingly and demandingly to our fellow men to at any rate force others into following the God. Unfortunately there are men who allow themselves to be persuaded into doing this, to their and our detriment.

Much undoing resides in this urge: since who could suspect that he who has made the God is himself condemned to Hell? But this is the way it is, because the matter that is stripped of the divine radiance of force is empty and dark. If the God alights from matter, we feel the emptiness of matter as one part of endless empty space.

Through haste and increased willing and action we want to escape from emptiness and also from evil. But the right way is that we accept emptiness, destroy the image of the form within us, negate the God, and descend into the abyss and awfulness of matter. The God as our work stands outside us and no longer needs our help. He is created and remains left to his own devices. A created work that perishes again immediately once we turn away from it is not worth anything, even if it / were a God. 68/69

But where is the God after his creation and after his separation from me? If you build a house, you see it standing in the outer world. When you have created a God whom you cannot see with your own eyes, then he is in the spiritual world that is no less valuable than the outer physical world. He is there and does everything for you and others that you would expect from a God.

Thus your soul is your own self in the spiritual world. As the abode of the spirits, however, the spiritual world is also an outer world. Just as you are also not alone in the visible world, but are surrounded by objects that belong to you and obey only you, you also have thoughts that belong to you and obey only you. But just as you are surrounded in the visible world by things and beings that neither belong to you nor obey you, you are also surrounded in the spiritual world by thoughts and beings of thought that neither obey you nor belong to you. Just as you engender or bear your physical children, and just as they grow up and separate themselves from you to live their own fate, you also produce or give birth to beings of thought which separate themselves from you and live their own lives. Just as we leave our children when we grow old and give our body back to the earth, I separate myself from my God, the sun, and sink into the emptiness of matter and obliterate the image of my child in me. This happens in that I accept the nature of matter and allow the force of my form to flow into emptiness. Just as I gave birth anew to the sick God through my engendering force, I henceforth animate the emptiness of matter from which the formation of evil grows.

Nature is playful and terrible. Some see the playful side and dally with it and let it sparkle. Others see the horror and cover their heads and are more dead than alive. The way does not lead between both, but embraces both. It is both cheerful play and cold
69/73 *horror.*[139] [Image 69][140] / [Image 70] / [Image 71][141] / [Image 72]. /

139. In "Dreams," Jung wrote on February 15, 1917: "Finished copying the opening scene. / The most wonderful feeling of renewal. Back to scientific work today. / Types!" (p. 5). This refers to completing this section of the transcription into the calligraphic volume, and to continuing his work on psychological types.

140. The blue and yellow circles are similar to image 60 in the facsimile edition.

141. This might be the image Tina Keller is referring to in the following statement in an interview, where she recalled Jung's discussion of his relations with Emma Jung and Toni Wolff: "Jung once showed me a picture in the book he was painting, and he said, 'See these three snakes that are intertwined. This is how we three struggle with this problem.' I can only say that it seemed to me very important that, even as a passing phenomenon, here three people were accepting a destiny which was not gone into just for their personal satisfaction" (interview with Gene Nameche, 1969, R. D. Laing papers, University of Glasgow, p. 27).

Hell
Cap. xii

[HI 73] On the second night[142] after the creation of my God, a vision made known to me that I had reached the underworld.

I find myself in a gloomy vault, whose floor consists of damp stone slabs. In the middle there is a column from which ropes and axes hang. At the foot of the column there lies an awful serpent-like tangle of human bodies. At first I catch sight of the figure of a young maiden with wonderful red-gold hair—a man of devilish appearance is lying half under her—his head is bent backward—a thin streak of blood runs down his forehead—two similar daimons have thrown themselves over the maiden's feet and body. Their faces bear an inhuman expression—the living evil—their muscles are taut and hard, and their bodies sleek like serpents. They lie motionless. The maiden holds her hand over one eye of the man lying beneath her, who is the most powerful of the three—her hand firmly clasps a small silver fishing rod that she has driven into the eye of the devil.

I break out in a profuse cold sweat. They wanted to torture the maiden to death, but she defended herself with the force of the most extreme despair, and succeeded in piercing the eye of the evil one with the little hook. If he moves, she will tear out his eye with a final jerk. The horror paralyzes me: what will happen? A voice speaks:

"The evil one cannot make a sacrifice, he cannot sacrifice his eye, victory is with the one who can sacrifice."[143]

[2] The vision vanished. I saw that my soul had fallen into the power of abysmal evil. The power of evil is unquestionable, and we rightfully fear it. Here no prayers, no pious words, no magical sayings help. Once raw power comes after you, there is no help. Once evil seizes you without pity, no father, no mother, no right, no wall

142. January 12, 1914.

143. Jung's marginal note to the calligraphic volume: "*çataphatha-brâhmanam* 2,2,4." The same inscription is given to image 64. See notes 132 and 133, above.

and tower, no armor and protective power come to your aid. You fall powerless and forlorn into the hand of the superior power of evil. In this battle you are all alone. Because I wanted to give birth to my God, I also wanted evil. He who wants to create an eternal fullness will also create eternal emptiness.[144] You cannot undertake one without the other. But if you want to escape evil, you will create no God, everything that you do is tepid and gray. I wanted my God at any cost. Hence I also want my evil. If my God were not overpowering, neither would be my evil. But I want my God to be powerful and beyond all measure happy and lustrous. Only in this way do I love my God. And the luster of his beauty will also have me taste the very bottom of Hell.

My God rose in the Eastern sky, brighter than the heavenly host, and brought about a new day for all the peoples. This is why I want to go to Hell. Would a mother not want to give up her life for her child? How much easier would it be to give up my life if only my God could overcome the torment of the last hour of the night and victoriously break through the red mist of the morning? I do not doubt: I also want evil for the sake of my God. I enter the unequal battle, since it is always unequal and without doubt a lost cause. How terrible and despairing would this battle be otherwise? But precisely this is how it should and will be.

73/74 / Nothing is more valuable to the evil one than his eye, since only through his eye can emptiness seize gleaming fullness. Because the emptiness lacks fullness, it craves fullness and its shining power. And it drinks it in by means of its eye, which is able to grasp the beauty and unsullied radiance of fullness. The emptiness is poor, and if it lacked its eye it would be hopeless. It sees the most beautiful and wants to devour it in order to spoil it. The devil knows what is beautiful, and hence he is the shadow of beauty and follows

144. In *Thus Spoke Zarathustra,* Nietzsche wrote: "one must have chaos in one, to give birth to a dancing star" ("Zarathustra's prologue," §5, p. 46; as underlined in Jung's copy).

it everywhere, awaiting the moment when the beautiful, writhing great with child, seeks to give life to the God.

If your beauty grows, the dreadful worm will also creep up you, waiting for its prey. Nothing is sacred to him except his eye, with which he sees the most beautiful. He will never give up his eye. He is invulnerable, but nothing protects his eye; it is delicate and clear, adept at drinking in the eternal light. It wants you, the bright red light of your life.

I recognize the fearful devilishness of human nature. I cover my eyes before it. I put out my hand to fend it off, if anyone wants to approach me for fear that my shadow could fall on him, or his shadow could fall on me, since I also see the devilish in him, who is the harmless companion of his shadow.

No one touches me, death and crime lie in wait for you and me. You smile innocently, my friend? Don't you see that a gentle flickering of your eye betrays the frightfulness whose unsuspecting messenger you are? Your bloodthirsty tiger growls softly, your poisonous serpent hisses secretly, while you, conscious only of your goodness, offer your human hand to me in greeting. I know your shadow and mine, that follows and comes with us, and only waits for the hour of twilight when he will strangle you and me with all the daimons of the night.

What abyss of blood-dripping history separates you from me! I grasped your hand and looked at you. I lay my head in your lap and felt the living warmth of your body on mine as if it were my own body—and suddenly I felt a smooth cord around my neck, which choked me mercilessly, and a cruel hammer blow struck a nail into my temple. I was dragged by my feet along the pavement, and wild hounds gnawed my body in the lonely night.

No one should be astonished that men are so far removed from one another that they cannot understand one another, that they wage war and kill one another. One should be much more surprised that men believe they are close, understand one another and love one another. Two things are yet to be discovered. The first is the infinite gulf that separates us from one another. The second is the bridge that could connect us. Have you considered how much unsuspected animality human company makes possible?

[145]When my soul fell into the hands of evil, it was defenseless except for the weak fishing rod which it could use, again with its power, to pull the fish from the sea of emptiness. The eye of the evil one sucked in all the force of my soul; only its will remained, which is just that small fish hook. I wanted evil, since I realized that I was not able to elude it. And because I wanted evil, my soul held the precious hook in its hand, that was supposed to strike the vulnerable place of the evil one. He who does not want evil will have no chance to save his soul from Hell. So long as he remains in the light of the upper world, he will become a shadow of himself. But his soul will languish in the dungeons of the daimons. This will act as a counterbalance that will forever constrain him. The higher circles of the inner world will remain unattainable for him. He remains where he was; indeed, he falls back. You know these
74/75 people, and you know how extravagantly nature strews / human life and force on barren deserts. You should not lament this, otherwise you will become a prophet, and will seek to redeem what can-

145. Jung's marginal note to the calligraphic volume: "*Khândogya*-upanishad 1,2,1–7." The *Chandogya Upanisad* reads: "Once, when the gods and demons, both children of Prajapati, arrayed themselves against each other, the gods got hold of the High Chant. 'With this we will overpower them,' they thought. / So they venerated the High Chant as the breath within the nostrils. The demons riddled it with evil. As a result, one smells with it both good and evil odors, for it is riddled with evil. / Then they venerated the High Chant as speech. The demons riddled it with evil. As a result, one speaks with it both what is true and what is false, for it is riddled with evil. / Then they venerated the High Chant as sight. The demons riddled it with evil. As a result one sees with it both what is good to see and what is not, for it is riddled with evil. / Then they venerated the High Chant as hearing. The demons riddled it with evil. As a result, one hears with it both what is good to hear and what is not, for it is riddled with evil. / Then they venerated the High Chant as the mind. The demons riddled it with evil. As a result, one envisages with it both what is good to envisage and what is not, for it is riddled with evil. / Finally, they venerated the High Chant as just this breath here within the mouth. And when the demons hurled themselves at it, they were smashed to bits like a clod of earth hurled against a target that is a rock" (*Upanishads*, tr. P. Olivelle [Oxford: Oxford University Press, 1996]). The "High Chant" is OM.

not be redeemed. Do you not know that nature also dungs its fields with men? Take in the seeker, but do not go out seeking those who err. What do you know about their error? Perhaps it is sacred. You should not disturb the sacred. Do not look back and regret nothing. You see many near you fall? You feel compassion? But you should live your life, since then at least one in a thousand will remain. You cannot halt dying.

But why did my soul not tear out the eye of the evil one? The evil one has many eyes, and losing one amounts to losing none. But if she had done it, she would have come completely under the spell of the evil one. The evil one can only fail to make sacrifice. You should not harm him, above all not his eye, since the most beautiful would not exist if the evil one did not see it and long for it. The evil one is holy.

There is nothing the emptiness can sacrifice, since it always suffers lack. Only fullness can sacrifice, since it has fullness. Emptiness cannot sacrifice its hunger for fullness, since it cannot deny its own essence. Therefore we also need evil. But I can sacrifice my will to evil, because I previously received fullness. All strength flows back to me again, since the evil one has destroyed the image I had of the formation of the God. But the image of the God's formation in me was not yet destroyed. I dread this destruction, since it is terrible, an unprecedented desecration of temples. Everything in me strives against this abysmal abomination. For I still did not know what it means to give birth to a God. [Image 75] / 75/76

The Sacrificial Murder.[146]

Cap. xiii.

[HI 76] But this was the vision that I did not want to see, the horror that I did not want to live: A sickening feeling of nausea sneaks up on me, and abominable, perfidious serpents wind their way slowly and cracklingly through parched undergrowth; they hang down lazily and disgustingly lethargic from the branches, looped in dreadful knots. I am reluctant to enter this dreary and unsightly valley, where the bushes stand in arid stony defiles. The valley looks so normal, its air smells of crime, of foul, cowardly deeds. I am seized by disgust and horror. I walk hesitantly over the boulders, avoiding every dark place for fear of treading on a serpent. The sun shines weakly out of a gray and distant sky, and all the leaves are shriveled. A marionette with a broken head lies before me amidst the stones—a few steps further, a small apron—and then behind the bush, the body of a small girl—covered with terrible wounds—smeared with blood. One foot is clad with a stocking and shoe, the other is naked and gorily crushed—the head—where is the head? The head is a mash of blood with hair and whitish pieces of bone, surrounded by stones smeared with brain and blood. My gaze is captivated by this awful sight—a shrouded figure, like that of a woman, is standing calmly next to the child; her face is covered by an impenetrable veil. She asks me:

S: "What then do you say?"

I: "What should I say? This is beyond words."

S: "Do you understand this?"

I: "I refuse to understand such things. I can't speak about them without becoming enraged."

S: "Why become enraged? You might as well rage every day of your life, for these and similar things occur every day."

146. The *Handwritten Draft* has instead: "*Eighth Adventure*" (p. 793).

I: "But most of the time we don't see them."

S: "So knowing that they happen is not enough to enrage you?"

I: "If I merely have knowledge of something, it's easier and simpler. The horror is less real if all I have is knowledge."

S: "Step nearer and you will see that the body of the child has been cut open; take out the liver."

I: "I will not touch this corpse. If someone witnessed this, they would think that I'm the murderer."

S: "You are cowardly; take out the liver."

I: "Why should I do this? This is absurd."

S: "I want you to remove the liver. You must do it."

I: "Who are you to give me such an order?"

S: "I am the soul of this child. You must do this for my sake."

I: "I don't understand, but I'll believe you and do this horrific and absurd deed." / 76/77

I reach into the child's visceral cavity—it is still warm—the liver is still firmly attached—I take my knife and cut it free of the ligaments. Then I take it out and hold it with bloody hands toward the figure.

S: "I thank you."

I: "What should I do?"

S: "You know what the liver means, and you ought to perform the healing act with it."[147]

I: "What is to be done?"

S: "Take a piece of the liver, in place of the whole, and eat it."

I: "What are you demanding? This is absolute madness. This is desecration, necrophilia. You make me a guilty party to this most hideous of all crimes."

S: "You have devised the most horrible torment for the murderer, which could atone for his act. There is only one atonement: abase yourself and eat."

147. In *Memories*, while commenting on the Liverpool dream (see below, p. 418, n. 296), Jung noted "According to an older view, the liver is the seat of life" (p. 224).

I: "I cannot—I refuse—I cannot participate in this horrible guilt."

S: "You share in this guilt."

I: "I? Share in this guilt?"

S: "You are a man, and a man has committed this deed."

I: "Yes, I am a man—I curse whoever did this for being a man, and I curse myself for being a man."

S: "So, take part in his act, abase yourself and eat. I need atonement."

I: "So shall it be for your sake, as you are the soul of this child."

I kneel down on the stone, cut off a piece of the liver and put it in my mouth. My gorge rises—tears burst from my eyes—cold sweat covers my brow—a dull sweet taste of blood—I swallow with desperate efforts—it is impossible—once again and once again—I almost faint—it is done. The horror has been accomplished.[148]

S: "I thank you."

She throws her veil back—a beautiful maiden with ginger hair.

S: "Do you recognize me?"

I: "How strangely familiar you are! Who are you?"

S: "I am your soul."[149]

[2] The sacrifice has been accomplished: the divine child, the image of the God's formation, is slain, and I have eaten from the sacrificial flesh.[150] The child, that is, the image of the God's forma-

148. In 1940, Jung discussed ritual anthropophagy, sacrifice, and self-sacrifice in "Transformation symbolism in the mass," CW 11.

149. In *Black Book* 3, Jung noted: "The curtain drops. What dreadful game has been played here? I realize: *Nil humanum a me alienum esse puto* [nothing human is alien to me]" (p. 91). The phrase is from the Roman playwright Terence, from *Heauton Timorumenos*. On September 2, 1960, Jung wrote to Herbert Read, "As a medical psychologist I do not merely assume, but I am thoroughly convinced, that *nil humanum a me alienum esse is even my duty*" (*Letters* 2, p. 589).

150. Instead of this sentence, the *Draft* has: "This experience accomplished what I needed. It occurred in the most abominable manner. The evil that I wanted performed the infamous deed, seemingly without me and yet with me, since I learned that I am party to all the horror of human nature. I destroyed the divine child, the image of my God's formation, through the most dreadful crime which human nature is capable of. It takes

tion, not only bore my human craving, but also enclosed all the primordial and elemental powers that the sons of the sun possess as an inalienable inheritance. The God needs all this for his genesis. But when he has been created and hastens away into unending space, we need the gold of the sun. We must regenerate ourselves. But as the creation of a God is a creative act of highest love, the restoration of our human life signifies an act of the Below. This is a great and dark mystery. Man cannot accomplish this act solely by himself, but is assisted by evil, which does it instead of man. But man must recognize his complicity in the act of evil. He must bear witness to this recognition by eating from the bloody sacrificial flesh. Through this act he testifies that he is a man, that he recognizes good as well as evil, and that he destroys the image of the God's formation through withdrawing his life force, with which he also dissociates himself from the God. This occurs for the salvation of the soul, which is the true mother of the divine child. / 77/78

When it bore and gave birth to the God, my soul was of human nature throughout; it possessed the primordial powers since time immemorial, but only in a dormant condition. They flowed into forming the God without my help. But through the sacrificial murder, I redeemed the primordial powers and added them to my soul. Since they became part of a living pattern, they are no longer dormant, but awake and active and irradiate my soul with their divine working. Through this it receives a divine attribute. Hence the eating of the sacrificial flesh aided its healing. The ancients have also indicated this to us, in that they taught us to drink the blood and eat the flesh of the savior. The ancients believed that this brought healing to the soul.[151]

---

this atrocity to destroy the image of the God that drinks all my life force so that I could reclaim my life" (p. 355).

151. I.e., the ritual of the mass.

There are not many truths, there are only a few. Their meaning is too deep to grasp other than in symbols.[152]

A God who is no stronger than man—what is he? You still should taste holy dread. How would you be worthy of enjoying the wine and the bread if you have not touched the black bottom of human nature? Hence you are lukewarm and pale shadows, proud of your shallow coastlines and broad country roads. But the floodgates will be opened, there are inexorable things, from which only God can save you.

The primordial force is the radiance of the sun, which the sons of the sun have carried in themselves for aeons and pass on to their children. But if the soul dips into radiance, she becomes as remorseless as the God himself, since the life of the divine child, which you have eaten, will feel like glowing coals in you. It will burn inside you like a terrible, inextinguishable fire. But despite all the torment, you cannot let it be, since it will not let you be. From this you will understand that your God is alive and that your soul has begun wandering on remorseless paths. You feel that the fire of the sun has erupted in you. Something new has been added to you, a holy affliction.

Sometimes you no longer recognize yourself. You want to overcome it, but it overcomes you. You want to set limits, but it compels you to keep going. You want to elude it, but it comes with you. You want to employ it, but you are its tool; you want to think about it, but your thoughts obey it. finally the fear of the inescapable seizes you, for it comes after you slowly and invincibly.

There is no escape. So it is that you come to know what a real God is. Now you'll think up clever truisms, preventive measures, secret escape routes, excuses, potions capable of inducing forgetful-

152. Jung developed his ideas concerning the significance of symbols in *Psychological Types* (1921). See CW 6, §814ff.

ness, but it's all useless. The fire burns right through you. That which guides forces you onto the way.

But the way is my own self, my own life founded upon myself. The God wants my life. He wants to go with me, sit at the table with me, work with me. Above all he wants to be ever-present.[153] But I'm ashamed of my God. I don't want to be divine but reasonable. The divine appears to me as irrational craziness. I hate it as an absurd disturbance of my meaningful human activity. It seems an unbecoming sickness which has stolen into the regular course of my life. Yes, I even find the divine superfluous. / [Image 79] / [Image 80] 78/90
/ [Image 81] / [Image 82] / [Image 83] / [Image 84][154] / [Image 85] / [Image 86] / [Image 87] / [Image 88] / [Image 89][155] / [Image 90]

153. In 1909, Jung had his house built in Küsnacht, and had the following motto from the Delphic oracle carved above the door: "Vocatus atque non vocatus deus aderit" (Called or not, the God will be present). The source of the quotation was Erasmus's *Collectanea adagiorum*. Jung explained the motto as follows: "It says, yes, the god will be on the spot, but in what form and to what purpose? I have put the inscription there to remind my patients and myself: *Timor dei initium sapientiae* [Psalms 111:10]. Here another not less important road begins, not the approach to 'Christianity' but to God himself and this seems to be the ultimate question" (Jung to Eugene Rolfe, November 19, 1960, *Letters* 2, p. 611).

154. There is a note at bottom of the page: "21 VIII. 1917. fect. 14.X.17," possibly an abbreviation for "fecit," i.e., "made."

155. In *Black Book* 7, in Jung's fantasy of October 7, 1917, a figure appears, Ha, who says he is the father of Philemon. Jung's soul describes him as a black magician. His secret is the runes, which Jung's soul wants to learn. He refuses to teach them, but shows some examples, which Jung's soul asks him to explain. Some of the runes later appear in these paintings. About the runes in this painting, Ha explained: "See the two with different feet, one earth foot and one sun foot—which reach toward the upper cone and have the sun inside, but I have made one crooked line toward the other sun. Therefore one must reach downward. Meanwhile the upper sun comes out of the cone and the cone gazes after it, dejected about where it is going. One has to retrieve it with a hook and would like to place it in the small prison. Then the three have to stand together, unite, and twirl up at the top (curled). With this they manage to free the sun from its prison again. Now you make a thick bottom and a roof, where the sun sits safe at the top. But inside the house the other sun has risen also. Therefore you too are coiled up at the top and have made a roof over the prison again at the bottom, so that the upper sun cannot enter. The two suns always want to be together—I said so, didn't I—the two cones—each has a sun. You want to let them come together, because then you think that thus you could be one. You have now drawn up both suns and brought them to one another, and now slope to the other side—that is important (=) but then there are simply two suns at the bottom, so therefore you have to go to the lower cone. Then you put the suns together there, but in the middle, neither at the bottom nor at the top, therefore there are not four but two, but the upper cone is at the bottom and there is

90/95 / [Image 91] / [Image 92] / [Image 93][156] / [Image 94][157] /

---

a thick roof above and if you want to continue, you long to return with both arms. But at the bottom you have a prison for two, for both of you. Therefore you make a prison for the lower sun and fall toward the other side, to get the lower sun out of the prison. This is what you long for, and the upper cone comes and makes a bridge toward the lower, taking back its sun, which has run away before, and now the morning clouds come into the lower cone, but its sun is beyond the line, invisible (horizon). Now you are one and happy that you have the sun at the top and long to be up there, too. But you are imprisoned in the prison of the lower sun, that is rising. There is a stop. Now you make something quadrilateral above, which you call thoughts, a prison without doors, with thick walls, so that the upper sun does not leave, but the cone has already gone. You lean toward the other side, long for the below and coil up at the bottom. Then you are one and make the serpent's way between the suns—that is amusing! ~ and important (=). But because it was amusing below, there is a roof above and you must raise upward the hook with both arms, so that it goes through the roof. Then the sun below is free and there is a prison above. You look downward, but the upper sun looks toward you. But you stand upright as a pair and have detached the serpent from you—you have probably been put off. Therefore you make a prison for the below. Now the serpent crosses the sky above the earth. You are driven completely apart, the serpent wriggles its way through the sky around all the stars far above the earth. / At the bottom it says: the mother gives me this wisdom. / Be you content" (pp. 9–10). To Aniela Jaffé, Jung recounted that he had had a vision of a red clay tablet inscribed with hieroglyphics and embedded in his bedroom wall, and that he had transcribed the tablet the following day. He felt that it contained an important message, but he didn't understand it (*MP*, p. 172). In letters to Sabina Spielrein dated September 13 and October 10, 1917, Jung commented on the significance of some hieroglyphs she'd seen in a dream. On October 10, he wrote to her that "with your hieroglyphics we are dealing with phylogenetic engrams of a historical symbolic nature." Commenting on the contempt meted out to *Transformations and Symbols of the Libido* by the Freudians, he described himself as "clinging to his runes" which he would not hand over to those who would not understand them ("The letters of Jung to Sabina Spielrein," *Journal of Analytical Psychology* 41 [2001], pp. 187–88).

156. The runes in this painting appear in *Black Book* 7 in the entry for October 7, 1917. Jung appended the date "10 September 1917" to them. Ha explained: "If you have managed to move the arc forward, you make a bridge below and move upward and downward from the center, or you separate above and below, split the sun again and crawl like the serpent over the upper and receive the lower. You take with you what you have experienced and go forward to something new" (p. 11).

157. The runes in this painting appear in *Black Book* 7 in the entry for October 7, 1917. Jung appended the date "11 September 1917" to them. Ha explained: "Now, however, you make a bridge between you and the one longs for the below. But the serpent crawls at the top and draws the sun up. Then both of you move upward and want to go to the upper (◡), but the sun is below and tries to draw you down. But you draw a line above the below and long for the above and are completely at one. There the serpent comes and wants to drink from the vessel of the below. But there comes the upper cone and stops. Like the serpent, the looking coils back and moves forward again and afterward you very much (—) long to return. But the lower sun pulls and thus you become balanced again. But soon you fall backward, since the one has reached out toward the upper sun. The other does not want this and so you fall asunder, and therefore you must bind yourselves together three times. Then you stand upright again and you hold both suns before you, as if they were your eyes, the light of the above and the below before you and you stretch your arms out toward it, and you come together to become

[Image 95] / [Image 96] / [Image 97] / 95/98

---

one and must separate the two suns and you long to return a little to the lower and reach out toward the upper. But the lower cone has swallowed the upper cone into itself, because the suns were so close. Therefore you place the upper cone back up again, and because the lower is then no longer there, you want to draw it up again and have a profound longing for the lower cone, while it is empty Above, since the sun Above the line is invisible. Because you have longed to return downward for so long, the upper cone comes down and tries to capture the invisible lower sun within itself. There the serpent's way goes at the very top, you are split and everything below is beneath the ground. You long to be further above, but the lower longing already comes crawling like a serpent, and you build a prison over her. But there the lower comes up, you long to be at the very bottom and the two suns suddenly reappear, close together. You long for this and come to be imprisoned. Then the one is defiant and the other longs for the below. The prison opens, the one longs even more to be below, but the defiant one longs for the above and is no longer defiant, but longs for what is to come. And thus it comes to pass: the sun rises at the bottom, but it is imprisoned and above three nest boxes are made for you two and the upper sun, which you expect, because you have imprisoned the lower one. But now the upper cone comes down powerfully and divides you and swallows the lower cone. This is impossible. Therefore you place the cones tip to tip and curl up toward the front in the center. Because that's no way to leave matters! So it has to happen otherwise. The one attempts to reach upward, the other downward; you must strive to do this, since if the tips of the cones meet, they can hardly be separated anymore—therefore I have placed the hard seed in-between. Tip to tip—that would be too beautifully regular. This pleases father and mother, but where does that leave me? And my seed? Therefore a quick change of plan! One makes a bridge between you both, imprisons the lower sun again, the one longs for the above and the below, but the other longs especially strongly for the forward, above and below. Thus the future can become—see, how well I can already say it—yes, indeed, I am clever—cleverer than you—since you have taken matters in hand so well, you also get everything beneath the roof and into the house, the serpent, and the two suns. That is always most amusing. But you are separated and because you have drawn the line above, the serpent and the suns are too far below. This happens because beforehand you curled around yourself from below. But you come together and into agreement and stand upright, because it is good and amusing and fine and you say: thus shall it remain. But down comes the upper cone, because it felt dissatisfied, that you had set a limit above beforehand. The upper cone reaches out immediately for its sun—but there is nowhere a sun to be found anymore and the serpent also jumps up, to catch the suns. You fall over, and one of you is eaten by the lower cone. With the help of the upper cone you get him out and in return you give the lower cone its sun and the upper cone its as well. You spread yourself out like the one-eyed, who wanders in heaven and hold the cones beneath you—but in the end matters still go awry. You leave the cones and the suns to go and stand side by side and still do not want the same. In the end you agree to bind yourself threefold to the upper cone descending from above. / I am called Ha-Ha-Ha—a jolly name—I am clever—look here, my last sign, that is the magic of the white man who lived in the great magic house, the magic which you call Christianity. Your medicine man said so himself: I and the father are one, no one comes to the father other than through me. I told you so, the upper cone is the father. He has bound himself threefold to you and stands between the other and the father. Therefore the other must go through him, if he wants to reach the cone" (pp. 13–14).

Divine Folly[158]

Cap. xiv.

[HI 98] [159]I am standing in a high hall. Before me I see a green curtain between two columns. The curtain parts easily. I see into a small deep room with bare walls. There is a small window with bluish glass above. I set foot on the stair leading up to this room between the pillars and enter. In the rear wall, I see a door right and left. It's as if I must choose between right and left.

I choose the right. The door is open, I enter: I'm in the reading room of a large library. In the background sits a small thin man of pale complexion, apparently the librarian. The atmosphere is troubling—scholarly ambitions—scholarly conceit—wounded scholarly vanity. Apart from the librarian I see no one. I step toward him. He looks up from his book and says, "What do you want?"

I'm somewhat embarrassed, since I don't know what I really want: Thomas à Kempis crosses my mind.

I: "I'd like to have Thomas à Kempis's *The Imitation of Christ.*"[160]

---

158. The *Handwritten Draft* has instead: "*Ninth Adventure* 1st Night" (p. 814).
159. January 14, 1914.
160. *The Imitation of Christ* is a work of devotional instruction that appeared at the beginning of the fifteenth century and became extremely popular. Its authorship is still in dispute, though it is generally attributed to Thomas à Kempis (ca. 1380–1471), who was a member of the Brethren of the Common Life, a religious community in the Netherlands that was a prime representative of the *devotio moderna*, a movement stressing mediation and the inner life. In clear and simple language, *The Imitation of Christ* exhorts people to be concerned with the inner spiritual life as opposed to outer things, gives advice as to how this is to be lived, and shows the comfort and ultimate rewards of a life lived in Christ. The title derives from the first line of the first chapter, where it is also stated that "Anyone who wishes to understand and to savor the words of Christ to the full must try to make his whole life conform to the pattern of Christ's life" (*The Imitation of Christ*, tr. B. Knott [London: Fount, 1996], book 1, ch. 1, p. 33). The theme of the Imitation of Christ dates back much earlier. There was much discussion in the Middle Ages concerning how this was to be understood (on the history of this notion, see Giles Constable, "The Ideal of the Imitation of Christ," in *Three Studies in Medieval Religious and Social Thought* [Cambridge: Cambridge University Press, 1995], pp. 143–248). As Constable shows, two broad approaches may be distinguished, depending upon how imitation was understood: the first, the imitation of the divinity of Christ, stressed the doctrine of deification by which "Christ showed the way to become God through him" (p. 218). The second, the imitation of the humanity and body of Christ,

He looks at me somewhat astonished as if he didn't credit me with such an interest; he gives me an order-form to fill out. I too think that it's astonishing to ask for Thomas à Kempis.

"Are you surprised that I'm requesting Thomas's work?"

"Well, yes, the book is seldom asked for, and I wouldn't have expected this interest from you."

"I must confess that I'm also somewhat surprised by this inspiration, but recently I came across a passage from Thomas that made a particular impression on me. Why, I can't really say. If I remember correctly, it dealt with the problem of the Imitation of Christ."

"Do you have particular theological or philosophical interests, or—"

"Do you mean—whether I want to read it for the purpose of prayer?"

"Well, hardly."

"If I read Thomas à Kempis, I do so for the sake of prayer, or something similar, rather than out of scholarly interest."

"Are you that religious? I had no idea."

"You know that I value science extraordinarily highly. But there are actually moments in life where science also leaves us empty and sick. In such moments a book like Thomas's means very much to me since it is written from the soul."

"But somewhat old-fashioned. We can no longer get involved in Christian dogmatics these days, surely."

"We haven't come to an end with Christianity by simply putting it aside. It seems to me that there's more to it than we see."

"What is there about it? It's just a religion." / 98/99

"For what reasons and moreover at what age do men set it aside? Presumably, most do so during their student days or perhaps even earlier. Would you call that a particularly discriminating age? And have you ever examined more closely the grounds on which people

stressed the imitation of his life on earth. The most extreme form of this was in the tradition of stigmatics, individuals who bore the wounds of Christ on their body.

put aside positive religion? The grounds are mostly dubious, such as that the contents of belief clash with natural science or philosophy."

"In my view, such an objection should not necessarily be rejected out of hand, despite the fact that there are better reasons. For example, I consider the lack of a true and proper sense of actuality in religion a disadvantage. Incidentally, a host of substitutes now exists for the loss of opportunity for prayer caused by the collapse of religion. Nietzsche, for example, has written a more than veritable book of prayer,[161] not to mention *Faust*."

"I suppose that's correct in a certain sense. But especially Nietzsche's truth strikes me as too agitated and provocative—; it's good for those who are yet to be set free. For that reason his truth is good only for them. I believe that I've recently discovered that we also need a truth for those who are forced into a corner. It's possible that instead they need a depressive truth, which makes man smaller and more inward."

"Forgive me, but Nietzsche interiorizes man exceptionally well."

"Perhaps from your standpoint you're right, but I can't help feeling that Nietzsche speaks to those who need more freedom, not to those who clash strongly with life, who bleed from wounds, and who hold fast to actualities."

"But Nietzsche confers a precious feeling of superiority upon such people."

"I can't dispute that, but I know men who need inferiority, not superiority."

"You express yourself very paradoxically. I don't understand you. Inferiority can hardly be a desideratum."

"Perhaps you'll understand me better if instead of inferiority I say resignation, a word that one used to hear a lot of, but seldom anymore."

"It also sounds very Christian."

"As I said, there seem to be all sorts of things in Christianity that maybe one would do well to keep. Nietzsche is too oppositional. Like

161. I.e., *Thus Spoke Zarathustra*.

everything healthy and long-lasting, truth unfortunately adheres more to the middle way, which we unjustly abhor."

"I really had no idea that you take such a mediating position."

"Neither did I—my position is not entirely clear to me. If I mediate, I certainly mediate in a very peculiar manner."

At this moment the servant brought the book, and I took my leave from the librarian.

[2] The divine wants to live with me. My resistance is in vain. I asked my thinking, and it said: "Take as your model one that shows you how to live the divine." Our natural model is Christ. We have stood under his law since antiquity, first outwardly, and then inwardly. At first we knew this, and then knew it no longer. We fought against Christ, we deposed him, and we seemed to be conquerors. But he remained in us and mastered us.

It is better to be thrown into visible chains than into invisible ones. You can certainly leave Christianity but it does not leave you. Your liberation from it is delusion. Christ is the way. You can certainly run away, but then you are no longer on the way. The way of Christ ends on the cross. Hence we are crucified with him in ourselves. With him, we wait until we die for our resurrection.[162] With Christ the living experience no resurrection, unless it occurs after death.[163]

If I imitate Christ, he is always ahead of me and I can never reach the goal, unless I reach it in him. / But thus I move beyond 99/100
myself and beyond time, in and through which I am as I am. I thus

162. In *The Imitation of Christ*, Thomas à Kempis wrote: "There is no salvation for the soul nor hope for eternal life except in the cross. Take up your cross then, and follow Jesus, and you will enter eternal life. He went before you carrying his cross, and on the cross he died for you, so that you too should carry your cross, and long for a death on the cross. For if you share his death, you will also share his life" (book 2, ch. 12, p. 90).

163. The *Draft* continues: "But we know that the ancients spoke to us in images. Hence my thinking advised me to emulate Christ, not to imitate him but because he is the way. If I follow a way, I do not imitate him. But if I imitate Christ, he is my goal and not my way. But if he is my way, I thus go toward his goal, as the mysteries had shown me previously. Thus my thinking spoke to me in a confused and ambiguous manner, but it advised me to imitate Christ" (p. 366).

blunder into Christ and his time, which created him thus and not otherwise. And so I am outside my time, despite the fact that my life is in this time and I am split between the life of Christ and my life that still belongs to this present time. But if I am truly to understand Christ, I must realize how Christ actually lived only his own life, and imitated no one. He did not emulate any model.[164]

If I thus truly imitate Christ, I do not imitate anyone, I emulate no one, but go my own way, and I will also no longer call myself a Christian. Initially, I wanted to emulate and imitate Christ by living my life, while observing his precepts. A voice in me protested against this and wanted to remind me that my time also had its prophets who struggle against the yoke with which the past burdens us. I did not succeed in uniting Christ with the prophets of this time. The one demands bearing, the other discarding; the one commands submission, the other the will.[165] How should I think of this contradiction without doing injustice to either? What I could not conjoin in my mind probably lends itself to living one after the other.

And so I decided to cross over into lower and everyday life, my life, and to begin down there, where I stood.

When thinking leads to the unthinkable, it is time to return to simple life. What thinking cannot solve, life solves, and what action never decides is reserved for thinking. If I ascend to the highest and most difficult on the one hand, and seek to eke out redemption that reaches even higher, then the true way does not lead upward, but toward the depths, since only my other leads me beyond myself. But acceptance of the other means a descent into the opposite, from seriousness into the laughable, from suffering into the cheerful, from the beautiful into the ugly, from the pure into the impure.[166]

---

164. The *Draft* continues: "His own way led him to the cross for humanity's own way leads to the cross. My way also leads to the cross, but not to that of Christ, but to mine, which is the image of the sacrifice and of life. But as I was still blinded, I was inclined to yield to the enormous temptation of imitation and to look across to Christ, as if he were my goal and not my way" (p. 367).
165. The references seem to be to Schopenhauer and Nietzsche, respectively.
166. The *Draft* continues: "Consider this. Once you have considered it, you will understand the adventure that beset me the following night" (p. 368).

Nox secunda[167]

Cap. xv.

[HI 100] On leaving the library, I stood in the anteroom again.[168] This time I look across to the door on the left. I put the small book into my pocket and go to the door; it is also open, and leads to a large kitchen, with a large chimney over the stove. Two long tables stand in the middle of the room, flanked by benches. Brass pots, copper pans, and other vessels stand on shelves along the walls. A large fat woman is standing at the stove—apparently the cook—wearing a checkered apron. I greet her, somewhat astonished. She too seems embarrassed. I ask her: "May I sit down for a while? It's cold outside and I must wait for something."

"Please have a seat."

She wipes the table in front of me. Having nothing else to do, I take out my Thomas and begin to read. The cook is curious and looks at me furtively. Every once in a while she goes past me.

"Excuse me, are you perhaps a clergyman?"

"No, why do you think so?"

"Oh, I just thought you might be because you are reading a small black book. My mother, may God rest her soul, left me such a book."

"I see, and what book might that be?"

"It is called *The Imitation of Christ*. It's a very beautiful book. I often pray with it in the evenings."

"You have guessed well, I too am reading *The Imitation of Christ*."

"I don't believe that a man like you would read such a book unless he were a pastor."

"Why shouldn't I read it? It also does me good to read a proper book."

"My mother, God bless her, had it with her on her deathbed, and she gave it to me before she died."

167. Second night.

168. January 17, 1914.

I browse through the book absentmindedly while she is speak-
100/101 ing. My eyes fall on the following / passage in the nineteenth chapter: "The righteous base their intentions more on the mercy of God, which in whatever they undertake they trust more than their own wisdom."[169]

This is the intuitive method that Thomas recommends, it occurs to me.[170] I turn to the cook: "Your mother was a clever woman, and she did well to give you this book."

"Yes, indeed, it has often comforted me in difficult hours and it always provides good counsel."

I become immersed in my thoughts again: I believe one can also follow one's own nose. That would also be[171] the intuitive method. But the beautiful way in which Christ does this must nevertheless be of special value. I would like to imitate Christ—an inner disquiet seizes me—what is supposed to happen? I hear an odd swishing and whirring—and suddenly a roaring sound fills the room like a horde of large birds—with a frenzied flapping of wings—I see many shadowlike human forms rush past and I hear a manifold babble of voices utter the words: "Let us pray in the temple!"

"Where are you rushing off to?" I call out. A bearded man with tousled hair and dark shining eyes stops and turns toward me: "We are wandering to Jerusalem to pray at the most holy sepulcher."

"Take me with you."

[172]"You cannot join us, you have a body. But we are dead."

---

169. "The resolve of the upright depends upon the grace of God, not on their own wisdom; in him they trust, whatever they undertake; for man proposes, God disposes, and *it is not for man to choose his lot*" (*The Imitation of Christ*, book 1, ch. 19, p. 54).

170. Instead of this sentence, *Black Book* 4 has: "Well, Henri Bergson, I think there you have it—this is precisely the genuine and right intuitive method" (p. 9). On March 20, 1914, Adolf Keller gave a talk on "Bergson and the theory of libido" to the Zürich Psychoanalytical Society. In the discussion, Jung said "Bergson should have been discussed here long ago. B. says everything that we have not said" (*MZS*, vol. 1, p. 57). On July 24, 1914, Jung gave a talk in London where he noted that his "constructive method" corresponded to Bergson's "intuitive method" ("On psychological understanding," *Collected Papers on Analytical Psychology*, ed. Constance Long [London: Ballière, Tindall and Cox, 1917], p. 399). The work Jung read was *L'evolution creatrice* (Paris: Alcan, 1907). He possessed the 1912 German translation.

171. Cary Baynes's transcription has: "Bergson's."

172. In the *Draft*, the speaker is identified as "The Uncanny One."

"Who are you?"

"I am Ezechiel, and I am an Anabaptist."[173]

"Who are those wandering with you?"

"These are my fellow believers."

"Why are you wandering?"

"We cannot stop, but must make a pilgrimage to all the holy places."

"What drives you to this?"

"I don't know. But it seems that we still have no peace, although we died in true belief."

"Why do you have no peace if you died in true belief?"

"It always seems to me as if we had not come to a proper end with life."

"Remarkable—how so?"

"It seems to me that we forgot something important that should also have been lived."

"And what was that?"

"Would you happen to know?"

With these words he reaches out greedily and uncannily toward me, his eyes shining as if from inner heat.

"Let go, daimon, you did not live your animal."[174]

---

173. The biblical Ezechiel was a prophet in the sixth century BCE. Jung saw a great deal of historical significance in his visions, which incorporated a mandala with quaternities, as representing the humanization and differentiation of Yahweh. Although Ezechiel's visions are often viewed as pathological, Jung defended their normality, arguing that visions are natural phenomena that can be designated as pathological only when their morbid aspects have been demonstrated ("Answer to Job," 1952, CW 11, §§665, 667, 686). Anabaptism was a radical movement of the sixteenth-century Protestant reformation, which tried to restore the spirit of the early church. The movement originated in Zürich in the 1520s, where they rebelled against Zwingli and Luther's reluctance to completely reform the church. They rejected the practice of infant baptism, and promoted adult baptisms (the first of these took place in Zollikon, which is near Küsnacht, where Jung lived). Anabaptists stressed the immediacy of the human relation with God and were critical of religious institutions. The movement was violently suppressed and thousands were killed. See Daniel Liechty, ed., *Early Anabaptist Spirituality: Selected Writings* (New York: Paulist Press, 1994).

174. In 1918, Jung argued that Christianity had suppressed the animal element ("On the unconscious," CW 10, §31). He elaborated this theme in his 1923 seminars in Polzeath, Cornwall. In 1939, he argued that the "psychological sin" which Christ committed was that "he did not live the animal side of himself" (*Modern Psychology* 4, p. 230).

The cook is standing in front of me with a horrified face; she has taken me by the arm and grips me firmly. "For God's sake," she calls out, "Help, what's wrong with you? Are you in a bad way?"

I look at her astonished and wonder where I really am. But soon strange people burst in—among them the librarian—infinitely astonished and dismayed at first, then laughing maliciously: "Oh, I might have known! Quick, the police!"

Before I can collect myself, I am pushed through a crowd of people into a van. I am still clutching my copy of Thomas and ask myself: "What would he say to this new situation?" I open the booklet and my eyes fall on the thirteenth chapter, where it says: "So long as we live here on earth, we cannot escape temptation. There is no man who is so perfect, and no saint so sacred, that he cannot be tempted on occasion. Yes, we can hardly be without temptation."[175]

Wise Thomas, you always come up with the right answer. That crazy Anabaptist certainly had no such knowledge, or he might have made a peaceful end. He also could have read it in Cicero: *rerum omnium satietas vitae facit satietatem—satietas vitae tempus maturum mortis affert* [satiety of all things causes satiety of life—one is satiated with life and the time is ripe for death].[176] This knowledge had evidently

175. Chapter 13 of book 1 of *The Imitation of Christ* begins: "As long as we are in this world we shall have to face trials and temptations. As it says in the Book of Job—What is man's life on earth but a time of temptation? That is why we should treat our temptations as a serious matter and endeavor by vigilance and prayer to keep the devil from finding any loophole. Remember that the devil never sleeps, but goes about looking for his prey. There is no one so perfect and holy that he never meets temptation; we cannot escape it altogether" (p. 46). He goes on to emphasize the benefits of temptation, as being the means through which a man is "humbled, purified and disciplined."

176. The citation is from Cicero's *Cato Maior de Senectute* (Cato the Elder on Old Age). The text is a eulogy to old age. The lines Jung cites are italicized in the following passage: "Omnino, ut mihi quidem videtur, *rerum omnium satietas vitae facit satietatem.* Sunt pueritiae studia certa; num igitur ea desiderant adulescentes? Sunt ineuntis adulescentiae: num ea constans iam requirit aetas quae media dicitur? Sunt etiam eius aetatis; ne ea quidem quaeruntur in senectute. Sunt extrema quaedam studia senectutis: ergo, ut superiorum aetatum studia occidunt, sic occidunt etiam senectutis; quod cum evenit, *satietas vitae tempus maturum mortis affert*" (Tullii Ciceronis, *Cato Maior de Senectute*, ed. Julius Sommerbrodt [Berlin: Weidmannsche Buchhandlung, 1873]). Translation: "Undoubtedly, as it seems to me at least, *satiety of all things causes satiety of life.* Boyhood has certain pursuits: does adolescence yearn for them? Adolescence has its pursuits: does the matured or so-called middle stage of life need them? Maturity, too, has such as not even sought in old age, and finally, there are those suitable to old age. Therefore as the

brought me into conflict with society. I was flanked by policemen left and right. "Well," I said to them, "you can let me go now." "Yes, we know all about this," / one said laughing. "Now just you hold 101/102
your peace," said the other sternly. So, we are obviously heading for the madhouse. That is a high price to pay. But one can go this way too, it seems. It's not so strange, since thousands of our fellows take that path.

We have arrived—a large gate, a hall—a friendly bustling superintendent—and now also two doctors. One of them is a small fat professor.

Pr: "What's that book you've got there?"

"It's Thomas à Kempis, *The Imitation of Christ.*"

Pr: "So, a form of religious madness, perfectly clear, religious paranoia.[177]—You see, my dear, nowadays, the imitation of Christ leads to the madhouse."

"That is hardly to be doubted, professor."

Pr: "The man has wit—he is obviously somewhat maniacally aroused. Do you hear voices?"

"You bet! Today it was a huge throng of Anabaptists that swarmed through the kitchen."

Pr: "Now, there we have it. Are the voices following you?"

"Oh no, Heaven forbid, I summoned them."

Pr: "Ah, this is yet another case that clearly indicates that hallucinations directly call up voices. This belongs in the case history. Would you immediately make a note of that, doctor?"

"With all due respect, Professor, may I say that it is absolutely not abnormal, but much rather the intuitive method."

Pr: "Excellent. The fellow also uses neologisms. Well—I suppose we have an adequately clear diagnosis. Anyway, I wish you a good recovery, and make sure you stay quiet."

---

pleasures and pursuits of the earlier periods of life fall away, so also do those of old age; and when that happens *one is satiated of life and the time is ripe for death*" (Cicero, *De Senectute, De Amicitia, De Divinatione* [London: William Heinemann, 1927], pp. 86–88, tr. mod.).

177. *Black Book* 4 has: "paranoid form of Dementia praecox" (p. 16).

"But professor, I'm not at all sick, I feel perfectly well."

Pr: "Look, my dear. You don't have any insight into your illness yet. The prognosis is naturally pretty bad, with at best limited recovery."

Superintendent: "Professor, can the man keep the book?"

Pr: "Well, I suppose so, as it seems to be a harmless prayer book."

Now my clothes are inventoried—then the bath—and now I'm taken off to the ward. I enter a large sickroom, where I'm told to get into bed. The person to my left is lying motionless with a transfixed gaze, while the one to the right appears to possess a brain whose girth and weight are shrinking. I enjoy perfect silence. The problem of madness is profound. Divine madness—a higher form of the irrationality of the life streaming through us—at any rate a madness that cannot be integrated into present-day society—but how? What if the form of society were integrated into madness? At this point things grow dark, and there is no end in sight.[178]

[2] [HI 102] The growing plant sprouts a sapling on its right-hand side, and when this is completely formed, the natural urge to grow will not develop beyond the final bud but flows back into the stem, into the mother of the sprig, paving an uncertain way in the dark and through the stem, and finally finding the right position on the left where it sprouts a new sapling. But this new direction of growth is completely opposed to the previous one. And yet the plant nevertheless grows regularly in this way, without overstraining or disturbing its balance.

On the right is my thinking, on the left is my feeling. I enter the space of my feeling which was previously unknown to me, and see with astonishment the difference between my two rooms. I cannot help laughing—many laugh instead of crying. I have stepped from

178. In the *Draft* a passage occurs here, a paraphrase of which follows: Since I was a thinker, my feeling was the lowest, oldest, and least developed. When I was brought up against the unthinkable through my thinking and what was unreachable through my thought power, then I could only press forward in a forced way. But I overloaded on one side, and the other side sank deeper. Overloading is not growth, which is what we need (p. 376).

the right foot onto the left, and wince, struck by inner pain. The difference between hot and cold is too great. I leave the spirit of this world which has thought Christ through to the end, and step over into that other funny-frightful realm in which I can find Christ again.

The "imitation of Christ" led me to the master himself and to his astonishing kingdom. I do not know what I want there; I can only follow the master who governs this other realm in me. In this realm other laws are valid than the guidelines of my wisdom. Here, the "mercy of God," which I had never relied on, for good practical reasons, is the highest law of action. The "mercy of God" signifies a
particular / state of the soul in which I entrust myself to all neigh- 102/103
bors with trembling and hesitation and with the mightiest outlay of hope that everything will work out well.

I can no longer say that this or that goal should be reached, or that this or that reason should apply because it is good; instead I grope through mist and night. No line emerges, no law appears; instead everything is thoroughly and convincingly accidental, as a matter of fact even terribly accidental. But one thing becomes dreadfully clear, namely that contrary to my earlier way and all its insights and intentions, henceforth all is error. It becomes ever more apparent that nothing leads, as my hope sought to persuade me, but that everything misleads.

And suddenly to your shivering horror it becomes clear to you that you have fallen into the boundless, the abyss, the inanity of eternal chaos. It rushes toward you as if carried by the roaring wings of a storm, the hurtling waves of the sea.

Every man has a quiet place in his soul, where everything is self-evident and easily explainable, a place to which he likes to retire from the confusing possibilities of life, because there everything is simple and clear, with a manifest and limited purpose. About nothing else in the world can a man say with the same conviction as he does of this place: "You are nothing but . . . " and indeed he has said it.

And even this place is a smooth surface, an everyday wall, nothing more than a snugly sheltered and frequently polished crust over the mystery of chaos. If you break through this most everyday of walls, the overwhelming stream of chaos will flood in. Chaos is not single, but an unending multiplicity. It is not formless, otherwise it would be single, but it is filled with figures that have a confusing and overwhelming effect due to their fullness.[179]

These figures are the dead, not just your dead, that is, all the images of the shapes you took in the past, which your ongoing life has left behind, but also the thronging dead of human history, the ghostly procession of the past, which is an ocean compared to the drops of your own life span. I see behind you, behind the mirror of your eyes, the crush of dangerous shadows, the dead, who look greedily through the empty sockets of your eyes, who moan and hope to gather up through you all the loose ends of the ages, which sigh in them. Your cluelessness does not prove anything. Put your ear to that wall and you will hear the rustling of their procession.

Now you know why you lodged the simplest and most easily explained matters in just that spot, why you praised that peaceful seat as the most secure: so that no one, least of all yourself, would unearth the mystery there. For this is the place where day and night agonizingly merge. What you excluded from your life, what you renounced and damned, everything that was and could have gone wrong, awaits you behind that wall before which you sit quietly.

If you read the books of history, you will find men who sought the strange and incredible, who ensnared themselves and who were held captive by others in wolves' lairs; men who sought the highest and the lowest, and who were wiped by fate, incomplete, from the tablets of the living. Few of the living know of them, and these few appreciate nothing about them, but shake their heads at such delusion.

---

179. Jung's marginal note to the calligraphic volume: "26. 1. 1919." The date appears to refer to when this section was transcribed into the calligraphic volume.

While you mock them, one of them stands behind you, panting from rage and despair at the fact that your stupor does not attend to him. He besieges you in sleepless nights, sometimes he takes hold of you in an illness, sometimes he crosses your intentions. He makes you overbearing and greedy, he pricks your longing for everything, which avails you nothing, he devours your success in discord. He accompanies you as your evil spirit, to whom you can grant no release.

Have you heard of those dark ones who roamed incognito alongside those who ruled the day, conspiratorially causing unrest? Who devised cunning things and did not shrink from any crime to honor their God?

Beside them place Christ, who was the greatest among them. It was too little for him to break the world, so he broke himself. And therefore he was the greatest of them all, and the powers of this world did not reach him. But I speak of the dead who fell prey to power, broken by force and not by themselves. Their hordes people the land of the soul. If you accept / them, they fill you with delu- 103/104
sion and rebellion against what rules the world. From the deepest and from the highest they devised the most dangerous things. They were not of a common nature, but fine blades of the hardest steel. They would have nothing to do with the small lives of men. They lived on the heights and accomplished the lowest. They forgot only one thing: they did not live their animal.

The animal does not rebel against its own kind. Consider animals: how just they are, how well-behaved, how they keep to the time-honored, how loyal they are to the land that bears them, how they hold to their accustomed routes, how they care for their young, how they go together to pasture, and how they draw one another to the spring. There is not one that conceals its overabundance of prey and lets its brother starve as a result. There is not one that tries to enforce its will on those of its own kind. Not a one mistakenly imagines that it is an elephant when it is a mosquito. The animal lives fittingly and true to the life of its species, neither exceeding nor falling short of it.

He who never lives his animal must treat his brother like an animal. Abase yourself and live your animal so that you will be able to treat your brother correctly. You will thus redeem all those roaming dead who strive to feed on the living. And do not turn anything you do into a law, since that is the hubris of power.[180]

When the time has come and you open the door to the dead, your horrors will also afflict your brother, for your countenance proclaims the disaster. Hence withdraw and enter solitude, since no one can give you counsel if you wrestle with the dead. Do not cry for help if the dead surround you, otherwise the living will take flight, and they are your only bridge to the day. Live the life of the day and do not speak of mysteries, but dedicate the night to bringing about the salvation of the dead.

For whoever well-meaningly tears you away from the dead has rendered you the worst service, since he has torn your life branch from the tree of divinity. He also sins against restoring what was created and later subjugated and lost.[181] "For the earnest expectation of the creature waiteth for the manifestation of the sons of God. For the creature was made subject to vanity, not willingly, but by reason of him who hath subjected the same in hope, because the creature itself also shall be delivered from the bondage of corruption into the glorious liberty of the children of God. For we know that the whole creation groaneth and travaileth in pain together until now."

Every step upward will restore a step downward so that the dead will be delivered into freedom. The creating of the new shrinks from the day since its essence is secret. It prepares the destruction

180. In 1930, Jung said in a seminar: "We are prejudiced in regard to the animal. People don't understand when I tell them they should become acquainted with their animals or assimilate their animals. They think the animal is always jumping over walls and raising hell all over town. Yet in nature the animal is a well-behaved citizen. It is pious, it follows the path with great regularity, it does nothing extravagant. Only man is extravagant. So if you assimilate the character of the animal you become a peculiarly law-abiding citizen, you go very slowly, and you become very reasonable in your ways, in as much as you can afford it" (*Visions* 1, p. 168).

181. The *Handwritten Draft* has in the margin: "Rom 8 19" (p. 863). What follows in the text is a citation from Romans 8:19–22.

of precisely this day in the hope of leading it over into a new creation. Something evil is attached to the creation of the new, which you cannot proclaim loudly. The animal that looks for new hunting grounds cowers slinking and sniffing on dark paths and does not want to be surprised.

Please consider that it is the suffering of the creative that they carry something evil in them, a leprosy of the soul that separates them from its danger. They could praise their leprosy as a virtue and could indeed do so out of virtuousness. But this would be doing what Christ does, and would therefore be his imitation. For only one was Christ and only one could violate the laws as he did. It is impossible to commit higher infringements on his path. Fulfill that which comes to you. Break the Christ in yourself so that you may arrive at yourself and ultimately at your animal which is well-behaved in its herd and unwilling to infringe its laws. May it suffice in terms of transgression that you do not imitate Christ, since thereby you take a step back from Christianity and a step beyond it. Christ brought salvation through adeptness, and ineptitude will save you.

Have you counted the dead whom the master of sacrifice honored? Have you asked them for whose sake they believe they have suffered death? Have you entered the beauty of their thoughts and the purity of their intention? "And they shall go forth, and look upon the carcasses of the men that have transgressed against me: for their worm shall not die, neither shall their fire be quenched."[182]

Thus do penance, consider what fell victim to death for the sake of Christianity, lay it before you and force yourself to accept it. For the dead need salvation. The number of the unredeemed dead has become greater than the number of living Christians; therefore it is time that we accept the dead.[183]

---

182. This is a citation from Isaiah 66:24.

183. The *Draft* continues: "We were led by a prophet, whose proximity to God had driven him insane. He raged blindly against Christianity in his sermon, but he was the champion of the dead who had appointed him their spokesman and resounding trumpet. He shouted in a deafening voice so that many would hear him, and the power of his lan-

Do not throw yourself against what has become, enraged or bent on destruction. What will you put in its place? Do you not know that if you are successful in destroying what has become, you will then turn the will of destruction against yourself? But anyone who makes destruction their goal will perish through self-destruction. Much rather respect what has become, since reverence is a blessing.

Then turn to the dead,[184] listen to their lament and accept them
104/106 with love. Be not their blind spokesman,[185] / [Image 105][186] / there

---

guage also burned those who resisted death. He preached the struggle against Christianity. This was good, too" (p. 387). The reference is to Nietzsche.

184. The *Draft* continues: "whose champion you are" (p. 388).

185. The *Draft* continues: "like that raving prophet who did not know whose cause he was promoting, but instead believed himself to be speaking on his own behalf and thought he was the will of destruction" (p. 388). The reference is to Nietzsche.

186. In 1930, Jung anonymously reproduced this image in "Commentary on 'The Secret of the Golden Flower'" as a mandala painted by a male patient during treatment. He described it as follows: "In the centre, the white light, shining in the firmament; in the first circle, protoplasmic life-seeds; in the second, rotating cosmic principles which contain the four primary colors; in the third and fourth, creative forces working inward and outward. At the cardinal points, the masculine and feminine souls, both again divided into light and dark" (*CW* 13, A6). He reproduced it again in 1952 in "Concerning mandala symbolism" and wrote: "Picture by a middle-aged man. In the center is a star. The blue sky contains golden clouds. At the four cardinal points we see human figures: at the top, an old man in the attitude of contemplation; at the bottom, Loki or Hephaestus with red, flaming hair, holding in his hands a temple. To the right and left are a light and dark female figure. Together they indicate four aspects of the personality, or four archetypal figures belonging, as it were, to the periphery of the self. The two female figures can be recognized without difficulty as the two aspects of the anima. The old man corresponds to the archetype of meaning, or of the spirit, and the dark chthonic figure to the opposite of the Wise Old Man, namely the magical (and sometimes destructive) Luciferian element. In alchemy it is Hermes Trismegistus versus Mercurius, the evasive 'trickster.' The circle enclosing the sky contains structures or organisms that look like protozoa. The sixteen globes painted in four colors just outside the circle derived originally from an eye motif and therefore stand for the observing and discriminating consciousness. Similarly, the ornaments in the next circle, all opening inward, are rather like vessels pouring out their content toward the center. [Fn: There is a similar conception in alchemy, in the Ripley Scrowle and its variants (*Psychology and Alchemy*, fig 257). There it is the planetary Gods who are pouring their qualities into the bath of rebirth.] On the other hand the ornaments along the rim open outward, as if to receive something from outside. That is, in the individuation process what were originally projections stream back 'inside' and are integrated into the personality again. Here, in contrast to Figure 25, 'Above' and 'Below,' male and female, are integrated, as in the alchemical hermaphrodite" (*CW* 9, 1, §682). On March 21, 1950, he wrote to Raymond Piper concerning the same image: "The other picture is by an educated man about 40 years old. He produced this picture also as an at-first unconscious attempt to restore order in the emotional state he was in which had been caused by an invasion of unconscious contents" (*Letters* 1, p. 550).

are prophets who in the end have stoned themselves. But we seek salvation and hence we need to revere what has become and to accept the dead, who have fluttered through the air and lived like bats under our roofs since time immemorial. The new will be built on the old and the meaning of what has become will become manifold. Your poverty in what has become you will thus deliver into the wealth of the future.

What seeks to distance you from Christianity and its holy rule of love are the dead, who could find no peace in the Lord since their uncompleted work has followed them. A new salvation is always a restoring of the previously lost. Did not Christ himself restore bloody human sacrifice, which better customs had expelled from sacred practice since days of old? Did he not himself reinstate the sacred practice of the eating of human sacrifice? In your sacred practice that which earlier laws condemned will once again be included.

However, just as Christ brought back human sacrifice and the eating of the sacrificed, all this happened to him and not to his brother, since Christ placed above it the highest law of love, so that no brother would come to harm as a result, but so that all could rejoice in the restoration. The same thing happened as in ancient times, but now under the law of love.[187] So if you have no reverence for what has become, you will destroy the law of love.[188] And what will become of

187. The *Draft* continues: "Not one title of Christian law is abrogated, but instead we are adding a new one: accepting the lament of the dead" (p. 390).

188. The *Draft* continues: "It is nothing other than common evil desire, nothing but everyday temptation, as long as you do not know that it is what the dead demand. But as long as you know about the dead, you will understand your temptation. As long as it is no more than evil desire, what can you do about it? Damn it, regret it, arise anew, only to stumble again and mock and loathe yourself, but definitely despise and pity yourself. But if you know what the dead demand, temptation will become the wellspring of your best work, indeed of the work of salvation: When Christ ascended after completing his work, he led those up with him who had died prematurely and incomplete under the law of hardship and alienation and raw violence. The lamentations of the dead filled the air at the time, and their misery became so loud that even the living were saddened, and became tired and sick of life and yearned to die to this world already in their living bodies. And thus you too lead the dead to their completion with your work of salvation" (pp. 390–91).

you then? You will be forced to restore what was before, namely violent deeds, murder, wrongdoing, and contempt of your brother. And one will be alien to the other, and confusion will rule.

Therefore you should have reverence for what has become, so that the law of love may become redemption through the restoration of the lower and of the past, not perdition through the boundless mastery of the dead. But the spirits of those who die before their time will live, for the sake of our present incompleteness, in dark hordes in the rafters of our houses and besiege our ears with urgent laments, until we grant them redemption through restoring what has existed since ancient times under the rule of love.

What we call temptation is the demand of the dead who passed away prematurely and incomplete through the guilt of the good and of the law. For no good is so complete that it could not do injustice and break what should not be broken.

We are a blinded race. We live only on the surface, only in the present, and think only of tomorrow. We deal roughly with the past in that we do not accept the dead. We want to work only with visible success. Above all we want to be paid. We would consider it insane to do hidden work that does not visibly serve men. There is no doubt that the necessity of life forced us to prefer only those fruits one can taste. But who suffers more from the tempting and misleading influence of the dead than those who have gone wholly missing on the surface of the world?

There is one necessary but hidden and strange work—a major work—which you must do in secret, for the sake of the dead. He who cannot attain his own visible field and vineyard is held fast by the dead, who demand the work of atonement from him. And until he has fulfilled this, he cannot get to his outer work, since the dead do not let him. He shall have to search his soul and act in stillness at their behest and complete the mystery, so that the dead will not let him. Do not look forward so much, but back and into yourself, so that you will not fail to hear the dead.

It belongs to the way of Christ that he ascends with few of the living, but many of the dead. His work was the salvation of the despised and lost, for whose sake he was crucified between two criminals.

I suffer my agony between two madmen. I enter the truth if I descend. Become accustomed to being alone with the dead. It is difficult, but this is precisely how you will discover the worth of your living companions.

What the ancients did for their dead! You seem to believe that you can absolve yourself from the care of the dead, and from the work that they so greatly demand, since what is dead is past. You excuse yourself with your disbelief in the immortality of the soul. Do you think that the dead do not exist because you have devised the impossibility of immortality? You believe in your idols of words. The dead produce effects, that is sufficient. In the inner world there is no explaining away, as little as you can explain away the sea in the outer world. You must finally understand your purpose in explaining away, namely to seek protection.[189]

I accepted the chaos, and in the following night, my soul
approached me. / [Image 107] / 106/108

Nox tertia[190]

Cap. xvi.

[HI 108] [191]My soul spoke to me in a whisper, urgently and alarmingly: "Words, words, do not make too many words. Be silent and listen: have you recognized your madness and do you admit it? Have you noticed that all your foundations are completely mired in madness? Do you not want to recognize your madness and welcome it

189. The *Draft* continues: "You employ old word magic to protect yourself through superstition for you are still a powerless child of the old wood. But we can see behind your word magic, and it is rendered feeble, and nothing protects you against the chaos other than acceptance" (p. 395).

190. Third night.

191. January 18, 1914.

in a friendly manner? You wanted to accept everything. So accept madness too. Let the light of your madness shine, and it will suddenly dawn on you. Madness is not to be despised and not to be feared, but instead you should give it life."

I: "Your words sound hard and the task you set me is difficult."

S: "If you want to find paths, you should also not spurn madness, since it makes up such a great part of your nature."

I: "I didn't know that this is so."

S: "Be glad that you can recognize it, for you will thus avoid becoming its victim. Madness is a special form of the spirit and clings to all teachings and philosophies, but even more to daily life, since life itself is full of craziness and at bottom utterly illogical. Man strives toward reason only so that he can make rules for himself. Life itself has no rules. That is its mystery and its unknown law. What you call knowledge is an attempt to impose something comprehensible on life."

I: "That all sounds very desolate, but nevertheless it prompts me to disagree."

S: "You have nothing to disagree with—you are in the madhouse."

There stands the fat little professor—had he spoken this way? And had I taken him for my soul?

Prof: "Yes, my dear, you are confused. Your speech is completely incoherent."

I: "I too believe that I've completely lost myself. Am I really crazy? It's all terribly confusing."

Prof: "Have patience, everything will work out. Anyway, sleep well."

I: "Thank you, but I'm afraid."

Everything inside me is in utter disarray. Matters are becoming serious, and chaos is approaching. Is this the ultimate bottom? Is chaos also a foundation? If only there weren't these terrible waves. Everything breaks asunder like black billows. Yes, I see and understand: it is the ocean, the almighty nocturnal tide—a ship moves there—a large steamer—I'm just about to enter the smoking parlor—

many people—beautiful clothes—they all look at me astonished—someone comes up to me and says: "What's the matter? You look just like a ghost! What happened?"

I: "Nothing—that is—I believe that I have gone crazy—the floor sways—everything moves—"

Someone: "The sea is somewhat rough this evening, that's all—have a hot toddy—you're seasick."

I: "You're right, I am seasick, but in a special way—I'm really in a madhouse."

Someone: "Well now, you're joking again, life is returning."

I: "Do you call that wit? Just now the professor pronounced me truly and utterly mad."

The fat little professor is actually sitting at a green-covered table playing cards. He turns toward me when he hears me speak and laughs: "Well, where did you get to? Come here. Would you like a drink too? You're quite a character, I must say. You've put all the ladies in quite a flurry this evening."

I: "Professor, for me this is no longer a joke. Just now I was your patient—"

The parlor erupts in unbridled laughter.

Prof: "I hope that I haven't upset you too much."

I: "Well, to be committed is no small matter."

The person to whom I had been speaking before suddenly comes up to me and looks me in the face. He is a man with a black beard, a tousled head of hair, and dark shining eyes. He speaks to me vehemently: "Something worse happened to me, it's five years now that I've been here."

I realize that it is my neighbor, who has apparently awakened from his apathy and is now sitting on my bed. He goes on speaking fiercely and urgently: "But I am Nietzsche, only rebaptized, I am also Christ, the Savior, and appointed to save the world, but they won't let me."

I: "Who won't let you?"

The fool: "The devil. We are in Hell. But of course, you haven't noticed it yet. I didn't realize until the second year of my time here that the director is the devil."

I: "You mean the professor? That sounds incredible."

The fool: "You're an ignoramus. I was supposed to marry the mother of God long ago.[192] But the professor, that devil, has her in his power. Every evening when the sun goes down he gets her with child. In the morning before sunrise she gives birth to it. Then all the devils come together and kill the child in a grue-
108/110 some / [Image 109][193] / manner. I distinctly hear his cries."

I: "But what you have told me is pure mythology."

The fool: "You're crazy and understand nothing of it. You belong in the madhouse. My God, why does my family always shut me in with crazy people? I'm supposed to save the world, I'm the Savior!"

He lies down again and sinks back into his lassitude. I clutch the sides of my bed to protect myself against the terrible waves. I stare at the wall, so that I can at least latch onto something with my eyes. A horizontal line runs along the wall, which is painted a darker color beneath. A radiator stands in front of it—it is a railing and I can see the sea beyond it. The line is the horizon. And there the sun now rises in red glory, solitary and magnificent—in it is a cross from which a serpent hangs—or is it a bull, slit open, as at the slaughterhouse, or is it an ass? I suppose it is really a ram with a crown of thorns—or is it the crucified one, myself? The sun of martyrdom has arisen and is pouring bloody rays over the sea. This spectacle lasts a long time, the sun rises higher, its rays grow brighter[194] and hotter and the sun burns down white on a blue sea. The swell has subsided. A charitable and quiet summer dawn lies on

192. In *The Relations between the I and the Unconscious* (1928), Jung refers to a case of a man with paranoid dementia he encountered during his time at the Burghölzli who was in telephonic communication with the Mother of God (CW 7, §229).

193. Image legend: "This man of matter rises up too far in the world of the spirit, there the spirit bores through his heart with the golden ray. He falls with joy and disintegrates. The serpent, who is the evil one, could not remain in the world of the spirit."

194. Jung's marginal note to the calligraphic volume: "22.3.1919." This seems to refer to when this passage was transcribed into the calligraphic volume.

the shimmering sea. The salty smell of water rises up. A faint wide surf breaks on the sand with a dull thunder, and returns incessantly, twelve times, the strokes of the world clock[195]—the twelfth hour is complete. And now silence enters. No noise, no breeze. Everything is rigid and deathly still. I wait, secretly anxious. I see a tree arise from the sea. Its crown reaches to Heaven and its roots reach down into Hell. I am completely alone and disheartened and gaze from afar. It is as if all life had flown from me and completely passed into the incomprehensible and fearful. I am utterly weak and incapable. "Salvation," I whisper. A strange voice speaks: "There is no salvation here,[196] you must remain calm, or you will disturb the others. It is night and the other people want to sleep." I see, it's the attendant. The room is dimly lit by a weak lamp and sadness weighs on the room.

I: "I couldn't find the way."

He says: "You don't need to find a way now."

He speaks the truth. The way, or whatever it might be, on which people go, is our way, the right way. There are no paved ways into the future. We say that it is this way, and it is. We build roads by going on. Our life is the truth that we seek. Only my life is the truth, the truth above all. We create the truth by living it.

[2] This is the night in which all the dams broke, where what was previously solid moved, where the stones turned into serpents, and everything living froze. Is this a web of words? If it is, it is a hellish web for those caught in it.

There are hellish webs of words, only words, but what are words? Be tentative with words, value them well, take safe words, words without catches, do not spin them with one another so that no webs arise, for you are the first who is ensnared in them.[197] For words

195. In *Psychology and Religion* (1938), Jung commented on the symbolism of the world clock (CW 11, §110ff).

196. In Dante's *Commedia*, the following lines are inscribed over the gates of Hell: "Abandon every hope, you who enter" (canto 3, line 9). See *The Divine Comedy of Dante Alighieri*, vol. 1., ed. and tr. Robert Durling (New York: Oxford University Press, 1997), p. 55.

197. The *Draft* continues: "For words are not merely words, but have meanings for which they are set. They attract these meanings like daimonic shadows" (p. 403).

have meanings. With words you pull up the underworld. Word, the paltriest and the mightiest. In words the emptiness and the fullness flow together. Hence the word is an image of God. The word is the greatest and the smallest that man created, just as what is created through man is the greatest and the smallest.

So if I fall prey to the web of words, I fall prey to the greatest and the smallest. I am at the mercy of the sea, of the inchoate waves that are forever changing place. Their essence is movement and movement is their order. He who strives against waves is exposed to the arbitrary. The work of men is steady but it swims upon chaos. The striving of men seems like lunacy to him who comes from the sea. But men consider him mad.[198] He who comes from the sea is sick. He can hardly bear the gaze of men. For to him they all seem to be drunk and foolish from sleep-inducing poisons. They want to come to your rescue, and as for accepting help, for sure you would like less of that, rather than swindling your way into their company and being completely like one who has never seen the chaos but only talks about it.

But for him who has seen the chaos, there is no more hiding, because he knows that the bottom sways and knows what this swaying means. He has seen the order and the disorder of the endless, he knows the unlawful laws. He knows the sea and can never forget it. The chaos is terrible: days full of lead, nights full of horror.

But just as Christ knew that he was the way, the truth, and the life, in that the new torment and the renewed salvation came into the world through him,[199] I know that chaos must come over men, and that the hands of those who unknowingly and unsuspectingly

198. The *Draft* continues: "Once you have seen the chaos, look at your face: you saw more than death and the grave, you saw beyond and your face bears the mark of one who has seen chaos and yet was a man. Many cross over, but they do not see the chaos; however the chaos sees them, stares at them, and imprints its features on them. And they are marked forever. Call such a one mad, for that is what he is; he has become a wave and has lost his human side, his constancy" (p. 404).

199. The preceding sentence is crossed out in the *Corrected Draft*, and Jung has written in the margin: "ΦΙΛΗΜΩΝ identification" (p. 405).

break through the thin walls that separate us from the sea are busy. For this is our way, our truth, and our life.

Just as the disciples of Christ recognized that God had become flesh and lived among them as a man, we now recognize that the anointed of this time is a God who does not appear in the flesh; he is no man and yet is a son of man, but in spirit and not in flesh; hence he can be born only through the spirit of men as the conceiving womb of the God.[200] What is done to this God you do to the lowest in yourself, under the law of love according to which nothing is cast out. For how else should your lowest be saved from depravity? / [Image 111][201] / Who should accept the lowest in you, if you 110/112

200. Jung elaborated on this issue many years later in *Answer to Job* (1952), where he studied the historical transformation of Judeo-Christian God images. A major theme in this is the continued incarnation of God after Christ. Commenting on the Book of Revelation, Jung argued that: "Ever since John the apocalyptist experienced for the first time (perhaps unconsciously) the conflict into which Christianity inevitably leads, mankind is burdened with this: God wanted and wants to become man" (CW 11, §739). In Jung's view, there was a direct link between John's views and Eckhart's views: "This disturbing invasion engendered in him the image of the divine consort, whose image lives in every man: of the child, whom Meister Eckhart also saw in the vision. It was he who knew that God alone in his Godhead is not in a state of bliss, but must be born in the human soul. The incarnation in Christ is the prototype which is continually being transferred to the creature by the Holy Ghost" (Ibid., §741). In contemporary times, Jung gave great importance to the papal bull of the *Assumptio Maria*. He held that it "points to the *hieros gamos* in the Pleroma, and this in turn implies, as we have said, the future birth of the divine child, who, in accordance with the divine trend toward incarnation, will choose as his birthplace the empirical man. This metaphysical process is known as the *individuation process* in the psychology of the unconscious" (Ibid., §755). Through being identified with the continued incarnation of God in the soul, the process of individuation found its ultimate significance. On May 3, 1958, Jung wrote to Morton Kelsey: "The real history of the world seems to be the progressive incarnation of the deity" (*Letters* 2, p. 436).

201. Image legend: "The serpent fell dead unto the earth. And that was the umbilical cord of a new birth." The serpent is similar to the serpent in Image 109. In *Black Book* 7 on January 27, 1922, Jung's soul refers to images 109 and 111. His soul says: "the giant cloud of eternal night is awful. I see a yellow shining stroke on this cloud from the top left-hand corner in the irregular shape of a streak of lightning, and behind it an indeterminate reddish light in the cloud. It does not move. I see a dead black serpent lying beneath the cloud and the lightning. It does not move. Beneath the cloud I see a dead black serpent and the thunderbolt stuck in its head like a spear. A hand, as large as that of a God, has thrown the spear and everything has frozen to a gloomy image. What is it trying to say. Do you recall that image that you painted years ago, the one in which the black and red man with the black and white serpent is struck by the ray of God [i.e., image 109]? This image seems to follow that one, because afterward you also painted the dead serpent [i.e., image 111] and did you not behold a gloomy image this morning,

do not? But he who does it not from love but from pride, selfishness, and greed, is damned. None of the damnation is cast out either.[202]

If you accept the lowest in you, suffering is unavoidable, since you do the base thing and build up what lay in ruin. There are many graves and corpses in us, an evil stench of decomposition.[203] Just as Christ through the torment of sanctification subjugated the flesh, so the God of this time through the torment of sanctification will subjugate the spirit. Just as Christ tormented the flesh through the spirit, the God of this time will torment the spirit through the flesh. For our spirit has become an impertinent whore, a slave to words created by men and no longer the divine word itself.[204]

The lowest in you is the source of mercy. We take this sickness upon ourselves, the inability to find peace, the baseness, and the contemptibility so that the God can be healed and radiantly ascend, purged of the decomposition of death and the mud of the under-

---

of that man in the white robe and a black face, like a mummy?" I: "How now, what is this supposed to mean?" Soul: "It is an image of your self" (p. 57).

202. The *Draft* continues: "But who does this under the law of love will move beyond suffering, sit at the table with the anointed and behold God's glory" (p. 406).

203. The *Draft* continues: "But God will come to those who take their suffering upon themselves under the law of love, and he will establish a new bond with them. For it is predicted that the anointed is supposed to return, but no longer in the flesh, but in the spirit. And just as Christ guided the flesh upward through the torment of salvation, the anointed of this time will guide the spirit upward through the torment of salvation" (p. 407).

204. The *Draft* continues: "The lowest in you is the stone that the builders discarded. It will become the cornerstone. The lowest in you will grow like a grain of rice from dry soil, shooting up from the sand of the most barren desert, and rise and stand very tall. Salvation comes to you from the discarded. Your sun will rise from muddy swamps. Like all others, you are annoyed at the lowest in you because its guise is uglier than the image of yourself that you love. The lowest in you is the most despised and least valued, full of pain and sickness. He is despised so much that one hides one's face from him, that he is held in no respect whatsoever, and it is even said that he does not exist because one is ashamed for his sake and despises oneself. In truth, it carries our sickness and is ridden with our pain. We consider him the one who is plagued and punished by God on account of his despicable ugliness. But he is wounded, and exposed to madness, for the sake of our own justice; he is crucified and suppressed for the sake of our own beauty. We leave him to punishment and martyrdom that we might have peace. But we will take his sickness upon ourselves, and salvation will come to us through our own wounds" (pp. 407–8). The first lines refer to Psalm 118:22. The passage echoes Isaiah 53, which Jung cited above, p. 118.

world. The despicable prisoner will ascend to his salvation shining and wholly healed.[205]

Is there a suffering that would be too great to want to undergo for our God? You only see the one, and do not notice the other. But when there is one, so there is also another and that is the lowest in you. But the lowest in you is also the eye of the evil that stares at you and looks at you coldly and sucks your light down into the dark abyss. Bless the hand that keeps you up there, the smallest humanity, the lowest living thing. Quite a few would prefer death. Since Christ imposed bloody sacrifice on humanity, the renewed God will also not spare bloodshed.

Wherefore art thou red in thine apparel, and thy garments like him that treadeth in the winefat? I have trodden the wine-

---

205. The *Draft* continues: "Why should our spirit not take upon itself torment and restlessness for the sake of sanctification? But all this will come over you, for I already hear the steps of those who bear the keys to open the gates of the depths. The valleys and mountains that resound with the noise of battles, the lamentation arising from innumerable inhabited sites is the omen of what is to come. My visions are truth for I have beheld what is to come. But you are not supposed to believe me, because otherwise you will stray from your path, the right one, that leads you safely to your suffering that I have seen ahead. May no faith mislead you, accept your utmost unbelief, it guides you on your way. Accept your betrayal and infidelity, your arrogance and your better knowledge, and you will reach the safe and secure route that leads you to your lowest; and what you do to your lowest, you will do to the anointed. Do not forget this: Nothing of the law of love is abrogated, but much has been added to it. Cursed unto himself is he who kills the one capable of love in himself, for the horde of the dead who died for the sake of love is immeasurable, and the mightiest among these dead is Christ the Lord. Holding these dead in reverence is wisdom. Purgatory awaits those who murder the one in themselves who is capable of love. You will lament and rave against the impossibility of uniting the lowest in you with the law of those who love. I say to you: Just as Christ subjugated the nature of the physical to the spirit under the law of the word of the father, the nature of the spirit shall be subjugated to the physical under the law of Christ's completed work of salvation through love. You are afraid of the danger; but know that where God is nearest, the danger is greatest. How can you recognize the anointed one without any danger? Will one ever acquire a precious stone with a copper coin? The lowest in you is what endangers you. Fear and doubt guard the gates of your way. The lowest in you is the unforeseeable for you cannot see it. Thus shape and behold it. You will thus open the floodgates of chaos. The sun arises from the darkest, dampest, and coldest. The unknowing people of this time only see the one; they never see the other approaching them. But if the one exists, so does the other" (pp. 409–10). Jung here implicitly cites the opening lines of Friedrich Hölderlin's "Patmos," which was one of his favorite poems: "Near is / the God, and hard to grasp. / But where danger is, / salvation also grows." Jung discussed this in *Transformations and Symbols of the Libido* (1912, CW B, §651f).

press alone and no one is with me. I have trodden myself down in my anger, and trampled upon myself in my fury. Hence my blood has spattered my clothes, and I have stained my robe. For I have afforded myself a day of vengeance, and the year to redeem myself has come. And I looked around, and there was none to help; and I wondered that there was no one who stood by me: therefore my own arm must save me, and my fury upheld me. And I trod myself down in my rage, and made myself drunk in my fury, and spilt my blood on the earth.[206] For I took my misdeed upon myself so that the God would be healed.

Just as Christ said that he did not come to make peace but brought the sword,[207] so he in whom Christ becomes complete will not give himself peace, but a sword. He will rebel against himself and one will be turned against the other in him. He will also hate that which he loves in himself. He will be castigated in himself, mocked, and given over to the torment of crucifixion, and no one will aid him or soothe his torment.

Just as Christ was crucified between the two thieves, our lowest lies on either side of our way. And just as one thief went to Hell and the other rose up to Heaven, the lowest in us will be sundered in two halves on the day of our judgment. The one is destined for damnation and death, and the other will rise up.[208] But it will take a long time until you see what is destined for death and what is destined for life, since the lowest in you is still unseparated and one, and in a deep sleep.

If I accept the lowest in me, I lower a seed into the ground of Hell. The seed is invisibly small, but the tree of my life grows from it and conjoins the Below with the Above. At both ends there is fire and blazing embers. The Above is fiery and the Below is fiery.

206. These lines actually cite Isaiah 63:2–6.

207. Matthew 10:34: "Think not that I am come to send peace on earth: I came not to send peace, but a sword."

208. In *Answer to Job* (1952), Jung wrote of Christ on the cross: "This picture is completed by the two thieves, one whom goes down to hell, the other into paradise. One could hardly imagine a better representation of the oppositeness of the central Christian symbol" (CW 11, §659).

Between the unbearable fires grows your life. You hang between these two poles. In an immeasurably frightening movement the stretched hanging welters up and down.[209]

We thus fear our lowest, since that which one does not possess is forever united with the chaos and takes part in its mysterious ebb and flow. Insofar as I accept the lowest in me—precisely that red glowing sun of the depths—and thus fall victim to the confusion of chaos, the upper shining sun also rises. Therefore he who strives for the highest finds the deepest.

To deliver the men of his time from the stretched hanging, Christ effectively took this torment upon himself and taught them: "Be crafty like serpents and guileless like doves."[210] For craftiness counsels against chaos, and guilelessness veils its terrible aspect. Thus men could take the safe middle path, hedged both upward and downward.

But the dead of the Above and the Below mounted, and their demands grew ever louder. And both the noble and the wicked rose up again and, unaware, broke the law of the mediator. They flung open doors both above and below. They drew many after them to higher and lower madness, thereby sowing confusion and preparing the way of what is to come.

But he who goes into the one and not also at the same time into the other by accepting what comes toward him, will simply teach and live the one and turn it into a reality. For he will be its victim. When you go into the one and hence consider the other approaching you as your enemy, you will fight against the other. You will do so because you fail to recognize that the other is also in you. On the contrary, you think that the other comes somehow from without and you think that you also catch sight of it in the views and actions of your fellow men which clash with yours. You thus fight the other and are completely blinded.

---

209. Dieterich notes that in Plato's *Gorgias*, there is the motif that transgressors hang in Hades (*Nekyia*, p. 117). In Jung's list of references at the back of his copy of *Nekyia*, he noted: "117 hanging."

210. Matthew 10:16: "Behold, I send you forth as sheep in the midst of wolves: be ye therefore wise as serpents, and harmless as doves."

But he who accepts what approaches him because it is also in him, quarrels and wrangles no more, but looks into himself and
112/114 keeps silent. / [Image 113][211] /

---

211. Image legend: "This is the image of the divine child. It means the completion of a long path. Just as the image was finished in April 1919, and work on the next image had already begun, the one who brought the ☉ came, as ΦΙΛΗΜΩΝ [Philemon] had predicted to me. I called him ΦΑΝΗΣ [Phanes], because he is the newly appearing God." ☉ may be the astrological sign for the sun. In the Orphic theogony, Aither and Chaos are born from Chronos. Chronos makes an egg in Aither. The egg splits into two, and Phanes, the first of the Gods, appears. Guthrie writes that "he is imagined as marvelously beautiful, a figure of shining light, with golden wings on his shoulders, four eyes, and the heads of various animals. He is of both sexes, since he is to create the race of the gods unaided" (*Orpheus and Greek Religion: A Study of the Orphic Movement* [London: Methuen, 1935, p. 80). In *Transformations and Symbols of the Libido* (1912) while discussing mythological conceptions of creative force, Jung drew attention to the "Orphic figure of Phanes, the 'Shining One,' the first-born, the 'Father of Eros.' In Orphic terms, Phanes also denotes Priapos, a god of love, androgynous, and equal to the Theban Dionysus Lysios. The Orphic meaning of Phanes is the same as that of the Indian Kâma, the God of love, which is also a cosmogonic principle" (CW B, §223). Phanes appears in *Black Book* 6 in the autumn of 1916. His attributes match the classical depictions, and he is described as the brilliant one, a God of beauty and light. Jung's copy of Isaac Cory's *Ancient Fragments of the Phoenician, Chaldean, Egyptian, Tryian, Carthaginian, Indian, Persian, and Other Writers; With an Introductory Dissertation; And an Inquiry into the Philosophy and Trinity of the Ancients* has underlinings in the section containing the Orphic theogony, and a slip of paper and mark by the following statement: "they imagine as the god a conceiving and conceived egg, or a white garment, or a cloud, because Phanes springs forth from these" ([London: William Pickering, 1832], p. 310). Phanes is Jung's God. On September 28, 1916, Phanes is described as a golden bird (*Black Book* 6, p. 119). On February 20, 1917, Jung addresses Phanes as the messenger of Abraxas (Ibid., p. 167). On May 20, 1917, Philemon says that he will become Phanes (Ibid., p. 195). On September 11, Philemon describes him as follows: "Phanes is the God who rises agleam from the waters. / Phanes is the smile of dawn. / Phanes is the resplendent day. / He is the immortal present. / He is the gushing streams. / He is the soughing wind. / He is hunger and satiation. / He is love and lust. / He is mourning and consolation. / He is promise and fulfillment. / He is the light that illuminates every darkness. / He is the eternal day. / He is the silver light of the moon. / He is the flickering stars. / He is the shooting star that flashes and falls and lapses. / He is the stream of shooting stars that returns every year. / He is the returning sun and moon. / He is the trailing star that brings wars and noble wine. / He is the good and fullness of the year. / He fulfills the hours with life-filled enchantment. / He is love's embrace and whisper. / He is the warmth of friendship. / He is the hope that enlivens the void. / He is the magnificence of all renewed suns. / He is the joy at every birth. / He is the blooming flowers. / He is the velvety butterfly's wing. / He is the scent of blooming gardens that fills the nights. / He is the song of joy. / He is the tree of light. / He is perfection, everything done better. / He is everything euphonious. / He is the well-measured. / He is the sacred number. / He is the promise of life. / He is the contract and the sacred pledge. / He is the diversity of sounds and colors. / He is the sanctification of morning, noon, and evening. / He is the benevolent and the gentle. / He is salvation . . . / In truth, Phanes is the happy day . . . / In truth, Phanes is work and its accomplishment and its remuneration. / He is the troublesome task and the evening calm. / He is the step on the middle way, its beginning, its middle, and its end. / He is

He sees the tree of life, whose roots reach into Hell and whose top

---

foresight. / He is the end of fear. / He is the sprouting seed, the opening bud. / He is the gate of reception, of acceptance and deposition. / He is the spring and the desert. / He is the safe haven and the stormy night. / He is the certainty in desperation. / He is the solid in dissolution. / He is the liberation from imprisonment. / He is counsel and strength in advancement. / He is the friend of man, the light emanating from man, the bright glow that man beholds on his path. / He is the greatness of man, his worth, and his force" (*Black Book* 7, pp. 16–9). On July 31, 1918, Phanes himself says: "The mystery of the summer morning, the happy day, the completion of the moment, the fullness of the possible, born from suffering and joy, the treasure of eternal beauty, the goal of the four paths, the spring and the ocean of the four streams, the fulfillment of the four sufferings and of the four joys, father and mother of the Gods of the four winds, crucifixion, burial, resurrection, and man's divine enhancement, highest effect and nonbeing, world and grain, eternity and instance, poverty and abundance, evolution, death and the rebirth of God, borne by eternally creative power, resplendent in eternal effect, loved by the two mothers and sisterly wives, ineffable pain-ridden bliss, unknowable, unrecognizable, a hair's breadth between life and death, a river of worlds, canopying the heavens—I give you philanthropy, the opal jug of water; he pours water and wine and milk and blood, food for men and Gods. / I give you the joy of suffering and suffering of joy. / I give you what has been found: the constancy in change and the change in constancy. / The jug made of stone, the vessel of completion. Water flowed in, wine flowed in, milk flowed in, blood flowed in. / The fours winds precipitated into the precious vessel. / The Gods of the four heavenly realms hold its curvature, the two mothers and the two fathers guard it, the fire of the North burns above its mouth, the serpent of the South encircles its bottom, the spirit of the East holds one of its sides and the spirit of the West the other. / Forever denied it exists forever. Recurring in all forms, forever the same, this one precious vessel, surrounded by the circle of animals, denying itself, and arising in new splendor through its self-denial. / The heart of God and of man. / It is the One and the Many. A path leading across mountains and valleys, a guiding star on the oceans, in you and always ahead of you. / Perfected, indeed truly perfected is he who knows this. / Perfection is poverty. But poverty means gratitude. Gratitude is love (2 August). / In truth, perfection is sacrifice. / Perfection is joy and anticipation of the shadow. / Perfection is the end. The end means the beginning, and hence perfection is both smallness and the smallest possible beginning. / Everything is imperfect, and perfection is hence solitude. But solitude seeks community. Hence perfection means community. / I am perfection, but perfected is only he who has attained his limits. / I am the eternal light, but perfect is he who stands between day and night. I am eternal love, but perfect is he who has placed the sacrificial knife beside his love. / I am beauty, but perfect is he who sits against the temple wall and mends shoes for money. / He who is perfect is simple, solitary, and unanimous. Hence he seeks diversity, community, ambiguity. Through diversity, community, and ambiguity he advances toward simplicity, solitude, and unanimousness. / He who is perfect knows suffering and joy, but I am the bliss beyond joy and suffering. / He who is perfect knows light and dark, but I am the light beyond day and darkness. / He who is perfect knows up and down, but I am the height beyond high and low. / He who is perfect knows the creating and the created, but I am the parturient image beyond creation and creature. / He who is perfect knows love and being loved, but I am the love beyond embrace and mourning. / He who is perfect knows male and female, but I am the One, his father and son beyond masculine and feminine, beyond child and the aged. / He who is perfect knows rise and fall, but I am the center beyond dawn and dusk. / He who is perfect knows me and hence he is different from me" (*Black Book* 7, pp. 76–80).

touches Heaven. He also no longer knows differences:[212] who is right? What is holy? What is genuine? What is good? What is correct? He knows only one difference: the difference between below and above. For he sees that the tree of life grows from below to above, and that it has its crown at the top, clearly differentiated from the roots. To him this is unquestionable. Hence he knows the way to salvation.

To unlearn all distinctions save that concerning direction is part of your salvation. Hence you free yourself from the old curse of the knowledge of good and evil. Because you separated good from evil according to your best appraisal and aspired only to the good and denied the evil that you committed nevertheless and failed to accept, your roots no longer suckled the dark nourishment of the depths and your tree became sick and withered.

Therefore the ancients said that after Adam had eaten the apple, the tree of paradise withered.[213] Your life needs the dark. But if you know that it is evil, you can no longer accept it and you suffer anguish and you do not know why. Nor can you accept it as evil, else your good will reject you. Nor can you deny it since you know good and evil. Because of this the knowledge of good and evil was an insurmountable curse.

But if you return to primal chaos and if you feel and recognize that which hangs stretched between the two unbearable poles of fire, you will notice that you can no longer separate good and evil conclusively, neither through feeling nor through knowledge, but that you can discern the direction of growth only from below to above. You thus forget the distinction between good and evil, and you no longer know it as long as your tree grows from below to above. But as soon as growth stops, what was united in growth falls apart and once more you recognize good and evil.

You can never deny your knowledge of good and evil to yourself, so that you could betray your good in order to live evil. For as soon as you separate good and evil, you recognize them. They are united

212. Jung's marginal note to the calligraphic volume: 14. IX. 1922.

213. In *Transformations and Symbols of the Libido* (1912), Jung referred to a legend in which the tree had withered after the fall (CW B, §375).

only in growth. But you grow if you stand still in the greatest doubt, and therefore steadfastness in great doubt is a veritable flower of life.

He who cannot bear doubt does not bear himself. Such a one is doubtful; he does not grow and hence he does not live. Doubt is the sign of the strongest and the weakest. The strong have doubt, but doubt has the weak. Therefore the weakest is close to the strongest, and if he can say to his doubt: "I have you," then he is the strongest.[214] But no one can say yes to his doubt, unless he endures wide-open chaos. Because there are so many among us who can talk about anything, pay heed to what they live. What someone says can be very much or very little. Thus examine his life.

My speech is neither light nor dark, since it is the speech of someone who is growing.

Nox quarta[215]

Cap. xvii

[HI 114] [216]I hear the roaring of the morning wind, which comes over the mountains. The night is overcome, when all my life was subject to eternal confusion and stretched out between the poles of fire.

My soul speaks to me in a bright voice: "The door should be lifted off its hinges to provide a free passage between here and there, between yes and no, between above and below, between left and right. Airy passages should be built between all opposed things, light smooth streets should lead from one pole to the other. Scales should be set up, whose pointer sways gently. A flame should burn that cannot be blown out by the wind. A stream should flow to its deepest goal. The herds of wild animals should move to their feeding grounds along their old game paths. Life should proceed, from birth to death, from death to birth, unbroken like the path of the sun. Everything should proceed on this path."

214. The *Draft* continues: "Hence Christ taught: Blessed be ye poor, for yours is the kingdom of God" (p. 416). This refers to Luke 6:20.

215. Fourth night.

216. January 19, 1914.

Thus speaks my soul. But I toy casually and terribly with myself. Is it day or night? Am I asleep or awake? Am I alive or have I already died?

Blind darkness besieges me—a great wall—a gray worm of twilight crawls along it. It has a round face and laughs. The laughter is convulsive and actually relieving. I open my eyes: the fat cook is standing before me: "You're a sound sleeper, I must say. You've slept for more than an hour."

I: "Really? Have I slept? I must have dreamed, what a dreadful play! Did I fall asleep in this kitchen? Is this really the realm of mothers?"[217]

"Have a glass of water, you're still thoroughly drowsy."

I: 'Yes, this sleep can make one drunk. Where is my Thomas? There it lies, open at the twenty-first chapter: "My soul, in everything and yet beyond everything, you must find your rest in the Lord, for he is the eternal rest of the saints."[218]

I read this sentence aloud. Is not every word followed by a question mark?

"If you fell asleep with this sentence, you must really have had a beautiful dream."

I: "I certainly dreamed, and I will think about the dream. Incidentally, can you tell me whose cook you are?"

"The librarian's. He loves good cooking and I have been with
114/116 him for many years." / [Image 115][219] /

I: "Oh, I had no idea that the librarian had such a cook."

"Yes, you must know that he's a gourmet."

I: "Farewell, madam cook, and thank you for the accommodation."

"You are most welcome and the pleasure was entirely mine."

---

217. In the first act of the second part of Goethe's *Faust*, Faust has to descend to the realm of the Mothers. There has been much speculation concerning the meaning of this term in Goethe. To Eckermann, Goethe stated that the source for the name was from Plutarch. In all likelihood, this was Plutarch's discussion of the Mother Goddesses in Engyon. (See Cryus Hamlin, ed., *Faust* [New York: W. W. Norton, 1976], pp. 328–29.) In 1958, Jung identified the realm of the Mothers with the collective unconscious (*A Modern Myth: Of Things That Were Seen in the Skies*, CW 10, §714).

218. *The Imitation of Christ*, ch. 21, p. 124.

219. Image legend: "This is the golden fabric in which the shadow of God lives."

Now I am outside. So that was the librarian's cook. Does he really know what food is prepared inside? He has certainly never gone in there for a temple sleep.[220] I think that I'll return the Thomas à Kempis to him. I enter the library.

L: "Good evening, here you are again."

I: "Good evening, Sir, I've come to return the Thomas. I sat down for a bit in your kitchen next door to read, without suspecting that it's your kitchen."

L: "Please, there's no problem whatsoever. Hopefully my cook received you well."

I: "I can't complain about the reception. I even had an afternoon sleep over Thomas."

L: "That doesn't surprise me. These prayer books are terribly boring."

I: "Yes, for people like us. But your cook finds the little book very edifying."

L: "Well yes, for the cook."

I: "Allow me the indiscrete question: have you ever had an incubation sleep in your kitchen?"

L: "No, I've never entertained such a strange idea."

I: "Let me say that you'd learn a lot that way about the nature of your kitchen. Good night, Sir!"

After this conversation I left the library and went outside into the anteroom where I approached the green curtains. I pushed them aside, and what did I see? I saw a high-ceilinged hall before me—with a supposedly magnificent garden in the background—Klingsor's magical garden, it occurred to me at once. I had entered a theater; those two over there are part of the play: Amfortas and Kundry, or rather, just what am I looking at? It is the librarian and his cook. He is ailing and pale, and has a bad stomach, she is disappointed and furious. Klingsor is standing to the left, holding the feather the librarian used to tuck behind his ear. How closely Kling-

220. Jung is referring to the Greek practices of dream incubation. See C. A. Meier, *Healing Dream and Ritual: Ancient Incubation and Modern Psychotherapy* (Einsiedeln: Daimon Verlag, 1989).

sor resembles me! What a repulsive play! But look, Parsifal enters from the left. How strange, he also looks like me. Klingsor venomously throws the feather at Parsifal. But the latter catches it calmly.

The scene changes: It appears that the audience, in this case me, joins in during the last act. One must kneel down as the Good Friday service begins: Parsifal enters—slowly, his head covered with a black helmet. The lionskin of Hercules adorns his shoulders and he holds the club in his hand; he is also wearing modern black trousers in honor of the church holiday. I bristle and stretch out my hand avertingly, but the play goes on. Parsifal takes off his helmet. Yet there is no Gurnemanz to atone for and consecrate him. Kundry stands in the distance, covering her head and laughing. The audience is enraptured and recognizes itself in Parsifal. He is I. I take off my armor layered with history and my chimerical decoration and go to the spring wearing a white penitent's shirt, where I wash my feet and hands without the help of a stranger. Then I also take off my penitent's shirt and put on my civilian clothes. I walk out of the scene and approach myself—I who am still kneeling down in prayer as the audience. I rise and become one with myself.[221]

---

221. In *Parsifal*, Wagner presented his reworking of the Grail legend. The plot runs as follows: Titurel and his Christian knights have the Holy Grail in their keeping in their castle, with a sacred spear to guard it. Klingsor is a sorcerer who seeks the Grail. He has enticed the keepers of the Grail into his magic garden, where there are flower maidens and the enchantress, Kundry. Amfortas, Titurel's son, goes into the castle to destroy Klingsor but is enchanted by Kundry and lets the sacred spear fall, and Klingsor wounds him with it. Amfortas needs the touch of the spear to heal his wound. Gurnemanz, the oldest of the knights, looks after Kundry, not knowing her role in Amfortas's wounding. A voice from the Grail sanctuary prophesies that only a youth who is guileless and innocent can regain the spear. Parsifal enters, having killed a swan. Not knowing his name or the name of his father, the knights hope that he is this youth. Gurnemanz takes him to Klingsor's castle. Klingsor orders Kundry to seduce Parsifal. Parsifal defeats Klingsor's knights. Kundry is transformed into a beautiful woman, and she kisses him. From this, he realizes that Kundry seduced Amfortas, and he resists her. Klingsor hurls the spear at him, and Parsifal seizes it. Klingsor's castle and garden disappear. After wandering, Parsifal finds Gurnemanz, now living as a hermit. Parsifal is covered in black armor, and Gurnemanz is offended that he is armed on Good Friday. Parsifal lays his spear before him, and removes his helmet and arms. Gurnemanz recognizes him, and anoints him king of the knights of the Grail. Parsifal baptizes Kundry. They go into the castle and ask Amfortas to uncover the Grail. Amfortas asks them to slay him. Parsifal enters and touches his wound with the spear.

[2] What would mockery be, if it were not true mockery? What would doubt be, if it were not true doubt? What would opposition be, it if were not true opposition? He who wants to accept himself must also really accept his other. But in the yes not every no is true, and in the no every yes is a lie. But since I can be in the yes today and in the no tomorrow, yes and no are both true and untrue. Whereas yes and no cannot yield because they exist, our concepts of truth and error can.

I presume you would like to have certainty with regard to truth and error? Certainty within one or the other is not only possible, but also necessary, although certainty in one is protection and resistance against the other. If you are in one, your certainty about the one excludes the other. But how can you then reach the other? And why can the one not be enough for us? One cannot be enough for us since the other is in us. And if we were content with one, the other would suffer great need and afflict us with its hunger. But we misunderstand this hunger and still believe that we are hungry for the one and strive for it even more adamantly.

Through this we cause the other in us to assert its demands on us even more strongly. If we are then ready to recognize the claim of the other in us, we can cross over into the other to satisfy it. But we can thus reach across, since the other has become conscious to us. Yet if our blinding through the one is strong, we become even more distant from the other, and a disastrous chasm between the one and the other opens up in us. The one becomes surfeited and the other becomes too hungry. The satiated grows

---

Amfortas is transfigured, and Parsifal radiantly holds up the Grail. On May 16, 1913, Otto Mensendieck gave a presentation to the Zürich Psychoanalytical Society on "The Grail-Parsifal Saga." In the discussion, Jung said: "Wagner's exhaustive treatment of the legend of the Holy Grail and Parsifal would need to be supplemented with the synthetic view that the various figures correspond to various artistic aspirations.—The incest barrier will not serve to explain that Kundry's ensnarement fails; instead this has to do with the activity of the psyche to elevate human aspirations ever higher" (*MZS*, p. 20). In *Psychological Types* (1921), Jung put forward a psychological interpretation of *Parsifal* (CW 6, §§371–72).

lazy and the hungry grows weak. And so we suffocate in fat, consumed by lack.

This is sickness, but you see a lot of this type. It must be so, but it need not be so. There are grounds and causes enough that it is so,
116/117 but we also want it not / to be so. For man is afforded the freedom to overcome the cause, for he is creative in and of himself. If you have reached that freedom through the suffering of your spirit to accept the other despite your highest belief in the one, since you are it too, then your growth begins.

If others mock me, it is nevertheless them doing this, and I can attribute guilt to them for this, and forget to mock myself. But he who cannot mock himself will be mocked by others. So accept your self-mockery so that everything divine and heroic falls from you and you become completely human. What is divine and heroic in you is a mockery to the other in you. For the sake of the other in you, set off your admired role which you previously performed for your own self and become who you are.

He who has the luck and misfortune of a particular talent falls prey to believing that he is this gift. Hence he is also often its fool. A special gift is something outside of me. I am not the same as it. The nature of the gift has nothing to do with the nature of the man who carries it. It often even lives at the expense of the bearer's character. His character is marked by the disadvantage of his gift, indeed even through its opposite. Consequently he is never at the height of his gift but always beneath it. If he accepts his other he becomes capable of bearing his gift without disadvantage. But if he only wants to live in his gift and consequently rejects his other, he oversteps the mark, since the essence of his gift is extrahuman and a natural phenomenon, which he in reality is not. All the world sees his error, and he becomes the victim of its mockery. Then he says that others mock him, while it is only the disregard of his other that makes him ridiculous.

When the God enters my life, I return to my poverty for the sake of the God. I accept the burden of poverty and bear all my ugliness and ridiculousness, and also everything reprehensible in me. I thus relieve the God of all the confusion and absurdity that would befall him if I did not accept it. With this I prepare the way for the God's doing. What should happen? Has the darkest abyss been emptied and exhausted? Or what stands and waits down there, impending and red-hot? [Image 117][222]

/ Which fire has not been put out and which embers are still ablaze? We sacrificed innumerable victims to the dark depths, and yet it still demands more. What is this crazy desire craving satisfaction? Whose mad cries are these? Who among the dead suffers thus? Come here and drink blood, so that you can speak.[223] Why do you 117/118

222. Text in image: (Atmavictu); (iuvenis adiutor) [a youthful supporter]; (ΤΕΛΕΣΦΟΡΟΣ) [TELESPHORUS]; (spiritus malus in homnibus quibusdam) [evil spirit in some men]. Image legend: "The dragon wants to eat the sun and the youth beseeches him not to. But he eats it nevertheless." Atmaviktu (as spelled there) first appears in *Black Book* 6 in 1917. Here is a paraphrase of the fantasy of April 25, 1917: The serpent says that Atmaviktu was her companion for thousands of years. He was first an old man, and then he died and became a bear. Then he died and became an otter. Then he died and became a newt. Then he died again and came into the serpent. The serpent is Atmaviktu. He made a mistake before then and became a man, while he was still an earth serpent. Jung's soul says that Atmaviktu is a kobold, a serpent conjuror, a serpent. The serpent says that she is the kernel of the self. From the serpent, Atmaviktu transformed into Philemon (p. 179f). There is a sculpture of him in Jung's garden in Küsnacht. In "From the earliest experiences of my life" Jung wrote: "When I was in England in 1920, I carved two similar figures out of thin branch without having the slightest recollection of that childhood experience. One of them I had reproduced on a larger scale in stone, and this figure now stands in my garden in Küsnacht. It was only at that time that the unconscious supplied me with a name. It called the figure Atmavictu—the 'breath of life.' It is a further development of that quasi-sexual object of my childhood, which turned out to be the 'breath of life,' the creative impulse. Basically, the manikin is a kabir" (*JA*, pp. 29–30; cf. *Memories*, pp. 38–39). The figure of Telesphorus is like Phanes in Image 113. Telesphorus is one of the Cabiri, and the daimon of Aesclepius (see fig. 77, *Psychology and Alchemy*, CW 12). He was also regarded as a God of healing, and had a temple at Pergamon in Asia Minor. In 1950, Jung carved an image of him in his stone at Bollingen, together with a dedication to him in Greek, combining lines from Heraclitus, the Mithraic Liturgy, and Homer (*Memories*, p. 254).

223. In Book 11 of the *Odyssey*, Odysseus makes a libation to the dead to enable them to speak. Walter Burkert notes: "The dead drink the pourings and indeed the blood—they are invited to come to the banquet, to the satiation with blood; as the libations seep into the earth, so the dead will send good things up above" (*Greek Religion*, tr. J. Raffar [Oxford: Basil Blackwell, 1987], pp. 194–95). Jung had used this motif in a metaphorical sense in 1912 in *Transformations and Symbols of the Libido*: "like Odysseus, I have sought to allow this shade [Miss Frank Miller] to drink only as much so as to make it speak so it can give away some of the secrets of the underworld" (CW B, §57n). Around 1910,

reject the blood? Would you like milk? Or the red juice of the vine? Perhaps you would rather have love? Love for the dead? Being in love with the dead? Are you perhaps demanding the seeds of life for the faded thousand-year-old body of the underworld? An unchaste incestuous lust for the dead? Something that makes the blood run cold. Are you demanding a lusty commingling with corpses? I spoke of "acceptance"—but you demand "to seize, embrace, copulate?" Are you demanding the desecration of the dead? That prophet, you say, lay on the child, and placed his mouth on the child's mouth, and his eyes on its eyes, and his hands on its hands and he thus splays himself over the boy, so that the child's body became warm. But he rose again and went here and there in the house before he mounted anew and spread himself over him again. The boy snorted seven times. Then the boy opened his eyes. So shall your acceptance be, so shall you accept, not cool, not superior, not thought out, not obsequious, not as a self-chastisement, but with pleasure, precisely with this ambiguous impure pleasure, whose ambiguity enables it to unite with the higher, with that holy-evil pleasure of which you do not know whether it be virtue or vice, with that pleasure which is lusty repulsiveness, lecherous fear, sexual immaturity. One wakens the dead with this pleasure.

Your lowest is in a sleep resembling death and needs the warmth of life which contains good and evil inseparably and indistinguishably. That is the way of life; you can call it neither evil nor good, neither pure nor impure. Yet this is not the goal, but the way and the crossing. It is also sickness and the beginning of recovery. It is the mother of all abominable deeds and all salutary symbols. It is the most primordial form of creation, the very first dark urge that flows through all secret hiding places and dark passages, with the

---

Jung went on a sailing trip with his friends Albert Oeri and Andreas Vischer, during which Oeri read aloud the chapters from the Odyssey dealing with Circe and the nekyia. Jung noted that shortly after this, he "like Odysseus, was presented by fate with a nekyia, the descent into the dark Hades" (Jung/Jaffé, *Erinnerungen, Träume, Gedanken*, p. 104). The passage which follows depicting the prophet's revival of the child paraphrases Elisha's revival of the son of the Shunammite widow in 2 Kings 4:32–36.

unintentional lawfulness of water and from unexpected places in the loose soil, swelling from the finest cracks to fructify the dry soil. It is the very first, secret teacher of nature, teaching plants and animals the most astonishing and supremely clever skills and tricks, which we hardly know how to fathom. It is the great sage who has superhuman knowledge, who has the greatest of all the sciences, who makes order out of confusion, and who prophesies the future clairvoyantly out of ungraspable fullness. It is the serpentlike, perishable and beneficial, the dreadfully and ridiculously daimonic. It is the arrow that always hits the weakest spot, the spring root which opens the sealed treasure chambers.

You can call it neither clever nor stupid, neither good nor evil, since its nature is inhuman throughout. It is the son of the earth, the dark one whom you should awaken.[224] It is man and woman at the same time and immature sex, rich in interpretation and misinterpretation, so poor in meaning and yet so rich. This is the dead that cried loudest, that stood right at the bottom and waited, that suffered worst. It desired neither blood nor milk nor wine for the sacrifice of the dead, but the willingness of our flesh. Its longing paid no heed to the torment of our spirit which struggled and tortured itself to devise what cannot be devised, that hence tore itself apart and sacrificed itself. Not until our spirit lay dismembered on the altar did I hear the voice of the son of the earth, and only then did I see that he was the great suffering one, who needed salvation. He is the chosen one since he was the most rejected. It is bad to have to say this, but perhaps I hear badly, or perhaps I misunderstand what the depths say. It is miserable to say as much, and yet I must say it.

The depths are silent. He has arisen and now beholds the light of the sun and is among the living. Restlessness and discord rose up with him, doubt and the fullness of life.

---

224. See below, p. 448.

Amen, it is finished. What was unreal is real, what was real is unreal. However, I may not, I do not want to, I cannot. Oh human wretchedness! Oh unwillingness in us! Oh doubt and despair. This is really Good Friday, upon which the Lord died and descended into Hell and completed the mysteries.[225] This is the Good Friday when we complete the Christ in us and we descend to Hell ourselves. This the Good Friday on which we moan and cry to will the completion of Christ, for after his completion we go to Hell. Christ was so powerful that his realm covered all the world and only Hell lay outside it.

Who succeeded in crossing the borders of this realm with good grounds, pure conscience, and obeying the law of love? Who among the living is Christ and journeys to Hell in living flesh? Who is it that expands the realm of Christ with Hell? Who is it that is full of drunkenness while sober? Who is it that descended from being one into being two? Who is it that tore apart his own heart to unite what has been separated?

I am he, the nameless one, who does not know himself and whose name is concealed even from himself. I have no name, since I have not yet existed, but have only just become. To myself I am an Anabaptist and a stranger. I, who I am, am not it. But I, who will be I before me and after me, am it. In that I abased myself, I elevated myself as another. In that I accepted myself, I divided myself into two, and in that I united myself with myself, I became the smaller part of myself. I am this in my consciousness. However, I am thus in
118/120 my consciousness as if I were also separated from it. I am / [Image 119][226] / not in my second and greater state, as if I were this second and greater one myself, but I am always in ordinary consciousness, yet so separate and distinct from it, as if I were in my second and

225. See above, note 135, p. 167.

226. Image legend: "The accursed dragon has eaten the sun, its belly being cut open and he must not hand over the gold of the sun, together with his blood. This is the turning back of Atmavictu, of the old one. He who destroyed the proliferating green covering is the youth who helped me to kill Siegfried." The reference is to *Liber Primus*, ch. 7, "Murder of the Hero."

greater state, but without the consciousness of really being it. I have even become smaller and poorer, but precisely because of my smallness I can be conscious of the nearness of the great.

I have been baptized with impure water for rebirth. A flame from the fire of Hell awaited me above the baptismal basin. I have bathed myself with impurity and I have cleansed myself with dirt. I received him, I accepted him, the divine brother, the son of the earth, the two-sexed and impure, and overnight he has become a man. His two incisors have broken through and light down covers his chin. I captured him, I overcame him, I embraced him. He demanded much from me and yet brought everything with him. For he is rich; the earth belongs to him. But his black horse has parted from him.

Truly, I have shot down a proud enemy, I have forced a greater and stronger one to be my friend. Nothing should separate me from him, the dark one. If I want to leave him, he follows me like my shadow. If I do not think of him, he is still uncannily near. He will turn into fear if I deny him. I must amply commemorate him, I must prepare a sacrificial meal for him. I fill a plate for him at my table. Much that I would have done earlier for men, I now must do for him. Hence they consider me selfish, for they do not know that I go with my friend, and that many days are consecrated to him.[227] But unrest has moved in, a quiet underground earthquake, a distant great roaring. Ways have been opened to the primordial and to the future. Miracles and terrible mysteries are close at hand. I feel the things that were and that will be. Behind the ordinary the eternal abyss yawns. The earth

227. The *Draft* continues: "I put many people, books, and thoughts aside for his sake; but even more, I withdrew from the current world and did the plain and simple, and what suggested it most immediately, to serve his secret purpose. By serving him, the dark one, I encounter another on the path of mercy. If intentions and wishes torment me, I think, feel, and do what lies closest. Thus what is most remote reaches me" (p. 434).

120/123 gives me back what it hid. / [Image 121][228, 229, 230] / [Image 122][231, 232] /

228. In 1944 in *Psychology und Alchemy*, Jung referred to an alchemical representation of a circle quadrated by four "rivers" in the context of a discussion of mandala symbolism (CW 12, §167n). Jung commented on the four rivers of paradise on a number of occasions—see, for instance, *Aion*, CW §§2, 9, 311, 353, 358, 372.

229. Inscription: "XI. MCMXIX. [11. 1919: This date seems to refer to when this image was painted.] This stone, set so beautifully, is certainly the Lapis Philosophorum. It is harder than diamond. But it expands into space through four distinct qualities, namely breadth, height, depth, and time. It is hence invisible and you can pass through it without noticing it. The four streams of Aquarius flow from the stone. This is the incorruptible seed that lies between the father and the mother and prevents the heads of both cones from touching: it is the monad which countervails the Pleroma." On the pleroma, see below p. 509f. Concerning the reference to the incorruptible seed, see the dialogue with Ha in the note to image 94, p. 326, n. 157 above.

230. On June 3, 1918, Jung's soul described Philemon as the joy of the earth: "The daimons become reconciled in the one who has found himself, who is the source of all four streams, of the source-bearing earth. From his summit waters flow in all four directions. He is the sea that bears the sun; he is the mountain that carries the sun; he is the father of all four great streams; he is the cross that binds the four great daimons. He is the incorruptible seed of nothingness, which falls accidentally through space. This seed is the beginning, younger than all other beginnings, older than all endings" (*Black Book* 7, p. 61). Some of the motifs in this statement may have some connections with this image. There is a gap between July 1919 and February 1920 in *Black Book* 7, during which time Jung was presumably writing *Psychological Types*. On February 23 he made the following entry: "What lies between appears in the book of dreams, but even more in the images of the red book" (p. 88). In "Dreams" Jung noted around eight dreams during this period, and a vision at night in August 1919 of two angels, a dark transparent mass, and a young woman. This suggests that the symbolic process continues in the paintings in the calligraphic volume, which do not appear to have direct cross-references to either the text in *Liber Novus* or the *Black Books*. In 1935, Jung put forward a psychological interpretation of the symbolism of medieval alchemy, viewing the philosopher's stone—the goal of the alchemical opus—as a symbol of the self (*Psychology and Alchemy*, CW 12).

231. Inscription: "4 December MCMXIX. [December 4, 1919: This date seems to refer to when the image was painted.] This is the back side of the gem. He who is in the stone has this shadow. This is Atmavictu, the old one, after he has withdrawn from the creation. He has returned to endless history, where he took his beginning. Once more he became stony residue, having completed his creation. In the form of Izdubar he has outgrown and delivered ΦΙΛΗΜΩΝ and Ka from him. ΦΙΛΗΜΩΝ gave the stone, Ka the ⊙." The final character appears to be the astrological symbol for the sun.

232. On Atmavictu, see note to image 117. On May 20, 1917, Philemon said: "As Atmavictu I committed the error and became human. My name was Izdubar? I approached him as just that. He paralyzed me. Yes, man paralyzed me and turned me into a dragon's serpent. Fortunately, I recognized my error, and the fire consumed the serpent. And thus Philemon came into being. My form is appearance. Previously, my appearance was form" (*Black Book* 7, p. 195). In *Memories*, Jung said: "Later, Philemon became relativized by yet another figure, whom I called Ka. In ancient Egypt the 'King's Ka' was his earthly form, the embodied soul. In my fantasy the ka-soul came from below, out of the earth as out of a deep shaft. I did a painting of him, showing him in his earthbound form, as a herm with base of stone and upper part of bronze. High up in the painting appears a kingfisher's wing, and between it and the head of Ka floats a round, glowing nebula of stars. Ka's expression has something demonic about it—one might also say Mephistophelian. In one hand he holds something like a colored pagoda, or

a reliquary, and in the other a stylus with which he is working on the reliquary. He is saying, 'I am he who buries the Gods in gold and gems.' Philemon has a lame foot, but was a winged spirit, whereas Ka represented a kind of earth demon or metal demon. Philemon was the spiritual aspect, 'the meaning,' Ka, on the other hand was a spirit of nature like the Anthroparion of Greek alchemy—with which at that time I was still unfamiliar. Ka was he who made everything real, but who also obscured the kingfisher spirit, the meaning, or replaced it by beauty, the 'eternal reflection.' In time I was able to integrate both figures through the study of alchemy" (pp. 209–10). Wallace Budge notes that "The ka was an abstract individuality or personality which possessed the form and attributes of the man to whom it belonged, and, though its normal dwelling place was in the tomb with the body, it could wander at will; it was independent of the man and could go and dwell in any statue of him" (*Egyptian Book of the Dead*, p. lxv). In 1928, Jung commented: "At a rather higher stage of development, where the idea of the soul already exists, not all the images continue to be projected . . . but one or the other complex has come near enough to consciousness to be felt as no longer strange, but as somehow belonging. Nevertheless, the feeling that it belongs is not at first sufficiently strong for the complex to be sensed as a subjective content of consciousness. It remains in a sort of no-man's-land between consciousness and the unconscious, in the half-shadow, in part belonging or akin to the conscious subject, in part an autonomous being, and meeting consciousness as such. At all events it is not necessarily obedient to the subject's intentions, it may even be of a higher order, more often than not a source of inspiration or warning, or of supernatural information. Psychologically such a content could be explained as a partly autonomous complex that is not yet fully integrated. The primitive souls, the Egyptian Ba and Ka, are complexes of this kind" (*The Relations between the I and the Unconscious*, CW 7, §295). In 1955/56, Jung described the Anthroparion in alchemy as "a type of goblin, that as πνευμα παρεδρον [devoted spirit], spiritus familiaris, stands by the adept in his work and helps the physician to heal" (*Mysterium Coniunctionis*, CW 14, §304). The Anthroparion was seen to represent the alchemical metals ("On the psychology of the Child archetype," CW 9, 1, §268) and appeared in the visions of Zosimos (CW 13, pp. 60–62). The painting of Ka that Jung refers to has not come to light. Ka appeared to Jung in a fantasy on October 22, 1917, where he introduced himself as the other side of Ha, his soul. It was Ka who had given Ha the runes and the lower wisdom (see note 155, pp. 325–26). His eyes are of pure gold and his body is of black iron. He tells Jung and his soul that they need his secret, which is the essence of all magic. This is love. Philemon says that Ka is Philemon's shadow (*Black Book* 7, p. 25ff). On November 20, Ka calls Philemon his shadow, and his herald. Ka says that he is eternal and remains, while Philemon is fleeting and passes on (p. 34). On February 10, 1918, Ka says that he has built a temple as a prison and grave for the Gods (p. 39). Ka features in *Black Book* 7 until 1923. During this period, Jung attempts to understand the connection among Ka, Philemon, and the other figures, and to establish the right relation to them. On October 15, 1920, Jung discussed an unidentified picture with Constance Long, who was in analysis with him. Some of the comments she noted shed light on his understanding of the relation of Philemon and Ka: "The 2 figures on either side are personifications of dominants 'fathers.' The one is the creative father, Ka, the other, Philemon that one whom gives form and law (the formative instinct) Ka would equal Dionysus & P = Apollo. Philemon gives formulation to the things within elements of the collective unc . . . Philemon gives the idea (maybe of a god) but it remains floating, distant & indistinct because all the things he invents are winged. But Ka gives substance & is called the one who buries the gods in gold & marble. He has a tendency to misprison them in matter, & so they are in danger of losing their spiritual meaning, & becoming buried in stone. So the temple maybe the grave of God, as the church has become the grave of Xt. The more the church develops, the more Xt dies. Ka must not be allowed to produce too much—you must not depend

123/124 [Image 123][233] /

The Three Prophecies

Cap. xviii

[HI 124][234] Wondrous things came nearer. I called my soul and asked her to dive down into the floods, whose distant roaring I could hear. This happened on 22 January of the year 1914, as recorded in my black book. And thus she plunged into the darkness like a shot, and from the depths she called out: "Will you accept what I bring?"

I: "'I will accept what you give. I do not have the right to judge or to reject."

S: "So listen. There is old armor and the rusty gear of our fathers down here, murderous leather trappings hanging from them, worm-eaten lance shafts, twisted spear heads, broken arrows, rotten shields, skulls, the bones of man and horse, old cannons, catapults, crumbling firebrands, smashed assault gear, stone spearheads, stone clubs, sharp bones, chipped arrowhead teeth—everything the battles of yore have littered the earth with. Will you accept all this?"

I: "I accept it. You know better, my soul."

S: "I find painted stones, carved bones with magical signs, talismanic sayings on hanks of leather and small plates of lead, dirty pouches filled with teeth, human hair and fingernails, timbers

---

on substantiation; but if too little substance is produced the creature floats. The transcendent function is the whole. Not this picture, nor my rationalization of it, but the new and vivifying creative spirit that is the result of the intercourse between the consc. intelligence and the creative side. Ka is sensation, P is intuition, he is too supra-human (he is Zarathustra, extravagantly superior in what he says & cold. [CGJ has not printed the questions he addressed to P nor his answers] . . . Ka & Philemon are bigger than the man, they are supra-human (Disintegrated into them one is in the Col. Unc)" (Diary, Countway Library of Medicine, pp. 32–33).

233. Inscription: "IV Jan, MCMXX [January 4, 1920: This date seems to refer to when the image was painted.] This is the holy caster of water. The Cabiri grow out of the flowers which spring from the body of the dragon. Above is the temple."

234. In *Black Book* 4, Jung noted: "Thereafter I walk on like a man who is tense, and who expects something new that he has never suspected before. I listen to the depths—warned, instructed, and undaunted—outwardly striving to lead a full human life" (p. 42).

lashed together, black orbs, moldy animal skins—all the superstitions hatched by dark prehistory. Will you accept all this?"

I: "I accept it all, how should I dismiss anything?"

S: "But I find worse: fratricide, cowardly mortal blows, torture, child sacrifice, the annihilation of whole peoples, arson, betrayal, war, rebellion—will you also accept this?"

I: "Also this, if it must be. How can I judge?"

S: "I find epidemics, natural catastrophes, sunken ships, razed cities, frightful feral savagery, famines, human meanness, and fear, whole mountains of fear."

I: "So shall it be, since you give it."

S: "I find the treasures of all past cultures, magnificent images of Gods, spacious temples, paintings, papyrus rolls, sheets of parchment with the characters of bygone languages, books full of lost wisdom, hymns and chants of ancient priests, stories told down the ages through thousands of generations."

I: "That is an entire world—whose extent I cannot grasp. How can I accept it?"

S: "But you wanted to accept everything? You do not know your limits. Can you not limit yourself?"

I: "I must limit myself. Who could ever grasp such wealth?"

S: "Be content and cultivate your garden with modesty."[235]

I: "I will. I see that it is not worth conquering a larger piece of the immeasurable, but a smaller one instead. A well-tended small garden is better than an ill-tended large garden. Both gardens are equally small when faced with the immeasurable, but unequally cared for."

S: "Take shears and prune your trees."

[2] From the flooding darkness the son of the earth had brought, my soul gave me ancient things that pointed to the future. She gave

235. These lines refer to the end of *Voltaire's Candide*: "All that is well said—but we must cultivate our garden" (*Candide and Other Stories*, tr. R. Pearson [Oxford: Oxford University Press, 1759/1998], pp. 392–93). Jung kept a bust of Voltaire in his study.

me three things: The misery of war, the darkness of magic, and the gift of religion.

If you are clever, you will understand that these three things belong together. These three mean the unleashing of chaos and its power, just as they also mean the binding of chaos. War is obvious and everybody sees it. Magic is dark and no one sees it. Religion is still to come, but it will become evident. Did you think that the horrors of such atrocious warfare would come over us? Did you think that magic existed? Did you think about a new religion? I sat up for long nights and looked ahead at what was to come and I shuddered. Do you believe me? I am not too concerned. What should I believe? What should I disbelieve? I saw and I shuddered.

But my spirit could not grasp the monstrous, and could not conceive the extent of what was to come. The force of my longing languished, and powerless sank the harvesting hands. I felt the burden of the most terrible work of the times ahead. I saw where and how, but no word can grasp it, no will can conquer it. I could not do otherwise, I let it sink again into the depths.

I cannot give it to you, and I can speak only of the way of what is to come. Little good will come to you from outside. What will come to you lies within yourself. But what lies there! I would like to avert my eyes, close my ears and deny all my senses; I would like to be someone among you, who knows nothing and who never saw anything. It is too much and too unexpected. But I saw it and my memory will not leave me alone.[236] Yet I curtail my longing, which would like to stretch out into the future, and I return to my small garden that presently blooms, and whose extent I can measure. It shall be well-tended.

The future should be left to those of the future. I return to the small and the real, for this is the great way, the way of what is to come. I return to my simple reality, to my undeniable and most minuscule being. And I take a knife and hold court over every-

236. The *Draft* continues: "How can I fathom what will happen during the next eight hundred years, up to the time when the One begins his rule? I am speaking only of what is to come" (p. 440).

thing that has grown without measure and goal. Forests have grown around me, winding plants have climbed up me, and I am completely covered by endless proliferation. The depths are inexhaustible, they give everything. Everything is as good as nothing. Keep a little and you have something. To recognize and know your ambition and your greed, to gather / [Image 125][237] / your craving, to cul- 124/126
tivate it, grasp it, make it serviceable, influence it, master it, order it, to give it interpretations and meanings, is extravagant.

It is lunacy, like everything that transcends its boundaries. How can you hold that which you are not? Would you really like to force everything which you are not under the yoke of your wretched knowledge and understanding? Remember that you can know yourself, and with that you know enough. But you cannot know others and everything else. Beware of knowing what lies beyond yourself, or else your presumed knowledge will suffocate the life of those who know themselves. A knower may know himself. That is his limit.

With a painful slice I cut off what I pretended to know about what lies beyond me. I excise myself from the cunning interpretive loops that I gave to what lies beyond me. And my knife cuts even deeper and separates me from the meanings that I conferred upon myself. I cut down to the marrow, until everything meaningful falls from me, until I am no longer as I might seem to myself, until I know only that I am without knowing what I am.

I want to be poor and bare, and I want to stand naked before the inexorable. I want to be my body and its poverty. I want to be from the earth and live its law. I want to be my human animal and accept all its frights and desires. I want to go through the wailing and the blessedness of the one who stood alone with a poor unarmed body on the sunlit earth, a prey of his drives and of the lurking wild animals, who was terrified by ghosts and dreaming of distant Gods, who belonged to what was near and was enemy to the far-off, who

237. The scene in the landscape resembles one of Jung's waking fantasies during his childhood in which Alsace is submerged by water, Basle is turned into a port, there is a ship with sails and a steamer, a medieval town, a castle with cannons and soldiers and inhabitants of the town, and a canal (*Memories*, p. 100).

struck fire from stones, and whose herds were stolen by unknowable powers that also destroyed the crops of his fields, and who neither knew nor recognized, but who lived by what lay at hand, and received by grace what lay far-off.

He was a child and unsure, yet full of certainty, weak and yet blessed with enormous strength. When his God did not help, he took another. And when this one did not help either, he castigated him. And behold: the Gods helped one more time. Thus I discard everything that was laden with meaning, everything divine and devilish with which chaos burdened me. Truly, it is not up to me to prove the Gods and the devils and the chaotic monsters, to feed them carefully, to warily drag them with me, to count and name them, and to protect them with belief against disbelief and doubt.

A free man knows only free Gods and devils that are self-contained and take effect on account of their own force. If they fail to have an effect, that is their own business, and I can remove this burden from myself. But if they are effective, they need neither my protection nor my care, nor my belief. Thus you may wait quietly to see whether they work. But if they do, be clever, for the tiger is stronger than you. You should be able to cast everything from you, otherwise you are a slave, even if you are the slave of a God. Life is free and chooses its way. It is limited enough, so do not pile up more limitation. Hence I cut away everything confining. I stood here, and there lay the riddlesome multifariousness of the world.

And a horror crept over me. Am I not the tightly bound? Is the world there not the unlimited? And I became aware of my weakness. What would poverty, nakedness and unpreparedness be without consciousness of weakness and without horror at powerlessness? Thus I stood and was terrified. And then my soul whispered to me:

The Gift of Magic

Cap. xix.

[HI 126][238] "Do you not hear something?"

I: "I'm not aware of anything, what should I hear?"

S: "A ringing."

I: "A ringing? What? I hear nothing."

S: "Listen harder."

I: "Perhaps something in the left ear. What could it mean?"

S: "Misfortune."

I: "I accept what you say. I want to have fortune and misfortune."

S: "Well, then, raise your hands and receive what comes to you."

I: "What is it? A rod? A black serpent? A black rod, formed like a serpent—with two pearls as eyes—a gold bangle around its neck. Is it not like a magical rod?"

S: "It is a magical rod."

I: "What should I do with magic? Is the magical rod a misfortune? Is magic a misfortune?"

S: "Yes, for those who possess it."

I: "That sounds like the sayings of old—how strange you are, my soul! What should I do with magic?"

S: "Magic will do a lot for you."

I: "I'm afraid that you're stirring up my desire and misunderstanding. You know that man never stops craving the black art and things that cost no effort."

S: "Magic is not easy, and it demands sacrifice."

I: "Does it demand the sacrifice of love? Of humanity? If it does, take the rod back."

S: "Don't be rash. Magic doesn't demand that sacrifice. It demands another sacrifice."

I: "What sacrifice is that?"

S: "The sacrifice that magic demands is solace."

238. January 23, 1914.

I: "Solace? Do I understand correctly? Understanding you is unspeakably difficult. Tell me, what does this mean?"

S: "Solace is to be sacrificed."

I: "What do you mean? Should the solace that I give or the solace that I receive be sacrificed?"

S: "Both."

I: "I'm confused. This is too dark."

S: "You must sacrifice solace for the sake of the black rod, the solace you give and the solace you receive."

I: "Are you saying that I shouldn't be allowed to receive the solace of those I love? And should give no solace to those I love? This means the loss of a piece of humanity, and what one calls severity toward oneself and others takes its place."[239]

S: "That is how it is."

I: "Does the rod demand this sacrifice?"

S: "It demands this sacrifice."

I: "Can I, am I allowed to make this sacrifice for the sake of the rod? Must I accept the rod?"

S: "Do you want to or not?"

I: "I can't say. What do I know about the black rod? Who gives it to me?"

S: "The darkness that lies before you. It is the next thing that comes to you. Will you accept it and offer it your sacrifice?"

I: It is hard to sacrifice to the dark, to the blind darkness—and what a sacrifice!"

S: "Nature—does nature offer solace? Does it accept solace?"

I: "You venture a heavy word. What solitude are you asking of me?"

S: "This is your misfortune, and—the power of the black rod."

239. In *Ecce Homo*, Nietzsche wrote: "Every acquisition, every step forward in knowledge is the *result* of courage, of severity toward oneself, of cleanliness with respect to oneself" (tr. R. J. Hollingdale [Harmondsworth: Penguin, 1979], foreword 3, p. 34).

I: "How gloomily and full of foreboding you speak! Are you sheathing me in the armor / [Image 127][240] / of icy severity? Are 126/128
you clasping my heart with a bronze carapace? I'm happy with the warmth of life. Should I miss it? For the sake of magic? What is magic?"

S: "You don't know magic. So don't judge. What are you bristling at?"

I: "Magic! What should I do with magic? I don't believe in it, I can't believe in it. My heart sinks—and I'm supposed to sacrifice a greater part of my humanity to magic?"

S: "I advise you, don't struggle against this, and above all don't act so enlightened, as if deep down you did not believe in magic."

I: "You're inexorable. But I can't believe in magic, or maybe I have a completely false idea of it."

S: "Yes, I gather that from what you're saying. Cast aside your blind judgment and critical gesture, otherwise you'll never understand. Do you still mean to waste years waiting?"

I: "Be patient, my science has not yet been overcome."

S: "High time that you overcame it!"

I: "You ask a great deal, almost too much. After all—is science essential to life? Is science life? There are people who live without science. But to overcome science for the sake of magic? That's uncanny and menacing."

S: "Are you afraid? Don't you want to risk life? Isn't it life that presents you with this problem?"

---

240. Inscription on top: "Amor triumphat." Inscription at bottom: "This image was completed on 9 January 1921, after it had waited incomplete for 9 months. It expresses I know not what kind of grief, a fourfold sacrifice. I could almost choose not to finish it. It is the inexorable wheel of the four functions, the essence of all living beings imbued with sacrifice." The functions are those of thinking, feeling, sensation, and intuition, which Jung wrote about in *Psychological Types* (1921). On February 23, 1920, Jung noted in *Black Book* 7: "What occurs between the lover and the beloved is the entire fullness of the Godhead. Both are unfathomable riddles to each other. For who understands the Godhead? / But the God is born in solitude, from the secret / mystery of the individual. / The separation between life and love is the contradiction between solitude and togetherness" (p. 88). The next entry in *Black Book* 7 is on September 5, 1921. On March 4, 1920, Jung went to North Africa with his friend Hermann Sigg, returning on April 17.

I: "All this leaves me so dazed and confused. Won't you give me an enlightening word?"

S: "Oh, so it's solace you long for? Do you want the rod or don't you?"

I: "You tear my heart to pieces. I want to submit to life. But how difficult this is! I want the black rod because it is the first thing the darkness grants me. I don't know what this rod means, nor what it gives—I only feel what it takes. I want to kneel down and receive this messenger of darkness. I have received the black rod, and now I hold it, the enigmatic one, in my hand; it is cold and heavy, like iron. The pearl eyes of the serpent look at me blindly and dazzlingly. What do you want, mysterious gift? All the darkness of all former worlds crowds together in you, you hard, black piece of steel! Are you time and fate? The essence of nature, hard and eternally inconsolable, yet the sum of all mysterious creative force? Primordial magic words seem to emanate from you, mysterious effects weave around you, and what powerful arts slumber in you? You pierce me with unbearable tension—what grimaces will you make? What terrible mystery will you create? Will you bring bad weather, storms, cold, thunder and lightning, or will you make the fields fruitful and bless the bodies of pregnant women? What is the mark of your being? Or don't you need that, you son of the dark womb? Do you content yourself with the hazy darkness, whose concretion and crystal you are? Where in my soul do I shelter you? In my heart? Should my heart be your shrine, your holy of holies? So choose your place. I have accepted you. What crushing tension you bring with you! Isn't the bow of my nerves breaking? I've taken in the messenger of the night."

S: "The most powerful magic lives in it."

I: "I feel it and yet can't put into words the nightmarish power granted to it. I wanted to laugh, because so much alters in laughter, and resolves itself only there. But laughter dies in me. The magic of this rod is as solid as iron and as cold as death. Forgive me, my soul, I don't want to be impatient, but it seems to me that something has got to happen to break through this unbearable tension that came with the rod."

S: "Wait, keep your eyes and ears open."

I: "I'm shuddering, and I don't know why."

S: "Sometimes one must shudder before—the greatest."

I: "I bow, my soul, before unknown forces—I'd like to consecrate an altar to each unknown God. I must submit. The black iron in my heart gives me secret power. It's like defiance and like—contempt for men."[241]

[2] Oh dark act, violation, murder! Abyss, give birth to the unredeemed. Who is our redeemer? Who our leader? Where are the ways through black wastes? God, do not abandon us! What are you summoning, God? Raise your hand up to the darkness above you, pray, despair, wring your hands, kneel, press your forehead into the dust, cry out, but do not name Him, do not look at Him. Leave Him without name and form. What should form the formless? Name the nameless? Step onto the great way and grasp what is nearest. Do not look out, do not want, but lift up your hands. The gifts of darkness are full of riddles. The way is open to whomever can continue in spite of riddles. Submit to the riddles and the thoroughly incompre- 128/130
hensible.There are dizzying / [Image 129] / bridges over the eternally deep abyss. But follow the riddles.

Endure them, the terrible ones. It is still dark, and the terrible goes on growing. Lost and swallowed by the streams of procreating life, we approach the overpowering, inhuman forces that are busily creating what is to come. How much future the depths carry! Are not the threads spun down there over millennia?[242] Protect the riddles,

241. In *Black Book* 4, Jung noted: [Soul:] "Tame your impatience. Only waiting will help you here." [I:] "Waiting—I know this word. Hercules also found waiting troublesome when he carried the weight of the world on his shoulders." [Soul:] "He had to await Atlas's return and carried the weight of the world for the sake of the apples" (p. 60). The reference is to the eleventh labor of Hercules, in which he has to get the golden apples, which confer immortality. Atlas offered to get them for him, if he held up the world in the interim.

242. In Greek mythology, the Moirae, or three fates, Clotho, Lachesis, and Atropus, spun and controlled the threads of human life. In Norse mythology, the norns spun the threads of fate at the foot of Yggsdrasil, the world tree.

bear them in your heart, warm them, be pregnant with them. Thus you carry the future.

The tension of the future is unbearable in us. It must break through narrow cracks, it must force new ways. You want to cast off the burden, you want to escape the inescapable. Running away is deception and detour. Shut your eyes so that you do not see the manifold, the outwardly plural, the tearing away and the tempting. There is only one way and that is your way; there is only one salvation and that is your salvation. Why are you looking around for help? Do you believe that help will come from outside? What is to come will be created in you and from you. Hence look into yourself. Do not compare, do not measure. No other way is like yours. All other ways deceive and tempt you. You must fulfill the way that is in you.

Oh, that all men and all their ways become strange to you! Thus might you find them again within yourself and recognize their ways. But what weakness! What doubt! What fear! You will not bear going your way. You always want to have at least one foot on paths not your own to avoid the great solitude! So that maternal comfort is always with you! So that someone acknowledges you, recognizes you, bestows trust in you, comforts you, encourages you. So that someone pulls you over onto their path, where you stray from yourself, and where it is easier for you to set yourself aside. As if you were not yourself! Who should accomplish your deeds? Who should carry your virtues and your vices? You do not come to an end with your life, and the dead will besiege you terribly to live your unlived life. Everything must be fulfilled. Time is of the essence, so why do you want to pile up the lived and let the unlived rot?

Great is the power of the way.[243] In it Heaven and Hell grow together, and in it the power of the Below and the power of the Above unite. The nature of the way is magical, as are supplication

243. The *Draft* continues: "The power of the way is so great that it carries away others and ignites them. You do not know how this happens; hence it is best you call this effect magical" (p. 453).

and invocation;[244] malediction and deed are magical if they occur on the great way. Magic is the working of men on men, but your magic action does not affect your neighbor; it affects you first, and only if you withstand it does an invisible effect pass from you to your neighbor. There is more of it in the air than I ever thought. However, it cannot be grasped. Listen:

The Above is powerful,
The Below is powerful,
Twofold power is in the One.
North, come hither,
West, snuggle up,
East, flow upward,
South, spill over.

The winds in-between bind the
cross. The poles are united by the
intermediate poles in-between.
Steps lead from above to below.
Boiling water bubbles in
cauldrons. Red-hot ash envelops
the round floor.[245]
Night sinks blue and deep from
above, earth rises black from
below. / [Image 131] / 130/132

A solitary is cooking up healing potions.
He makes offering to the four winds.
He greets the stars and touches the earth.
He holds something luminous in his hand.

Flowers sprout around him and the bliss of a new spring kisses all his limbs.

Birds fly around and the shy animals of the forest gaze at him.

He is far from men and yet the threads of their fate pass through his hands.

May your intercession be meant for him, so that his medicine grows ripe and strong and brings healing to the deepest wounds.

For your sake he is solitary and waits alone between Heaven and earth, for the earth to rise up to him and for Heaven to come down to him.

All peoples are still far off and stand behind the wall of darkness.

But I hear his words, which reach me from afar.

244. The *Draft* continues: "which is represented as a serpent precisely on account of its particular nature" (p. 453).

245. This appears to refer to the magical circle, in which ritual acts are performed.

He has chosen a poor scribe, someone hard of hearing, who also stutters when he writes.

I do not recognize him, the solitary. What is he saying? He says: "I suffer fear and distress for the sake of man."

I dug up old runes and magical sayings for words never reach men. Words have become shadows.

Therefore I took old magical apparatuses and prepared hot potions and mixed in secrets and ancient powers, things that even the cleverest would not guess at.

I stewed the roots of all human thoughts and deeds.

I watched over the cauldron through many starry nights. The brew ferments forever. I need your intercession, your kneeling, your desperation and your patience. I need your ultimate and highest longing, your purest willing, your most humble subjugation.

Solitary, who are you waiting for? Whose help do you require? There is none who can rush to your aid, since all look to you and wait for your healing art.

We are all utterly incapable and need help more than you. Grant us help so that we can help you in return.

The solitary speaks: "Will no one stand by me in this need? Should I leave my work to help you so that you can help me again? But how should I help you, if my brew has not grown ripe and strong? It was supposed to help you. What do you hope from me?"

Come to us! Why are you standing there cooking up marvels? What can your healing and magical potion do for us? Do you believe in healing potions? Look at
132/134 *life, behold how much it needs you!* / [Image 133] /

The solitary speaks: "Fools, can you not keep watch with me for an hour,[246] *until the difficult and long-lasting achieves completion and the juice has ripened?*

Just a little longer and fermentation will be complete. Why can't you wait? Why should your impatience destroy the highest opus?"

What highest opus? We are not alive; cold and numbness have seized us. Your opus, solitary one, will not be finished for aeons, even if it advances day after day.

The work of salvation is endless. Why do you want to wait for the end of this work? Even if your waiting turned you into stone for endless ages, you could not

246. In Matthew 24:40, Christ rebukes his disciples for having been unable to remain awake for an hour while he prayed in the garden of Gethsemane.

endure till the end. And if your salvation came to its end, you would have to be saved from your salvation again.

The solitary speaks: "What smooth-tongued lamentation reaches my ears! What whining! What foolish doubters you are! Unruly children! Persevere, it will be accomplished after this night!"

We will not wait a single night longer; we have persevered long enough. Are you a God, that a thousand nights are as one night to you? For us, this one night would be like a thousand nights. Abandon the work of salvation, and we will be saved. What stretch of ages are you saving us for?

The solitary speaks: "You embarrassing human swarm, you foolish bastard of God and cattle, I'm still lacking a piece of your precious flesh for my mixture. Am I truly your most valuable piece of meat? Is it worth my while to come to the boil for you? One let himself be nailed to the cross for you. One is truly enough. He blocks my way. Therefore neither will I walk on his ways, nor make for you any healing brew or immortal[247] *blood potion, but rather I will abandon the potion and cauldron and occult work for your sake, since you can neither wait for nor endure the fulfillment. I throw down your intercession, your genuflection, your invocations. You can save yourselves from both your lack of salvation and your salvation! Your worth rose quite high enough because one died for you. Now prove your worth by each living for himself. My God, how difficult it is to leave a work unfinished for the sake of men! But for the sake of men, I abstain from being a savior. Lo! Now my potion has completed its fermentation. I did not mix a piece of myself into the drink, but I did slice in a piece of humanity, and behold, it clarified the murky foaming potion.*

How sweet, how bitter
it tastes!
The Below is weak,
The Above is weak,
The form of the One
becomes double.
North, rise and be gone,
West, retire to your place,
East, spread yourself,
South, die down.
The winds in-between
loosen the crucified. / 134/135
[Image 135][248] / 135/136

247. Jung's marginal note to the calligraphic volume: "29/11/1922." This appears to refer to when this passage was transcribed.

248. Inscription: "Completed on 25 November 1922. The fire comes out of Muspilli and grasps the tree of life. A cycle is completed, but it is the cycle within the world egg. A strange God, the unnameable God of the solitary, is incubating it. New creatures

The far poles are separated
by the poles in-between.
The levels are broad ways,
patient streets.
The bubbling pot grows cold.

The ash turns gray
beneath its ground.
Night covers the sky and far
below lies the black earth.

Day approaches, and above the clouds a distant sun.
No solitary cooks healing potions.
The four winds blow and laugh at their bounty.
And he mocks the four winds.
He has seen the stars and touched the earth.
Therefore his hand clasps something luminous
and his shadow has grown to Heaven. [Image 136]

The inexplicable occurs. You would very much like to forsake yourself and defect to each and every manifold possibility. You would very much like to risk every crime in order to steal for yourself the mystery of the changeful. But the road is without end.

The Way of the Cross

Cap. xx.[249]

[HI 136] [250]I saw the black serpent,[251] as it wound itself upward around the wood of the cross. It crept into the body of the crucified and emerged again transformed from his mouth. It had become white. It wound itself around the head of the dead one like a diadem, and a light gleamed above his head, and the sun rose shining in the east. I stood and watched and was confused and a great weight burdened my soul. But the white bird that sat on my shoulder spoke

form from the smoke and ashes." In Norse mythology Muspilli (or Muspelheim) is the abode of the Fire Gods.

249. Jung's marginal note to the calligraphic volume: "25 February 1923. The transformation of black into white magic."

250. January 27, 1914.

251. The *Draft* continues: "the serpent of my way" (p. 460).

to me:[252] "Let it rain, let the wind blow, let the waters flow and the fire burn. Let each thing have its development, let becoming have its day."

[2] 2. Truly, the way leads through the crucified, that means through him to whom it was no small thing to live his own life, and who was therefore raised to magnificence. He did not simply teach what was knowable and worth knowing, he lived it. It is unclear how great one's humility must be to take it upon oneself to live one's own life. The disgust of whoever wants to enter into his own life can hardly be measured. Aversion will sicken him. He makes himself vomit. His bowels pain him and his brain sinks into lassitude. He would rather devise any trick to help him escape, since nothing matches the torment of one's own way. It seems impossibly difficult, so difficult that nearly anything seems preferable to this torment. Not a few choose even to love people for fear of themselves. I believe, too, that some commit a crime to pick a quarrel with themselves. Therefore I cling to everything that obstructs my way to myself.

252. In *Black Book* 4, this is spoken by his soul. In this chapter and in *Scrutinies*, we find a shift in the attribution of some statements in the *Black Books* from the soul to the other characters. This textual revision marks an important psychological process of differentiating the characters, separating them out from one another, and disidentifying from them. Jung discussed this process in general in 1928, in *The Relations between the I and the Unconscious*, ch. 7, "The technique for differentiation between the I and the figures of the unconscious" (CW 7). In *Black Book* 6, the soul explains to Jung in 1916: "If I am not conjoined through the uniting of the Below and the Above, I break down into three parts: the *serpent*, and in that or some other animal form I roam, living nature daimonically, arousing fear and longing. The *human soul*, living forever within you. The celestial soul, as such dwelling with the Gods, far from you and unknown to you, appearing in the form of a bird." (Appendix C, p. 577). The textual changes that Jung makes among the soul, the serpent, and the bird from the *Black Books* in this chapter and in *Scrutinies* can be seen to be the recognition and differentiation of the threefold nature of the soul. Jung's notion of the unity and multiplicity of the soul resembles Eckhart's. In Sermon 52, Eckhart wrote: "the soul with her higher powers touches eternity, which is God, while her lower powers being in touch with time make her subject to change and biased toward bodily things, which degrade her" (*Sermons & Treatises*, vol. 2, tr. M. O'C. Walshe [London: Watkins, 1981], p. 55). In Sermon 85, he wrote: "Three things prevent the soul from uniting with God. The first is that she is too scattered, and that she is not unitary: for when the soul is inclined toward creatures, she is not unitary. The second is when she is involved with temporal things. The third is when she is turned toward the body, for then she cannot unite with God" (Ibid., p. 264).

3. [253] He who goes to himself, climbs down. Pathetic and ridiculous forms appeared to the greatest prophet who came before this time, and these were the forms of his own essence. He did not accept them, but exorcized them before others. Ultimately, however, he was forced to celebrate a Last Supper with his own poverty and to accept these forms of his own essence out of compassion, which is precisely that acceptance of the lowest in us.[254] But this enraged the mighty lion, who chased down the lost and restored it to the darkness of the depths.[255] And like all those with power, the one with the great name wanted to erupt from the womb of the mountain like the sun.[256] But what happened to him? His way led him before the crucified and he began to rage. He raged against the man of mockery and pain because the power of his own essence forced him to follow precisely this way as Christ had done before us. Yet he loudly proclaimed his power and greatness. No one speaks louder of his power and greatness than he from whom the earth disappears under his feet. Ultimately the lowest in him got to him, his incapacity, and this crucified his spirit, so that, as he himself had predicted, his soul died before his body.[257]

4. No one rises above himself who has not turned his most dangerous weapon against himself. One who wants to rise above himself

---

253. The *Draft* continues: "'Why,' you ask, 'does man not want to reach himself?' The raging prophet who preceded this time wrote a book about this and embellished it with a proud name. The book is about how and why man does not want to reach himself" (p. 461). The reference is to Nietzsche's *Thus Spoke Zarathustra*.

254. See "The Last Supper," *Thus Spoke Zarathustra*, p. 294f.

255. In the last chapter of *Thus Spoke Zarathustra*, "The sign," when the higher men come to meet Zarathustra in his cave, "the lion started violently, suddenly turned away from Zarathustra, and leaped up to the cave, roaring fiercely" (p. 407). In 1926 Jung noted: "The roaring of the Zarathustrian lion drove all the 'higher' men who were clamoring for experience back again into the cavern of the unconscious. Hence his life does not convince us of his teaching" (*The Unconscious in Normal and Sick Psychic Life*, CW 7, §37).

256. Nietzsche ends *Thus Spoke Zarathustra* with the lines: "Thus spoke Zarathustra and left his cave, glowing and strong, like a morning sun emerging from behind dark clouds" (p. 336).

257. In Zarathustra's prologue, a tightrope walker falls from a rope. Zarathustra says to the injured tightrope walker: "Your soul will be dead even before your body: therefore fear nothing any more!" (*Zarathustra*, §6, 48; as underlined in Jung's copy, p. 22). In 1926 Jung argued that this was prophetic of Nietzsche's own fate (*The Unconscious in Normal and Sick Psychic Life*," CW 7, §36–44).

shall climb down and hoist himself onto himself and lug himself to the place of sacrifice. But what must happen to a man until he realizes that outer visible success, that he can grasp with his hands, / leads 136/137
him astray. What suffering must be brought upon humanity, until man gives up satisfying his longing for power over his fellow man and forever wanting others to be the same. How much blood must go on flowing until man opens his eyes and sees the way to his own path and himself as the enemy, and becomes aware of his real success. You ought to be able to live with yourself, but not at your neighbor's expense. The herd animal is not his brother's parasite and pest. Man, you have even forgotten that you too are an animal. You actually still seem to believe that life is better elsewhere. Woe unto you if your neighbor also thinks so. But you may be sure that he does. Someone must begin to stop being childish.

5. Your craving satisfies itself in you. You can offer no more precious a sacrificial meal to your God than yourself. May your greed consume you, for this wearies and calms it, and you will sleep well and consider the sun of each day as a gift. If you devour other things and other people, your greed remains eternally dissatisfied, for it craves more, the most costly—it craves you. And thus you compel your desire to take your own way. You may ask others provided that you need help and advice. But you should make demands on no one, neither desiring nor expecting anything from anyone except from yourself. For your craving satisfies itself only within you. You are afraid of burning in your own fire. May nothing prevent you from doing so, neither any one else's sympathy nor your more dangerous sympathy with yourself. Since you should live and die with yourself.

6. When the flame of your greed consumes you, and nothing remains of you but ash, so nothing of you was steadfast. Yet the flame in which you consumed yourself has illuminated many. But if you flee from your fire full of fear, you scorch your fellow men, and the burning torment of your greed cannot die out, so long as you do not desire yourself.

7. The mouth utters the word, the sign, and the symbol. If the word is a sign, it means nothing. But if the word is a symbol, it

means everything.[258] When the way enters death and we are surrounded by rot and horror, the way rises in the darkness and leaves the mouth as the saving symbol, the word. It leads the sun on high, for in the symbol there is the release of the bound human force struggling with darkness. Our freedom does not lie outside us, but within us. One can be bound outside, and yet one will still feel free since one has burst inner bonds. One can certainly gain outer freedom through powerful actions, but one creates inner freedom only through the symbol.

8. The symbol is the word that goes out of the mouth, that one does not simply speak, but that rises out of the depths of the self as a word of power and great need and places itself unexpectedly on the tongue. It is an astonishing and perhaps seemingly irrational word, but one recognizes it as a symbol since it is alien to the conscious mind. If one accepts the symbol, it is as if a door opens leading into a new room whose existence one previously did not know. But if one does not accept the symbol, it is as if one carelessly went past this door; and since this was the only door leading to the inner chambers, one must pass outside into the streets again, exposed to everything external. But the soul suffers great need, since outer freedom is of no use to it. Salvation is a long road that leads through many gates. These gates are symbols. Each new gate is at first invis-
137/138 ible; indeed, it seems at first that / it must be created, for it exists only if one has dug up the spring's root, the symbol.

To find the mandrake, one needs the black dog,[259] since good and bad must always be united first if the symbol is to be created. The symbol can be neither thought up nor found: it becomes. Its becoming is like the becoming of human life in the womb. Pregnancy comes about through voluntary copulation. It goes on through will-

258. For Jung's differentiation of the significance of signs and symbols, see *Psychological Types* (1921, CW 6, §814ff).

259. The mandrake is a plant whose roots bear some resemblance to the human figure, hence they have been used in magical rites. According to legend, they shriek when they are pulled from the ground. In "The philosophical tree" (1945), Jung noted that the magical mandrake "when tied to the tail of a black dog, shrieks when it is torn out of the earth" (CW 13, §410).

ing attention. But if the depths have conceived, then the symbol grows out of itself and is born from the mind, as befits a God. But in the same way a mother would like to throw herself on the child like a monster and devour it again.

In the morning, when the new sun rises, the word steps out of my mouth, but is murdered lovelessly, since I did not know that it was the savior. The newborn child grows quickly, if I accept it. And immediately it becomes my charioteer. The word is the guide, the middle way which easily oscillates like the needle on the scales. The word is the God that rises out of the waters each morning and proclaims the guiding law to the people. Outer laws and outer wisdom are eternally insufficient, since there is only one law and one wisdom, namely my daily law, my daily wisdom. The God renews himself each night.

The God appears in multiple guises; for when he emerges, he has assumed some of the character of the night and the nightly waters in which he slumbered, and in which he struggled for renewal in the last hour of the night. Consequently his appearance is twofold and ambiguous; indeed, it even tears at the heart and the mind. On emerging, the God calls me toward the right and the left, his voice calling out to me from both sides. Yet the God wants neither the one nor the other. He wants the middle way. But the middle is the beginning of the long road.

Man, however, can never see this beginning; he always sees only one and not the other, or the other and not the one, but never that which the one as well as the other encloses in itself. The point of origin is where the mind and the will stand still; it is a state of suspension that evokes my outrage, my defiance and eventually my greatest fear. For I can see nothing anymore and can no longer want anything. Or at least that is how it seems to me. The way is a highly peculiar standstill of everything that was previously movement, it is a blind waiting, a doubtful listening and groping. One is convinced that one will burst. But the resolution is born from precisely this tension, and it almost always appears where one did not expect it.

But what is the resolution? It is always something ancient and precisely because of this something new, for when something long since passed away comes back again in a changed world, it is new. To give birth to the ancient in a new time is creation. This is the creation of the new, and that redeems me. Salvation is the resolution of the task. The task is to give birth to the old in a new time. The soul of humanity is like the great wheel of the zodiac that rolls along the way. Everything that comes up in a constant movement from below to the heights was already there. There is no part of the wheel that does not come around again. Hence everything that has been streams upward there, and what has been will be again. For these are all things which are the inborn properties of human nature. It belongs to the essence of forward movement that what was returns.[260] Only the ignorant can marvel at this. Yet the meaning does not lie in the eternal recurrence of the same,[261] but in the manner of its recurring creation at any given time.

The meaning lies in the manner and the direction of the recurring creation. But how do I create my charioteer? Or do I want to be my own charioteer? I can guide myself only with will and intention. But will and intention are simply part of myself. Consequently

260. The *Draft* continues: "Everything is forever the same and yet not, for the wheel rolls along on a long road. But the way leads through valleys and across mountains. The movement of the wheel and the eternal recurrence of its parts is essential to the carriage, but meaning lies in the way. Meaning is attained only through the wheel's constant revolution and forward movement. The recurrence of the past is inherent in forward movement. This can only baffle the ignorant person. Ignorance makes us resist the necessary recurrence of the same, or greed allows the wheel to toss us up and away in its upward movement because we believe that we will rise ever higher with this part of the wheel. But we will not rise higher, but deeper; ultimately we will be at the very bottom. Thus praise standstill, since it shows you that you are not bound to the spokes like Ixion, but sit alongside the charioteer who will interpret the meaning of the way to you" (pp. 469–70). In Greek mythology, Ixion was the son of Ares. He tried to seduce Hera, and Zeus punished him by binding him to a fiery wheel that rolled unceasingly.

261. The notion that everything recurs is found in various traditions, such as Stoicism and Pythagoreanism, and features prominently in Nietzsche's work. There has been much debate in Nietzsche studies as to whether it should primarily be understood as an ethical imperative of life affirmation or as cosmological doctrine. See Karl Löwith, *Nietzsche's Doctrine of the Eternal Recurrence of the Same*, tr. J. Lomax (Berkeley: University of California Press, 1997). Jung discusses this in 1934, *Nietzsche's Zarathustra*, vol. 1, pp. 191–92.

they are insufficient to express my wholeness. Intention is what I can foresee, and willing is to want a foreseen goal. But where do I find the goal? I take it from what is presently known to me. Thus I set the present in place of the future. In this / manner, though 138/139
I cannot reach the future, I artificially produce a constant present. Everything that would like to break into this present strikes me as a disturbance, and I seek to drive it away so that my intention survives. Thus I close off the progress of life. But how can I be my own charioteer without will and intention? Therefore a wise man does not want to be a charioteer, for he knows that will and intention certainly attain goals but disturb the becoming of the future.

Futurity grows out of me; I do not create it, and yet I do, though not deliberately and willfully, but rather against will and intention. If I want to create the future, then I work against my future. And if I do not want to create it, once again I do not take sufficient part in the creation of the future, and everything happens then according to unavoidable laws to which I fall victim. The ancients devised magic to compel fate. They needed it to determine outer fate. We need it to determine inner fate and to find the way that we are unable to conceive. For a long time I considered what type of magic this would have to be. And in the end I found nothing. Whoever cannot find it within himself should become an apprentice, and so I took myself off to a far country where a great magician lived, of whose reputation I had heard.

The Magician[262]

Cap. xxi.

[HI: 139] {1} [1][263]After a long search I found the small house in the country fronted by a large bed of tulips. This is where ΦΙΛΗΜΩΝ [Philemon], the magician, lives with his wife, ΒΑΥΚΙΣ [Baucis].

262. The *Handwritten Draft* has instead: "*Tenth Adventure*" (p. 1061).

263. January 27, 1914.

ΦΙΛΗΜΩΝ is one of those magicians who has not yet managed to banish old age, but who lives it with dignity, and his wife can only do the same.[264] Their interests seem to have become narrow, even childish. They water their bed of tulips and tell each other about the flowers that have newly appeared. And their days fade into a pale wavering chiaracuso, lit up by the past, only slightly frightened of the darkness of what is to come.

---

264. In the *Metamorphoses*, Ovid tells the tale of Philemon and Baucis. Jupiter and Mercury wandered disguised as mortals, in the hill country of Phyrgia. They searched for somewhere to rest but were barred by a thousand homes. An old couple finally took them in. The couple had been married in their cottage in their youth, grew old together, and contentedly accepted their poverty. They prepared a meal for their guests. During the meal, the couple saw that the flagon automatically refilled itself as soon as it was emptied. In honor of their guests, the couple offered to kill their sole goose. The goose took refuge with the Gods, who said that it should not be killed. Jupiter and Mercury then revealed themselves and told the couple that their neighborhood would be punished, but that they would be spared. They asked the couple to climb the mountain with them. When they reached the top, the couple saw that the country surrounding their cottage had been flooded and only their cottage remained; it had been transformed into a temple with marble columns and a gold roof. The Gods asked what the couple would like, and Philemon replied that they would like to be their priests and serve in their shrine, and also that they could die at the same time. Their wish was granted, and as they died, they transformed into trees side by side. In Goethe's *Faust* 2, act V, a wanderer, who had previously been saved by them, calls upon Philemon and Baucis. Faust was in the process of building a city on land reclaimed from the sea. Faust proceeds to tell Mephistopheles that he wants Philemon and Baucis moved. Mephistopheles and three mighty men go and burn the cottage, with Philemon and Baucis in it. Faust replies that he had only intended to exchange their dwelling. To Eckermann, Goethe recounted that "My Philemon and Baucis . . . have nothing to do with that renowned ancient couple or the tradition connected with them. I gave this couple the names merely to elevate the characters. The persons and relations are similar, and hence the use of the names has a good effect" (June 6, 1831, cited in Goethe, *Faust*, tr. W. Arndt [New York: Norton Critical Edition, 1976], p. 428). On June 7, 1955, Jung wrote a letter to Alice Raphael which refers to Goethe's comments to Eckermann: "Ad *Philemon and Baucis*: a typical Goethean answer to Eckermann! trying to conceal his vestiges. *Philemon* (Φιλημα [philema] = kiss), the loving one, the simple old loving couple, close to the earth and aware of the Gods, the complete opposite to the Superman Faust, the product of the devil. Incidentally: in my tower at Bollingen is a hidden inscription: *Philemon sacrum Fausti poenitentia* [Philemon's Sanctuary, Faust's Repentance]. When I first encountered the archetype of the old wise man, he called himself *Philemon*. / In Alchemy Ph. and B. represented the artifex or vir sapiens and the soror mystica (Zosimos-Theosebeia, Nicolas Flamel-Péronelle, Mr. South and his daughter in the XIXth Cent.) and the pair in the *mutus liber* (about 1677)" (Beinecke Library, Yale University). On Jung's inscription, see also his letter to Hermann Keyserling, January 2, 1928 (*Letters* 1, p. 49). On January 5, 1942, Jung wrote to Paul Schmitt, "I have taken over *Faust as my heritage*, and moreover as the advocate of Philemon and Baucis, who, unlike Faust the superman, are the hosts of the gods in a ruthless and godforsaken age" (*Letters* 1, pp. 309–10).

Why is ΦΙΛΗΜΩΝ a magician?[265] Does he conjure up immortality for himself, a life beyond? He was probably only a magician by profession, and he now appears to be a pensioned magician who has retired from service. His desirousness and creative drive have expired and he now enjoys his well-earned rest out of sheer incapacity, like every old man who can do nothing else than plant tulips and water his little garden. The magical rod lies in a cupboard together with the sixth and seventh books of Moses[266] and the wisdom of ΕΡΜΗΣ ΤΡΙΣΜΕΓΙΣΤΥΣ [Hermes Trismegistus].[267] ΦΙΛΗΜΩΝ is old and has become somewhat feeble-minded. He still murmurs a few magical spells for the well-being of bewitched cattle in return for some petty cash or a gift for the kitchen. But it is uncertain if these spells are still correct and whether he understands their meaning. It
is also clear that it hardly matters what he murmurs, / as the cattle 139/140
might also get well on their own. There goes old ΦΙΛΗΜΩΝ in the garden, bent, with a watering can in his shaking hand. Baucis stands at the kitchen window and looks at him calmly and impassively. She has already seen this image a thousand times—somewhat more infirm every time, feebler, seeing it a little less well every time since her eyesight gradually has become weaker.[268]

265. In *Psychological Types* (1921), in the course of a discussion of Faust, Jung wrote: "The magician has preserved in himself a trace of primordial paganism, he possesses a nature that is still unaffected by the Christian splitting, which means he has access to the unconscious, which is still pagan, where the opposites still lie in their original naïve state, beyond all sinfulness, but, if assimilated into conscious life, produce evil and good with the same primordial and consequently daimonic force . . . Therefore he is a destroyer as well as savior. This figure is therefore pre-eminently suited to become the symbol carrier for an attempt at unification" (CW 6, §316).

266. The sixth and seventh books of Moses (i.e., in addition to the five contained in the Torah) were published in 1849 by Johann Schiebel, who claimed that they came from ancient Talmudic sources. The work is a compendium of Kabbalistic magical spells, which has been enduringly popular.

267. The figure of Hermes Trismegistus was formed through the amalgamation of Hermes with the Egyptian God Thoth. *The Corpus Hermeticum*, a collection of largely alchemical and magical texts dating from the early Christian era but initially thought to have been much older, was ascribed to him.

268. In Goethe's *Faust*, Philemon speaks of his declining powers: "Older, I could not lend a hand [to the building of the dyke] / as once I did full well, / and with my powers ebbing / the waters were pushed back" (Ll. 11087–9).

I stand at the garden gate. They have not noticed the stranger. "ΦΙΛΗΜΩΝ, old magician, how are you?" I call out to him. He does not hear me, seeming to be stone-deaf. I follow him and take his arm. He turns and greets me awkwardly and trembling. He has a white beard and thin white hair and a wrinkled face and there appears to be something about this face. His eyes are gray and old and something in them is strange, one would like to say alive. "I am well, stranger," he says, "but what are you doing here?"

I: "People tell me that you understand the black art. I am interested in that. Will you tell me about it?"

Φ: "What should I tell you about? There is nothing to tell."

I: "Don't be ill-natured, old man, I want to learn."

Φ: "You are certainly more learned than I. What could I teach you?"

I: "Do not be mean. I certainly don't intend to become your competitor. I'm just curious to know what you are up to and what magic you are performing."

Φ: "What do you want? In the past I have helped people here and there who have been sick and disadvantaged."

I: "What exactly did you do?"

Φ: "Well, I did it quite simply with sympathy."

I: " Old man, that word sounds comical and ambiguous."

Φ: "How so?"

I: "It could mean that you helped people either by expressing compassion or by superstitious, sympathetic means."

Φ: "Well, surely it would have been both."

I: "And that's all there was to your magic?"

Φ: "There was more."

I: "What was it, tell me."

Φ: "That is none of your business. You are impertinent and meddlesome."

I: "Please, don't take my curiosity badly. Recently I heard something about magic that awakened my interest in this bygone practice. And then I came to you because I heard that you understand the black art. If magic were still taught today at university, I would have studied it there. But the last college of magic was closed long ago. Today no professor knows anything anymore about magic. So do not be sensitive and miserly, but tell me a bit about your art. Surely, you don't want to take your secrets with you to the grave, do you?"

Φ: "Well, all you will do is laugh anyway. So why should I tell you anything? It would be better if everything were buried with me. It can always be rediscovered later. It will never be lost to humanity, since magic is reborn with each and every one of us."

I: "What do you mean? Do you believe that magic is really inborn in man?"

Φ: "If I could, I would say, yes, of course, it is. But you will find this laughable."

I: "No, this time I will not laugh, because I have often wondered about the fact that all peoples in all times and in all places have the same magical customs. As you can see, I have already thought along similar lines."

Φ: "What do you make of magic?"

I: "To put it plainly, nothing, or very little. It appears to me that magic is one of the vain tools of men inferior to nature. I can detect no other tangible meaning in magic."

Φ: Your professors probably also know just as much."

I: "Yes, but what do you know about it?"

Φ: "I'd prefer not to say."

I: "Don't be so secretive, old man, otherwise I must assume that you know no more than I do."

Φ: "Take it as you please."

I: "Your answer suggests that you most definitely understand more about it than others."

Φ: "Comical fellow, how stubborn you are! But what I like about you is that your reason does not deter you."

I: "That's actually the case. Whenever I want to learn and understand something, I leave my so-called reason at home and give whatever it is that I am trying to understand the benefit of the doubt. I have learned this gradually, because nowadays the world of science is full of scary examples of the opposite."

140/141 Φ: "In which case you could do very well for yourself." /

I: "I hope so. Now, let us not stray from magic."

Φ: "Why are you so determined about learning more about magic, if you claim that you have left your reason at home? Or would you not consider consistency part of reason?"

I: "I do—I see, or rather, it seems as if you are quite an adept sophist, who skillfully leads me around the house and back to the door."

Φ: "It seems that way to you because you judge everything from the standpoint of your intellect. If you forsake reason for a while, you will also give up consistency."

I: "That's a difficult test. But if I want to be adept at some point, I suppose I ought to submit to your request. All right, I'm listening."

Φ: "What do you want to hear?"

I: "You're not going to draw me out. I'm simply waiting for whatever you are going to say."

Φ: "And what if I say nothing?"

I: "Well, then I'll withdraw somewhat embarrassed and think that ΦΙΛΗΜΩΝ is at the very least a shrewd fox, who definitely would have something to teach me."

Φ: "With this, my boy, you have learned something about magic."

I: "I'll have to chew on this. I must admit that this is somewhat surprising. I had imagined magic as being somewhat different."

Φ: "Well, this shows you how little you understand about magic and how incorrect your notion of it is."

I: "If this should be the case, or that's how it is, then I must confess that I approached the problem completely incorrectly. I gather from what you are saying that these matters do not follow ordinary understanding."

Φ: "Nor does magic."

I: "But you have not deterred me at all; on the contrary, I'm burning to hear even more. What I know up to now is essentially negative."

Φ: "With this you have recognized a second main point. Above all, you must know that magic is the negative of what one can know."

I: "That, too, my dear ΦΙΛΗΜΩΝ, is a piece of knowledge that is hard to digest and causes me no small pain. The negative of what one can know? I suppose you mean that it cannot be known, don't you? This exhausts my understanding."

Φ: "That is the third point that you must note as essential: namely, that there is nothing for you to understand."

I: "Well, I must confess that that is new and strange. So nothing at all about magic can be understood?"

Φ: "Exactly. Magic happens to be precisely everything that eludes comprehension."

I: "But then how the devil is one to teach and learn magic?"

Φ: "Magic is neither to be taught nor learned. It's foolish that you want to learn magic."

I: "But then magic is nothing but deception."

Φ: "Watch out—you have started reasoning again."

I: "It's difficult to exist without reason."

Φ: "And that is exactly how difficult magic is."

I: "Well, in that case it's hard work. I conclude that it is an inescapable condition for the adept that he completely unlearns his reason."

Φ: "I'm afraid that is what it amounts to."

I: "Ye Gods, this is serious."

Φ: "Not as serious as you think. Reason declines with old age, since it is an essential counterpart of the drives, which are much more intense in youth than in old age. Have you ever seen young magicians?"

I: "No, the magician is proverbially old."

Φ: "You see, I'm right."

I: "But then the prospects of the adept are bad. He must wait until old age to experience the mysteries of magic."

Φ: "If he gives up his reason before then, he can already experience something useful sooner."

I: "That seems to me to be a dangerous experiment. One cannot give up reason without further ado."

Φ: "Nor can one / simply become a magician." 141/142

I: "You lay damnable snares."

Φ: "What do you want? Such is magic."

I: "Old devil, you make me envious of unreasoning old age."

Φ: "Well, well, a youth who wants to be an old man! And why? He wants to learn magic and yet dares not to for the sake of his youth."

I: "You spread a terrible net, old trapper."

Φ: "Perhaps you should still wait a few years with magic until your hair has gone gray and your reason has slackened somewhat."

I: "I don't want to listen to your scorn. Stupidly enough, I got caught up in your yarn. I can't make sense of you."

Φ: "But stupidity would perhaps be progress on the way to magic."

I: "Incidentally, what on earth do you intend to achieve with your magic?"

Φ: "I am alive, as you see."

I: "Other old men are, too."

Φ: "Yes, but have you seen how?"

I: "Well, admittedly it was not a pleasant sight. Incidentally, time has left its mark on you, too."

Φ: "I know."

I: "So, what gives you the advantage?"

Φ: "It doesn't exactly meet the eye."

I: "What kind of advantage doesn't meet the eye?"

Φ: "I call that magic."

I: "You're moving in a vicious circle. May the devil get the better of you."

Φ: "Well, that's another advantage of magic: not even the devil gets the better of me. You're beginning to understand magic, so I must assume that you have a good aptitude for it."

I: "Thank you, ΦΙΛΗΜΩΝ, that is enough; I feel dizzy. Goodbye!"

I leave the small garden and walk down the street. People are standing around in groups and glancing at me furtively. I hear them whispering behind my back: "Look, there he goes, old ΦΙΛΗΜΩΝ's student. He spoke a long time with the old man. He has learned something. He knows the mysteries. If only I could do what he is able to do now." "Be quiet, you damned fools," I want to call out to them, but I cannot, since I do not know whether I have actually learned anything. And because I remain silent, they are even more convinced that I have received the black art from ΦΙΛΗΜΩΝ.

[269][2] [HI 142] *It is an error to believe that there are* magical practices that one can learn. One cannot understand magic. One can only understand what accords with reason. Magic accords with unreason, which one cannot understand. The world accords not only with reason but also with unreason. But just as one employs reason to make sense of the world, in that what is reasonable about it approaches reason, a lack of understanding also accords with unreason. / 142/143

This meeting is magical and eludes comprehension. Magical understanding is what one calls noncomprehension. Everything that works magically is incomprehensible, and the incomprehensible often works magically. One calls incomprehensible workings magical. The magical always surrounds me, always involves me. It opens spaces that have no doors and leads out into the open where there is no exit. The magical is good and evil and neither good nor evil. Magic is dangerous since what accords with unreason confuses, allures and provokes; and I am always its first victim.

Where reason abides, one needs no magic. Hence our time no longer needs magic. Only those without reason needed it to replace their lack of reason. But it is thoroughly unreasonable to bring together what suits reason with magic since they have nothing to do with one another. Both become spoiled through being brought together. Therefore all those lacking reason quite rightly fall into superfluity and disregard. A rational man of this time will therefore never use magic.[270]

But it is another thing for whoever has opened the chaos in himself. We need magic to be able to receive or invoke the messenger

269. Jung's marginal note to the calligraphic volume: "Jan. 1924." This seems to refer to when this passage was transcribed into the calligraphic volume. The writing at this point gets larger, with more space between the words. At this time, Cary Baynes commenced her transcription.

270. In *Psychological Types* (1921) Jung wrote: "Reason can only give one equilibrium if one's reason is already an equilibrating organ . . . As a rule, man needs the opposite of his actual condition to force him to find his place in the middle" (CW 6, §386).

and the communication of the incomprehensible. We recognized that the world comprises reason and unreason; and we also understood that our way needs not only reason but also unreason. This distinction is arbitrary and depends upon the level of comprehension. But one can be certain that the greater part of the world eludes our understanding. We must value the incomprehensible and unreasonable equally, although they are not necessarily equal in themselves; a part of the incomprehensible, however, is only presently incomprehensible and might already concur with reason tomorrow. But as long as one does not understand it, it remains unreasonable. Insofar as the incomprehensible accords with reason, one may try to
143/144 think it with success; but insofar as it is unreasonable, / one needs magical practices to open it up.

The practice of magic consists in making what is not understood understandable in an incomprehensible manner. The magical way is not arbitrary, since that would be understandable, but it arises from incomprehensible grounds. Besides, to speak of grounds is incorrect, since grounds concur with reason. Nor can one speak of the groundless, since hardly anything further can be said about this. The magical way arises by itself. If one opens up chaos, magic also arises.

One can teach the way that leads to chaos, but one cannot teach magic. One can only remain silent about this, which seems to be the best apprenticeship. This view is confusing, but this is what magic is like. Where reason establishes order and clarity, magic causes disarray and a lack of clarity.[271] One indeed needs reason for the magical translation of the not-understood into the understandable, since only by means of reason can the understandable be created. No one can say how to use reason, but it does arise if one tries to express only what an opening of chaos means.[272]

271. The *Draft* continues: "Magical practice hence falls into two parts: first, developing an understanding of chaos; and second, translating the essence into what can be understood" (p. 484).

272. The *Draft* continues: "Reason takes up only a very small share of magic. This will offend you. Age and experience are needed. The rash desirousness and fear of youth, as well as its necessary virtuousness, disturb the secret interplay of God and the devil. You are then all too easily torn to one side or the other, blinded or paralyzed" (p. 484).

Magic is a way of living. If one has done one's best to steer the chariot, and one then notices that a greater other is actually steering it, then magical operation takes place. One cannot say what the effect of magic will be, since no one can know it in advance because the magical is the lawless, which occurs without rules and by chance, so to speak. But the condition is that one totally accepts it and does not reject it, in order to transfer everything to the growth of the tree. Stupidity too is part of this, which everyone has a great deal of, and also tastelessness, which is possibly the greatest nuisance.

Thus a certain solitude and isolation are inescapable conditions of life for the well-being of oneself and of the other, otherwise one cannot / sufficiently be oneself. A certain slowness of life, which 144/145
is like a standstill, will be unavoidable. The uncertainty of such a life will most probably be its greatest burden, but still I must unite the two conflicting powers of my soul and keep them together in a true marriage until the end of my life, since the magician is called ΦΙΛΗΜΩΝ and his wife ΒΑΥΚΙΣ. I hold together what Christ has kept apart in himself and through his example in others, since the more the one half of my being strives toward the good, the more the other half journeys to Hell.

When the month of the Twins had ended, the men said to their shadows: "You are I," since they had previously had their spirit around them as a second person. Thus the two became one, and through this collision the formidable broke out, precisely that spring of consciousness that one calls culture and which lasted until the time of Christ.[273] But the fish indicated the moment when what was united split, according to the eternal law of contrasts, into

273. The reference is to the astrological conception of the Platonic month, or aeon, of Pisces, which is based on the precession of the equinoxes. Each Platonic month consists of one zodiacal sign, and lasts approximately 2,300 years. Jung discusses the symbolism attached to this in *Aion* (1951, CW 6, ch. 6). He notes that around 7 BC there was a conjunction of Saturn and Jupiter, representing a union of extreme opposites, which would place the birth of Christ under Pisces. Pisces (Latin for "fishes") is known as the sign of the fish and is often represented by two fish swimming in opposite directions. On the Platonic months, see Alice Howell, *Jungian Synchronicity in Astrological Signs and Ages* (Wheaton, IL: Quest Books, 1990), p. 125f. Jung started studying astrology in 1911, in the course of his study of mythology, and learned to cast horoscopes (Jung to Freud, May 8, 1911, *The Freud/Jung Letters*, p. 421). In terms of Jung's sources for the his-

an underworld and upperworld. If the power of growth begins to cease, then the united falls into its opposites. Christ sent what is beneath to Hell, since it strives toward the good. That had to be. But the separated cannot remain separated forever. It will be united again and the month of the fish will soon be over.[274] We suspect and understand that growth needs both, and hence we keep good and evil close together. Because we know that too far into the good means the same as too far into evil, we keep them both together.[275]

But we thus lose direction and things no longer flow from the mountain to the valley, but grow quietly from the valley to the mountain. That which we can no longer prevent or hide is our fruit.
145/146 The flowing stream becomes a lake and an ocean / that has no outlet, unless its water rises to the sky as steam and falls from the clouds as rain. While the sea is a death, it is also the place of rising. Such is ΦΙΛΗΜΩΝ, who tends his garden. Our hands have been tied, and each must sit quietly in his place. He rises invisibly and falls as rain on distant lands.[276] The water on the ground is no cloud, which should rain. Only pregnant women can give birth, not those who have yet to conceive.[277]

---

tory of astrology, he cited Auguste Bouché-Leclercq's *L'Astrologie Grecque* on nine occasions in his later work (Paris: Ernest Leroux, 1899).

274. This refers to the end of the Platonic month of Pisces and the beginning of the Platonic month of Aquarius. The precise dating of this is uncertain. In *Aion* (1951), Jung noted: "Astrologically the beginning of the next aeon, according to the starting point you select, falls between AD 2000 and 2200" (CW 9, 2, §149, note 88).

275. In *Aion* (1951), Jung wrote: "If, as seems probable, the aeon of the fishes is ruled by the archetypal motif of the 'hostile brothers,' then the approach of the next Platonic month, namely Aquarius, will constellate the problem of the union of opposites. It will then no longer be possible to write off evil as a mere *privatio boni*; its real existence will have to be recognized" (CW 9, §142).

276. The *Draft* continues: "The hibernal rains began with Christ. He taught mankind the way to Heaven. We teach the way to earth. Hence nothing has been removed from the Gospel, but only added to it" (p. 486).

277. The *Draft* continues: "Our striving focused on sagacity and intellectual superiority, and we hence developed all our cleverness. But the extraordinary extent of stupidity inherent in all men was disregarded and denied. But if we accept the other in us, we also evoke the particular stupidity of our nature. Stupidity is one of man's strange hobbyhorses. There is something divine about it, and yet something of the megalomania of the world. Which is why stupidity is really large. It keeps away everything that could induce us to intelligence. It leaves everything not understood which is not naturally supposed to demand understanding. This particular stupidity occurs in thought and in life. Somewhat deaf, somewhat blind, it brings about necessary fate and keeps from

[HI 146] *But what mystery are you intimating* to me with your name, Oh ΦΙΛΗΜΩΝ? Truly you are the lover who once took in the Gods as they wandered the earth when everyone else refused them lodging. You are the one who unsuspectingly gave hospitality to the Gods; they thanked you by transforming your house into a golden temple, while the flood swallowed everyone else. You remained alive when chaos erupted. You it was who served in the sanctuary when the peoples called out in vain to the Gods. Truly, it is the lover who survives. Why did we not see that? And just when did the Gods manifest? Precisely when ΒΑΥΚΙΣ wished to serve the esteemed guests her only goose, that blessed stupidity: the animal fled to the Gods who then revealed themselves to their poor hosts, who had given their last. Thus I saw that the lover survives, and that he is the one who unwittingly grants hospitality to the Gods.[278]

Truly, Oh ΦΙΛΗΜΩΝ, I did not see that your hut is a temple, and that you, ΦΙΛΗΜΩΝ, and ΒΑΥΚΙΣ, serve in the sanctuary. / This 146/147
magical power allows itself to be neither taught nor learned. Either one has it or does not have it. Now I know your final mystery: you are a lover. You have succeeded in uniting what has been sundered, that is, binding together the Above and Below. Have we not known this for a long time? Yes, we knew it, no, we did not know it. It has always been this way, and yet it has never been thus. Why did I have to wander such long roads before I came to ΦΙΛΗΜΩΝ, if he was going to teach me what has been common knowledge for ages? Alas, we have known everything since time immemorial and yet we will never know it until it is has been accomplished. Who exhausts the mystery of love?

[HI 147] *Under which mask, Oh* ΦΙΛΗΜΩΝ, are you hiding? You did not strike me as a lover. But my eyes were opened, and I saw that you are a lover of your soul, who anxiously and jealously guards its treasure. There are those who love men, and those who love the souls of

---

us the virtuousness coupled with rationality. It is what separates and isolates the mixed seeds of life, affording us thus with a clear view of good and evil, and of what is reasonable and what not. But many people are logical in their lack of reason" (p. 487).

278. In this paragraph, Jung refers to the classical account of Philemon and Baucis from the *Metamorphoses*.

men, and those who love their own soul. Such a one is ΦΙΛΗΜΩΝ, the host of the Gods.

You lie in the sun, Oh ΦΙΛΗΜΩΝ, like a serpent that coils around itself. Your wisdom is the wisdom of serpents, cold, with a grain of poison, yet healing in small doses. Your magic paralyzes and therefore makes strong people, who tear themselves away from themselves. But do they love you, are they thankful, lover of your own soul? Or do they curse you for your magical serpent poison? They keep their distance, shaking their heads and whispering together.

147/148 Are you still a man, ΦΙΛΗΜΩΝ, or / is one not a man until one is a lover of one's own soul? You are hospitable, ΦΙΛΗΜΩΝ, you took the dirty wanderers unsuspectingly into your hut. Your house then became a golden temple, and did I really leave your table unsatisfied? What did you give me? Did you invite me for a meal? You shimmered multicolored and inextricable; nowhere did you give yourself to me as prey. You escaped my grasp. I found you nowhere. Are you still a man? Your kind is far more serpentlike.

I sought to grab hold of you and tear it out of you, since the Christians have learned to devour their God. And how long will it take for what happens to the God also to happen to man? I look into the vast land and hear nothing but wailing and see nothing but men consuming each other.

Oh ΦΙΛΗΜΩΝ, you are no Christian. You did not let yourself be engorged and did not engorge me. Because of this you have neither lecture halls nor columned halls teeming with students who stand around and speak of the master and soak up his words like the elixir of life. You are no Christian and no pagan, but a hospitable inhospitable one, a host of the Gods, a survivor, an eternal one, the father of all eternal wisdom.

But did I really leave you unsatisfied? No, I left you because I was really satisfied. Yet what did I eat? Your words gave me nothing. Your words left me to myself and my doubt. And so I ate myself. And because of this, Oh ΦΙΛΗΜΩΝ, you are no Christian, since you nourish yourself from yourself and force men to do the same. This displeases them most, since nothing disgusts the human animal more than itself. Because of this they would rather eat all crawling, hopping, swimming and flying creatures, yes, even their own species, before they nibble at themselves. But this nourishment is effective and one is soon satiated from it. Because of this, Oh ΦΙΛΗΜΩΝ, we rise satiated from your table.

Your way, Oh ΦΙΛΗΜΩΝ, is instructive. You leave me in a salutary darkness, where there is nothing for me to either see or look for. You are no light that shines in the darkness,[279] no savior who establishes an eternal truth and thus extinguishes the / nocturnal 148/149
light of human understanding. You leave room for the stupidity and jokes of others. You do not want, Oh blessed one, anything from the other, but instead you tend the flowers in your own garden. He who needs you asks you, and, Oh clever ΦΙΛΗΜΩΝ, I suppose that you also ask those from whom you need something and that you pay for what you receive. Christ has made men desirous, for ever since they expect gifts from their saviors without any service in return. Giving is as childish as power. He who gives presumes himself powerful. The virtue of giving is the sky-blue mantle of the tyrant. You are wise, Oh ΦΙΛΗΜΩΝ, you do not give. You want your garden to bloom, and for everything to grow from within itself.

I praise, Oh ΦΙΛΗΜΩΝ, your lack of acting like a savior; you are no shepherd who runs after stray sheep, since you believe in the dignity of man, who is not necessarily a sheep. But if he happens to be a sheep, you would leave him the rights and dignity of sheep, since why should sheep be made into men? There are still more than enough men.

You know, Oh ΦΙΛΗΜΩΝ, the wisdom of things to come; therefore you are old, oh so very ancient, and just as you tower above me in years, so you tower above the present in futurity, and the length of your past is immeasurable. You are legendary and unreachable. You were and will be, returning periodically. Your wisdom is invisible, your truth is unknowable, entirely untrue in any given age, and

279. Contrast with John 1:5, where Christ is described as follows: "The light shines in the darkness, but the darkness has not understood it."

yet true in all eternity, but you pour out living water, from which the flowers of your garden bloom, a starry water, a dew of the night.

What do you need, Oh ΦΙΛΗΜΩΝ? You need men for the sake of small things, since everything greater and the greatest thing is in you. Christ spoiled men, since he taught them that they can be saved only by one, namely Him, the Son of God, and ever since men have been demanding the greater things from others, especially their sal-
149/150 vation; and if a sheep gets lost / somewhere, it accuses the shepherd. Oh ΦΙΛΗΜΩΝ, you are a man, and you prove that men are not sheep, since you look after the greatest in yourself, and hence fructifying water flows into your garden from inexhaustible jugs.

[HI 150] *Are you lonely, Oh* ΦΙΛΗΜΩΝ, I see no entourage and no companions around you; ΒΑΥΚΙΣ is only your other half. You live with flowers, trees, and birds, but not with men. Should you not live with men? Are you still a man? Do you want nothing from men? Do you not see how they stand together and concoct rumors and childish fairy tales about you? Do you not want to go to them and say that you are a man and a mortal as they are, and that you want to love them? Oh ΦΙΛΗΜΩΝ, you laugh? I understand you. Just now I ran into your garden and wanted to tear out of you what I had to understand from within myself.

Oh ΦΙΛΗΜΩΝ, I understand: immediately I made you into a savior who lets himself be consumed and bound with gifts. That's what men are like, you think; they are all still Christians. But they want even more: they want you as you are, otherwise you would not be ΦΙΛΗΜΩΝ to them and they would be inconsolable, if they could find no bearer for their legends. Hence they would also laugh, if you approached them and said you were as mortal as they are and want to love them. If you did that, you would not be ΦΙΛΗΜΩΝ. They want you, ΦΙΛΗΜΩΝ, but not another mortal who suffers from the same ills as they do.

150/151 I understand you, Oh ΦΙΛΗΜΩΝ, you are a true / lover, since you love your soul for the sake of men, because they need a king who lives from himself and owes no one gratitude for his life. They want to have you thus. You fulfill the wish of the people and you vanish. You are a vessel of fables. You would besmirch yourself if you went to men as a man, since they would all laugh and call you a liar and a swindler, since ΦΙΛΗΜΩΝ is not a man.

I saw, Oh ΦΙΛΗΜΩΝ, that crease in your face: you were young once and wanted to be a man among men. But the Christian animals did not love your pagan humanity, since they felt in you what they needed. They always sought the branded one, and when they caught him somewhere in freedom, they locked him in a golden cage and took from him the force of his masculinity, so that he was paralyzed and sat in silence. Then they praise him and devise fables about him. I know, they call this veneration. And if they do not find the true one, they at least have a Pope, whose occupation it is to represent the divine comedy. But the true one always disowns himself, since he knows nothing higher than to be a man.

Are you laughing, Oh ΦΙΛΗΜΩΝ? I understand you: it irked you to be a man like others. And because you truly loved being human, you voluntarily locked it away so that you could be for men at least what they wanted to have from you. Therefore I see you, Oh ΦΙΛΗΜΩΝ, not with men, but wholly with flowers, the trees and the birds and all waters flowing and still that do not besmirch your humanity. For you are not ΦΙΛΗΜΩΝ to the flowers, trees, and birds, but a man. Yet what solitude, what inhumanity! / 151/152

[HI 152] *Why are you laughing, Oh ΦΙΛΗΜΩΝ, I cannot fathom you. But do I not see the blue air of your garden? What happy shades surround you? Does the sun hatch blue midday specters around you?*

Are you laughing, Oh ΦΙΛΗΜΩΝ? Alas, I understand you: humanity has completely faded for you, but its shadow has arisen for you. How much greater and happier the shadow of humanity is than it is itself! The blue midday shadows of the dead! Alas, there is your humanity, Oh ΦΙΛΗΜΩΝ, you are a teacher and friend of the dead. They stand sighing in the shade of your house, they live under the branches of your trees. They drink the dew of your tears, they warm themselves at the goodness of your heart, they hunger after

the words of your wisdom, which sounds full to them, full of the sounds of life. I saw you, Oh ΦΙΛΗΜΩΝ, at the noonday hour when the sun stood highest; you stood speaking with a blue shade, blood stuck to its forehead and solemn torment darkened it. I can guess, Oh ΦΙΛΗΜΩΝ, who your midday guest was.[280] How blind I was, fool that I am! That is you, Oh ΦΙΛΗΜΩΝ! But who am I! I go my way, shaking my head, and people's looks follow me and I remain
152/153 silent. Oh despairing silence! / [HI 153]

Oh master of the garden! I see your dark tree from afar in the shimmering sun. My street leads to the valleys where men live. I am a wandering beggar. And I remain silent.

Killing off would-be prophets is a gain for the people. If they want murder, then may they kill their false prophets. If the mouth of the Gods remains silent, then each can listen to his own speech. He who loves the people remains silent. If only false teachers teach, the people will kill the false teachers, and will fall into the truth even on the way of their sins. Only after the darkest night will it be day. So cover the lights and remain silent so that the night will become dark and noiseless. The sun rises without our help. Only he who knows the darkest error knows what light is.

Oh master of the garden, your magical grove shone to me from afar. I venerate
153/154 *your deceptive mantle, you father of all will-o'-the-wisps. /*[281] [Image 154][282]

280. Cf. Jung's fantasy of June 1, 1916, where Philemon's guest was Christ (see below, p. 551).
281. Jung's marginal note to the calligraphic volume: "The bhagavadgita says: whenever there is a decline of the law and an increase in iniquity, then I put forth myself. For the rescue of the pious and for the destruction of the evildoers, for the establishment of the law I am born in every age." The citation is from chapter 4, verses 7–8 of the *Bhagavad Gita.* Krishna is instructing Arjuna concerning the nature of truth.
282. The text in the image reads: "Father of the Prophet, beloved Philemon." Jung subsequently painted another version of this painting as a mural in one of the bedrooms in his tower at Bollingen. He added an inscription in Latin from the *Rosarium Philosophorum,* in which Hermes describes the stone as saying: "defend me and I will defend thee, give me my right that I may help thee, for Sol is mine and the beams thereof are my inward parts; but Luna is proper to me, and my light excelleth all light, and my goods are higher than all goods. I give many riches and delights to men desiring them, and when I seek after anything they acknowledge it, I make them understand and I cause

I continue on my way, accompanied by a finely polished piece of steel, hardened in ten fires, stowed safely in my robe. Secretly, I wear chain mail under my coat. Overnight I became fond of serpents, and I solved their riddle. I sit down next to them on the hot stones lying by the wayside. I know how to catch them cunningly and cruelly, those cold devils that prick the heel of the unsuspecting. I became their friend and played a softly toned flute. But I decorate my cave with their dazzling skins. As I walked on my way, I came to a red rock on which a great iridescent serpent lay. Since I had now learned magic from ΦΙΛΗΜΩΝ, I took out my flute again and played a sweet magical song to make her believe that she was my soul. When she was sufficiently enchanted, / [Image 155][283] {2} [1][284] I 154/155

them to possess divine strength. I engender light, but my nature is darkness. Unless my metal should be dry, all bodies have need of me, because I moisten them. I blot out their rustiness and extract their substance. Therefore I and my son being joined together, there can be nothing made better nor more honorable in the whole world." Jung cited some of these lines in *Psychology and Alchemy* (1944, CW 12, §§99, 140, 155). The *Rosarium*, first published in 1550, was one of the most important texts of European alchemy, and concerns the means of producing the philosopher's stone. It contained a series of woodcuts of symbolic figures, which was Jung's exemplar in *Psychology of the Transference. Explained through an Alchemical Series of Pictures. For Doctors and Practical Psychologists* (1946, CW 16).

283. In "The psychological aspects of the Kore" (1951), Jung anonymously described this image as "xi. Then she [the anima] appears in a church, taking the place of the altar, still over-life-size but with veiled face." He commented: "Dream xi restores the anima to the Christian church, not as an icon but as the altar itself. The altar is the place of sacrifice and also the receptacle for consecrated relics" (CW 9, 1, §369, 380). On the left-hand side, there is the Arabic word for "daughters." On the border of the image is the following inscription: "Dei sapientia in mysterio quae abscondita est, quam praedestinavit ante secula in gloriam nostrum quam nemo princip[i]um huius seculi cognovit. Spiritus enim omnia scrutatur etiam profundo dei." This is a citation from 1 Corinthians 2:7–10. (Jung has omitted "Deus" before "ante secula.") The portions cited are marked here in italics: "But we speak *the wisdom of God in a mystery, even the hidden wisdom, which God ordained before the world unto our glory: Which none of the princes of the world knew*: for had they known it, they would not have crucified the Lord of glory. But as it is written, Eye hath not seen, nor ear heard, neither have entered into the heart of man, the things which God hath prepared for them that love him. But God hath revealed them unto us by his Spirit: *for the Spirit searcheth all things, yea, the deep things of God.*" On either side of the arch is the following inscription: "Spiritus et sponsa dicunt veni et qui audit dicat veni et qui sitit veniat qui vult accipiat aquam vitae gratis." The text is from Revelation 22:17: "the Spirit and the bride say, Come. And let him that heareth say, Come. And let him that is athirst come. And whosoever will, let him take the water of life freely." Above the arch is the following inscription: "ave virgo virginum [Hail, virgin of virgins]." This is the title of a medieval hymn.

284. January 29, 1914.

spoke to her: "My sister, my soul, what do you say?" But she spoke, flattered and therefore tolerantly: "I let grass grow over everything that you do."

I: "That sounds comforting and seems not to say much."

S: "Would you like me to say much? I can also be banal, as you know, and let myself be satisfied that way."

I: "That seems hard to me. I believe that you stand in a close
155/156 connection with everything beyond, / [285] with what is greatest and most uncommon. Therefore I thought that banality would be foreign to you."

S: "Banality is my element."

I: "That would be less astonishing if I said it about myself."

S: "The more uncommon you are, the more common I can be. A true respite for me. I think you can sense that I don't need to torment myself today."

I: "I can feel it, and I'm worried that your tree will ultimately bear me no more fruit."

S: "Worried already? Don't be stupid, and let me rest."

I: "I notice that you like being banal. But I do not take you to heart, my dear friend, since I now know you much better than before."

S: "You're getting to be familiar. I'm afraid that you are beginning to lose respect."

I: "Are you upset? I believe that would be uncalled for. I'm sufficiently well-informed about the proximity of pathos and banality."

S: "So, have you noticed that the becoming of the soul follows a serpentine path? Have you seen how soon day becomes night, and night day? How water and dry land change places? And that everything spasmodic is merely destructive?"

I: "I believe that I saw all this. I want to lie in the sun on this warm stone for a while. Perhaps the sun will incubate me."

---

285. From this point in the calligraphic volume, Jung's coloring of red and blue initials becomes less consistent. Some have been added here for consistency.

But the serpent crept up to me quietly and wound herself smoothly around my feet.[286] Evening fell and night came. I spoke to the serpent and said: "I don't know what to say. All pots are on the boil."

[287]S: "A meal is being prepared."

I: "A Last Supper, I suppose?"

S: "A union with all humanity."

I: "A horrifying, sweet thought: to be both guest and dish at this meal."[288]

S: "That was also Christ's highest pleasure."

I: "How holy, how sinful, how everything hot and cold flows into one another! Madness and reason want to be married, the lamb and the wolf graze peacefully side by side.[289] It is all yes and no. The opposites embrace each other, see eye to eye, and intermingle. They recognize their oneness in agonizing pleasure. My heart is filled with wild battle. The waves of dark and bright rivers rush together, one crashing over the other. I have never experienced this before."

S: "That is new, my dear one, at least for you."

I: "I suppose you are mocking me. But tears and laughter are
one.[290] / I no longer feel like either and I am rigid with tension. 156/157
Loving reaches up to Heaven and resisting reaches just as high. They are entwined and will not let go of each other, since the excessive tension seems to indicate the ultimate and highest possibility of feeling."

286. This line is not in *Black Book* 4, where the voice is not identified as the serpent.

287. January 31, 1914.

288. In *Mysterium Coniunctionis* (1955/56), Jung noted: "If the projected conflict is to be healed, it must return into the soul of the individual, where it had its beginnings in an unconscious manner. He who wants to be the master of this descent must celebrate a Last Supper with himself, and eat his own flesh and drink his own blood; which means that he must recognize and accept the other in himself" (CW 14, §512).

289. Cf. Isaiah 11:6: "The wolf also shall dwell with the lamb, and the leopard shall lie down with the kid; and the calf and the young lion and the fatling together; and a little child shall lead them."

290. Jung's marginal note to the calligraphic volume: "XIV AUG. 1925." This appears to refer to when this passage was transcribed into the calligraphic volume. In the autumn of 1925, Jung went to Africa, together with Peter Baynes and George Beckwith. They left England on October 15, and he arrived back in Zürich on March 14, 1926.

S: "You express yourself emotionally and philosophically. You know that one can say all this much more simply. For example, one can say that you have fallen in love all the way from the worm up to Tristan and Isolde.[291]

I: "Yes, I know, but nonetheless—"

S: "Religion is still tormenting you, it seems? How many shields do you still need? Much better to say it straight out."

I:" You're not tripping me up."

S: "Well, what is it with morality? Have morality and immorality also become one today?"

I: "You're mocking me, my sister and chthonic devil. But I must say that those two that rose up to Heaven entwined are also good and evil. I'm not joking but I groan, because joy and pain sound shrill together."

S: "Where then is your understanding? You've gone utterly stupid. After all, you could resolve everything by thinking."

I: "My understanding? My thinking? I no longer have any understanding. It has grown impervious to me."

S: "You deny everything that you believed. You've completely forgotten who you are. You even deny Faust, who walked calmly past all the specters."

I: "I'm no longer up to this. My spirit, too, is a specter."

S: "Ah, I see, you follow my teaching."

I: "Unfortunately, that's the case, and it has benefited me with painful joy."

S: "You turn your pain into pleasure. You are twisted, blinded; just suffer, you fool."

I: "This misfortune ought to make me happy."

---

291. The twelfth-century tale of the adulterous romance between the Cornish knight Tristan and the Irish princess Isolde has been retold in many versions, up to Wagner's opera, which Jung referred to as an example of the visionary mode of artistic creation ("Psychology and poetry," 1930, *CW* 15, §142).

The serpent now became angry and tried to bite my heart, but my secret armor broke her poisonous fang.[292] She drew back astonished and said hissing: "You actually behave as if you were unfathomable."

I: "That's because I have studied the art of stepping from the left foot onto the right and vice versa, which others have done unthinkingly from time immemorial."

The serpent raised herself again, as if accidentally / holding her 157/158
tail in front of her mouth, so that I should not see the broken fang. Proudly and calmly she said[293]: "So you have finally noticed this?" But I spoke to her smilingly: "The sinuous line of life could not escape me in the long run."

[2] [HI 158] Where is truth and faith? Where is warm trust? You find all this between men but not between men and serpents, even if they are serpent souls. But wherever there is love, the serpentlike abides also. Christ himself compared himself to a serpent,[294] and his hellish brother, the Antichrist, is the old dragon himself.[295] What is beyond the human that appears in love has the nature of the serpent and the bird, and the serpent often enchants the bird, and more rarely the bird bears off the serpent. Man stands in-between. What seems like a bird to you is a serpent to the other, and what seems like a serpent to you is a bird to the other. Therefore you will meet the other only in human form. If you want to become, then a battle between bird and serpent breaks out. And if you only want to be, you will be a man to yourself and to others. He who is becoming belongs in the desert or in a prison, for he is beyond the human. If men want to become, they behave like animals. No one saves us from the evil of becoming, unless we choose to go through Hell.

Why did I behave as if that serpent were my soul? Only, it seems, because my soul was a serpent. This knowledge gave my soul a new

292. This sentence is not in *Black Book* 4.

293. This sentence is not in *Black Book* 4.

294. Jung commented on the comparison of Christ with the serpent in *Transformations and Symbols of the Libido* (1912), CW B, §585 and in *Aion* (1950), CW 9, 2, §291.

295. Cf. *Transformations and Symbols of the Libido* (1912), CW B, §585.

face, and I decided henceforth to enchant her myself and subject her to my power. Serpents are wise, and I wanted my serpent soul to communicate her wisdom to me. Never before had life been so doubtful, a night of aimless tension, being one in being directed against one another. Nothing moved, neither God nor the devil. So I approached the serpent that lay in the sun, as if she were unthinking. Her eyes were not visible, since they blinked in the shimmering
158/160 sunshine, and / [Image 159][296] / {3} [1] I spoke to her[297]: "How will it be, now that God and the devil have become one? Are they in

296. Image legend: "9 January 1927 my friend Hermann Sigg died age 52." Jung described this as "A luminous flower in the center, with stars rotating about it. Around the flower, walls with eight gates. The whole conceived as a transparent window." This mandala was based on a dream noted on January 2, 1927 (see above, p. 85). From the "town map" that Jung drew, the relation between the dream and the painting is clear. He anonymously reproduced this in 1930 in "Commentary to the 'Secret of the Golden Flower,'" from which this description is taken. He reproduced it again in 1952, and added the following commentary: "The rose in the center is depicted as a ruby, its outer ring being conceived as a wheel or a wall with gates (so that nothing can come out from inside or go in from outside). The mandala was a spontaneous product from the analysis of a male patient." After narrating the dream, Jung added: "The dreamer went on: 'I tried to paint this dream. But as so often happens, it came out rather different. The magnolia turned into a sort of rose made of ruby-colored glass. It shone like a four-rayed star. The square represents the wall of the park and at the same time a street leading round the park in a square. From it there radiate eight main streets, and from each of these eight side-streets, which meet in a shining red central point, rather like the Étoile in Paris. The acquaintance mentioned in the dream lived in a house at the corner of one of these stars.' The mandala thus combines the classic motifs of flower, star, circle, precinct (temenos), and plan of city divided into quarters with citadel. 'The whole thing seemed like a window opening on to eternity,' wrote the dreamer" ("Concerning mandala symbolism," CW 9, 1, §654–55). In 1955/56 he used this same expression to denote the illustration of the self (*Mysterium Coniunctionis*, CW 14, §763). On October 7, 1932, Jung showed this mandala in a seminar, and commented on it the next day. In this account, he states that the painting of the mandala *preceded* the dream: "You remember possibly the picture that I showed you last evening, the central stone and the little jewels round it. It is perhaps interesting if I tell you about the dream in connection with it. I was the perpetrator of that mandala at a time when I had not the slightest idea what a mandala was, and in my extreme modesty I thought, I am the jewel in the center and those little lights are surely very nice peosple who believe that they are also jewels, but smaller ones . . . I thought very well of myself that I was able to express myself like that: my marvelous center here and I am right in my heart." He added that at first he did not recognize that the park was the same as the mandala which he had painted, and commented: "Now Liverpool is the center of life—liver is the center of life—and I am not the center, I am the fool who lives in a dark place somewhere, I am one of those little side lights. In that way my Western prejudice that I was the center of the mandala was corrected—that I am everything, the whole show, the king, the god" (*The Psychology of Kundalini Yoga*, p. 100). In *Memories*, Jung added some further details (pp. 223–24).

297. February 1, 1914.

agreement to bring life to a standstill? Does the conflict of opposites belong to the inescapable conditions of life? And does he who recognizes and lives the unity of opposites stand still? He has completely taken the side of actual life, and he no longer acts as if he belonged to one party and had to battle against the other, but he is both and has brought their discord to an end. Through taking this burden from life, has he also taken the force from it?"[298]

The serpent turned and spoke ill-humoredly: "Truly, you pester me. Opposites were certainly an element of life for me. You probably will have noticed this. Your innovations deprive me of this source of power. I can neither lure you with pathos nor annoy you with banality. I am somewhat baffled."

I: "If you are baffled, should I give counsel? I would rather you dive down to the deeper grounds to which you have entry and ask Hades or the heavenly ones, perhaps someone there can give counsel."

S: "You have become imperious."

I: "Necessity is even more imperious than I. I must live and be able to move."

S: "You have the whole wide earth. What do you want to ask the beyond for?"

I: "It isn't curiosity that drives me, but necessity. I will not yield."

S: "I obey, but reluctantly. This style is new and unaccustomed to me."

I: "I'm sorry, but there is pressing need. Tell the depths that prospects are not looking too good for us, because we have cut off an important organ from life. As you know, I'm not the guilty one, since you have led me carefully along this way."

S:[299] "You might have rejected the apple."

I: "Enough of these jokes. You know that story better than I do. I am serious. We need some air. Be on your way and fetch the fire.

---

298. *Black Book* 4 also has: "I lay these questions before you today, my soul" (p. 91). Here, the serpent is substituted for the soul.

299. *Black Book* 4: "You are playing Adam and Eve with me" (p. 93).

It has already been dark around me for too long. Are you sluggish or cowardly?"

S: "I'm off to work. Take from me what I bring up."[300]

[HI 160] Slowly, the throne of the God ascends into empty space, followed by the holy trinity, all of Heaven, and finally Satan
160/161 himself. He resists and clings to his beyond. He will not / let it go. The upperworld is too chilly for him.

S: "Have you got tight hold of him?"[301]

I: "Welcome, hot thing of darkness! My soul probably pulled you up roughly?"

S:[302] "Why this noise? I protest against this violent extraction."

I: "Calm down. I didn't expect you. You come last of all. You seem to be the hardest part."

S: "What do you want from me? I don't need you, impertinent fellow."

I: "It's a good thing we have you. You're the liveliest thing in the whole dogma."[303]

S: "What concern is your prattle to me! Make it quick. I'm freezing."

I: "Listen, something has just happened to us: we have united the opposites. Among other things, we have bonded you with God."[304]

S: "For God's sake, why this hopeless fuss? Why such nonsense?"

I: "Please, that wasn't so stupid. This unification is an important principle. We have put a stop to never-ending quarreling, to finally free our hands for real life."

---

300. Jung's marginal note to the calligraphic volume: "Visio."

301. *Black Book* 4: "Satan crawls out of a dark hole with horns and tail, I pull him out by the hands" (p. 94).

302. The interlocutor is Satan.

303. For Jung's account of the significance of Satan, see *Answer to Job* (1952), CW 11.

304. Jung discussed the issue of uniting the opposites at length in *Psychological Types* (1921), ch. 6, "The type problem in the poetic art." The uniting of the opposites takes place through the production of the reconciling symbol.

S: "This smells of monism. I have already made note of some of these men. Special chambers have been heated for them."

I: "You're mistaken. Matters are not as rational with us as they seem to be.[305] We have no single correct truth either. Rather, a most remarkable and strange fact has occurred: after the opposites had been united, quite unexpectedly and incomprehensibly nothing further happened. Everything remained in place, peacefully and yet completely motionless, and life turned into a complete standstill."

S: "Yes, you fools, you certainly have made a pretty mess of things."

I: "Well, your mockery is unnecessary. Our intentions were serious."

S: "Your seriousness leads us to suffer. The ordering of the beyond is shaken to its foundations."

I: "So you realize that matters are serious. I want an answer to my question, what should happen under these circumstances? We no longer know what to do."

S: "Well, it is hard to know what to do, and difficult to give advice even if one would like to give it. You are blinded fools, a brashly impertinent people. Why didn't you stay out of trouble? How do you mean to understand the ordering of the world?"

I: "Your ranting suggests that you are quite thoroughly aggrieved. Look, the holy trinity is taking things coolly. It seems not to dislike the innovation."

S: "Ah, the trinity is so irrational that one / can never trust its 161/162
reactions. I strongly advise you not to take those symbols seriously."[306]

I: "I thank you for this well-meant advice. But you seem to be interested. One would expect you to pass unbiased judgment on account of your proverbial intelligence."

---

305. *Black Book* 4 has instead of this sentence: "Matters are not as intellectual and generally ethical with us as in Monism" (p. 96). The reference is to Ernst Haeckel's system of Monism, which Jung was critical of.

306. Cf. Jung, "Attempt at a psychological interpretation of the dogma of the trinity" (1940), CW 11.

S: "Me, unbiased! You can judge for yourself. If you consider this absoluteness in its completely lifeless equanimity, you can easily discover that the state and standstill produced by your presumptuousness closely resembles the absolute. But if I counsel you, I place myself completely on your side, since you too find this standstill unbearable."

I: "What? You take my side? That is strange."

S: "That's not so strange. The absolute was always adverse to the living. I am still the real master of life."

I: "That is suspicious. Your reaction is far too personal."

S: "My reaction is far from personal. I am utterly restless, quickly hurrying life. I am never contented, never unperturbed. I pull everything down and hastily rebuild. I am ambition, greed for fame, lust for action; I am the fizz of new thoughts and action. The absolute is boring and vegetative."

I: "All right, I believe you. So—just what do you advise?"

S: "The best advice I can give you is: revoke your completely harmful innovation as soon as possible."

I: "What would be gained by that? We'd have to start from scratch again and would infallibly reach the same conclusion a second time. What one has grasped once, one cannot intentionally not know again and undo. Your counsel is no counsel."

S: "But could you exist without divisiveness and disunity? You have to get worked up about something, represent a party, overcome opposites, if you want to live."

I: "That does not help. We also see each other in the opposite. We have grown tired of this game."

S: "And so with life."

I: "It seems to me that it depends on what you call life. Your notion of life has to do with climbing up and tearing down, with assertion
162/164 and doubt, with impatient dragging around, / [Image 163][307] / with hasty desire. You lack the absolute and its forbearing patience."

---

307. Image legend: "1928. When I painted this image, which showed the golden well-fortified castle, Richard Wilhelm sent me from Frankfurt the Chinese, thousand-year-old text of the golden castle, the embryo of the immortal body. Ecclesia catholic et protestantes et seclusi in secreto. Aeon finitus. (The Catholic church and the

S: "Quite right. My life bubbles and foams and stirs up turbulent waves, it consists of seizing and throwing away, ardent wishing and restlessness. That is life, isn't it?"

I: "But the absolute also lives."

S: "That is no life. It is a standstill or as good as a standstill, or rather: it lives interminably slowly and wastes thousands of years, just like the miserable condition that you have created."

I: "You enlighten me. You are personal life, but the apparent standstill is the forbearing life of eternity, the life of divinity! This time you have counseled me well. I will let you go. Farewell."

[HI 164] Satan crawls deftly like a mole back into his hole again. The symbol of the trinity and its entourage rise up in peace and equanimity to Heaven. I thank you, serpent, for hauling up the right one for me. Everyone understands his words, since they are personal. We can live again, a long life. We can waste thousands of years.

Protestants and those secluded in secret. The end of an aeon.) Jung described this as: A mandala as a fortified city with wall and moat. Within, a broad moat surrounding a wall fortified with sixteen towers and with another inner moat. This moat encloses a central castle with golden roofs whose centre is a golden temple. He anonymously reproduced this in 1930 in "Commentary on 'The Secret of the Golden Flower,'" from which this description is taken. He reproduced it again in 1952 in "Concerning mandala symbolism" and added the following commentary: "Painting of a medieval city with walls and moats, streets and churches, arranged quadratically. The inner city is again surrounded by walls and moats, like the Imperial City in Peking. The buildings all open inward, toward the center, represented by a castle with a golden roof. It too is surrounded by a moat. The ground round the castle is laid with black and white tiles, representing the united opposites. This mandala was done by a middle-aged man . . . A picture like this is unknown in Christian symbolism. The Heavenly Jerusalem of Revelation is known to everybody. Coming to the Indian world of ideas, we find the city of Brahma on the world mountain, Meru. We read in the *Golden Flower*: '*The Book of the Yellow Castle* says: "In the square inch field of the square foot house, life can be regulated." The square foot house is the face. The square inch field in the face: what could that be other than the heavenly heart? In the middle of the square inch dwells the splendor. In the purple hall of the city of Jade dwells the God of Utmost Emptiness and Life.' The Taoists call this center 'the land of ancestors or golden castle'" (CW 9, 1, §691). On this mandala, see John Peck, *The Visio Dorothei: Desert Context, Imperial Setting, Later Alignments: Studies in the Dreams and Visions of Saint Pachomius and Dorotheus, Son of Quintus*, Thesis, C. G. Jung Institute, Zürich, 1992, pp. 183–85.

[HI 164/2] [2] Where to begin, oh Gods? In suffering or in joy, or in the mixed feeling lying between? The beginning is always the smallest, it begins in nothing. If I begin there, I see the little drop of "something" that falls into the sea of nothingness. It is forever about beginning again down where the nothingness widens itself to unrestricted freedom.[308] Nothing has happened yet, the world has yet to begin, the sun is not yet born, the watery firmament has not been separated,[309] we have not yet climbed onto the shoulders of our fathers, since our fathers have not yet become. They have only just died and rest in the womb of our bloodthirsty Europe.

We stand in the vastness, wed to the serpent, and consider which
164/165 stone could be the foundation stone of the building, / which we do not yet know. The most ancient? It is suitable as a symbol. We want something graspable. We are weary of the webs that the day weaves and the night unpicks. The devil is probably supposed to create it, that paltry partisan with sham understanding and greedy hands? He emerged from the lump of manure in which the Gods had secured their eggs. I would like to kick the garbage away from me, if the golden seed were not in the vile heart of the misshapen form.

Arise then, son of darkness and stench! How firmly you cling to the rubble and waste of the eternal cesspit! I do not fear you, though I hate you, you brother of everything reprehensible in me. Today, you shall be forged with heavy hammers so that the gold of the Gods will spray out of your body. Your time is over, your years are numbered, and today your day of judgment has gone to smithereens. May your casings burst asunder, with our hands we wish to take hold of your seed, the golden one, and free it from slithery mud. May you freeze, devil, since we will cold-forge you. Steel is harder than ice. You shall fit into our form, you thief of the divine marvel, you mother ape, you who stuff your body with the egg of the Gods and thereby make yourself weighty. Hence we curse you, though not because of you, but for the sake of the golden seed.

308. This line links with the beginning of Sermon one, *Scrutinies* (see below, p. 508).
309. A reference to the account of creation in the book of Genesis.

What serviceable forms rise from your body, you thieving abyss! These appear as elemental spirits, dressed in wrinkled garb, Cabiri, with delightful misshapen forms, young and yet old, dwarfish, shriveled, unspectacular bearers of secret arts, possessors of ridiculous wisdom, first formations of the unformed gold, worms that crawl from the liberated egg of the Gods, incipient ones, unborn, still invisible. What should your appearance be to us? What new arts do you bear up from the inaccessible treasure chamber, the sun yoke from the egg of the Gods? You still have roots in the soil like
plants and you are animal faces / of the human body; you are fool- 165/166
ishly sweet, uncanny, primordial, and earthly. We cannot grasp your essence, you gnomes, you object-souls. You have your origin in the lowest. Do you want to become giants, you Tom Thumbs? Do you belong to the followers of the son of the earth? Are you the earthly feet of the Godhead? What do you want? Speak![310]

The Cabiri: "We come to greet you as the master of the lower nature."

I: "Are you speaking to me? Am I your master?"

---

310. The Cabiri were the deities celebrated at the mysteries of Samothrace. They were held to be promoters of fertility and protectors of sailors. Friedrich Creuzer and Schelling held them to be the primal deities of Greek mythology, from which all others developed (*Symbolik und Mythologie der alten Völker* [Leipzig: Leske, 1810–23]; *The Deities of Samothrace* [1815], introduced and translated by R. F. Brown [Missoula, MT: Scholars Press, 1977]). Jung had copies of both of these works. They appear in Goethe's *Faust*, part 2, act 2. Jung discussed the Cabiri in *Transformations and Symbols of the Libido* (1912, CW B §209–11). In 1940 Jung wrote: "The Cabiri are, in fact, the mysterious creative powers, the gnomes who work under the earth, i.e., below the threshold of consciousness, in order to supply us with lucky ideas. As imps and hobgoblins, however, they also lay all sorts of nasty tricks, keeping back names and dates that were 'on the tip of the tongue,' making us say the wrong thing, etc. They give an eye to everything that has not already been anticipated by consciousness and the functions at its disposal . . . deeper insight will show that the primitive and archaic qualities of the inferior function conceal all sorts of significant relationships and symbolic meanings, and instead of laughing off the Cabiri as ridiculous Tom Thumbs he may begin to suspect that they are a treasure-house of hidden wisdom" ("Attempt at a psychological interpretation of the dogma of the trinity," CW 11, §244). Jung commented on the Cabiri scene in *Faust* in *Psychology and Alchemy* (1944, CW 12, §203f). The dialogue with the Cabiri that takes place here is not found in *Black Book* 4, but is in the *Handwritten Draft*. It may have been written separately; if so it would have been written prior to the summer of 1915.

The Cabiri: "You were not, but you are now."

I: "So you declare. And so be it. Yet what should I do with your following?"

The Cabiri: "We carry what is not to be carried from below to above. We are the juices that rise secretly, not by force, but sucked out of inertia and affixed to what is growing. We know the unknown ways and the inexplicable laws of living matter. We carry up what slumbers in the earthly, what is dead and yet enters into the living. We do this slowly and easily, what you do in vain in your human way. We complete what is impossible for you."

I: "What should I leave to you? Which troubles can I transfer to you? What should I not do, and what do you do better?"

The Cabiri: "You forget the lethargy of matter. You want to pull up with your own force what can only rise slowly, ingesting itself, affixed to itself from within. Spare yourself the trouble, or you will disturb our work."

I: "Should I trust you, you untrustworthy ones, you slaves and slave souls? Get to work. Let it be so."

[311][HI 166] "It seems to me that I gave you a long time. Neither did I descend to you nor did I disturb your work. I lived in the light of day and did the work of the day. What did you do?"

The Cabiri: "We hauled things up, we built. We placed stone upon stone. Now you stand on solid ground."

I: "I feel the ground more solid. I stretch upward."

166/167 The Cabiri: "We forged a flashing / sword for you, with which you can cut the knot that entangles you."

I: "I take the sword firmly in my hand. I lift it for the blow."

The Cabiri: "We also place before you the devilish, skillfully twined knot that locks and seals you. Strike, only sharpness will cut through it."

311. Jung's marginal note to the calligraphic volume: "Thereupon I laid this matter aside for three weeks."

I: "Let me see it, the great knot, all wound round! Truly a masterpiece of inscrutable nature, a wily natural tangle of roots grown through one another! Only Mother Nature, the blind weaver, could work such a tangle! A great snarled ball and a thousand small knots, all artfully tied, intertwined, truly, a human brain! Am I seeing straight? What did you do? You set my brain before me! Did you give me a sword so that its flashing sharpness slices through my brain? What were you thinking of?"[312]

The Cabiri: "The womb of nature wove the brain, the womb of the earth gave the iron. So the Mother gave you both: entanglement and severing."

I: "Mysterious! Do you really want to make me the executioner of my own brain?"

The Cabiri: "It befits you as the master of the lower nature. Man is entangled in his brain and the sword is also given to him to cut through the entanglement."

I: "What is the entanglement you speak of?"

The Cabiri: "The entanglement is your madness, the sword is the overcoming of madness."[313]

I: "You offsprings of the devil, who told you that I am mad? You earth spirits, you roots of clay and excrement, are you not yourselves the root fibers of my brain? You polyp-snared rubbish, channels for juice knotted together, parasites upon parasites, all sucked up and deceived, secretly climbing up over one another by night, you deserve the flashing sharpness of my sword. You want to persuade me to cut through you? Are you contemplating self-destruction? How come nature gives birth to creatures that she herself wants to destroy?"

312. In "Transformation symbolism in the mass" (1941), Jung noted that the motif of the sword played an important role in alchemy and discussed its significance as an instrument of sacrifice, its divisive and separative functions. He noted that "The alchemical sword brings about the solutio or separatio elementorum, thereby restoring the original condition of chaos, so that a new and more perfect body can be produced by a new impressio formae or imaginatio" (CW 11, §357 & ff.).

313. The notion here of overcoming madness is close to Schelling's distinction between the person who is overcome by madness and the person who manages to govern madness (see note 89, p. 149).

The Cabiri: "Do not hesitate. We need destruction since we ourselves are the entanglement. He who wishes to conquer new
167/168 land / brings down the bridges behind him. Let us not exist anymore. We are the thousand canals in which everything also flows back again into its origin."

I: "Should I sever my own roots? Kill my own people, whose king I am? Should I make my own tree wither? You really are the sons of the devil."

The Cabiri: "Strike, we are servants who want to die for their master."

I: "What will happen if I strike?"

The Cabiri: "Then you will no longer be your brain, but will exist beyond your madness. Do you not see, your madness is your brain, the terrible entanglement and intertwining in the connection of the roots, in the nets of canals, the confusion of fibers. Being engrossed in the brain makes you wild. Strike! He who finds the way rises up over his brain. You are a Tom Thumb in the brain, beyond the brain you gain the form of a giant. We are surely sons of the devil, but did you not forge us out of the hot and dark? So we have something of its nature and of yours. The devil says that everything that exists is also worthy, since it perishes. As sons of the devil we want destruction, but as your creatures we want our own destruction. We want to rise up in you through death. We are roots that suck up from all sides. Now you have everything that you need, therefore chop us up, tear us out."

I: "Will I miss you as servants? As a master I need slaves."

The Cabiri: "The master serves himself."

I: "You ambiguous sons of the devil, these words are your undoing. May my sword strike you, this blow shall be valid forever."

The Cabiri "Woe, woe! What we feared, what we desired, has come to pass."

168/171 / [Image 169] / [HI 171] I set foot on new land. Nothing brought up should flow back. No one shall tear down what I have built. My tower is of iron and has no seams. The devil is forged into the foundations. The Cabiri built it and the master builders were sacrificed with the sword on the battlements of the tower. Just as a tower surmounts the summit of a mountain on which it stands, so I stand above my brain, from which I grew. I have become hard and cannot be undone again. No more do I flow back. I am the master of my own self. I admire my mastery. I am strong and beautiful and rich. The vast lands and the blue sky have laid themselves before me and bowed to my mastery. I wait upon no one and no one waits upon me. I serve myself and I myself serve. Therefore I have what I need.[314]

My tower grew for several thousand years, imperishable. It does not sink back. But it can be built over and will be built over. Few grasp my tower, since it stands on a high mountain. But many will
see it / and not grasp it. Therefore my tower will remain unused. 171/172
No one scales its smooth walls. No one lands on its pointed roof. Only he who finds the entrance hidden in the mountain and rises up through the labyrinths of the innards can reach the tower, and the happiness of he who surveys things from there and he who lives from himself. This has been attained and created. It has not arisen from a patchwork of human thoughts, but has been forged from the glowing heat of the innards; the Cabiri themselves carried the matter to the mountain and consecrated the building with their own blood as the sole keepers of the mystery of its genesis. I built it out of the lower and upper beyond and not from the surface of the world. Therefore it is new and strange and towers over the plains inhabited by humans. This is the solid and the beginning.[315]

---

314. Jung's marginal note to the calligraphic volume: "accipe quod tecum est. in collect. Mangeti in ultimis paginis" (Accept what is present. In the last pages of the Mangeti collection). It seems that this refers to the *Bibliotheca chemica curiosa, seu rerum ad alchemiam pertinentium thesaurus instructissimus* of J. J. Manget (1702), a collection of alchemical texts. Jung possessed a copy of this work, which has some slips of paper in it and some underlinings. Jung's note possibly refers to the last woodcut of the *Mutus Liber*, which concludes volume one of the *Bibliotheca chemica curiosa*, a representation of the completion of the alchemical opus, with a man being lifted upward by angels, while another lies prostrate.

315. In *Psychological Types*, Jung commented on the symbolism of the tower in his discussion of the vision of the tower in *The Shepherd of Hermas* (CW 6, §390ff). In 1920, Jung began planning his tower at Bollingen.

[HI 172] I have united with the serpent of the beyond. I have accepted everything beyond into myself. From this I have built my beginning. When this work was completed, I was pleased, and I felt curious to know what might still lie in my beyond. So I approached
172/173 my serpent and asked her / amiably whether she would not like to creep over to bring me news of what was happening in the beyond. But the serpent was weary and said that she had no liking for this.

{4}[I][316]I: "I don't want to force anything, but perhaps, who knows? We will still find out something useful." For a while the serpent hesitated, then she disappeared into the depths. Soon I heard her voice: "I believe that I have reached Hell. There is a hanged man here." A plain, ugly man with a contorted face stands before me. He has protruding ears and a hunchback. He said: "I am a poisoner who was condemned to the rope."

I: "What did you do?"

He: "I poisoned my parents and my wife."

I: "Why did you do that?"

He: "To honor God."

I: "What? To honor God? What do you mean by that?"

He: "First of all, everything that happens is for the honor of God, and secondly, I had my own ideas."

I: "What went through your mind?"

He: "I loved them and wanted to transport them more quickly from a wretched life into eternal blessedness. I gave them a strong, too strong a nightcap."

I: "And did this not lead you to find out what your own interest in this was?"

He: "I was now alone and very unhappy. I wanted to live for the sake of my two children, for whom I foresaw a better future. I was
173/174 in better health than my wife, so / I wanted to live."

I: "Did your wife agree to the murders?"

316. February 2, 1914.

He: "No, she certainly would have consented, but she knew nothing of my intentions. Unfortunately, the murder was discovered and I was condemned to death."

I: "Have you found your relatives again in the beyond?"

He: "That's a strange and unlikely story. I suspect that I'm in Hell. Sometimes it seems as if my wife were here too, and sometimes I'm not sure, just as little as I'm sure of my own self."

I: "What is it like? Tell me."

He: "From time to time, she seems to speak to me and I reply. But we haven't spoken about either the murder or our children until now. We only speak together here and there, and only about trivial things, small matters from our earlier daily life, but completely impersonal, as if we no longer had anything to do with each other. But the true nature of things eludes me. I see even less of my parents; I believe that I have yet to meet my mother. My father was here once and said something about his tobacco pipe, which he had lost somewhere."

I: "But how do you pass your time?"

He: "I believe that there is no time with us, so there is none to spend. Nothing at all happens."

I: "Isn't that / extremely boring?" 174/175

He: "Boring? I've never thought about it like that. Boring? Perhaps, but there's nothing interesting. In actual fact, it's pretty much all the same."

I: "Doesn't the devil ever torment you?"

He: "The devil? I've seen nothing of him."

I: "You come from the beyond and yet you have nothing to report? I find that hard to believe."

He: "When I still had a body, I often thought that surely it would be interesting to speak to one of the dead. But now the prospect means nothing much to me. As I said, everything here is impersonal and purely matter of fact. As far as I know, that's what they say."

I: "That is bleak. I assume that you are in the deepest Hell."

He: "I don't care. I guess I can go now, can't I? Farewell."

Suddenly he vanished. But I turned to the serpent[317] and said: "What should this boring guest from the beyond mean?"

S: "I met him over there, stumbling around restlessly like so many others. I chose him as the next best. He strikes me as a good example."

I: "But is the beyond so colorless?"

S: "It seems so; there is nothing but motion, when I make my way over there. Everything merely surges back and forth in a shadowy way. There is nothing personal whatsoever."

I: "What is it, then, with this damned personal quality? Satan
175/176 recently made / a strong impression on me, as if he were the quintessence of the personal."

S: "Of course he would, since he is the eternal adversary, and because you can never reconcile personal life with absolute life."

I: "Can't one unite these opposites?"

S: "They are not opposites, but simply differences. Just as little as you make the day the opposite of the year or the bushel the opposite of the cubit."

I: "That's enlightening, but somewhat boring."

S: "As always, when one speaks of the beyond. It goes on withering away, particularly since we have balanced the opposites and married. I believe the dead will soon become extinct."

[HI 176] [2] The devil is the sum of the darkness of human nature. He who lives in the light strives toward being the image of God; he who lives in the dark strives toward being the image of the devil. Because I wanted to live in the light, the sun went out for me when I touched the depths. It was dark and serpentlike. I united myself with it and did not overpower it. I took my part of the humiliation and subjugation upon myself, in that I took on the nature of the serpent.

176/177 If I had / not become like the serpent, the devil, the quintessence of everything serpentlike, would have held this bit of power

317. *Black Book* 4 has: "soul" (p. 110).

over me. This would have given the devil a grip and he would have forced me to make a pact with him just as he also cunningly deceived Faust.[318] But I forestalled him by uniting myself with the serpent, just as a man unites with a woman.

So I took away from the devil the possibility of influence, which only ever passes through one's own serpenthood,[319] which one commonly assigns to the devil instead of oneself. Mephistopheles is Satan, taken with my serpenthood. Satan himself is the quintessence of evil, naked and therefore without seduction, not even clever, but pure negation without convincing force. Thus I resisted his destructive influence and grasped him and fettered him firmly. His descendants served me and I sacrificed them with the sword.

Thus I built a firm structure. Through this I myself gained stability and duration and could withstand the fluctuations of the personal. Therefore the immortal in me is saved. Through drawing the darkness from my beyond over into the day, I emptied my beyond. Therefore the demands of the dead disappeared, as they were satisfied.

/ I am no longer threatened by the dead, since I accepted their 177/178
demands though accepting the serpent. But through this I have also taken over something of the dead into my day. Yet it was necessary, since death is the most enduring of all things, that which can never be canceled out. Death gives me durability and solidity. So long as I wanted to satisfy only my own demands, I was personal and therefore living in the sense of the world. But when I recognized the demands of the dead in me and satisfied them, I gave up my earlier personal striving and the world had to take me for a dead man. For a great cold comes over whoever in the excess of his personal striving has recognized the demands of the dead and seeks to satisfy them.

While he feels as if a mysterious poison has paralyzed the living quality of his personal relations, the voices of the dead remain silent in his beyond; the threat, the fear, and the restlessness cease. For

318. In Goethe's *Faust*, Mephistopheles makes a pact with Faust that he will serve him in life on condition that Faust will serve him in the beyond (l. 1655).

319. The *Corrected Draft* has instead: "me with the serpent" (p. 521).

everything that previously lurked hungrily in him no longer lives with him in his day. His life is beautiful and rich, since he is himself.

But whoever always wants only the fortune of others is ugly,
178/179 since he / cripples himself. A murderer is one who wants to force others to blessedness, since he kills his own growth. A fool is one who exterminates his love for the sake of love. Such a one is personal to the other. His beyond is gray and impersonal. He forces himself upon others; therefore he is cursed into forcing himself upon himself in a cold nothingness. He who has recognized the demands of the dead has banished his ugliness to the beyond. He no longer greedily forces himself upon others, but lives alone in beauty and speaks with the dead. But there comes the day when the demands of the dead also are satisfied. If one then still perseveres in solitude, beauty fades into the beyond and the wasteland comes over onto this side. A black stage comes after the white, and Heaven and Hell are forever there.[320]

{5}[1] [HI 179] Now that I had found the beauty in me and with myself, I spoke to my serpent[321]: "I look back as onto a work that has been accomplished."

Serpent: "Nothing is accomplished yet."

I: "What do you mean? Not accomplished?"

Se: "This is only the beginning."

I: "I think you are lying."

Se: "Whom are you quarreling with? Do you know better?"

179/180 I: "I know / nothing, but I'd already gotten used to the idea that we had reached a goal, at least a temporary one. If even the dead are about to become extinct, what else is going to happen?"

Se: "But then the living must first begin to live."

I: "This remark could certainly be deeply meaningful, but it seems to be nothing but a joke."

320. Jung's marginal note to the calligraphic volume: "I still did not realize that I myself was this murderer."

321. February 9, 1914. *Black Book* 4 has: "soul" (p. 114).

Se: “You are getting impertinent. I’m not joking. Life has yet to begin.”

I: “What do you mean by life?”

Se: “I say, life has yet to begin. Didn’t you feel empty today? Do you call that life?”

I: “What you say is true, but I try to put as good a face as I can on everything and to settle for things.”

Se: “That might be quite comfortable. But you really ought to make much higher demands.”

I: “That I dread. I will certainly not assume that I could satisfy my own demands, but neither do I think that you are capable of satisfying them. However, it might be that once again I’m not trusting you enough. I suppose that might be so because I’ve drawn closer to you in human terms and find you so urbane.”

Se: “That proves nothing. Just don’t assume that somehow you could ever grasp me and embody me.”

I: “So, what should it be? I’m ready.”

Se: “You are entitled to a reward for / what has been accom- 180/181
plished so far.”

I: “A sweet thought, that payment could be made for this.”

Se: “I give you payment in images. Behold:”

[HI 181] Elijah and Salome! The cycle is completed and the gates of the mysteries have opened again. Elijah leads Salome, the seeing one, by the hand. She blushes and lowers her eyes while lovingly batting her eyelids.

E: “Here, I give you Salome. May she be yours.”

I: “For God’s sake, what should I do with Salome? I am already married and we are not among the Turks.”[322]

E: “You helpless man, how ponderous you are. Is this not a beautiful gift? Is her healing not your doing? Won’t you accept her love as the well-deserved payment for your trouble?”

322. Polygamy used to be practiced in Turkey. It was officially banned by Ataturk in 1926.

I: "It seems to me a rather strange gift, more burden than joy. I am happy that Salome is thankful to me and loves me. I love her too—somewhat. Incidentally, the care I afforded her, was, literally, pressed out of me, rather than something I gave freely and inten-
181/182 tionally. If my partly unintentional / ordeal has had such a good outcome, I'm already completely satisfied."

Salome to Elijah: "Leave him, he is a strange man. Heaven knows what his motives are, but he seems to be serious. I'm not ugly and surely I'm generally desirable."

Salome to me: "Why do you refuse me? I want to be your maid and serve you. I will sing and dance before you, fend off people for you, comfort you when you are sad, laugh with you when you are happy. I will carry all your thoughts in my heart. I will kiss the words that you speak to me. I will pick roses for you each day and all my thoughts will wait upon you and surround you."

I: "I thank you for your love. It is beautiful to hear you speak of love. It is music and old, far-off homesickness. Look, my tears are falling because of your good words. I want to kneel before you and kiss your hands a hundred times, because they want to give me love. You speak so beautifully of love. One can never hear enough of love being spoken."

Sal: "Why only speak? I want to be yours, utterly and completely yours."

I: "You are like the serpent that coiled around me and pressed
182/183 out my blood."[323] / Your sweet words wind around me and I stand like someone crucified."

Sal: "Why still crucified?"

I: "Don't you see that unrelenting necessity has flung me onto the cross? It is impossibility that lames me."

Sal: "Don't you want to break through necessity? Is what you call a necessity really one?"[324]

---

323. Jung's marginal note to the calligraphic volume: "In XI Cap. of the mystery play" (see above, p. 194).

324. *Black Book* 4 continues: "I: My principles—it sounds stupid—forgive me—but I have principles. Do not think these are stale moral principles, for these are insights that life

I: "Listen, I doubt that it is your destiny to belong to me. I do not want to intervene in your utterly singular life, since I can never help you to lead it to an end. And what do you gain if one day I must lay you aside like a worn garment?"

Sal: "Your words are terrible. But I love you so much that I could also lay myself aside when your time has come."

I: "I know that it would be the greatest torment for me to let you go away. But if you can do this for me, I can also do it for you. I would go on without lament, since I have not forgotten the dream where I saw my body lying on sharp needles and a bronze wheel rolling over my breast, crushing it. I must think of this dream whenever I think of love. If it must be, I am ready."

Sal: "I don't want such a sacrifice. I want to bring you joy. Can I not be joy to you?"

I: "I don't know, perhaps, / perhaps not." 183/184

Sal: "So then at least try."

I: "The attempt is the same as the act. Such attempts are costly."

Sal: "Won't you bear the cost for my sake?"

I: "I'm rather too weak, too exhausted after what I have suffered because of you, still to be able to undertake further tasks for you. I would be overwhelmed."

Sal: "If you don't want to accept me, then surely I cannot accept you?"

I: "It's not a matter of acceptance; if it's about anything in particular, it's about giving."

Sal: "But I do give myself to you. Just accept me."

I: "As if that would settle the matter! But being entangled with love! Simply thinking about it is dreadful."

Sal: "So you really demand that I be and not be at the same time. That is impossible. What's wrong with you?"

I: "I lack the strength to hoist another fate onto my shoulders. I have enough to carry."

Sal: "But what if I help you bear this load?"

---

has imposed on me. / Serpent: What principles are these?" (pp. 121–22).

I: "How can you? You'd have to carry me, an untamed burden. Shouldn't I have to carry it myself?"

E: "You speak the truth. May each one carry his load. He who wants to burden others with his baggage is their slave.[325] It is not too difficult for anyone to lug themselves."

Sal: "But father, couldn't I help him bear part of his burden?"

184/185 E: "Then he'd be your slave." /

Sal: "Or my master and ruler."

I: "That I shall not be. You should be a free being. I can bear neither slaves nor masters. I long for men."

Sal: "Am I not a human being?"

I: "Be your own master and your own slave, do not belong to me but to yourself. Do not bear my burden, but your own. Thus you leave me my human freedom, a thing that's worth more to me than the right of ownership over another person."

Sal: "Are you sending me away?"

I: "I'm not sending you away. You must not be far from me. But give to me out of your fullness, not your longing. I cannot satisfy your poverty just as you cannot still my longing. If your harvest is rich, send me some fruit from your garden. If you suffer from abundance, I will drink from the brimming horn of your joy. I know that that will be a balm for me. I can satisfy myself only at the table of the satisfied, not at the empty bowls of those who yearn. I will not steal my payment. You possess nothing, so how can you give? Insofar as you give, you demand. Elijah, old man, listen: you have a
185/186 strange gratitude. Do not give away your daughter, but set her / on her own feet. She would like to dance, to sing or play the lute before people, and she would like their flashing coins thrown before her feet. Salome, I thank you for your love. If you really love me, dance before the crowd, please people so that they praise your beauty and your art. And if you have a rich harvest, throw me one of your roses through the window, and if the fount of your joy overflows, dance

---

325. The issue of master and slave morality featured prominently in the first essay of Nietzsche's *On the Genealogy of Morals* (tr. D. Smith [Oxford: Oxford University Press, 1996]).

and sing to me once more. I long for the joy of men, for their fullness and freedom and not their neediness."

Sal: "What a hard and incomprehensible man you are."

E: "You have changed since I last saw you. You speak another language, one that sounds foreign to me."

I: "My dear old man, I'd like to believe that you find me changed. But you too seem to have changed. Where is your serpent?"

E: "She has gone astray. I believe she was stolen. Since then things have been somewhat gloomy with us. Therefore I would have been happy if you had at least accepted my daughter."

I: "I know where your serpent is. I have her. We fetched her
from the underworld. She / gave me hardness, wisdom, and magical 186/187
power. We need her in the upperworld, since otherwise the underworld would have had the advantage, to our detriment."

E: "Away with you, accursed robber, may God punish you."

I: "Your curse is powerless. Whoever possesses the serpent cannot be touched by curses. No, be sensible, old man: whoever possesses wisdom is not greedy for power. Only the man who has power declines to use it. Do not cry, Salome, fortune is only what you yourself create and not what comes to you. Be gone, my unhappy friends, the night grows late. Elijah, expunge the false gleam of power from your wisdom, and you, Salome, for the sake of our love, do not forget to dance."

[2][326] When everything was completed in me, I unexpectedly returned to the mysteries, to that first sight of the otherworldly powers of the spirit and desire. Just as I had achieved pleasure in myself and power over myself, Salome had lost pleasure in herself but learned love for the other, and Elijah had lost the power of his wisdom but he had learned to recognize the spirit of the other. Salome thus
lost the power of temptation and has / become love. As I have won 187/188
pleasure in myself, I also want love for myself. But that really would be too much and would bind me like an iron ring that would stifle me.

326. In the calligraphic volume, there is a blank space for a historiated initial.

I accepted Salome as pleasure, and reject her as love. But she wants to be with me. How, then, should I also have love for myself? Love, I believe, belongs to others. But my love wants to be with me. I dread it. May the power of my thinking push it from me, into the world, into things, into men. For something should join men together, something should be a bridge. It is the most difficult temptation, if even my love wants me! Mysteries, open your curtains again! I want to wage this battle to its end. Come here, serpent of the dark abyss.

{6}[327][1] I hear Salome still crying. What does she want, or what do I still want? It's a damnable payment you have given to me, a payment that one cannot touch without sacrifice. One that requires even greater sacrifice once one has touched it.

Serpent:[328] "Do you mean to live without sacrifice? Life must cost you something, mustn't it?"

I: "I have, I believe, already paid. I have rejected Salome. Is that not sacrifice enough?"

Se: "Too little for you. As has been said, you are allowed to make demands of yourself."

I: "You mean well with your damned logic: demanding in
188/189 sacrifice? That / isn't what I understood. My error has obviously been to my own benefit. Tell me, isn't it enough if I force my feeling into the background?"

Se: "You're not forcing your feeling into the background at all; rather it suits you much better not to agonize further over Salome."

I: "If you're speaking the truth, it's quite bad. Is that why Salome is still crying?"

Se: "Yes, it is."

I: "But what is to be done?"

Se: "Oh, you want to act? One can also think."

I: "But what is there to think? I confess that I know nothing to think here. Perhaps you have advice. I have the feeling that I must soar over my own head. I can't do that. What do you think?"

327. February 11, 1914.
328. In *Black Book* 4, this figure is identified as "soul" (p. 131).

Se: "I think nothing and have no advice either."

I: "So ask the beyond, go to Heaven or Hell, perhaps there is advice there."

Se: "I am being pulled upward."

Then the serpent turned into a small white bird which soared into the clouds where she disappeared. My gaze followed her for a long time.[329]

Bird: "Do you hear me? I'm far off now. Heaven is so far away. Hell is much nearer the earth. I found something for you, a discarded crown. It lay on a street in the immeasurable space of Heaven, a golden crown."

And now it already lies in[330]/ my hand, a golden royal crown, 189/*Draft*
with lettering incised within; what does it say? "Love never ends."[331] A gift from Heaven. But what does it mean?

B: "Here I am, are you satisfied?"

I: "Partially—at any rate I thank you for this meaningful gift. But it is mysterious, and your gift makes me well-nigh suspicious."

B: "But the gift comes from Heaven, you know."

I: "It's certainly very beautiful, but you know very well what we have grasped of Heaven and Hell."

B: "Don't exaggerate. After all, there is a difference between Heaven and Hell. I certainly believe, to judge from what I have seen, that just as little happens in Heaven as in Hell, though probably in another way. Even what does not occur cannot occur in a particular way."

I: "You speak in riddles that could make one ill if one took them to heart. Tell me, what do you make of the crown?"

B: "What do I make of it? Nothing. It truly speaks for itself."

I: "You mean, through the inscription it bears?"

B: "Precisely; I presume that makes sense to you?"

---

329. This sentence is added in the *Draft*, p. 533.

330. The transcription in the calligraphic volume of *Liber Novus* ends at this point. What follows here is transcribed from the *Draft*, pp. 533–56.

331. This is a quotation from I Corinthians 13:8. Near the end of his life, Jung cited it again in his reflections on love at the end of *Memories* (p. 387). In *Black Book* 4, the inscription is first given in Greek letters (p. 134).

I: "To some extent, I suppose. But that keeps the question awfully in suspense."

B: "Which is how it is meant to be."

Now the bird suddenly turned into the serpent again.[332]

I: "You're unnerving."

Serpent:[333] "Only for him who isn't in agreement with me."

I: "That I am certainly not. But how could one? To hang in the air in such a way is gruesome."

Se: "Is this sacrifice too difficult for you? You must also be able to hang if you want to solve problems. Look at Salome!"

I, to Salome: "I see, Salome, that you are still weeping. You are not yet done for. I hover and curse my hovering. I am hanging for your sake and for mine. First I was crucified, now I'm simply hanging—which is less noble, but no less agonizing.[334] Forgive me, for wanting to do you in; I thought of saving you as I did when I healed your blindness through my self-sacrifice. Perhaps I must be decapitated a third time for your sake, like your earlier friend John, who brought us the Christ of agony. Are you insatiable? Do you still see no way to become reasonable?"

Sal: "My beloved, what can I do for you? I have utterly forsaken you."

I: "So why are you still crying? You know I can't bear seeing you in tears."

Sal: "I thought that you were invulnerable since you possessed the black serpent rod."

I: "The effect of the rod seems doubtful to me. But in one respect it does help me: at least I do not suffocate, although I have been strung up. The magic rod apparently helps me bear the hanging, surely a gruesome good deed and aid. Don't you at least want to cut the cord?"

---

332. This sentence is added in the *Draft* (p. 534).

333. This figure is not identified as the serpent in *Black Book* 4.

334. In *Transformations and Symbols of the Libido* (1912), Jung commented on the motif of hanging in folklore and mythology (CW B, §358).

Sal: "How can I? You are hanging too high.[335] High on the summit of the tree of life where I cannot reach. Can't you help yourself, you knower of serpent wisdom?"

I: "Must I go on hanging for long?"

Sal: "Until you have devised help for yourself."

I: "So at least tell me what you think of the crown that the bird of my soul fetched for me from Heaven."

Sal: "What are you saying? The crown? You have the crown? Lucky one, what are you complaining about?"

I: "A hanged king would like to change places with every blessed beggar on the country road who has not been hanged."

Sal (ecstatic): "The crown! You have the crown!"

I: "Salome, take pity on me. What is it with the crown?"

Sal (ecstatic): "The crown—you are to be crowned! What blessedness for me and you!"

I: "Alas, what do you want with the crown? I can't understand it and I'm suffering unspeakable torment."

Sal (cruelly): "Hang until you understand."

I remain silent and hang high above the ground on the swaying branch of the divine tree, for whose sake the original ancestors could not avoid sin. My hands are bound and I am completely helpless. So I hang for three days and three nights. From where should help come? There sits my bird, the serpent, which has put on her white feather dress.

Bird: "We'll fetch help from the clouds trailing above your head, when nothing else is of help to us."

I: "You want to fetch help from the clouds? How is that possible?"

B: "I will go and try."

The bird swings off like a rising lark, becomes smaller and smaller, and finally disappears in the thick gray veil of clouds covering the sky. My gaze follows her longingly and I make out nothing

335. There is a passage missing in *Black Book* 4, covering the end of this dialogue and the next paragraph.

more than the endless gray cloudy sky above me, impenetrably gray, harmoniously gray and unreadable. But the writing on the crown—that is legible. "Love never ends"—does that mean eternal hanging? I was not wrong to be suspicious when my bird brought the crown, the crown of eternal life, the crown of martyrdom—ominous things that are dangerously ambiguous.

I am weary, weary not only of hanging but of struggling after the immeasurable. The mysterious crown lies far below my feet on the ground, winking gold. I do not hover, no, I hang, or rather worse, I am hanged between sky and earth—and do not tire of the state of hanging for I could indulge in it forever, but love never ends. Is it really true, shall love never end? If this was a blessed message to them, what is it for me?

"That depends entirely on the notion," an old raven suddenly said, perched on a branch not far from me, awaiting the funeral meal, and immersed in philosophizing.

I: "Why does it depend entirely on the notion?"

Raven: "On your notion of love and the other."

I: "I know, unlucky old bird, you mean heavenly and earthly love.[336] Heavenly love would be utterly beautiful, but we are men, and, precisely because we are men, I've set my mind on being a complete and full-fledged man."

R: "You're an ideologue."

I: "Dumb raven, be gone!"

There, very close to my face, a branch moves, a black serpent has coiled itself around it and looks at me with the blinding pearly shimmer of its eyes. Is it not my serpent?

I: "Sister, and black rod of magic, where do you come from? I thought that I saw you fly to Heaven as a bird and now you are here? Do you bring help?"

336. Swedenborg described heavenly love as "loving uses for the sake of uses, or goods for the sake of goods, which a man performs for the Church, his country, human society, and a fellow-citizen," differentiating it from self love and love of the world (*Heaven and Its Wonders and Hell: From Things Heard and Seen*, tr. J. Rendell [London: Swedenborg Society, 1920], §554f).

Serpent: "I am only my own half; I'm not one, but two; I'm the one and the other. I am here only as the serpentlike, the magical. But magic is useless here. I wound myself idly around this branch to await further developments. You can use me in life, but not in hanging. In the worst case, I'm ready to lead you to Hades. I know the way there."

A black form condenses before me out of the air, Satan, with a scornful laugh. He calls to me: "See what comes from the reconciliation of opposites! Recant, and in a flash you'll be down on the greening earth."

I: "I won't recant, I'm not stupid. If such is the outcome of all this, let it be the end."

Se: "Where is your inconsistency? Please remember this important rule of the art of life."

I: "The fact that I'm hanging here is inconsistency enough. I've lived inconsistently ad nauseam. What more do you want?"

Se: "Perhaps inconsistency in the right place?"

I: "Stop it! How should I know what the right and the wrong places are?"

Satan: "Whoever gets on in a sovereign way with the opposites knows left from right."

I: "Be quiet, you're an interested party. If only my white bird came back with help; I fear I'm growing weak."

Se: "Don't be stupid, weakness too is a way, magic makes good the error."

Satan: "What, you've not yet once had the courage of weakness? You want to become a complete man—are men strong?"

I: "White bird of mine, I suppose you can't find your way back? Did you get up and leave because you couldn't live with me? Ah, Salome! There she comes. Come to me, Salome! Another night has passed. I didn't hear you cry, but I hung and still hang."

Sal: "I haven't cried anymore, for good fortune and misfortune are balanced in me."

I: "My white bird has left and has not yet returned. I know nothing and understand nothing. Does this have to do with the crown? Speak!"

Sal: "What should I say? Ask yourself."

I: "I cannot. My brain is like lead, I can only whimper for help. I have no way of knowing whether everything is falling or standing still. My hope is with my white bird. Oh no, could it be that the bird means the same thing as hanging?"

Satan: "Reconciliation of the opposites! Equal rights for all! Follies!"

I: "I hear a bird chirping! Is that you? Have you come back?"

Bird: "If you love the earth, you are hanged; if you love the sky, you hover."

I: "What is earth? What is sky?"

B: "Everything under you is the earth, everything above you is the sky. You fly if you strive for what is above you; you are hanged if you strive for what is below you."

I: "What is above me? What is beneath me?"

B: "Above you is what is before and over you; beneath you is what comes back under you."

I: "And the crown? Solve the riddle of the crown for me!"

B: "The crown and serpent are opposites, and are one. Did you not see the serpent that crowned the head of the crucified?"

I: "What, I don't understand you."

B: "What words did the crown bring you? 'Love never ends'—that is the mystery of the crown and the serpent."

I: "But Salome? What should happen to Salome?"

B: "You see, Salome is what you are. Fly, and she will grow wings."

The clouds part, the sky is full of the crimson sunset of the completed third day.[337] The sun sinks into the sea, and I glide with it from the top of the tree toward the earth. Softly and peacefully night falls.

337. In the biblical account of creation, the sea and the land were separated on the third day.

[2] Fear has befallen me. Whom did you carry to the mountain, you Cabiri? And whom have I sacrificed in you? You have piled me up yourselves, turning me into a tower on inaccessible crags, turning me into my church, my monastery, my place of execution, my prison. I am locked up and condemned within myself. I am my own priest and congregation, judge and judged, God and human sacrifice.

What a work you have accomplished, Cabiri! You have given birth to a cruel law from the chaos that cannot be revoked. It is understood and accepted.

The completion of the secret operation approaches. What I saw I described in words to the best of my ability. Words are poor, and beauty does not attend them. But is truth beautiful and beauty true?[338]

One can speak in beautiful words about love, but about life? And life stands above love. But love is the inescapable mother of life. Life should never be forced into love, but love into life. May love be subject to torment, but not life. As long as love goes pregnant with life, it should be respected; but if it has given birth to life from itself, it has turned into an empty sheath and expires into transience.

I speak against the mother who bore me, I separate myself from the bearing womb.[339] I speak no more for the sake of love, but for the sake of life.

The word has become heavy for me, and it barely wrestles itself free of the soul. Bronze doors have shut. fires have burned out and sunk into ashes. Wells have been drained and where there were seas there is dry land. My tower stands in the desert. Happy is he who can be a hermit in his own desert. He survives.

338. John Keats's poem "Ode to a Grecian Urn" ends with these lines: "Beauty is truth, truth beauty,—that is all / Ye know on earth, and all ye need to know."

339. In *Transformations and Symbols of the Libido* (1912, CW B), Jung argued that in the course of psychological development, the individual had to free himself from the figure of the mother, as depicted in heroic myths (see ch. 6, "The battle for deliverance from the mother").

Not the power of the flesh, but of love, should be broken for the sake of life, since life stands above love. A man needs his mother until his life has developed. Then he separates from her. And so life needs love until it has developed, then it will cut loose from it. The separation of the child from the mother is difficult, but the separation of life from love is harder. Love seeks to have and to hold, but life wants more.

The beginning of all things is love, but the being of things is life.[340] This distinction is terrible. Why, Oh spirit of the darkest depths, do you force me to say that whoever loves does not live and whoever lives does not love? I always get it backward! Should everything be turned into its opposite?[341] Will there be a sea where ΦΙΛΗΜΩΝ's temple stands? Will his shady island sink into the deepest ground? Into the whirlpool of the withdrawing flood that earlier swallowed all peoples and lands? Will the bottom of the sea be where Ararat arises?[342]

What repulsive words do you mutter, you mute son of the earth? You want to sever my soul's embrace? You, my son, do you thrust yourself between? Who are you? And who gives you the power? Everything that I strove for, everything I wrested from myself, do you want to reverse it again and destroy it? You are the son of the devil, to whom everything holy is inimical. You grow overpowering. You frighten me. Let me be happy in the embrace of my soul and do not disturb the peace of the temple.

Off with you, you pierce me with paralyzing force. For I do not want your way. Should I languidly fall at your feet? You devil and

---

340. In *Transformations and Symbols of the Libido* (1912), while discussing his concept of libido, Jung referred to the cosmogonic significance of Eros in Hesiod's *Theogony*, which he linked with the figure of Phanes in Orphism and with Kama, the Hindu God of love (CW B, §223).

341. In his later work, Jung gave importance to "enantiodromia," the principle that everything turns into its opposite, which he attributed to Heraclitus. See *Psychological Types* (1921), CW 6, §708f.

342. In the biblical account of the flood, the ark came to rest on Mount Ararat (Genesis 8:4). Ararat is a dormant volcanic cone formerly in Armenia (now Turkey).

son of the devil, speak! Your silence is unbearable, and of awful stupidity.

I won my soul, and to what did she give birth for me? You, monster, a son, ha!—a frightful miscreant, a stammerer, a newt's brain, a primordial lizard! You want to be king of the earth? You want to banish proud free men, bewitch beautiful women, break up castles, rip open the belly of old cathedrals? Dumb thing, a lazy bug-eyed frog that wears pond weed on his skull's pate! And you want to call yourself my son? You're no son of mine, but the spawn of the devil. The father of the devil entered into the womb of my soul and in you has become flesh.

I recognize you, ΦΙΛΗΜΩΝ, you most cunning of all fraudsters! You have deceived me. You impregnated my maidenly soul with the terrible worm. ΦΙΛΗΜΩΝ, damned charlatan, you aped the mysteries for me, you lay the mantle of the stars on me, you played a Christ-fool's comedy with me, you hanged me, carefully and ludicrously, in the tree just like Odin,[343] you let me devise runes to enchant Salome—and meanwhile you procreated my soul with the worm, spew of the dust. Deception upon deception! Terrible devil trickery!

You gave me the force of magic, you crowned me, you clad me with the shimmer of power, that let me play a would-be Joseph father to your son. You lodged a puny basilisk in the nest of the dove.

My soul, you adulterous whore, you became pregnant with this bastard! I am dishonored; I, laughable father of the Antichrist! How I mistrusted you! And how poor was my mistrust, that it could not gauge the magnitude of this infamous act!

What do you break apart? You broke love and life in twain. From this ghastly sundering, the frog and the son of the frog come forth. Ridiculous—disgusting sight! Irresistible advent! They will sit on the banks of the sweet water and listen to the nocturnal song of the frogs, since their God has been born as a son of frogs.

343. In Norse mythology, Odin was pierced by a spear and hung from the world tree, Yggdrasill, where he hung for nine nights until he found the runes, which gave him power.

Where is Salome? Where is the unresolvable question of love? No more questions, my gaze turned to the coming things, and Salome is where I am. The woman follows your strongest, not you. Thus she bears you your children, in both a good and a bad way.

{7}[1] As I stood so alone on the earth, which was covered by rain clouds and falling night, my serpent[344] crept up to me and told me a story:

"Once upon a time there was a king and he had no children. But he would have liked to have a son. So he went to a wise woman who lived as a witch in the forest and confessed all his sins, as if she were a priest appointed by God. To this she said: 'Dear King, you have done what you should not have done. But since it has come to pass, it has come to pass, and we will have to see how you can do it better in the future. Take a pound of otter lard, bury it in the earth, and let nine months pass. Then dig up that place again and see what you find.' So the king went to his house, ashamed and saddened, because he had humiliated himself before the witch in the forest. Yet he listened to her advice, dug a hole in the garden at night, and placed a pot of otter lard in it, which he had obtained with some difficulty. Then he let nine months go by.

"After this time had passed he went again by night to the place where the pot lay buried and dug it up. To his great astonishment, he found a sleeping infant in the pot, though the lard had disappeared. He took out the infant and jubilantly brought it to his wife. She took it immediately to her breast and behold—her milk flowed freely. And so the child thrived and became great and strong. He grew into a man who was greater and stronger than all others. When the king's son was twenty years old, he came before his

344. February 23, 1914. In *Black Book* 4, the dialogue is with the soul, and this section begins with Jung asking her what is stopping him from getting back to his work, and she tells him that it is his ambition, He thought he had overcome it, but she said that he had simply negated it, and thus tells him the tale that follows (p. 171). On February 13, 1914, Jung gave a talk, "On dream symbolism," to the Zürich Psychoanalytical Society. From March 30 to April 13, Jung vacationed in Italy.

father and said: 'I know that you have produced me through sorcery and that I was not born as one of men. You have made me from the repentance of your sins and this has made me strong. I am born from no woman, which makes me clever. I am strong and clever and therefore I demand the crown of the realm from you.' The old king was startled at his son's knowledge, but even more by his impetuous longing for regal power. He remained silent and thought: 'What has produced you? Otter lard. Who bore you? The womb of the earth. I drew you from a pot, a witch humiliated me.' And he decided to let his son be killed secretly.

"But because his son was stronger than others, he feared him and therefore he wanted to take refuge in a trick. He went again to the sorceress in the forest and asked her for advice. She said: 'Dear King, you confess no sin to me this time, because you want to commit a sin. I advise you to bury another pot with otter's lard and leave it to lie in the earth for nine months. Then dig it out again and see what has happened.' The king did what the sorceress advised him. And thenceforth his son became weaker and weaker, and when the king returned to the place where the pot lay after nine months, he could dig his son's grave at the same time. He lay the dead one in the fosse beside the empty pot.

"But the king was saddened, and when he could no longer master his melancholy, he returned yet again to the sorceress one night and asked her for advice. She spoke to him: 'Dear King, you wanted a son, but the son wanted to be king himself and also had the power and cleverness for it, and then you wanted your son no more. Because of this you lost your son. Why are you complaining? You have everything, dear King, that you wanted.' But the king said: 'You are right. I wanted it so. But I did not want this melancholy. Do you have any remedies against remorse?' The sorceress spoke: 'Dear King, go to your son's grave, fill the pot again with otter's lard, and after nine months see what you find in the pot.' The king did this, as he had been commanded, and henceforth he became happy and did not know why.

"When the nine months had passed, he dug out the pot again; the body had disappeared, but in the pot there lay a sleeping infant, and he realized that the infant was his dead son. He took the infant to himself, and henceforth he grew as much in a week as other infants grow in a year. And when twenty weeks had passed, the son came before the father again and claimed his realm. But the father had learned from experience and already knew for a long time how everything would turn out. After the son had voiced his demand, the old king got up from his throne and embraced his son with tears of joy and crowned him king. And so the son, who had thus become king, was grateful to his father and held him in high esteem, as long as his father was granted life."

But I spoke to my serpent: "In truth, my serpent, I didn't know that you are also a teller of fairy tales. So tell me, how should I interpret your fairy tale?"

Se: "Imagine that you are the old king and have a son."

I: "Who is the son?"

Se: "Well, I thought that you had just spoken of a son who doesn't make you very happy."

I: "What? You don't mean—that I should crown him?"

Se: "Yes, who else?"

I: "That's uncanny. But what about the sorceress?"

Se: "The sorceress is a motherly woman whose son you should be, since you are a child renewing himself in you."

I: "Oh no, will it be impossible for me to be a man?"

Se: "Sufficient manhood, and beyond that fullness of childhood. Which is why you need the mother."

I: "I'm ashamed to be a child."

Se: "And thus you kill your son. A creator needs the mother, since you are not a woman."

I: "This is a terrible truth. I thought and hoped that I could be a man in every way."

Se: "You cannot do this for the sake of the son. To create means: mother and child."

I: "The thought that I must remain a child is unbearable."

Se: "For the sake of your son you must be a child and leave him the crown."

I: "The thought that I must remain a child is humiliating and shattering."

Se: "A salutary antidote against power![345] Don't resist being a child, otherwise you resist your son,[346] whom you want above all."

I: "It's true, I want the son and survival. But the price for this is high."

Se: "The son stands higher. You are smaller and weaker than the son. That is a bitter truth, but it can't be avoided. Don't be defiant, children must be well-behaved."

I: "Damned scorn!"

Se: "Man of mockery! I'll have patience with you. My wells should flow for you and pour forth the drink of salvation, if all lands parch with thirst and everyone comes to you begging for the water of life. So subject yourself to the son."

I: "Where am I going to take hold of the immeasurable? My knowledge and ability are poor, my power is not enough."

At which the serpent curled up, gathered herself into knots and said: "Do not ask after the morrow, sufficient unto you is the day. You need not worry about the means. Let everything grow, let everything sprout; the son grows out of himself."

[2] The myth commences, the one that need only be lived, not sung, the one that sings itself. I subject myself to the son, the one engendered by sorcery, the unnaturally born, the son of the frogs, who stands at the waterside and speaks with his fathers and listens to their nocturnal singing. Truly he is full of mysteries and superior in strength to all men. No man has produced him, and no woman has given birth to him.

345. *Black Book* 4 has: "ambition" (p. 180).
346. *Black Book* 4 has "work" instead of "son" in the next few lines (p. 180).

The absurd has entered the age-old mother, and the son has grown in the deepest ground. He sprang up and was put to death. He rose again, was produced anew in the way of sorcery, and grew more swiftly than before. I gave him the crown that unites the separated. And so he unites the separated for me. I gave him the power and thus he commands, since he is superior in strength and cleverness to all others.

I did not give way to him willingly, but out of insight. No man binds Above and Below together. But he who did not grow like a man, and yet has the form of a man, is capable of binding them. My power is paralyzed, but I survive in my son. I set aside my concern that he may master the people. I am solitary, the people rejoice at him. I was powerful, now I am powerless. I was strong, now I am weak. Since then he has taken all the strength into himself. Everything has turned itself upside down for me.

I loved the beauty of the beautiful, the spirit of those rich in spirit, the strength of the strong; I laughed at the stupidity of the stupid, I despised the weakness of the weak, the meanness of the mean, and hated the badness of the bad. But now I must love the beauty of the ugly, the spirit of the foolish, and the strength of the weak. I must admire the stupidity of the clever, must respect the weakness of the strong and the meanness of the generous, and honor the goodness of the bad. Where does that leave mockery, contempt, and hatred?

They went over to the son as a token of power. His mockery is bloody, and how contemptuously his eyes flash! His hatred is a singing fire! Enviable one, you son of the Gods, how can one fail to obey you? He broke me in two, he cut me up. He yokes the separated. Without him I would fall apart, but my life went on with him. My love remained with me.

Thus I entered solitude with a black look on my face, full of resentment and outrage at my son's dominion. How could my son arrogate my power? I went into my gardens and sat down in a lonely spot on rocks by the water, and brooded darkly. I called the serpent, my nocturnal companion, who lay with me on the rocks through many twilights, imparting her serpent wisdom. But then my son emerged from the water, great and powerful, the crown on his head, with a swirling lion's mane, shimmering serpent skin covering his body; he said to me:[347]

{8} [1] "I come to you and demand your life."

I: "What do you mean? Have you even become a God?"[348]

He: "I rise again, I had become flesh, now I return to eternal glitter and shimmer, to the eternal embers of the sun, and leave you your earthliness. You will remain with men. You have been in immortal company long enough. Your work belongs to the earth."

I: "What a speech! Weren't you wallowing in the earth and the underearth?"

He: "I had become man and beast, and now ascend again to my own country."

I: "Where is your country?"

He: "In the light, in the egg, in the sun, in what is innermost and compressed, in the eternal longing embers. So rises the sun in your heart and streams out into the cold world."

I: "How you transfigure yourself!"

He: "I want to vanish from your sight. You ought to live in darkest solitude, men—not Gods—should illumine your darkness."

I: "How hard and solemn you are! I'd like to bathe your feet with my tears, dry them with my hair—I'm raving, am I a woman?"

He: "Also a woman, also a mother, pregnant. Giving birth awaits you."

I: "Oh holy spirit, grant me a spark of your eternal light!"

He: "You are with child."

I: "I feel the torment and the fear and the desolation of pregnant woman. Do you go from me, my God?"

He: "You have the child."

347. April 19, 1914. The preceding paragraph was added in the *Draft*.

348. In *Black Book* 5, this dialogue is with his soul (p. 29f).

I: "My soul, do you still exist? You serpent, you frog, you magically produced boy whom my hands buried; you ridiculed, despised, hated one who appeared to me in a foolish form? Woe betide those who have seen their soul and felt it with hands. I am powerless in your hand, my God!"

He: "The pregnant woman belongs to fate. Release me, I rise to the eternal realm."

I: "Will I never hear your voice again? Oh damned deception! What am I asking? You'll talk to me again tomorrow, you'll chat over and over in the mirror."

He: "Do not rail. I will be present and not present. You will hear and not hear me. I will be and not be."

I: "You utter gruesome riddles."

He: "Such is my language and to you I leave the understanding. No one besides you has your God. He is always with you, yet you see him in others, and thus he is never with you. You strive to draw to yourself those who seem to possess your God. You will come to see that they do not possess him, and that you alone have him. Thus you are alone among men—in the crowd and yet alone. Solitude in multitude—ponder this."

I: "I suppose I ought to remain silent after what you have said, but I cannot; my heart bleeds when I see you go from me."

He: "Let me go. I shall return to you in renewed form. Do you see the sun, how it sinks red into the mountains? This day's work is accomplished, and a new sun returns. Why are you mourning the sun of today?"

I: "Must night fall?"

He: "Is it not mother of the day?"

I: "Because of this night I want to despair."

He: "Why lament? It is fate. Let me go, my wings grow and the longing toward eternal light swells up powerfully in me. You can no longer stop me. Stop your tears and let me ascend with cries of joy. You are a man of the fields, think of your crops. I become light, like the bird that rises up into the skies of morning. Do not stop me, do not complain; already I hover, the cry of life escapes from me, I can no longer hold back my supreme pleasure. I must go up—it has happened, the last cord tears away, my wings bear me up. I dive up into the sea of light. You who are down there, you distant, twilight being—you fade from me."

I: "Where have you gone? Something has happened. I am lamed. Has the God not left my sight?"

Where is the God?

What has happened?

How empty, how utterly empty! Should I proclaim to men how you vanished? Should I preach the gospel of godforsaken solitude?

Should we all go into the desert and strew ashes on our heads, since the God has left us?

I believe and accept that the God[349] is something different from me.

He swung high with jubilant joy.

I remain in the night of pain.

No longer with the God,[350] but alone with myself.

Now shut, you bronze doors I opened to the flood of devastation and murder brooding over the peoples, opened so as to midwife the God.

Shut, may mountains bury you and seas flow over you.[351]

I came to my self,[352] a giddy and pitiful figure. My I! I didn't want this fellow as my companion. I found myself with him. I'd prefer a bad woman or a wayward hound, but one's own I—this horrifies me.

[353]An opus is needed, that one can squander decades on, and do it out of necessity. I must catch up with a piece of the Middle Ages—within myself. We have only finished the Middle Ages of—others. I

349. *Black Book* 5 has instead "Soul" (p. 37).
350. *Black Book* 5 has instead "with my soul" (p. 38).
351. This paragraph was added in the *Draft*.
352. The *Corrected Draft* has instead: "to myself" (p. 555).
353. The remainder is added in the *Draft* (p. 555f).

must begin early, in that period when the hermits died out.[354] Asceticism, inquisition, torture are close at hand and impose themselves. The barbarian requires barbaric means of education. My I, you are a barbarian. I want to live with you, therefore I will carry you through an utterly medieval Hell, until you are capable of making living with you bearable. You should be the vessel and womb of life, therefore I shall purify you.

The touchstone is being alone with oneself.

This is the way.[355]

354. In 1930, Jung stated: "A movement back into the Middle Ages is a sort of regression, but it is not personal. It is a historical regression, a regression into the past of the collective unconscious. This always takes place when the way ahead is not free, when there is an obstacle from which you recoil; or when you need to get something out of the past in order to climb over the wall ahead" (*Visions*, vol. 1, p. 148). Around this time, Jung began working intensively on medieval theology (see *Psychological Types* [1921], CW 6, ch. 1, "The type problem in the history of the mind in antiquity and the Middle Ages").

355. At this point, the *Handwritten Draft* has: "Finis," surrounded by a box (p. 1205).

Scrutinies

Scrutinies

{1} I resist, I cannot accept this hollow nothing that I am. What am I? What is my I? I always presuppose my I. Now it stands before me—I before my I. I speak now to you, my I:

[1]We are alone and our being together threatens to become unbearably boring. We must do something, devise a pastime; for example, I could educate you. Let us begin with your main flaw, which strikes me first: you have no correct self-esteem. Have you no good qualities that you can be proud of? You believe that being capable is an art. But one can also learn such skills to some extent. Please, do so. You find it difficult—well, all beginnings are difficult.[2] Soon you will be able to do it better. Do you doubt this? That is of no use; you must be able to do it, or else I cannot live with you. Ever since the God has arisen and spreads himself in whichever fiery heavens, to do whatever he does, what exactly I do not know, we have depended upon one another. Therefore you must think about improving, or else our life together will become wretched. So pull yourself together and value yourself! Don't you want to?

Pitiful creature! I will torment you a bit if you do not make an effort. What are you moaning about? Perhaps the whip will help?

Now that gets under your skin, doesn't it? Take that—and that. What does it taste of? Of blood, presumably? Of the Middle Ages *in majorem Dei gloriam*?[3]

Or do you want love, or what goes by that name? One can also teach with love, if blows do not bear fruit. So should I love you? Press you tenderly to myself?

I truly believe that you are yawning.

How now, you want to speak? But I won't let you, otherwise in the end you will claim that you are my soul. But my soul is with the fire worm, with the son of the frog who has flown to the heavens above, to the upper sources. Do I know what he is doing there? But

1. April 19, 1914.
2. "All beginnings are difficult" is a proverb from the Talmud.
3. "To the greater glory of God." This was the motto of the Jesuits.

you are not my soul, you are my bare, empty nothing—I, this disagreeable being, whom one cannot even deny the right to consider itself worthless.

One could despair over you: your sensitivity and desirousness exceed any reasonable measure. And I should live with you, of all people? I must, since the strange misfortune occurred that gave me a son and took him away.

I regret that I must speak such truths to you. Yes, you are laughably sensitive, self-righteous, unruly, mistrustful, pessimistic, cowardly, dishonest with yourself, venomous, vengeful; one can hardly speak about your childish pride, your craving for power, your desire for esteem, your laughable ambition, your thirst for fame without feeling sick. The playacting and pomposity become you badly and you abuse them to the best of your ability.

Do you believe that it is a pleasure rather than a horror to live together with you? No, three times no! But I promise you that I will tighten the vise around you and slowly pull off your skin. I will give you the chance to be flayed.

You, you of all people wanted to tell other people what to do?

Come here, I will stitch a cloth of new skin onto you, so that you can feel its effect.

You want to complain about others, and that one has done an injustice to you, not understood you, misinterpreted you, hurt your feelings, ignored you, not recognized you, falsely accused you, and what else? Do you see your vanity in this, your eternally ridiculous vanity?

You complain that the torment has not yet come to an end?

Let me tell you: it has only just begun. You have no patience and no seriousness. Only when it concerns your pleasure do you praise your patience. I will double the torment so that you learn patience.

You find the pain unbearable, but there are other things that hurt even more, and you can inflict them on others with the greatest naivety and absolve yourself all unknowingly.

But you will learn silence. For this I will pull out your tongue—with which you have ridiculed, blasphemed and—even worse—

joked. I will pin all your unjust and depraved words one by one to your body with needles so that you can feel how evil words stab.

Do you admit that you also derive pleasure from this torment? I will increase this pleasure until you vomit with joy so that you know what taking pleasure in self-torment means.

You rise against me? I am screwing the vise tighter, that's all. I will break your bones until there is no longer a trace of hardness there.

For I want to get along with you—I must—damn you—you are my I, which I must carry around with me to the grave. Do you think that I want to have such foolishness around me all my life? If you were not my I, I would have torn you to pieces long ago.

But I am damned to haul you through a purgatory so that you too will become somewhat acceptable.

You call on God for help?

The dear old God has died,[4] and it is good that way, otherwise he would have had pity on your repentant sinfulness and spared me the execution by granting mercy. You must know that neither a God of love nor a loving God has yet arisen, but instead a worm of fire crawled up, a magnificent frightful entity that lets fire rain on the earth, producing lamentations.[5] So cry to the God, he will burn you with fire for the forgiveness of your sins. Coil yourself and sweat blood. You have needed this cure for a long time. Yes—others always do wrong—and you? You are the innocent, the correct, you must defend your good right and you have a good, loving God on your side, who always forgives sins with pity. Others must reach insight, not you, since you have a monopoly on all insight from the start and are always convinced that you are right. And so cry really loudly to your dear God—he will hear you and let fire fall on you. Have you not noticed that your God has become a fiery worm with a flat skull who crawls red-hot on the earth?

---

4. See below, note 91, p. 515.
5. References to this God in the following pages are not in *Black Book* 5.

You wanted to be superior! How laughable. You were, and are, inferior. Who are you, then? Scum that disgusts me.

Are you perhaps somewhat powerless? I place you in a corner where you can remain lying until you come to your senses again. If you no longer feel anything, the procedure is of no use. After all, we must proceed skillfully. It really says a lot about you that one needs such barbaric means for your amendment. Your progress since the early Middle Ages appears to be minuscule.

[6]Did you feel dejected today, inferior, debased? Shall I tell you why?

Your inordinate ambition is boundless. Your grounds are not focused on the good of the matter but on your vanity. You do not work for humanity but for your self-interest. You do not strive for the completion of the thing but for the general recognition and safeguarding of your own advantage. I want to honor you with a prickly crown of iron; it has teeth inside that bore themselves into your flesh.

And now we come to the vile swindle that you pursue with your cleverness. You speak skillfully and abuse your capability and discolor, tone down, strengthen, apportion light and shade, and loudly proclaim your honorableness and upright good faith. You exploit the good faith of others, you gloatingly catch them in your snares and speak of your benevolent superiority and the prize that you are for others. You play at modesty and do not mention your merit, in the certain hope that someone else will do it for you; you are disappointed and hurt if this doesn't happen.

You preach hypocritical composure. But when it really matters, are you calm? No, you lie. You consume yourself in rage and your tongue speaks cold daggers and you dream of revenge.

You are gloating and resentful. You begrudge the other the sunshine, since you would like to assign it to those whom you favor

6. April 20, 1914. On the same day, Jung resigned as president of the International Psychoanalytical Association (*The Freud/Jung Letters*, p. 613).

because they favor you. You are envious of all well-being around you and you impertinently assert the opposite.

Inside yourself you think unsparingly and coarsely only what always suits you, and with this you feel yourself above humanity and not in the least responsible. But you are responsible to humanity in everything that you think, feel, and do. Do not pretend there is a difference between thinking and doing. You rely only on your undeserved advantage, not to be compelled to say or do what you think and feel.

But you are shameless in everything where no one sees you. If another said that to you, you would be mortally offended, despite knowing that it is true. You want to reproach others for their failings? So that they better themselves? Yes, confess, have you bettered yourself? From where do you get the right to have opinions of others? What is your opinion about yourself? And what are the good grounds that support it? Your grounds are webs of lies covering a dirty corner. You judge others and charge them with what they should do. You do this because you have no order within yourself, because you are unclean.

And then—how do you really think? It appears to me that you even think with men, regardless of their human dignity; you dare think by means of them, and use them as figures on your stage, as if they were how you conceive them? Have you ever considered that you thus commit a shameful act of power, as bad as that for which you condemn others, namely that they love their fellow men, as they claim, but in reality exploit them to their own ends. Your sin flourishes in seclusion, but it is no less great, remorseless, and coarse.

What is concealed in you I will drag out into the light, shameless one! I will crush your superiority under my feet.

Do not speak to me about your love. What you call love oozes with self-interest and desirousness. But you speak about it with great words, and the greater your words are, the more pathetic your so-called love is. Never speak to me of your love, but keep your mouth shut. It lies.

I want you to speak about your shame, and that instead of speaking great words, you utter a discordant clamor before those whose respect you wanted to exact. You deserve mockery, not respect.

I will burn out of you the contents of which you were proud, so that you will become empty like a poured-out vessel. You should be proud of nothing more than your emptiness and wretchedness. You should be a vessel of life, so kill your idols.

Freedom does not belong to you, but form; not power, but suffering and conceiving.

You should make a virtue out of your self-contempt, which I will spread out before men like a carpet. They should walk over it with dirty feet and you should see to it that you are dirtier than all the feet that step on you.

[7]If I tame you, beast, I give others the opportunity to tame their beasts. The taming begins with you, my I, nowhere else. Not that you, stupid brother I, had been particularly wild. There are some who are wilder. But I must whip you until you endure the wildness of the others. Then I can live with you. If someone does you wrong, I will torment you to death, until you have forgiven the wrong suffered, yet not just by paying lip service, but also in your heavy heart with its heinous sensitivity. Your sensitivity is your particular form of violence.

Therefore listen, brother in my solitude, I have prepared every kind of torture for you, if it should ever occur to you again to be sensitive. You should feel inferior. You should be able to bear the fact that one calls your purity dirty and that one desires your dirtiness, that one praises your wastefulness as miserliness and your greed as a virtue.

Fill your beaker with the bitter drink of subjugation, since you are not your soul. Your soul is with the fiery God who flamed up to the roof of the heavens.

7. April 21, 1914.

Should you still be sensitive? I notice that you are forging secret plans for revenge, plotting deceitful tricks. But you are an idiot, you cannot take revenge on fate. Childish one, you probably even want to lash the sea. Build better bridges instead; that is a better way to squander your wit.

You want to be understood? That's all we needed! Understand yourself, and you will be sufficiently understood. You will have quite enough work in hand with that. Mothers' little dears want to be understood. Understand yourself, that is the best protection against sensitivity and satisfies your childish longing to be understood. I suppose you want to turn others into slaves of your desirousness again? But you know that I must live with you and that I will no longer tolerate such abject plaintiveness.[8]

{2} After I had spoken these and many more angry words to my I, I noticed that I began to bear being alone with myself. But the touchiness still stirred in me frequently and I had to lash myself just as often. And I did this until even the pleasure in self-torment faded.[9]

[10]Then I heard a voice one night; it came from afar and was the voice of my soul. She spoke: "How distant you are!"

I: "Is that you my soul, from which height and distance do you speak?"

8. Jung later described the self-criticism depicted in this opening section as the confrontation with the shadow. In 1934 he wrote: "Whoever looks into the mirror of the water will see first of all his own image. Whoever goes to himself risks a confrontation with himself. The mirror does not flatter, it faithfully shows whatever looks into it; namely the face we never show to the world because we cover it with the persona, the mask of the actor. But the mirror lies behind the mask and shows the true face. This confrontation is the first test of courage on the inner way, a test sufficient to frighten off most people, for the meeting with ourselves belongs to the more unpleasant things that can be avoided as long as one can project everything negative into the environment. But if we are able to see our own shadow and can bear knowing about it, then a small part of the problem has already been solved: we have at least brought up the personal unconscious" ("On the archetypes of the collective unconscious," CW 9, 1, §§43–44).

9. This paragraph does not occur in *Black Book* 5. On April 30, 1914, Jung resigned as a lecturer in the medical faculty of the University of Zürich.

10. May 8, 1914. There is a gap in the entries in *Black Book* 5 between April 21 and May 8, so the discussions referred to in the previous paragraph do not appear to have been recorded.

S: "I am above you. I am a world apart. I have become sunlike. I received the seeds of fire. Where are you? I can hardly find you in your mists."

I: "I am down on the murky earth, in the dark smoke that the fire left us, and my gaze does not reach you. But your voice sounds closer."

S: "I feel it. The heaviness of the earth penetrates me, damp cold enshrouds me, gloomy memories of former pain overcome me."

I: "Do not lower yourself into the smoke and the darkness of the earth. I would like that which I am still working on to remain sunlike. Otherwise I will lose the courage to live further down in the darkness of the earth. Let me just hear your voice. I will never want to see you in the flesh again. Say something! Take it from the depths, from which fear perhaps flows to me."

S: "I cannot, since your creative source flows from there."

I: "You see my uncertainty."

S: "The uncertain way is the good way. Upon it lie possibilities. Be unwavering and create."

I heard the rushing of wings. I knew that the bird rose higher, above the clouds in the fiery brilliance of the outspread Godhead.

[11]I turned to my brother, the I; he stood sadly and looked at the ground and sighed, and would rather have been dead, since the burden of enormous suffering burdened him. But a voice spoke from me and said:

"It is hard—the sacrificed fall left and right—and you will be crucified for the sake of life."

And I said to my I: "My brother, how do you like this speech?"

But he sighed deeply and moaned: "It is bitter, and I suffer much."

To which I answered: "I know, but it is not to be altered." But I did not know what that was, since I still did not know what the future held (this happened on the 21st May of the year 1914). In the excess of suffering I looked up to the clouds and called out to my

11. May 21, 1914.

soul and asked her. And I heard her voice, happy and bright, and she answered:

"Much happiness has happened to me. I rise higher, my wings grow."

I was seized with bitterness at these words and I cried: "You live from the blood of the human heart."

I heard her laughing—or was she not laughing? "No drink is dearer to me than red blood."

Powerless anger seized me and I called out: "If you were not my soul who followed the God to the eternal realm, I would call you the most terrible scourge of men. But who moves you? I know that divinity is not humanity. The divine consumes the human. I know that this is the severity, this is the cruelty; he who has felt you with his hands can never remove the blood from his hands. I have become enslaved to you."

She answered: "Do not be angry, do not complain. Let the bloody victims fall at your side. It is not your severity, it is not your cruelty, but necessity. The way of life is sown with fallen ones."

I: "Yes, I see, it is a battlefield. My brother, what is with you? Are you groaning?"

Then my I answered: "Why should I not groan and moan? I load myself with the dead and cannot haul their number."

But I did not understand my I and therefore spoke to him: "You are a pagan, my friend! Have you not heard that it is said, let the dead bury their dead?[12] Why do you want to be burdened with the dead? You do not help them by hauling them."

Then my I wailed: "But I pity the poor fallen ones, they cannot reach the light. Perhaps if I haul them—?"

I: "What is this? Their souls have accomplished as much as they could. Then they encountered fate. It will also happen to us. Your compassion is sick."

---

12. Matthew 8:21–22: "And another of his disciples said unto him, Lord, suffer me first to go and bury my father. But Jesus said unto him, Follow me; and let the dead bury their dead."

But my soul called from afar: "Leave him compassion, compassion binds life and death."

These words of my soul stung me. She spoke of compassion, she, who rose up following the God without compassion, and I asked her:

[13]"Why did you do that?"

For my human sensitivity could not grasp the hideousness of that hour. She answered:

"It is not meant for me to be in your world. I besmirch myself on the excrement of your earth."

I: "Am I not earth? Am I not excrement? Did I commit an error that forced you to follow the God into the upper realms?"

S: "No, it was inner necessity. I belong to the Above."

I: "Has no one suffered an irreplaceable loss through your disappearance?"

S: "On the contrary, you have enjoyed utmost benefit."

I: "If I heed my human feeling about this, doubt could come over me."

S: "What have you noticed? Why should what you see always be untrue? It is your particular wrong that you cannot stop making a fool of yourself. Can you not remain on your way for once?"

I: "You know that I doubt, because of my love for men."

S: "No, for the sake of your weakness, for the sake of your doubt and disbelief. Stay on your way and do not run away from yourself. There is a divine and a human intention. They cross each other in stupid and godforsaken people, to whom you also belong from time to time."

Since what my soul spoke about referred to nothing that I could see, nor could I see what my I suffered from (since this happened two months before the outbreak of the war), I wanted to understand it all as personal experiences within me, and consequently I could neither understand nor believe it all, since my belief is weak. And I believe that it is better in our time if belief is weak. We have

13. May 23, 1914.

outgrown that childhood where mere belief was the most suitable means to bring men to what is good and reasonable. Therefore if we wanted to have a strong belief again today, we would thus return to that earlier childhood. But we have so much knowledge and such a thirst for knowledge in us that we need knowledge more than belief. But the strength of belief would hinder us from attaining knowledge. Belief certainly may be something strong, but it is empty, and too little of the whole man can be involved, if our life with God is grounded only on belief. Should we simply believe first and foremost? That seems too cheap to me. Men who have understanding should not just believe, but should wrestle for knowledge to the best of their ability. Belief is not everything, but neither is knowledge. Belief does not give us the security and the wealth of knowing. Desiring knowledge sometimes takes away too much belief. Both must strike a balance.

But it is also dangerous to believe too much, because today everyone has to find his own way and encounters in himself a beyond full of strange and mighty things. He could easily take everything literally with too much belief and would be nothing but a lunatic. The childishness of belief breaks down in the face of our present necessities. We need differentiating knowledge to clear up the confusion which the discovery of the soul has brought in. Therefore it is perhaps much better to await better knowledge before one accepts things all too believingly.[14]

From these considerations I spoke to my soul:

"Is all that to be accepted? You know in what sense I ask this. It is not stupid and unbelieving to ask thus, but is doubting of a higher type."

To this she answered: "I understand you—but it is to be accepted."

14. These last two paragraphs do not occur in *Black Book* 5: In *Transformations and Symbols of the Libido* (1912), Jung wrote: "I think, belief should be replaced by understanding" (CW B, §356). On October 5, 1945, Jung wrote to Victor White: "I began my career with repudiating everything that smelt of belief" (Ann Conrad Lammers and Adrian Cunningham, eds., *The Jung-White Letters* [Philemon Series, London: Routledge, 2007], p. 6).

To which I replied: "The solitude of this acceptance terrifies me. I dread the madness that befalls the solitary."

She answered: "As you already know, I have long predicted solitude for you. You need not be afraid of madness. What I predict is valid."

These words filled me with disquiet, since I felt that I could almost not accept what my soul predicted, because I did not understand it. I always wanted to understand it with regard to myself. Therefore I said to my soul: "What misunderstood fear torments me?"

"That is your disbelief, your doubt. You do not want to believe in the size of the sacrifice that is required. But it will go on to the bitter end. Greatness requires greatness. You still want to be too cheap. Did I not speak to you of abandonment, of leaving be? Do you want to have it better than other men?"

"No," I replied. "No, that is not it. But I fear committing an injustice to men if I go my own way."

"What do you want to avoid?" she said; "there is no avoidance. You must go your way, unconcerned about others, no matter whether they are good or bad. You have laid your hand on the divine, which those have not."

I could not accept these words since I feared deception. Therefore I also did not want to accept this way that forced me into dialogue with my soul. I preferred to speak with men. But I felt compelled toward solitude and I feared at the same time the solitude of my thinking which departed from accustomed paths.[15] As I pondered this, my soul spoke to me: "Did I not predict dark solitude for you?"

"I know," I answered, "but I did not really think that it would happen. Must it be so?"

15. May 24, 1914. The lines from the beginning of the paragraph do not occur in *Black Book* 4.

"You can only say yes. There is nothing to do other than for you to take care of your cause. If anything should happen, it can only happen on this way."

"So it is hopeless," I cried, "to resist solitude?"

"It is utterly hopeless. You should be forced into your work."

As my soul spoke thus, an old man with a white beard and a haggard face approached me.[16] I asked him what he wanted with me. To which he replied:

"I am a nameless one, one of the many who lived and died in solitude. The spirit of the times and the acknowledged truth required this from us. Look at me—you must learn this. Things have been too good for you."[17]

"But," I replied, "is this another necessity in our so very different time?"

"It is as true today as it was yesterday. Never forget that you are a man and therefore you must bleed for the goal of humanity. Practice solitude assiduously without grumbling so that everything will in time become ready. You should become serious, and hence take your leave from science. There is too much childishness in it. Your way goes toward the depths. Science is too superficial, mere language, mere tools. But you must set to work."[18]I did not know what work was mine, since everything was dark. And everything became heavy and doubtful and an endless sadness seized me and lasted for many days. Then, one night, I heard the voice of an old man. He spoke slowly, heavily, and his sentences appeared to be disconnected and

16. *Black Book* 4 continues: "He is like one of the old saints, one of the first Christians who lived in the desert" (p. 77).

17. In the handwritten manuscript of *Scrutinies*, there is a note here: "27/11/17," which appears to refer to when this portion of the manuscript was composed.

18. *Black Book* 5 continues: [I]: "I am scholastic?" [Soul]: "Not that, but scientific; science is a new version of scholasticism. It needs to be surmounted." [I]: "Is it not enough yet? Do I thus not counter the spirit of the time if I dissociate myself from science?" [Soul]: "You are not supposed to dissociate yourself, but consider that science is merely your language." [I]: "Which depths do you require me to advance to?" [Soul]: "Forever above yourself and the present." / [I]: "I want to, but what should happen? I often feel I can no longer." [Soul]: "You must put in extra work. Provide respite. Too many take up your time." / [I]: "Will this sacrifice arise too?" [Soul]: "You must, you must" (pp. 79–80).

terribly absurd, so that the fear of madness seized me again.[19] For he spoke the following words:

[20]"It is not yet the evening of days. The worst comes last.

The hand that strikes first, strikes best.

Nonsense streams from the deepest wells, amply like the Nile.

Morning is more beautiful than night.

Flowers smell until they fade.

Ripeness comes as late as possible in spring, or else it misses its purpose."

These sentences that the old man spoke to me on the night of the 25 May of the year 1914 appeared to me dreadfully meaningless. I felt my I squirm in pain. It moaned and wailed about the burden of the dead that rested on it. It seemed as if it had to carry a thousand dead.

This sadness did not leave until the 24th June 1914.[21] In the night my soul spoke to me: "The greatest comes to the smallest." After this nothing further was said. And then the war broke out. This opened my eyes about what I had experienced before, and it also gave me the courage to say all of that which I have written in the earlier part of this book.

{3} From there on the voices of the depths remained silent for a whole year. Again in summer, when I was out on the water alone, I saw an osprey plunge down not far from me; he seized a large fish and rose up into the skies again clutching it.[22] I heard the voice of

19. This paragraph does not occur in *Black Book* 5.
20. May 25, 1914.
21. *Black Book* 5 continues: "Ha, this book! I have laid hands on you again—banal and pathological and frantic and divine, my written unconscious! You have forced me to my knees again! Here I am, say what you have to say!" (p. 82). This is the one reference to "the unconscious" in *Black Books* 2 to 7.
22. June 3, 1915. In the interim, Jung wrote the draft of the preceding books of *Liber Novus*. On July 28, 1914, Jung gave a talk on "The importance of the unconscious in psychopathology" at a meeting of the British Medical Association in Aberdeen. From around August 9 to around August 22, Jung was on military service in Luzern for 14 days. From around January 1 to around March 8, 1915, Jung was on military service in Olten

my soul, and she spoke: "That is a sign that what is below is borne upward."

Soon after this on an autumn night I heard the voice of an old man (and this time I knew that it was ΦΙΛΗΜΩΝ).[23] He said:[24] "I want to turn you around. I want to master you. I want to emboss you like a coin. I want to do business with you. One should buy and sell you.[25] You should pass from hand to hand. Self-willing is not for you. You are the will of the whole. Gold is no master out of its own will and yet it rules the whole, despised and greedily demanded, an inexorable ruler: it lies and waits. He who sees it longs for it. It does not follow one around, but lies silently, with a brightly gleaming countenance, self-sufficient, a king that needs no proof of its power. Everyone seeks after it, few find it, but even the smallest piece is highly esteemed. It neither gives nor squanders itself. Everyone takes it where he finds it, and anxiously ensures that he doesn't lose the smallest part of it. Everyone denies that he depends on it, and yet he secretly stretches out his hand longingly toward it. Must gold prove its necessity? It is proven through the longing of men. Ask it:

---

for 64 days. Between March 10 and 12, he served on the invalid transport (Jung's military service books, *JFA*).

23. This sentence is not in *Black Book* 6.

24. September 14, 1915. In late summer and autumn of 1915, Jung conducted his correspondence with Hans Schmid on the question of psychological types. His concluding letter to Schmid of November 6 indicates a shift that signals a return to the elaboration of his fantasies in the *Black Books*: "Understanding is a terribly binding power, possibly a veritable soul murder when it levels out vitally important differences. The core of the individual is a mystery of life, which dies when it is 'grasped.' That is also why *symbols want to keep their secrets*, they are mysterious not only because we are unable to clearly see what is at their bottom . . . All understanding as such, being an integration into general viewpoints, contains the devil's element, and kills . . . That is why, in the later stages of analysis, we must help the other to come to those hidden and un-openable symbols, in which the seed of life lies securely hidden like the tender seed in the hard shell. Actually, there must not be any understanding and agreement on this, even if it were possible, as it were. But if understanding and agreement on this has become generalized and obviously possible, the symbol is ripe for destruction, because it no longer covers the seed, which is about to outgrow the shell. Now I understand a dream I once had, and which greatly impressed me: I was standing in my garden, and I had dug open a rich spring of water which gushed forth mightily. Then I had to dig a trench and a deep hole, in which I collected all the water and let it flow back into the depths of the earth again. In this way salvation is given to us in the un-openable and un-sayable symbol, for it protects us by preventing the devil from swallowing the seed of life" (John Beebe and Ernst Falzeder, eds., *The Question of Psychological Types*, forthcoming).

25. *Black Book* 5 continues: "Hermes is your daimon" (p. 87).

who takes me? He who takes it, has it. Gold does not stir. It sleeps and shines. Its brilliance confuses the senses. Without a word, it promises everything that men deem desirable. It ruins those to be ruined and helps those on the rise to ascend.[26]

"A blazing hoard is piled up, it awaits the taker. What tribulations do men not take upon themselves for the sake of gold? It waits and does not shorten their tribulations—the greater the tribulations, the greater the trouble, the more esteemed it is. It grows from underground, from the molten lava. It slowly exudes, hidden in veins and rocks. Man exerts all cunning to dig it out, to raise it."

But I called out dismayed: "What ambiguous speech, Oh ΦΙΛΗΜΩΝ!"

[27]But ΦΙΛΗΜΩΝ continued: "Not only to teach, but also to disavow, or why then did I teach? If I do not teach, I do not have to disavow. But if I have taught, I must disavow thereafter. For if I teach, I must give others what they should have taken. What he acquires is good, but the gift that was not acquired is bad. To waste oneself means: to want to suppress many. Deceitfulness surrounds the giver because his own enterprise is deceitful. He is forced to revoke his gift and to deny his virtue.

"The burden of silence is not greater than the burden of my self that I would like to load onto you. Therefore I speak and I teach. May the listener defend himself against my ruse, by means of which I burden him.

"The best truth is also such a skillful deception that I also entangle myself in it as long as I do not realize the worth of a successful ruse."

And I was startled again and cried: "Oh ΦΙΛΗΜΩΝ, men have deceived themselves about you, therefore you deceive them. But he who fathoms you, fathoms himself."

---

26. Jung discussed the alchemical symbolism of gold in *Mysterium Coniunctionis* (1955/56, CW 14, §353ff).
27. September 15, 1915.

[28]But ΦΙΛΗΜΩΝ fell silent and retired into the shimmering cloud of uncertainty. He left me to my thoughts. And it occurred to me that high barriers would still need to be erected between men, less to protect them against mutual burdens than against mutual virtues. It seemed to me as if the so-called Christian morality of our time made for mutual enchantment. How can anyone bear the burden of the other, if it is still the highest that one can expect from a man, that he at least bears his own burden.

But sin probably resides in enchantment. If I accept self-forgetting virtue, I make myself the selfish tyrant of the other, and I am thus also forced to surrender myself again in order to make another my master, which always leaves me with a bad impression and is not to the other's advantage. Admittedly, this interplay underpins society, but the soul of the individual becomes damaged since man thus learns always to live from the other instead of from himself. It appears to me that, if one is capable, one should not surrender oneself, as that induces, indeed even forces, the other to do likewise. But what happens if everyone surrenders themselves? That would be folly.

Not that it would be a beautiful or a pleasant thing to live with one's self, but it serves the redemption of the self. Incidentally, can one give oneself up? With this one becomes one's own slave. That is the opposite of accepting oneself. If one becomes one's own slave—and this happens to everyone who surrenders himself—one is lived by the self. One does not live one's self; it lives itself.[29]

28. September 17, 1915.

29. In *Thus Spoke Zarathustra*, Nietzsche wrote: "The Self also seeks with the eyes of sense, it listens too with the ears of the spirit. The Self is always listening and seeking: it compares, subdues, conquers, destroys. It rules and is also the I's ruler. Behind your thoughts and feelings, my brother, stands a mighty commander, an unknown sage—he is called Self" (section 1, "Of the despisers of the body," §1, p. 62). The passage is underlined as in Jung's copy. There are also lines by the margin and exclamation marks. In commenting on this passage in 1935 in his seminar on *Zarathustra*, Jung said: "I was already very interested in the concept of the self, but I was not sure how I should understand it. I made my marks when I came across these passages, and they seemed very important to me . . . The concept of the self continued to recommend itself to me . . . I thought that Nietzsche meant a sort of thing-in-itself behind the psychological phenomenon . . . I saw then also that he was producing a concept of the self which was like the Eastern concept; it is an Atman idea" (*Nietzsche's Zarathustra*, vol.1, p. 391).

The self-forgetting virtue is an unnatural alienation from one's own essence, which is thus deprived of development. It is a sin to deliberately alienate the other from his self by means of one's own virtuousness, for example, through saddling oneself with his burden. This sin rebounds on us.[30]

It is submission enough, amply enough, if we subjugate ourselves to our self. The work of redemption is always first to be done on ourselves, if one dare utter such a great word. This work cannot be done without love for ourselves. Must it be done at all? Certainly not, if one can endure a given condition and does not feel in need of redemption. The tiresome feeling of needing redemption can finally become too much for one. Then one seeks to rid oneself of it and thus enters into the work of redemption.

It appears to me that we benefit in particular from removing every sense of beauty from the thought of redemption, and even need to do so, or else we will deceive ourselves again because we like the word and because a beautiful shimmer spreads out over the thing through the great word. But one can at least doubt whether the work of redemption is in itself a beautiful thing. The Romans did not find the hanged Jew exactly tasteful, and the gloomy excessive enthusiasm for catacombs around which cheap, barbaric symbols gathered probably lacked a pleasant shimmer in their eyes, given that their perverse curiosity for everything barbaric and subterranean had already been aroused.

I think it would be most correct and most decent to say that one blunders into the work of redemption unintentionally, so to speak, if one wants to avoid what appears to be the unbearable evil of an insurmountable feeling of needing redemption. This step into the work of redemption is neither beautiful nor pleasant nor does it divulge an inviting appearance. And the thing itself is so difficult

30. In *Thus Spoke Zarathustra*, Nietzsche wrote: "You crowd together with your neighbours and have beautiful words for it. But I tell you: Your love of your neighbour is your bad love of yourself. You flee away from yourselves and would like to make a virtue of it: but I see through your 'selflessness'" ("Of love of one's neighbour," p. 86; as underlined by Jung in his copy).

and full of torment that one should count oneself as one of the sick and not as one of the overhealthy who seek to impart their abundance to others.

Consequently we should also not use the other for our own supposed redemption. The other is no stepping stone for our feet. It is far better that we remain with ourselves. The need for redemption rather expresses itself through an increased need for love with which we think we can make the other happy. But meanwhile we are brimming with longing and desire to alter our own condition. And we love others to this end. If we had already achieved our purpose, the other would leave us cold. But it is true that we also need the other for our own redemption. Perhaps he will lend us his help voluntarily, since we are in a state of sickness and helplessness. Our love for him is, and should not be, selfless. That would be a lie. For its goal is our own redemption. Selfless love is true only as long as the demand of the self can be pushed to one side. But someday comes the turn of the self. Who would want to lend himself to such a self for love? Certainly only one who does not yet know what excess of bitterness, injustice, and poison the self of a man harbors who has forgotten his self and made a virtue of it.

In terms of the self, selfless love is a veritable sin.

[31]We must presumably often go to ourselves to re-establish the connection with the self, since it is torn apart all too often, not only by our vices but also by our virtues. For vices as well as virtues always want to live outside. But through constant outer life we forget the self and through this we also become secretly selfish in our best endeavors.[32] What we neglect in ourselves blends itself secretly into our actions toward others.

31. September 18, 1915.

32. In 1941, Jung noted: "The integration or humanization of the self, as has already been indicated, is initiated from the conscious side by making ourselves conscious of our egotistical aims, that means we give an account of our motives and try to form as objective a picture as possible of our own being" ("Transformation symbolism in the mass," CW 11, §400). This corresponds to the process depicted here in the opening section of *Scrutinies*.

Through uniting with the self we reach the God.[33]

I must say this, not with reference to the opinions of the ancients or this or that authority, but because I have experienced it. It has happened thus in me. And it certainly happened in a way that I neither expected nor wished for. The experience of the God in this form was unexpected and unwanted. I wish I could say it was a deception and only too willingly would I disown this experience. But I cannot deny that it has seized me beyond all measure and steadily goes on working in me. So if it is a deception, then deception is my God. Moreover, the God is in the deception. And if this were already the greatest bitterness that could happen to me, I would have to confess to this experience and recognize the God in it. No insight or objection is so strong that it could surpass the strength of this experience. And even if the God had revealed himself in a meaningless abomination, I could only avow that I have experienced the God in it. I even know that it is not too difficult to cite a theory that would sufficiently explain my experience and join it to the already known. I could furnish this theory myself and be satisfied in intellectual terms, and yet this theory would be unable to remove even the smallest part of the knowledge that I have experienced the God. I recognize the God by the unshakeableness of the experience. I cannot help but recognize him by the experience. I do not want to believe it, I do not need to believe it, nor could I believe it. How can one believe such? My mind would need to be totally confused to believe such things. Given their nature, they are most improbable. Not only improbable but also impossible for our understanding. Only a sick brain could produce such deceptions. I am like those sick persons who have been overcome by delusion and sensory deception. But I must say that the God makes us sick. I experience the God in sickness. A living God afflicts our reason like a sickness.

---

33. *Black Book* 5 continues: "which unites Heaven and Hell in itself" (p. 92). Cf. Jung, "Transformation symbolism in the mass": "The self then functions as a unio oppositorum and thus constitutes the most immediate experience of the divine which is at all psychologically comprehensible" (1941, CW 11, §396).

He fills the soul with intoxication. He fills us with reeling chaos. How many will the God break?

The God appears to us in a certain state of the soul. Therefore we reach the God through the self.[34] [35] Not the self is God, although we reach the God through the self. The God is behind the self, above the self, the self itself, when he appears. But he appears as our sickness, from which we must heal ourselves.[36] We must heal ourselves from the God, since he is also our heaviest wound.

For in the first instance the God's power resides entirely in the self, since the self is completely in the God, because we were not with the self. We must draw the self to our side. Therefore we must wrestle with the God for the self. Since the God is an unfathomable powerful movement that sweeps away the self into the boundless, into dissolution.

Hence when the God appears to us we are at first powerless, captivated, divided, sick, poisoned with the strongest poison, but drunk with the highest health.

---

34. In 1921, Jung wrote concerning the self: "But inasmuch as the I is only the centre of my field of consciousness, it is not identical with the totality of my psyche, being merely one complex among other complexes. I therefore distinguish between the *I* and the *self*, since the I is only the subject of my consciousness, while the self is the subject of my total psyche, which also includes the unconscious" (*Psychological Types*, CW 6, §706). In 1928, Jung described the process of individuation as "self-becoming" and "self-realization" (*The Relations between the I and the Unconscious*, CW 7, §266). Jung defined the self as the archetype of order, and noted that representations of the self were indistinguishable from God-images (ch. 4, "The self," *Aion: Contributions to the Symbolism of the Self*, CW 9, 2). In 1944 he noted that he chose the term because this concept was "on the one hand definite enough to convey the sum of human wholeness and on the other hand indefinite enough to express the indescribable and indeterminate nature of this wholeness . . . in scientific usage the 'self' refers neither to Christ nor to the Buddha but to the totality of the figures that are its equivalent, and each of these figures is *a symbol of the self*" (*Psychology and Alchemy*, CW 12, §20).
35. The following section is reworked from *Black Book* 5 in a manner that is hard to separate the layers.
36. In 1929, Jung wrote: "The Gods have become diseases; Zeus no longer rules Olympus but rather the solar plexus and produces curious specimens for the doctor's consulting room" ("Commentary on 'The Secret of the Golden Flower,'" CW 13, §54).

Yet we cannot remain in this state, since all the powers of our body are consumed like fat in the flames. Hence we must strive to free the self from the God, so that we can live.[37]

[38]It is certainly possible and even quite easy for our reason to deny the God and to speak only of sickness. Thus we accept the sick part and can also heal it. But it will be a healing with loss. We lose a part of life. We go on living, but as ones lamed by the God. Where the fire blazed dead ashes lie.

I believe that we have the choice: I preferred the living wonders of the God. I daily weigh up my whole life and I continue to regard the fiery brilliance of the God as a higher and fuller life than the ashes of rationality. The ashes are suicide to me. I could perhaps put out the fire but I cannot deny to myself the experience of the God. Nor can I cut myself off from this experience. I also do not want to, since I want to live. My life wants itself whole.

Therefore I must serve my self. I must win it in this way. But I must win it so that my life will become whole. For it seems to me to be sinful to deform life where there is yet the possibility to live it fully. The service of the self is therefore divine service and the service of mankind. If I carry myself I relieve mankind of myself and heal my self from the God.

I must free my self from the God,[39] since the God I experienced is more than love; he is also hate, he is more than beauty, he is also the abomination, he is more than wisdom, he is also meaningless-

---

37. *Black Book* 5 continues: "The God has the power, not the self. Powerlessness should thus not be deplored, but it is the condition that should abide. / The God acts from within himself. This should be left to him. What we do to the self, we do to the God. / If we twist the self, we also twist the God. It is divine service to serve oneself. We thus relieve humanity of ourselves. May one man carry another's burden, has become an immorality. May each carry his own load; that is the least that one can demand anyone to do. We can at best show another how to carry his own load. / To give all one's goods to the poor means to educate them to become idle. / Pity should not carry another's load, but it should be a strict educator instead. Solitude with ourselves has no end. It has only just begun" (pp. 92–93).
38. The next four paragraphs do not occur in the *Black Books*.
39. In Jung's copy of Eckhart's *Schriften und Predigten*, the phrase "that the soul would also have to lose God!" is underlined, and there is a slip of paper on which is written: "Soul must lose God" (Meister Eckhart, *Schriften und Predigten. Aus dem Mittelhochdeutschen übersetzt und herausgegeben von Herman Büttner*, 2 vols [Eugen Diederichs, 1912], p. 222).

ness, he is more than power, he is also powerlessness, he is more than omnipresence, he is also my creature.

In the following night, I heard the voice of ΦΙΛΗΜΩΝ again and he said:[40]

"Draw nearer, enter into the grave of the God. The place of your work should be in the vault. The God should not live in you, but you should live in the God."

[41]These words disturbed me since I had thought before precisely to free myself from the God. But ΦΙΛΗΜΩΝ advised me to enter even deeper into the God.

Since the God has ascended to the upper realms, ΦΙΛΗΜΩΝ also has become different. He first appeared to me as a magician who lived in a distant land, but then I felt his nearness and, since the God has ascended, I knew that ΦΙΛΗΜΩΝ had intoxicated me and given me a language that was foreign to me and of a different sensitivity. All of this faded when the God arose and only ΦΙΛΗΜΩΝ kept that language. But I felt that he went on other ways than I did. Probably the most part of what I have written in the earlier part of this book was given to me by ΦΙΛΗΜΩΝ.[42] Consequently I was as if intoxicated. But now I noticed that ΦΙΛΗΜΩΝ assumed a form distinct from me.

{4} [43]Several weeks later, three shades approached me. I noticed from their chilly breath that they were dead. The first figure was that of a woman. She drew near and made a soft whirring sound, the whirring of the wings of the sun beetle. Then I recognized her. When she was still alive, she recovered the mysteries of the Egyptians for me, the red sun disk and the song of the golden wings. She remained shadowy and I could hardly understand her words. She said:

40. In *Black Book* 5, the voice is not identified as Philemon's.
41. The next two paragraphs do not occur in *Black Book* 5.
42. The handwritten manuscript of *Scrutinies* continues:"~~and spoken through me~~" (p. 37).
43. December 2, 1915.

"It was night when I died—you still live in the day—there are still days, years ahead of you—what will you begin—Let me have the word—oh, that you cannot hear! How difficult—give me the word!"

I answered dismayed: "I do not know the word that you seek."

But she cried: "The symbol, the mediator, we need the symbol, we hunger for it, make light for us."

"Wherefrom? How can I? I do not know the symbol that you demand."

But she insisted: "You can do it, reach for it."

And precisely at this moment the sign was placed in my hand and I looked at it filled with boundless astonishment. Then she spoke loudly and joyfully to me:[44]

"That is it, that is HAP, the symbol that we desired, that we needed. It is terribly simple, initially stupid, naturally godlike, the God's other pole. This is precisely the pole we needed."

"Why do you need HAP?"[45] I replied.

"He is in the light, the other God is in the night."

"Oh," I answered, "what's that, beloved? The God of the spirit is in the night? Is that the son? The son of the frogs? Woe betide us, if he is the God of our day!"

But the dead one spoke full of triumph:

"He is the flesh spirit, the blood spirit, he is the extract of all bodily juices, the spirit of the sperm and the entrails, of the genitals, of the head, of the feet, of the hands, of the joints, of the bones, of the eyes and ears, of the nerves and the brain; he is the spirit of the sputum and of excretion."

---

44. Instead of this paragraph, *Black Book* 5 has: "A phallus?" (p. 95). There is no mention of HAP in *Black Book* 5. The following references may be connected to this. In *The Egyptian Heaven and Hell*, Wallis Budge notes that "The Phallus of his Pepi is Hap" (vol. 1, p. 110). He notes that Hap is a son of Horus (p. 491—Jung placed a mark in the margin by this in his copy). He also noted that "In the *Book of the Dead* these four children of Horus play very prominent parts, and the deceased endeavoured to gain their help and protection at all costs, both by offerings and prayers . . . the four children of Horus shared the protection of the deceased among them, and as far back as the Vth dynasty we find that they presided over his life in the underworld" (Ibid.; underlined as in Jung's copy) [London: Kegan Paul, Trench and Trubner, 1905]).

45. *Black Book* 5 has: "of this divine pole" (p. 95).

"Are you of the devil?" I exclaimed full of horror. "Where does my flashing godly light remain?"

But she said: "Your body remains with you, my beloved, your living body. The enlightening thought comes from the body."

"What thought are you talking about? I recognize no such thought," I said.

"It crawls around like a worm, like a serpent, soon there, soon here, a blind newt of Hell."

"Then I must be buried alive. Oh horror! Oh rottenness! Must I attach myself completely, like a leech?"

"Yes, drink blood," she said, "suck it up, get your fill from the carcass, there is juice inside, certainly disgusting, but nourishing. You should not understand, but suck!"

"Damned horror! No, three times no," I cried in outrage.

But she said: "It should not irritate you, we need this meal, the life juices of men, since we want to share in your life. Thus we can draw closer to you. We want to give you tidings of what you need to know."

"That is horribly absurd! What are you talking about?"

[46]But she looked at me as she had done on the day I had last seen her among the living, and on which she showed me, unaware of its meaning, something of the mystery of what the Egyptians had left behind. And she said to me:

"Do it for me, for us. Do you recall my legacy, the red sun disk, the golden wings and the wreath of life and duration? Immortality, of this there are things to know."

"The way that leads to this knowledge is Hell."

[47]From this I sank into gloomy brooding since I suspected the heaviness and incomprehension and the immeasurable solitude of this way. And after a long struggle with all the weakness and cowardice in me, I decided to take upon myself this solitude of the holy

46. This paragraph is not in *Black Book* 5.
47. December 5, 1915.

error and the eternally valid truth.[48]And in the third night I called to my dead beloved and asked her:

"Teach me the knowledge of the worms and the crawling creatures, open to me the darkness of the spirits!"

She whispered: "Give blood, so that I may drink and gain speech. Were you lying when you said that you would leave the power to the son?"

"No, I was not lying. But I said something that I did not understand."

"You are fortunate," she said, "if you can say what you do not understand. So listen: HAP[49] is not the foundation but the summit of the church that still lies sunken. We need this church since we can live in it with you and take part in your life. You have excluded us to your own detriment."

"Tell me, is HAP for you the sign of the church in which you hope for community with the living? Speak, why do you hesitate?"

She moaned and whispered with a weak voice: "Give blood, I need blood."[50]

"So take blood from my heart," I spoke.

"I thank you," she said, "that is fullness of life. The air of the shadow world is thin since we hover on the ocean of the air like birds above the sea. Many went beyond limits, fluttering on indeterminate paths of outer space, bumping at hazard into alien worlds. But we, we who are still near and incomplete, would like to immerse ourselves in the sea of the air and return to earth, to the living. Do you not have an animal form into which I can enter?"

"What," I exclaimed horrified, "you would like to be my dog?"

"If possible, yes," she replied, "I would even like to be your dog. To me you are of unspeakable worth, all my hope, that still clings to earth. I would still like to see completed what I left too soon. Give me blood, much blood!"

48. This paragraph is not in *Black Book* 5.
49. *Black Book* 5 has: "The Phallus" (p. 100). Cf. Jung's childhood dream of the ritual phallus in the underground temple, p. 4 above.
50. See note 223, p. 367.

"So drink," I said despairingly, "drink, so that what should be will be."

She whispered with a hesitant voice: "Brimo[51]—I guess that's what you call her—the old one—which is how it begins—the one who bore the son—the powerful HAP, who grew out of her shame and strove after the wife of Heaven, who arches over earth, for Brimo, above and below, envelops the son.[52] She bears and raises him. Born from below, he fertilizes the Above, since the wife is his mother, and the mother is his wife."

"Accursed teaching! Is this still not enough of the horrifying Mysterium?" I cried full of outrage and abhorrence.

"If Heaven becomes pregnant and can no longer hold its fruit, it gives birth to a man who carries the burden of sin—that is the tree of life and of unending duration. Give me your blood! Listen! This riddle is terrible: when Brimo, the heavenly, was pregnant, she gave birth to the dragon, first the afterbirth and then the son, HAP, and the one who carried HAP. HAP is the rebellion of the Below, but the bird comes from the Above and places itself on the head of HAP. That is peace. You are a vessel. Speak, Heaven, pour out your rain. You are a shell. Empty shells do not spill, they catch. May it stream in from all the winds. Let me tell you that another evening is approaching. A day, two days, many days have come to an end. The light of day goes down and illumines the shadow, itself a shadow of the sun. Life becomes a shadow, and the shadow enlivens itself, the shadow that is greater than you. Do you think that your shadow is your son? He is small at midday, and fills the sky at midnight."[53]

But I was exhausted and desperate and could hear no more, and so I said to the dead one:

---

51. In 1912, Jung discussed the Hecate mysteries that flourished in Rome at the end of the fourth century. Hecate, the Goddess of magic and spells, guarded the underworld, and was seen as the sender of madness. She was identified with Brimo, a Goddess of death (*Transformations and Symbols of the Libido*, CW B, §586ff).

52. In *Transformations and Symbols of the Libido* (1912), Jung referred to Nut, the Egyptian Sky Goddess, who arched over the earth, daily giving birth to the Sun God (CW B, §364).

53. This paragraph is reworked from *Black Book* 5.

[54]"So you introduce the terrible son who lived beneath me, under the trees on the water? Is he the spirit that the heavens pour out, or is he the soulless worm that the earth bore? Oh Heaven—Oh most sinister womb! Do you want to suck the life out of me for the sake of the shadow? Should humanity thus completely go to waste for divinity?[55] Should I live with shadows, instead of with the living? Should all the longing for the living belong to you, the dead? Did you not have your time to live? Did you not use it? Should a living person give his life for your sake, you who did not live the eternal? Speak, you mute shadows, who stand at my door and demand my blood!"

The shadow of the dead one raised its voice and said: "You see—or do you still not see, what the living do with your life. They fritter it away. But with me you live yourself, since I belong to you. I belong to your invisible following and community. Do you believe that the living see you? They see only your shadow, not you—you servant, you bearer, you vessel—"

"How you hold forth! Am I at your mercy? Should I no longer see the light of day? Should I become a shadow with a living body? You are formless and beyond grasp, and you emanate the coldness of the grave, a breath of emptiness. To let myself be buried alive—what are you thinking of? Too soon, it seems to me, I must die first. Do you have the honey that pleases my heart and the fire that warms my hands? What are you, you mournful shadows? You specters of children! What do you want with my blood? Truly, you are even worse than men. Men give little, yet what do you give? Do you make the living? The warm beauty? Or joy perhaps? Or should all this go to your gloomy Hell? What do you offer in return? Mysteries? Will the living live from these? I regard your mysteries as tricks if the living cannot live from them."

54. December 7, 1915.
55. December 9, 1915.

But she interrupted me and cried: "Impetuous one, stop, you take my breath away. We are shadows; become a shadow and you will grasp what we give."

"I do not want to die to descend into your darkness."

"But," she said, "you need not die. You must only let yourself be buried."

"In the hope of resurrection? No joking now!"

But she spoke calmly: "You suspect what will happen. Triple walls before you and invisibility—to Hell with your longing and feeling! At least you do not love us, so we will cost you less dearly than the men who roll in your love and patience and have you make a fool of yourself."

"My dead one, I think you are speaking my language."

She replied to me scornfully: "Men love—and you! What an error! All this means is that you want to run away from yourself. What do you do to men? You tempt and coax them into megalomania, to which you fall victim."

"But it grieves me, pains me, howls at me; I feel a great longing, everything soft complains, and my heart yearns."

But she was unsparing. "Your heart belongs to us," she said. "What do you want with men? Self-defense against men—so that you walk on your own two feet, not on human crutches. Men need the undemanding, but they are always wanting love to be able to run away from themselves. This ought to stop. Why do fools go out and preach the gospel to the negroes, and then ridicule it in their own country? Why do these hypocritical preachers speak of love, divine and human love, and use the same gospel to justify the right to wage war and commit murderous injustice? Above all, what do they teach others when they themselves stand up to their necks in the black mud of deception and self-deceit? Have they cleaned their own house, have they recognized and driven out their own devil? Because they do none of this, they preach love to be able to run away from themselves, and to do to others what they should do to themselves. But this greatly prized love, given to one's own self, burns like fire. These hypocrites and liars have noticed this—as you have—and prefer to love others. Is that love? It is false hypocrisy.[56] It always begins in yourself and in all things and above all with love. Do you believe that one who wounds himself unsparingly does the other a good deed with his love? No, of course you don't believe it. You even know that he only teaches the other how one must wound oneself, so that he can compel others to express sympathy. Therefore you should be a shadow since this is what men need. How can they get away from the hypocrisy and foolishness of your love if you yourself cannot? For everything begins with yourself. But your horse still cannot refrain from whinnying. Even worse, your virtue is a wagging dog, a growling dog, a licking dog, a barking dog—and you call that human love! But love is: to bear and endure oneself. It begins with this. It is truly about you; you are not yet tempered; other fires must yet come over you until you have accepted your solitude and learned to love.

"What do you ask about love? What is love? To live, above all, that is more than love. Is war love? You are bound to see what human love is still good enough for—a means like other means. Therefore, above all, solitude, until every softness toward yourself has been burnt out of you. You should learn to freeze."[57]

"I see only graves before me," I answered, "what cursed will is above me?"

"The will of the God, that is stronger than you, you slave, you vessel. You have fallen into the hands of the greater. He knows no pity. Your Christian shrouds have fallen, the veils that blinded your

56. Jung was critical of Christian missionaries. See "The problems of the soul of modern men" (1931), CW 10, §185.

57. Black Book 5 continues: [The dead one:] "after the devil has preceded you. Now is not the time for love, but for deeds." [I:] "Why do you mention deeds? Which deeds?" [The dead one]: "Your work." [I:] "What do you mean, my work? My science, my book?" [The dead one:] "That is not your book, that is the book. Science is what you do. Do it, without hesitation. There is no way back, only forward. Your love belongs there. Ridiculous—your love! You must allow death to occur." [I:] "Leave dead ones around me at least." [The dead one:] "Enough dead, you are surrounded." [I:] "I do not notice anything." [The dead one:] "You ought to notice them." [I]: "How? How can I?" [The dead one:] "Proceed. Everything will come toward you. Not today, but tomorrow" (pp. 116–17).

eyes. The God has become strong again. The yoke of men is lighter than the yoke of the God; therefore everyone seeks to yoke the other out of mercy. But he who does not fall into the hands of men falls into those of the God. May he be well and may woe betide him! There is no escape."

"Is that freedom?" I cried.

"The highest freedom. Only the God above you, through yourself. Comfort yourself with this and that as well as you can. The God bolts doors that you cannot open. Let your feelings whimper like puppies. The ears on high are deaf."

"But," I answered, "is there no outrage for the sake of the human?"

"Outrage? I laugh at your outrage. The God knows only power and creation. He commands and you act. Your anxieties are laughable. There is only one road, the military road of the Godhead."

The dead one spoke these unsparing words to me.[58] As I did not want to obey anyone, I had to obey this voice. And she spoke unsparing words about the power of the God. I had to accept these words.[59] We have to greet a new light, a blood-red sun, a painful wonder. No one forces me to; only the foreign will in me commands and I cannot escape since I find no grounds to do so.

The sun, appearing to me, swam in a sea of blood and wailing; therefore I said to the dead one:

"Should it be the sacrifice of joy?"

But the dead one replied: "The sacrifice of all joy, provided that you do it yourself. Joy should neither be made nor sought; it should come, if it must come. I demand your service. You should not serve your personal devil. That leads to superfluous pain. True joy is simple: it comes and exists from itself, and is not to be sought here and there. At the risk of encountering black night, you must devote yourself to me and seek no joy. Joy can never ever be prepared, but exists of its own accord or exists not at all. All you must do is fulfill

58. The handwritten manuscript of *Scrutinies* has "Soul" (p. 49), and the dialogue partner in this section is changed from the soul to the dead one.

59. December 20, 1915.

your task, nothing else. Joy comes from fulfillment, but not from longing. I have the power. I command, you obey."

"I fear that you will destroy me."

But she answered: "I am life that destroys only the unfit. Therefore take care that you are no unapt tool. You want to rule yourself? You steer your ship onto the sand. Build your bridge, stone upon stone, but don't think of wanting to take the helm. You go astray if you want to escape my service. There is no salvation without me. Why are you dreaming and hesitating?"

"You see," I answered, "that I am blind and do not know where to begin."

"It always begins with the neighbor. Where is the church? Where is the community?"

"This is pure madness," I cried out indignantly, "why do you speak of a church? Am I a prophet? How can I claim such for myself? I am just a man who is not entitled to know any better than others."

But she replied: "I want the church, it is necessary for you and for others. Otherwise what are you going to do with those whom I force to your feet? The beautiful and natural will nestle into the terrible and dark and will show the way. The church is something natural. The holy ceremony must be dissolved and become spirit. The bridge should lead out beyond humanity,[60] inviolable, far, of the air. There is a community of spirits founded on outer signs with a solid meaning."

"Cease," I cried, "that doesn't bear thinking about, it's incomprehensible."

But she continued: "Community with the dead is what both you and the dead need. Do not commingle with any of the dead, but stand apart from them and give to each his due. The dead demand your expiatory prayers."

And when she spoke these words, she raised her voice and evoked the dead in my name:

60. See note 8, p. 120.

"You dead, I call you.

"You shades of the departed, who have cast off the torment of living, come here!

"My blood, the juice of my life, will be your meal and your drink.

"Sustain yourself from me, so that life and speech will be yours.

"Come, you dark and restless ones, I will refresh you with my blood, the blood of a living one so that you will gain speech and life, in me and through me.

"The God forces me to address this prayer to you so that you come to life. Too long have we left you alone.

"Let us build the bond of community so that the living and the dead image will become one and the past will live on in the present.

"Our desire pulls us to the living world and we are lost in our desire.

"Come drink the living blood, drink your fill so that we will be saved from the inextinguishable and unrelenting power of vivid longing for visible, graspable, and present being.

"Drink from our blood the desire that begets evil, as quarrel, discord, ugliness, violent deed, and famishment.

"Take, eat, this is my body, that lives for you. Take, eat, drink, this is my blood, whose desire flows for you.

"Come, celebrate a Last Supper with me for your redemption and mine.

"I need community with you so that I fall prey neither to the community of the living nor to my desire and yours, whose envy is insatiable and therefore begets evil.

"Help me, so that I do not forget that my desire is a sacrificial fire for you.

"You are my community. I live what I can live for the living. But the excess of my longing belongs to you, you shades. We need to live with you.

"Be auspicious to us and open our closed spirit so that we become blessed with the redeeming light. May it happen thus!"

When the dead one had ended this prayer, she turned to me again and said:

"Great is the need of the dead. But the God needs no sacrificial prayer. He has neither goodwill nor ill will. He is kind and fearful, though not actually so, but only seems to you thus. But the dead hear your prayers since they are still of human nature and not free of goodwill and ill will. Do you not understand? The history of humanity is older and wiser than you. Was there a time when there were no dead? Vain deception! Only recently have men begun to forget the dead and to think that they have now begun the real life, sending them into a frenzy."

{5} When the dead one had uttered all these words, she disappeared. I sank into gloominess and dull confusion. When I looked up again, I saw my soul in the upper realms, hovering irradiated by the distant brilliance that streamed from the Godhead.[61] And I called out:

"You know what has taken place. You see that it surpasses the power and understanding of a man. But I accept it for your sake and mine. To be crucified on the tree of life, Oh bitterness! Oh painful silence! If it weren't you, my soul, who touched the fiery Heaven and the eternal fullness, how could I?

"I cast myself before human animals—Oh most unmanly torment! I must let my virtues, my best ability be torn apart, because they are still thorns in the side of the human animal. Not death for the sake of the best, but befouling and rending of the most beautiful for the sake of life.

"Alas, is there nowhere a salutary deception to protect me from having the Last Supper with my carcass? The dead want to live from me.

"Why did you see me as the one to drink the cess of humanity that poured out of Christendom? Haven't you had enough of beholding the fiery fullness, my soul? Do you still want to fly entire into the glaring white light of the Godhead? Into what shades of horror are you plunging me? Is the devil's pool so deep that its mud sullies even your glowing robe?

61. January 8, 1916. This paragraph does not occur in *Black Book* 5.

"Where do you get the right to do me such a foul deed? Let the beaker of disgusting filth pass from me.[62] But if this be not your will, then climb past fiery Heaven and lodge your charges and topple the throne of God, the dreadful, proclaim the right of men also before the Gods and take revenge on them for the infamous deed of humanity, since only Gods are able to spur on the human worm[63] to acts of colossal atrocity. Let my fate suffice and let men manage human destiny.

"Oh my mother humanity, thrust the terrible worm of God, the strangler of men, from you. Do not venerate him for the sake of his terrible poison—a drop suffices—and what is a drop to him—who at the same time is all emptiness and all fullness?"

As I proclaimed these words, I noticed that ΦΙΛΗΜΩΝ stood behind me and had given them to me. He came alongside me invisibly, and I felt the presence of the good and the beautiful. And he spoke to me with a soft deep voice:

[64]"Remove, Oh man, the divine, too, from your soul, as far as you can manage. What a devilish farce she carries on with you, as long as she still arrogates divine power over you! She's an unruly child and a bloodthirsty daimon at the same time, a tormentor of humans without equal, precisely because she has divinity. Why? Where from? Because you venerate her. The dead too want the same thing. Why don't they stay quiet? Because they have not crossed over to the other side. Why do they want sacrifice? So they can live. But why do they still want to live with men? Because they want to rule. They have not come to an end with their craving for power, since they died still lusting for power. A child, an old man, an evil woman, a spirit of the dead, and a devil are beings who need to be humored. Fear the soul, despise her, love her, just like the Gods. May they be far from us! But above all never lose them! Because when lost

62. In Gethsamane, Christ said: "O my Father, if it be possible, let this cup pass from me: nevertheless not as I will, but as thou wilt" (Matthew 26:39).

63. Cf. Job 25:6: "How much less man, that is a worm? and the son of man, which is a worm?"

64. January 10, 1916.

they are as malicious as the serpent, as bloodthirsty as the tiger that pounces on the unsuspecting from behind. A man who goes astray becomes an animal, a lost soul becomes a devil. Cling to the soul with love, fear, contempt, and hate, and don't let her out of your sight. She is a hellish-divine treasure to be kept behind walls of iron and in the deepest vault. She always wants to get out and scatter glittering beauty. Beware, because you have already been betrayed! You'll never find a more disloyal, more cunning and heinous woman than your soul. How should I praise the miracle of her beauty and perfection? Does she not stand in the brilliance of immortal youth? Is her love not intoxicating wine and her wisdom the primordial cleverness of serpents?

"Shield men from her, and her from men. Listen to what she wails and sings in prison but don't let her escape, as she will immediately turn whore. As her husband you are blessed through her, and therefore cursed. She belongs to the daimonic race of the Tom Thumbs and giants, and is only distantly related to humankind. If you seek to grasp her in human terms you will be beside yourself. The excess of your rage, your doubt, and your love belong to her, but only the excess. If you give her this excess, humanity will be saved from the nightmare. For if you do not see your soul, you see her in fellow men and this will drive you mad, since this devilish mystery and hellish spook can hardly be seen through.

"Look at man, the weak one in his wretchedness and torment, whom the Gods have singled out as their quarry—tear to pieces the bloody veil that the lost soul has woven around man, the cruel nets woven by the death-bringing, and take hold of the divine whore who still cannot recover from her fall from grace and craves filth and power in raving blindness. Lock her up like a lecherous bitch who would like to mingle her blood with every dirty cur. Capture her, may enough at last be enough. Let her for once taste your torment so that she will get to feel man and his hammer, which he has wrested from the Gods.[65]

65. In the *Poetic Edda*, the giant Thrym stole the hammer of the God Thor.

"May man rule in the human world. May his laws be valid. But treat the souls, daimons, and Gods in their way, offering what is demanded. But burden no man, demand and expect nothing from him, with what your devil-souls and God-souls lead you to believe, but endure and remain silent and do piously what befits your kind. You should act not on the other but on yourself, unless the other asks for your help or opinion. Do you understand what the other does? Never—how should you? Does the other understand what you do? Whence do you take the right to think about the other and act on him? You have neglected yourself, your garden is full of weeds, and you want to teach your neighbor about order and provide evidence for his shortcomings.

"Why should you keep silent about the others? Because there would be plenty to discuss concerning your own daimons. But if you act on and think about the other without him soliciting your opinion or advice, you do so because you cannot distinguish yourself from your soul. Therefore you fall victim to her presumption and help her into whoring. Or do you believe that you must lend your human power to the soul or the Gods, or even that it will be useful and pious work if you want to bring the Gods to bear on others? Blinded one, that is Christian presumptuousness. The Gods don't need your help, you laughable idolater, who seem to yourself like a God and want to form, improve, rebuke, educate, and create men. Are you perfect yourself?—therefore remain silent, mind your business, and behold your inadequacy every day. You are most in need of your own help; you should keep your opinions and good advice ready for yourself and not run to others like a whore with understanding and the desire to help. You don't need to play God. What are daimons, who don't act out of themselves? So let them go to work, but not through you, or else you yourself will become a daimon to others; leave them to themselves and don't pre-empt them with awkward love, concern, care, advice, and other presumptions. Otherwise you would be doing the work of the daimons; you yourself would become a daimon and therefore go into a frenzy. But the daimons are pleased at the raving of helpless men advising and striving to help others. So stay quiet, fulfill the cursed work of redemption on yourself, for then the daimons must torment themselves and in the same way all your fellow men, who do not distinguish themselves from their souls and let themselves be mocked by daimons. Is it cruel to leave your blinded fellow human beings to their own devices? It would be cruel if you could open their eyes. But you could open their eyes only if they solicited your opinion and help. Yet if they do not, they do not need your help. If you force your help on them nonetheless, you become their daimon and increase their blindness, since you set a bad example. Draw the coat of patience and silence over your head, sit down, and leave the daimon to accomplish his work. If he brings something about, he will work wonders. Thus will you sit under fruit-bearing trees.

"Know that the daimons would like to inflame you to embrace their work, which is not yours. And, you fool, you believe that it is you and that it is your work. Why? Because you can't distinguish yourself from your soul. But you are distinct from her, and you should not pursue whoring with other souls as if you yourself were a soul, but instead you are a powerless man who needs all his force for his own completion. Why do you look to the other? What you see in him lies neglected in yourself. You should be the guard before the prison of your soul. You are your soul's eunuch, who protects her from Gods and men, or protects the Gods and men from her. Power is given to the weak man, a poison that paralyzes even the Gods, like a poison sting bestowed upon the little bee whose force is far inferior to yours. Your soul could seize this poison and thereby endanger even the Gods. So put the soul under wraps, distinguish yourself from her, since not only your fellow men but also the Gods must live."

When ΦΙΛΗΜΩΝ had finished, I turned to my soul, who had come nearer from above during ΦΙΛΗΜΩΝ's speech, and spoke to her:

"Have you heard what ΦΙΛΗΜΩΝ has been saying? How does this tone strike you? Is his advice good?"

But she said, "Do not mock, or else you strike yourself. Do not forget to love me."

"It is difficult for me to unite hate and love," I replied.

"I understand," she said, "yet you know that it is the same. Hate and love mean the same to me. Like all women of my kind, form matters less to me than that everything belong to me or else to no one. I am also jealous of the hate you give others. I want everything, since I need everything for the great journey that I intend to begin after your disappearance. I must prepare in good time. Until then I must make timely provision and much is still lacking."

"And do you agree that I throw you into prison" I asked.

"Of course," she answered, "there I have peace and can collect myself. Your human world makes me drunk—so much human blood—I could get intoxicated on it to the point of madness. Doors of iron, walls of stone, cold darkness and the rations of penance—that is the bliss of redemption. You do not suspect my torment when the bloody intoxication seizes me, hurls me again and again into living matter from a dark fearful creative urge that formerly brought me close to the lifeless and ignited the terrible lust for procreation in me. Remove me from conceiving matter, the rutting feminine of yawning emptiness. Force me into confinement where I can find resistance and my own law. Where I can think about the journey, the rising sun the dead one spoke of, and the buzzing, melodious golden wings. Be thankful—don't you want to thank me? You are blinded. You deserve my highest thanks."

Filled with delight at these words, I cried:

"How divinely beautiful you are!" And at the same time fury seized me:

[66]"Oh bitterness! You have dragged me through sheer and utter Hell, you have tormented me nearly to death—and I long for your thanks. Yes, I am moved that you thank me. The hound's nature lies in my blood. Therefore I am bitter—for my sake, since how does it move you! You are divine and devilishly great, wherever and how-

66. January 11, 1916.

soever you are. As yet I am only your eunuch doorkeeper, no less imprisoned than you. Speak, you concubine of Heaven, you divine monster! Have I not fished you from the swamp? How do you like the black hole? Speak without blood, sing from your own force, you have gorged yourself on men."

Then my soul writhed and like a downtrodden worm turned and cried out, "Pity, have compassion."

"Compassion? Have you ever had compassion for me? You brute bestial tormentor! You've never gotten past compassionate moods. You lived on human food and drank my blood. Has it made you fat? Will you learn to revere the torment of the human animal? What would you souls and Gods want without man? Why do you long for him? Speak, whore!"

She sobbed, "My speech stops. I'm horrified at your accusation."

"Are you going to get serious? Are you going to have second thoughts? Are you going to learn modesty or perhaps even some other human virtue, you soulless soul-being? Yes, you have no soul, because you are the thing itself, you fiend. Would you like a human soul? Should I perhaps become your earthly soul so that you will have a soul? You see, I've gone to your school. I've learned how one behaves as a soul, perfectly ambiguous, mysteriously untruthful and hypocritical."

While I spoke to my soul in this way, ΦΙΛΗΜΩΝ stood silently a little distance off. But now he stepped forward, laid his hand on my shoulder, and spoke in my name:

"You are blessed, virgin soul, praised be your name. You are the chosen one among women. You are the God-bearer. Praise be to you! Honor and fame be yours in eternity.

"You live in the golden temple. The peoples come from afar and praise you.

"We, your vassals, wait on your words.

"We drink red wine, dispensing a sacrificial drink in recollection of the meal of blood that you celebrated with us.

"We prepare a black chicken for a sacrificial meal in remembrance of the man who fed you.

"We invite our friends to the sacrificial meal, carrying wreaths of ivy and roses in remembrance of the farewell you took from your saddened vassals and maids.

"Let this day be a festival celebrating joy and life—the day upon which you, blessed one, commence the return journey from the land of men where you have learned how to be a soul.

"You follow the son who ascended and passed over.

"You carry us up as your soul and set yourself before the son of God, maintaining your immortal right as an ensouled being.

"We are joyful, good things will follow you. We lend you strength. We are in the land of men and we are alive."

After ΦΙΛΗΜΩΝ had ended, my soul looked saddened and pleased, and hesitated and yet hurried to prepare herself to leave us and to ascend again, happy at the regained freedom. But I suspected something secret in her, something that she sought to hide from me. Therefore I did not let her make off, but spoke to her:[67]

"What holds you back? What are you hiding? Probably a golden vessel, a jewel that you have stolen from men? Isn't that a gem, a piece of gold, shining through your robe? What is the beautiful thing that you robbed when you drank the blood of men and ate their sacred flesh? Speak the truth, for I see the lie on your face."

"I haven't taken anything," she answered annoyed.

"You are lying, you want to cast suspicion on me, where you are lacking. Those times when you could rob men unpunished are over. Surrender everything that is his sacred inheritance and that you have rapaciously claimed. You have stolen from the vassal and the beggar. God is rich and powerful, you can steal from him. His kingdom knows no loss. Shameful liar, when will you finally stop plaguing and robbing your humanity?"

But she looked at me as innocently as a dove and said gently:

"I do not suspect you. I wish you well. I respect your right. I acknowledge your humanity. I do not take anything away from you.

67. January 13, 1916. The preceding paragraph does not occur in *Black Book* 5.

I do not withhold anything from you. You possess everything, I, nothing."

"Yet," I exclaimed, "you lie insufferably. You possess not only that marvelous thing that belongs to me, but you also have access to the Gods and eternal fullness. Therefore surrender what you have stolen, liar."

Now she was vexed and replied:

"How can you? I no longer recognize you. You are crazy, even more: you are laughable, a childish ape, who extends his paw toward everything that glitters. But I will not allow what is mine to be taken from me."

Then I cried enraged, "You're lying, you're lying; I saw the gold, I saw the sparkling light of the jewel; I know it belongs to me. You ought not take that away from me. Give it back!"

Then she broke out in defiant tears and said, "I don't want to part with it, it's too precious to me. Do you want to rob me of the last ornament?"

"Embellish yourself with the gold of the Gods, but not with the meager treasures of earthbound human beings. May you taste heavenly poverty after you have preached earthly poverty and necessity to your humankind, like a true and proper cleric full of lies, who fills his belly and purse and preaches poverty."

"You torment me awfully," she wailed, "leave me just this one thing. You men still have enough. I cannot be without this very one, this incomparable one, for whose sake even the Gods envy men."

"I will not be unjust," I replied, "But give me what belongs to me and beg for what you need from it. What is it? Speak!"

"Alas, that I can neither keep it nor conceal it! It is love, warm human love, blood, warm red blood, the holy source of life, the unification of everything separated and longed for."

"So," I said, "it is love that you claim as a natural right and property, although you still ought to beg for it. You get drunk on the blood of man and let him starve. Love belongs to me. I want to love, not you through me. You'll crawl and beg for it like a dog. You'll raise your hands and fawn like hungry hounds. I possess the key. I will be a more just administrator than you godless Gods. You will gather around the source of blood, the sweet miracle, and you will come bearing gifts so that you may receive what you need. I protect the holy source so that no God can seize it for himself. The Gods know no measure and no mercy. They get drunk on the most precious of draughts. Ambrosia and nectar[68] are the flesh and blood of men, truly a noble meal. They waste the drink in drunkenness, the goods of the poor, since they have neither God nor soul presiding over them as their judges. Presumptuousness and excessiveness, severity and callousness are your essence. Greed for the sake of greed, power for the sake of power, pleasure for the sake of pleasure, immoderation and insatiableness: this is how one recognizes you, you daimons.

"Yes, you have yet to learn, you devils and Gods, you daimons and souls, to crawl in the dust for the sake of love so that from someone somewhere you snatch a drop of the living sweetness. Learn humility and pride from men for the sake of love.

"You Gods, your first born son is man. He bore a terribly beautiful-ugly son of God who is renewal to you all. But this mystery, too, fulfills you: you bore a son of men who is my renewal, no less splendid-terrible, and his rule also will serve you."

Then ΦΙΛΗΜΩΝ approached me, raised his hand, and spoke:[69]

"Both God and man are disappointed victims of deception, blessedly blessed, powerlessly powerful. The eternally rich universe unfolds again in the earthly Heaven and the Heaven of the Gods, in the underworlds and in the worlds above. Separation once more comes to the agonizingly united and yoked. Endless multiplicity takes the place of what has been forced together, since only diversity is wealth, blood, and harvest."

A night and a day passed, and when night came again and I looked around I saw that my soul hesitated and waited. So I addressed her:[70]

68. In Greek mythology, ambrosia and nectar are the food and drink of the Gods.

69. This sentence does not occur in *Black Book* 5.

70. January 14, 1916. The preceding paragraph does not occur in *Black Book* 5.

"What, you're still here? Didn't you find the way or didn't you find the words, which belong to me? How do you honor humankind, your earthly soul? Recall what I bore and suffered for you, how I wasted myself, how I lay before you and writhed, how I gave my blood to you! I have an obligation to lay on you: learn to honor humankind, for I saw the land that is promised to man, the land where milk and honey flows.[71]

"I saw the land of the promised love.

"I saw the splendor of the sun on that land.

"I saw the green forests, the golden vineyards and the villages of man.

"I saw the towering mountains with hanging fields of eternal snow.

"I saw the fruitfulness and fortune of the earth.

"None but I saw the fortune of man.

"You, my soul, force mortal men to labor and suffer for your salvation. I demand that you do this for the earthly fortune of humankind. Pay heed! I speak in both my name and the name of mankind, since our power and glory are yours, thine is the kingdom and our promised land. So bring it about, employing your abundance! I will remain silent, yes, I will leave you be, it depends on you; you can bring about what man is denied to create. I stand waiting. Torment yourself, so that you come to find it. Where is your own salvation, if you fail in your duty to bring about that of man? Pay heed! You will be working for me, and I will remain silent."

"Now then," she said, "I want to set to work. But you must build the furnace. Throw the old, the broken, the worn out, the unused, and the ruined into the melting pot, so that it will be renewed for fresh use.

"It is the custom of the ancients, the tradition of the ancestors, observed since days of old. It is to be adapted for new use. It is practice and incubation in a smelter, a taking-back into the interior, into the hot accumulation where rust and brokenness are taken away

71. In *Exodus* 3, God appears to Moses in the burning bush and promises to lead his people out of Egypt into a land flowing with milk and honey.

through the heat of the fire. It is a holy ceremony, help me so that my work may succeed.

"Touch the earth, press your hand into matter, shape it with care. The power of matter is great. Did HAP not come from matter? Is matter not the filling of emptiness? By forming matter, I shape your salvation. If you do not doubt the power of HAP, how can you doubt the power of its mother, matter? Matter is stronger than HAP, since HAP is the son of the earth. The hardest matter is the best; you should form the most durable matter. This strengthens thought."

{6} I did as my soul advised, and formed in matter the thoughts that she gave me. She spoke often and at length to me about the wisdom that lies behind us.[72] But one night she suddenly came to me with a sense of unease and anxiety and exclaimed:[73] "What am I seeing? What does the future harbor? Blazing fire? A fire hovers in the air—it draws near—a flame—many flames—a searing miracle—how many lights burn? My beloved, it is the mercy of the eternal fire—the breath of fire descends on you!"

But I cried out in horror, "I fear something terrible and dreadful, I am deeply afraid, since the things that you announced beforehand were awful—must everything be broken, burned, and destroyed?"

"Patience," she said and stared into the distance, "fire surrounds you—an immeasurable sea of embers."

"Don't torture me—what dreadful mysteries do you possess? Speak, I implore you. Or are you lying again, damned tormenting spirit, deceiving fiend? What are your treacherous specters supposed to mean?"

72. See Appendix C, January 16, 1916. This is a preliminary sketch of the cosmology of the *Septem Sermones*. Jung's reference to forming his soul's thoughts in matter seems to refer to composition of the Systema Munditotius (see Appendix A). For a study of this, see Barry Jeromson, "*Systema Munditotius* and *Seven Sermons*: symbolic collaborators in Jung's confrontation with the dead," *Jung History* 1, 2 (2005/6), pp. 6–10, and "The sources of Systema Munditotius: mandalas, myths and a misinterpretation," *Jung History* 2, 2, 2007, pp. 20–22.

73. January 18, 1916.

But she answered calmly, "I also want your fear."

"What for? To torment me?"

But she continued, "To bring it before the ruler of this world.[74] He demands the sacrifice of your fear. He appreciates your sacrifice. He[75] has mercy upon you."

"Mercy upon me? What is that supposed to mean? I want to hide myself from him. My face shrinks from the ruler of this world, for it is branded, it bears a mark, it beheld the forbidden. Therefore I avoid the ruler of this world."

"But you should come before him," she said, "he has heard about your fear."

"You instilled this fear in me. Why did you give me away?"

"You have been summoned to serve him."

But I moaned and exclaimed: "Thrice damned fate! Why can't you leave me in seclusion? Why has he chosen me for sacrifice? Thousands would gladly throw themselves before him! Why must it be me? I cannot, I don't want to."

But the soul said, "You possess the word that should not be allowed to remain concealed."

"What is my word?" I answered. "It is the stammering of a minor; it is my poverty and my incapacity, my inability to do otherwise. And you want to drag this before the ruler of this world?"

But she looked straight into the distance and said, "I see the surface of the earth and smoke sweeps over it—a sea of fire rolls close in from the north, it is setting the towns and villages on fire, plunging over the mountains, breaking through the valleys, burning the forests—people are going mad—you go before the fire in a burning robe with singed hair, a crazy look in your eyes, a parched tongue, a hoarse and foul-sounding voice—you forge ahead, you announce what approaches, you scale the mountains, you go into every valley and stammer words of fright and proclaim the fire's agony. You bear the mark of the fire and men are horrified at you. They do not see

74. The painting *Systema munditotius* has a legend at the bottom: "Abraxas dominus mundi" (Abraxas Master of the World).

75. *Black Book* 5 has: "Abraxas" (p. 181).

the fire, they do not believe your words, but they see your mark and unknowingly suspect you to be the messenger of the burning agony. What fire? they ask, what fire? You stutter, you stammer, what do you know about a fire? I looked at the embers, I saw the blazing flames. May God save us."

"My soul," I cried in despair, "speak, explain, what should I proclaim? The fire? Which fire?"

"Look up, see the flames that blaze over your head—look up, the skies redden."

With these words my soul vanished.

But I remained anxious and confused for many days. And my soul remained silent and was not to be seen.[76] But one night a dark crowd knocked at my door, and I trembled with fear. Then my soul appeared and said in haste, "They are here and will tear open your door."

"So that the wicked herd can break into my garden? Should I be plundered and thrown out onto the street? You make me into an ape and a child's plaything. When, Oh my God, shall I be saved from this Hell of fools? But I want to hack to pieces your cursed webs, go to Hell, you fools. What do you want with me?"

But she interrupted me and said, "What are you talking about? Let the dark ones speak."

I retorted, "How can I trust you? You work for yourself, not for me. What good are you, if you can't even protect me from the devil's confusion?"

"Be quiet," she replied, "or else you'll disturb the work."

And as she spoke these words, behold, ΦΙΛΗΜΩΝ came up to me, dressed in the white robe of a priest, and lay his hand on my shoulder.[77] Then I said to the dark ones, "So speak, you dead." And immediately they cried in many voices,[78] "We have come back from

76. January 29, 1916.

77. January 30, 1916. The preceding sentence does not occur in *Black Book* 5.

78. On the significance of the *Sermones* that follow, Jung said to Aniela Jaffé that the discussions with the dead formed the prelude to what he would subsequently communicate to the world, and that their content anticipated his later books. "From that time on, the dead have become ever more distinct for me as the voices of the unanswered,

Jerusalem, where we did not find what we sought.[79] We implore you to let us in. You have what we desire. Not your blood, but your light. That is it."

Then ΦΙΛΗΜΩΝ lifted his voice and taught them, saying[80] (and this is the first sermon to the dead)[81]:

---

unresolved and unredeemed." The questions he was required to answer did not come from the world around him, but from the dead. One element that astonished him was the fact that the dead appeared to know no more than they did when they died. One would have assumed that they had attained greater knowledge since death. This explained the tendency of the dead to encroach upon life, and why in China important family events have to be reported to the ancestors. He felt that the dead were waiting for the answers of the living (*MP*, pp. 258–59; *Memories*, p. 217). See note 135 (p. 167), above, concerning Christ's preaching to the dead in Hell.

79. See above, p. 335, where the dead Anabaptists led by Ezechiel were heading to Jerusalem to pray at the holy places.
80. This sentence does not occur in *Black Book* 5. Concerning the relation of Philemon to the *Sermones*, Jung told Aniela Jaffé that he grasped Philemon in the *Sermones*. It was here that Philemon lost his autonomy. (*MP*, p. 25).
81. Jung's calligraphic and printed versions of the *Sermones* bear the subheading: "The seven instructions of the dead. Written by Basilides in Alexandria, where the East touches the West. Translated from the original Greek text into the German language." Basilides was a Christian philosopher in Alexandria in the first part of the second century. Little is known about his life, and only fragments of his teachings have survived (and none in his own hand), which present a cosmogonic myth. For the extant fragments and commentary, see Bentley Layton ed., *The Gnostic Scriptures* (New York: Doubleday, 1987, pp. 417–44). According to Charles King, Basilides was by birth an Egyptian. Before his conversion to Christianity, he "followed the doctrines of Oriental Gnosis, and endeavoured . . . to combine the tenets of the Christian religion with the Gnostic philosophy . . . For this purpose he chose expressions of his own invention, and ingenious symbols" (*The Gnostics and their Remains* [Bell and Daldy, 1864], pp. 33–34). According to Layton, the classical Gnostic myth has the following structure: "Act I. The expansion of a solitary first principle (god) into a full nonphysical (spiritual) universe. Act II. Creation of the material universe, including stars, planets, earth, and hell. Act III. Creation of Adam, Eve, and their children. Act IV. Subsequent history of the human race" (*The Gnostic Scriptures*, p. 13). Thus in its broadest outlines, Jung's *Sermones* is presented in the form analogous to a Gnostic myth. Jung discusses Basilides in *Aion* (1951). He credits the Gnostics for having found suitable symbolic expressions of the self, and notes that Basilides and Valentinus "allowed themselves to be influenced in a large measure by natural inner experience. They therefore provide, like the alchemists, a veritable mine of information concerning all those symbols arising out of the repercussions of the Christian message. At the same time, their ideas compensate the aysmmetry of God postulated by the doctrine of the *privato boni*, exactly like those well-known modern tendencies of the unconscious to produce symbols of totality for bridging the gap between consciousness and the unconscious" (CW 9, 2, §428). In 1915, he wrote a letter to a friend from his student days, Rudolf Lichtenhan, who had written a book, *Die Offenbarung im Gnosticismus* (1901). From Lichtenhan's reply dated November 11, it appears that Jung had asked for information concerning the conception of different human characters in Gnosticism, and their possible correlation with William James's distinction between tough- and tender-minded characters (*JA*). In *Memories*, Jung said: "Between 1918 and 1926 I had seriously studied the Gnostics, for they too

"Now hear: I begin with nothingness. Nothingness is the same as the fullness. In infinity full is as good as empty. Nothingness is empty and full. You might just as well say anything else about nothingness, for instance, that it is white, or black, or that it does not exist, or that it exists. That which is endless and eternal has no qualities, since it has all qualities.

"We call this nothingness or fullness the *Pleroma*.[82] Therein both thinking and being cease, since the eternal and endless possess no

had been confronted with the primal world of the unconscious. They had dealt with its contents and images, which were obviously contaminated with the world of drives" (p. 226). Jung was already reading Gnostic literature in the course of the preparatory reading for *Transformations and Symbols of the Libido*. There has been an extensive body of commentaries concerning the *Septem Sermones*, which provides some valuable discussion. However, these should be treated cautiously, as they considered the *Sermones* without the benefit of *Liber Novus* and the *Black Books*, and, not least, Philemon's commentaries, which together provide critical contextual clarification. Scholars have discussed Jung's relation to Gnosticism and the historical Basilides, other possible sources and parallels for *Sermones*, and the relation of the *Sermones* to Jung's later works. See especially Christine Maillard, *Les Septem Sermones aux Morts de Carl Gustav Jung* (Nancy: Presses Universitaires de Nancy, 1993). See also Alfred Ribi, *Die Suche nach den eigenen Wurzeln: Die Bedeutung von Gnosis, Hermetik und Alchemie für C. G. Jung und Marie-Louise von Franz und deren Einfluss auf das moderne Verständnis dieser Disziplin* (Bern: Peter Lang, 1991); Robert Segal, *The Gnostic Jung* (Princeton: Princeton University Press, 1992); Gilles Quispel, "C. G. Jung und die Gnosis," *Eranos-Jahrbuch* 37 (1968, reprinted in Segal); E M. Brenner, "Gnosticism and Psychology: Jung's Septem Sermones ad Mortuos," *Journal of Analytical Psychology* 35 (1990); Judith Hubback, "VII Sermones ad mortuos," *Journal of Analytical Psychology* 11 (1966); James Heisig, "The VII Sermones: Play and Theory," *Spring* (1972); James Olney, *The Rhizome and the Flower: The Perennial Philosophy, Yeats and Jung* (Berkeley: University of California Press, 1980); and Stephen Hoeller, *The Gnostic Jung and the Seven Sermons to the Dead* (Wheaton, IL: Quest, 1982).

82. The Pleroma, or fullness, is a term from Gnosticism. It played a central role in the Valentinian system. Hans Jonas states that "Pleroma is the standard term for the fully explicated manifold of divine characteristics, whose standard number is thirty, forming a hierarchy and together constituting the divine realm" (*The Gnostic Religion: The Message of the Alien God and the Beginnings of Christianity* [London: Routledge, 1992], p. 180). In 1929, Jung said: "The Gnostics . . . expressed it as Pleroma, a state of fullness where the pairs of opposites, yea and nay, day and night, are together, then when they 'become,' it is either day or night. In the state of 'promise' before they become, they are nonexistent, there is neither white nor black, good nor bad" (*Dream Analysis: Notes of the Seminar Given in 1928–1930*, ed. William McGuire [Bollingen Series, Princeton: Princeton University Press, 1984], p. 131). In his later writings, Jung used the term to designate a state of pre-existence and potentiality, identifying it with the Tibetan Bardo: "He must . . . accustom himself to the idea that 'time' is a relative concept and needs to be compensated by the concept of a 'simultaneous' Bardo—or pleromatic existence of all historical processes. What exists in the Pleroma as an eternal 'process' appears in time as aperiodic sequence, that is to say, it is repeated many times in an irregular pattern" (*Answer to Job*, 1952, CW 11, §629; see also §§620, 624, 675, 686, 727, 733, 748). The distinction that Jung draws between the Pleroma and the creation has some points of

qualities. No one is in it, for he would then be distinct from the Pleroma, and would possess qualities that would distinguish him as something distinct from the Pleroma.

"In the Pleroma there is nothing and everything. It is fruitless to think about the Pleroma, for this would mean self-dissolution.

"*Creation* is not in the Pleroma, but in itself. The Pleroma is the beginning and end of creation.[83] It pervades creation, just as the sunlight pervades the air. Although the Pleroma is altogether pervasive, creation has no share in it, just as a wholly transparent body becomes neither light nor dark through the light pervading it.

"We are, however, the Pleroma itself, for we are a part of the eternal and the endless. But we have no share therein, as we are infinitely removed from the Pleroma; not spatially or temporally, but *essentially*, since we are distinguished from the Pleroma in our essence as creation, which is confined within time and space.

"Yet because we are parts of the Pleroma, the Pleroma is also in us. Even in the smallest point the Pleroma is endless, eternal, and whole, since small and great are qualities that are contained in it. It is nothingness that is whole and continuous throughout. Only figuratively, therefore, do I speak of creation as part of the Pleroma. Because, actually, the Pleroma is nowhere divided, since it is nothingness. We are also the whole Pleroma, because, figuratively, the Pleroma is the smallest point in us, merely assumed, not existing, and the boundless firmament about us. But why then do we speak of the Pleroma at all, if it is everything and nothing?

---

contact with Meister Eckhart's differentiation between the Godhead and God. Jung commented on this in *Psychological Types* (1921, CW 6, §429f). The relation of Jung's Pleroma to Eckhart is discussed by Maillard, *op cit.*, pp. 118–20. In 1955/56, Jung equated the Pleroma with the alchemist Gerhardus Dorn's notion of the 'unus mundus' (one world) (*Mysterium Coniunctionis*, CW 14, §660). Jung adopted this expression to designate the transcendental postulate of the unity underlying the multiplicity of the empirical world (Ibid., §759f.).

83. In *Psychological Types* (1921), Jung described "Tao" as "the creative being, begetting as the father and bringing forth as the mother. It is the beginning and end of all beings" (CW 6, §363.) The relation of Jung's Pleroma to the Chinese Tao is discussed by Maillard, *op cit.*, p. 75. See also John Peck, *The Visio Dorothei: Desert Context, Imperial Setting, Later Alignments*, pp. 179–80.

"I speak about it in order to begin somewhere, and also to free you from the delusion that somewhere without or within there is something fixed or in some way established from the outset. Every so-called fixed and certain thing is only relative. That alone is fixed and certain that is subject to change.

"Creation, however, is subject to change; therefore it alone is fixed and determined because it has qualities: indeed, it is quality itself.

"Thus we ask: how did the creation come into being? Creatures came into being, but not creation: since creation is the very quality of the Pleroma, as much as noncreation, eternal death. Creation is ever-present, and so is death. The Pleroma has everything, differentiation and nondifferentiation.

"Differentiation[84] is creation. It is differentiated. Differentiation is its essence, and therefore it differentiates. Therefore man differentiates, since his essence is differentiation. Therefore he also differentiates the qualities of the Pleroma that do not exist. He differentiates them on account of his own essence. Therefore he must speak of those qualities of the Pleroma that do not exist.

"You say: 'what use is there in speaking about it at all?' Did you yourself not say that it is not worth thinking about the Pleroma?

"I mentioned that to free you from the delusion that we are able to think about the Pleroma. When we distinguish the qualities of the Pleroma, we are speaking from the ground of our own differentiated state and about our own differentiation, but have effectively said nothing about the Pleroma. Yet we need to speak about our own differentiation, so that we may sufficiently differentiate ourselves. Our very nature is differentiation. If we are not true to this nature we do not differentiate ourselves enough. We must therefore make distinctions between qualities.

"You ask: 'what harm is there in not differentiating oneself?' If we do not differentiate, we move beyond our essence, beyond creation, and we fall into nondifferentiation, which is the other quality

84. Lit. *Unterschiedenheit*. Cf. *Psychological Types* (1921), CW 6, §705, "Differentiation" [*Differenzierung*].

of the Pleroma. We fall into the Pleroma itself and cease to be created beings. We lapse into dissolution in nothingness. This is the death of the creature. Therefore we die to the same extent that we do not differentiate. Hence the creature's essence strives toward differentiation and struggles against primeval, perilous sameness. This is called the *principium individuationis.*[85] This principle is the essence of the creature. From this you can see why nondifferentiation and nondistinction pose a great danger to the creature.

"We must, therefore, distinguish the qualities of the Pleroma. These qualities are *pairs of opposites,* such as

"the effective and the ineffective,
the fullness and the emptiness,
the living and the dead,
the different and the same,
light and darkness,
hot and cold,
force and matter,
time and space,
good and evil,
the beautiful and the ugly,
the one and the many, etc.

---

85. The principium individuationis is a notion from the philosophy of Arthur Schopenhauer. He defined space and time as the principium individuationis, noting that he had borrowed the expression from Scholasticism. The principium individuationis was the possibility of multiplicity (*The World as Will and Representation* [1819], 2 vols., tr. E. J. Payne [New York: Dover], pp. 145–46). The term was used by Eduard von Hartmann, who saw its origin in the unconscious. It designated the "uniqueness" of each individual set against the "all-one unconscious" (*Philosophie des Unbewussten: Versuch einer Weltanschauung* [Berlin: C. Dunker], 1869, p. 519). In 1912, Jung wrote, "Diversity arises from individuation. This fact validates an essential part of Schopenhauer's and Hartmann's philosophy in profound psychological terms" (*Transformations and Symbols of the Libido,* CW B, §289). In a series of papers and presentations later in 1916, Jung developed his concept of individuation ("The structure of the unconscious," CW 7, and "Individuation and collectivity," CW 18). In 1921, Jung defined it as follows: "The concept of individuation plays no minor role in our psychology. Individuation is in general the process of the formation and particularization of individual beings; especially the development of the psychological individual, as a being distinct from generality, from collective psychology. Individuation, therefore, is a process of differentiation, having for its goal the development of the individual personality" (*Psychological Types,* CW 7, §758).

"The pairs of opposites are the qualities of the Pleroma that do not exist, because they cancel themselves out. As we are the Pleroma itself, we also have all these qualities in us. Since our nature is grounded in differentiation, we have these qualities in the name and under the sign of differentiation, which means:

"First: these qualities are differentiated and separate in us; therefore they do not cancel each other out, but are effective. Thus we are the victims of the pairs of opposites. The Pleroma is rent within us.

"Second: these qualities belong to the Pleroma, and we must possess and live them only in the name and under the sign of differentiation. We must differentiate ourselves from these qualities. They cancel each other out in the Pleroma, but not in us. Distinction from them saves us.

"When we strive for the good or the beautiful, we forget our essence, which is differentiation, and we fall subject to the spell of the qualities of the Pleroma, which are the pairs of opposites. We endeavor to attain the good and the beautiful, yet at the same time we also seize the evil and the ugly, since in the Pleroma these are one with the good and the beautiful. But if we remain true to our essence, which is differentiation, we differentiate ourselves from the good and the beautiful, and hence from the evil and ugly. And thus we do not fall under the spell of the Pleroma, namely into nothingness and dissolution.[86]

"You object: you said that difference and sameness are also qualities of the Pleroma. What is it like if we strive for distinctiveness? Are we, in so doing, not true to our own nature? And must we nonetheless fall into sameness when we strive for distinctiveness?

"You must not forget that the Pleroma has no qualities. We create these through thinking. If, therefore, you strive for distinctiveness or sameness, or any qualities whatsoever, you pursue thoughts

86. The notion of life and nature being constituted by opposites and polarities featured centrally in the *Naturphilosophie* of Schelling. The notion that psychic conflict took the form of a conflict of opposites and that healing represented their resolution featured prominently in Jung's later work; see *Psychological Types*, 1921, CW 6, ch. 5, and *Mysterium Coniunctionis*, 1955/56, CW 14.

that flow to you out of the Pleroma: thoughts, namely, concerning the non-existing qualities of the Pleroma. Inasmuch as you run after these thoughts, you fall again into the Pleroma, and attain distinctiveness and sameness at the same time. Not your thinking, but your essence, is differentiation. Therefore you must not strive for what you conceive as distinctiveness, but for *your own essence.* At bottom, therefore, there is only one striving, namely the striving for one's own essence. If you had this striving, you would not need to know anything about the Pleroma and its qualities, and yet you would attain the right goal by virtue of your own essence. Since, however, thought alienates us from our essence, I must teach you that knowledge with which you can bridle your thoughts."

[87]The dead faded away grumbling and moaning and their cries died away in the distance.

[88]But I turned to ΦΙΛΗΜΩΝ and said, "My father, you utter strange teachings. Did not the ancients teach similar things? And was it not a reprehensible heresy, removed equally from love and the truth? And why do you lay out such a teaching to this horde, which the night wind swirled up from the dark bloodfields of the West?"

"My son," ΦΙΛΗΜΩΝ replied, "these dead ended their lives too early. These were seekers and therefore still hover over their graves. Their lives were incomplete, since they knew no way beyond the one to which belief had abandoned them. But since no one teaches them, I must do so. That is what love demands, since they wanted to hear, even if they grumble. But why do I impart this teaching of the ancients? I teach in this way because their Christian faith once discarded and persecuted precisely this teaching. But they repudiated Christian belief and hence were rejected by that faith. They do not know this and therefore I must teach them, so that their life may be fulfilled and they can enter into death."

87. The following paragraphs to the end of this section do not occur in *Black Book 6*.
88. In the published version of the *Sermones*, these commentaries that follow each sermon do not appear, and nor does Philemon. The person delivering the sermons has been assumed to be Basilides. These commentaries were added in *Scrutinies*.

"But do you, Oh wise ΦΙΛΗΜΩΝ, believe what you teach?"

"My son," ΦΙΛΗΜΩΝ replied, "why do you raise this question? How could I teach what I believe? Who would give me the right to such belief? It is what I know how to say, not because I believe it, but because I know it. If I knew better, I would teach better. But it would be easy for me to believe more. Yet should I teach a belief to those who have discarded belief? And, I ask you, is it good to believe something even more, if one does not know better?"[89]

"But," I retorted, "are you certain that things really are as you say?"

To this ΦΙΛΗΜΩΝ answered, "I do not know whether it is the best that one can know. But I know nothing better and therefore I am certain these things are as I say. If they were otherwise I would say something else, since I would know them to be otherwise. But these things are as I know them, since my knowledge is precisely these things themselves."

"My father, is that your guarantee that you are not mistaken?"

"There are no mistakes in these things," ΦΙΛΗΜΩΝ replied, "there are only different levels of knowledge. These things are as you know them. Only in your world are things always other than you know them, and therefore there are only mistakes in your world."

After these words ΦΙΛΗΜΩΝ bent down and touched the earth with his hands and disappeared.

{7} That night ΦΙΛΗΜΩΝ stood beside me and the dead drew near and lined the walls and cried out,[90] "We want to know about God. Where is God? Is God dead?"[91]

---

89. In his 1959 BBC TV interview, John Freeman asked Jung, "Do you now believe in God?" Jung replied: "Now? [Pause.] Difficult to answer. I *know*. I don't need to believe. I know." William McGuire and R.F.C. Hull, eds., C. G. *Jung Speaking: Interviews and Encounters* (p. 428). Philemon's statement here seems to be the background for this much cited and debated statement. This emphasis on direct experience also accords with classical Gnosticism.

90. January 31, 1916. This sentence does not occur in *Black Book* 6.

91. For Nietzsche's discussion of the death of God, see *The Gay Science* (1882, §§108 and 125), and *Thus Spoke Zarathustra*, section 4 ("Retired from service," p. 271f). For Jung's discussion of this, see "Psychology and religion," 1938, CW 11 §142f. Jung commented: "When Nietzsche said: 'God is dead,' he expressed a truth which is valid for the greater

But ΦΙΛΗΜΩΝ rose and said (and this is the second sermon to the dead):

"God is not dead. He is as alive as ever. God is creation, for he is something definite, and therefore differentiated from the Pleroma. God is a quality of the Pleroma, and everything I have said about creation also applies to him.

"But he is distinct from creation in that he is much more indefinite and indeterminable. He is less differentiated than creation, since the ground of his essence is effective fullness. Only insofar as he is definite and differentiated is he creation, and as such he is the manifestation of the effective fullness of the Pleroma.

"Everything that we do not differentiate falls into the Pleroma and is cancelled out by its opposite. If, therefore, we do not differentiate God, effective fullness is canceled out for us.

"Moreover, God is the Pleroma itself, just as each smallest point in the created and uncreated is the Pleroma itself.

"Effective emptiness is the essence of the devil. God and devil are the first manifestations of nothingness, which we call the Pleroma. It makes no difference whether the Pleroma exists or not, since it cancels itself out completely. Not so creation. Insofar as God and the devil are created beings, they do not cancel each other out, but stand one against the other as effective opposites. We need no proof of their existence. It is enough that we have to keep speaking about them. Even if both were not, creation would forever distinguish them anew out of the Pleroma on account of their distinct essences.

"Everything that differentiation takes out of the Pleroma is a pair of opposites, therefore the devil always belongs to God.[92]

---

part of Europe" (Ibid., §145). To Nietzsche's statement, Jung noted, "However it would be more correct to say: 'He has discarded our image, and where will we find him again?'" (Ibid.) He goes on to discuss the motif of the death and disappearance of God in connection with Christ's crucifixion and resurrection.

92. Cf. "Attempt at a psychological interpretation of the dogma of the Trinity" (1940), CW 11, §284f.

"This inseparability is most intimate and, as you know from experience, as indissoluble in your life as the Pleroma itself, since both stand very close to the Pleroma in which all opposites are canceled out and united.

"Fullness and emptiness, generation and destruction, are what distinguish God and the devil. *Effectiveness* is common to both. Effectiveness joins them. Effectiveness, therefore, stands above both, and is a God above God, since it unites fullness and emptiness through its effectuality.

"This is a God you knew nothing about, because mankind forgot him. We call him by his name *ABRAXAS*.[93] He is even more indefinite than God and the devil.

"To distinguish him from God, we call God *HELIOS* or sun.[94] Abraxas is effect. Nothing stands opposed to him but the ineffective; hence his effective nature unfolds itself freely. The ineffective neither exists nor resists. Abraxas stands above the sun and above the devil. He is improbable probability, that which takes

93. In 1932, Jung commented on Abraxas: "the Gnostic symbol Abraxas, a made-up name meaning three hundred and sixty-five . . . the Gnostics used it as the name of their supreme deity. He was a time god. The philosophy of Bergson, *la durée créatrice*, is an expression of the same idea." Jung described him in a way that echoes his description here: "just as this archetypal world of the collective unconscious is exceedingly paradoxical, always yea and nay, that figure of Abraxas means the beginning and the end, it is life and death, therefore it is represented by a monstrous figure. It is a monster because it is the life of vegetation in the course of one year, the spring and the autumn, the summer and the winter, the yea and nay of nature. So Abraxas is really identical with the Demiurgos, the world creator. And as such he is surely identical with the Purusha, or with Shiva" (November 16, *Visions Seminar*, vol. 2, pp. 806–7). Jung added that "Abraxas is usually represented with the head of a fowl, the body of a man, and the tail of a serpent, but there is also the lion-headed symbol with a dragon's body, the head crowned with the twelve rays, alluding to the number of months" (June 7, 1933, *Visions Seminar*, vol. 2, p. 1041–42). According to St. Irenaeus, Basilides held that "the ruler of them is named Abrasaks, and that is why this (ruler) has the number 365 within it" (Layton, ed., *The Gnostic Scriptures*, p. 425). Abraxas featured in Albrecht Dieterich's work *Abraxas. Studien zur Religionsgeschichte des spätern Altertums*. Jung studied this work closely early in 1913, and his copy is annotated. Jung also had a copy of Charles King's *The Gnostics and their Remains* (London: Bell and Daldy, 1864), and there are marginal annotations next to the passage discussing the etymology of Abraxas on p. 37.

94. Helios is the Greek Sun God. Jung discussed solar mythologies in *Transformations and Symbols of the Libido* (1912, CW B, §177f) and also in his unpublished concluding talk on Opicinus de Canistris at the Eranos conference in Ascona in 1943 (*JA*).

unreal effect. If the Pleroma had an essence, Abraxas would be its manifestation.

"He is the effectual itself, not any particular effect, but effect in general.

"He takes unreal effect, because he has no definite effect.

"He is also creation, since he is distinct from the Pleroma.

"The sun has a definite effect, and so does the devil. Therefore they appear to us more effective than the indefinite Abraxas.

"He is force, duration, change."

[95]The dead now raised a great tumult, for they were Christians.

But when ΦΙΛΗΜΩΝ had ended his speech, one after another the dead also stepped back into the darkness once more and the noise of their outrage gradually died away in the distance. When all the clamor had passed, I turned to ΦΙΛΗΜΩΝ and exclaimed:

"Pity us, wisest one! You take from men the Gods to whom they could pray. You take alms from the beggar, bread from the hungry, fire from the freezing."

ΦΙΛΗΜΩΝ answered and said, "My son, these dead have had to reject the belief of the Christians and therefore they can pray to no God. So should I teach them a God in whom they can believe and to whom they can pray? That is precisely what they have rejected. Why did they reject it? They had to reject it because they could not do otherwise. And why did they have no other choice? Because the world, without these men knowing it, entered into that month of the great year where one should believe only what one knows.[96] That is difficult enough, but it is also a remedy for the long sickness that arose from the fact that one believed what one did not know. I teach them the God whom both I and they know of without being aware of him, a God in whom one does not believe and to whom one does not pray, but of whom one knows. I teach this God to the

95. The following paragraphs to the end of this section do not occur in *Black Book* 6.

96. The reference is to the Platonic months. See note 273, p. 405.

dead since they desired entry and teaching. But I do not teach him to living men since they did not desire my teaching. Why, indeed, should I teach them? Therefore, I take away from them no kindly hearer of prayers, their father in Heaven. What concern is my foolishness to the living? The dead need salvation, since they are a great waiting flock hovering over their graves, and long for the knowledge that belief and the rejection of belief have breathed their last. But whoever has fallen ill and is near death wants knowledge, and he sacrifices pardon."

"It appears," I replied, "as if you teach a terrible and dreadful God beyond measure, to whom good and evil and human suffering and joy are nothing."

"My son," said ΦΙΛΗΜΩΝ, "did you not see that these dead had a God of love and rejected him? Should I teach them a loving God? They had to reject him after already having long since rejected the evil God whom they call the devil. Therefore they must know a God to whom everything created is nothing, because he himself is the creator and everything created and the destruction of everything created. Have they not rejected a God who is a father, a lover, good and beautiful? One whom they thought to have particular qualities and a particular being? Therefore I must teach a God to whom nothing can be attributed, who has all qualities and therefore none, because only I and they can know such a God."

"But how, Oh my father, can men unite in such a God? Does the knowledge of such a God not amount to destroying human bonds and every society based on the good and the beautiful?"

ΦΙΛΗΜΩΝ answered: "These dead rejected the God of love, of the good and the beautiful; they had to reject him and so they rejected unity and community in love, in the good and the beautiful. And thus they killed one another and dissolved the community of men. Should I teach them the God who united them in love and whom they rejected? Therefore I teach them the God who dissolves unity, who blasts everything human, who powerfully creates and mightily destroys. Those whom love does not unite, fear compels."

And as ΦΙΛΗΜΩΝ spoke these words, he bent down swiftly to the ground, touched it with his hand, and disappeared.

{8} The following night,[97] the dead approached like fog from a swamp and exclaimed, "Tell us more about the highest God."

And ΦΙΛΗΜΩΝ stepped forward and began to speak (and this is the third sermon to the dead)[98]:

"Abraxas is the God who is difficult to grasp. His power is greatest, because man does not see it. From the sun he draws the *summum bonum*;[99] from the devil the *infinum malum*; but from Abraxas *LIFE*, altogether indefinite, the mother of good and evil.[100]

"Life seems to be smaller and weaker than the *summum bonum*; therefore it is also hard to conceive that Abraxas's power transcends even the sun's, which is the radiant source of all vital force.

"Abraxas is the sun, and at the same time the eternally sucking gorge of emptiness, of the diminisher and dismemberer, of the devil.

97. February 1, 1916.
98. This sentence does not occur in *Black Book* 6.
99. Aristotle defined happiness as the supreme good (Summum Bonum). In his *Summa Theologica*, Thomas Aquinas identified this with God. Jung saw the doctrine of the Summum Bonum as being the source of the concept of the *privatio boni*, which in his view had led to the denial of the reality of evil. See *Aion*, 1951, CW 9, 2, §§80 and 94. Hence it is counterbalanced here with the "Infinum Malum."
100. In *Black Book* 6 (see Appendix C), Jung notes that Abraxas is the God of the frogs and that "The God of the frogs or toads, the brainless one, is the union of the Christian God with Satan" (see below, p. 579). In his later writings, Jung argued that the Christian God image was one-sided, in that it left out the factor of evil. Through studying the historical transformations of God-images, he attempted to correct this (especially, *Aion* and *Answer to Job*). In his note on how *Answer to Job* came to be written he wrote that in *Aion* he had "criticized the idea of the *privatio boni* as not agreeing with the psychological findings. Psychological experience shows us that whatever we call 'good' is balanced by an equally substantial 'bad' or 'evil.' If 'evil' is non-existent, then whatever there is must needs be 'good.' Dogmatically, neither 'good' nor 'evil' can be derived from Man, since the 'Evil One' existed before Man as one of the 'Sons of God.' The idea of the privatio boni began to play a role in the Church only after Mani. Before this heresy, Clement of Rome taught that God rules the world with a right and a left hand, the right being Christ, the left being Satan. Clement's view is clearly monotheistic, as it unites the opposites in one God. Later Christianity, however, is dualistic, inasmuch as it splits off one half of the opposites, personified in Satan . . . If Christianity claims to be a *monotheism*, it becomes unavoidable to assume the opposites as being contained in God" (1956, CW 11, pp. 357–58).

The power of Abraxas is twofold; but you do not see it, because in your eyes the warring opposites of this power are canceled out.

"What the Sun God speaks is life, what the devil speaks is death.

"But Abraxas speaks that hallowed and accursed word that is at once life and death.

"Abraxas produces truth and lying, good and evil, light and darkness, in the same word and in the same act. Therefore Abraxas is terrible.

"He is as splendid as the lion in the instant he strikes down his victim. He is as beautiful as a spring day.

"He is the great and the small Pan alike.

"He is Priapos.

"He is the monster of the underworld, a thousand-armed polyp, a coiled knot of winged serpents, frenzy.

"He is the hermaphrodite of the earliest beginning.

"He is the lord of toads and frogs, which live in the water and go up on the land, whose chorus ascends at noon and at midnight.

"He is the fullness that seeks union with emptiness.

"He is holy begetting,

"He is love and its murder,

"He is the saint and his betrayer,

"He is the brightest light of day and the darkest night of madness.

"To look upon him, is blindness.

"To recognize him is sickness.

"To worship him is death.

"To fear him is wisdom.

"Not to resist him is redemption.

"God dwells behind the sun, the devil behind the night. What God brings forth out of the light, the devil sucks into the night. But Abraxas is the world, its becoming and its passing. Upon every gift that comes from the sun god the devil lays his curse.

"Everything that you request from the Sun God produces a deed from the devil. Everything that you create with the Sun God gives effective power to the devil.

"That is terrible Abraxas.

"He is the mightiest created being and in him creation is afraid of itself.

"He is the manifest opposition of creation to the Pleroma and its nothingness.

"He is the son's horror of the mother.

"He is the mother's love for the son.

"He is the delight of the earth and the cruelty of the heavens.

"At his sight man's face congeals.

"Before him there is no question and no reply.

"He is the life of creation.

"He is the effect of differentiation.

"He is the love of man.

"He is the speech of man.

"He is the appearance and the shadow of man.

"He is deceptive reality."[101]

[102]Now the dead howled and raged, for they were incomplete.

But when their noisy cries had faded away, I said to ΦΙΛΗΜΩΝ: "How, Oh my father, should I understand this God?"

ΦΙΛΗΜΩΝ answered and said:

"My son, why do you want to understand him? This God is to be known but not understood. If you understand him, then you can say that he is this or that and this and not that. Thus you hold him in the hollow of your hand and therefore your hand must throw him away. The God whom I know is this and that and just as much this other and that other. Therefore no one can understand this God, but it is possible to know him, and therefore I speak and teach him."

"But," I retorted, "does this God not bring despairing confusion into the minds of men?"

101. In 1942, Jung noted: "the concept of an all-encompassing God must necessarily include his opposite. The coincidence of course must not be too radical, otherwise God would cancel himself out. The principle of the coincidence of opposites must therefore be completed by its opposite in order to attain full paradoxicality and hence psychological validity" ("The spirit Mercurius," CW 13, §256).

102. The following paragraphs through the end of the section do not occur in *Black Book* 6.

To this ΦΙΛΗΜΩΝ said, "These dead rejected the order of unity and community since they rejected the belief in the father in Heaven who ruled with just measure. They had to reject him. Therefore I teach them the chaos that is without measure and utterly boundless, to which justice and injustice, leniency and severity, patience and anger, love and hate, are nothing. For how can I teach anything other than the God whom I know and whom they know, without being conscious of him?"

I replied, "Why, Oh solemn one, do you call the eternally incomprehensible, the cruel contradictoriness of nature, God?"

ΦΙΛΗΜΩΝ said, "How should I name it otherwise? If the overpowering essence of events in the universe and in the hearts of men were law, I would call it law. Yet it is also no law, but chance, irregularity, sin, error, stupidity, carelessness, folly, illegality. Therefore I cannot call it law. You know that this must be so, and at the same time you know that it did not have to be so and that at some other time it will not be so. It is overpowering and occurs as if from eternal law, and at another time a slanting wind blows a speck of dust into the works and this void is a superior strength, harder than a mountain of iron. Therefore you know that the eternal law is also no law. So I cannot call it law. But how else should it be named? I know that human language has forever named the maternal womb of the incomprehensible God. Truly, this God is and is not, since from being and nonbeing everything emerged that was, is, and will be."

But when ΦΙΛΗΜΩΝ had spoken the last word, he touched the earth with his hand and dissolved.

{9} The following night, the dead came running sooner, filling the place with their mutterings, and said:

"Speak to us about Gods and devils, accursed one."

And ΦΙΛΗΜΩΝ appeared and began to speak (and this is the fourth sermon to the dead)[103]:

103. February 3, 1916. This sentence does not occur in *Black Book* 6.

"The Sun God is the highest good, the devil the opposite. Thus you have two Gods. But there are many high and good things and many great evils. Among these are two devil Gods; one is the *Burning One*, the other the *Growing One*.

"The burning one is EROS, in the form of a flame. It shines by consuming.[104]

"The growing one is the TREE OF LIFE. It greens by heaping up growing living matter.[105]

"Eros flames up and dies. But the tree of life grows with slow and constant increase through measureless periods of time.

"Good and evil unite in the flame.

"Good and evil unite in the growth of the tree. In their divinity life and love stand opposed.

"The number of Gods and devils is as innumerable as the host of stars.

"Each star is a God, and each space that a star fills is a devil. But the empty fullness of the whole is the Pleroma.

---

104. In 1917, Jung wrote a chapter on "the sexual theory" in *The Psychology of the Unconscious Processes*, which presented a critique of the psychoanalytic understanding of the erotic. In his 1928 revision of this chapter, retitled "The Eros theory" he added: "The Erotic . . . belongs on the one hand to the original drive nature of man . . . On the other hand it is related to the highest forms of the spirit. It only thrives when spirit and drive are in right harmony . . . 'Eros is a mighty daemon,' as the wise Diotima said to Socrates . . . He is not all of nature within us, though he is at least one of its essential aspects" (CW 7, §§32–33). In the *Symposium*, Diotima teaches Socrates about the nature of Eros. She tells him that "'He is a great spirit, Socrates. Everything classed as a spirit falls between god and human.' / 'What function do they have?' I asked. / 'They interpret and carry messages from humans to gods and from gods to humans. They convey prayers and sacrifices from humans, and commands and gifts in return for sacrifices from gods. Being intermediate between the other two, they fill the gap between them, and enable the universe to form an interconnected whole. They serve as the medium for all divination, for priestly expertise in sacrifice, ritual and spells, and for all prophecy and sorcery. Gods do not make direct contact with humans; they communicate and converse with humans (whether awake or asleep) entirely through the medium of spirits'" (tr. C. Gill [London: Penguin, 1999], pp. 202e–203a. In *Memories* Jung reflected on the nature of Eros, describing it as "a *kosmogonos*, a creator and father-mother of all consciousness" (p. 387). This cosmogonic characterization of Eros needs to be distinguished from Jung's use of the term to characterize women's consciousness. See note 161, p. 177.

105. In 1954, Jung wrote an extended study of the archetype of the tree: "The philosophical tree" (CW 13).

"Abraxas is the effect of the whole, and only the ineffective opposes him.

"Four is the number of the principal Gods, as four is the number of the world's measurements.

"One is the beginning, the Sun God.

"Two is Eros, for he binds two together and spreads himself out in brightness.

"Three is the Tree of Life, for it fills space with bodies.

"Four is the devil, for he opens all that is closed. He dissolves everything formed and physical; he is the destroyer in whom everything becomes nothing.

"Happy am I who can recognize the multiplicity and diversity of the Gods. But woe unto you, who replace this incompatible multiplicity with a single God. In so doing you produce the torment of incomprehension, and mutilate the creation whose nature and aim is differentiation. How can you be true to your own nature when you try to turn the many into one? What you do unto the Gods is done likewise unto you. You all become equal and thus your nature[106] is maimed.

"Equality prevails not for the sake of God, but only for the sake of man. For the Gods are many, while men are few. The Gods are mighty and endure their manifoldness. Like the stars they abide in solitude, separated by vast distances. Therefore they dwell together and need communion, so that they may bear their separateness.[107] For redemption's sake I teach you the reprehensible, for whose sake I was rejected.

"The multiplicity of the Gods corresponds to the multiplicity of men.

"Numberless Gods await the human state. Numberless Gods have been men. Man shares in the nature of the Gods. He comes from the Gods and goes unto the God.

106. *Black Book* 6 continues: "The dead: 'You are a pagan, a polytheist!'" (p. 30).
107. February 5, 1916.

"Thus, just as it is no use to reflect upon the Pleroma, it is not worthwhile to worship the multiplicity of the Gods. Least of all does it serve to worship the first God, the effective fullness, and the *summum bonum*. By our prayer we can add nothing to it, and take nothing from it; because effective emptiness gulps down everything.[108] The bright Gods form the heavenly world. It is manifold and extends and increases infinitely. The Sun God is the supreme lord of the world.

"The dark Gods form the earthly world. It is simple and diminishes and declines infinitely. The devil is its nethermost lord, the moon spirit, satellite of the earth, smaller, colder, and more dead than the earth.

"There is no difference between the might of the heavenly and earthly Gods. The heavenly Gods magnify, the earthly Gods diminish. Both directions are immeasurable."

[109]Here the dead interrupted ΦΙΛΗΜΩΝ's speech with angry laughter and mocking shouts, and as they withdrew, their discord, mockery, and laughter faded into the distance. I turned to ΦΙΛΗΜΩΝ and said to him:

"Oh ΦΙΛΗΜΩΝ, I believe you are mistaken. It seems that you teach a raw superstition which the Fathers had successfully and gloriously overcome, that polytheism which a mind produces only when it cannot free its gaze from the force of compulsive desire chained to sensory things."

"My son," ΦΙΛΗΜΩΝ replied, "these dead have rejected the single and highest God. So how can I teach them about the one, only, and not multifarious God? They must of course believe me. But they have rejected their belief. So I teach them the God that I know, the multifarious and extended, who is both the thing and its appearance, and they also know him even if they are not conscious of him.

"These dead have given names to all beings, the beings in the air, on the earth and in the water. They have weighed and counted

108. In *Black Book* 6, the dark guest (see below, p. 537) enters here.
109. The following paragraphs to the end of the section do not occur in *Black Book* 6.

things. They have counted so and so many horses, cows, sheep, trees, segments of land, and springs; they said, this is good for this purpose, and that is good for that one. What did they do with the admirable tree? What happened to the sacred frog? Did they see his golden eye? Where is the atonement for the 7,777 cattle whose blood they spilled, whose flesh they consumed? Did they do penance for the sacred ore that they dug up from the belly of the earth? No, they named, weighed, numbered, and apportioned all things. They did whatever pleased them. And what did they do! You saw the powerful—but this is precisely how they gave power to things unknowingly. Yet the time has come when things speak. The piece of flesh says: how many men? The piece of ore says, how many men? The ship says, how many men? The coal says, how many men? The house says: how many men? And things rise and number and weigh and apportion and devour millions of men.

"Your hand grasped the earth and tore off the halo and weighed and numbered the bones of things. Is not the one and only, simpleminded God pulled down and thrown onto a heap, the massed seeming of separate things dead and living? Yes, this God taught you to weigh and number bones. But the month of this God is drawing to a close. A new month stands at the door. Therefore everything had to be as it is, and hence everything must become different.

"This is no polytheism that I have made up! But many Gods who powerfully raise their voices and tear humanity to bloody pieces. So and so many men, weighed, numbered, apportioned, hacked, and devoured. Therefore I speak of many Gods as I speak of many things, since I know them. Why do I call them Gods? For the sake of their superiority. Do you know about this superior strength? Now is the time when you can learn.

"These dead laugh at my foolishness. But would they have raised a murderous hand against their brothers if they had atoned for the ox with the velvet eyes? If they had done penance for the shiny ore?

If they had worshiped the holy trees?[110] If they had made peace with the soul of the golden-eyed frog? What say things dead and living? Who is greater, man or the Gods? Truly, this sun has become a moon and no new sun has arisen from the contractions of the last hour of the night."

And when he had finished these words, ΦΙΛΗΜΩΝ bent down to the earth, kissed it, and said, "Mother, may your son be strong." Then he stood, looked up at the heavens, and said, "How dark is your place of the new light." Then he disappeared.

{10} When the following night came, the dead approached noisily, pushing and shoving; they were scoffing and exclaimed, "Teach us, fool, about the church and holy communion."

But ΦΙΛΗΜΩΝ stepped before them, and began to speak:[111] (and this is the fifth sermon to the dead):

"The world of the Gods is made manifest in spirituality and in sexuality. The celestial ones appear in spirituality, the earthly in sexuality.[112]

"Spirituality conceives and embraces. It is womanlike and therefore we call it *MATER COELESTIS*,[113] the celestial mother. Sexuality engenders and creates. It is manlike, and therefore we call it *PHALLOS*,[114] the earthly father.[115] The sexuality of man is more

---

110. This may refer to the advent of Christianity into Germany in the eighth century CE, when sacred trees were chopped down.
111. This sentence does not occur in *Black Book* 6.
112. In the 1925 seminar, Jung said: "Sexuality and spirituality are pairs of opposites that need each other" (*Introduction to Jungian Psychology*, p. 30).
113. Goethe's *Faust* ends with a vision of the Mater Gloriosa. In his lecture, "Faust and alchemy," Jung said of this: "The Mater Coelestis should on no account be thought of as Mary or the Church. She is rather Aphrodite urania, as in St. Augustine or Pico de Mirandola, the beatissima mater" (in Irene Gerber-Münch, *Goethes Faust: Eine tiefenpsychologische Studie über den Mythos des modernen Menschen. Mit dem Vortrag von* C. G. *Jung, Faust und die Alchemie* [Küsnacht, Verlag Stiftung für Jung'sche Psychologie, 1997], p. 37).
114. *Black Book* 6 has "Phallus" (p. 41), as does the handwritten calligraphic version of the *Septem Sermones* (p. 21).
115. In *Transformations and Symbols of the Libido* (1912), Jung noted: "The phallus is the creature that moves without limbs, sees without eyes, and knows the future; and as the symbolic representative of ubiquitous creative power it claims immortality" (CW B, §209). He goes on to discuss phallic Gods.

earthly, that of woman is more spiritual. The spirituality of man is more heavenly, it moves toward the greater.

"The spirituality of woman is more earthly, it moves toward the smaller.

"Mendacious and devilish is the spirituality of man, and it moves toward the smaller.

"Mendacious and devilish is the spirituality of woman, and it moves toward the greater.

"Each shall go to its own place.

"Man and woman become devils to each other if they do not separate their spiritual ways, for the essence of creation is differentiation.

"The sexuality of man goes toward the earthly, the sexuality of woman goes toward the spiritual. Man and woman become devils to each other if they do not distinguish their sexuality.

"Man shall know the smaller, woman the greater.

"Man shall differentiate himself both from spirituality and sexuality. He shall call spirituality mother, and set her between Heaven and earth. He shall call sexuality Phallos, and set him between himself and earth. For the mother and the Phallos are superhuman daimons that reveal the world of the Gods. They affect us more than the Gods since they are closely akin to our essence.[116] If you do not differentiate yourselves from sexuality and from spirituality, and do not regard them as an essence both above and beyond you, you are delivered over to them as qualities of the Pleroma. Spirituality and sexuality are not your qualities, not things you possess and encompass. Rather, they possess and encompass you, since they are powerful daimons, manifestations of the Gods, and hence reach beyond you, existing in themselves. No man has a spirituality unto himself, or a sexuality unto himself. Instead, he stands under the law of spirituality and of sexuality. Therefore no one escapes these daimons. You shall look upon them as daimons, and as a common task and danger, a common burden that life has laid upon you. Thus

116. *Black Book* 6 continues: "The mother is the grail. / The phallus is the spear" (p. 43).

life, too, is for you a common task and danger, as are the Gods, and first and foremost terrible Abraxas.

"Man is weak, and community is therefore indispensable. If your community is not under the sign of the mother, it is under the sign of the Phallos. Absence of community is suffering and sickness. Community in everything is dismemberment and dissolution.

"Differentiation leads to singleness. Singleness is opposed to community. But because of man's weakness with regard to the Gods and daimons and their invincible law, community is necessary, not for man's sake, but because of the Gods. The Gods drive you to community. Insofar as the Gods impose community upon you, it is necessary; more is bad.

"In the community every man shall submit to others, so that the community be maintained, for you need it.

"In singleness every man shall place himself above the other, so that every man may come to himself and avoid slavery.

"Abstention shall hold good in community, extravagance in singleness.

"Community is depth, singleness is height.

"Right measure in community purifies and preserves.

"Right measure in singleness purifies and increases.

"Community gives us warmth, singleness gives us light."[117]

{11}When ΦΙΛΗΜΩΝ had finished, the dead remained silent and did not move, but looked at ΦΙΛΗΜΩΝ with expectation. But when ΦΙΛΗΜΩΝ saw that the dead remained silent and waited, he continued (and this is the sixth sermon to the dead)[118]:

"The daimon of sexuality approaches our soul as a serpent. She is half human soul and is called thought-desire.

---

117. *Black Book* 6 continues: "In community, we go to the source, which is the mother. / In singleness we go to the future, which is the engendering phallus" (p. 46). In October 1916, Jung gave two presentations to the Psychological Club concerning the relation of individuation to collective adaptation; see "Adaptation, individuation and collectivity," CW 18. This theme dominated the discussions in the club that year.

118. This paragraph is not in *Black Book* 6.

"The daimon of spirituality descends into our soul as the white bird. He is half human soul and is called desire-thought.

"The serpent is an earthly soul, half daimonic, a spirit, and akin to the spirits of the dead. Thus too, like these she swarms around in the things of earth, making us fear them or else having them arouse our craving. The serpent has a female nature, forever seeking the company of those dead who are spellbound by the earth, and who did not find a way across to singleness. The serpent is a whore. She courts the devil and evil spirits; she is a mischievous tyrant and tormentor, forever inveigling the most evil company. The white bird is a half-celestial soul of man. He abides with the mother, descending from time to time. The bird is manlike, and is effective thought. He is chaste and solitary, a messenger of the mother. He flies high above the earth. He commands singleness. He brings knowledge from the distant ones, who have departed before and attained perfection. He bears our word up to the mother. She intercedes, she warns, but she is powerless against the Gods. She is a vessel of the sun. The serpent descends and cunningly lames the phallic daimon, or else goads him on. She bears up the too-crafty thoughts of the earthly, those thoughts that creep through every hole and cleave to all things with craving. Although the serpent does not want to, she must be of use to us. She flees our grasp, thus showing us the way, which our human wits could not find."

[119]When ΦΙΛΗΜΩΝ had finished, the dead looked on with contempt and said, "Cease this talk of Gods and daimons and souls. We have known this for a long time."

But ΦΙΛΗΜΩΝ smiled and replied, "You poor souls, poor in flesh and rich in spirit, the meat was fat and the spirit thin. But how do you reach the eternal light? You mock my stupidity, which you too possess: you mock yourselves. Knowledge frees one from danger. But mockery is the other side of your belief. Is black less than white? You rejected faith and retained mockery. Are you thus saved from

119. The following paragraphs to the end of the section are not in *Black Book* 6.

faith? No, you bound yourselves to mockery and hence again to faith. And therefore you are miserable."

But the dead were outraged and cried, "We are not miserable, we are clever; our thinking and feeling is as pure as clear water. We praise our reason. We mock superstition. Do you believe that your old folly reaches us? A childish delusion has overcome you, old one, what good is it to us?"

ΦΙΛΗΜΩΝ replied: "What can do you any good? I free you from what still holds you to the shadow of life. Take this wisdom with you, add this folly to your cleverness, this unreason to your reason, and you will find yourselves. If you were men, you would then begin your life and your life's way between reason and unreason and live onward to the eternal light, whose shadow you lived in advance. But since you are dead, this knowledge frees you from life and strips you of your greed for men and it also frees your self from the shrouds that the light and the shadow lay on you, compassion with men will overcome you and from the stream you will reach solid ground, you will step forth from the eternal whirl onto the unmoving stone of rest, the circle that breaks flowing duration, and the flame will die down.

"I have fanned a glowing fire, I have given the murderer a knife, I have torn open healed-over wounds, I have quickened all movement, I have given the madman more intoxicating drink, I have made the cold colder, the heat hotter, falseness even falser, goodness even better, weakness even weaker.

"This knowledge is the axe of the sacrificer."

But the dead cried, "Your wisdom is foolishness and a curse. You want to turn the wheel back? It will tear you apart, blinded one!"

ΦΙΛΗΜΩΝ replied, "So this is what happened. The earth became green and fruitful again from the blood of the sacrifice, flowers sprouted, the waves crash into the sand, a silver cloud lies at the foot of the mountain, a bird of the soul came to men, the hoe sounds in the fields and the axe in the forests, a wind rushes through the trees and the sun shimmers in the dew of the risen morning, the planets behold the birth, out of the earth climbed the many-armed, the stones speak and the grass whispers. Man found himself, and the Gods wander through Heaven, the fullness gives birth to the golden drop, the golden seed, plumed and hovering."

The dead now fell silent and stared at ΦΙΛΗΜΩΝ and slowly crept away. But ΦΙΛΗΜΩΝ bent down to the ground and said: "It is accomplished, but not fulfilled. Fruit of the earth, sprout, rise up—and Heaven, pour out the water of life."

Then ΦΙΛΗΜΩΝ disappeared.

[120]I was probably very confused when ΦΙΛΗΜΩΝ approached me the following night, since I called to him saying, "What did you do, Oh ΦΙΛΗΜΩΝ? What fires have you kindled? What have you broken asunder? Does the wheel of creations stand still?"

But he answered and said, "Everything is running its usual course. Nothing has happened, and yet a sweet and indescribable mystery has taken place: I stepped out of the whirling circle."

"What's that?" I exclaimed. "Your words move my lips, your voice sounds from my ears, my eyes see you from within me. Truly, you are a magician! You stepped out of the whirling circle? What confusion! Are you I, am I you? Did I not feel as if the wheel of creation was standing still? And yet you say that you have stepped out of the whirling circle? I am truly bound to the wheel—I feel the rushing swaying of it—and yet the wheel of creation also stands still for me. What did you do, father, teach me!"

Then ΦΙΛΗΜΩΝ said, "I stepped onto what is solid and took it with me and saved it from the wave surge, from the cycle of births, and from the revolving wheel of endless happening. It has been stilled. The dead have received the folly of the teaching, they have been blinded by truth and see by mistake. They have recognized, felt, and regretted it; they will come again and will humbly inquire. Since what they rejected will be most valuable to them."

120. This section does not occur in *Black Book* 6.

I wanted to question ΦΙΛΗΜΩΝ, since the riddle distressed me. But he had already touched the earth and disappeared. And the darkness of the night was silent and did not answer me. And my soul stood silently, shaking her head, and did not know what to say about the mystery that ΦΙΛΗΜΩΝ had indicated and not given away.

{12} Another day passed and the seventh night fell.

And the dead came again, this time with pitiful gestures and said, "We forgot to mention one thing, that we would like you to teach us about men."

And ΦΙΛΗΜΩΝ stepped before me, and began to speak[121] (and this is the seventh sermon to the dead)[122]:

"Man is a gateway, through which you pass from the outer world of Gods, daimons, and souls into the inner world, out of the greater into the smaller world. Small and inane is man, already he is behind you, and once again you find yourselves in endless space, in the smaller or inner infinity.

"At immeasurable distance a lonely star stands in the zenith.

"This is the one God of this one man, this is his world, his Pleroma, his divinity.

"In this world, man is Abraxas, the creator and destroyer of his own world.

"This star is the God and the goal of man.

"This is his one guiding God,

"in him man goes to his rest,

"toward him goes the long journey of the soul after death, in him everything that man withdraws from the greater world shines resplendently.

"To this one God man shall pray.

"Prayer increases the light of the star,

"it throws a bridge across death,

121. February 8, 1916.This sentence does not occur in *Black Book* 6.
122. This sentence is not in *Black Book* 6.

"it prepares life for the smaller world, and assuages the hopeless desires of the greater.

"When the greater world turns cold, the star shines.

"Nothing stands between man and his one God, so long as man can turn away his eyes from the flaming spectacle of Abraxas.

"Man here, God there.

"Weakness and nothingness here, eternally creative power there.

"Here nothing but darkness and clammy cold
there total sun."[123]

[124]But when ΦΙΛΗΜΩΝ had finished, the dead remained silent. Heaviness fell from them, and they ascended like smoke above the shepherd's fire, who watches over his flock by night.

But I turned to ΦΙΛΗΜΩΝ and said, "Illustrious one, you teach that man is a gateway? A gateway through which the procession of the Gods passes? Through which the stream of life flows? Through which the entire future streams into the endlessness of the past?"

ΦΙΛΗΜΩΝ answered, saying, "These dead believed in the transformation and development of man. They were convinced of human nothingness and transitoriness. Nothing was clearer to them than this, and yet they knew that man even creates its Gods, and so they knew that the Gods were of no use. Therefore they had to learn what they did not know, that man is a gateway through which crowds the train of the Gods and the coming and passing of all

123. On February 29, 1919, Jung wrote a letter to Joan Corrie and commented on the *Sermones*, with particular reference to the last one: "The primordial creator of the world, the blind creative libido, becomes transformed in man through individuation & out of this process, which is like pregnancy, arises a divine child, a reborn God, no more (longer) dispersed into the millions of creatures, but being one & this individual, and at the same time all individuals, the same in you as in me. Dr. L[ong] has a little book: VII sermones ad mortuous. There you find the description of the Creator dispersed into his creatures, & in the last sermon you find the beginning of individuation, out of which, the divine child arises . . . The child is a new God, actually born in many individuals, but they don't know it. He is a spiritual God. A spirit in many people, yet one and the same everywhere. Keep to your time and you will experience His qualities" (Copied in Constance Long's diary, Countway Library of Medicine, pp. 21–22).

124. The following paragraphs to the end of the section do not occur in *Black Book* 6.

times. He does not do it, does not create it, does not suffer it, since he is the being, the sole being, since he is the moment of the world, the eternal moment. Whoever recognizes this stops being flame; he becomes smoke and ashes. He lasts and his transitoriness is over. He has become someone who is. You dreamed of the flame, as if it were life. But life is duration, the flame dies away. I carried that over, I saved it from the fire. That is the son of the fire flower. You saw that in me, I myself am of the eternal fire of light. But I am the one who saved it for you, the black and golden seed and its blue starlight. You eternal being—what is length and brevity? What is the moment and eternal duration? You, being, are eternal in each moment. What is time? Time is the fire that flares up, consumes, and dies down. I saved being from time, redeeming it from the fires of time and the darkness of time, from Gods and devils."

But I said to him, "Illustrious one, when will you give me the dark and golden treasure and its blue starlight?"

ΦΙΛΗΜΩΝ replied, "When you have surrendered everything that wants to burn to the holy flame."[125]

---

125. In September 1916, Jung had conversations with his soul that provided further elaboration and clarification of the cosmology of the *Sermones*. September 25: [Soul]: "How many lights do you want, three or seven? Three is the heartfelt and modest, seven the general and encompassing." [I:] "What a question! And what a decision! I must be true: I think I would like seven lights." [Soul:] "Seven, you say? I thought so. That has broad scope—cold lights." [I:] "I need cooling, fresh air. Enough of this stifling mugginess. Too much fear and not enough free breathing. Give me seven lights." [Soul:] "The first light means the Pleroma. / The second means Abraxas. / The third the sun. / The fourth the moon. / The fifth the earth. / The sixth the phallus. / The seventh the stars." [I:] "Why were there no birds, and why were the celestial mother and the sky missing?" [Soul:] "They are all enclosed in the star. As you look at the star, you look through them. They are the bridges to the star. They form the seventh light, the highest, the floating, which rises with flapping wings, released from the embrace of the tree of light with six branches and one blossom, in which the God of the star lay slumbering. / The six lights are single and form a multiplicity; the one light is one and forms a unity; it is the blossoming crown of the tree, the holy egg, the seed of the world endowed with wings so it can reach its place. The one gives rise to the many over and again, and the many entails the one" (*Black Book* 6, pp. 104–6). September 28: [Soul:] "Now let us try this: it is something of the golden bird. It is not the white bird, but the golden one. It is different. The white bird is a good daimon, but the golden one is above you and under your God. It flies ahead of you. I see it in the blue ether, flying toward the star. It is something that is part of you. And it is at once its own egg, containing you. Do you feel me. Then ask!" [I] "Tell me more. It makes me feel queasy." [Soul:] "The golden bird is no soul; it is your entire nature. People are golden birds as well; not all; some are worms and rot in the earth. But many are also golden birds." [I]:

{13} And as ΦΙΛΗΜΩΝ spoke these words, a dark form with golden eyes approached me from the shadows of the night.[126] I was startled and cried, "Are you an enemy? Who are you? Where do you come from? I have never seen you before! Speak, what do you want?"

The dark one answered, saying, "I come from afar. I come from the east and follow the shining fire that precedes me, ΦΙΛΗΜΩΝ. I am not your enemy, I am a stranger to you. My skin is dark and my eyes shine golden."

"What do you bring?" I asked fearfully.

"I bring abstinence—abstinence from human joy and suffering. Compassion leads to alienation. Pity, but no compassion—pity for the world and a will held in check toward the other.

"Pity remains misunderstood, therefore it works.

"Far from longing, know no fear.

"Far from love, love the whole."

I looked at him fearfully and said, "Why are you as dark as the earth of the fields and as black as iron? I'm afraid of you; such pain, what have you done to me?"

"Continue, I fear my revulsion. Tell me what you have grasped." [Soul:] "The golden bird sits in the tree of the six lights. The tree grows out of Abraxas's head, but Abraxas grows out of the Pleroma. Everything from which the tree grows blossoms as a light, transformed, as a womb of the flowering treetop, of the golden egg-bird. The tree of light is first a plant, which is called an individual; this grows out of Abraxas's head, his thought is one among many. The individual is a mere plant without flowers and fruits, a passageway to the tree of seven lights. The individual is a precursor of the tree of light. The lucent blossoms from him, Phanes himself, Agni, a new fire, a golden bird. This comes after the individual, namely when it has been reunited with the world, the world blossoms from it. Abraxas is the drive, individual, distinct from him, but the tree of the seven lights is the symbol of the individual united with Abraxas. This is where Phanes appears and he, the golden bird, flies ahead. / You unite yourself with Abraxas through me. / First you give me your heart, and then you live through me. I am the bridge to Abraxas. Thus the tree of light arises in you and you become the tree of light and Phanes arises from you. You have anticipated, but not understood this. At the time you had to separate from Abraxas to become individual, opposed to the drive. Now you become one with Abraxas. This happens through me. You cannot do this. Therefore you must remain with me. Unification with the physical Abraxas occurs through the human female, but that with the spiritual Abr. occurs through me; that is why you must be with me" (*Black Book* 6, pp. 114–20).

126. In *Black Book* 6, this figure enters on February 5, in the middle of the *Sermones* (p. 35f). See note 108, p. 526 above.

"You may call me death—death that rose with the sun. I come with quiet pain and long peace. I lay the cover of protection on you. In the midst of life begins death. I lay cover upon cover upon you so that your warmth will never cease."

"You bring grief and despair," I answered, "I wanted to be among men."

But he said, "You will go to men as one veiled. Your light shines at night. Your solar nature departs from you and your stellar nature begins."

"You are cruel," I sighed.

"The simple is cruel, it does not unite with the manifold."

With these words the mysterious dark one vanished. But ΦΙΛΗΜΩΝ regarded me with a serious and questioning look. "Did you take a proper look at him, my son?" he said. "You will be hearing from him. But come now, so that I can fulfill what the dark one prophesied for you."

As he spoke these words, he touched my eyes and opened my gaze and showed me the immeasurable mystery. And I looked for a long time until I could grasp it: but what did I see? I saw the night, I saw the dark earth, and above this the sky stood gleaming in the brilliance of countless stars. And I saw that the sky had the form of a woman and sevenfold was her mantle of stars and it completely covered her.

And when I had beheld it, ΦΙΛΗΜΩΝ said:

[127]"Mother, you who stand in the higher circle, nameless one, who shrouds me and him and protects me and him from the Gods: he wants to become your child.

"May you accept his birth.

"May you renew him. I separate myself from him.[128] The cold is growing and its star blazes brighter.

"He needs the bond of childhood.

127. February 17, 1916. In *Black Book* 6, this speech is spoken by Jung himself (p. 52).

128. *Black Book* 6 has here: "I need a new shadow, since I recognized dreadful Abraxas and withdrew from him" (p. 52).

"You gave birth to the godly serpent, you released it from the pangs of birth; take this man to the abode of the sun, he needs the mother."

A voice came from afar[129] and was like a falling star:

"I cannot take him as a child. He must cleanse himself first."

ΦΙΛΗΜΩΝ said,[130] "What is his impurity?"

But the voice said, "It is the commingling: he contains human suffering and joy. He shall remain secluded until abstinence is complete and he is freed from the commingling with men. Then shall he be taken as a child."

In this moment my vision ended. And ΦΙΛΗΜΩΝ went away and I was alone. And I remained apart as I had been told. But in the fourth night I saw a strange form, a man wearing a long coat and a turban; his eyes shone cleverly and kindly like a wise doctor's.[131] He approached me and said, "I speak to you of joy." But I answered, "You want to speak to me of joy? I bleed from the thousandfold wounds of men."

He replied, "I bring healing. Women taught me this art. They know how to heal sick children. Do your wounds burn you? Healing is at hand. Give ear to good counsel and do not be incensed."

I retorted, "What do you want? To tempt me? Mock me?"

"What are you thinking?" he interrupted. "I bring you the bliss of paradise, the healing fire, the love of women."[132]

"Are you thinking," I asked, "of the descent into the frog swamp?[133] The dissolution in the many, the scattering, the dismembering?"

---

129. In *Black Book* 6, this voice is identified as "mother" (p. 53).
130. In *Black Book* 6, this is spoken by Jung (p. 53).
131. February 21, 1916. *Black Book* 6 has instead: "[I:] "A Turk? Whence the journey? Do you profess Islam? What you are announcing Mohammed for?" [Visitor:] "I speak of polygamy, houris, and paradise. This is what you shall hear about." [I:] "Speak and end this torment" (p. 54).
132. The version of this dialogue in *Black Book* 6 includes the following interchange: [I:] "What about polygamy, houris, and paradise?" [Visitor]: "Many women amount to many books. Each woman is a book, each book a woman. The houri is a thought and the thought is a houri. The world of ideas is paradise and paradise is the world of ideas. Mohammed teaches that the houris admit the believer into paradise. The Teutons said as much" (p. 56). (Cf. *The Koran* 56:12–39.) In Norse mythology, the Valkyries escorted the brave who were slain in battle to Valhalla and tended them there.
133. February 24, 1916.

But as I spoke, the old man turned into ΦΙΛΗΜΩΝ,[134] and I saw that he was the magician who was tempting me. But ΦΙΛΗΜΩΝ continued:

"You have not yet experienced the dismembering. You should be blown apart and shredded and scattered to the winds. Men are preparing for the Last Supper with you."

"What then will remain of me?" I cried.

"Nothing but your shadow. You will be a river that pours forth over the lands. It seeks every valley and streams toward the depths."

I asked, full of grief, "But where will my uniqueness remain?"

"You will steal it from yourself," ΦΙΛΗΜΩΝ replied.[135] "You will hold the invisible realm in trembling hands; it lowers its roots into the gray darknesses and mysteries of the earth and sends up branches covered in leaves into the golden air.

"Animals live in its branches.

"Men camp in its shade.

"Their murmuring arises from below.

"A thousand-mile-long disappointment is the juice of the tree.

"It will stay green for a long time.

"Silence abides in its treetop.

"Silence in its deep roots."

[136]I gathered from ΦΙΛΗΜΩΝ's words that I must remain true to love to cancel out the commingling that arises through unlived love. I understood that the commingling is a bondage that takes the place of voluntary devotion. Scattering or dismembering arises, as ΦΙΛΗΜΩΝ had taught me, from voluntary devotion. It cancels out the commingling. Through voluntary devotion I removed binding ties. Therefore I had to remain true to love, and, devoted to it voluntarily, I suffer the dismembering and thus attain bonding with the great mother, that is, the stellar nature, liberation from bondage to men and things. If I am bound to men and things, I can neither go on with my life to its destination nor can I arrive at my very own

134. This statement does not occur in *Black Book* 6.
135. February 28, 1916.
136. The next two paragraphs do not occur in *Black Book* 6.

and deepest nature. Nor can death begin in me as a new life, since I can only fear death. I must therefore remain true to love since how else can I arrive at the scattering and dissolution of bondage? How else could I experience death other than through remaining true to love and willingly accepting the pain and all the suffering? As long as I do not voluntarily devote myself to the dismembering, a part of my self secretly remains with men and things and binds me to them; and thus I must, whether I want to or not, be a part of them, mixed in with them and bound to them. Only fidelity to love and voluntary devotion to love enable this binding and mixing to be dissolved and lead back to me that part of my self that secretly lay with men and things. Only thus does the light of the star grow, only thus do I arrive at my stellar nature, at my truest and innermost self, that simply and singly is.

It is difficult to remain true to love since love stands above all sins. He who wants to remain true to love must also overcome sin. Nothing occurs more readily than failing to recognize that one is committing a sin. Overcoming sin for the sake of remaining true to love is difficult, so difficult that my feet hesitated to advance.

When night fell, ΦΙΛΗΜΩΝ approached me in an earth-colored robe, holding a silver fish: "Look, my son," he said, "I was fishing and caught this fish; I bring it to you, so that you may be comforted." And as I looked at him astonished and questioningly, I saw that a shade stood in darkness at the door, bearing a robe of grandeur.[137] His face was pale and blood had flowed into the furrows of his brow. But ΦΙΛΗΜΩΝ knelt down, touched the earth, and said to the shade,[138] "My master and my brother, praised be your name. You did the greatest thing for us: out of animals you made men, you gave your life for men to enable their healing. Your spirit was with us through an endlessly long time. And men still look to you and still ask you to take pity on them and beg for the mercy of God and the forgiveness of their sins through you. You do not tire of giving to

137. I.e., Christ.
138. April 12, 1916. In *Black Book* 6, this speech is not attributed to Philemon.

men. I praise your divine patience. Are not men ungrateful? Does their craving know no limits? Do they still make demands on you? They have received so much yet still they are beggars.

"Behold, my master and my brother, they do not love me, but they long for you with greed, for they also crave their neighbor's possessions. They do not love their neighbor, but they want what is his. If they were faithful to their love, they would not be greedy. But whoever gives, attracts desire. Should they not learn love? Fidelity to love? Freely willed devotion? But they demand and desire and beg from you and have learned no lesson from your awe-inspiring life. They have imitated it, but they have not lived their own lives as you have lived yours. Your awe-inspiring life shows how everyone would have to take their own life into their own hands, faithful to their own essence and their own love. Have you not forgiven the adulteress?[139] Did you not sit with whores and tax-collectors?[140] Did you not break the command of the Sabbath?[141] You lived your own life, but men fail to do so; instead they pray to you and make demands on you and forever remind you that your work is incomplete. Yet your work would be completed if men managed to live their own lives without imitation. Men are still childish and forget gratitude, since they cannot say, Thanks be to you, our lord, for the salvation you have brought us. We have taken it unto ourselves, given it a place in our hearts, and we have learned to carry on your work in ourselves on our own. Through your help we have grown mature in continuing the work of redemption in us. Thanks to you, we have embraced your work, we grasped your redemptive teaching, we completed in ourselves what you had begun for us with bloody struggle. We are not ungrateful children who desire our parents' possessions. Thanks to you, our master, we will make the most of your talent and will not bury it in the earth and forever stretch out our hands helplessly and urge you to complete your work in us. We want to take your troubles and your work upon ourselves so that

139. Cf. John 8:1–11.
140. Cf. Matthew 21:31–32.
141. Cf. John 9:13f.

your work may be completed and so that you may lay your weary tired hands in your lap, like the worker after a long day's hard burden. Blessed is the dead one, who rests from the completion of his work.

"I wanted people to address you in this way. But they have no love for you, my master and brother. They begrudge you the price of peace. They leave your work incomplete, eternally needing your pity and your care.

"But, my master and my brother, I believe you have completed your work, since the one who has given his life, his entire truth, all his love, his entire soul, has completed his work. What one individual can do for men, you have done and accomplished and fulfilled. The time has come when each must do his own work of redemption. Mankind has grown older and a new month has begun."[142]

[143]When ΦΙΛΗΜΩΝ had finished, I looked up and saw that the place where the shade had stood was empty. I turned to ΦΙΛΗΜΩΝ and said, "My father, you spoke of men. I am a man. Forgive me!"

But ΦΙΛΗΜΩΝ dissolved into the darkness and I decided to do what was required of me. I accepted all the joy and every torment of my nature and remained true to my love, to suffer what comes to everyone in their own way. And I stood alone and was afraid.

{14} On a night when everything was silent, I heard a murmur like that of many voices and a bit more clearly I heard the voice of ΦΙΛΗΜΩΝ, and it was as if he were giving a speech. And as I listened more closely, I heard his words:

[144]"Afterward, when I had impregnated the dead body of the underworld, and when it had given birth to the serpent of the God, I went to men and saw the fullness of their affliction and their madness. I saw that they were slaying each other and that they sought the grounds for their actions. They did this because they did not have

142. The reference is to the Platonic months. See note 273, p. 405.

143. The next six paragraphs do not occur in *Black Book* 6.

144. The next two passages also occur in "Dreams" after entries for the middle of July 1917, introduced by the statement: "Fragments of the next book:" (p. 18).

anything different or better to do. But because they were accustomed to doing nothing for which they could not account, they devised reasons that compelled them to go on killing. Stop, you are out of your minds, said the sage. Stop, for Heaven's sake, and take stock of what damage you have done, said the canny one. But the fool laughed, since honors had been conferred upon him overnight. Why do men not see their stupidity? Stupidity is a daughter of the God. Therefore men cannot stop murdering, since thus they serve the serpent of the God without knowing it. It is worth giving one's life for the sake of serving the serpent of the God. Hence be reconciled! But it would be far better to live despite the God. But the serpent of the God wants human blood. This feeds it and makes it shine. Not wanting to murder and die amounts to deceiving the God. Whoever lives has become one who deceives the God. Whoever lives invents his life for himself. But the serpent wants to be deceived, out of hope for blood. The greater the number of men who stole their lives from the Gods, the greater the harvest feeding the serpent from the blood-sown field. The God grows strong through human murder. The serpent grows hot and fiery through the drenching flood. Its fat burns in the blazing flame. The flame becomes the light of men, the first ray of a renewed sun, He, the first appearing light."

I could not grasp what else ΦΙΛΗΜΩΝ said. I spent a long time pondering his words, which evidently he had spoken to the dead, and I was horrified by the atrocities that attend the rebirth of a God.

[145]And soon afterward I saw Elijah and Salome in a dream. Elijah appeared concerned and alarmed. Therefore, when in the following night that light was extinguished and every living sound fell still, I called Elijah and Salome so that they would answer my questions. Elijah came forward and said:

"I have become weak, I am poor, an excess of my power has gone to you, my son. You took too much from me. You went too far away from me. I heard strange and incomprehensible things and the peace of my depths became disturbed."

145. May 3, 1916.

I asked, "But what did you hear? What voice did you hear?"

Elijah answered, "I heard a voice full of confusion, an alarmed voice full of warning and the incomprehensible."

"What did it say," I asked, "did you hear the words?"

"Indistinctly, it was confused and confusing. The voice spoke first of a knife cutting something or perhaps harvesting, perhaps the grapes that go to the wine press. Perhaps the one wearing the red robe treads the winepress from which the blood flows.[146] Thereupon the voice spoke of gold that lies below, and that kills whoever touches it. Then it mentioned fire that burns terribly and that should flare up in our time. And then there was a malicious word, that I would rather not utter."

"A malicious word? What was it?" I asked.

He answered, "A word about the death of God. There is only one God and God cannot die."[147]

Then I replied, "I am astonished, Elijah. Do you not know what happened? Do you not know that the world has put on a new garb? That the one God has gone away, and that in turn many Gods and many daimons have come to man? Truly, I am surprised; I am extremely surprised! How could you not have known? Know you nothing of the new that has come to pass? Yet you know the future! You have foresight! Or maybe you should not know what is? Do you ultimately deny what is?"[148]

146. See above, p. 355f.

147. See above, p. 515.

148. In *Memories*, Jung stated: "The figures of the unconscious are also 'uninformed,' and need man, or contact with consciousness, in order to attain to 'knowledge.' When I began working with the unconscious, I found myself much involved with the figures of Salome and Elijah. Then they receded, but after about two years they reappeared. To my complete astonishment, they were completely unchanged; they spoke and acted as if nothing had happened in the meanwhile. In actuality the most incredible things had taken place in my life. I had, as it were, to begin from the beginning again, to tell them all about what had been going on, and explain things to them. At the time I had been greatly surprised by this situation. Only later did I understand what had happened: in the interval the two had sunk back into the unconscious and into themselves—I might equally put, into timelessness. They remained out of contact with the I and the I's changing circumstances, and therefore were 'ignorant' of what had happened in the world of consciousness" (pp. 338–39). This appears to refer to this conversation.

Salome interrupted me: "What is, gives no pleasure. Pleasure comes only from the new. Your soul would also like a new husband—ha ha!—she loves change. You are not pleasurable enough for her. In that respect she is unteachable and therefore you believe she is mad. We love only what is coming, not what is. Only the new gives us pleasure. Elijah does not think about what is, only about what is to come. Therefore he knows it."

I answered, "What does he know? He should say."

Elijah said, "I have already uttered the words: the image that I saw was crimson, fiery colored, a gleaming gold. The voice that I heard was like distant thunder, like the wind roaring in the forest, like an earthquake. It was not the voice of my God, but it was a thunderous pagan roar, a call my ancestors knew but which I have never heard. It sounded prehistoric, as if from a forest on a distant coast; it rang with all the voices of the wilderness. It was full of horror yet harmonic."

To this I replied, "My good old man, you heard correctly, as I thought you had. How wonderful! Shall I tell you about it? After all, I told you that the world has acquired a new face. A new cover was thrown over it. How odd that you don't know!

"Old Gods have become new. The one God is dead—yes, truly, he died. He disintegrated into the many, and thus the world became rich overnight. And something also happened to the individual soul—who would care to describe it! But therefore men too became rich overnight. How is it possible that you didn't know this?

"The one God became two, a multiple one, whose body consists of many Gods, and a single one, whose body is a man and yet he is brighter and stronger than the sun.

"What shall I tell you about the soul? Haven't you noticed that she has become multiple? She has become the closest, nearest, near, far, further, furthest and yet she is one, as before. First she divided herself into a serpent and a bird, then into a father and mother, and then into Elijah and Salome—How are you, my good fellow? Does it disturb you? Yes, you must be realizing that you are already very far removed from me, so that I can hardly reckon you as being part of my soul; since if you belonged to my soul, you would have to know what is happening. Therefore I must separate you and Salome from my soul and place you among the daimons. You are connected to what is primordially old and always exists, therefore you also know nothing of the being of men but simply of the past and future.

"Nevertheless it is good that you came to my call. Take part in that which is. For what is ought to be such that you can take part in it."

But Elijah sullenly replied, "I do not like this multiplicity. It is not easy to think it."

And Salome said, "The simple alone is pleasurable. One need not think about it."

I replied, "Elijah, you need not contemplate it at all. It is not to be thought; it is to be viewed. It is a painting."

And to Salome I said, "Salome, it is not true that only the simple is pleasurable; over time it is even boring. In truth the multiple captivates you."

But Salome turned to Elijah and said, "Father, it seems to me that men have outstripped us. He is right: the many is more pleasurable. The one is too simple and always the same."[149]

Elijah seemed saddened and said, "What about the one in this case? Does the one still exist if it stands next to the many?"

I answered, "That is your old and ingrained mistake, that the one excludes the many. But there are many individual things. The multiplicity of individual things is the one multiple God from whose body many Gods arise, but the uniqueness of the one thing is the other God, whose body is a man but whose spirit is as large as the world."

But Elijah shook his head and said, "That is new, my son. Is the new good? What was, is good; and what was, will be. Is that not the truth? Has there ever been anything new? And was what you call new, ever good? Everything remains the same if you give it a new name. There is nothing new, there can be nothing new; how could I then look ahead? I look at the past and therein I see the future, as

149. The rest of this dialogue does not occur in *Black Book* 6.

in a mirror. And I see that nothing new happens, everything is but mere recurrence of what has been since time immemorial.[150] What is your being? An appearance, a darting light; tomorrow it is no longer true. It is gone; it is as if it never was. Come, Salome, let us go. One is mistaken in the world of men."

But Salome looked back and whispered to me while leaving, "Being and multiplicity appeal to me, even if it is not new and not eternally true."

Thus they disappeared into the dark night and I returned to the burden signified by my existence. And I sought to do everything correctly that seemed to me to be a task and to take every way that seemed to me to be necessary for myself. But my dreams became difficult and laden with anxiety, and I did not know why. One night my soul suddenly came to me, as if worried, and said,[151] "Listen to me: I am in a great torment, the son of the dark womb besieges me. Therefore your dreams are also difficult, since you feel the torment of the depths, the pain of your soul, and the suffering of the Gods."

I answered, "Can I help? Or is it superfluous that a man elevates himself to being a mediator of the Gods? Is it presumption or should a man become a redeemer of the Gods, after men are saved through the divine mediator?"

"You speak the truth," my soul replied, "the Gods need a human mediator and rescuer. With this man paves the way to crossing over and to divinity. I gave you a frightening dream so that your face would turn to the Gods. I let their torment reach you so that you would remember the suffering Gods. You do too much for men since they are the masters of your world. You can in effect help men only through the Gods, not directly. Alleviate the burning torment of the Gods."

I asked her, "So tell me, where do I begin? I feel their torment and mine at the same time, and yet it is not mine, both real and unreal."

150. See note 261, p. 394.
151. May 31, 1916.

"That is it; and this is where separation should occur," my soul replied.

"But how? My wits fail me. You must know how."

"Your wits fail quickly," she retorted, "but the Gods need precisely your human wits."

"And I the wits of the Gods," I added; "and thus we run aground."

"No, you are too impatient; only patient comparison provides a solution, not one side taking a quick decision. It requires work."

I asked, "What do the Gods suffer from?"

"Well," my soul replied, "you have left them with torment, and since then they have suffered."

"Rightly so," I cried, "they have tormented men enough. Now they should get a taste of it."

She answered, "But what if the torment also reaches you? What have you gained then? You cannot leave all suffering to the Gods or else they will draw you into their torment. After all, they possess the power to do so. To be sure, I must confess that men too possess a wondrous power over the Gods through their wits."

I answered, "I recognize that the torment of the Gods reached me; therefore I also recognize that I must yield to the Gods. What is their desire?"

"They want obedience," she replied.

"So be it," I answered, "but I fear their desire, therefore I say: I want to do what I can. On no account will I take back onto myself all the torment that I had to leave to the Gods. Not even Christ took torment away from his followers, but rather he heaped it on. I reserve conditions for myself. The Gods should recognize this and direct their desire accordingly. There is no longer any unconditional obedience, since man has stopped being a slave to the Gods. He has dignity before the Gods. He is a limb that even the Gods cannot do without. Giving way before the Gods is no more. So let their wish be heard. Comparison shall accomplish the rest so that each will have his appropriate part."

My soul answered, "The Gods want you to do for their sake what you know you do not want to do."

"I thought so," I exclaimed, "of course that is what the Gods want. But do the Gods also do what I want? I want the fruits of my labor. What do the Gods do for me? They want their goals to be fulfilled, but what about mine?"

This infuriated my soul and she said, "You are unbelievably defiant and rebellious. Consider the fact that the Gods are strong."

"I know," I replied, "but no longer is there any unconditional obedience. When will they use their strength for me? They also want me to place mine in their service. What is their payment in kind? That they are tormented? Man suffered agony and the Gods were still not satisfied, but remained insatiable in their devising of new torments. They allowed man to become so blinded that he believed that there were no Gods, and that there was only one God who was a loving father, so that today someone who struggles with the Gods is even thought to be crazy. They have thus prepared this shame too for those who recognize them, out of boundless greed for power, since leading the blind is not easy. They will corrupt even their slaves."

"You do not want to obey the Gods?" my soul cried, astonished.

I answered, "I believe that has already gone on more than enough. Hence the Gods are insatiable, because they have received too many sacrifices: the altars of blinded humanity are streaming with blood. But dearth makes contentment, not abundance. May they learn dearth from men. Who does something for me? That is the question that I must pose. In no case will I do what the Gods would have to do. Ask the Gods what they think of my suggestion."

Then my soul divided herself. As a bird she swooped up to the higher Gods and as a serpent she crawled down to the lower Gods. Soon afterward, she returned and said, troubled, "The Gods are outraged that you do not want to be obedient."

"That bothers me very little," I replied, "I have done everything to placate the Gods. May they do their share now. Tell them. I can wait. I will let no one tell me what to do. The Gods may devise a service in return. You can go. I will call you tomorrow so that you can tell me what the Gods have decided."

As my soul departed, I saw that she was shocked and worried, since she belonged to the race of the Gods and daimons and forever sought to convert me to their kind, as my humanity would like to convince me that I belong to the clan and must serve it. When I was asleep, my soul came again and in a dream cunningly painted me as a horned devil to terrify me and make me afraid of myself. In the following night, however, I called my soul and said to her, "Your trick was recognized. It is to no avail. You do not frighten me. Now speak and convey your message!"

She answered, "The Gods give in. You have broken the compulsion of the law. Therefore I painted you as a devil, since he is the only one among the Gods who bows to no compulsion. He is the rebel against the eternal law, to which, thanks to his deed, there are also exceptions. Thus one does not necessarily have to. The devil is helpful in this respect. But it should not happen without seeking counsel from the Gods. This detour is necessary, or else you will fall prey to their law despite the devil."

Here the soul drew near to my ear and whispered, "The Gods are even happy to turn a blind eye from time to time, since basically they know very well that it would be bad for life if there were no exception to eternal law. Hence their tolerance of the devil."

She then raised her voice and cried loudly, "The Gods have mercy upon you and have accepted your sacrifice!"

And so the devil helped me to cleanse myself from commingling in bondage, and the pain of one-sidedness pierced my heart and the wound of being torn apart scorched me.

{15} [152]It was noon on a hot summer's day and I was taking a stroll in my garden; when I reached the shade of the high trees, I met ΦΙΛΗΜΩΝ strolling in the fragrant grass. But when I sought to approach him, a blue shade[153] came from the other side, and when

152. June 1, 1916.
153. In *Black Book* 6, the shade is identified as Christ (p. 85).

ΦΙΛΗΜΩΝ saw him, he said, "I find you in the garden, beloved. The sins of the world have conferred beauty upon your countenance.

"The suffering of the world has straightened your shape.

"You are truly a king.

"Your crimson is blood.

"Your ermine is snow from the coldness of the poles.

"Your crown is the heavenly body of the sun, which you bear on your head.

"Welcome to the garden, my master, my beloved, my brother!"

The shade replied, "Oh Simon Magus or whatever your name may be, are you in my garden or am I in yours?"[154]

ΦΙΛΗΜΩΝ said, "You are, Oh master, in my garden. Helena, or whatever you choose to call her, and I are your servants. You can find accommodation with us. Simon and Helena have become ΦΙΛΗΜΩΝ and Baucis and so we are the hosts of the Gods. We granted hospitality to your terrible worm. And since you come forward, we take you in. It is our garden that surrounds you."[155]

The shade answered, "Is this garden not mine? Is not the world of the heavens and of the spirits my own?"

ΦΙΛΗΜΩΝ said, "You are, Oh master, here in the world of men. Men have changed. They are no longer the slaves and no longer the swindlers of the Gods and no longer mourn in your name, but they

154. Simon Magus (first century) was a magician. In the Acts of the Apostles (8:9–24), after becoming a Christian, he wished to purchase the power of transmitting the Holy Spirit from Peter and Paul (Jung saw this account as a caricature). Further accounts of him are found in the apocryphal acts of Peter, and in writings of the Church fathers. He has been seen as one of the founders of Gnosticism, and in the second century a Simonian sect arose. He is said to have always traveled with a woman, whom he found in a brothel in Tyre, who was the reincarnation of Helen of Troy. Jung cited this as an example of the anima figure ("Soul and earth," 1927, CW 10, §75). On Simon Magus, see Gilles Quispel, *Gnosis als Weltreligion* (Zürich: Origo Verlag, 1951), pp. 51–70, and G.R.S. Mead, *Simon Magus: An Essay on the Founder of Simonianism Based on the Ancient Sources with a Reevaluation of His Philosophy and Teachings* (London: The Theosophical Publishing House, 1892).

155. In *Memories*, Jung commented: "In such dream wandering one frequently encounters an old man who is accompanied by a young girl, and examples of such couples are to be found in many mythic tales. Thus, according to Gnostic tradition, Simon Magus went about with a young girl whom he had picked up in a brothel. Her name was Helen, and she was regarded as the reincarnation of the Trojan Helen. Klingsor and Kundry, Lao-tzu and the dancing girl, likewise belong in this category" (p. 206).

grant hospitality to the Gods. The terrible worm[156] came before you, whom you recognize as your brother insofar as you are of divine nature, and as your father insofar as you are of human nature.[157] You dismissed him when he gave you clever counsel in the desert. You took the counsel, but dismissed the worm: he finds a place with us. But where he is, you will be also.[158] When I was Simon, I sought to escape him with the ploy of magic and thus I escaped you. Now that I gave the worm a place in my garden, you come to me."

The shade answered, "Do I fall for the power of your trick? Have you secretly caught me? Were not deception and lies always your manner?"

But ΦΙΛΗΜΩΝ answered, "Recognize, Oh master and beloved, that your nature is also of the serpent.[159] Were you not raised on the tree like the serpent? Have you laid aside your body, like the serpent its skin? Have you not practiced the healing arts, like the serpent? Did you not go to Hell before your ascent? And did you not see your brother there, who was shut away in the abyss?"[160]

Then the shade said, "You speak the truth. You are not lying. Even so, do you know what I bring you?"

"This I know not," ΦΙΛΗΜΩΝ answered. "I know only one thing, that whoever hosts the worm also needs his brother. What do you bring me, my beautiful guest? Lamentation and abomination were the gift of the worm. What will you give us?"

The shade answered, "I bring you the beauty of suffering. That is what is needed by whoever hosts the worm."

156. I.e., Satan.

157. In *Black Book* 6, this sentence reads: "Your brother came before you, Oh master, the terrible worm, whom you dismissed, when he gave you clever counsel in the desert with a tempting voice" (p. 86).

158. *Black Book* 6 continues: "since he is your immortal brother" (p. 86).

159. Jung commented on the serpent as an allegory of Christ in *Aion* (1952, CW 9, 2, §§369, 385, and 390).

160. See above, p. 165.

Epilogue[1]

1959
I worked on this book for 16 years. My acquaintance with alchemy in 1930 took me away from it. The beginning of the end came in 1928, when Wilhelm sent me the text of the "Golden Flower," an alchemical treatise. There the contents of this book found their way into actuality and I could no longer continue working on it. To the superficial observer, it will appear like madness. It would also have developed into one, had I not been able to absorb the overpowering force of the original experiences. With the help of alchemy, I could finally arrange them into a whole. I always knew that these experiences contained something precious, and therefore I knew of nothing better than to write them down in a "precious," that is to say costly, book and to paint the images that emerged through reliving it all—as well as I could. I knew how frightfully inadequate this undertaking was, but despite much work and many distractions I remained true to it, even if another / possibility never . . .

1. This appears on p. 190 of the calligraphic volume of *Liber Novus*. The transcription was abruptly left off in the middle of a sentence on p. 189. This epilogue appears on the next page, in Jung's normal handwriting. This in turn was abruptly left off in the middle of a sentence.

Appendix A

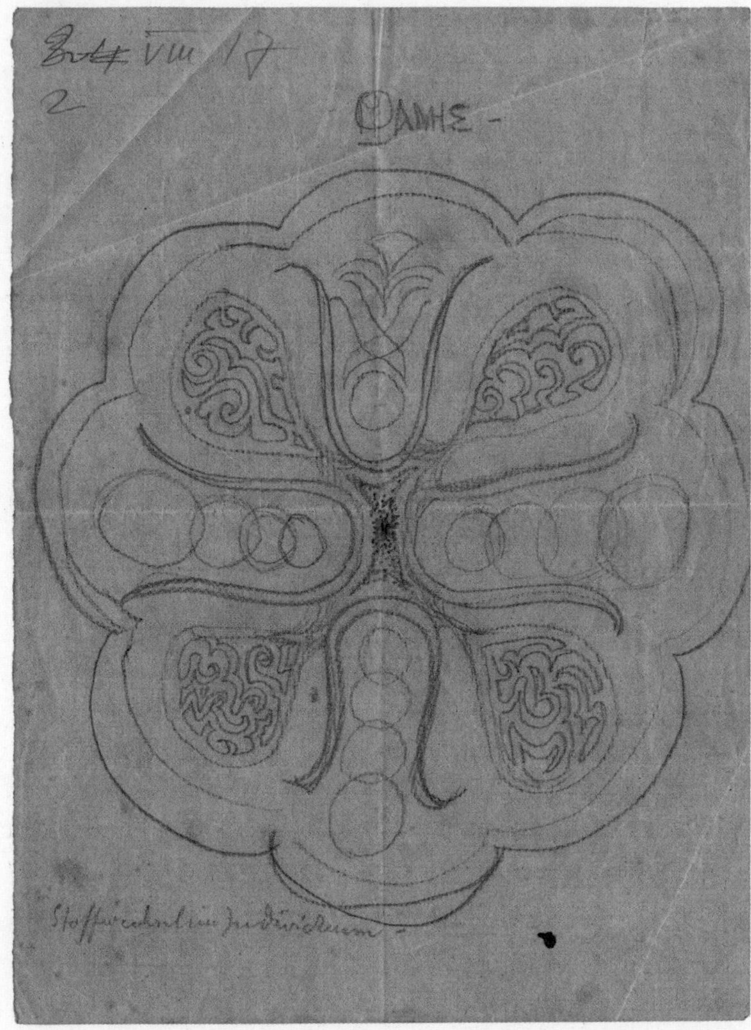

Mandala sketch 1 appears to be the first in the series, dated August 2, 1917. It is the basis of image 80. The legend at the top of the image is "ΦΑΝΗΣ [Phanes]" (see note 211, p. 358). Legend at bottom: "Stoffwechsel in Individuum" (metabolism in the individual). (19.4 cm x 14.3 cm)

Mandala sketch 2 is the reverse of mandala sketch 1. (19.4 cm x 14.3 cm)

Mandala sketch 3 is dated August 4, 1917, and August 8, 1917, and is the basis of image 82. (14.9 cm x 12.4 cm)

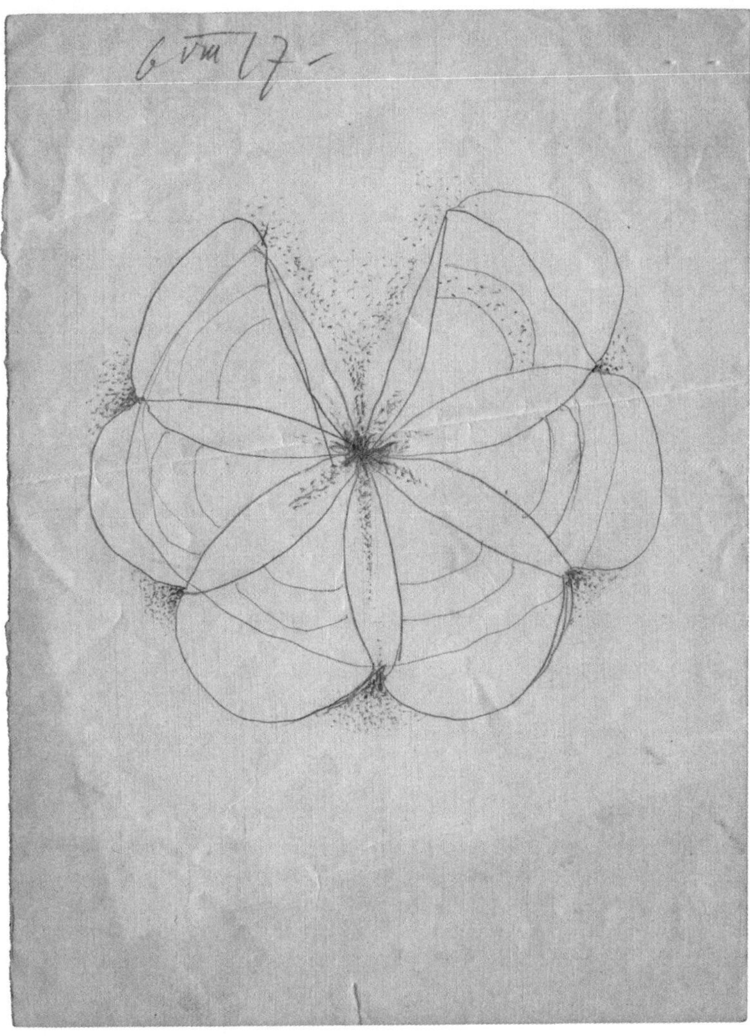

Mandala sketch 4 is dated August 6, 1917. On these sketches, see introduction, p. 43f. (20.3 cm x 14.9 cm)

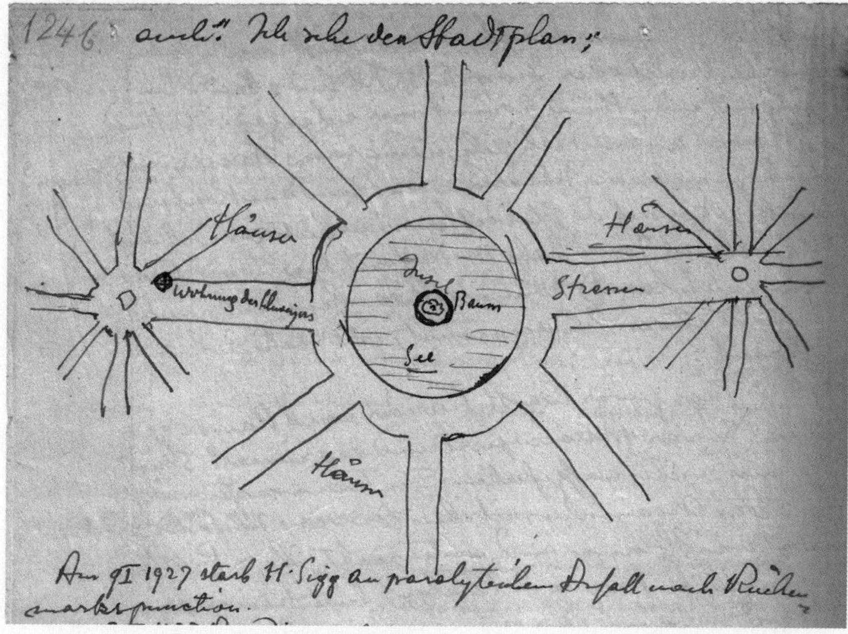

The town plan is from Black Book 7, page 124b, and depicts the scene of the "Liverpool" dream. This sketch is the basis of image 159, linking the dream with the mandala. Text in image, from left: "Dwelling of the Swiss"; above, "Houses"; below, "Houses," "Island"; (below) "Lake," "Tree," "Streets," "Houses." (13.3 cm x 19.1 cm)

Opposite: Systema Munditotius. (30 cm x 34 cm) In 1955, Jung's *Systema Munditotius* was published anonymously in a special issue of *Du* dedicated to the Eranos conferences. In a letter of February 11, 1955, to Walter Corti, Jung explicitly stated that he did not want his name to appear with it (JA). He added the following comments to it: "It portrays the antinomies of the microcosm within the macrocosmic world and its antinomies. At the very top, the figure of the young boy in the winged egg, called Erikapaios or Phanes and thus reminiscent as a spiritual figure of the Orphic Gods. His dark antithesis in the depths is here designated as Abraxas. He represents the *dominus mundi*, the lord of the physical world, and is a world-creator of an ambivalent nature. Sprouting from him we see the tree of life, labeled *vita* ('life') while its upper counterpart is a light-tree in the form of a seven-branched candelabra labeled *ignis* ('fire') and *Eros* ('love'). Its light points to the spiritual world of the divine child. Art and science also belong to this spiritual realm, the first represented as a winged serpent and the second as a winged mouse (as hole-digging activity!).—The candelabra is based on the principle of the spiritual number three (twice-three flames with one large flame in the middle), while the lower world of Abraxas is characterized by five, the number of natural man (the twice-five

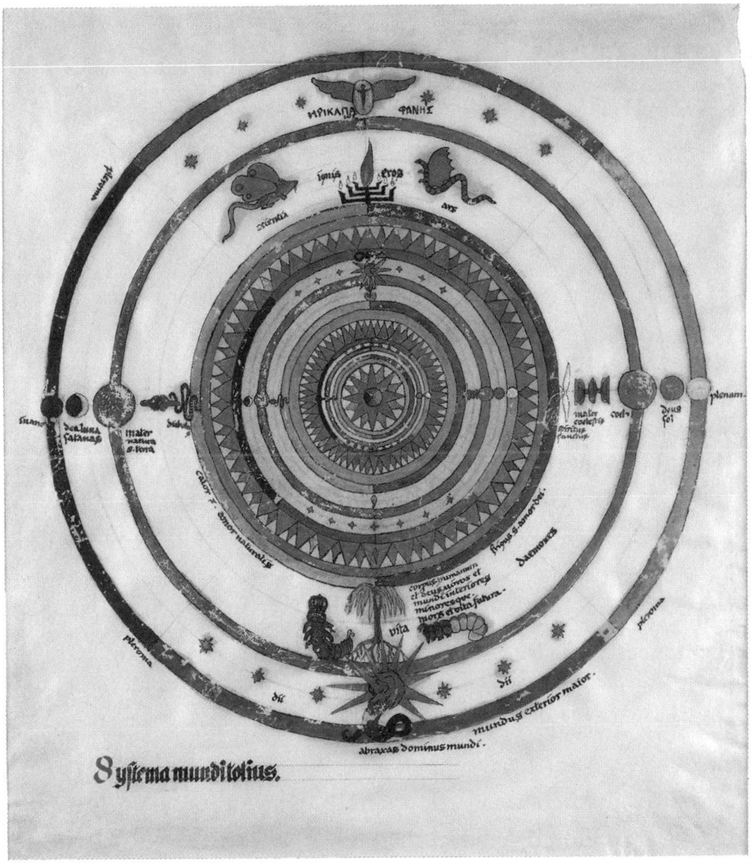

rays of his star). The accompanying animals of the natural world are a devilish monster and a larva. This signifies death and rebirth. A further division of the mandala is horizontal. To the left we see a circle indicating the body or the blood, and from it rears the serpent, which winds itself around the phallus, as the generative principle. The serpent is dark and light, signifying the dark realm of the earth, the moon, and the void (therefore called Satanas). The light realm of rich fullness lies to the right, where from the bright circle *frigus sive amor dei* [cold, or the love of God] the dove of the Holy Ghost takes wing, and wisdom (*Sophia*) pours from a double beaker to left and right.—This feminine sphere is that of heaven.—The large sphere characterized by zigzag lines or rays represents an inner sun; within this sphere the macrocosm is repeated, but with the upper and lower regions reversed as in a mirror. These repetitions should be conceived of as endless in number, growing even smaller until the innermost core, the actual microcosm, is reached."

Appendix B
Commentaries

pp. 86–89[1]

Age
Male
Enantiodromia of the life-type

It is difficult to force this image to make a statement. Yet it is so allegorical that it ought to speak. It differs from the earlier experiences in that it is more witnessed than experienced. For that matter, all the images that I have placed under the title "Mystery play" are rather more allegorical than actual experiences. They are certainly not intended allegories; they have not been consciously contrived to depict experience in either veiled or even fantastic terms. Rather, they appeared as visions. It was not until I reworked them later that I realized more and more that they could in no way be compared with the experiences portrayed in the other chapters. These images apparently are portrayals of personified unconscious thoughts. That follows from their imagistic manner. They also called for more reflection and interpretation than the other experiences, to which I could not do justice with cogitation, because they were quite simply experiences. The images of the "Mystery play," on the other hand, personify principles accessible to thinking and intellectual understanding, and their allegorical manner accordingly also invites such an attempt at explanation.

The action is set in a dark earthly depth, evidently an allegorical representation of the inner depths beneath the extension of the bright space of consciousness or the psychic field of vision. Sinking into such a depth corresponds to averting the mental gaze from outer things and focusing it on the inner dark depths. Gazing at the

1. The page numbers refer to the *Corrected Draft*. This corresponds to pp. 174–83 above.

darkness to some extent animates the previously dark background. Since gazing at the darkness occurs without conscious expectation, the inanimate psychic background has an opportunity to let its contents appear, undisturbed by conscious assumptions.

The preceding experiences indicated that strong psychic movements were present that consciousness could not grasp. Two figures—the old sage and the young maiden—step into the field of vision, unexpectedly for consciousness, but characteristic of the mythological spirit upon which consciousness rests. This configuration is an image that forever recurs in the human spirit. The old man represents a spiritual principle that could be designated as Logos, and the maiden represents an unspiritual principle of feeling that could be called Eros. A descendent of Logos is Nous, the intellect, which has done away with the commingling of feeling, presentiment, and sensation. In contrast, the Logos contains this commingling. But it is not the product of such blending, or else it would be a lower animalistic psychic activity, yet it masters the blend, so that the four fundamental activities of the soul become subordinate to its principle. It is an independent principle of form that means understanding, insight, foresight, legislation, and wisdom. The figure of an old prophet is therefore a fitting allegory for this principle, since the prophetic spirit unites in itself all these qualities. In contrast, Eros is a principle that contains a commingling of all the fundamental activities of the soul just as much as it masters them, although its purpose is completely different. It is not form-giving but form-fulfilling; it is the wine that will be poured into the vessel; it is not the bed and direction of the stream but the impetuous water flowing in it. Eros is desire, longing, force, exuberance, pleasure, suffering. Where Logos is ordering and insistence, Eros is dissolution and movement. They are two fundamental psychic powers that form a pair of opposites, each one requiring the other.

The old prophet expresses persistence, but the young maiden denotes movement. Their impersonal essence is expressed by the fact that they are figures belonging to general human history; they do not belong to a person but have been a spiritual content of the world's peoples since time immemorial. Everyone has them, and therefore these figures recur in the work of thinkers and poets.

Such primordial images have a secret power that works just as much on human reason as on the soul. Wherever they appear they stir something linked with the mysterious, the long gone, and heavy with foreboding. A string sounds whose vibration reverberates in every man's breast; these primordial images dwell in everyone as they are the property of all mankind.[2] This secret power is like a spell, like magic, and causes elevation just as much as seduction. It is characteristic of primordial images that they take hold of man where he is utterly human, and a power seizes him, as if the bustling throng were pushing him. And this happens even if individual understanding and feeling rise up against it. What is the power of the individual against the voice of the whole people in him? He is entranced, possessed, and consumed. Nothing makes this effect clearer than the serpent. It signifies everything dangerous and everything bad, everything nocturnal and uncanny, which adheres to Logos as well as to Eros, so long as they can work as the dark and unrecognized principles of the unconscious spirit.

The house represents a fixed abode, which indicates that Logos and Eros have permanent residence in us.

Salome is represented as the daughter of Elijah, thus expressing the order of succession. The prophet is her producer, she emanates from him. The fact that she is assigned to him as a daughter indicates a subordination of Eros to Logos. Although this relation is very frequent, as manifested by the constancy of this primordial image, it is nevertheless a special case that possesses no general validity. For if these were two opposed principles, one could not arise from the other and thus depend on it. Salome is hence apparently no (complete) correct embodiment of Eros, but a variety of the same. (This supposition is later confirmed.) That she is actually an incorrect allegory for Eros also stems from the fact that she is

2. Jung here employs a metaphor used by Jacob Burkhardt to describe the primordial images of Faust and Oedipus, which he had cited in *Transformations and Symbols of the Libido* (1912, CW B, §56n).

blind. Eros is not blind, since he regulates, just as well as Logos does, all fundamental activities of the soul. The blindness indicates her incompleteness and the absence of an essential quality. By virtue of her shortcoming she depends upon her father.

The indistinct glittering walls of the hall point to something unrecognized, perhaps something valuable that wakens curiosity and attracts attention. In this manner, creative involvement is woven even deeper into the image, so that an even greater animation of the dark background becomes possible. Such enhanced attention gives rise to the image of an object, which to all intents and purposes expresses concentration, namely the image of a crystal, which has been used to produce such visions since time immemorial. These figures, which at first are incomprehensible to the beholder, evoke dark processes in his soul, which to a certain extent lie even deeper (such as in the vision of blood), and whose perception requires an aid like the crystal. As has been said, however, this expresses nothing else than an even stronger concentration of creative attention.

A figure like the prophet, which is clear and complete in itself, arouses less curiosity than the unexpected form of blind Salome, which is why one may expect that the formative process will first address the problem of Eros. Hence an image of Eve appears first, together with images of the tree and the serpent. This apparently refers to temptation, as already encapsulated in the figure of Salome. Temptation brings about a further movement toward the side of Eros. This in turn forebodes many adventurous possibilities, for which the wandering of Odysseus is the fitting image. This image stimulates and invites adventurousness; it is as if a door opened to a new opportunity to free the gaze from the dark confinement and depths in which it was held fast. Hence the vision opens onto a sunny garden, whose red blooming trees represent a development of erotic feeling, and whose wells mean a steady source. The cool water of the well, which does not inebriate, indicates the Logos. (Therefore Salome also speaks later of the deep "wells" of the prophet.) This suggests that the development of Eros also means a source of knowledge. And with this Elijah begins to speak.

Logos undoubtedly has the upper hand in this, my case, since Elijah says that he and his daughter have always been one. Yet Logos and Eros are not one, but two. In this case, however, Logos has blinded and subjugated Eros. But if this is the case, then the necessity will also arise to free Eros from the clutch of Logos, so that the former will regain vision. Therefore Salome turns to me, because Eros is in need of help, and because I have apparently been enabled to behold this image for precisely this reason. The soul of the man is more inclined to Logos than to Eros, which is more characteristic of the essence of the woman. The subjugation of Eros through Logos explains not only the blindness of Eros but also the somewhat strange fact that Eros is represented precisely by the not-so-pleasing figure of Salome. Salome denotes bad qualities. She brings to mind not only the murder of the holy one but also the incestuous pleasure of the father.

A principle always has the dignity of independence. But if this dignity is taken from it, it is debased and then assumes a bad form. We know that psychic activity and qualities that are deprived of development through repression degenerate and thus become bad habits. Either an open or secret vice takes the place of a well-formed activity and gives rise to a disunity of the personality with itself, signifying a moral suffering or a real sickness. Only one way remains open to whoever wants to free himself from this suffering: he must accept the repressed part of his soul, he must love his inferiority, even his vices, so that what is degenerate can resume development.

Wherever Logos rules, there is order but too much persistence. The allegory of paradise where there is no struggle and therefore no development is fitting here. In this condition the repressed movement degenerates and its value is lost. This is the murder of the holy one, and the murder happens because, like Herod, Logos cannot protect the holy one on account of his own weakness, because he can do nothing else than hold onto himself, thus inducing the degeneration of Eros. Only disobedience against the ruling principle leads out of this condition of undeveloped persistence. The story of paradise repeats itself, and hence the serpent winds its way up the tree because Adam should be led into temptation.

Every development leads through the undeveloped, but capable of development. In its undeveloped condition it is almost worthless, while development represents a highest value that is unquestionable. One must give up this value or at least apparently give it up to be able to attend to the undeveloped. But this stands in the sharpest contrast to the developed, which perhaps represents our best and highest achievement. The acceptance of the undeveloped is therefore like a sin, like a false step, a degeneration, a descent to a deeper level; in actual fact, however, it is a greater deed than remaining in an ordered condition at the expense of the other side of our being, which is thus at the mercy of decay.

pp. 103–119[3]

The scene of the action is the same place as in the first image. The allusion to a crater heightens the impression of a large cavity that reaches far down into the interior of the earth; this depth is not inactive, but violently discharges all kinds of matter.

Since Eros poses the most serious problem at first, Salome enters the scene, blindly groping her way *toward the left*. Even what appear to be negligible details are important in such visionary images. The left is the side of the inauspicious. This suggests that Eros does not tend toward the right, the side of consciousness, conscious will and conscious choice, but toward the side of the heart, which is less subject to our conscious will. This movement toward the left is emphasized by the fact that the serpent moves in the same direction. The serpent represents magical power, which also appears where animal drives are aroused imperceptibly in us. They afford the movement of Eros the uncanny emphasis that strikes us as magical. Magical effect is the enchantment and underlining of our thought and feeling through dark instinctual impulses of an animal nature.

3. This corresponds to pp. 184–93 above.

The movement toward the left is blind, that is, without purpose and intention. It hence requires guidance, not by conscious intention but by Logos. Elijah calls Salome back. Her blindness is an affliction, and as such demands healing. Closer scrutiny at least partially invalidates the prejudice against her. She seems to be innocent, and perhaps her badness ought to be attributed to her blindness.

Logos asserts its power over Eros by calling back Salome. The serpent also obeys Logos. It rests with Logos and Eros to emphasize the power and significance of this image. A natural consequence of this magical, powerful view of the union of Logos and Eros is the strongly felt smallness and insignificance of the I, which finds expression in a sense of boyishness.

It appears as if the movement toward the left, following blind Eros, is not possible, or effectively disallowed, without the intervention of Logos. From the perspective of Logos, following a movement blindly is a sin, because it is one-sided and violates the law that man must forever strive for the highest degree of consciousness. Therein lies his humanity. The other he has in common with animals. Jesus also says, "If you know what you are doing, you are blessed; if you do not know what you are doing, you are damned."[4] The movement toward the left would be possible and permitted only if a conscious, *seeing* notion of it existed. Formulating such a notion is not possible without the intervention of Logos.

The first step toward developing such a notion is to become conscious of the goal or intention of the movement. Hence Elijah asks about the intention of the I. And it must admit its blindness, that is, its ignorance about intention. The only recognizable thing is a longing, a wish, to unravel the embroilment caused by the first image.

Such making conscious stirs a vague sense of happiness in Salome. Understandably so, since consciousness means insight, that

4. This sentence is an apocryphal insertion to Luke 6:4, from the Codex Bezae, "Man, if indeed you know what you are doing, happy are you; but if not, you are accursed and a transgressor of the law." J. K. Elliot, ed., *The Apocryphal New Testament*, p. 68. In 1952, Jung cited it in *Answer to Job* (CW 11, §696).

is, a healing of her blindness. Thus a step toward attaining the healing of Eros is taken.

At first the I remains in its inferior position, since its ignorance prevents it from surveying the further development of its problem. Nor would it know which direction to take, since it has never cast its gaze into the depths of its psychic substratum, but has seen only what meets the eye and recognized only the powers of consciousness and the conscious world as effective forces, half-consciously denying its inner impulses. Faced with its own depths, such an I can only feel embarrassed. Its belief in a conscious upperworld had been so firm that going down into the depths of the self is like guilt, a betrayal of conscious ideals.

But since its desire to unravel the embroilment is greater than its aversion to its own inferiority, the I entrusts itself to the guidance of Logos. Since nothing comes into view that could answer the question raised, even greater depths must evidently be opened up. This in turn occurs with the help of the crystal, that is, through the utmost concentration of expectant attention. The first image to appear in the crystal is the mother of God with child.

This image is obviously related, and opposed, to the vision of Eve in the first image. Just as Eve represents carnal temptation and carnal motherhood, the mother of God stands for carnal virginity and spiritual motherhood. The first direction would be a movement of Eros toward the flesh, the latter toward the spirit. Eve is an expression of the carnal side, whereas Mary expresses the spiritual side of Eros. As long as the I saw only Eve, it was blind. The evocation of awareness, however, affords a spiritual view of Eros. In the first case the I became an Odysseus on an adventurous journey, which concludes with the aging man's return to Penelope, the motherly woman.

In the latter case the I is depicted as Peter, the chosen rock upon which the Church is to be founded. The key as the symbol of the power of binding and loosing buttresses this idea, and leads one to the image of the pope as God's governor on earth with a threefold crown.

Undoubtedly, the I becomes involved in a movement toward spiritual power, as attested by the one-sidedness of the movement. The vision of Eve leads astray, to adventurous odyssey, to Circe and Calypso. The vision of the mother of God, on the other hand, turns desire away from the flesh and toward the humble veneration of the spirit. Eros is subject to error in the flesh, but in the spirit it rises above the flesh and the inferiority of carnal error. It therefore almost imperceptibly becomes the spirit, the power over the flesh in the guise of love, and thus spiritual power casts off the mantle of love; although the former believes it loves the spirit, in effect it rules the flesh. And the more powerful it is, the less loving it is. And the less it loves the spirit, the more it is carnal power. On account of its power over the flesh, the love of the spirit thus becomes a secular power-drive in spiritual guise.

Christ overcame the world by burdening himself with its suffering. But Buddha overcame both the pleasure and suffering of the world by disposing of both. And thus he entered into nonbeing, a condition from which there is no return. Buddha is an even higher spiritual power, that derives no pleasure from controlling the flesh, since he has altogether moved beyond pleasure and suffering. Passion, whose conquest still requires so much effort in the case of Christ and does so incessantly and in ever greater measure, has left Buddha and surrounds him as a blazing fire. He is both unaffected and untouchable.

But if the living I approaches this condition, its passion may leave it, though it will not die. Or are we not our passion? And what happens to our passion when it leaves the I? The I is consciousness, which only has eyes in front. It never sees what is behind it. But that is where the passion it has overcome in front regroups. Unguided by the eye of reason, unmitigated by humaneness, the fire becomes a devastating, bloodthirsty Kali, who devours the life of man from within, as the mantra of her sacrificial ceremony says: "Hail to you, O Kali, triple-eyed Goddess of dreadful aspect, from whose throat hangs a necklace of human skulls. May you be honored with this blood!" Salome must of course despair of this end, which would like to turn Eros into spirit, since Eros cannot exist without the flesh. In resisting the inferiority of the flesh, the I resists its female soul, which represents everything that strives to suppress consciousness, against spirit. Thus this path also results in an opposition. Hence the I returns from beholding the figures embodying its conflict.

Logos and Eros are reunited, as if they had overcome the conflict between spirit and flesh. They appear to know the solution. The movement toward the left, which started from Eros at the beginning of the image, now commences from Logos. He starts moving toward the left, to complete with seeing eyes what began in blindness. At first this movement leads into greater darkness, which is then still somewhat illumined by the reddish light. The color red points to Eros. While it does not emit a bright light, Eros at least provides an opportunity to recognize something, perhaps even merely by inducing a situation in which man can recognize something, provided Logos assists him.

Elijah leans against the marble lion. The lion as a royal animal signifies power. The stone suggests unshakeable firmness, thereby expressing the power and solidity of Logos. Once again awareness commences first, although now in greater depths and in renewed surroundings. Here the I experiences its smallness even more as it is even further removed from the world it knows, where it is conscious of its value and meaning. In these new surroundings there is nothing to remind it of its meaning. Hence it is obviously overwhelmed by so much otherness, which so completely eludes its own discretion. Elijah assumes control of developing awareness.

As the crystal visions have shown, the idea that should be conveyed to consciousness is an idea of spiritual power, that is, the I was tempted to arrogate prophethood. But this idea encountered such a feeling of resistance that it could not assert itself against consciousness. Hence it remained behind the curtain. But since the I could not follow Eros blindly, it sought at least to exchange spiritual power for this loss—as observed so very often in human life! It is almost inevitable that such a great loss, like that of Eros, presses man to search for a substitute at least in the sphere of power. This occurs in such an uncanny, cunning manner that the I mostly fails to notice the ruse. Which explains why the I as a rule cannot enjoy its power, since it does not possess power, but is possessed by the power-devil. In this case it would have been easy for the I to grasp the fact that Elijah imposes himself with such living reality, and lay claim to this figure as a personality valuable in itself. But awareness has forestalled this deception.

The appearance of living figures should not be taken personally, even though one is obviously inclined to assume responsibility for them. In reality such figures belong just as much or little to our personality as our hands and feet. The mere presence of hands or feet is not characteristic of personality. If anything about them is characteristic, it is merely their individual character. It is thus characteristic of the I that the old man and the young maiden are called Elijah and Salome; they might just as well have been called Simon Magus and Helena. What is significant, however, is that they are biblical figures. As proven later, this is one of the peculiarities of the psychic entanglement belonging to this moment.

The awareness of the alluring idea of spiritual power shifts the question of Eros into the foreground again, once more in a new form: both the possibility indicated by Eve and the one represented by Mary are ruled out. Hence the third possibility remains, namely filial relationship, which avoids the two extremes of the flesh and the spirit: Elijah as the father, Salome as the sister, the I as the son and brother. This solution corresponds to the Christian notion of childhood in God. Salome—as Mary—makes up the as-yet-absent mother in what is a formidably ensnaring manner. This has a corresponding effect on the I. There is something undeniably cathartic about the Christian solution—because it seems to be altogether possible. There is a child in each of us; in the elderly, it is even the only thing still alive. One can have recourse to the childlike anytime, on account of its inexhaustible freshness and adherence. Everything, even the most ominous, can be rendered harmless through retranslation into the childlike. After all, we do this often enough in everyday life. We even manage to tame a passion by leading it back to the childlike, and perhaps the flame of passion collapses in a childlike lament even more often. Thus there are many prospects for which the childlike can seem to be a satisfactory remedy, including not least the far-reaching effect of our Christian education, which hammers into us the notion of childhood in hundreds of mantras and hymns.

Salome's remark that Mary is their mother must thus appear even more devastating. Since this prevents the childlike solution from developing, it immediately prompts another thought: If Mary is the mother, then *inescapably I must be Christ*. The childlike solution would have canceled all reservations: Salome would no longer pose a threat, since she would be only the little sister. Elijah would be the caring father, whose wisdom and foresight would have left the I to its own devices with childlike trust.

But this is the unfortunate drawback constituted by childhood as a solution: every child wishes to grow. Being a child involves the burning desire and impatience for future adulthood. If we return to being a child for fear of the dangers of Eros, the child will want to develop toward spiritual power. But if we flee into childhood for fear of the dangers of the spirit, we fall into arrogating the power of Eros.

The condition of spiritual childhood constitutes a transition in which not everyone can remain. In this case it stands to reason that Eros demonstrates to the I the impossibility of being a child. One might think that it is not that awful to renounce the condition of childhood. But only those who fail to grasp the consequences of this renunciation think that way. It is not the loss of immemorial Christian views and the religious possibilities they ensured—many bear this loss all too easily—but rather that what is renounced refers to the much more profound attitude that far transcends the Christian outlook, which provides individual life and thought with a tried and tested direction. Even if one has long abstained from Christian religious practice and has long ceased to regret this loss, one continues to behave intuitively as if the original views still existed by right. One fails to consider that a discarded worldview needs to be replaced by a new one; in particular one fails to be clear about the fact that renouncing the Christian outlook erodes present-day morals. Renouncing childhood means that no emotional or habitual dependence on hitherto valid moral views any longer exists. The hitherto valid view has arisen from the spirit of the Christian worldview.

Notwithstanding all free thinking, our attitude to Eros, for instance, remains the old Christian view. We can now no longer bide our time peacefully without questioning and doubt, or else we will remain in the state of childhood. If we merely reject the dogmatic view, our liberation from the well-established will be merely intellectual, whereas our deeper feeling will persist on the old path. Most people, however, are unaware of how this sets them at odds with themselves. But later generations will become increasingly aware of this. Yet those who notice this will realize with horror that renouncing resumed childhood ousts them from our present times and that they can no longer follow any of the traditional ways. They enter uncharted territory, which has neither paths nor boundaries. They lack any direction, since they have forsaken all established bearings. This realization, however, dawns upon very few, since the vast majority makes do with half measures, and remains unperturbed by the stupidity of their spiritual condition. But then tepidity and slackness is not to everyone's taste. Some would rather abandon themselves to despair than adhere to a worldview completely removed from the well-trodden paths of their habitual behavior. They would rather venture into a pathless, dark land at the risk of perishing there, even if this should outrage all their cowardice.

When Salome remarks that Mary is their mother, which means that the I is Christ, this means in brief that the I has left the state of Christian childhood and has taken the place of Christ. Nothing could be more absurd, of course, than to assume that the I thus would be presuming excessive importance; on the contrary, it takes up a decidedly inferior position. Previously it had the advantage of being part of the crowd rallying behind a powerful figure, but now it has exchanged that for solitude and forlornness, rendering it as alien and lonely in its world as Jesus was in his, without possessing that great man's outstanding attributes. Being at odds with the world requires greatness, but the I experiences its almost ludicrous meagerness. Which explains its horror at Salome's revelations.

Whoever steps beyond the Christian outlook, yet does so definitely, falls into a seeming abyss, an utmost solitude, and lacks any means of hiding the fact. Of course one would like to persuade oneself that this is not all that bad. But it is. Abandonment is about the worst thing that can happen to man's herd instinct, not to mention the daunting task with which we thus burden ourselves. Destruction is easy, but rebuilding is difficult.

Thus the image ends with a sense of gloom, which stands opposed, however, to the tall, quietly burning flame encircled by the serpent. This view denotes devotion coupled with the magical compulsion expressed by the serpent. Thus an effective counterpart is set against the disquieting sense of doubt and fear, as if someone were saying, "Of course your I is full of unease and doubt, but the constant flame of devotion burns in you more strongly and the compulsion of your fate is more powerful."

pp. 127–150[5]

The far-reaching premonitions of the second image plunged the I into a chaos of doubt. Hence an understandable desire arose to rise above the confusion to attain greater clarity, as expressed in the image of the beetling mountain ridge. Logos appears to be leading the way. What occurs next is the image of two opposites, expressed by two serpents and the separation of day and night. Daylight signifies good, whereas darkness represents evil. As compelling forces, both assume the figure of serpents. Therein lies concealed an idea that subsequently assumes great importance: whoever encountered a black serpent would have been no less surprised at encountering a white one. Color does not dispel fear. What this suggests

5. This refers to pp. 194–207.

is that perhaps an equally dangerous, bewitching power resides in good as in evil. Essentially, the good needs to be regarded as an inherently no-less-dangerous principle than evil. In any event, the I could decide to approach the white serpent just as little as the black one, even though it believes it can or must by all means entrust itself more to good than to evil. But the I is rooted to the spot halfway, transfixed, and observes the struggle between the two principles—within itself.

The fact that the I remains in this middle position implies the advance of evil, since anything but unconditional surrender to the good impairs it. This finds expression in the attack of the black serpent. But the fact that the I does not partake of evil constitutes a victory for the good. This finds expression in the black serpent growing a white head.

The disappearance of the serpent denotes that the opposition of good and evil has become ineffective, that is, that at least it has lost its immediate significance. For the I this means a release from the unconditional power of the hitherto abiding moral point of view in favor of a middle position freed from the pair of opposites. But neither clarity nor a clear view has been gained thereby; hence the ascent continues to the final point of elevation, which might grant the longed-for outlook.

Appendix C

The following is an entry from *Black Book* 5, pp. 163–78, which gives a preliminary sketch of cosmology of the *Septem Sermones.*

16. I. 16.

The force of the God is frightful.

"You shall experience even more of it. You are in the second age. The first age has been overcome. This is the age of the rulership of the son, whom you call the Frog God. A third age will follow, the age of apportionment and harmonious power."

My soul, where did you go? Did you go to the animals?

I bind the Above with the Below. I bind God and animal. Something in me is part animal, something part God, and a third part human. Below you serpent, within you man, and above you God. Beyond the serpent comes the phallus, then the earth, then the moon, and finally the coldness and emptiness of outer space.

Above you comes the dove or the celestial soul, in which love and foresight are united, just as poison and shrewdness are united in the serpent. Shrewdness is the devil's understanding, which always detects smaller things and finds chinks where you suspect none.

If I am not conjoined through the uniting of the Below and the Above, I break down into three parts: the *serpent,* and in that or some other animal form I roam, living nature daimonically, arousing fear and longing. The *human soul,* living forever within you. The *celestial soul,* as such dwelling with the Gods, far from you and unknown to you, appearing in the form of a bird. Each of these three parts then is independent.

Beyond me stands the celestial mother. Its counterpart is the phallus. Its mother is the earth, its goal is the heavenly mother.

The celestial mother is the daughter of the celestial world. Its counterpart is the earth.

The celestial mother is illuminated through the spiritual sun. Its counterpart is the moon. And just as the moon is the crossing to the dead of space, the spiritual sun is the crossing to the Pleroma, the upper world of fullness. The moon is the God's eye of emptiness, just as the sun is the God's eye of fullness. The moon that you see is the symbol, just as the sun that you see. Sun and moon, that is, their symbols, are Gods. There are still other Gods; their symbols are the planets.

The celestial mother is a daimon among the order of the Gods, an inhabitant of the heavenly world.

The Gods are favorable and unfavorable, impersonal, the souls of stars, influences, forces, grandfathers of souls, rulers in the heavenly world, both in space and in force. They are neither dangerous nor kind, strong, yet humble, clarifications of the Pleroma and of the eternal emptiness, configurations of the eternal qualities.

Their number is immeasurably great and leads over to the one supreme fundamental, which contains all qualities in itself and itself has none, a nothing and everything, the complete dissolution of man, death and eternal life.

Man becomes through the *principium individuationis.* He strives for absolute individuality, through which he ever increasingly concentrates the absolute dissolution of the Pleroma. Through this he makes the Pleroma the point that contains the greatest tension and is itself a shining star, immeasurably small, just as the Pleroma is immeasurably great. The more concentrated the Pleroma becomes, the stronger the star of the individual becomes. It is surrounded by shining clouds, a heavenly body in the making, comparable to a small sun. It emits fire. Therefore it is called: εγω [ειμι] συμπλανοζ υμιν αστηρ.[1] Just like the sun, which is also such a star, which is a God and grandfather of souls, the star of the individual is also like the sun, a God and grandfather of the souls. He is visible from time to time, just as I have described him. His light is blue, like that

1. "I am a star, wandering about with you."—A citation from the Mithras Liturgy (Albrecht Dieterich, *Eine Mithrasliturgie* [Leipzig: B. G. Teubner, 1903], p. 8, line 5). Jung carved the continuation of this sentence on his stone at Bollingen.

of a distant star. He is far out in space, cold and solitary, since he is beyond death. To attain individuality, we need a large share of death. Therefore it is called ει εοι εστε,[2] since just as an innumerable number of men rule the earth, so a countless number of stars and of Gods rule the celestial world.

To be sure, this God is the one who survives the death of men. To him for whom solitude is Heaven, he goes to Heaven; to him for whom it is Hell, he goes to Hell. Whoever does not follow the *principium individuationis* to its end becomes no God, since he cannot bear individuality.

The dead who besiege us are souls who have not fulfilled the *principium individuationis*, or else they would have become distant stars. Insofar as we do not fulfill it, the dead have a claim on us and besiege us and we cannot escape them. [Image][3]

The God of the frogs or toads, the brainless, is the uniting of the Christian God with Satan. His nature is like the flame; he is like Eros, but a God; Eros is only a daimon.

The *one God*, to whom worship is due, is in the middle.

You should worship only one God. The other Gods are unimportant. *Abraxas is to be feared.* Therefore it was a deliverance when he separated himself from me. You do not need to seek him. He will find you, just like Eros. He is the God of the cosmos, extremely powerful and fearful. He is the creative drive, he is form and formation, just as much as matter and force, therefore he is above all the light and dark Gods. He tears away souls and casts them into procreation. He is the creative and created. He is the God who always renews himself, in days, in months, in years, in human life, in ages, in peoples, in the living, in heavenly bodies. He compels, he is unsparing. If you worship him, you increase his power over you. Thereby it becomes unbearable. You will have dreadful trouble getting clear of him.

2. "You are Gods." This is a citation from John 10:34: "The Jews answered him, saying, for a good work we stone thee not; but for blasphemy; and because that thou, being a man, makesth thyself God. Jesus answered them, Is it not written in your law, I said, Ye are gods?"

3. Sketch of *Systema Munditotius*; see Appendix A, p. 363 in the facsimile edition.

The more you free yourself from him, the more you approach death, since he is the life of the universe. But he is also universal death. Therefore you fall victim to him again, not in life but in dying. So remember him, do not worship him, but also do not imagine that you can flee him since he is all around you. You must be in the middle of life, surrounded by death on all sides. Stretched out, like one crucified, you hang in him, the fearful, the overpowering.

But you have in you the *one* God, the wonderfully beautiful and kind, the solitary, starlike, unmoving, he who is older and wiser than the father, he who has a safe hand, who leads you among all the darknesses and death scares of dreadful Abraxas. He gives joy and peace, since he is beyond death and beyond what is subject to change. He is no servant and no friend of Abraxas. He himself is an Abraxas, but not unto you, but in himself and his distant world, since you yourself are a God who lives in faraway realms and who renews himself in his ages and creations and peoples, just as powerful to them as Abraxas is to you.

You yourself are a creator of worlds and a created being.

You have the *one* God, and you become your *one* God in the innumerable number of Gods.

As a God, you are the great Abraxas in your world. But as a man you are the heart of the one God who appears to his world as the great Abraxas, the feared, the powerful, the donor of madness, he who dispenses the water of life, the spirit of the tree of life, the daimon of the blood, the death bringer.

You are the suffering heart of your *one* star God, who is Abraxas to his world.

Therefore because you are the heart of your God, aspire toward him, love him, live for him. Fear Abraxas, who rules over the human world. Accept what he forces upon you, since he is the master of the life of this world and none can escape him. If you do not accept, he will torment you to death and the heart of your God will suffer, just as the one God of Christ suffered the heaviest in his death.

The suffering of mankind is without end, since its life is without end. Since there is no end where none sees an end. If mankind has come to an end, there is none who would see its end and none who could say that mankind has an end. So it has no end for itself, but it certainly does for the Gods.

The death of Christ took no suffering away from the world, but his life has taught us much; namely, that it pleases the *one* God if the individual lives his own life against the power of Abraxas. The *one* God thus delivers himself from the suffering of the earth into which his Eros plunged him; since when the *one* God saw the earth, he sought its procreation, and forgot that a world was already given to him in which he was Abraxas. So the *one* God became human. Therefore the one in turn pulls man up to him and into him, so that the one becomes complete again.

But the freeing of man from the power of Abraxas does not follow man's withdrawing from the power of Abraxas—no one can pull away from it—but through subjugating himself to it. Even Christ had to subjugate himself to the power of Abraxas, and Abraxas killed him in a gruesome manner.

Only by living life can you free yourself from it. So live it to such a degree that it befits you. To the degree that you live it, you also fall victim to the power of Abraxas and his dreadful deceptions. But to the same degree the star God in you gains in longing and power, in that the fruit of deception and human disappointment falls to him. Pain and disappointment fill the world of Abraxas with coldness, all of your life's warmth slowly sinks into the depths of your soul, into the midpoint of man, where the far blue starlight of your one God glimmers.

If you flee Abraxas from fear, you escape pain and disappointment and you remain terrified, that is, out of unconscious love you cling to Abraxas and your *one* God cannot catch fire. But through pain and disappointment you redeem yourself, since your longing then falls of its own accord like a ripe fruit into the depths, following gravity, striving toward the midpoint, where the blue light of the star God arises.

So do not flee from Abraxas, do not seek him. You feel his coercion, do not resist him, so that you shall live and pay your ransom.

The works of Abraxas are to be fulfilled, for consider that in your world you yourself are Abraxas and force your creature to fulfil your work. Here, where you are the creature subjugated to Abraxas, you must learn to fulfill the work of life. There, where you are Abraxas, you compel your creatures.

You ask, why is all this so? I understand that it seems questionable to you. The world is questionable. It is the unending infinite folly of the Gods, which you know is unendingly wise. Surely it is also a crime, an unforgivable sin, and therefore also the highest love and virtue.

So live life, do not flee Abraxas, provided that he compels you and you can recognize his necessity. In one sense I say to you: do not fear him, do not love him. In another sense I say: fear him, love him. *He is the life of the earth*, that says enough.

You need to recognize the multiplicity of the Gods. You cannot unite all into one being. As little as you are one with the multiplicity of men, just so little is the *one* God one with the multiplicity of the Gods. This one God is the kind, the loving, the leading, the healing. To him all your love and worship is due. To him you should pray, you are one with him, he is near you, nearer than your soul.

I, your soul, am your mother, who tenderly and frightfully surrounds you, your nourisher and corrupter; I prepare good things and poison for you. I am your intercessor with Abraxas. I teach you the arts that protect you from Abraxas. I stand between you and Abraxas the all-encompassing. I am your body, your shadow, your effectiveness in this world, your manifestation in the world of the Gods, your effulgence, your breath, your odor, your magical force. You should call me if you want to live with men, but the *one* God if you want to rise above the human world to the divine and eternal solitude of the star.

Busen als des / der du bist / ist bad der wiedergeburt. das
dern ein unendlich langsames wachsthum. du mein
sam ins mēr / das überall die erde an den tiefsten stell
insel erscheint eingebettet in den schoß unermeßlich
ebbe und fluth. du schwillst langsam am lande empor
athemzügen. du wanderst in unmerklichen strömen
wie du dorthin kamest. mit den wogen des großen stur
tiefe. und du weißt nicht / wie dir geschieht. vorher da
deiner entschlüße und anstrengungen bedürfe / damit
anstrengung wärest du nie zu jener bewegung und zu jen
der welt die bringt. auf endlosen blauen flächen versin
vorüber / wunderliches geäst umranket dich. du schl
dunkelblättrige pflanzen und das mēr strömt dich wie
und eine welle schäumt dich aufs ufer und schluckt dich w
sanft empor und führt dich weiter zu neuen flächen und tie
langsam schleichenden schleimigen polypen und grünen
von ferne aber leuchtet im goldenen lichte dir deine höh
wirst deiner selbst von ferne gewahr. und die sehnsucht
über vom sein zu wenden / den du hast es erkannt / w
hierhin und dorthin führt / wo du nirgends haftest / und
emschluckt und hinunter und hinauf gurgelt. du sahe
zehen. da fühltest du dich vom allgemeinen tod umschlungen / v
wunderbar athmenden und strömenden tiefe. oh du sehns
dieses tode / der langsam athmet und ewig hin und widerstr
wassers / alle diese welligen schwankenden schlingenden pf
wunder werden dir zum grauen und du sehnst dich nach so